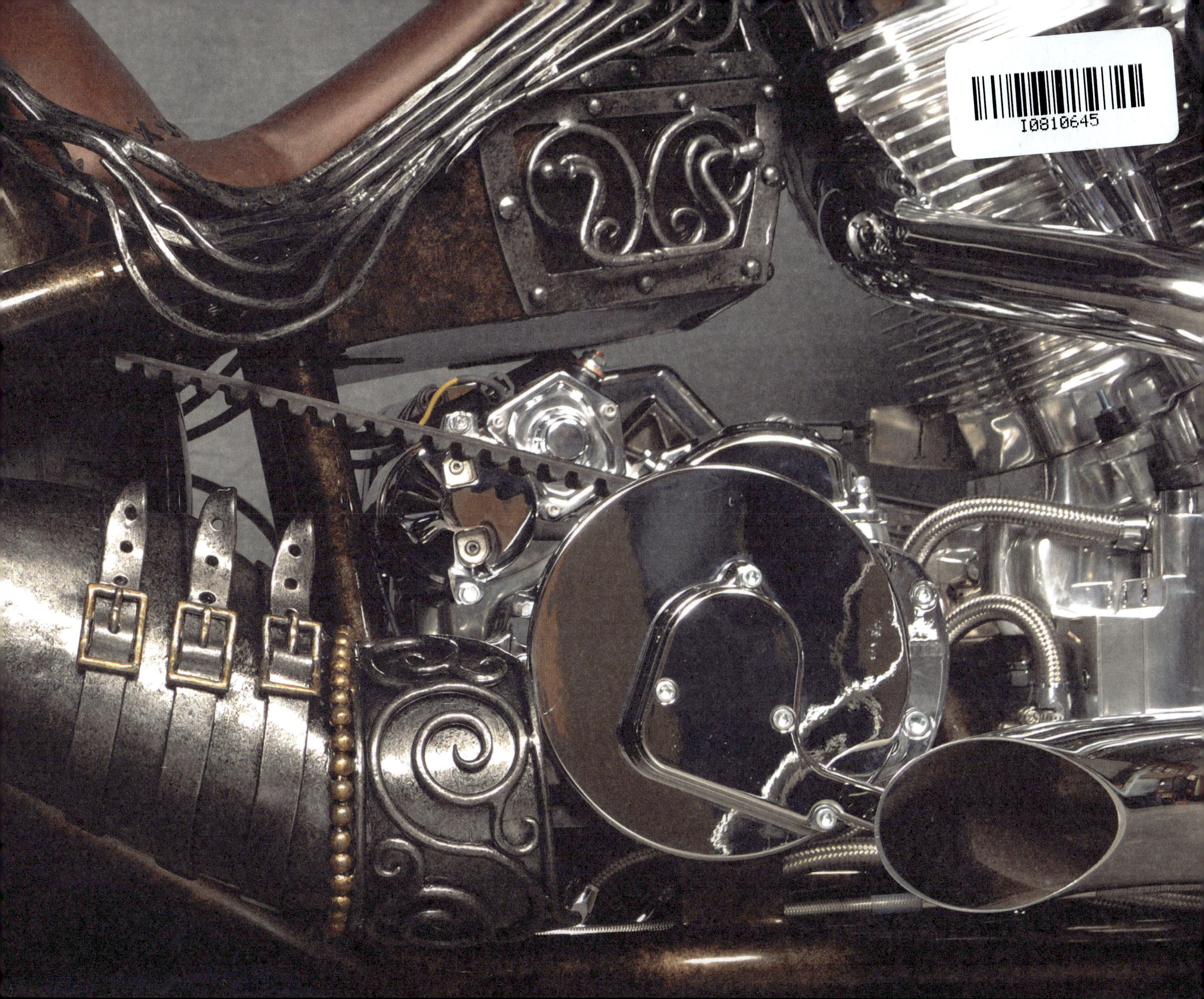

From Fire to Form

Sculpture from the Modern Blacksmith and Metalsmith

Mathew S. Clarke

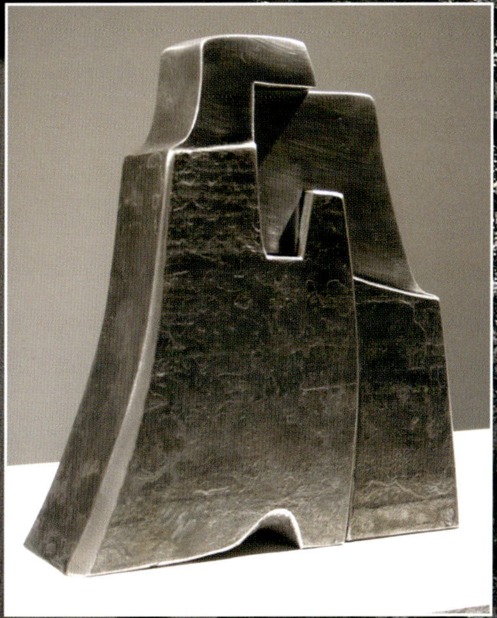

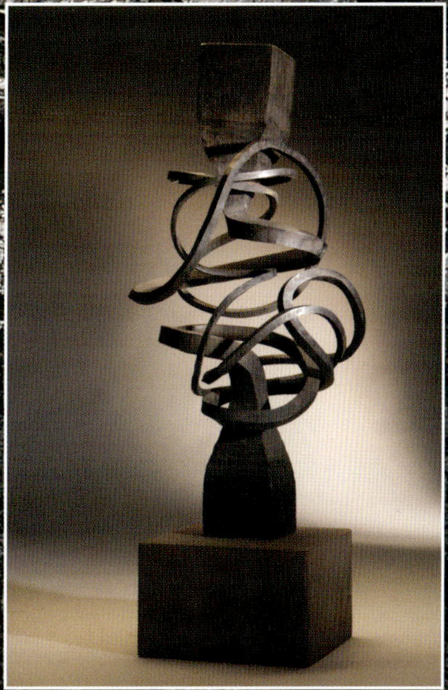

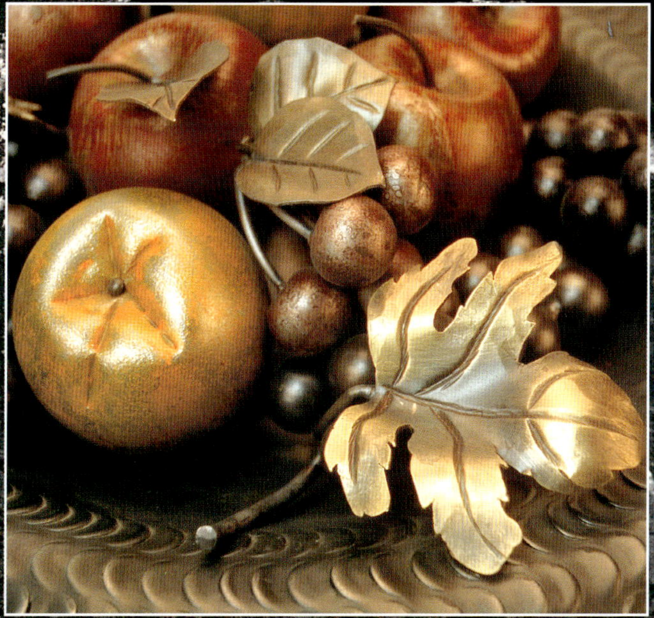

Schiffer Publishing Ltd
380 Lower Valley Road, Atglen, PA 19310

Other Schiffer Books on Related Subjects

Architectural Ironwork. Dona Z. Meilach. ISBN: 076431324X. $49.95

Art Deco Ironwork & Sculpture. "Jerry" S. F Cook III & Tina Skinner. ISBN: 0764322923. $49.95

Art Nouveau Ironwork of Austria & Hungary. Federico Santi & John Gacher. ISBN: 0764324365. $49.95

The Contemporary Blacksmith. Dona Z. Meilach. ISBN: 0764311069. $49.95

Decorative & Sculptural Ironwork: Tools, Techniques & Inspiration. Revised and Expanded 2nd Edition. Dona Z. Meilach. ISBN: 0764307908. $34.95

Decorative Architectural Ironwork: Featuring Wrought & Cast Designs. Diana Stuart. ISBN: 0764321927. $39.95

Decorative Ironwork: Wrought Iron Gratings, Gates and Railings. Margarete Baur-Heinhold. ISBN: 0764301535. $49.95

Ironwork: Dynamic Details. Dona Z. Meilach. ISBN: 0764325493. $39.95

Ironwork Today: Inside & Out. Dona Z. Meilach. ISBN: 0764323903. $49.95

Ironwork Today 2. Jeffrey B. Snyder. ISBN: 9780764330643. $50.00

Library of Congress Control Number: 2008939041

Designed by John P. Cheek
Cover design by Bruce Waters
Type set in Kabel Dm BT/New Baskerville BT

ISBN: 978-0-7643-3247-0
Printed in China

Cover photo: "Foundry Workman" © Steve Lovegrove. Image from BigStockPhoto.com

Published by Schiffer Publishing Ltd.
4880 Lower Valley Road
Atglen, PA 19310
Phone: (610) 593-1777; Fax: (610) 593-2002
E-mail: Info@schifferbooks.com

In Europe, Schiffer books are distributed by
Bushwood Books
6 Marksbury Ave.
Kew Gardens
Surrey TW9 4JF England
Phone: 44 (0) 20 8392-8585; Fax: 44 (0) 20 8392-9876
E-mail: info@bushwoodbooks.co.uk
Website: www.bushwoodbooks.co.uk
Free postage in the U.K., Europe; air mail at cost.

Contents

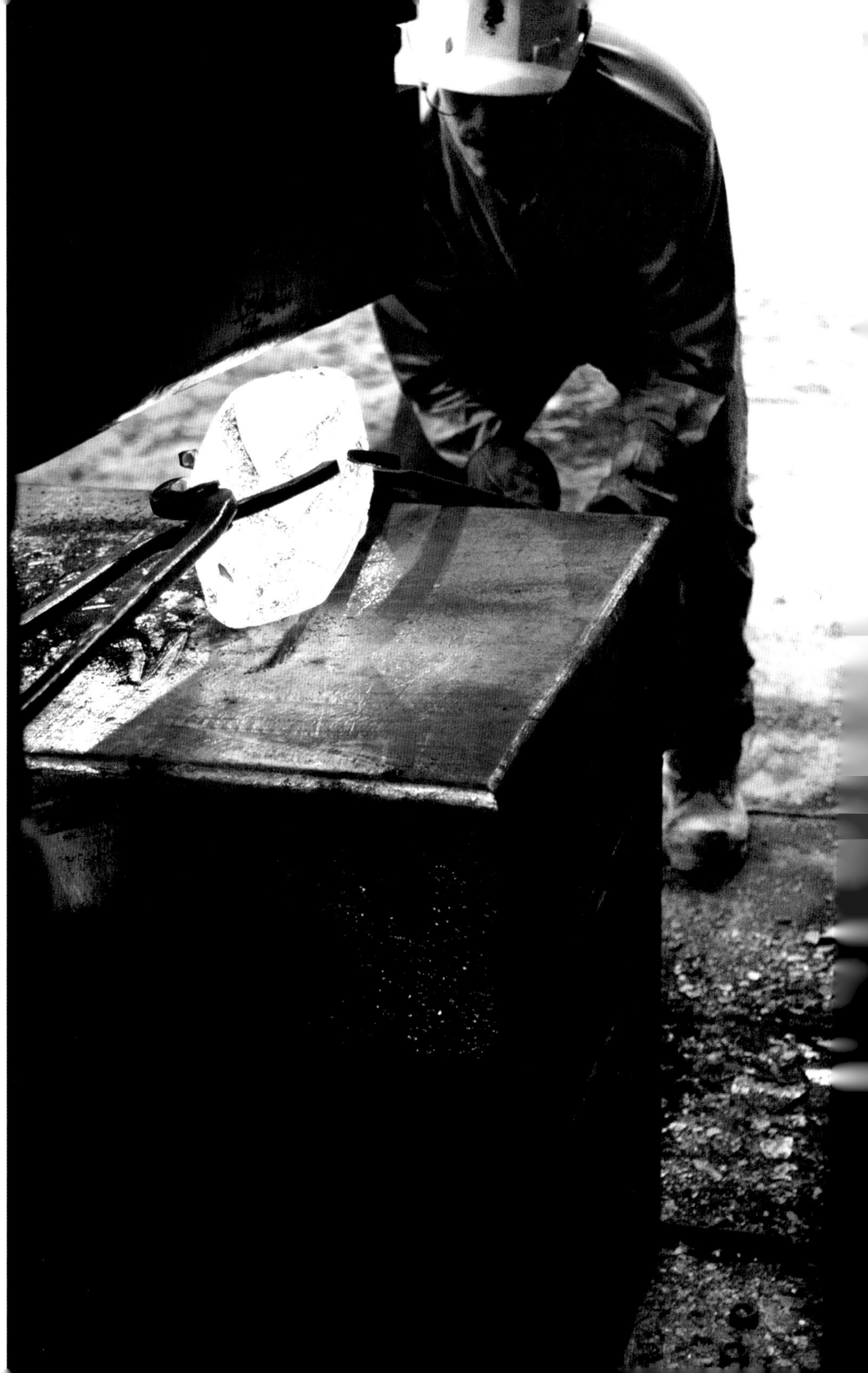

Acknowledgments

To all the artists who have generously contributed photographs of their work and to the photographers who have taken many of the magnificent photos presented in this book, I am tremendously grateful.

Special thanks goes to John Medwedeff for writing the foreword. His knowledge and experience lends great insight to the field of sculptural blacksmithing and metalsmithing.

I am particularly grateful to Elizabeth Brim for taking time from her busy schedule to help select from the approximately 6,700 photos I have received.

I am appreciative to everyone who helped in my research, including all those at ABANA (Artist Blacksmith Association of North America), and the many affiliates for working with me to extend my request for photos through their websites and publications. To BABA (British Artists Blacksmiths Association) and Tobias Schumacher, chief editor, and Peter Elgaß, publisher of *HEPHAISTOS* for their help in reaching out internationally. To all the smiths, galleries, and collectors who have contacted me with referrals, to Peter Pelletier for constructing and maintaining the website with the utmost efficiency, and to Peter Schiffer and his staff for opportunity to publish this book. Thanks to you all.

To my wife and children for the time, space, patience, and support given to me from the beginning of this project through to the end, I am truly grateful.

Foreword

There must have been something in the water. The first time I struck a piece of hot steel on an anvil with a hammer, I instantly recognized a connection between metalsmithing and sculpture. Instinctively I felt that I had just found my life's work. I had bought my first anvil at fourteen in 1976, but at that time I did not know what to do with it. By 1981, I was nineteen years old and had begun to forge iron. Without knowing it, I was stumbling into the early years of the renaissance in contemporary blacksmithing. Less than a year later, I was living and working as an apprentice to Director James Wallace at the Metal Museum in Memphis, Tennessee. At the Museum I had a front-row seat to learn and watch the movement unfold, and over the following years I went on to graduate school at Southern Illinois University Carbondale, before starting my career as a studio blacksmith. I have been fortunate to have found opportunities to contribute to the field and participated in the emergence of blacksmithing as sculptural medium.

The subject of how this movement came about is too complex and involves too many talented people to fully explain within the confines of a brief introduction. But with a blend of firsthand experience, stories told by my older friends and mentors, spiced with a dash of art history, I will try to illustrate the trajectory that this book represents.

The tradition of decorative ironwork in the United States had largely been lost in the mid-twentieth century's international mix of economic, political, and social upheaval that ultimately affected design styles in art and architecture. The sleek lines of modernism and the deliberate move away from ornamentation all but eliminated the blacksmith's role in architecture. For decades, Carl Jennings (1910-2003) may have been the only artist-blacksmith working in his own contemporary style in the United States. Then, in the late 1960s and early 1970s, a scattered and isolated handful of individual artists started to experiment with blacksmithing techniques, often blending functional and sculptural work. While the 1967 movie *The Graduate* proclaimed the age of plastics, and NASA was preparing to send astronauts to the moon, the counter-culture movement of the time helped fuel an interest in handmade objects. These artists had relatively little awareness of the history of ironwork, and most were working in a vacuum without technical instruction from a previous generation of master smiths. They were unrestrained by tradition. The result was an infusion of new ideas to a centuries-old craft.

That was the generation of artists I learned from, studied, and consider to be the pioneers of the contemporary movement of forged sculptural ironwork. They raised the bar and made the work we engage in now possible. Brent Kington introduced blacksmithing into the MFA program at Southern Illinois University Carbondale (SIUC) in 1969. Albert Paley's 1974 commission for the Portal Gates at the Renwick Gallery in Washington, DC, was the first high-profile public commission by an artist-blacksmith in the United States in decades. SIUC then hosted the 1976 Artist-Blacksmiths' Association of North America (ABANA) Conference, an international event that British artist-blacksmith Richard Quinnell called "the Woodstock of Iron" and said that it inspired (on the flight home) the creation of the British Artists Blacksmiths organization, which in turn spawned the start of contemporary blacksmithing organizations across the world.

Associated with that ABANA conference and the American Bicentennial Celebration, SIUC University Museum curator Evert Johnson (1929-2006), a visionary in his own right, organized the ground-breaking exhibition "Iron Solid Wrought." This exhibition brought together both historical and contemporary ironwork. The exhibition subsequently traveled to the Museum of Contemporary Craft in New York City and the Renwick Gallery of American Craft in Washington, DC. The high profile exposure fueled new interest in and helped to establish forged iron as legitimate art. Johnson's assistant, Jim Wallace, went on to become the first director of the Metal Museum in Memphis, Tennessee, which opened in 1979. Under Wallace's direction, the museum became an internationally recognized institution in the field of metalwork.

These are just a few examples of events that had a tremendous impact on blacksmithing's emergence from obsolete craft to relevant contemporary art form. Since then, the worldwide exchange of ideas among blacksmithing communities has encouraged a new generation of smiths to experiment with innovative design styles created with both historic and modern metal working methods. Computer technology developed for industry has continued to offer new possibilities of scale and efficiency, even for small studios, and some artists, such as Tom Joyce, have teamed with industry to execute monumental scale work. Equally important, a regained sense of professionalism coupled with an increasingly mainstream acceptance of the art of the blacksmith has made it possible to actually earn a living in the field.

In the 1980s, a common topic of conversation among artists whose chosen media were traditional craft materials such as fiber, glass, ceramic, wood, and metal was "Is it craft or is it art?" Certainly the tide was turning and craft media was gradually being accepted by artists, collectors, and curators alike as legitimate fine art. Blacksmithing may have been behind the curve in making this transition, considering its historical origins were almost entirely based on utilitarian and decorative objects fashioned in iron or steel, while sculpture was historically closely associated with stone, wood, and bronze.

History will always change course when there is a convergence of new material, technology, and creative minds. In this case it was economically mass-produced iron and steel, the acetylene welding torch, and some (now) very familiar names. Iron did not begin to emerge as a respected material for sculpture in the Western European tradition until the early twentieth century, through the works of Spain's Julio Gonzalez (1876-1966), the son of a metalsmith. Gonzalez initially introduced welded steel sculpture to Pablo Picasso (1881-1973). Their work, in turn, inspired the next generation of sculptors, including the American artists Alexander Calder (1898-1976) and David Smith (1906-1965).

By mid-century, their generation collectively produced an important body of work, including welded steel sculpture that ranged in style from Cubism to Abstract Expressionism to Modernism. The early work was expressive and not necessarily governed by a tidy sense of traditional craftsmanship. Steel is essentially a modern building material produced in a variety of structural cross sections and thickness of plates. It is no coincidence that the beginning of the twentieth century, with its new industrialism and emerging technology for welding iron, produced artists who quickly adapted the new tools of the day to create a revolutionary art form. In the hands of these artists, their contemporaries, and the generations they inspired, the stock industrial shapes were seldom or minimally altered. It was and remains typical to see fabricated steel sculpture in which structural beams, pipe, found objects, and cut out sections of plate are welded together to create the artist's desired composition.

I believe that these artists played an important role in the acceptance of iron and steel as equal to the established traditional materials for sculpture, but they are not the source of the contemporary movement of sculpture inspired by the process of forging. The art of Gonzalez and those that he inspired appears to have been realized mostly through additive processes, with direct manipulation of the material secondary. Although the medium is the same and nobody doubts these artists' passion for iron, the difference lies in inherent philosophies between work created primarily with a welder's torch and that which is shaped by hammer.

In contrast, it is the artist-blacksmiths' understanding of the inherent malleability of steel and their desire to reshape the metal—to make the surfaces their own and achieve an aesthetic that is based on their own visual language rather than found industrial parts—which marks the difference in the artist-blacksmiths' approach to creating sculpture.

Embedded in blacksmithing are the traditions of metalsmithing: attention to design detail, a value placed on craftsmanship, and a familiarity with the making of functional objects. These factors unquestionably influence and inform the work. As I mentioned earlier, there was a groundswell from which the 1970s interest in forging seemed to spontaneously emerge, but nothing happens in a vacuum. For every one of us involved we have our own stories with unique and crisscrossing lineages of inspiration and influence.

Ironically, there are even very interesting parallels between the history of welded sculpture and forged sculpture. For example, in the early 1970s blacksmith Steve Bondi (1948 - 2004) traveled to Italy to study and work with Simon Benetton, a prominent artist working with forged steel on a monumental scale to create sculpture. Steve and his brother Mike were, in turn, quick to begin groundbreaking experimentation with heavy power-hammer work in their California studio. In a 1997 interview, Steve described the modern look of the 1920s work of the Italian smiths, including Simon's father Toni Benetton (1910 - 1996), as a "tie between early twentieth century–which was Tony's work–to the end of the twentieth century."[1] Curiously, he went on to say that Tony Benetton's work was an extension of the architectural work of Allessandro Mazzuctelli (1865 - 1938), a contemporary of Gonzalez (but a century ahead of his time). Mazzuctelli chose a different path, concentrating on the hot manipulation of iron.

Today's blacksmiths, comfortable with purely sculptural forms and personal expression, will frequently and freely blend the making of functional objects with sculptural qualities, or vice versa. Quite often working on a very large scale, the artist-blacksmith's designs may be more informed by the forge than forged, borrowing technique from the fabricator but staying true to the mindset of the smith. Many public and private sculpture commissions for monuments, seating, gates, entryways, and fountains are perfectly suited to the particular perspective of an artist-blacksmith. While many now hold advanced degrees in art, the blacksmith's knowledge base is still part designer, mechanic, engineer, and inventor. As we start this new century, there is an emerging collective body of work, which has as many variations as practitioners who are redefining the possibilities of metal sculpture from the forge.

1. Rob Edwards, "Anvil Interview with Stephen Bondi at the California Blacksmith Association Spring Conference, Vista, CA," *Anvil Magazine*, June 1998, http://www.anvilmag.com/smith/bondi.htm, and conversations with Mike Bondi, James Wallace, Brent Kington, and Evert Johnson.

John Medwedeff
2008

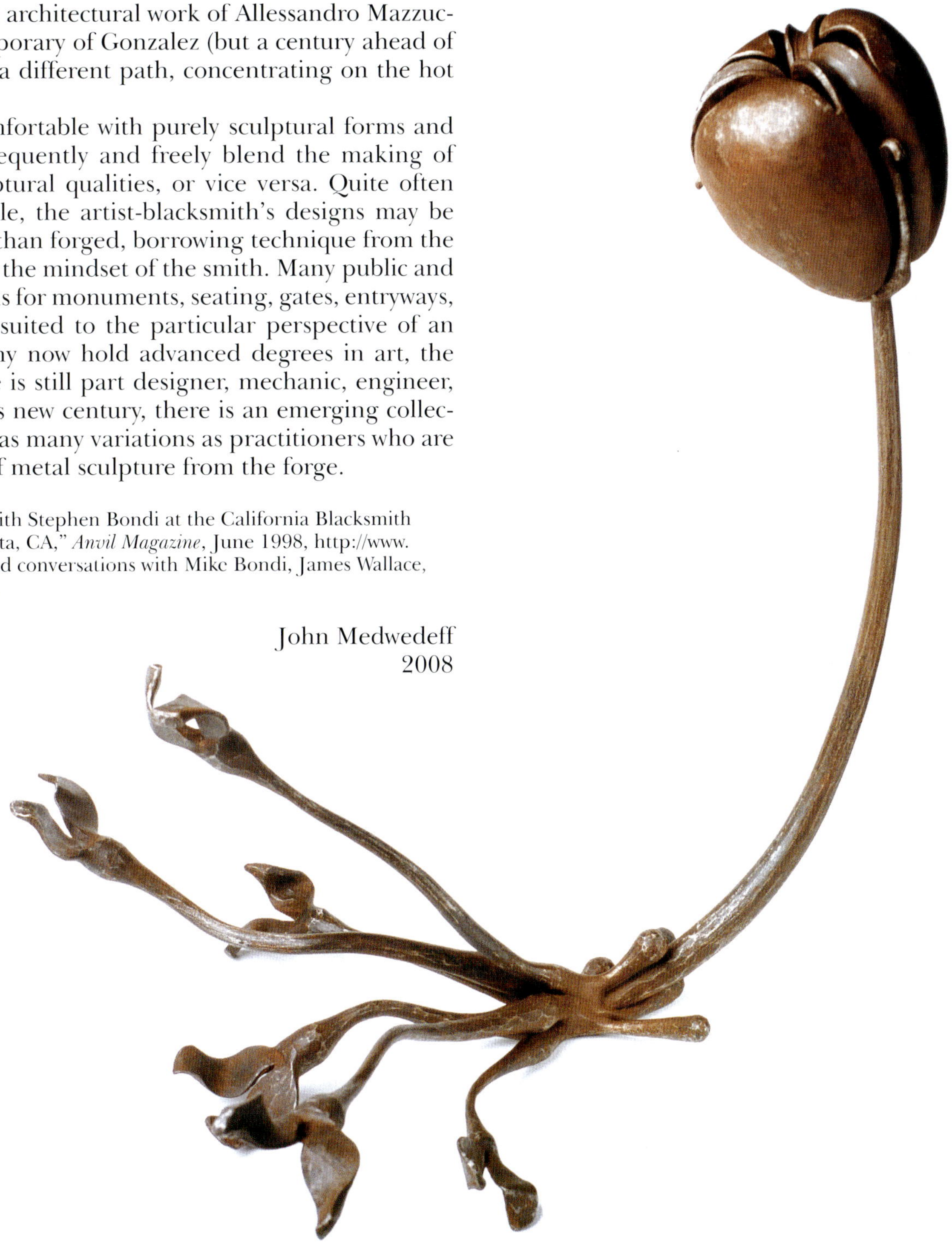

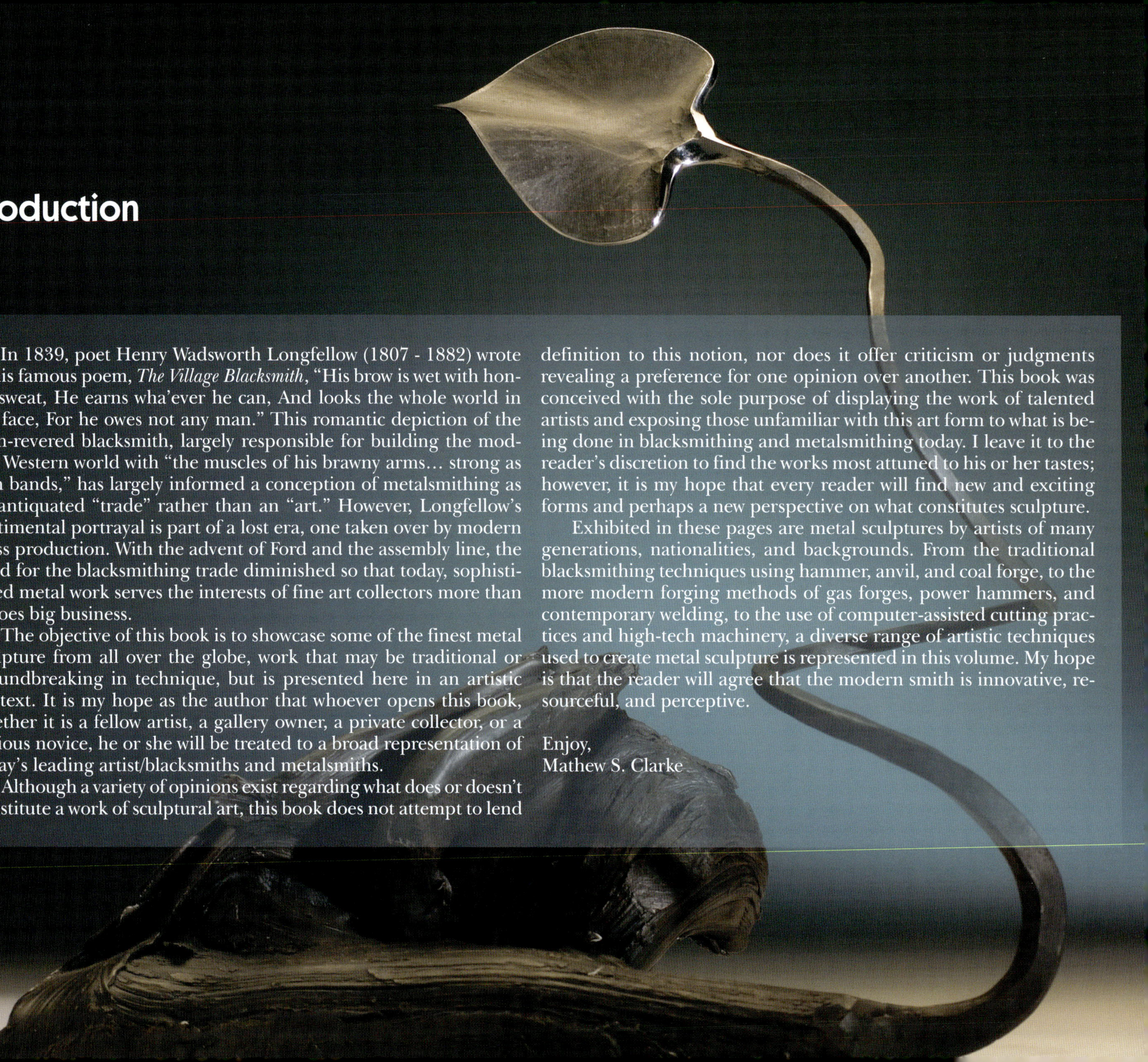

Introduction

In 1839, poet Henry Wadsworth Longfellow (1807 - 1882) wrote in his famous poem, *The Village Blacksmith*, "His brow is wet with honest sweat, He earns wha'ever he can, And looks the whole world in the face, For he owes not any man." This romantic depiction of the then-revered blacksmith, largely responsible for building the modern Western world with "the muscles of his brawny arms… strong as iron bands," has largely informed a conception of metalsmithing as an antiquated "trade" rather than an "art." However, Longfellow's sentimental portrayal is part of a lost era, one taken over by modern mass production. With the advent of Ford and the assembly line, the need for the blacksmithing trade diminished so that today, sophisticated metal work serves the interests of fine art collectors more than it does big business.

The objective of this book is to showcase some of the finest metal sculpture from all over the globe, work that may be traditional or groundbreaking in technique, but is presented here in an artistic context. It is my hope as the author that whoever opens this book, whether it is a fellow artist, a gallery owner, a private collector, or a curious novice, he or she will be treated to a broad representation of today's leading artist/blacksmiths and metalsmiths.

Although a variety of opinions exist regarding what does or doesn't constitute a work of sculptural art, this book does not attempt to lend definition to this notion, nor does it offer criticism or judgments revealing a preference for one opinion over another. This book was conceived with the sole purpose of displaying the work of talented artists and exposing those unfamiliar with this art form to what is being done in blacksmithing and metalsmithing today. I leave it to the reader's discretion to find the works most attuned to his or her tastes; however, it is my hope that every reader will find new and exciting forms and perhaps a new perspective on what constitutes sculpture.

Exhibited in these pages are metal sculptures by artists of many generations, nationalities, and backgrounds. From the traditional blacksmithing techniques using hammer, anvil, and coal forge, to the more modern forging methods of gas forges, power hammers, and contemporary welding, to the use of computer-assisted cutting practices and high-tech machinery, a diverse range of artistic techniques used to create metal sculpture is represented in this volume. My hope is that the reader will agree that the modern smith is innovative, resourceful, and perceptive.

Enjoy,
Mathew S. Clarke

Chapter One

The Sculptural Form

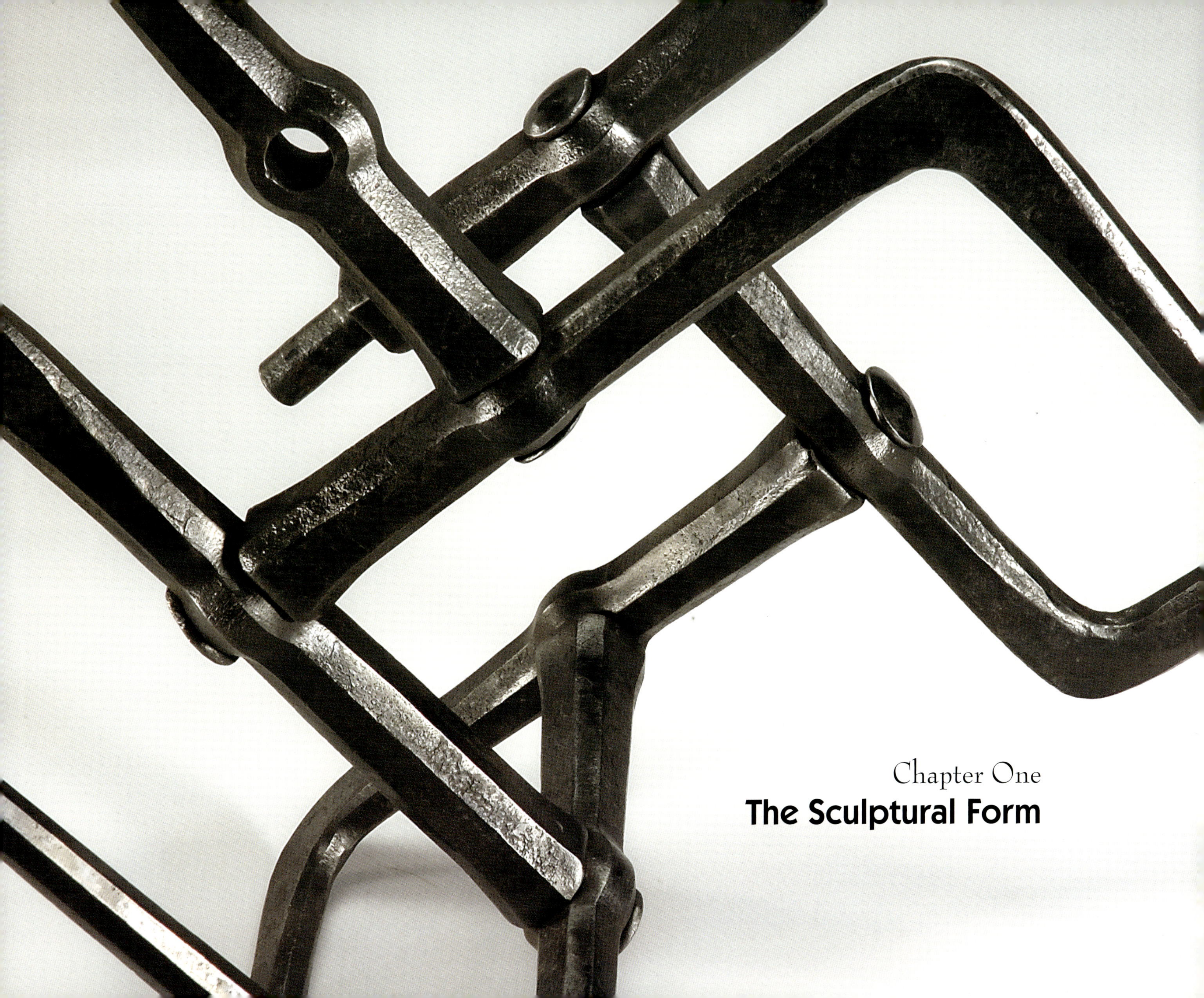

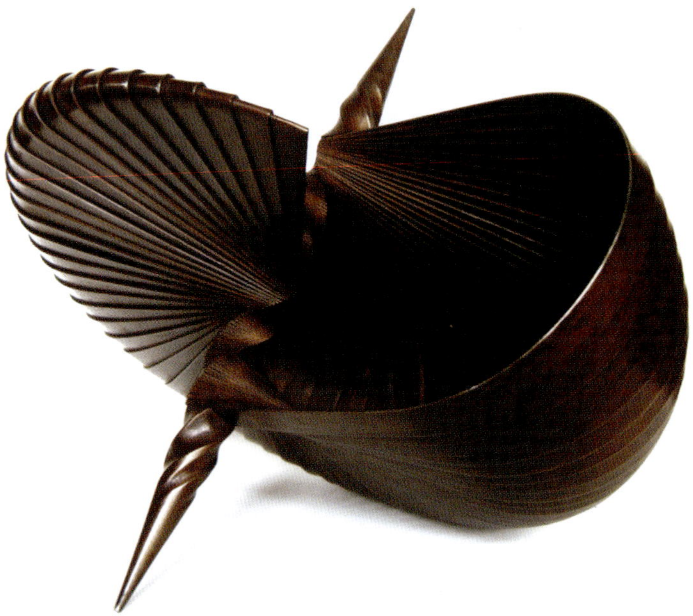

Michael Kaczmar. *Evolution,* 2006. Iron. 18" x 18". *Photo, artist*

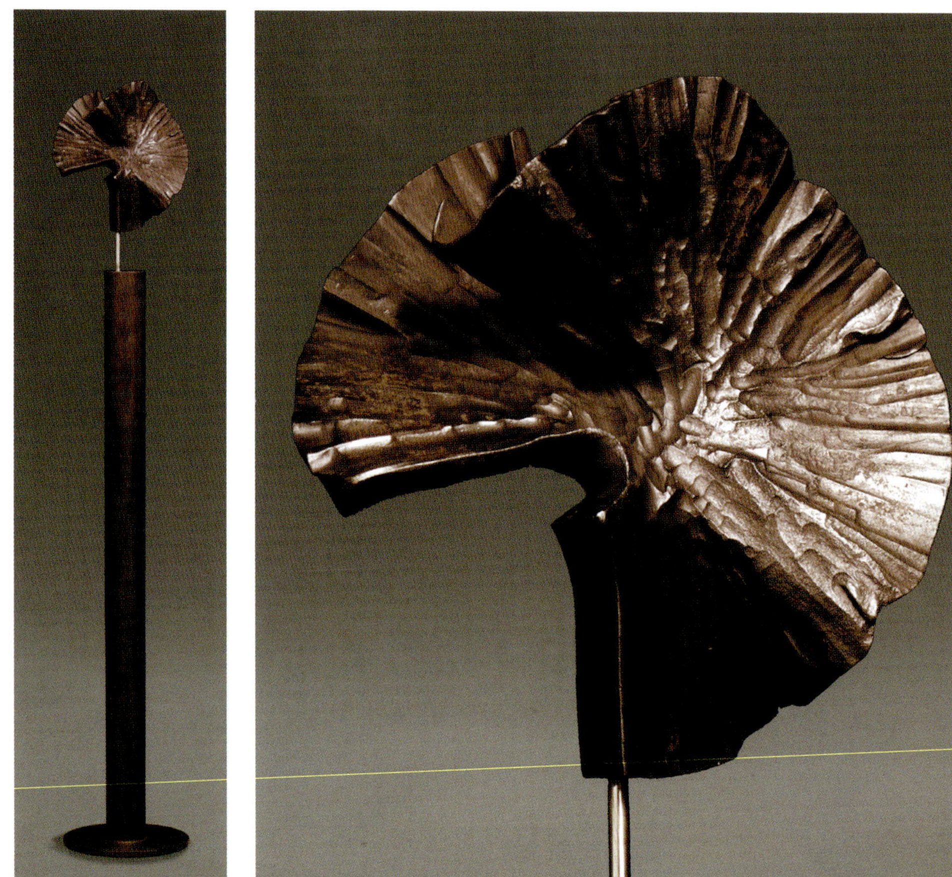

Michael Kaczmar. *Phönix*, 2002. Wrought iron. 14" x 14". *Photo, artist*

Nathan Blank. *Horizon.* Detail image.
Photo, Tom Mills

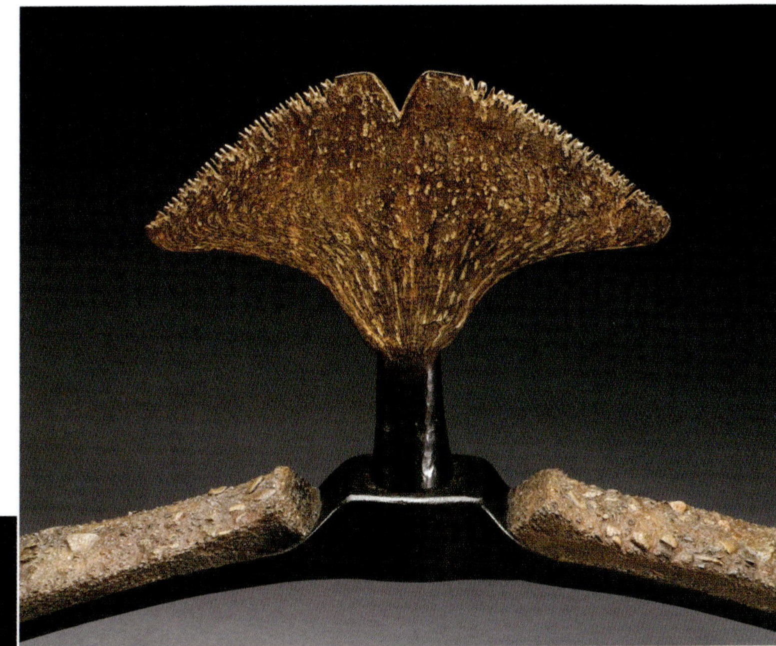

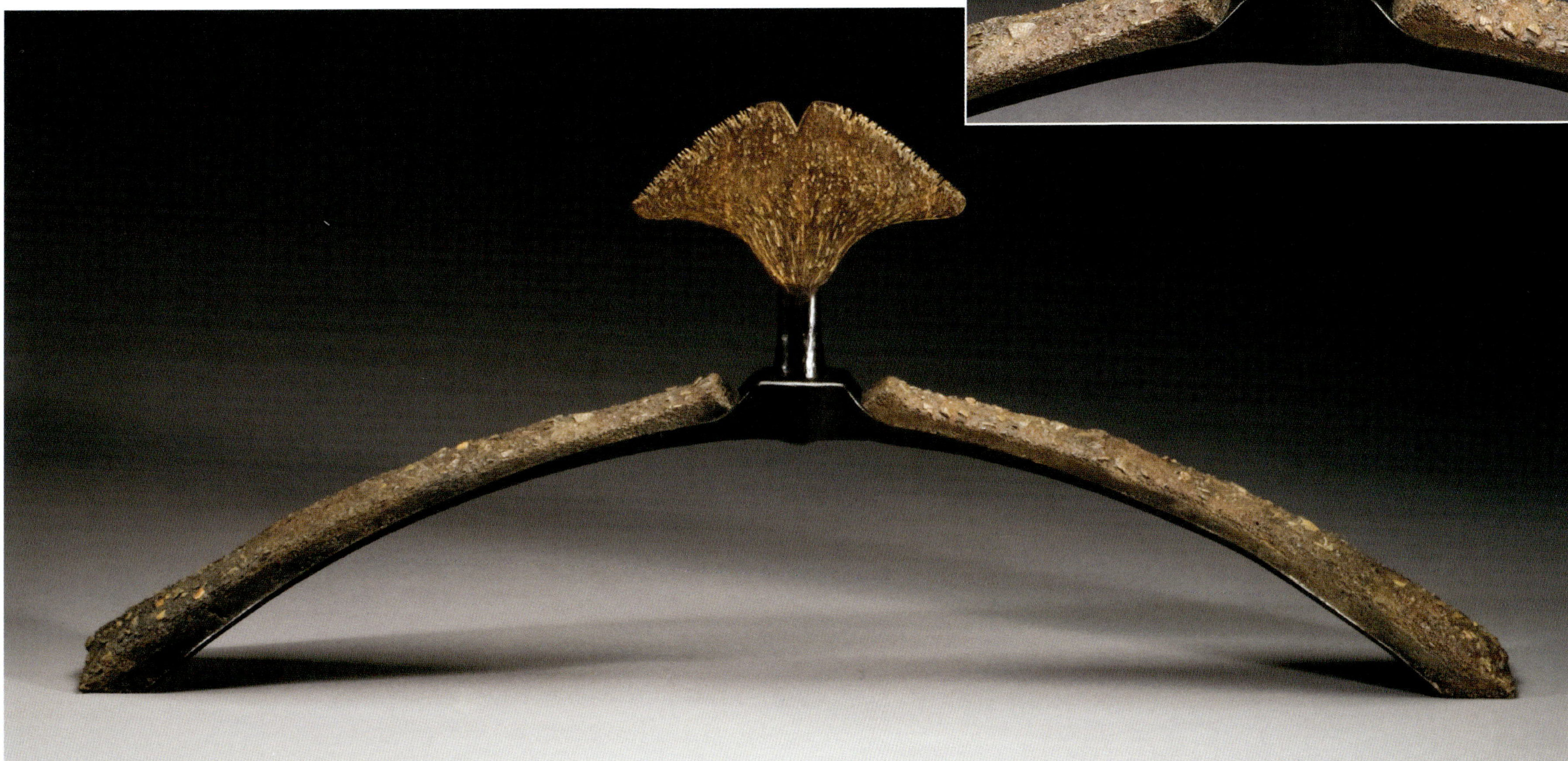

Nathan Blank. *Horizon.* Steel, wrought iron, and concrete. 43" x 17" x 4". Forged steel with forge welded wrought iron details combined with concrete, colored with patinas and masonry dyes. *Photo, Tom Mills*

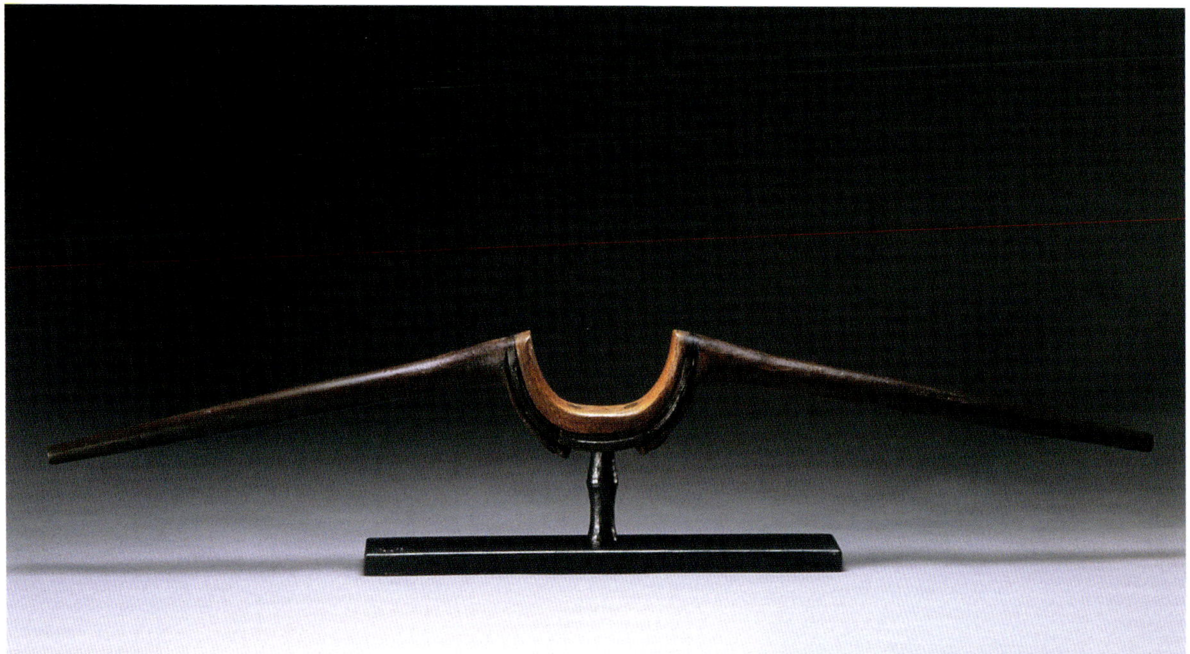

Nathan Blank. *Xyloid.* Steel and wrought iron. 32" x 8" x 3". Forged and fabricated with forge welded details, finished with patinas. *Photo, Tom Mills*

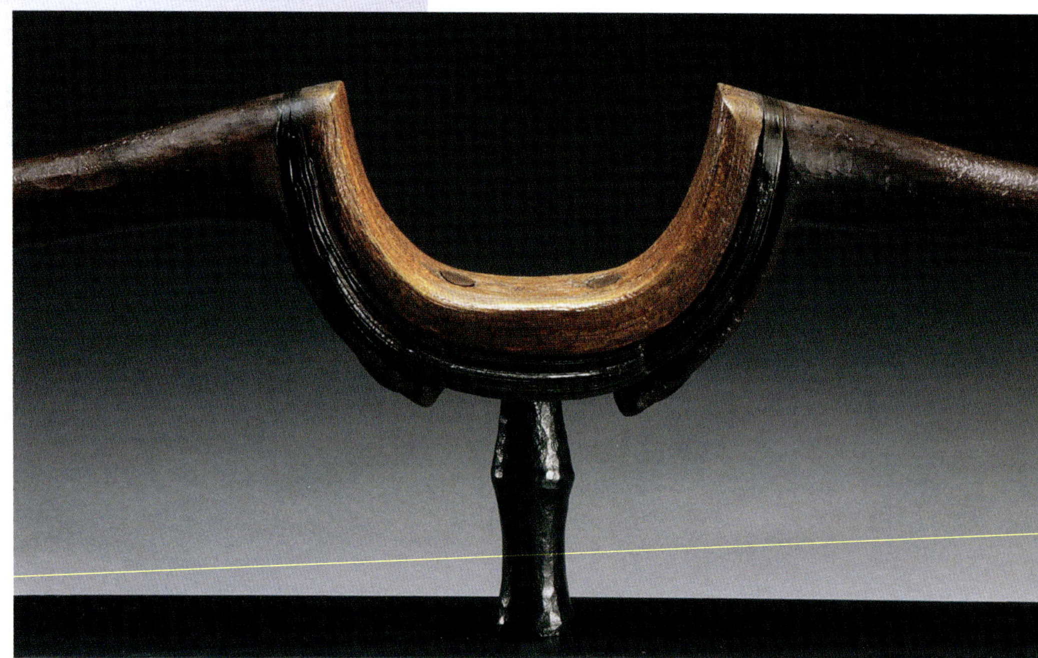

Nathan Blank. *Xyloid.* Detail image. *Photo, Tom Mills*

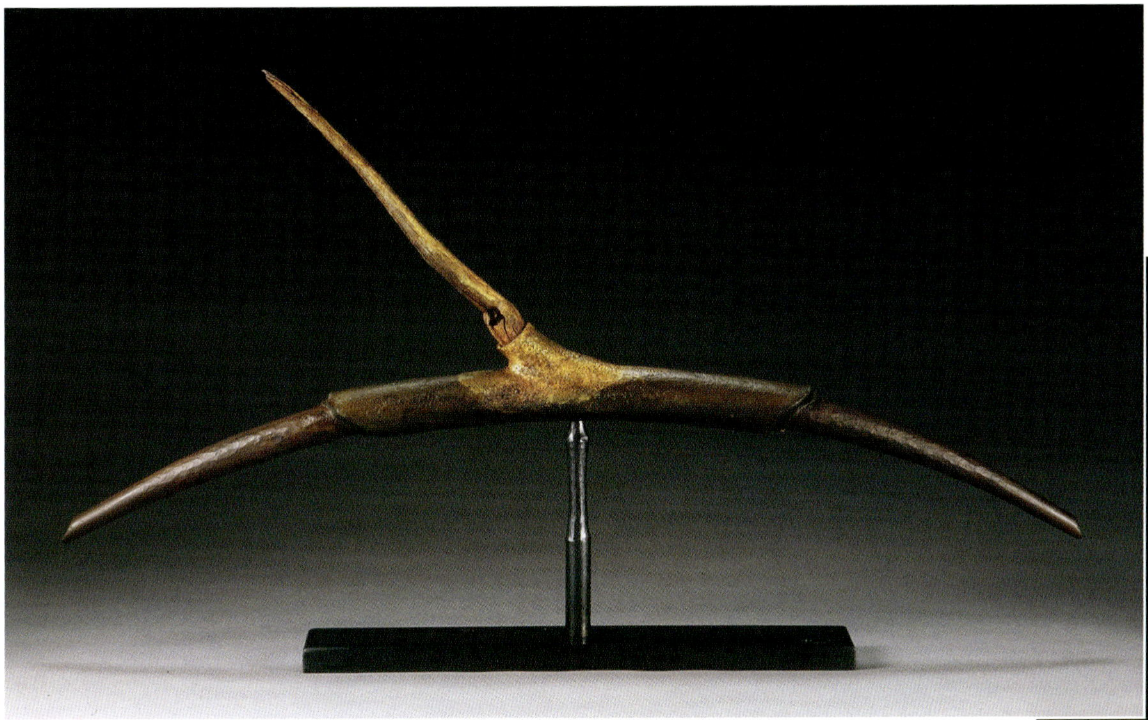

Nathan Blank. *Ligniform.* Steel and wrought iron. 31" x 17" x 3". Forged and fabricated with forge welded details, finished with patinas. *Photo, Tom Mills*

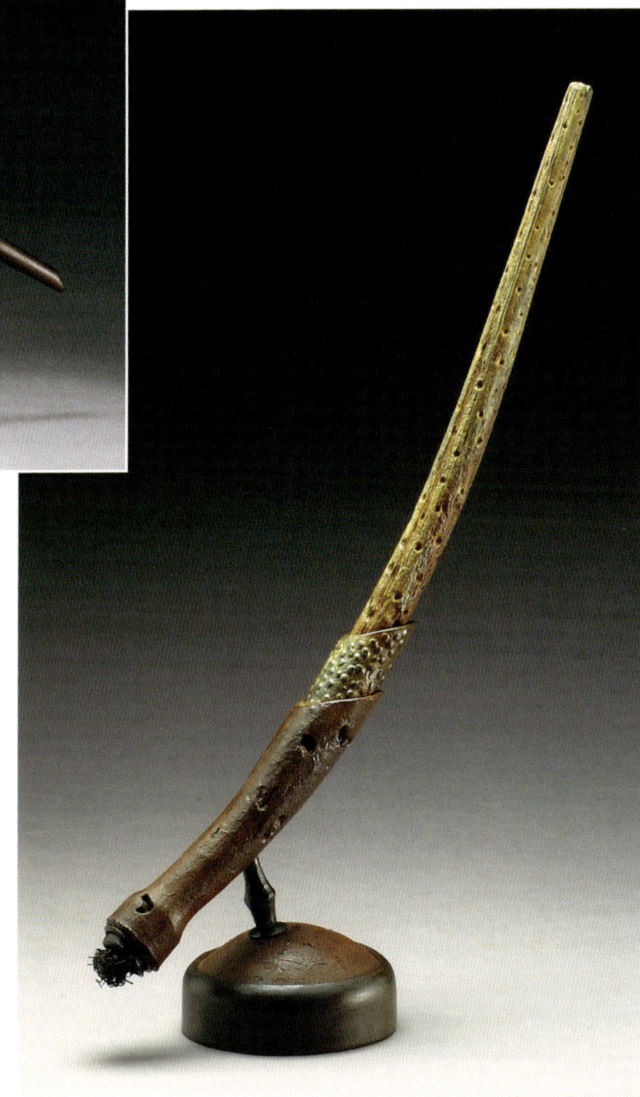

Nathan Blank. *Seedling.* Steel and wrought iron. 24" x 8" x 6". Forged and fabricated with forge welded details, finished with patinas. *Photo, Tom Mills*

Nathan Blank. *Arborea.* Steel and wrought iron. 84" x 18" x 2". Forged and fabricated with forge welded details, finished with patinas. *Photo, Tom Mills*

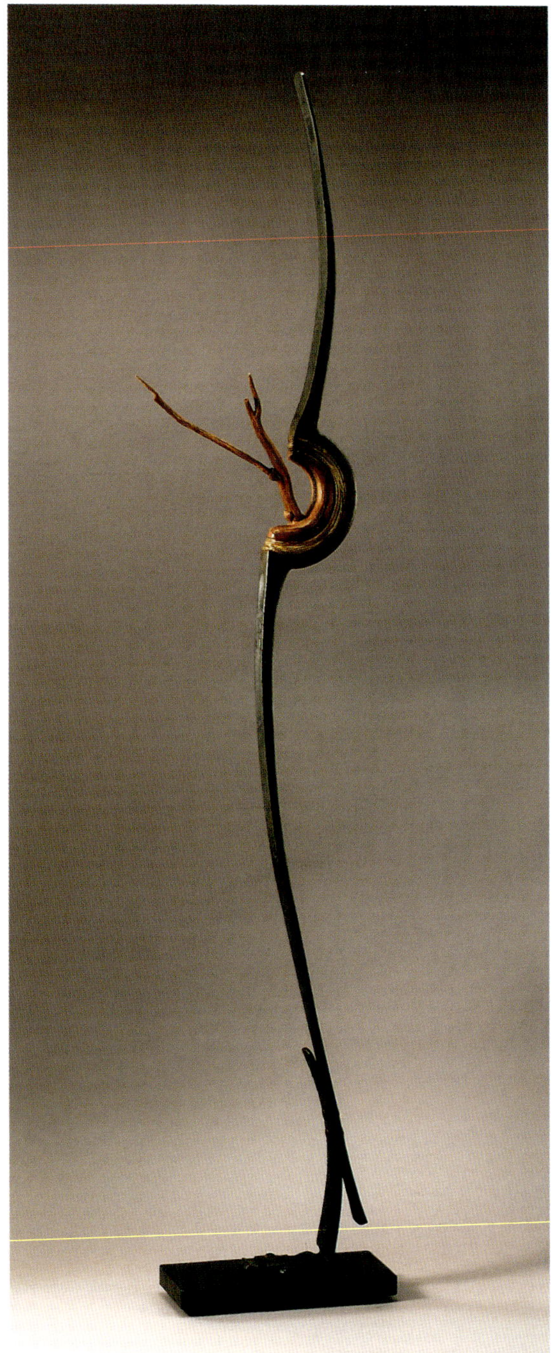

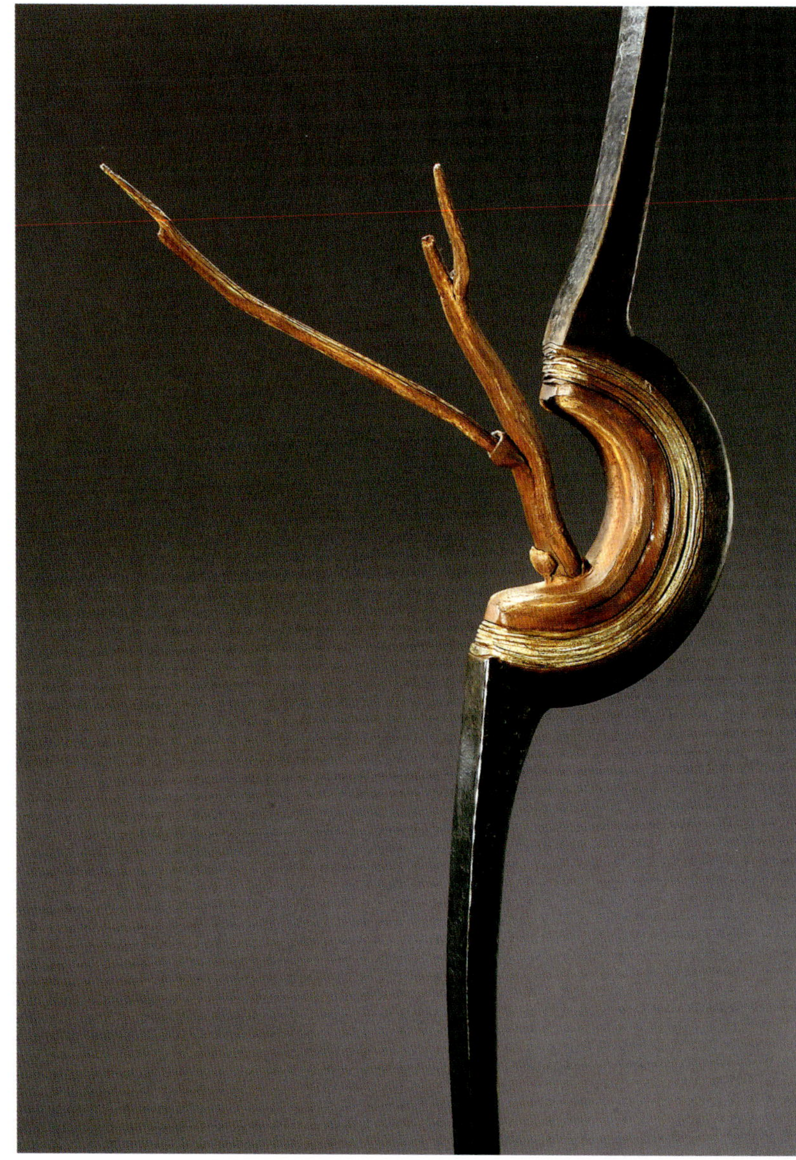

Nathan Blank. *Arborea.* Detail image. *Photo, Tom Mills*

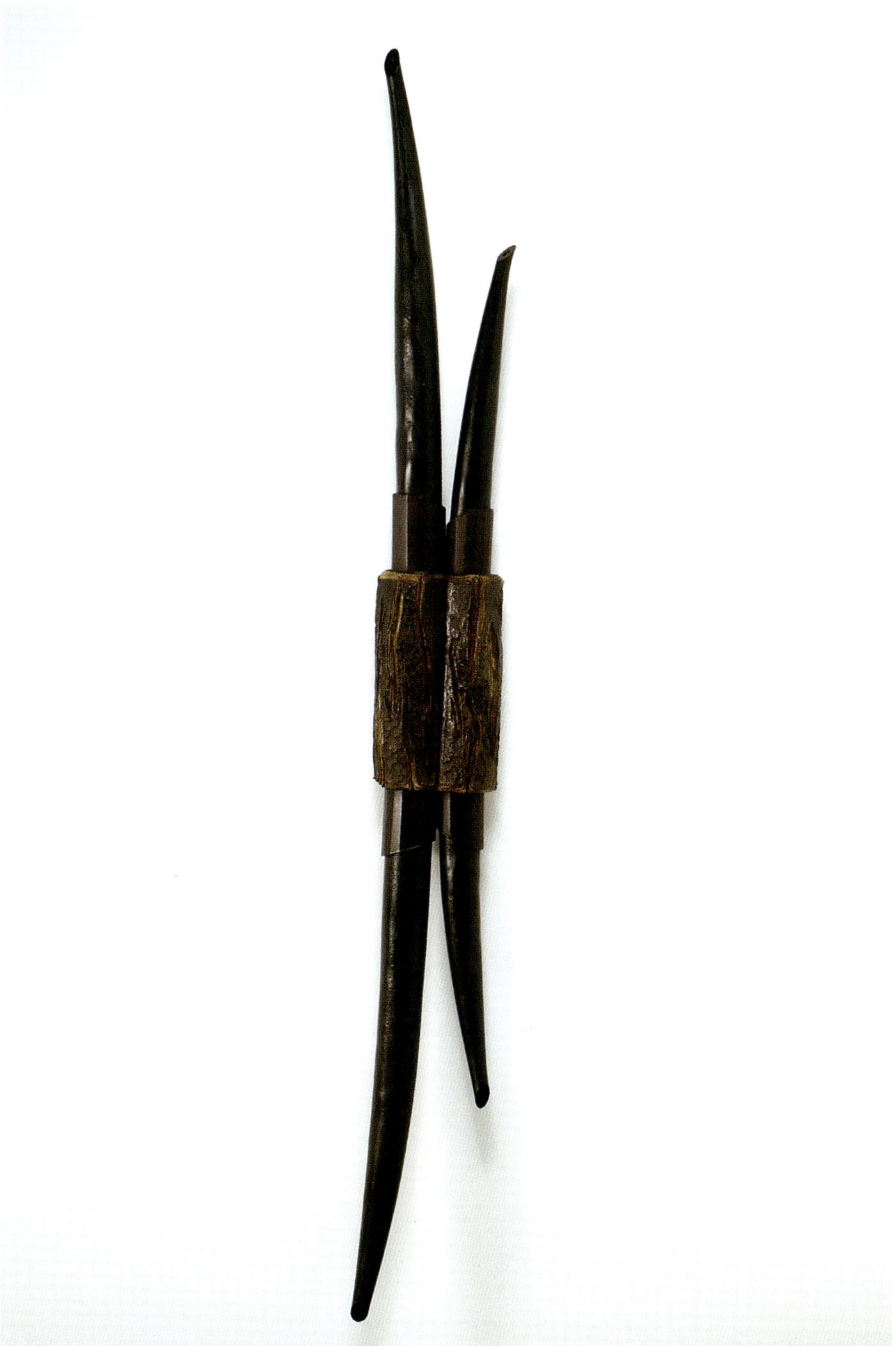

Nathan Blank. *Bound.* Wall piece, steel. 56" x 6" x 3".
Forged and fabricated with chiseled details. *Photo, Tom Mills*

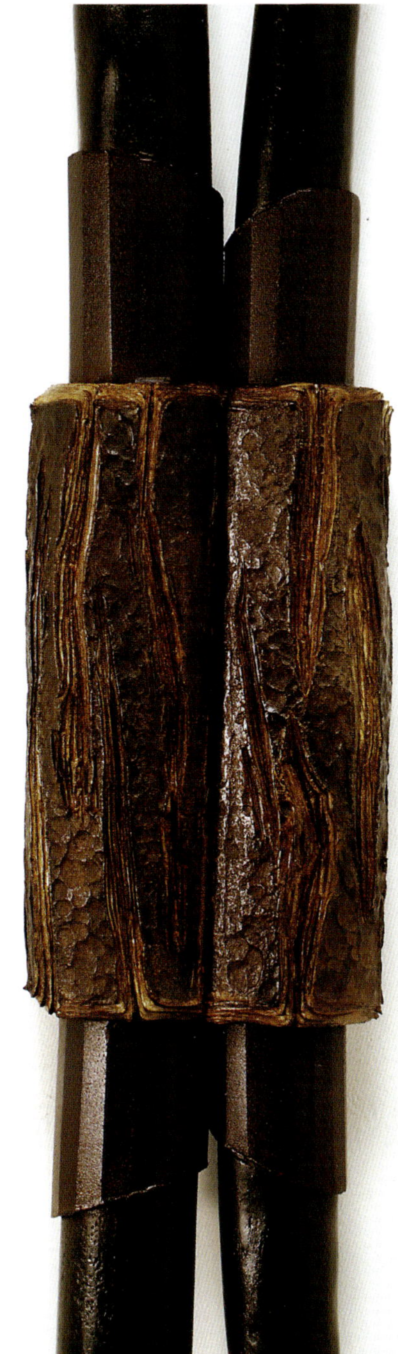

Nathan Blank. *Bound.*
Detail image. *Photo, Tom Mills*

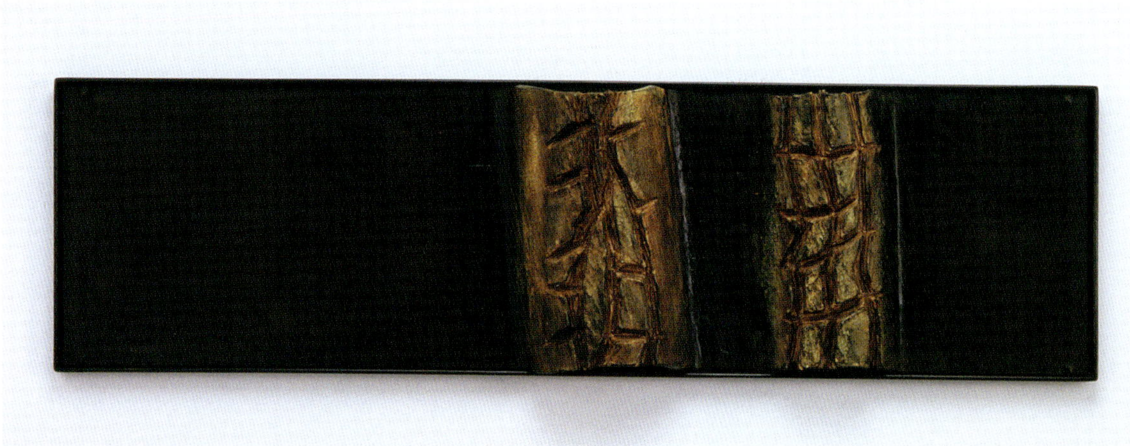

Nathan Blank. *Glimpse.* Wall piece, steel. 26" x 7" x 2". Forged and fabricated with chiseled details.
Photo, Tom Mills

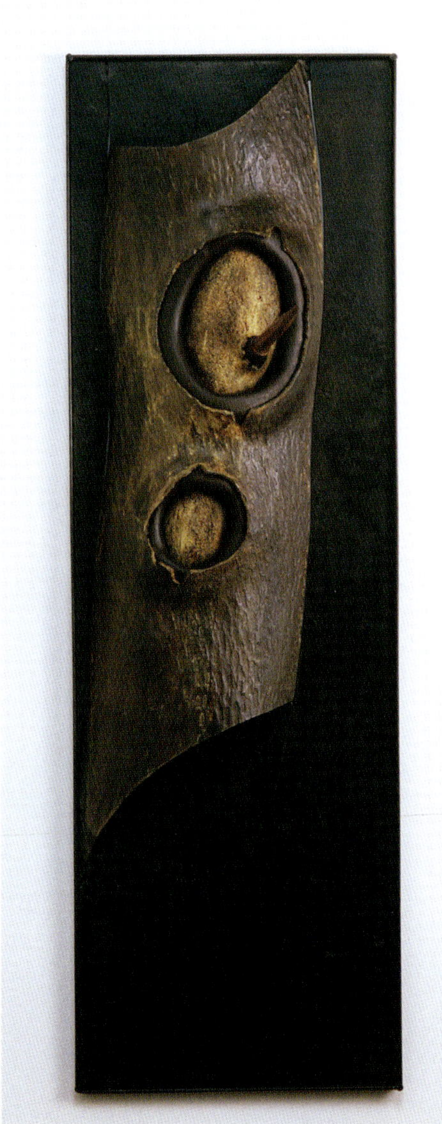

Nathan Blank. *Reminiscence.* Wall piece, steel and wrought iron. 29" x 11" x 3". Forged and fabricated with forge welded details, finished with patinas. *Photo, Tom Mills*

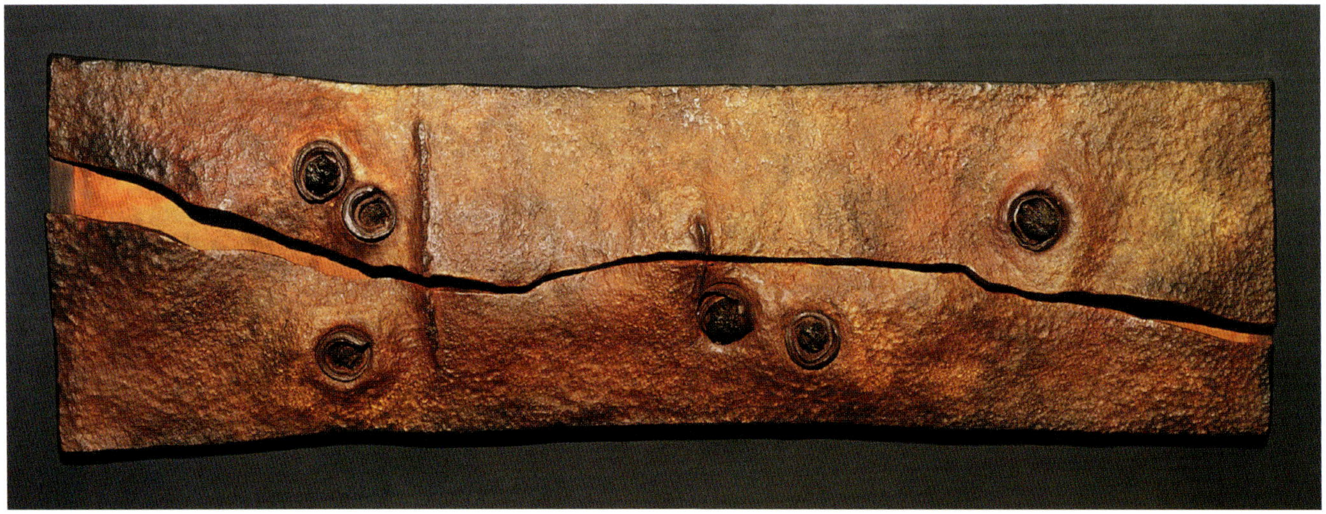

Nathan Blank. *Lichen.* Wall piece, steel. 35" x 11" x 1". Forged and fabricated with forge welded details, finished with patinas.
Photo, artist

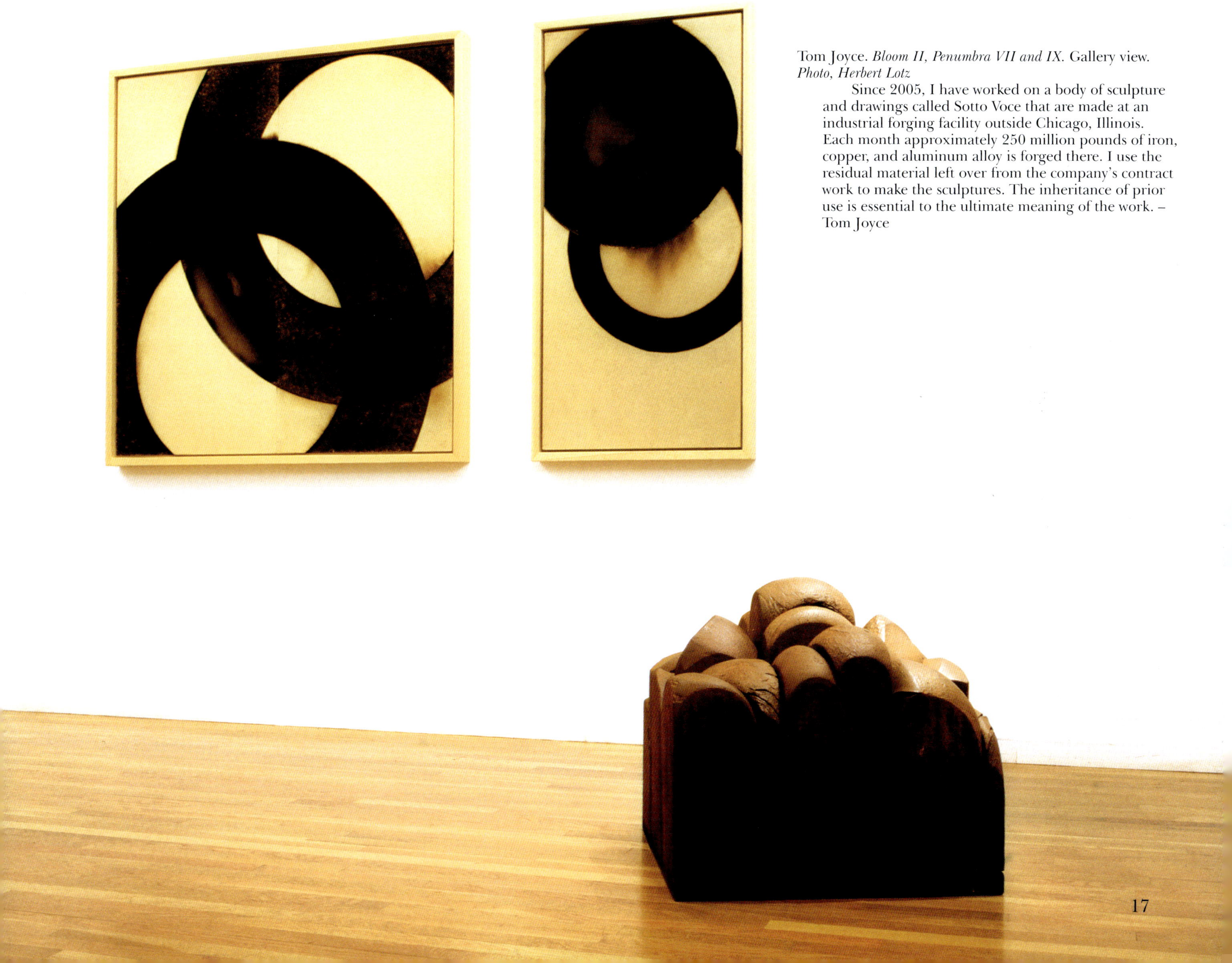

Tom Joyce. *Bloom II, Penumbra VII and IX.* Gallery view. *Photo, Herbert Lotz*

Since 2005, I have worked on a body of sculpture and drawings called Sotto Voce that are made at an industrial forging facility outside Chicago, Illinois. Each month approximately 250 million pounds of iron, copper, and aluminum alloy is forged there. I use the residual material left over from the company's contract work to make the sculptures. The inheritance of prior use is essential to the ultimate meaning of the work. – Tom Joyce

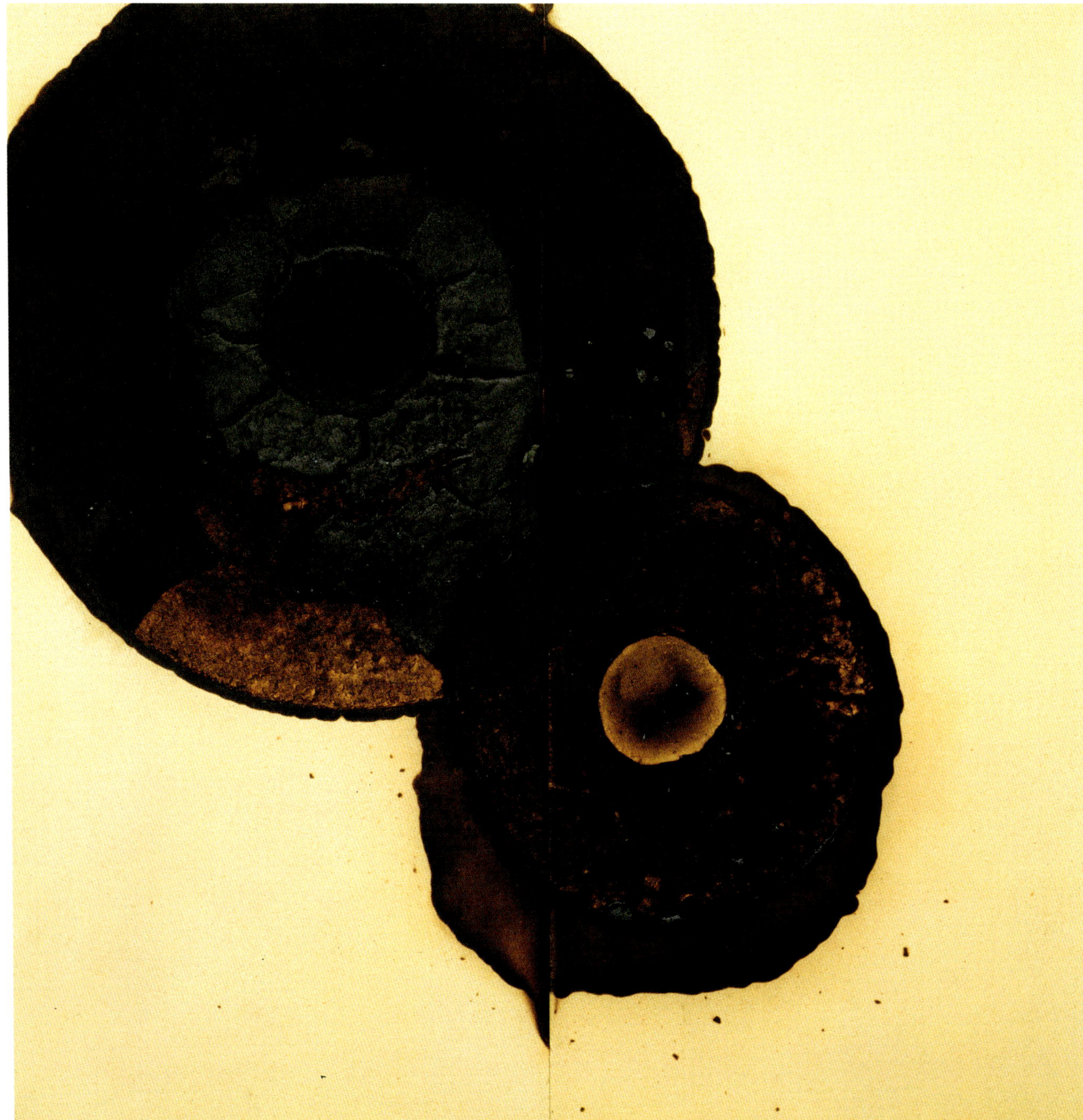

Tom Joyce. *Penumbra I,* 2005. Charred impression on wood. 48" x 48" x 3". *Photo, Herbert Lotz*

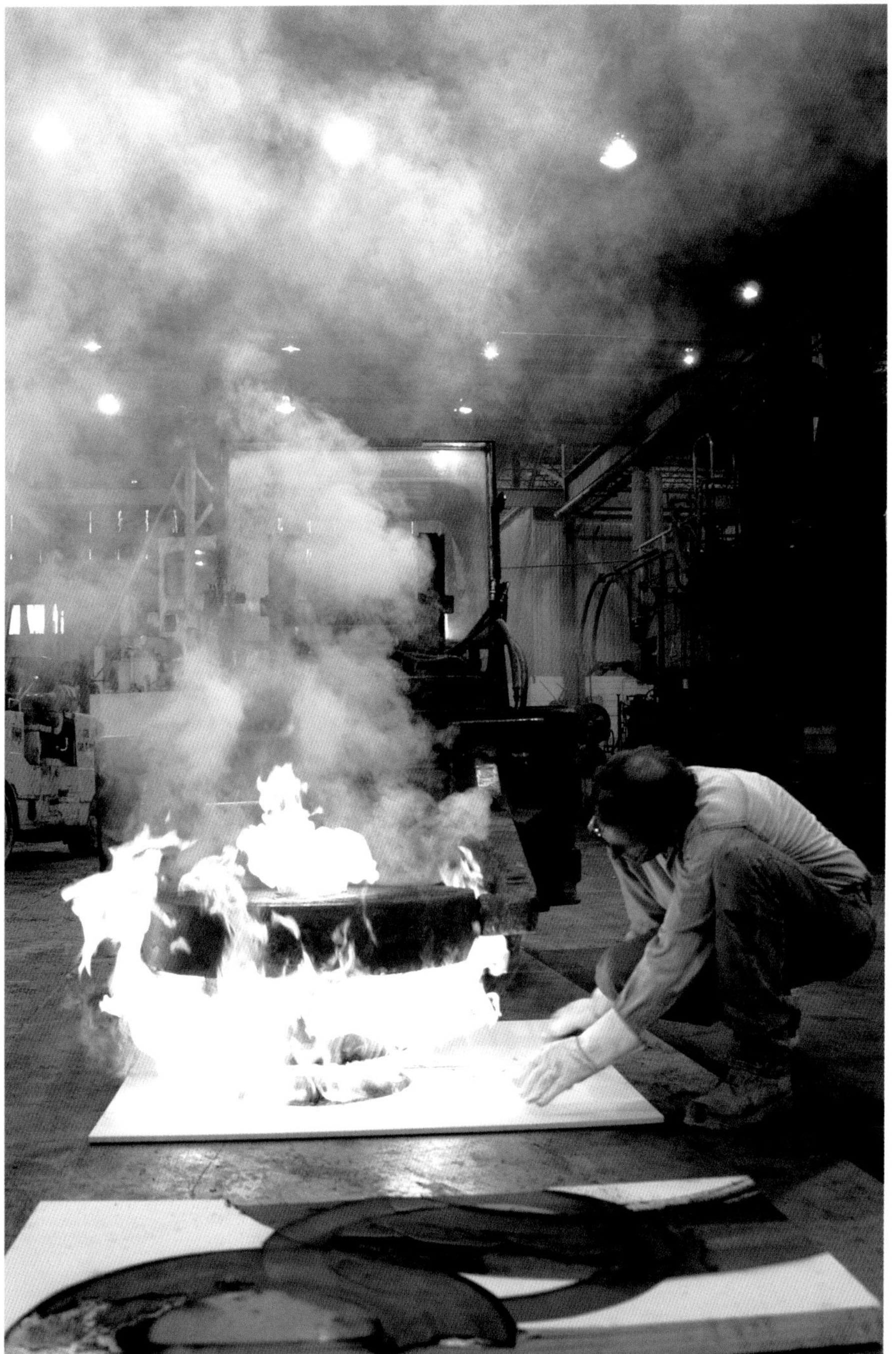

Tom Joyce. Process, Charring *Penumbra. Photo, Kate Joyce*

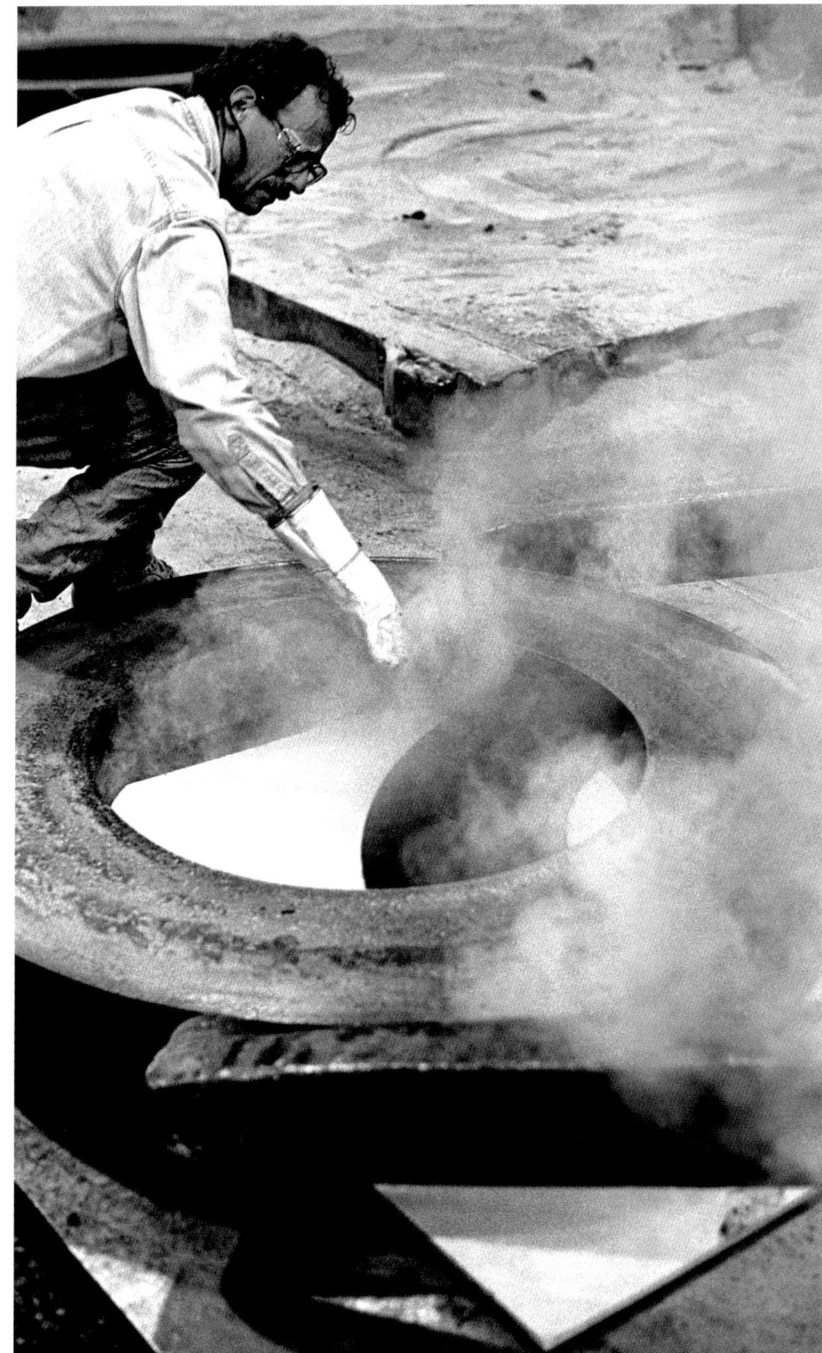

Tom Joyce. Process, Charring *Penumbra. Photo, Kate Joyce*

Tom Joyce. *Bloom III*, 2005. Forged iron. 28" x 30" x 30", 4079 lbs. *Photo, artist*

Bloom is forged from various industrial remnants that were turned inside out by forging and folding so that their original, recognizable skin is now hidden inside its folds. In smelting terminology, a bloom is the raw, sponge-like iron mass before refining into bar or plate. In many small-scale indigenous smelting traditions, a bloom is considered a child awaiting a future that is determined by the blacksmith. Among some traditional cultures in Africa, human creation and fertility is implied at every step of iron's manufacture. A bloom, as available material, is poised to become anything a blacksmith desires. – Tom Joyce

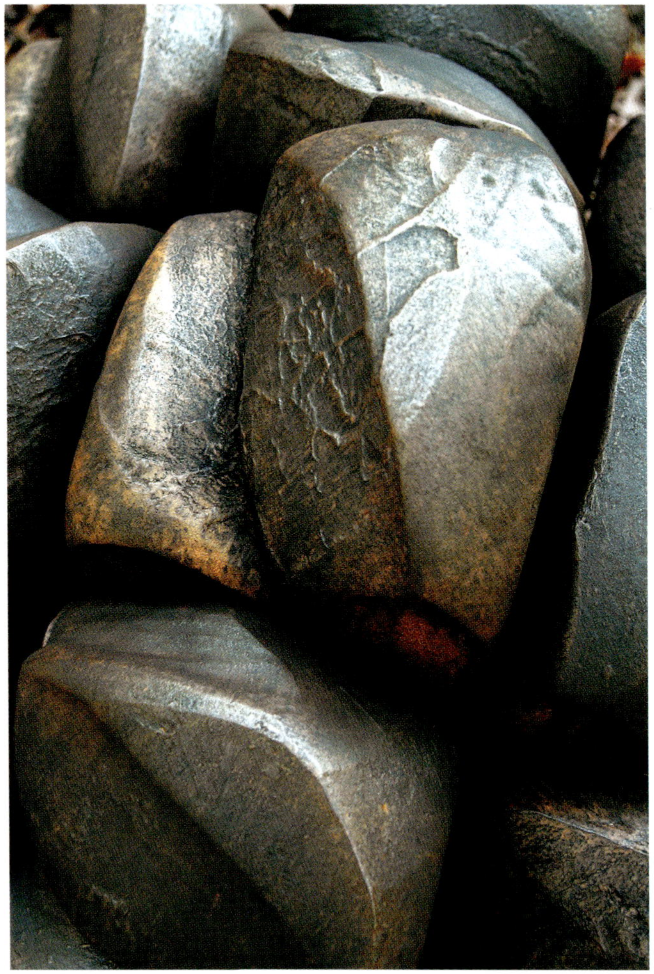

Tom Joyce. *Bloom III*, 2005. Detail. *Photo, artist*

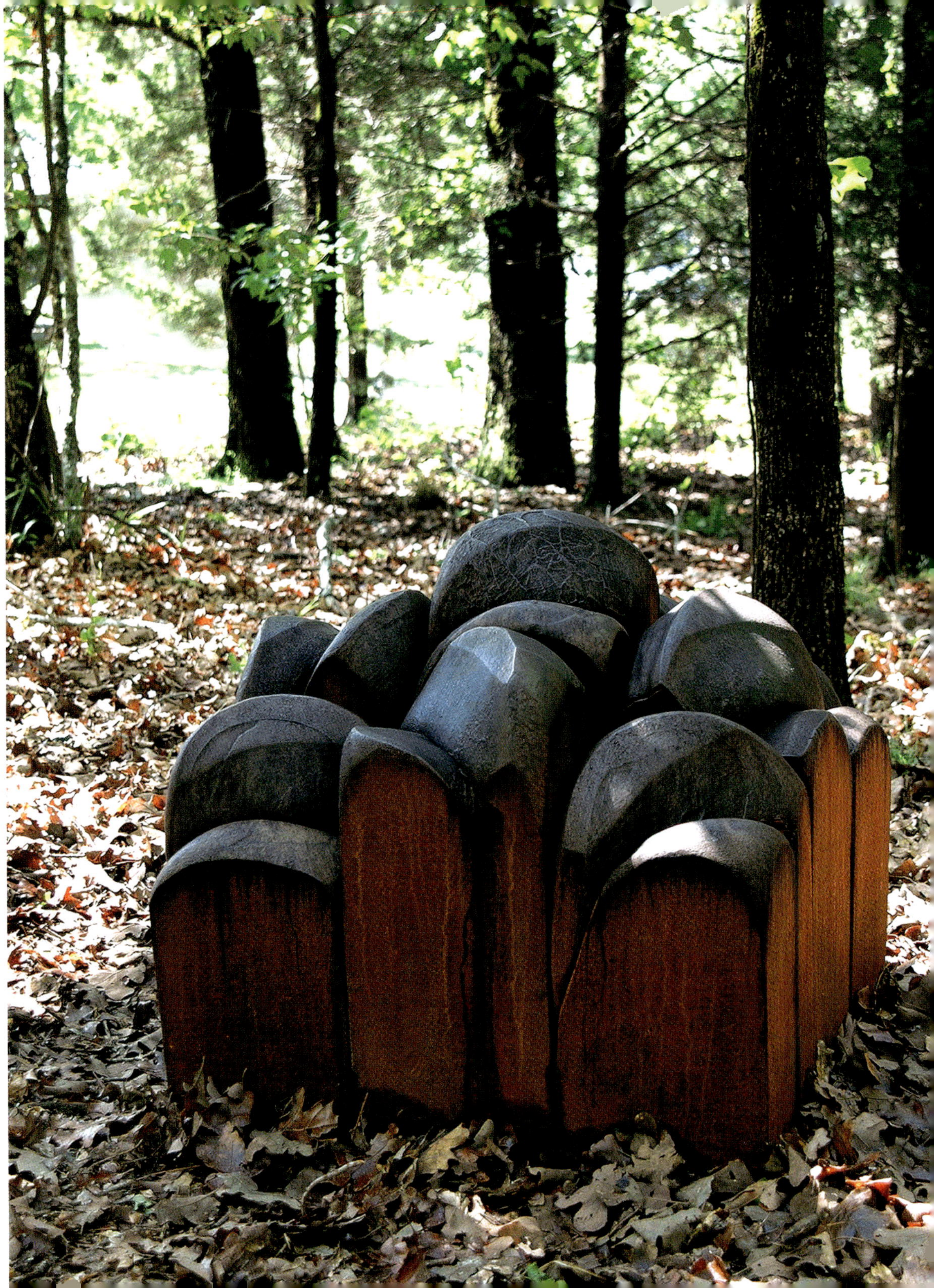

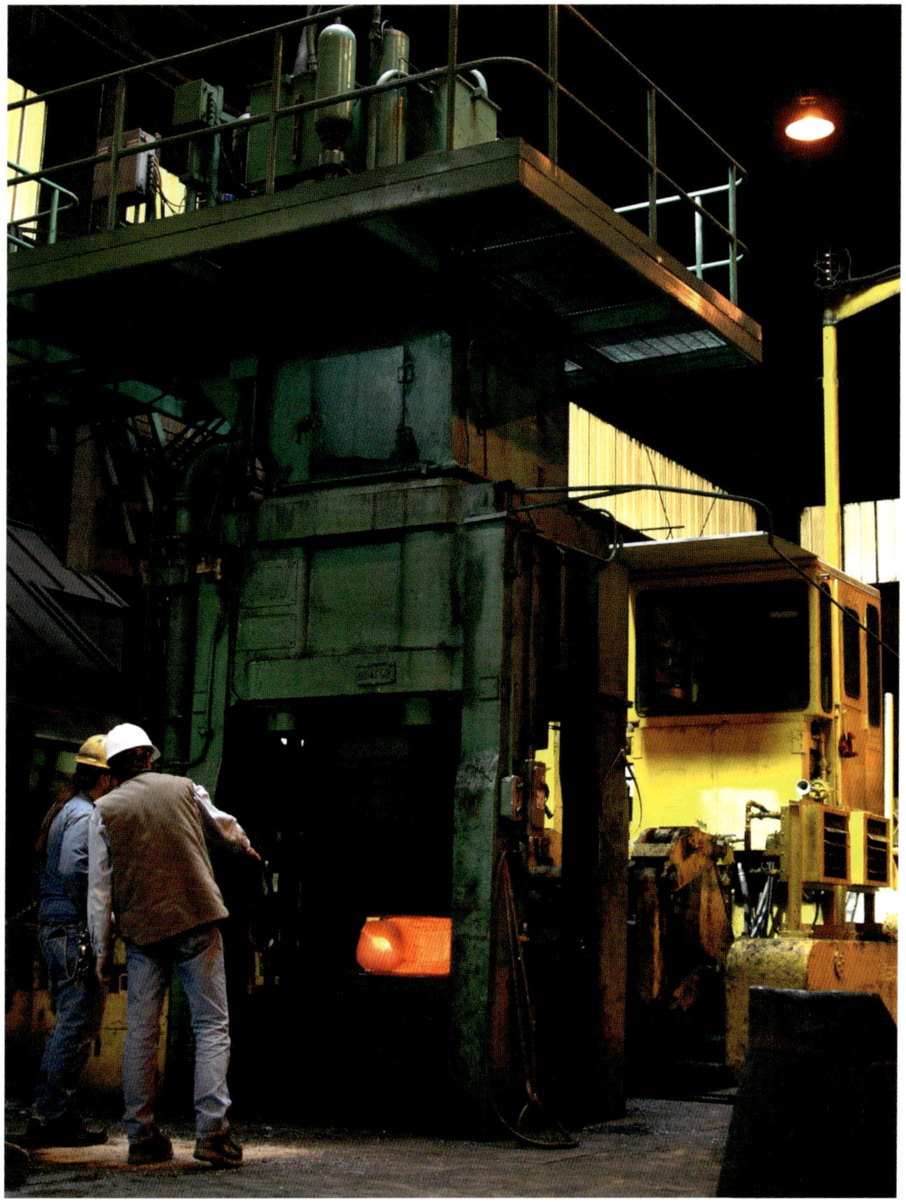

Tom Joyce. Process, Forging *Bloom* elements at 750-ton press. *Photo, Kate Joyce*

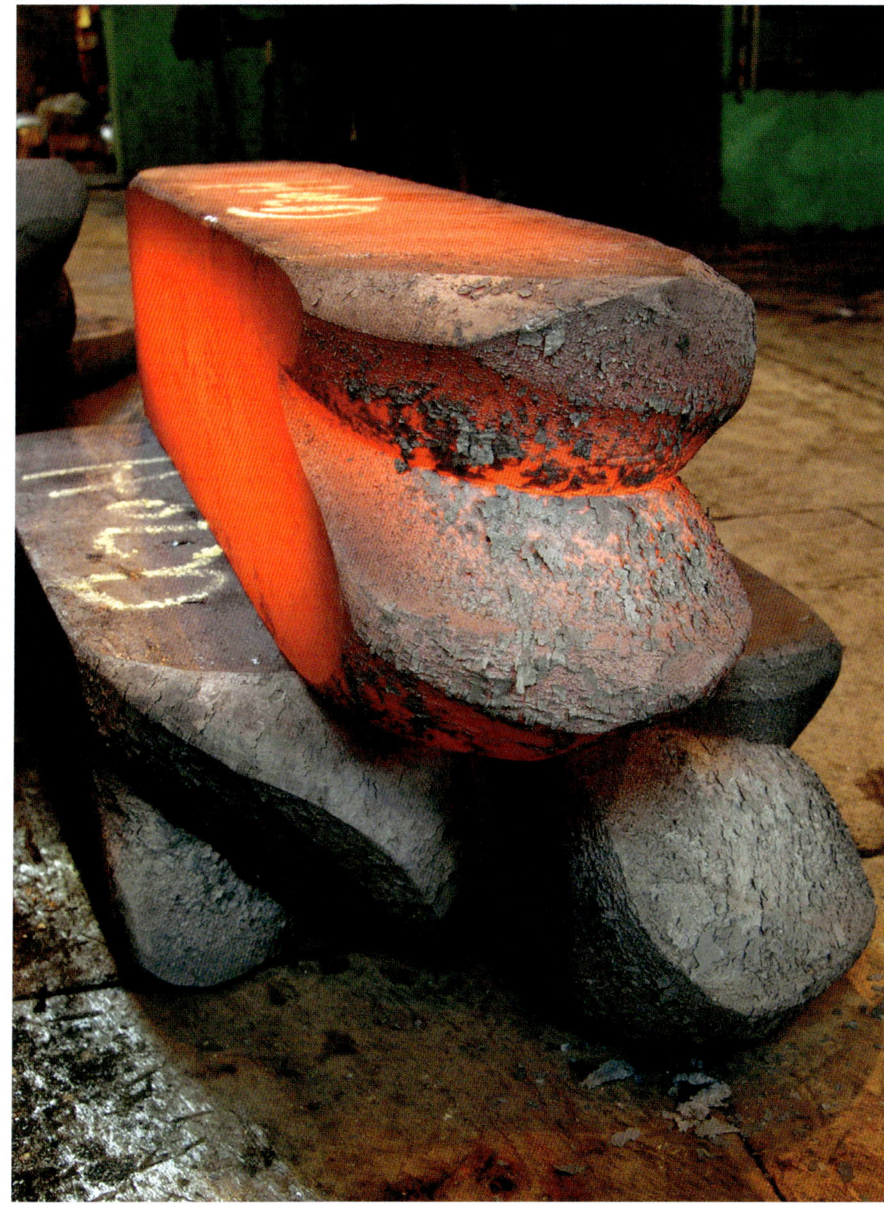

Tom Joyce. Process, Forging *Bloom* elements. *Photo, Kate Joyce*

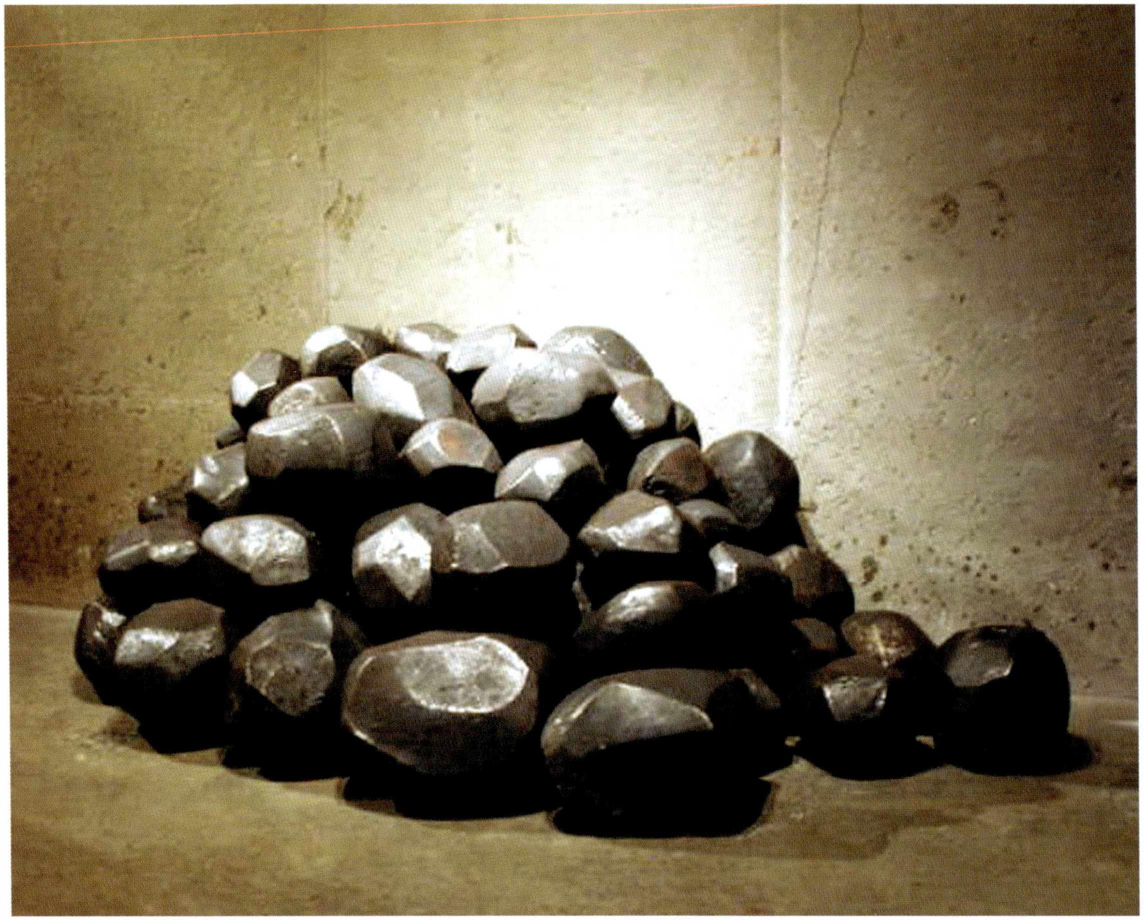

Tom Joyce. *Iron Cairn.* Forged iron, battlefield soil, dimensions variable. *Photo, artist*

Iron Cairn is a reliquary-like international war memorial, constructed from forged iron "boulders" made from salvaged industrial scrap. In the spirit of global collaboration, citizens in every region of the world are encouraged to participate in this ongoing project by contributing soil samples gathered from battlefields around the world. Eventually hundreds of "boulders" will hold small quantities of donated soil, concealed behind a plaque that identifies when and where the battle was fought and between what peoples. The battles date from the earliest recorded history through the present day.

Like travelers or pilgrims that make offerings of a stone onto a growing pile on mountain passes or at significant landmarks, participants in this project will offer up collected soil to acknowledge that no one is unscathed by acts of war. – Tom Joyce

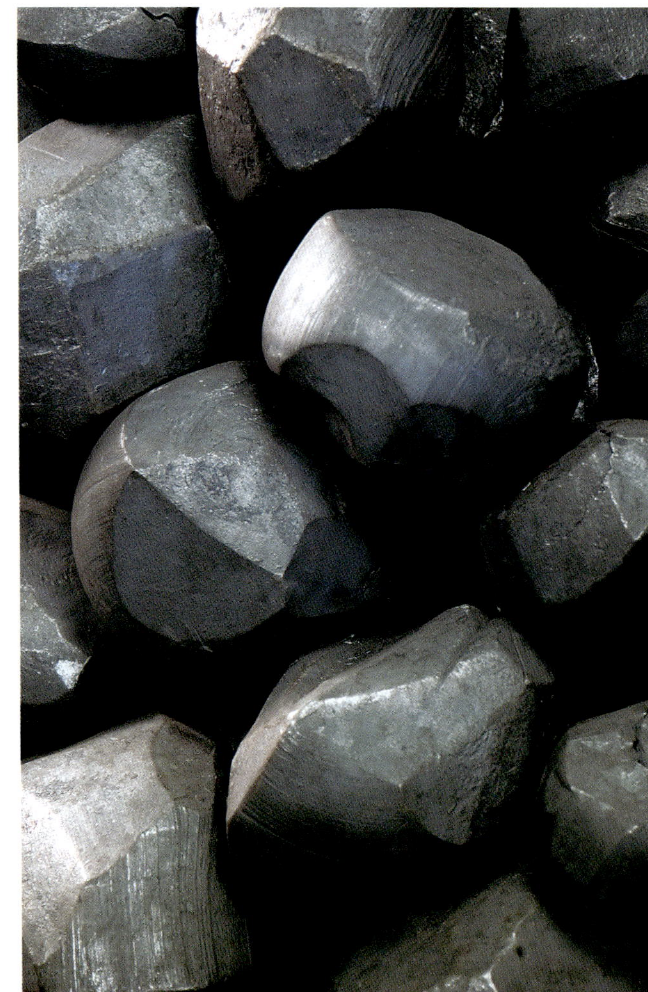

Tom Joyce. *Iron Cairn.* Detail. *Photo, artist*

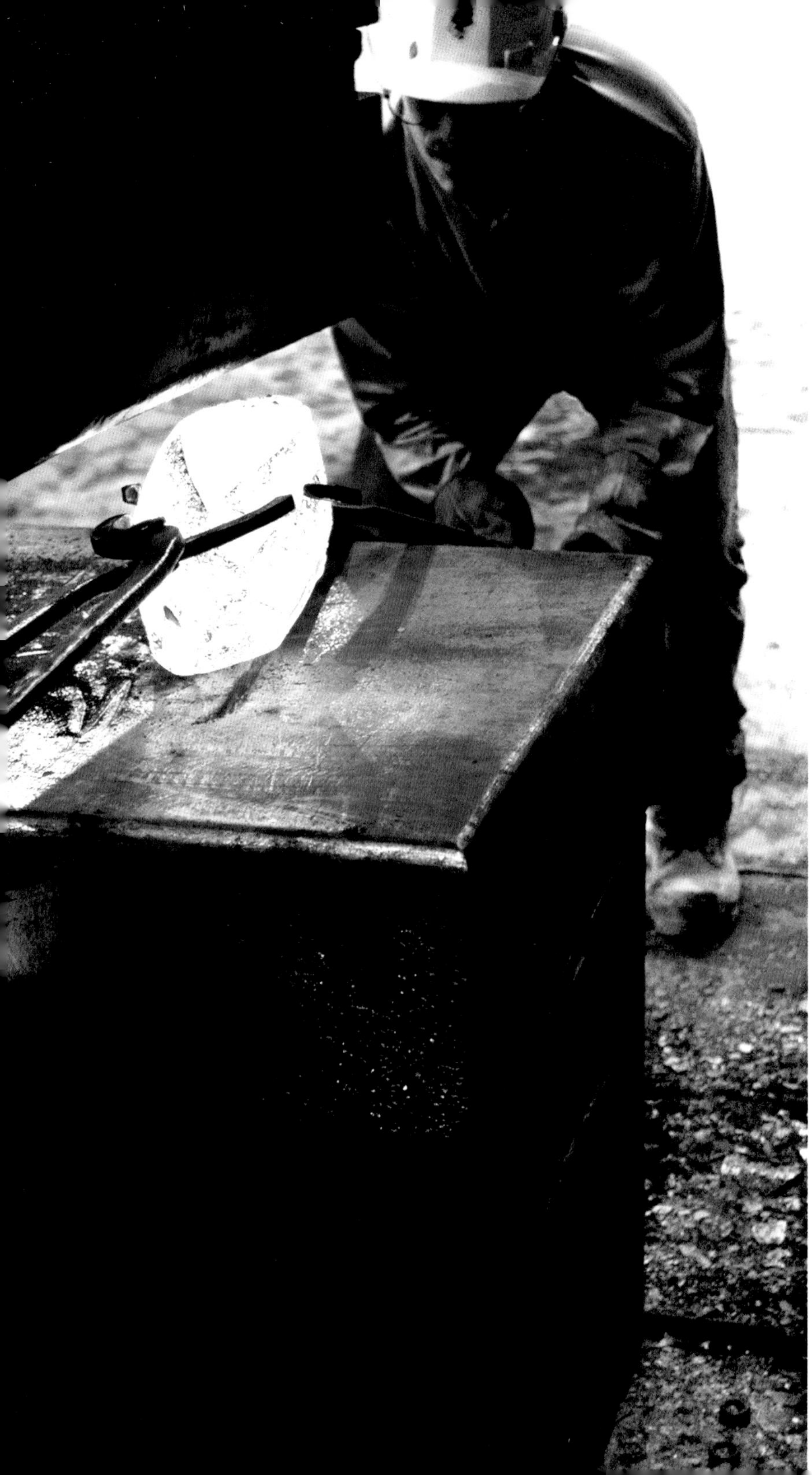

Tom Joyce. Process, Forging *Cairn*.
Photo, Kate Joyce

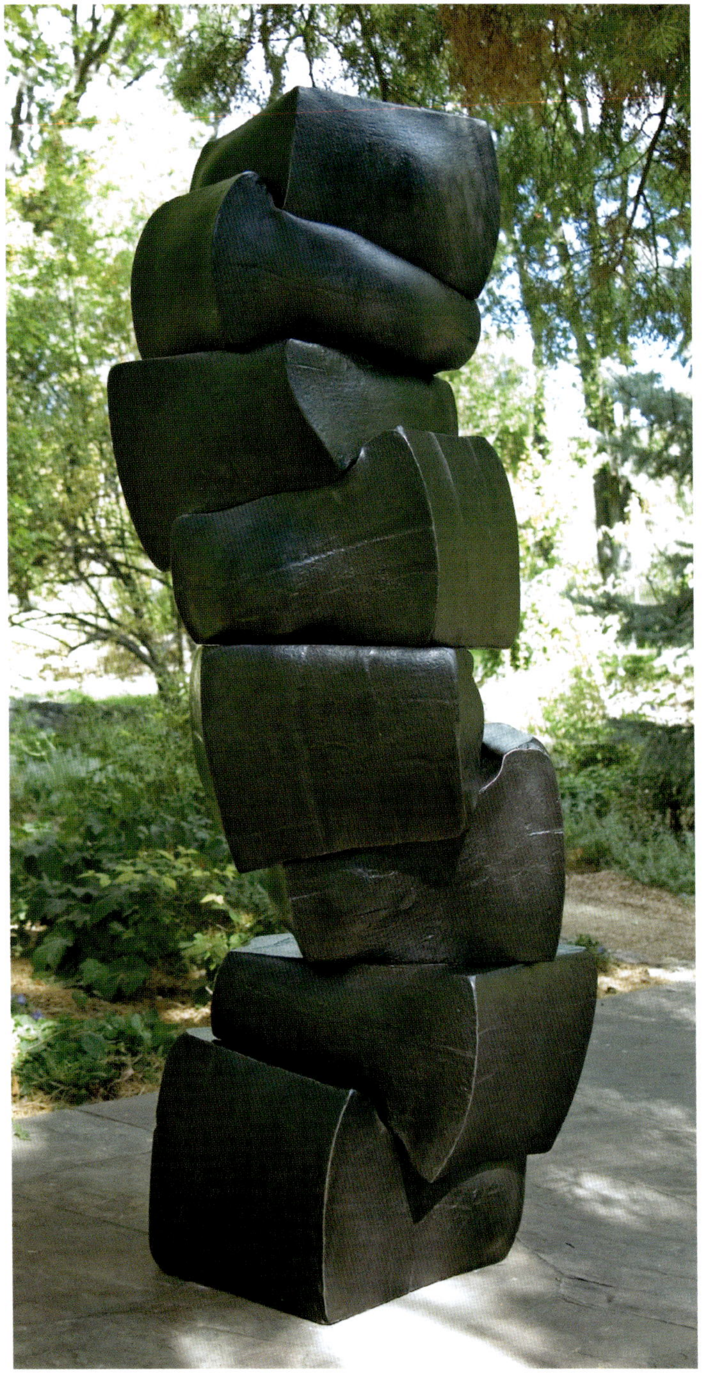

Tom Joyce. *Stacked,* 2006/2007. Forged iron. 74" h x 34" w x 32" d, 5507 lbs. *Photo, artist*

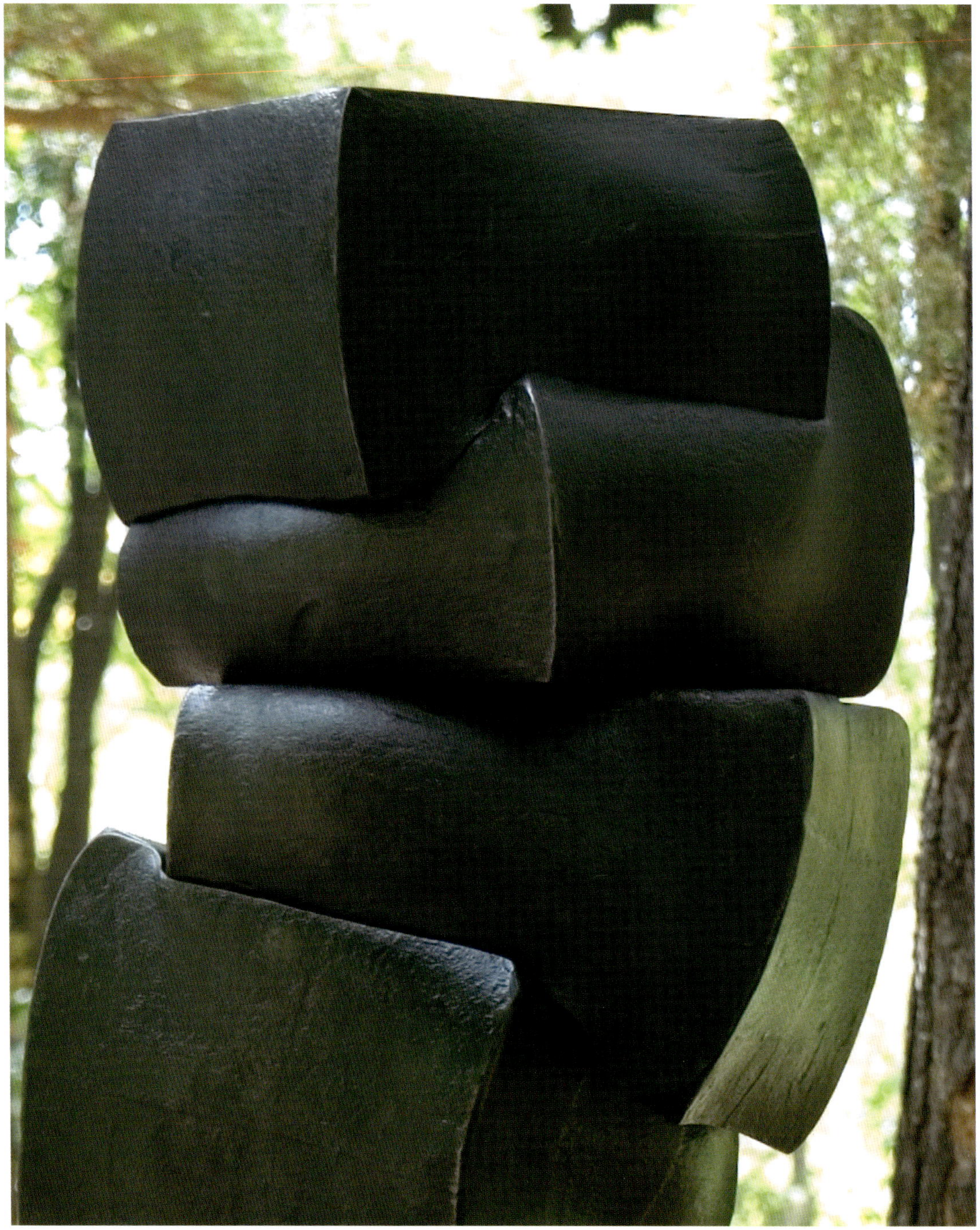

Tom Joyce. *Stacked,* 2006/2007. Detail. *Photo, artist*

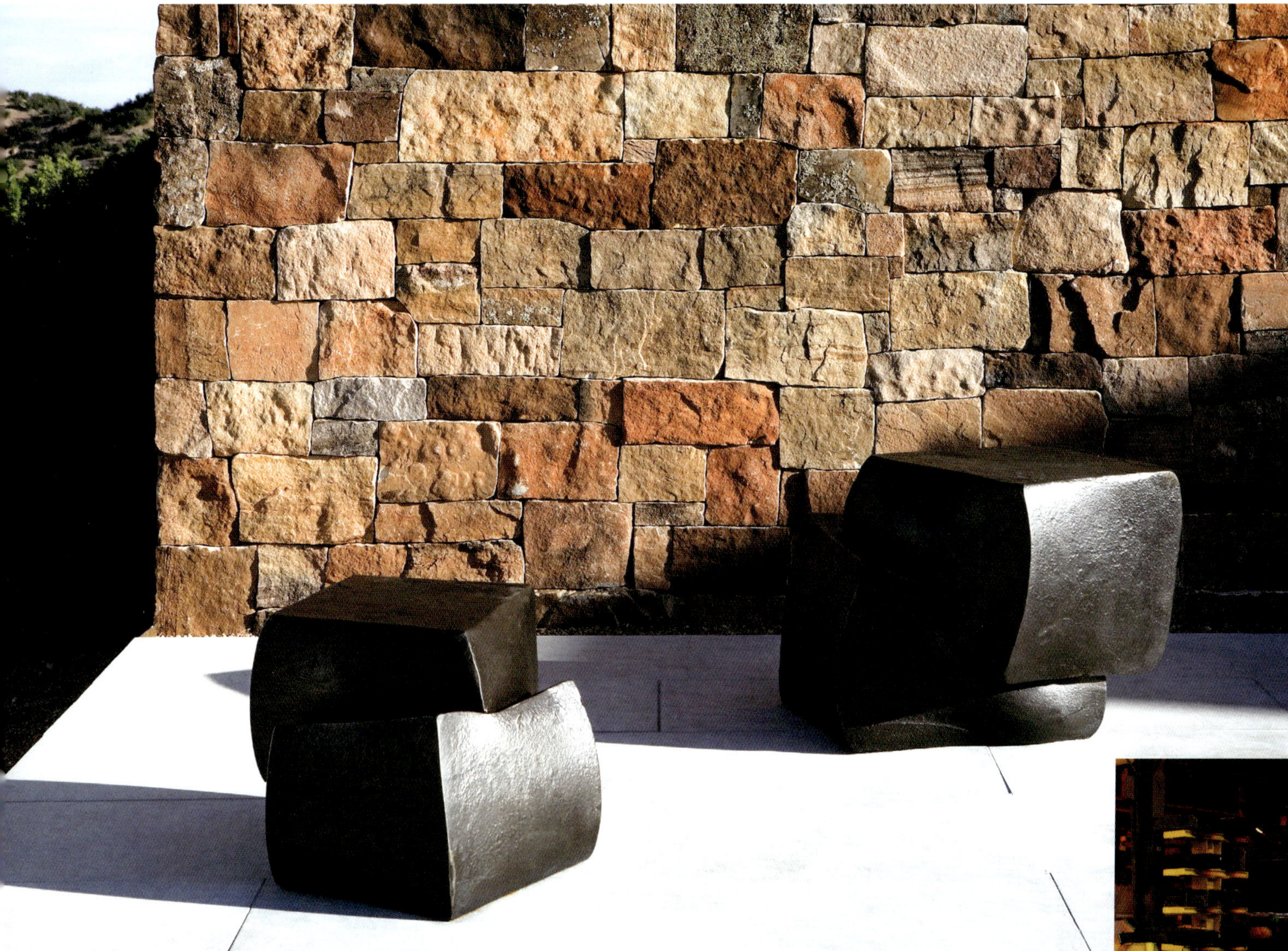

Tom Joyce. *Two to One*, 2005. Forged iron, Left – 1140 lbs. 15.5" h x 20.5" w x 19.5" d, Right – 1923 lbs, 19.5" h x 24.5" w x 23.5" d. *Photo, Robert Reck*

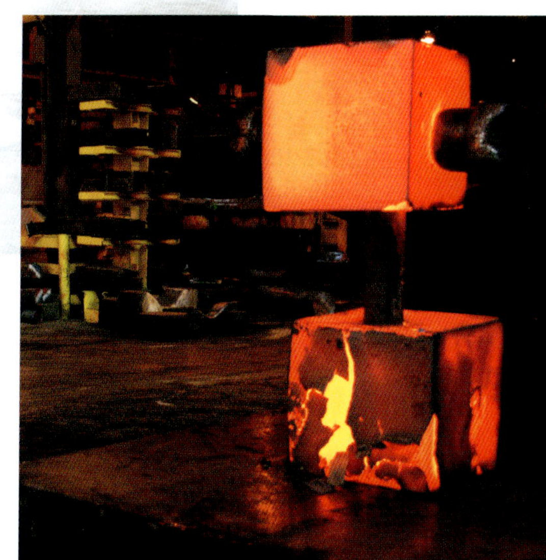

Tom Joyce. Process, forging *Two to One* at 3000 Ton Press. *Photo, Kate Joyce*

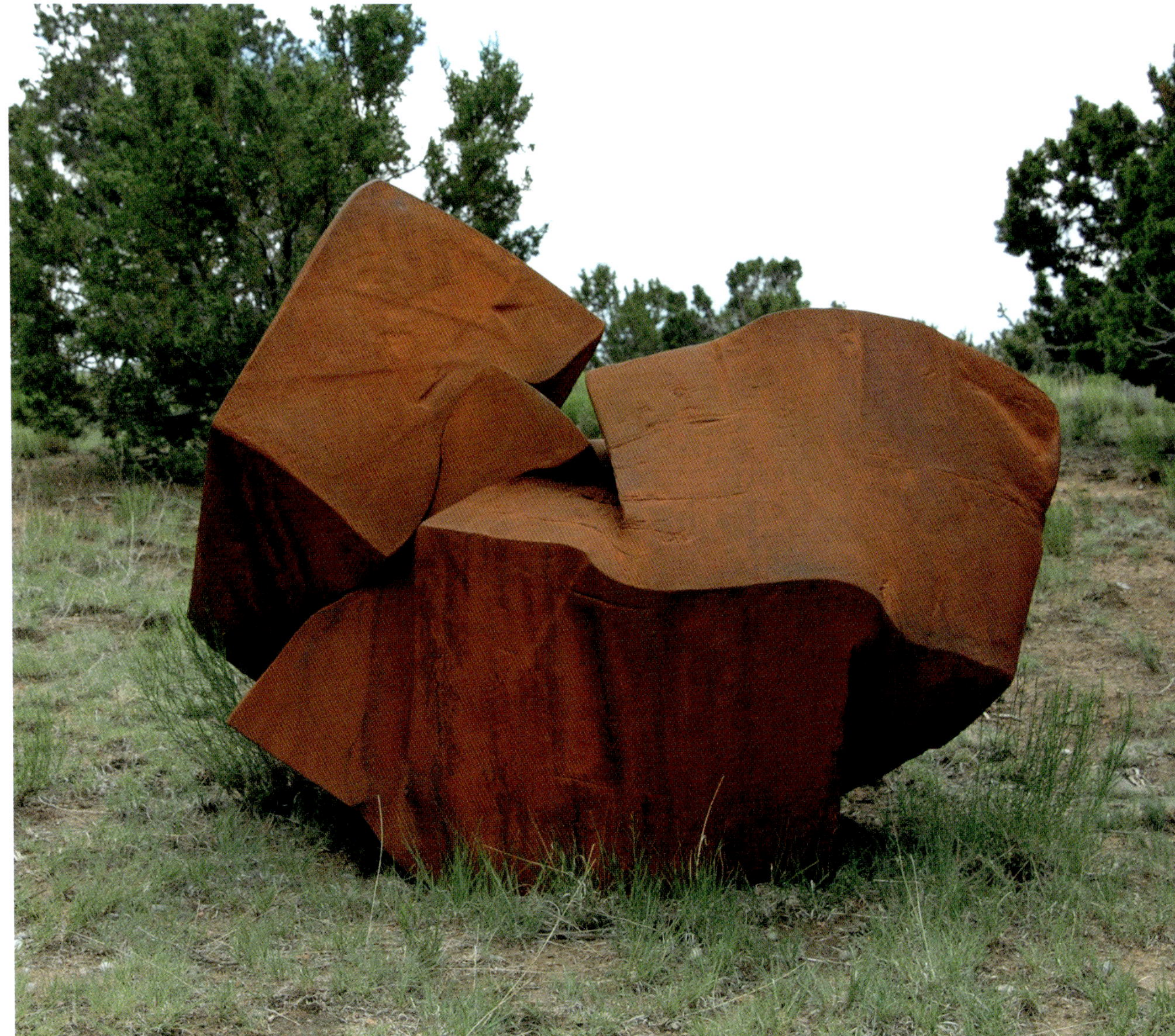

Tom Joyce. *Berg XV*, 2006/2007. Forged iron. 35" h x 51" w x 35.5" d, 6683 lbs. *Photo, artist*

Berg was forged from a scrap ingot and literally refers to the tip remaining of a much larger piece of iron that is now incorporated into an industrial purpose somewhere in the world. After forging the remnant down into a large square bar, it is cut almost all the way through on each of its four faces as it's rotated to reference the cardinal directions. While clamping one end securely, the bar is twisted by machine clockwise 120°. It was then turned up on end and upset between the 5500-ton hydraulic press dies, and squeezed almost to the breaking point. Each section hangs on by a thin web. – Tom Joyce

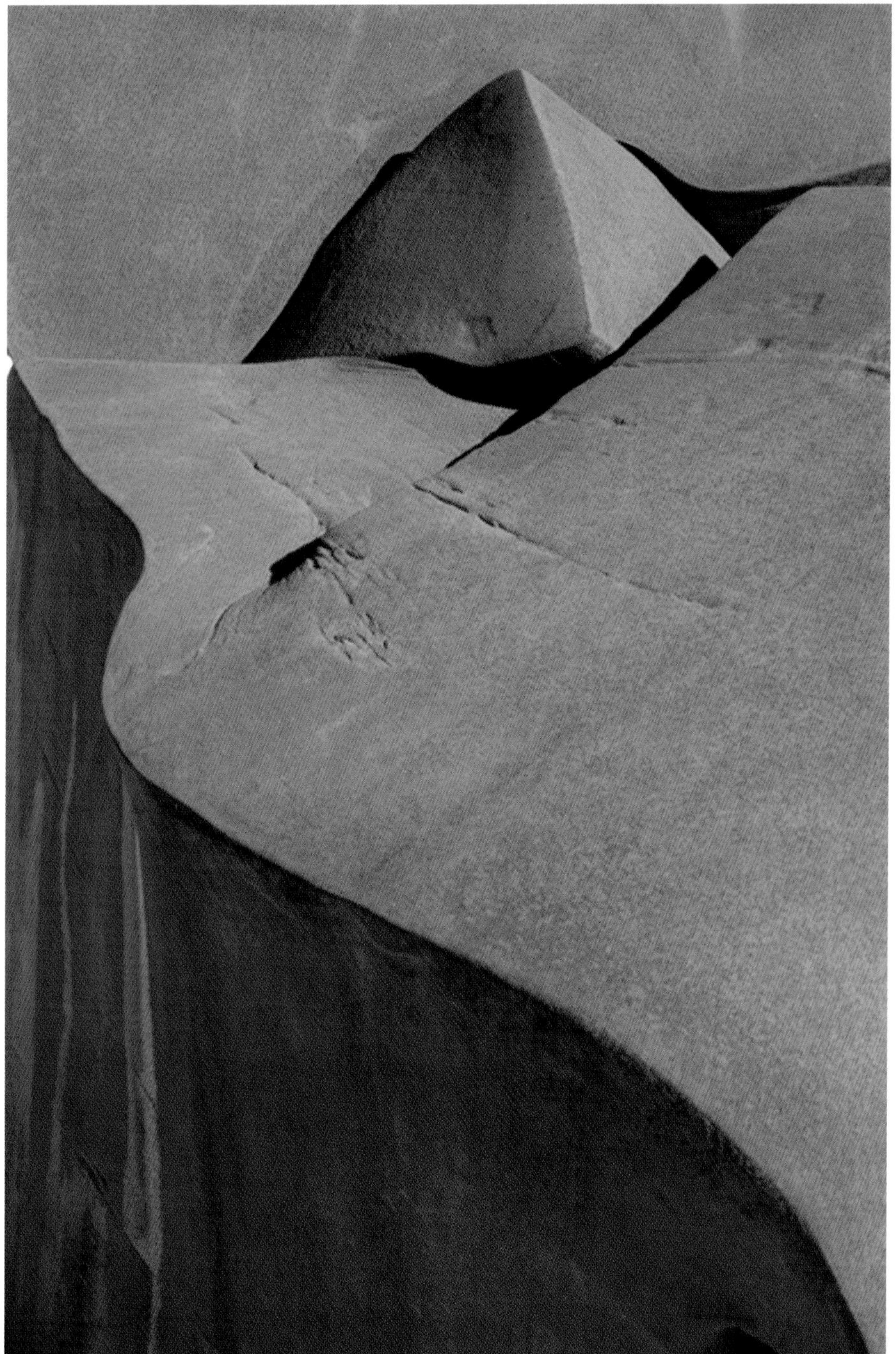

Tom Joyce. *Berg XV*, 2006/2007. Detail. *Photo, artist*

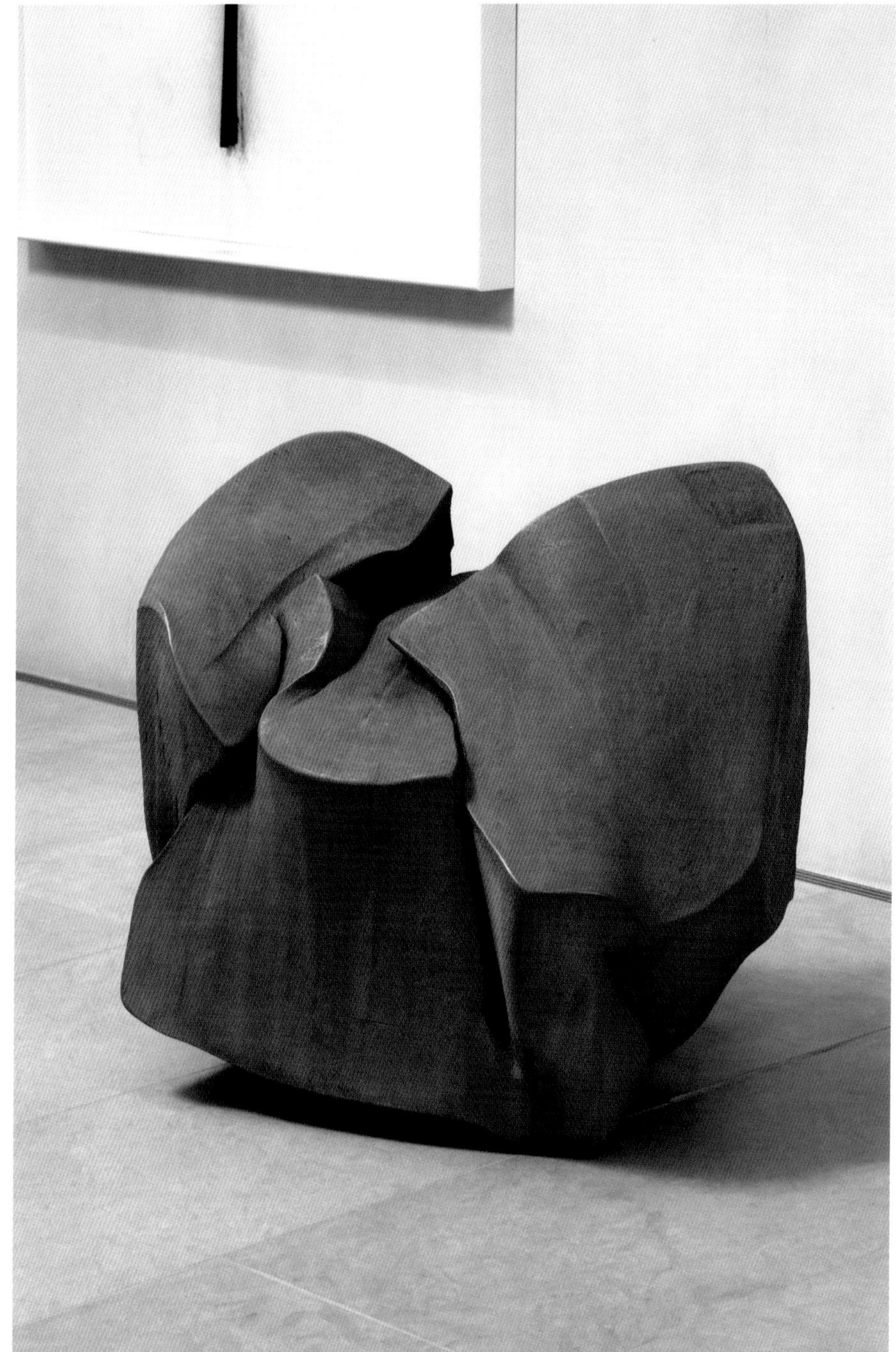

Tom Joyce. *Berg IV*, 2005. Forged iron. 32" h x 36" w x 24" d, 2354 lbs. *Photo, Robert Reck*

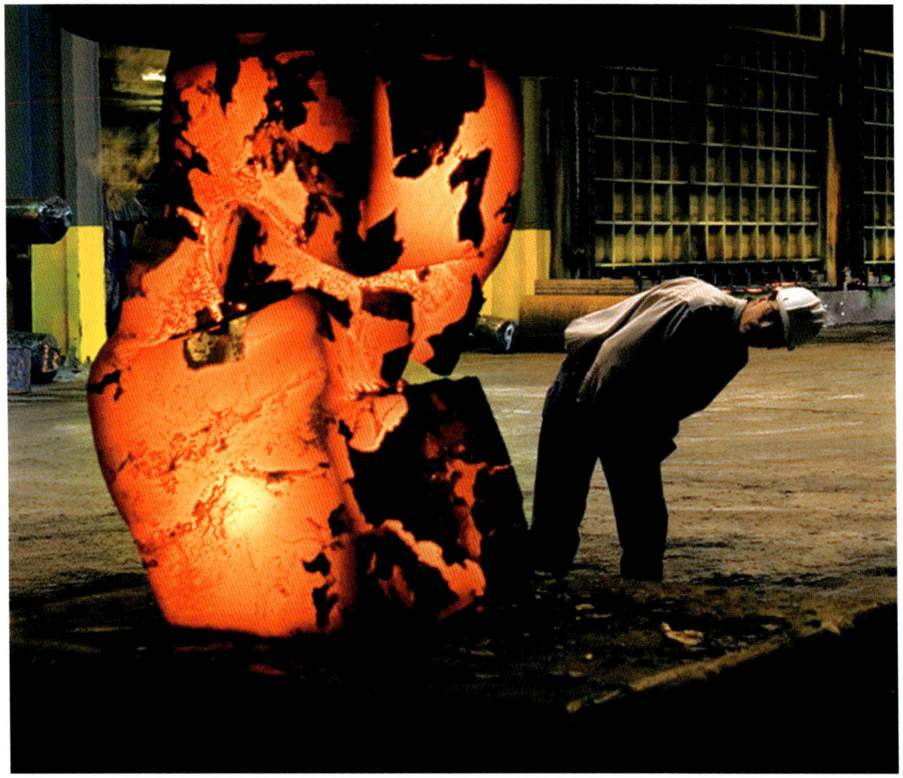

Tom Joyce. Process, Forging *Berg* at 5500-ton press. *Photo, Nigel Noble*

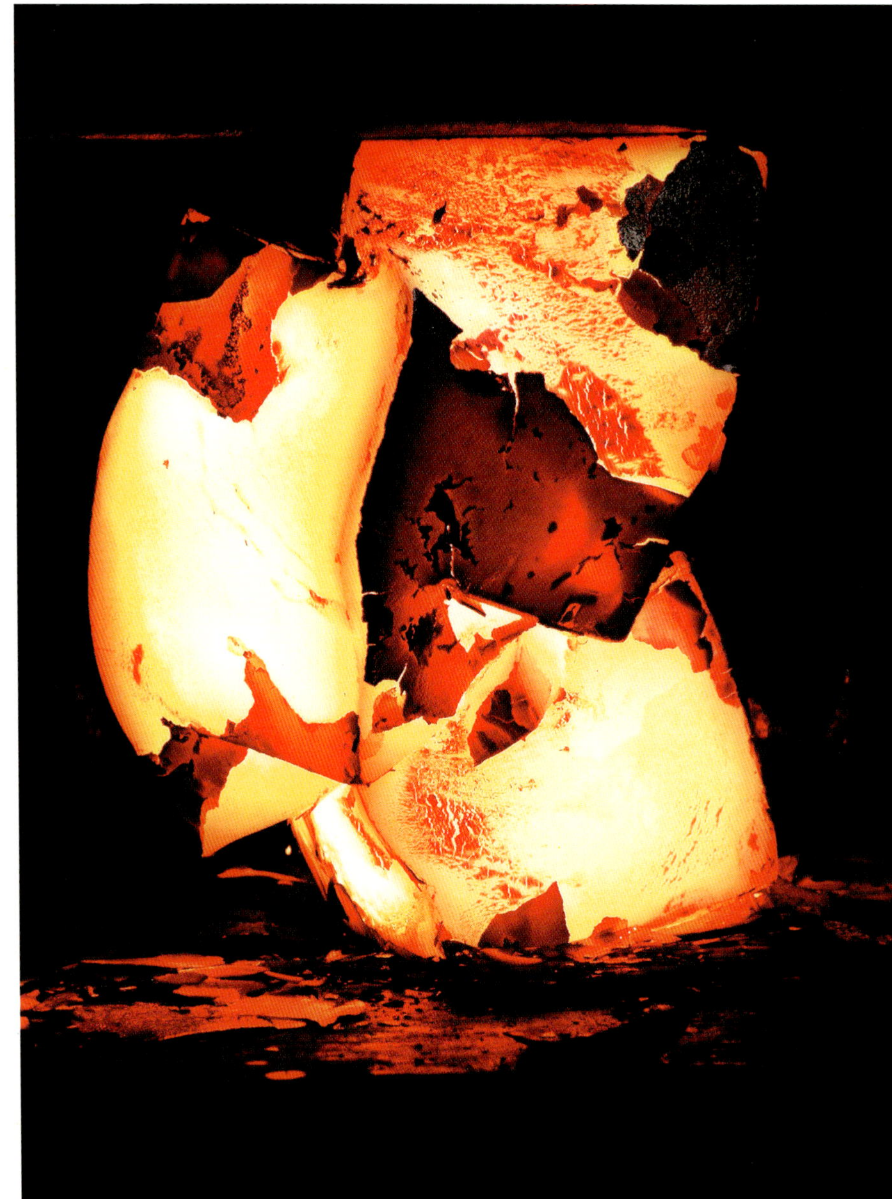

Tom Joyce. Process, Forging *Berg*. *Photo, Kate Joyce*

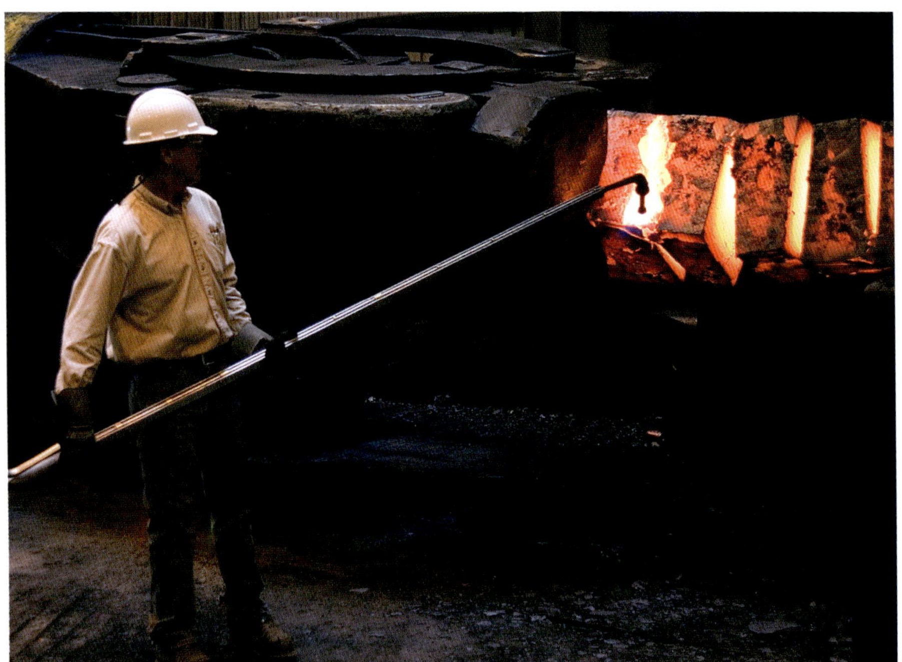

Tom Joyce. Process, Heating *Berg* at 5500-ton press while twisting. *Photo, Nigel Noble*

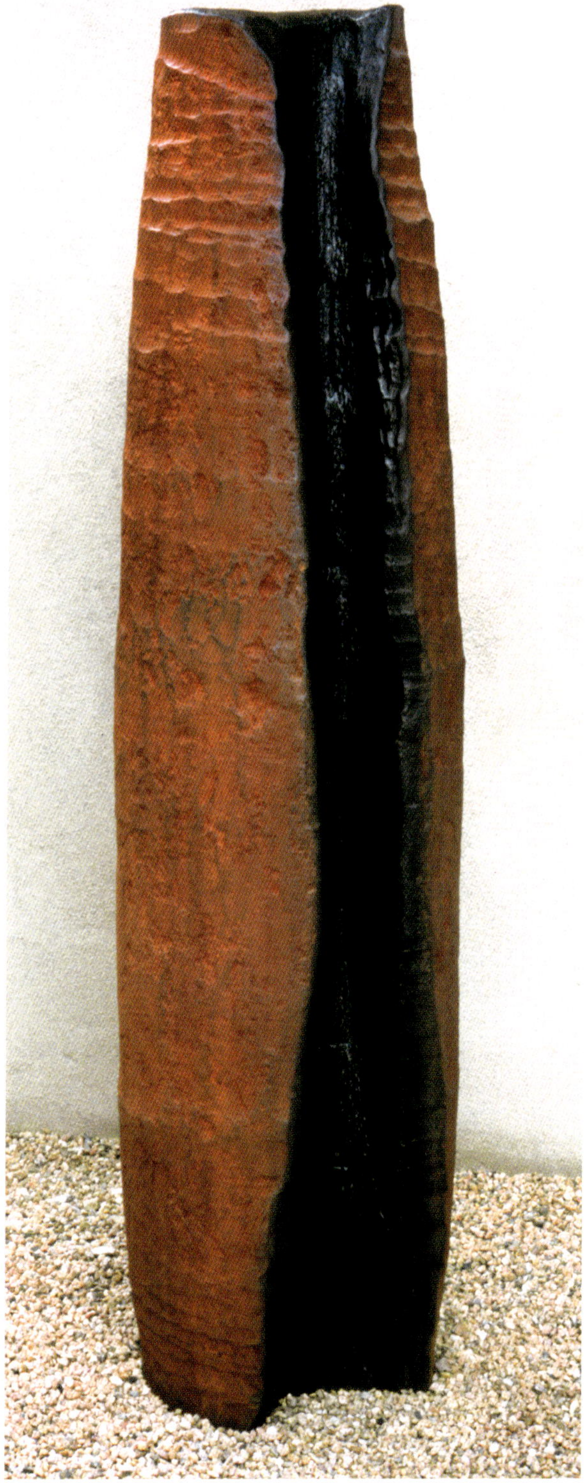

Tom Joyce. *Bifid II,* 2005. Forged iron. 65" h x 16.5" w x 15" d, 2856 lbs. *Photo, artist*

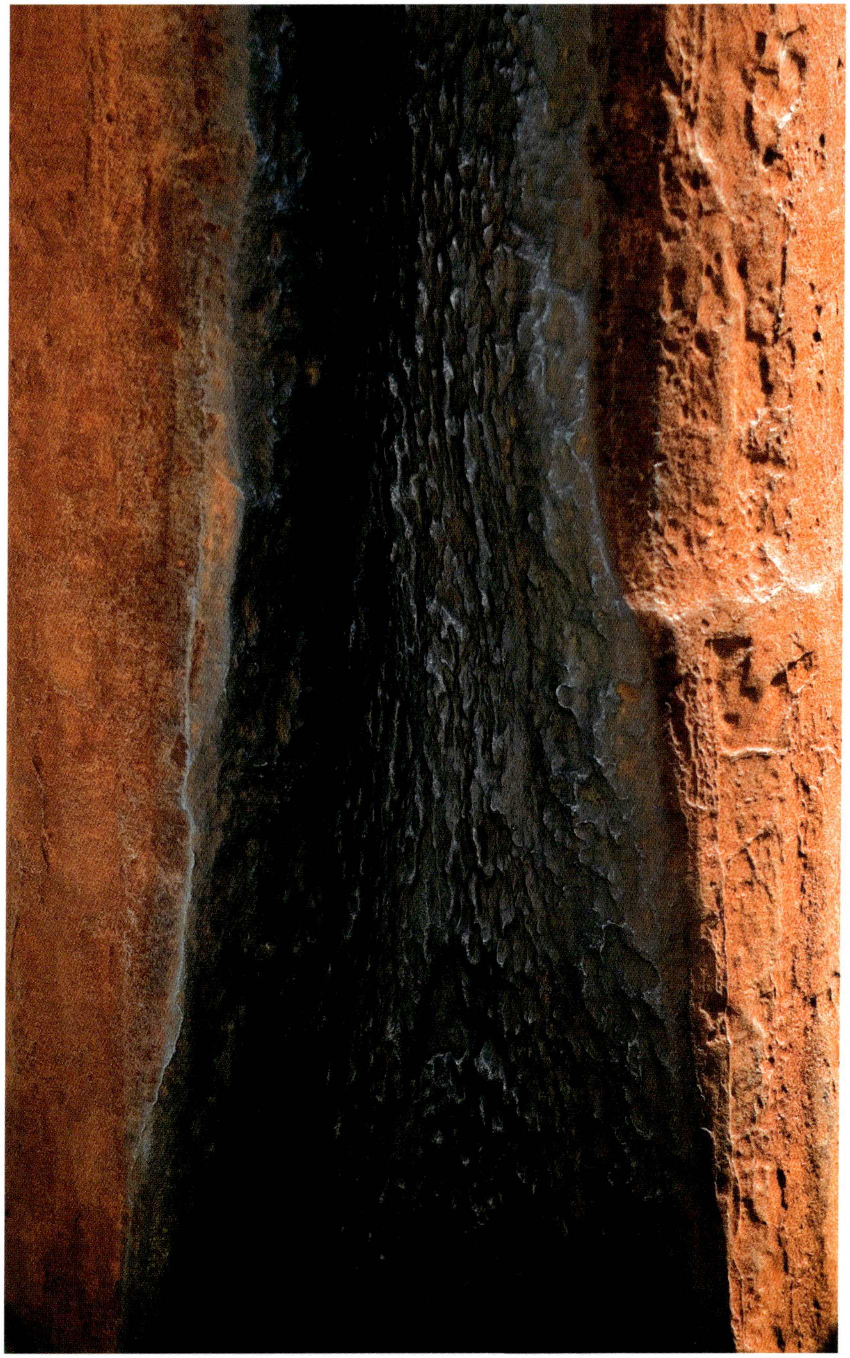

Tom Joyce. *Bifid II,* 2005. Detail. *Photo, artist*

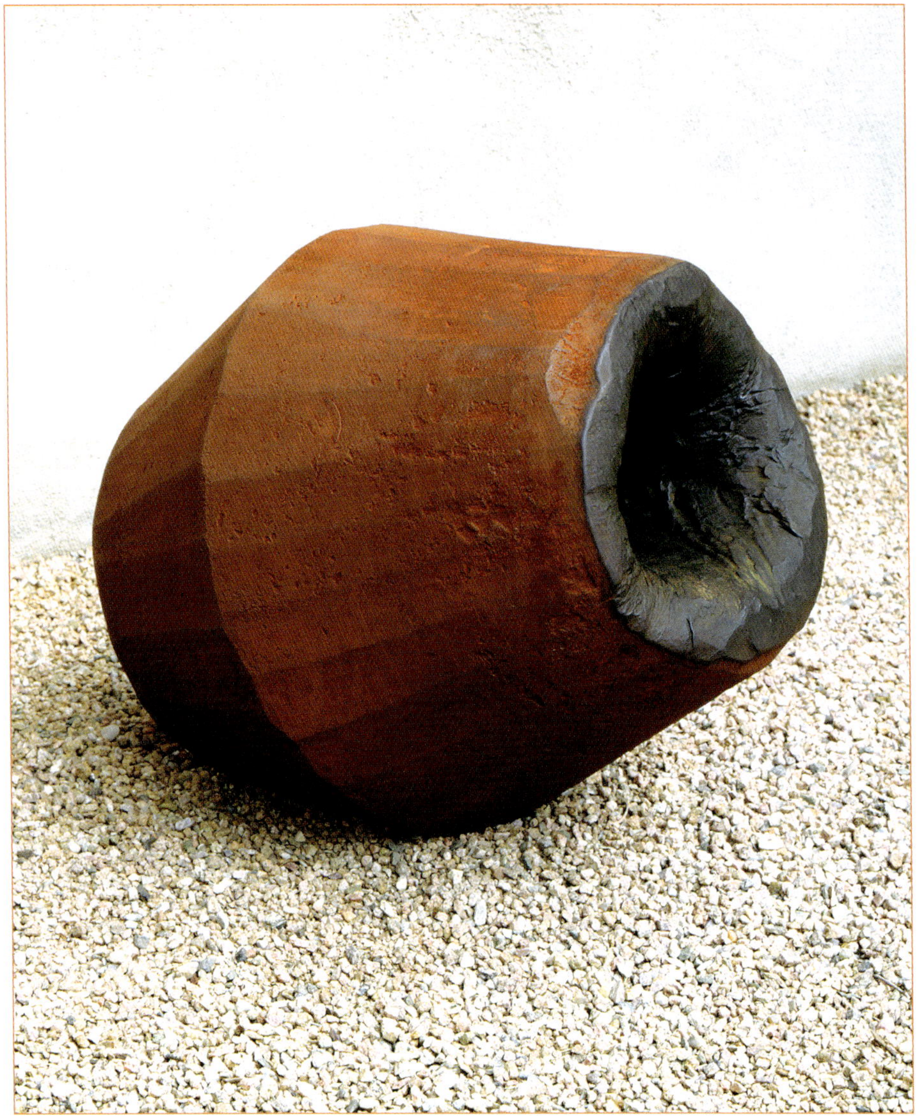

Tom Joyce. *Ootid,* 2005. Forged iron. 21.5" h x 20" w x 21" d, 1408 lbs. *Photo, artist*

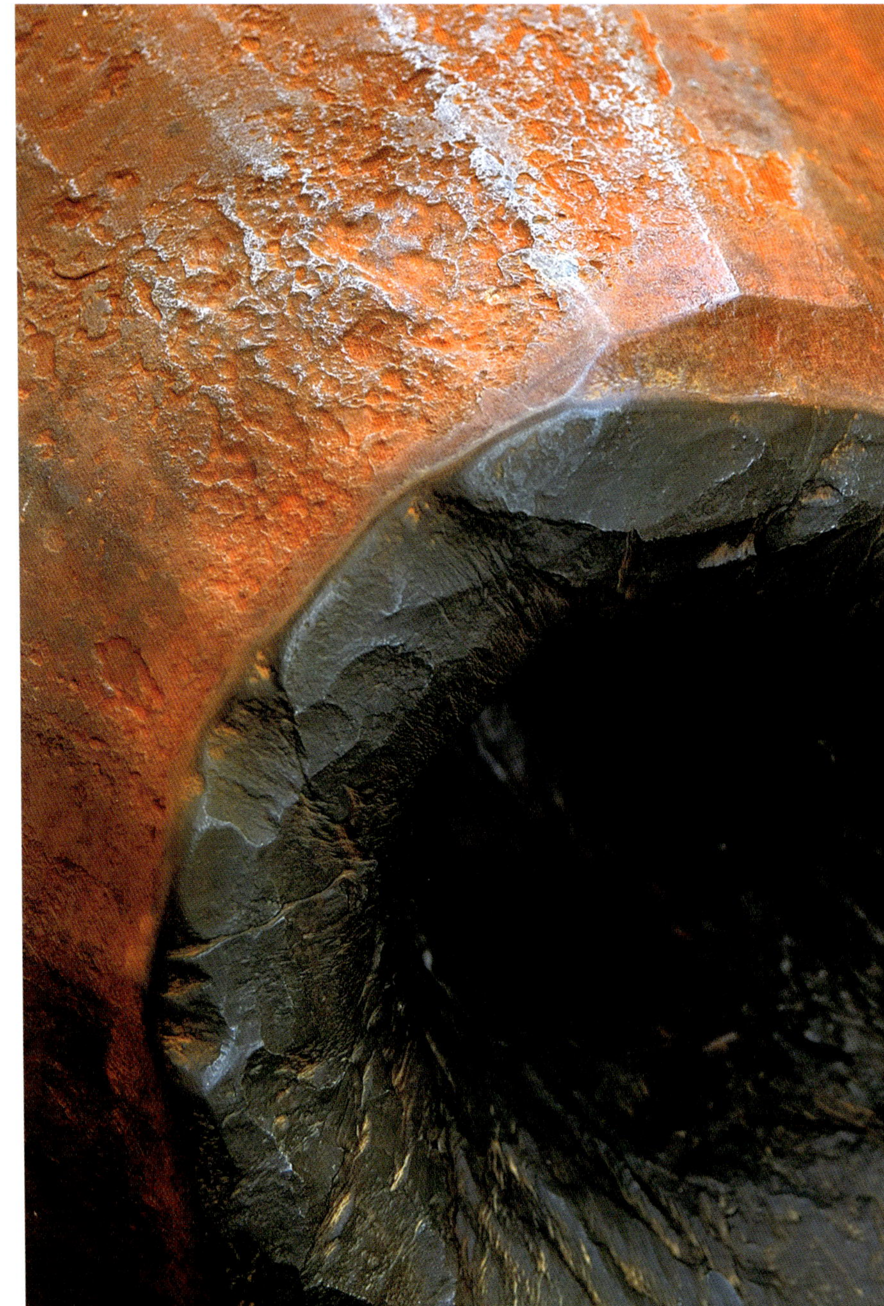

Tom Joyce. *Ootid,* 2005. Detail. *Photo, artist*

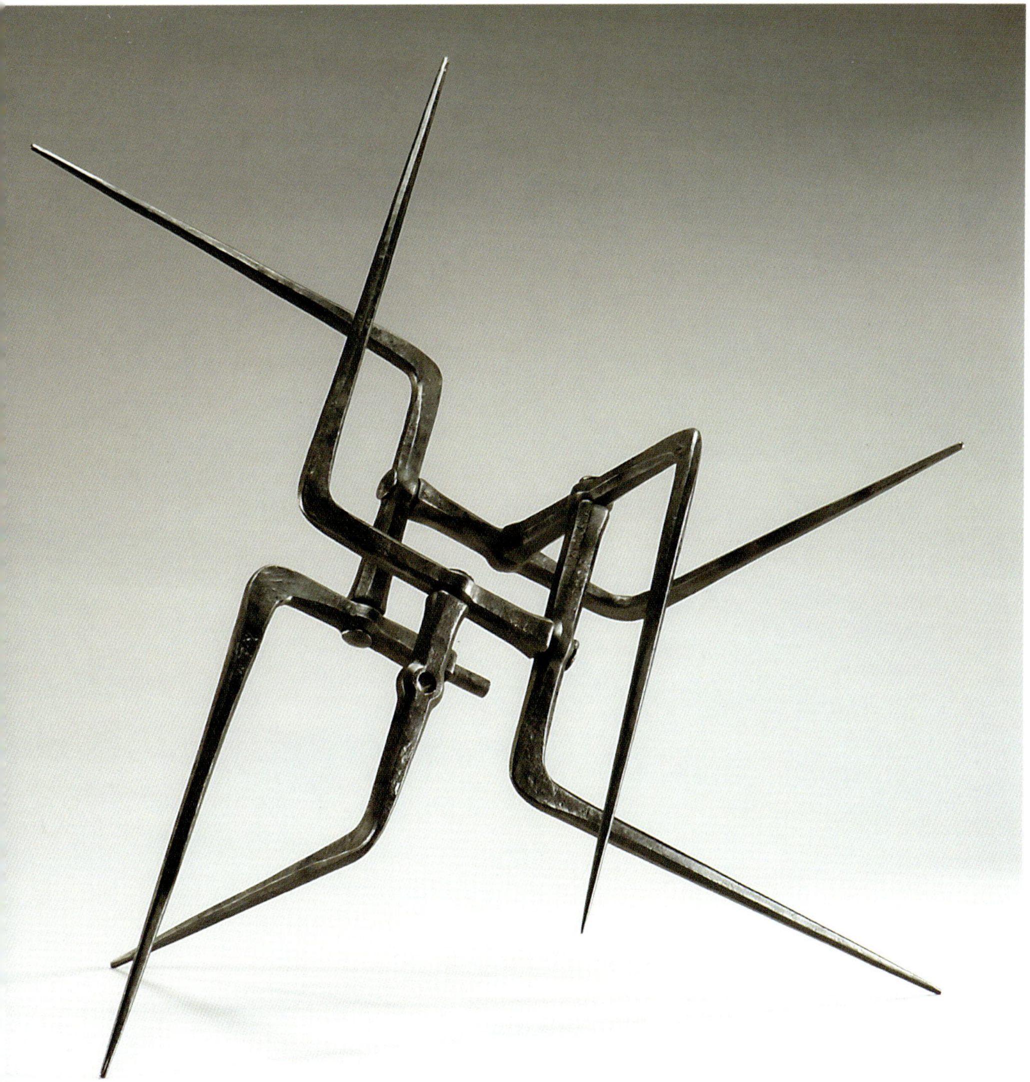

Zachary Noble. *Nodus #1,* 2007. Forged steel. 28" x 32" x 26". "Nodus" is from the words "knot or node," also meaning complication or difficulty. *Photo, Tom Mills*

Zachary Noble. *Nodus #1*. Detail image. *Photo, Tom Mills*

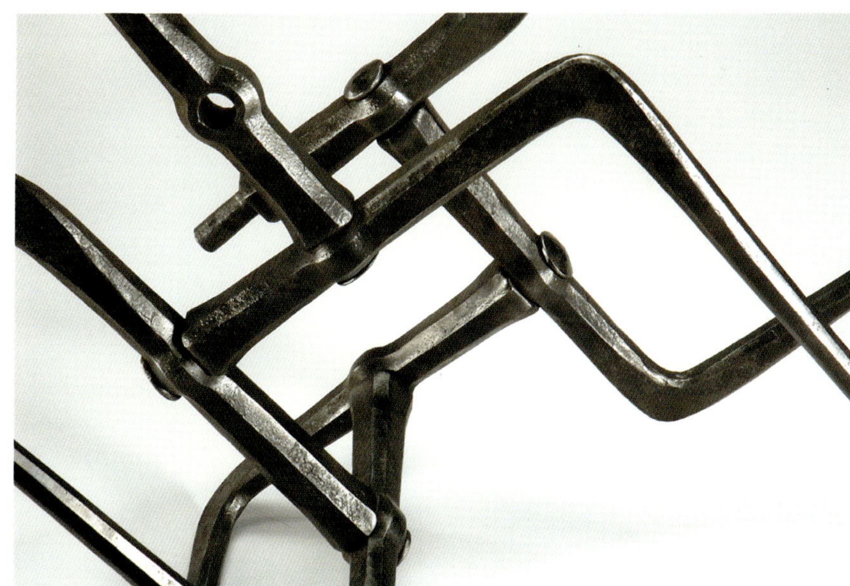

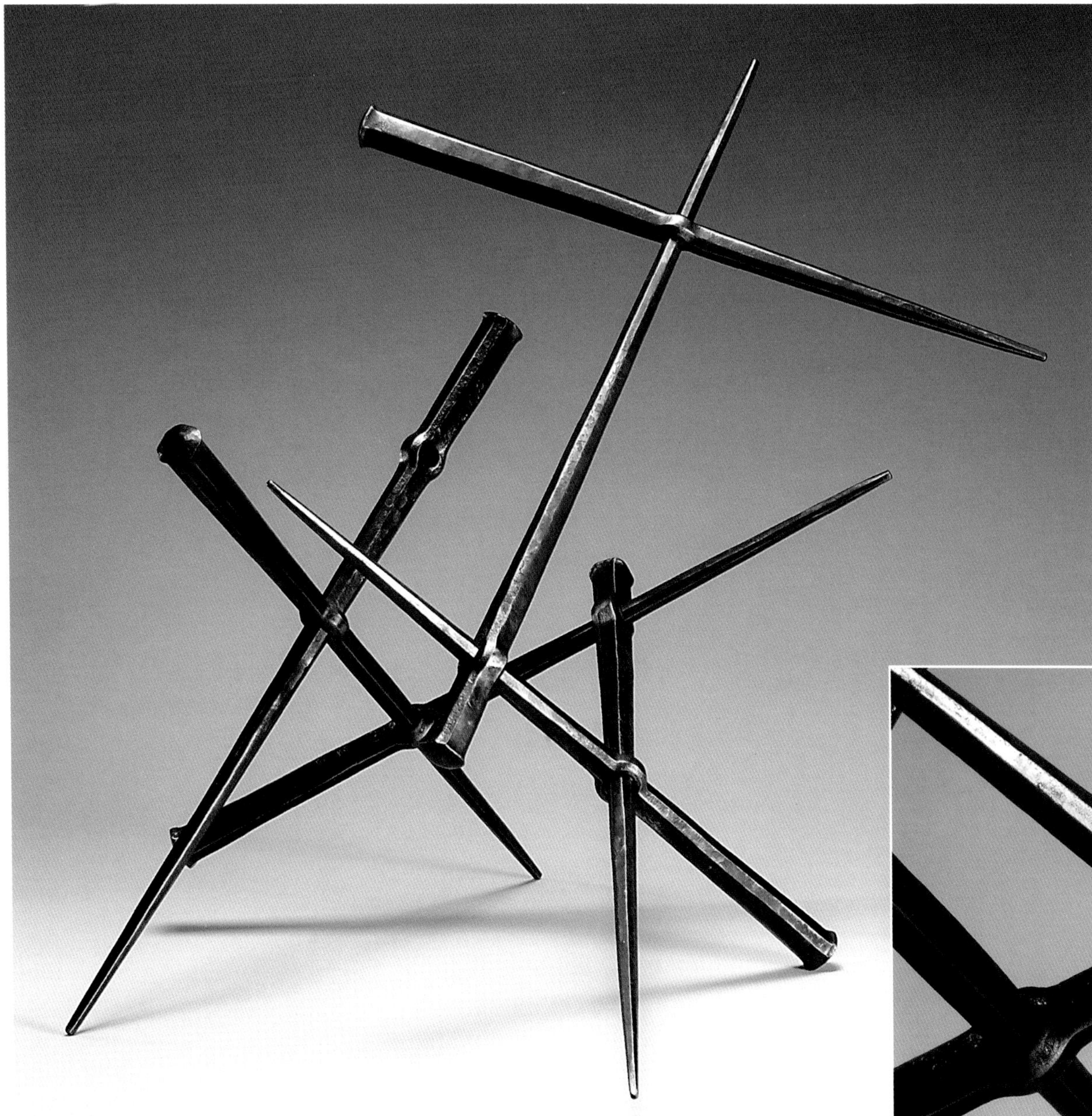

Zachary Noble. *Nodus #2*, 2007.
Forged steel. 28" x 22" x 30".
Photo, Tom Mills

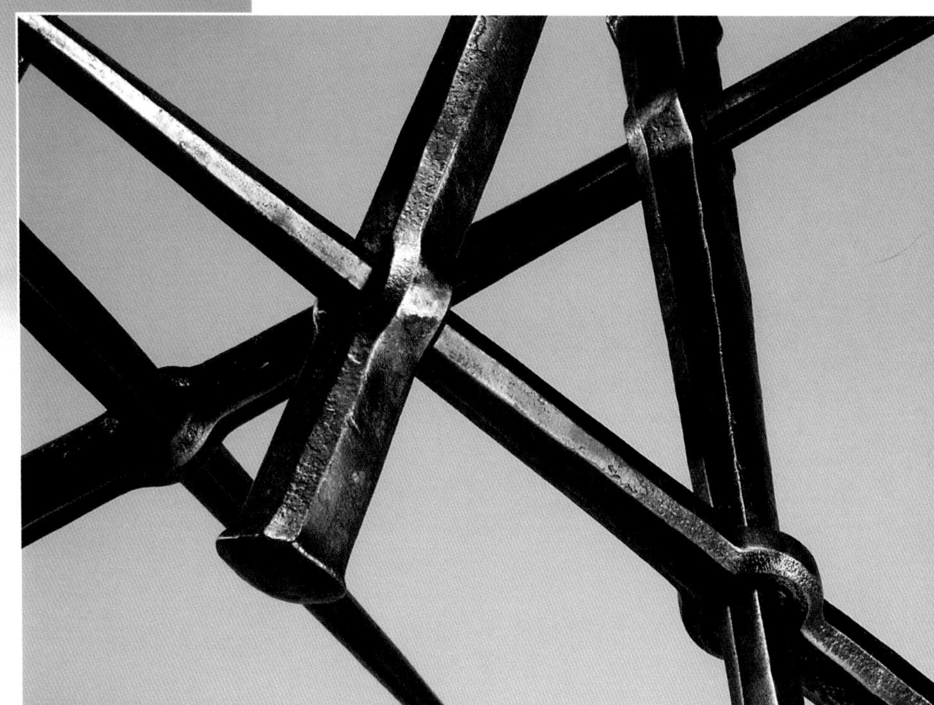

Zachary Noble. *Nodus #2*. Detail Image. *Photo, Tom Mills*

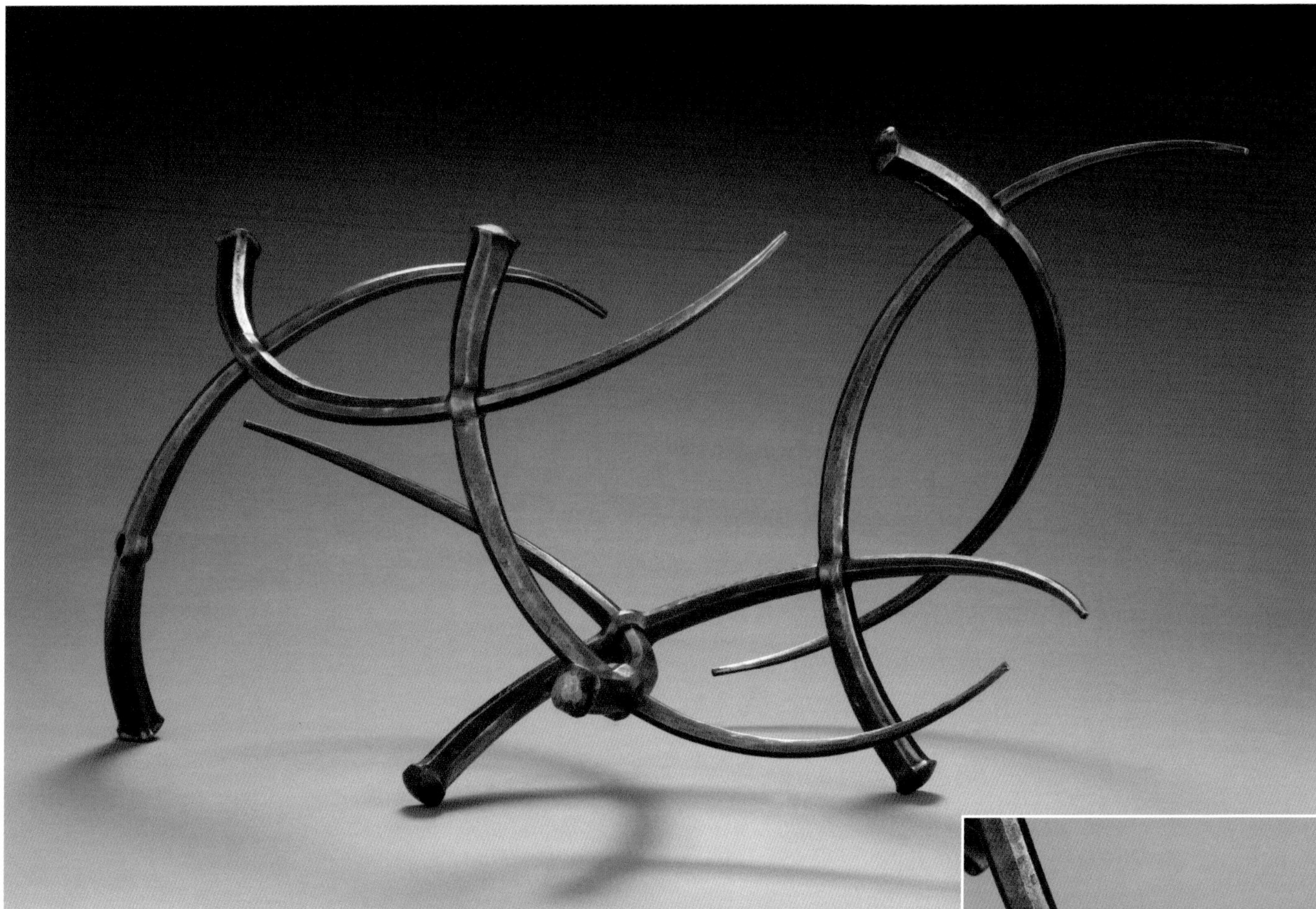

Zachary Noble. *Nodus #4*, 2007.
Forged steel. 38" x 22" x 22".
Photo, Tom Mills

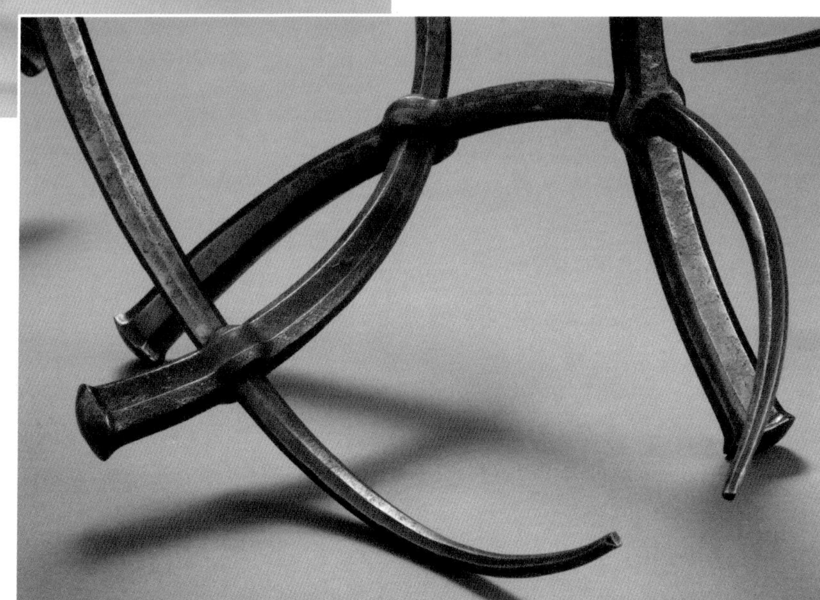

Zachary Noble. *Nodus #4*. Detail image. *Photo, Tom Mills*

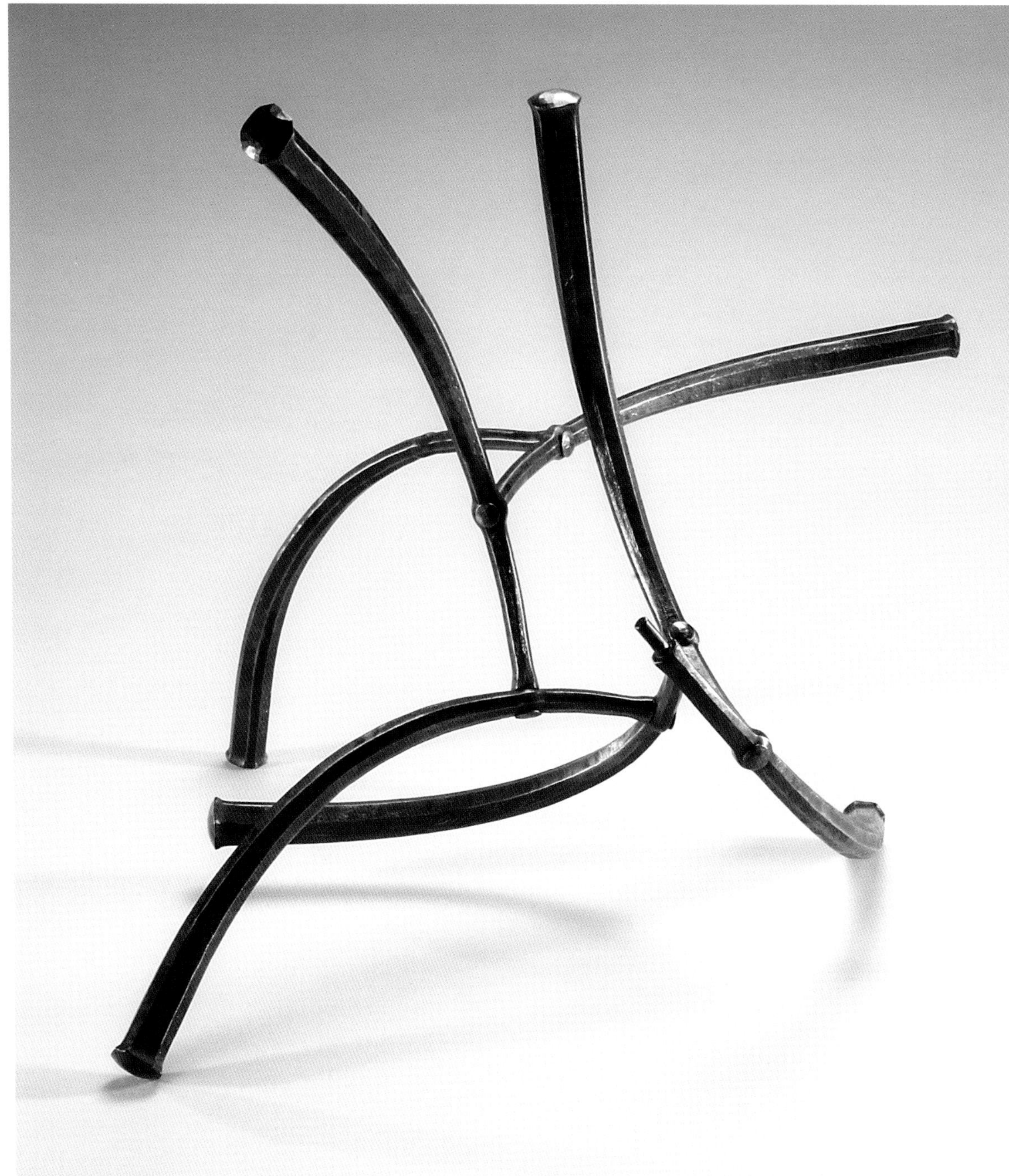

Zachary Noble. *Nodus #3*, 2007. Forged steel.
24" x 22" x 30". *Photo, Tom Mills*

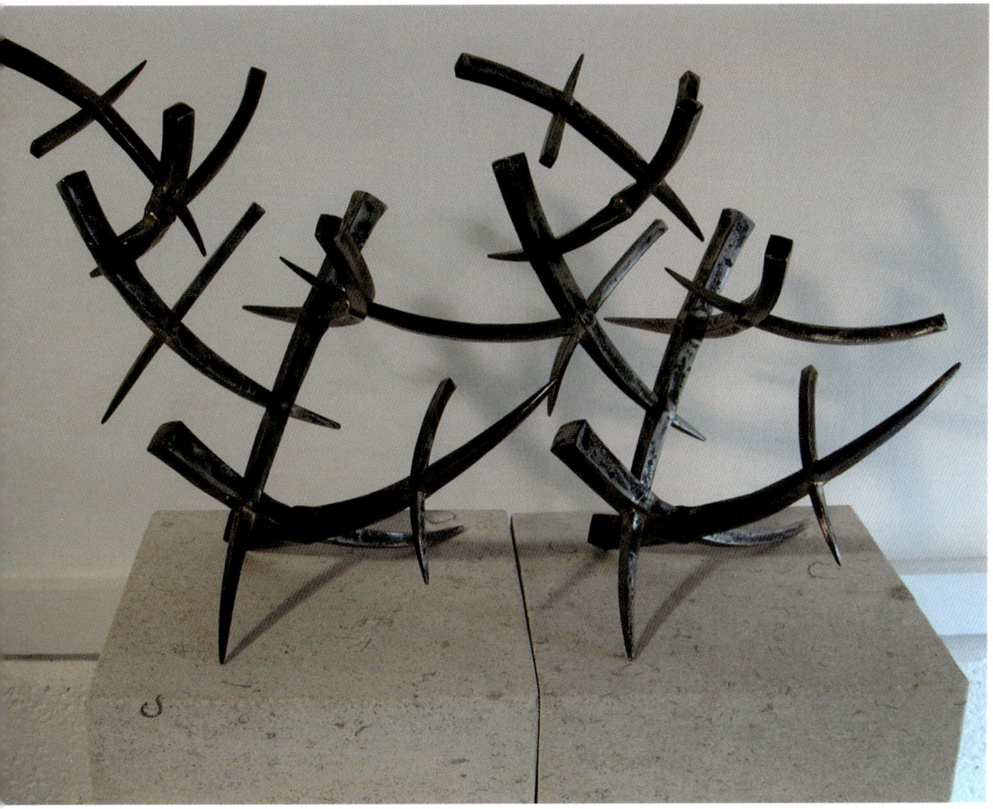

Melissa Cole. *Spinosity,* 2005. (12 points, 14 holes) forged steel, lacquer, Bath stone, 8" x 14", two identical pieces of work.

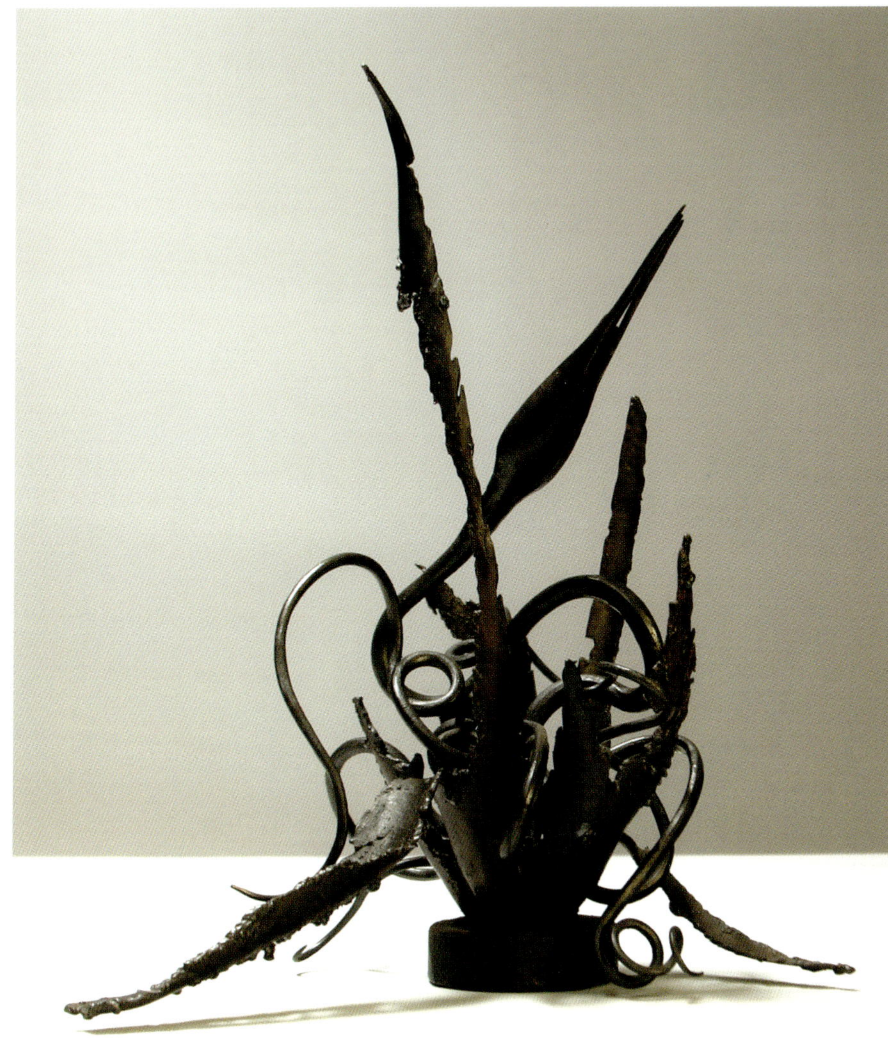

Jake James. *Alien Seed Pod #4*. Forged mild steel bar and sheet. This is the final in a series of three 'pods'. Exploring themes of birth, death, and regeneration, with a touch of sci-fi homage for good measure. The pods start fully closed and as the shell decays, so the new life form emerged from its ruins. *Photo, Doug Gilbert*

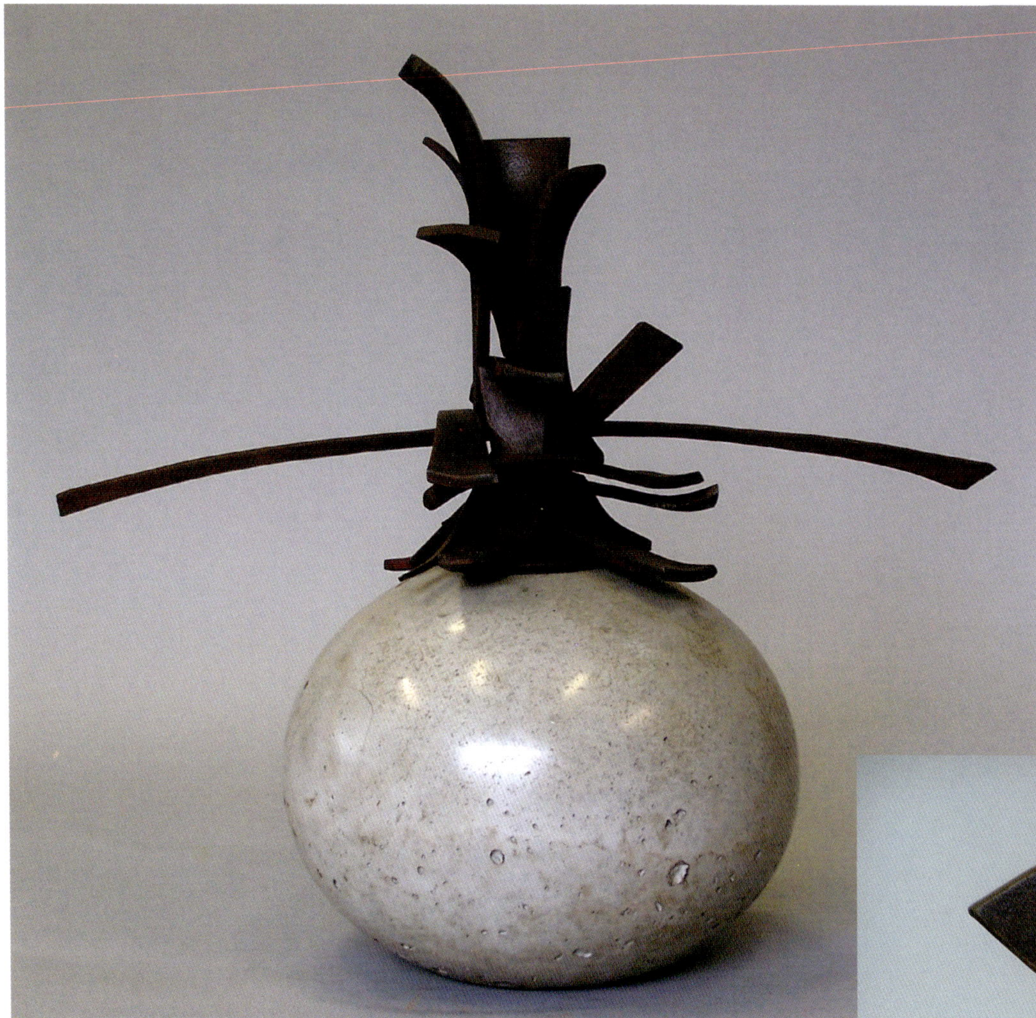

Mike Suri. *Artifact.* Steel and concrete. 20" x 10" x 20". Formed and patina steel, cast concrete. *Photo, artist*

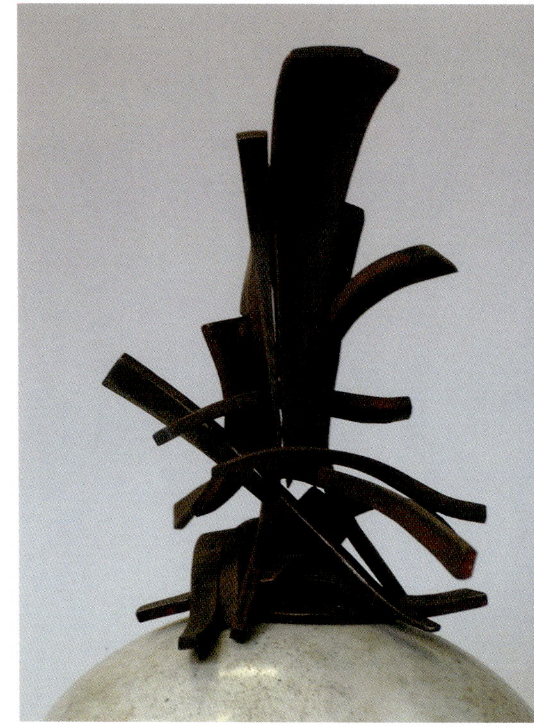

Mike Suri. *Artifact.* Detail image. *Photo, artist*

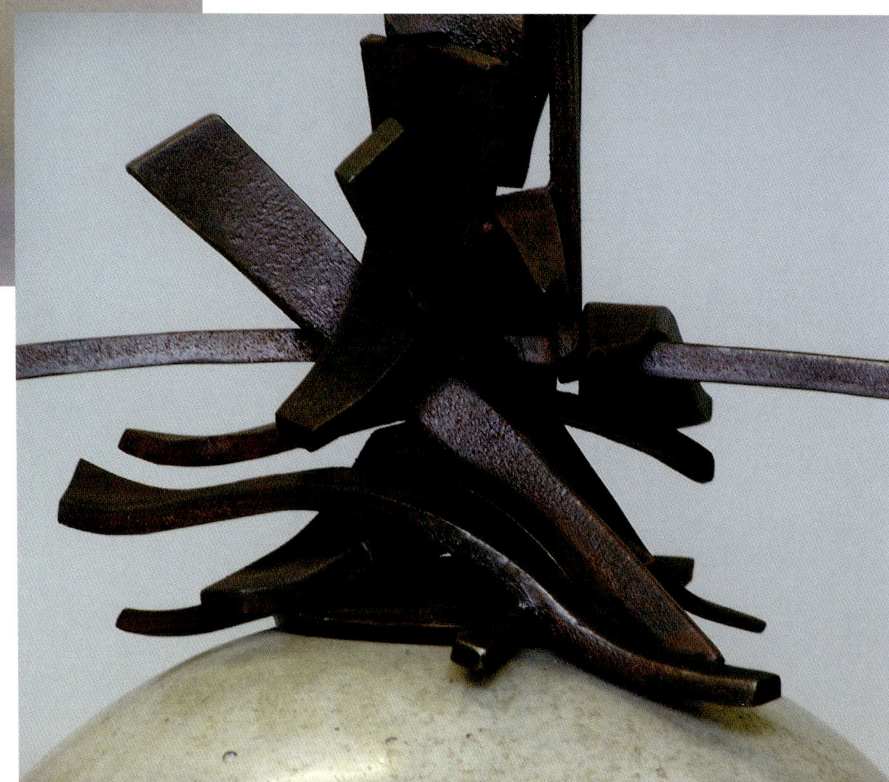

Mike Suri. *Artifact.* Detail image. *Photo, artist*

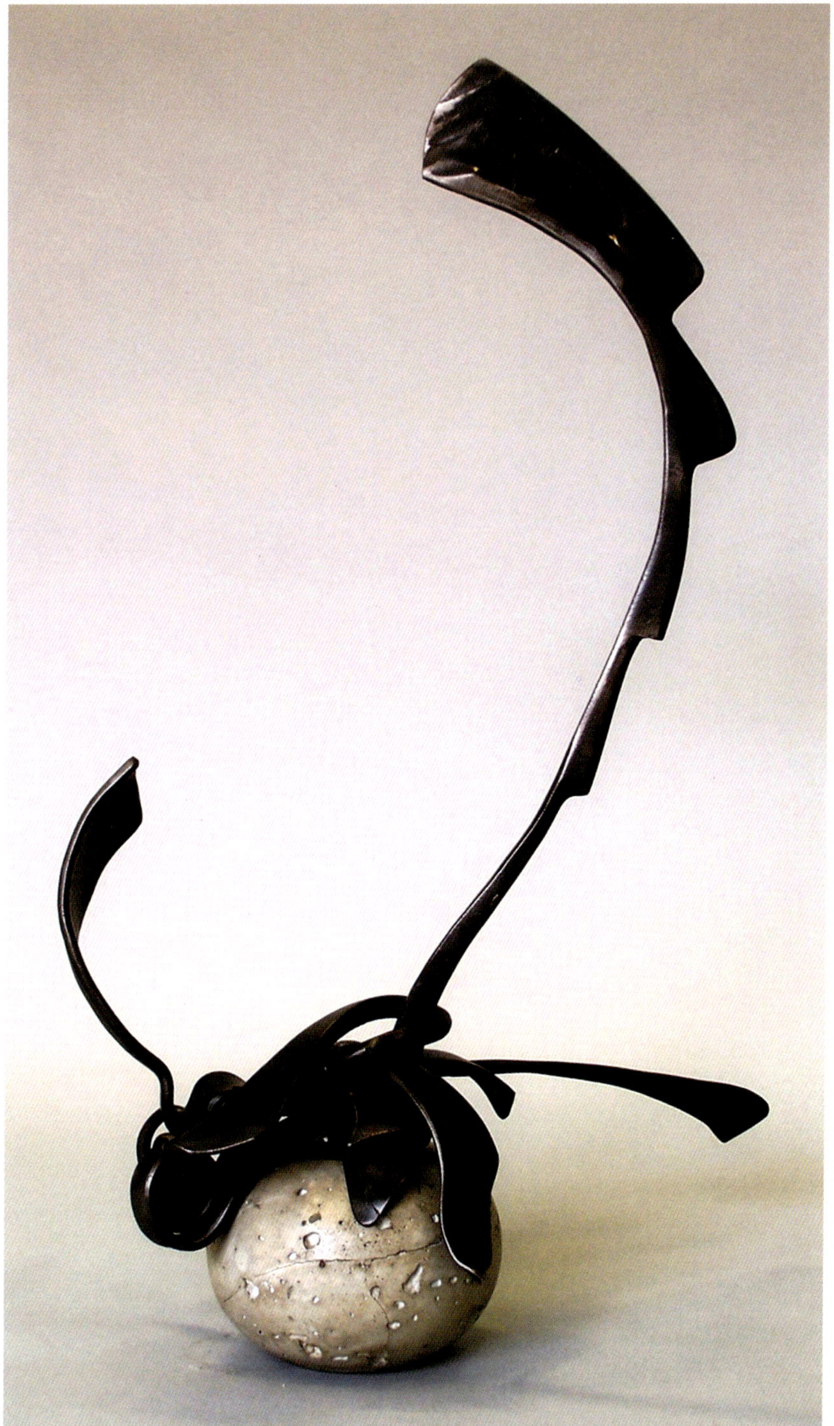

Mike Suri. *Black Plant Form*. Steel and concrete. 24" x 16" x 8". Formed and forged steel, cast concrete.

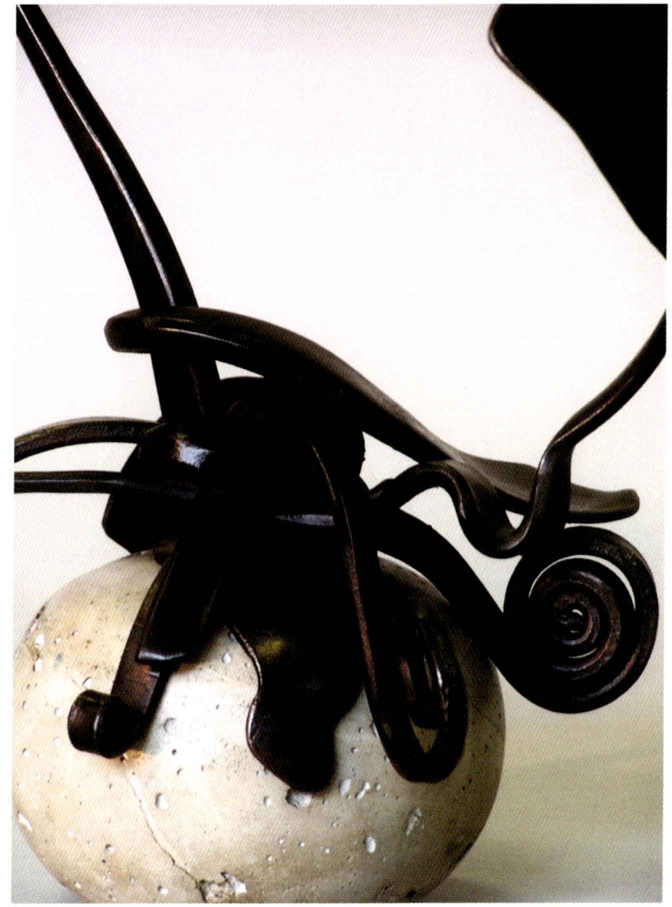

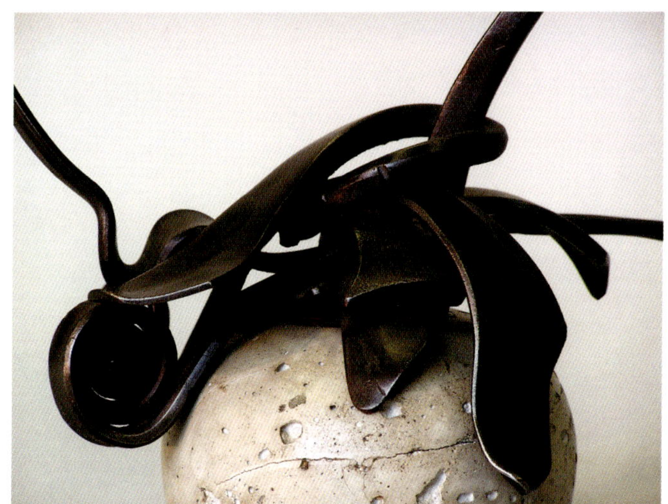

Mike Suri. *Black Plant Form*. Detail images. *Photo, artist*

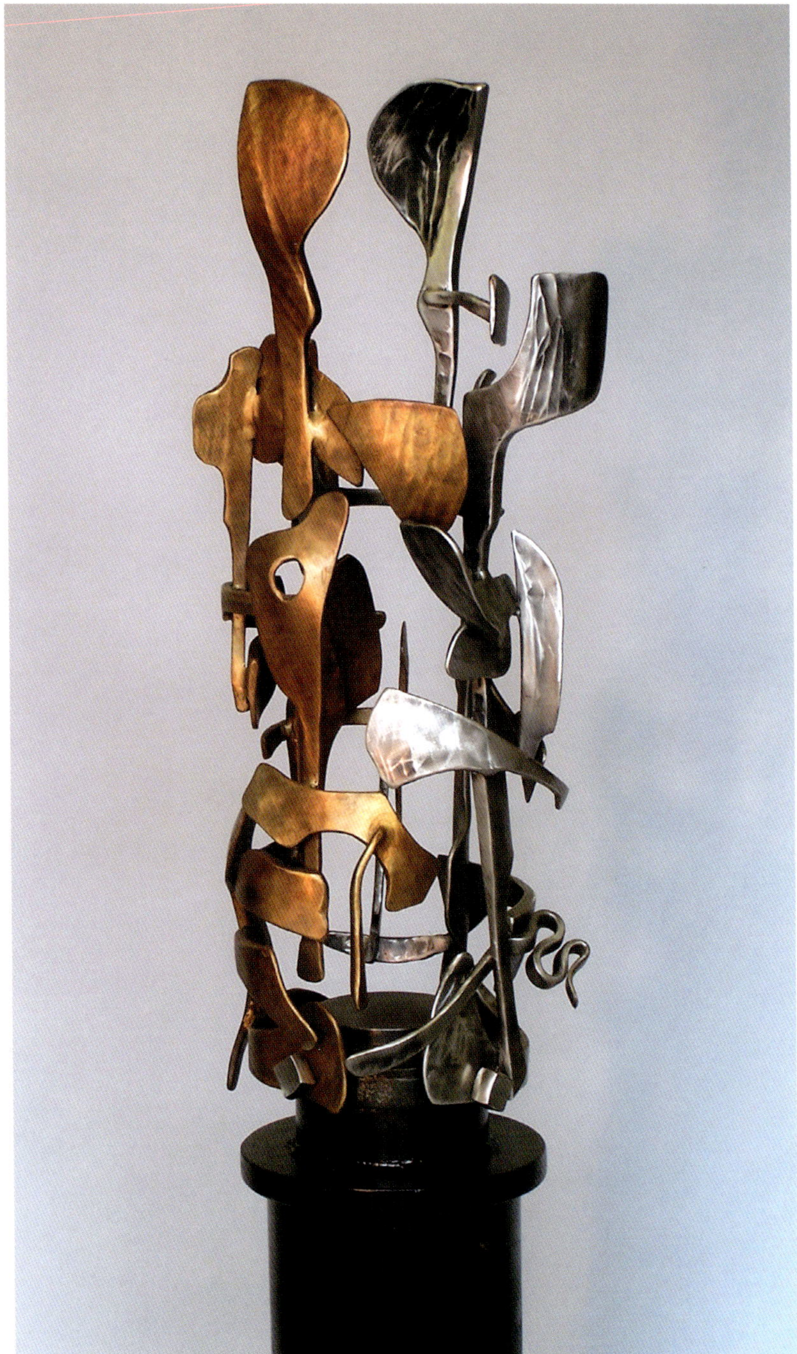

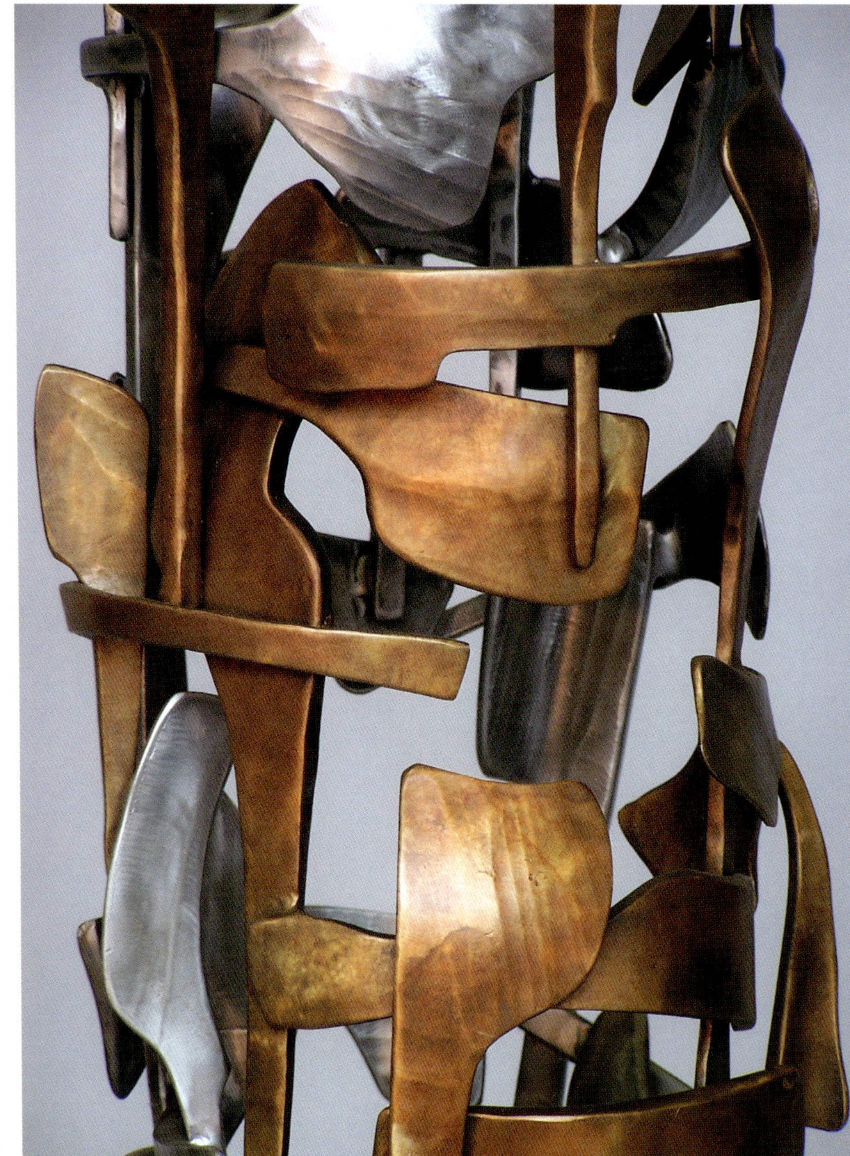

Mike Suri. *Ode.* Detail image. *Photo, artist*

Mike Suri. *Ode.* Steel, stainless steel, bronze. 10" x 10" x 36". Formed and forged. *Photo, artist*

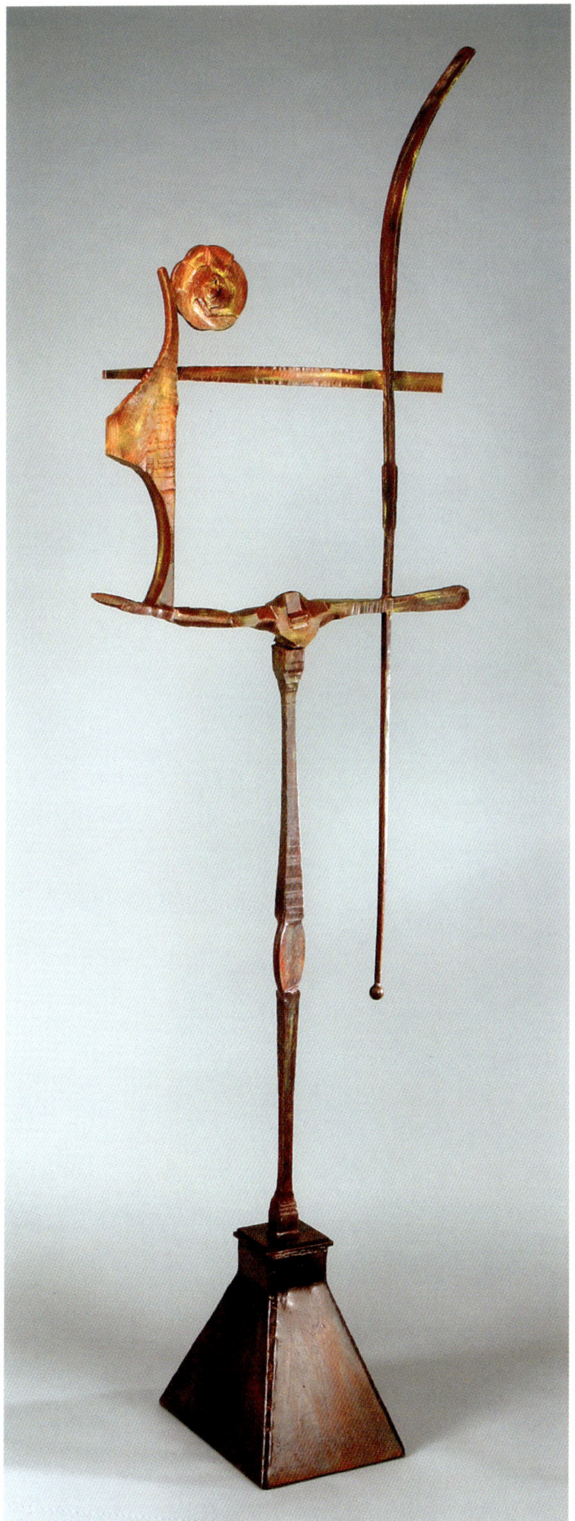

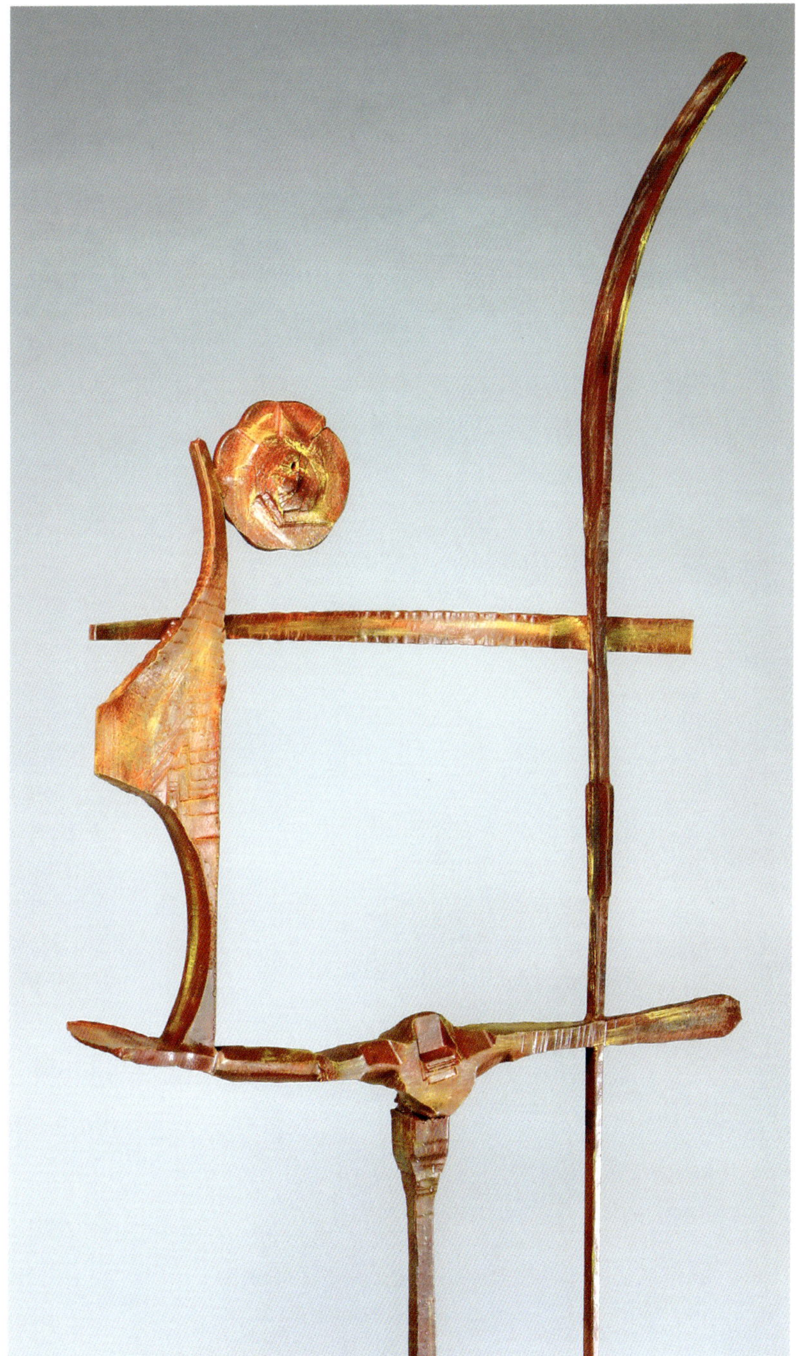

Bill Brown. *Desert Traveler*. Detail. *Photo, Tim Barnwell*

Bill Brown. *Desert Traveler,* 2001. Forged steel w/ acrylic enamel. 106" x 31" x 19". *Photo, Tim Barnwell*

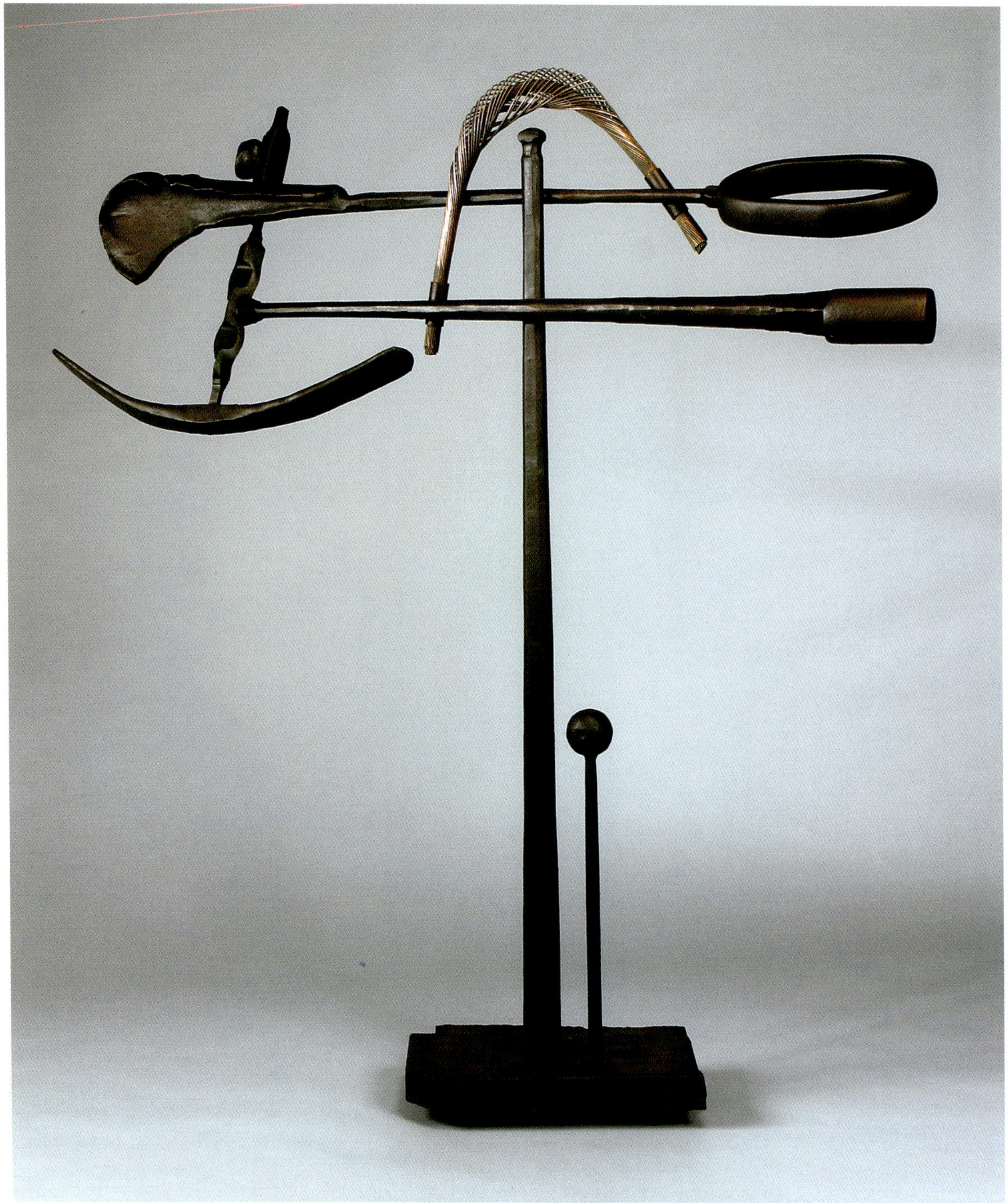

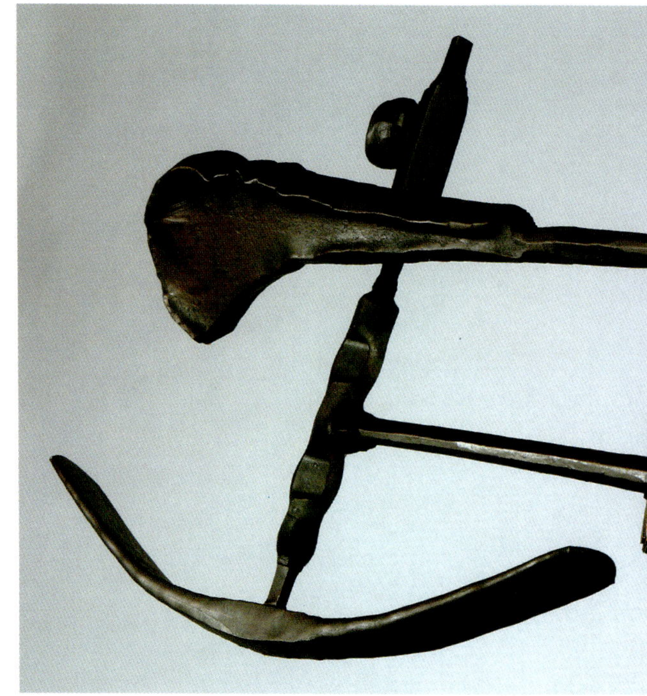

Bill Brown. *Guilty Bystander.* Detail. *Photo, Tim Barnwell*

Bill Brown. *Guilty Bystander,* 2002. Forged steel & copper. 61" x 57" x 14". *Photo, Tim Barnwell*

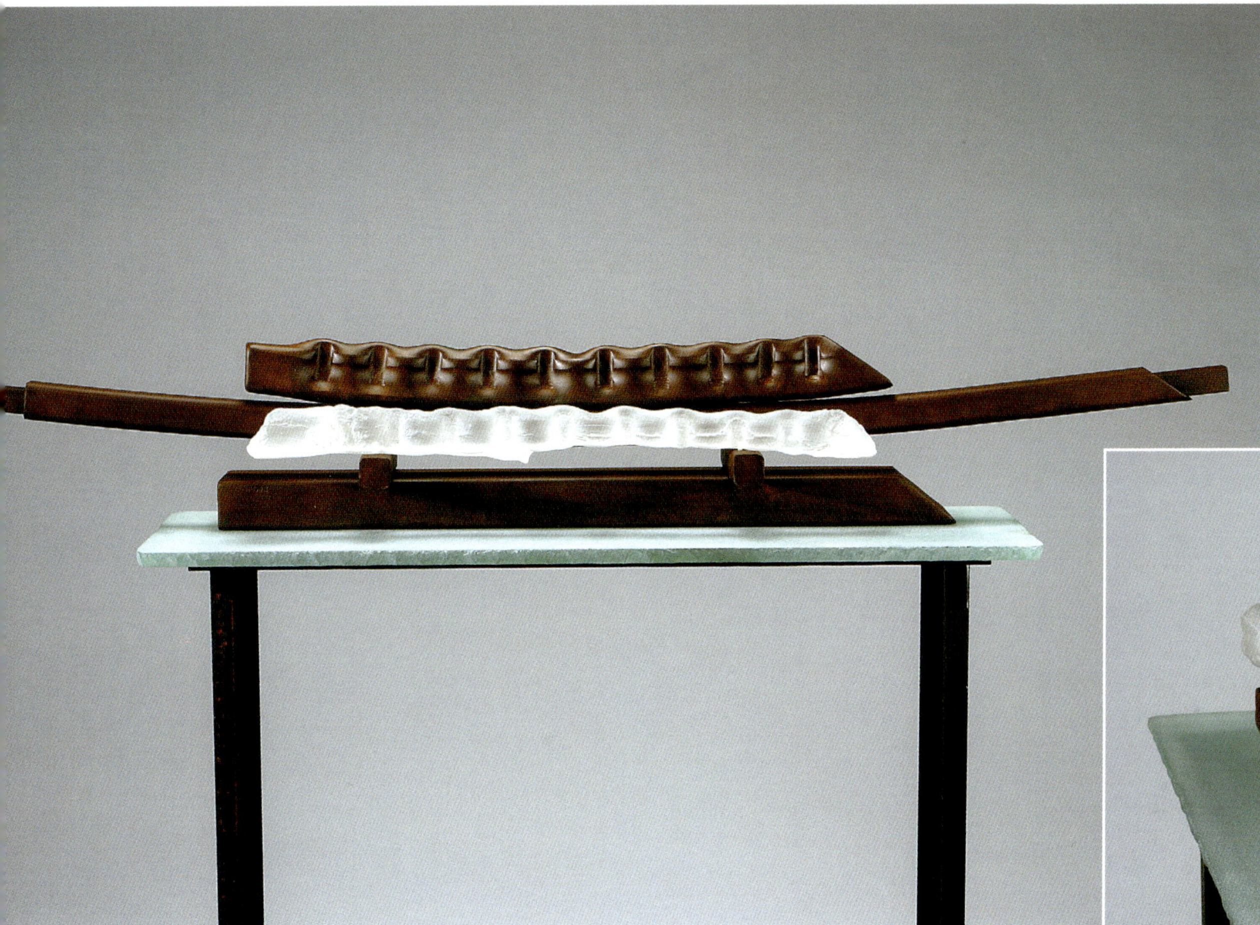

Bill Brown. *Samurai,* 2006. Glass & Steel. 9" x 52" x 12". *Photo, Tim Barnwell*

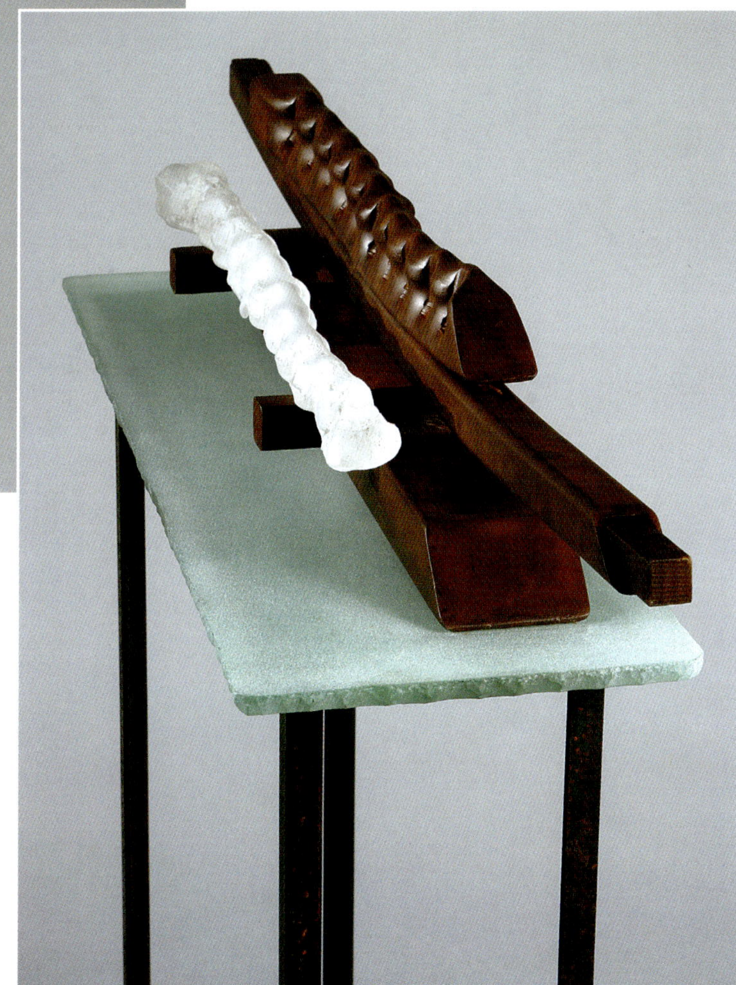

Bill Brown. *Samurai.* Side view. *Photo, Tim Barnwell*

Bill Brown. *A Bridge of Consciousness*, 2007.
Steel and Acrylic. 26" x 12" x 9".
Photo, Fanjoy-Labrenz

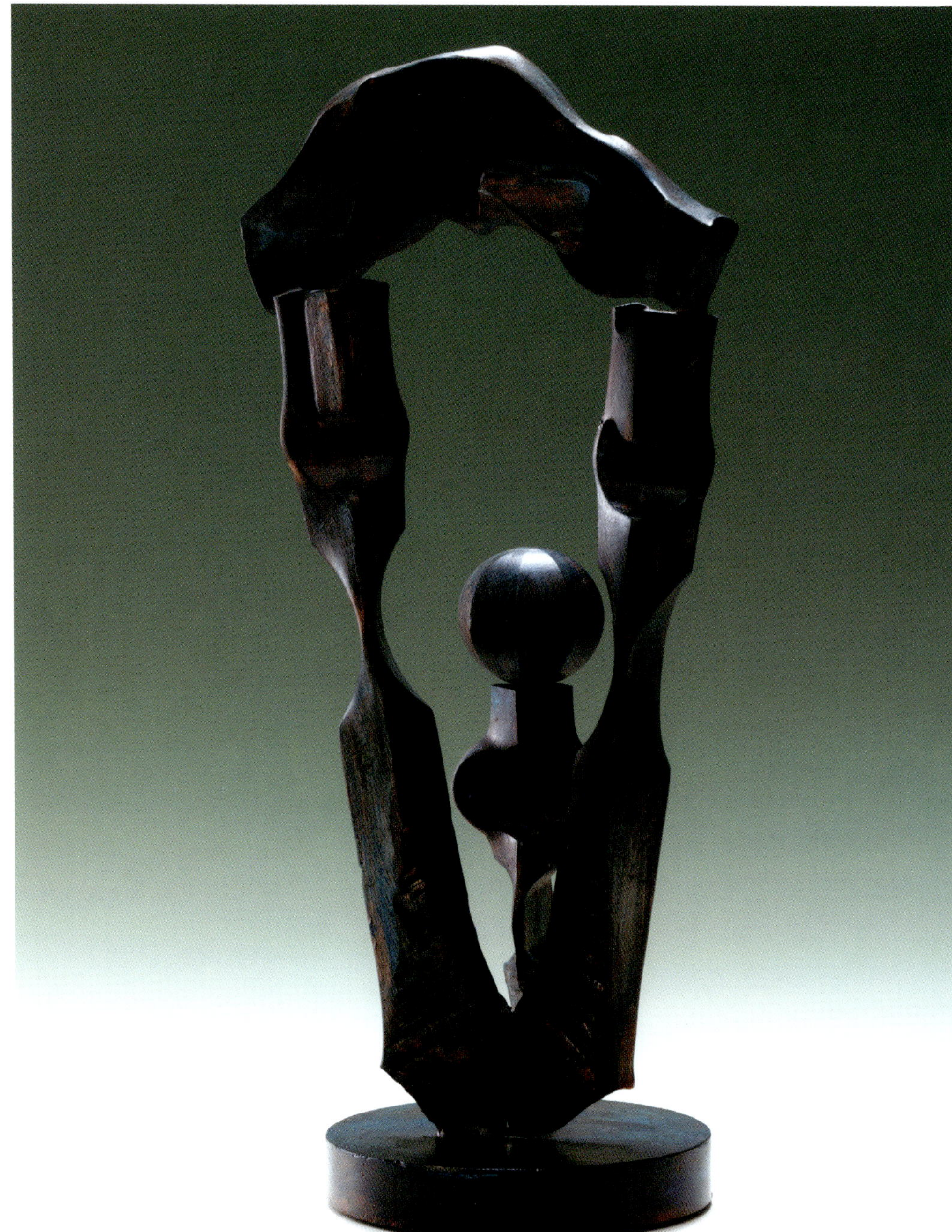

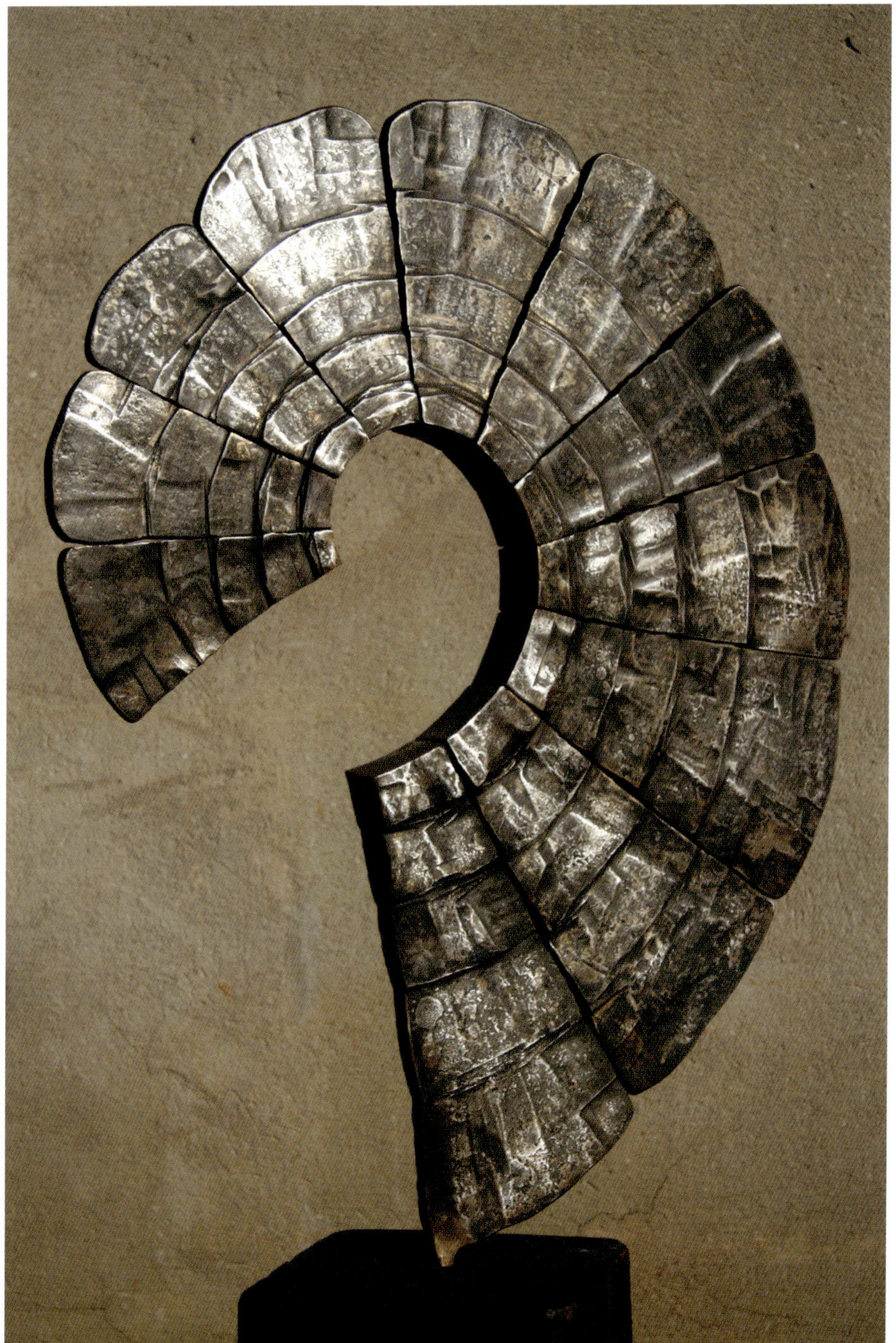

Claudio Bottero. *Giulio Cesare.* 39". *Photo, artist*

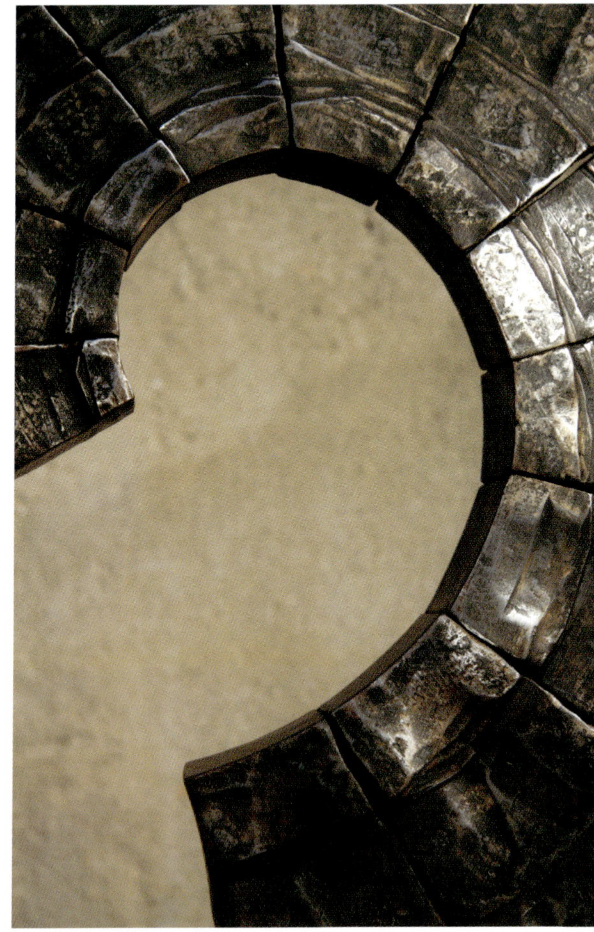

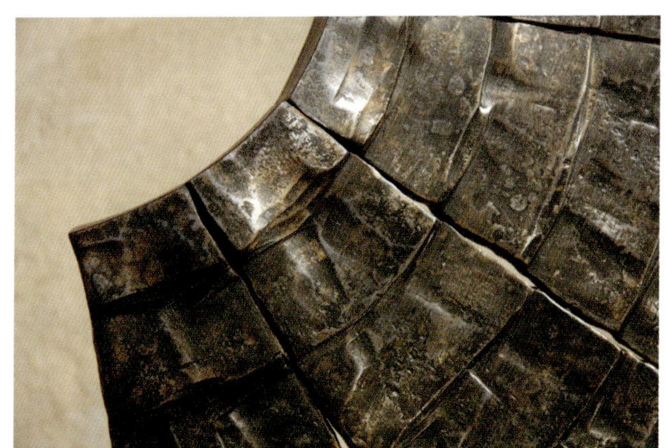

Claudio Bottero. *Giulio Cesare.* Details. *Photo, artist*

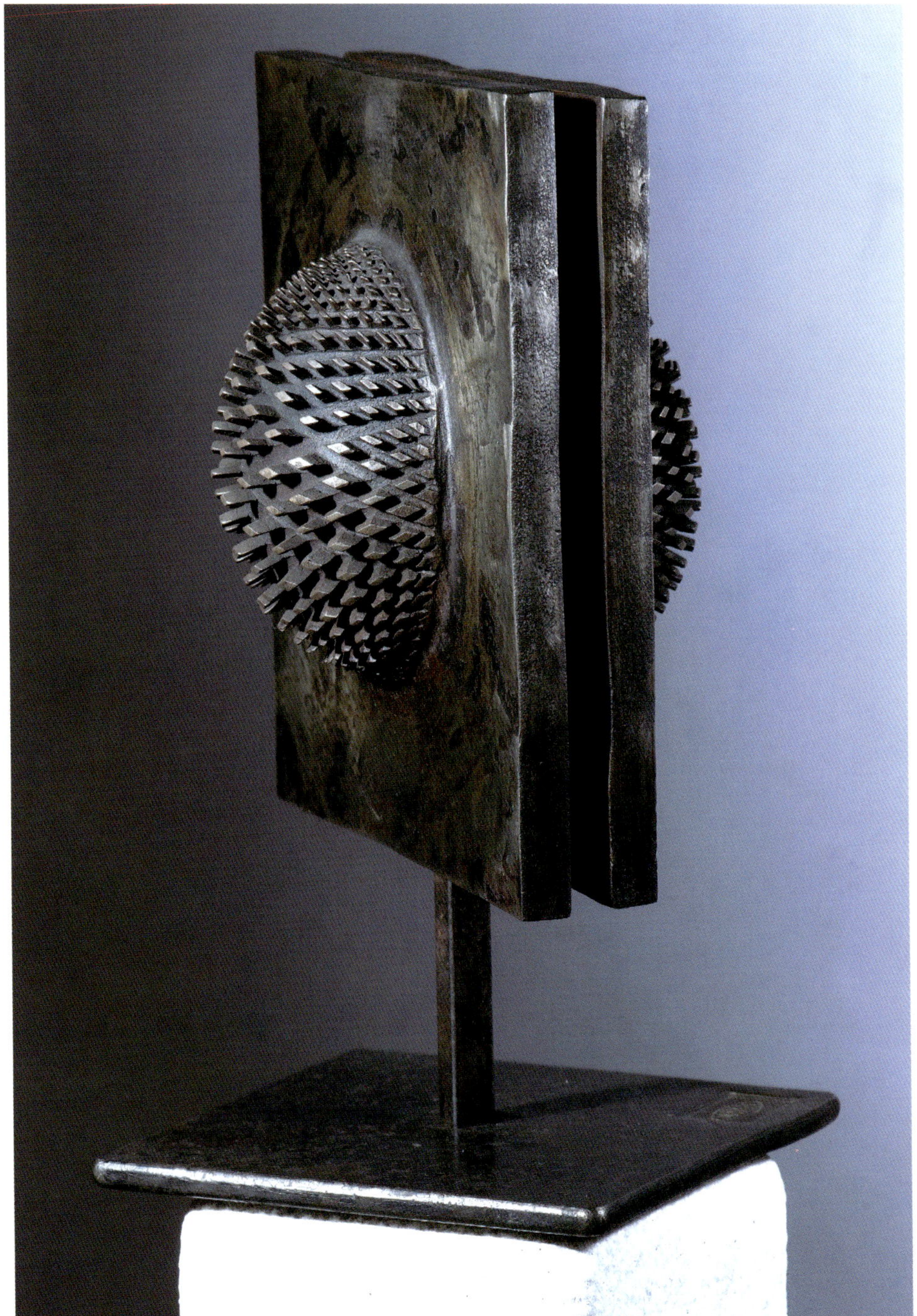

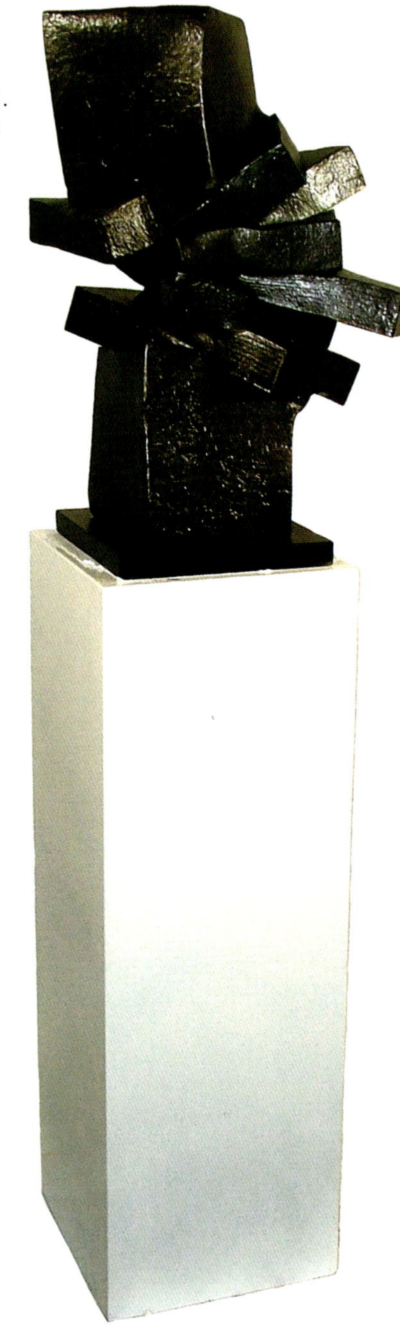

Frederic A. Crist. *Stacked Pillar #1*. Forged steel. 22" x 14" x 16" on a 36" pedestal. *Photo, artist*

Claudio Bottero. *Untitled*. 39" x 39" x 1", 881 lbs. Forged wrought iron. *Private collection. Photo, artist*

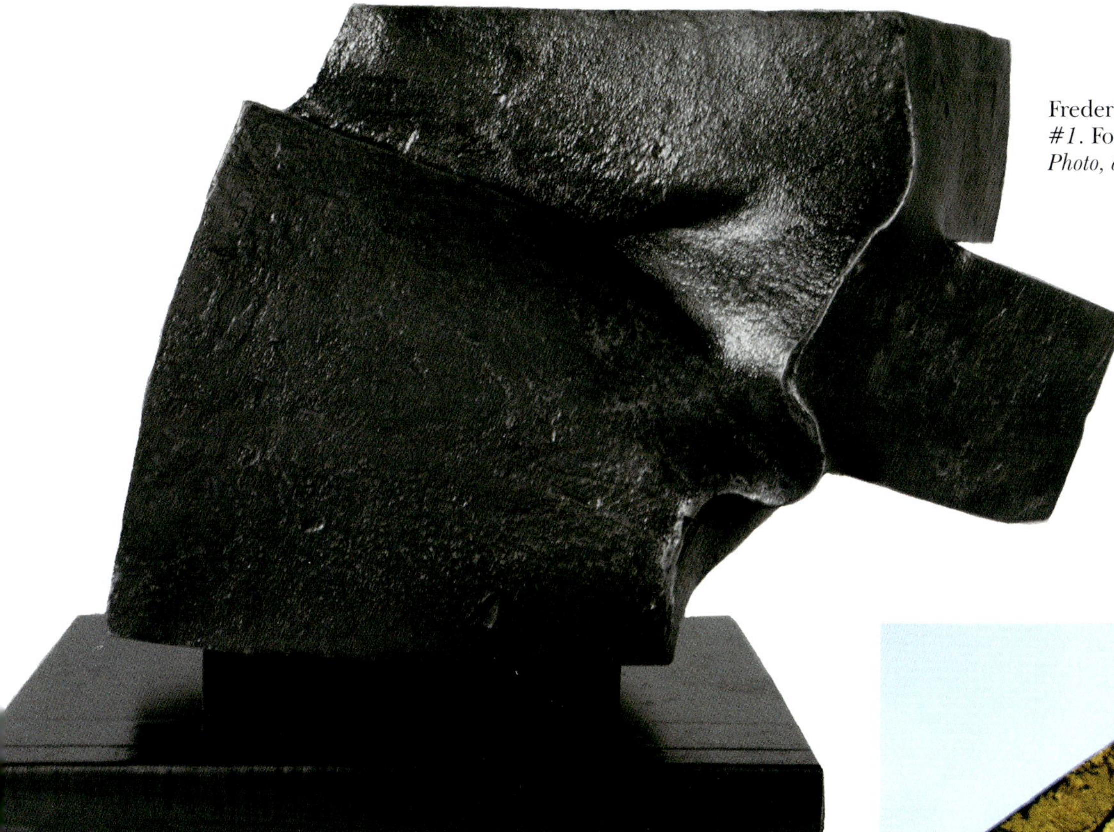

Frederic A. Crist. *Twisted Pillar #1*. Forged steel. 10" x 12" x 12". *Photo, artist*

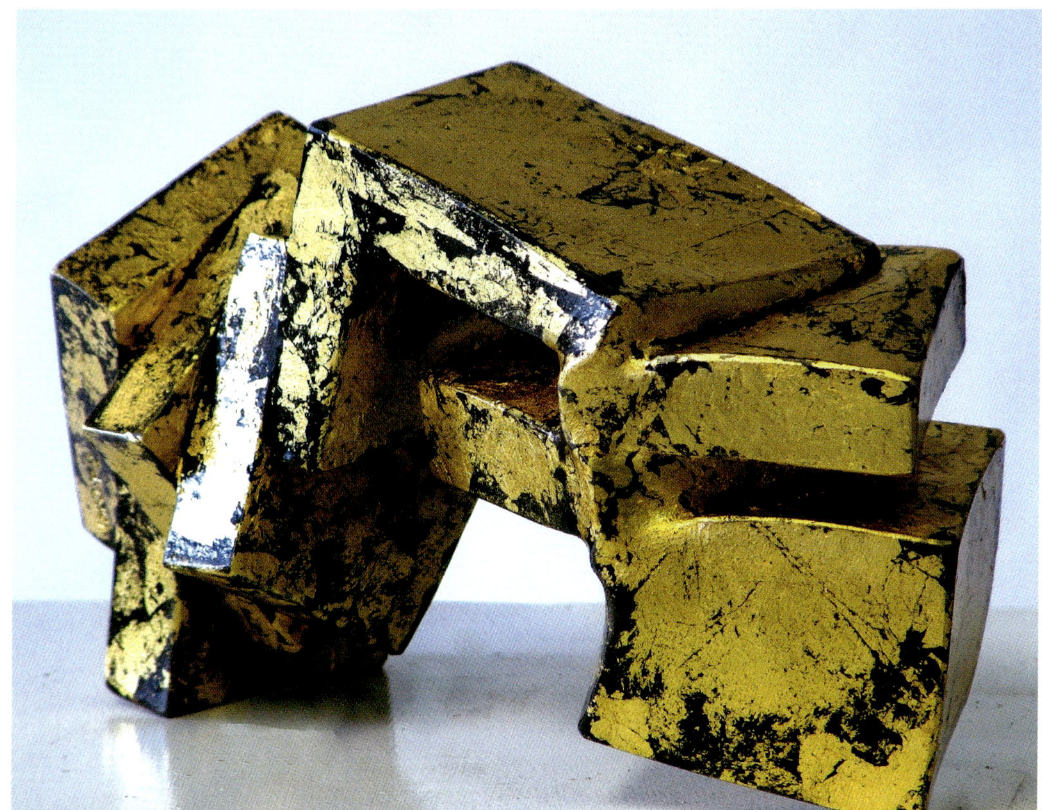

Frederic A. Crist. *Gold Leaf Pillar #2*, 2005. Forged steel with gold leaf. 5" x 10" x 4". *Photo, artist*

Frederic A. Crist. *Phoenix*. Cast Bronze. 15" x 10" x 12". *Photo, artist*

"Evolution of an Idea" Seven years ago I started working on a sculptural series entitled "The Pillars." I began by making small studies in forged steel and evolved into larger scale forgings, which were made in Cleveland, Ohio, at Rose industries. With the support of Melvin and Bob Rose and assistance of their blacksmiths, we forged five sculptures out of 18" x 6" x 6" solid stock using a 6B Nazel power hammer and a 250 ton press and a lot of heat and sweat. Five years latter and many small pieces of similar character, I still had two of the pieces left, which I was in no hurry to sell.

Up to this point I had always looked at the series as forged pieces. Over time though many discussions with Robert Bricker, who owns a fine art foundry near my studio, we decided to make castings of the remaining ones in bronze. As I had explored forging smaller pieces in brass and was quite pleased with the result, the idea seemed reasonable to investigate. Once we had made molds and waxes from forgings, I decided I did not want to reproduce what I had already done, I wanted to take the series in another direction. I began assembling the waxes together and modelling the joints to create a new single piece. In the series of photos you can see the progression from forging, to wax, to molds, to casting then to bronze.

In the blacksmithing community casting is a bad word and brings up the decline of the craft brought about by the casting of multiple cheap reproductions at the turn of the last century. In fact, Samuel Yellin made a casting from a forging he had done to show the inferior quality of cast iron to his clients. This in fact is another time and approach, plus the level of refinement in casting today is remarkable. Through the reproduction of these forms in wax, I am able to create new pieces in bronze, which I would not be able to create through forging, though forging is the primary directive to achieve the initial forms. In the future I will continue to explore the two processes more closely. – Frederic A. Crist

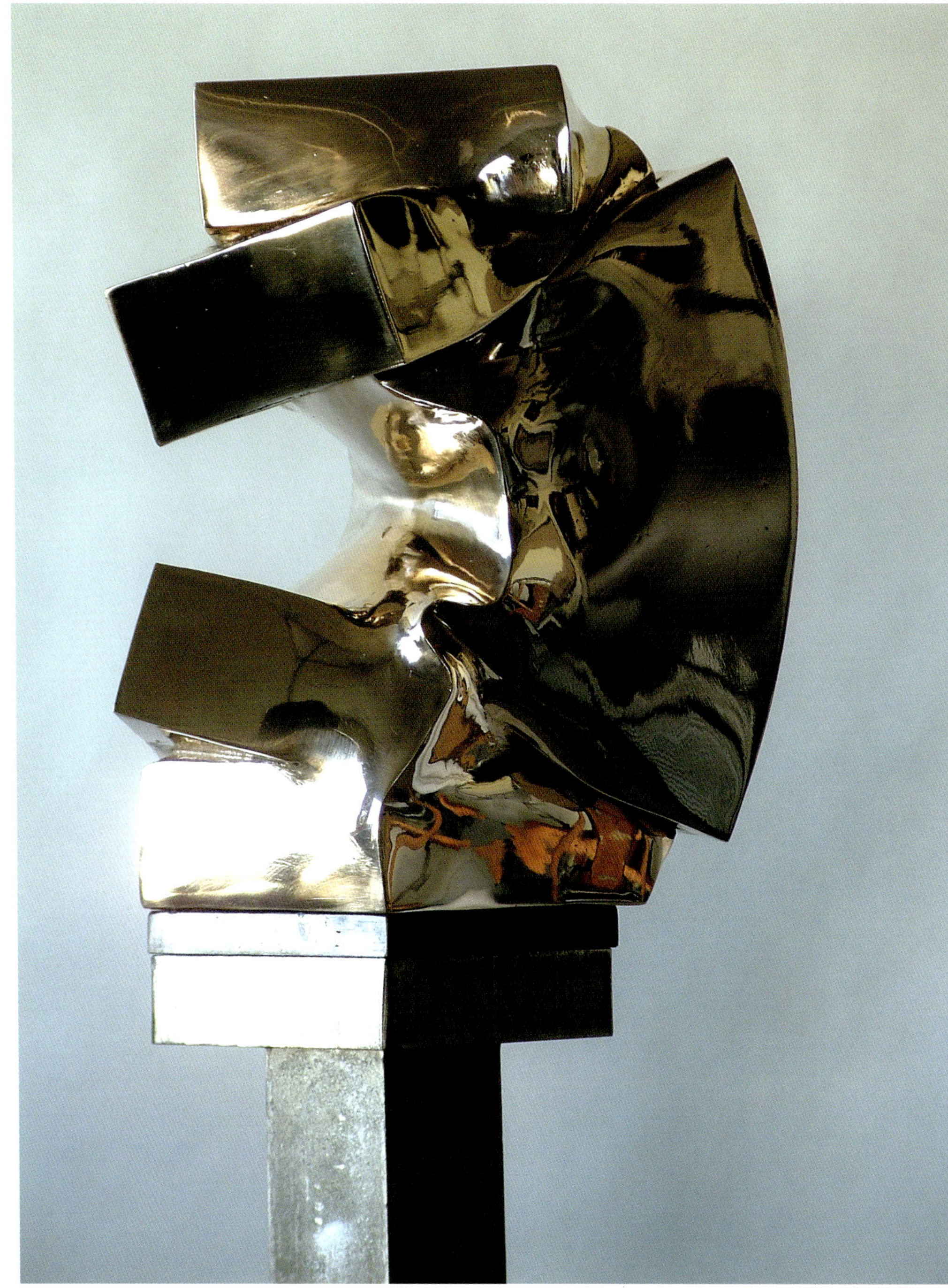

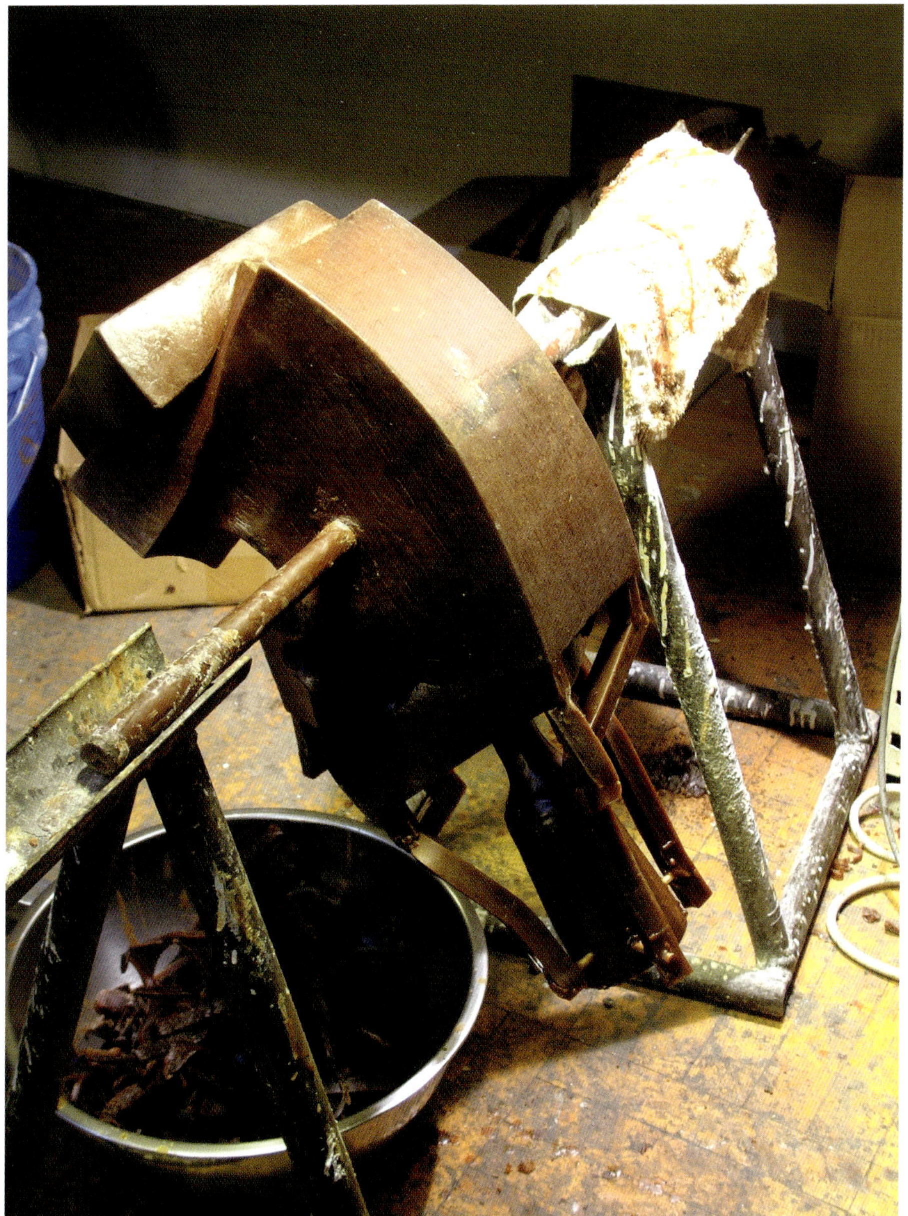

Frederic A. Crist. *Phoenix*. Spurring of the *Phoenix* in preparation for casting.
Photo, artist

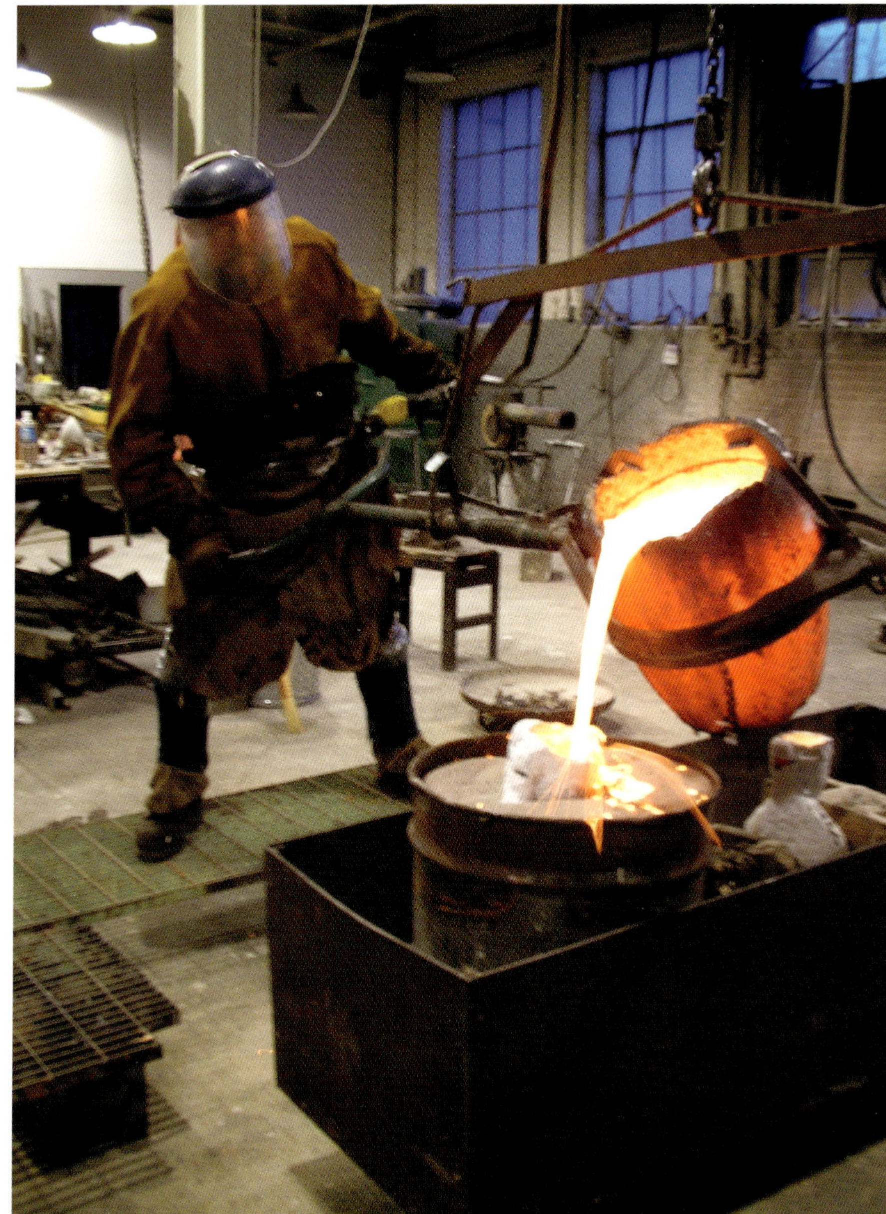

Frederic A. Crist. *Phoenix*. Fred Crist and assistant pouring the bronze.
Photo, artist

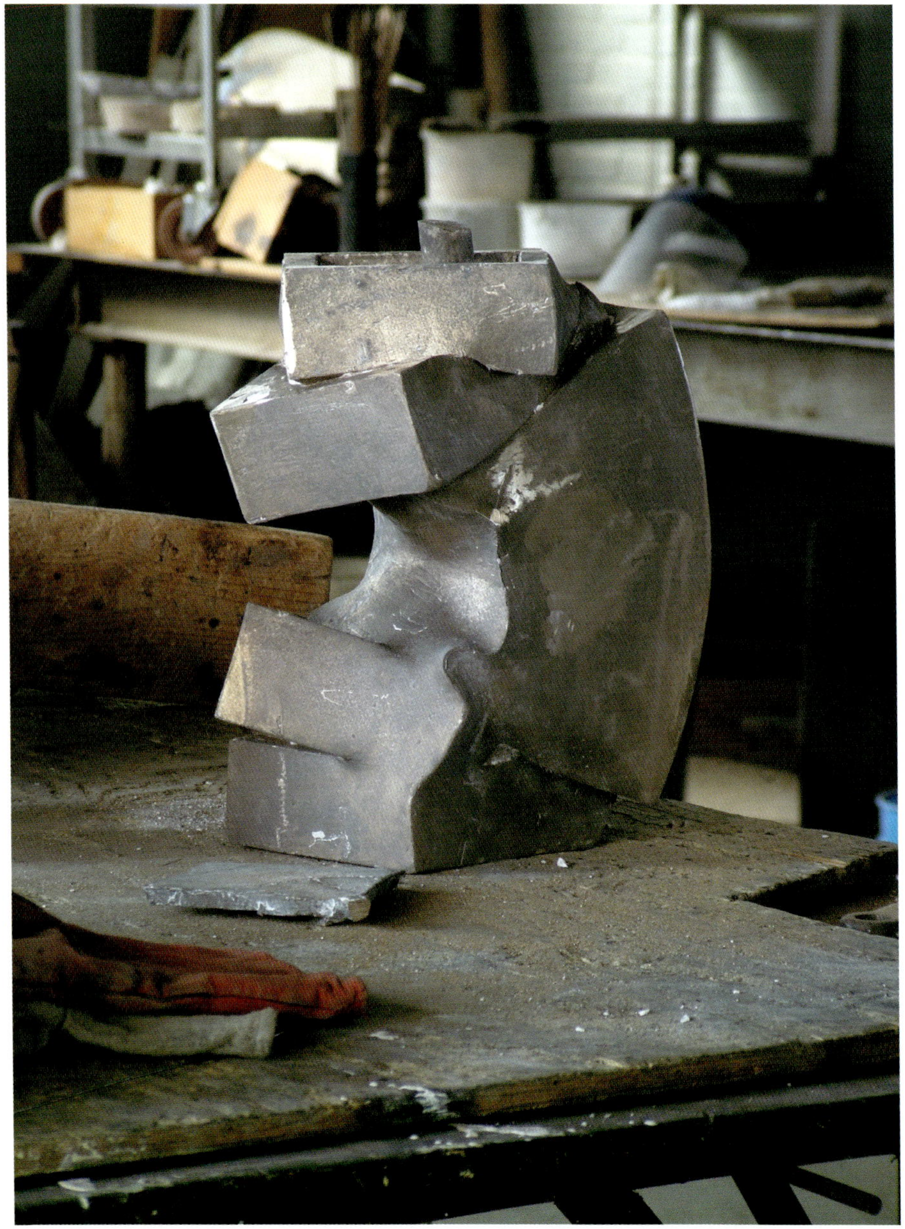

Frederic A. Crist. *Phoenix.* Raw casting fresh out of the mold. *Photo, artist*

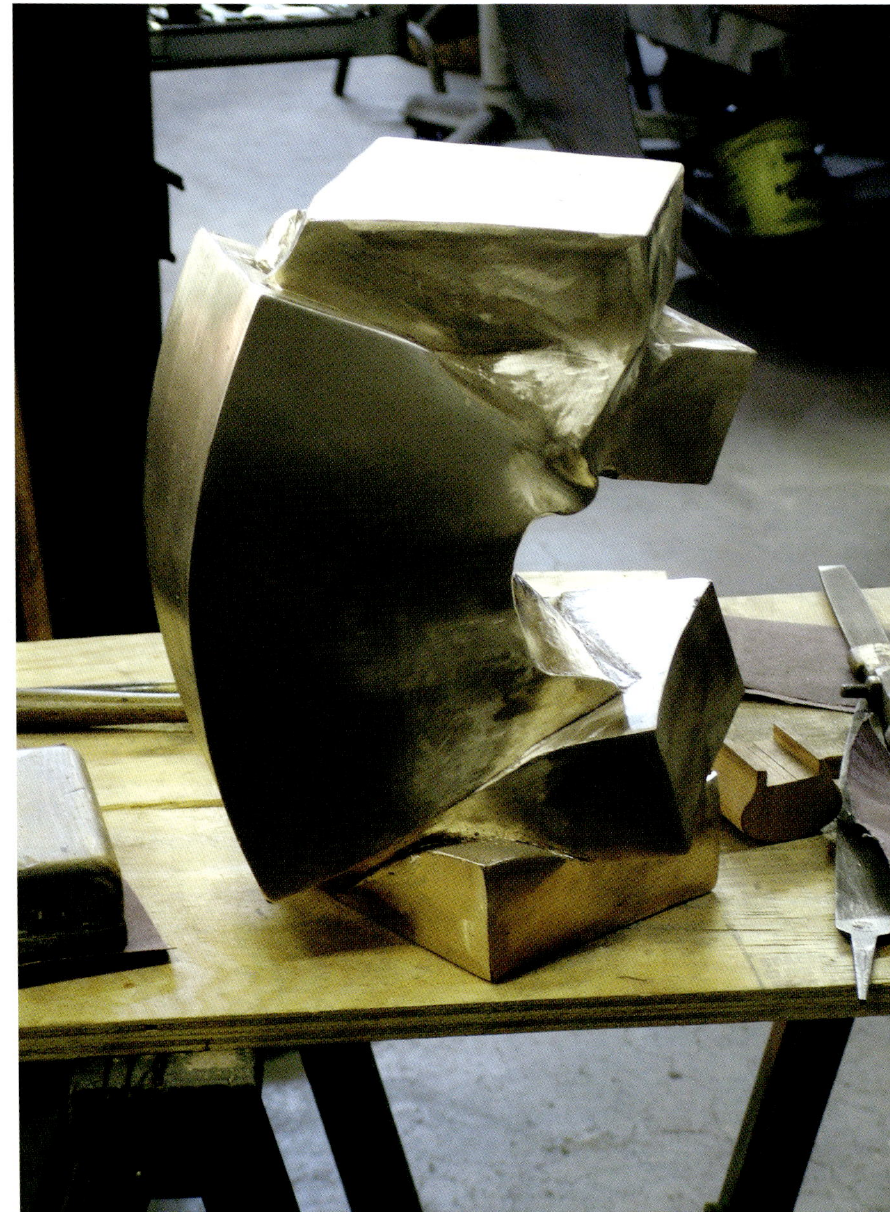

Frederic A. Crist. *Phoenix.* Polishing the Phoenix. *Photo, artist*

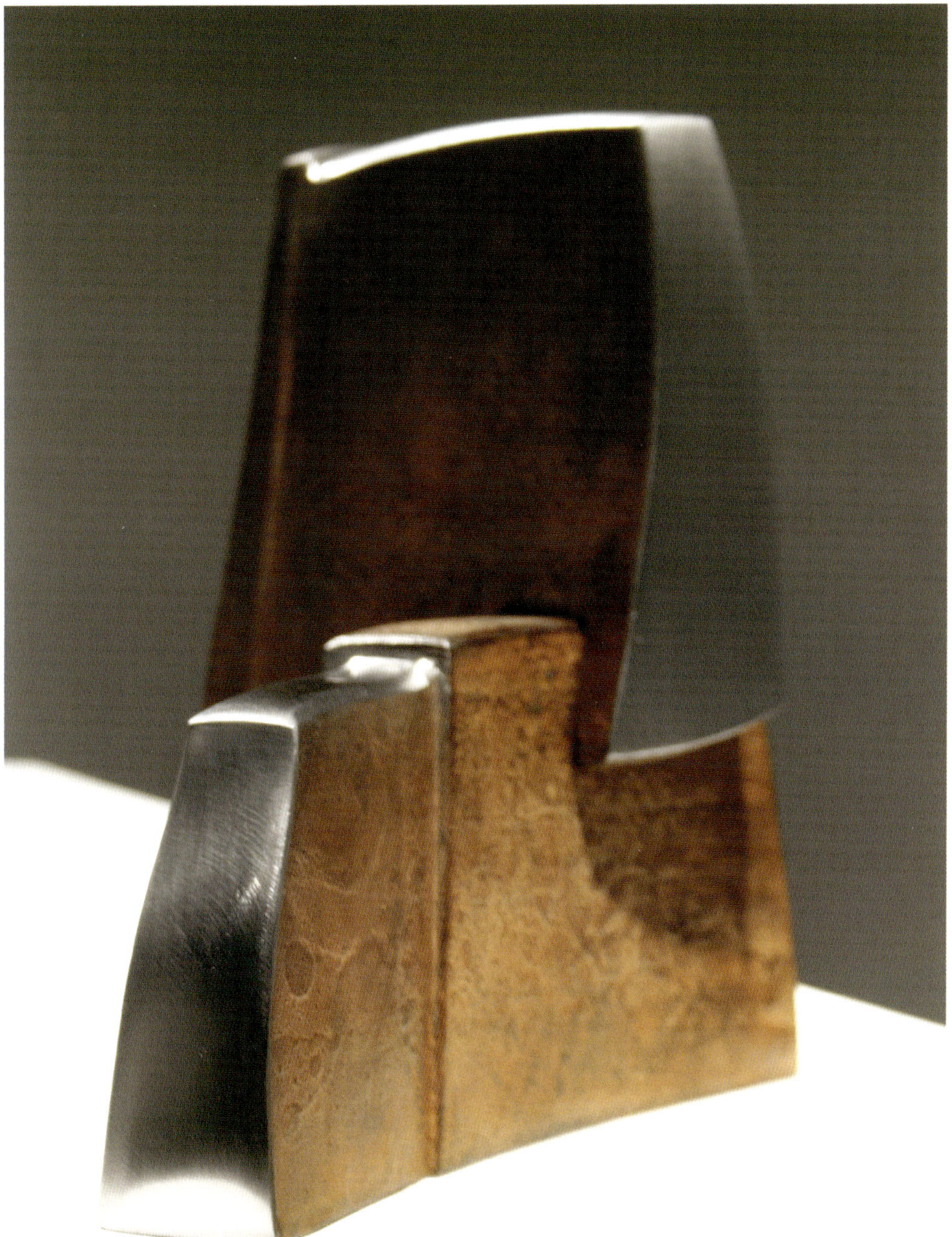

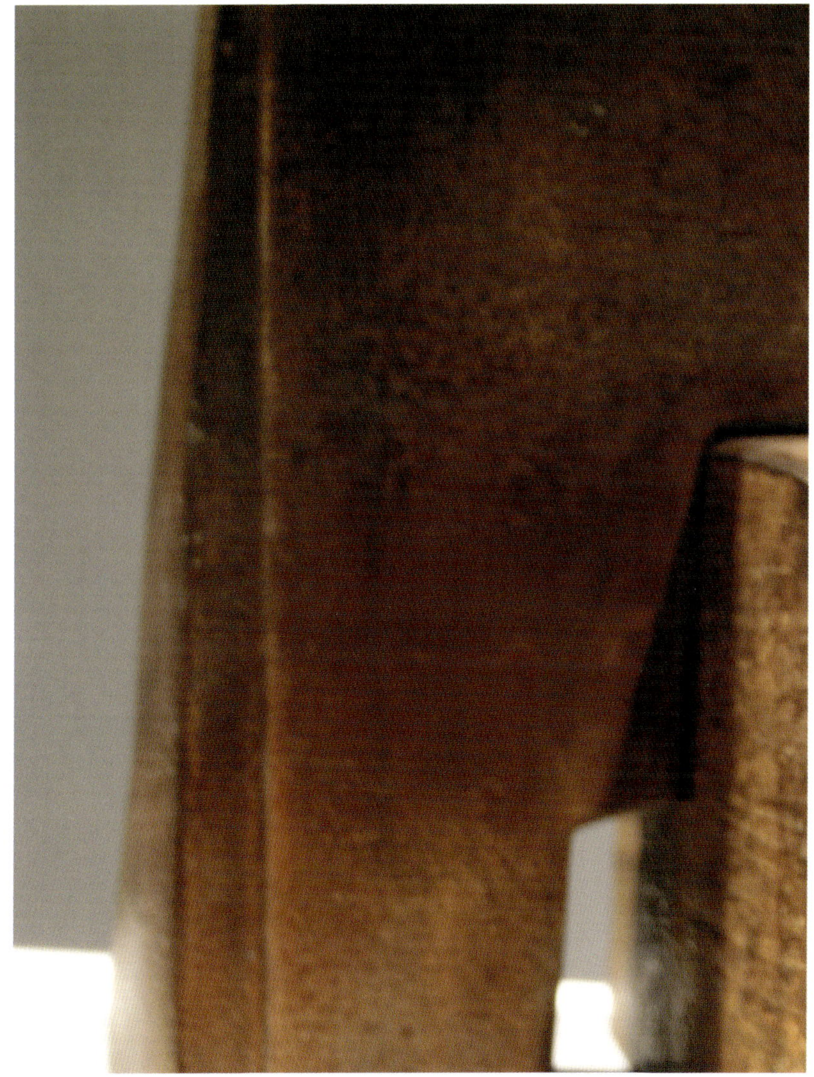

Matt Haugh. *Dave*, 2007. Second view. *Photo, artist*

Matt Haugh. *Dave*, 2007. Forged iron. 10" h x 10" w x 7" l. *Photo, artist*

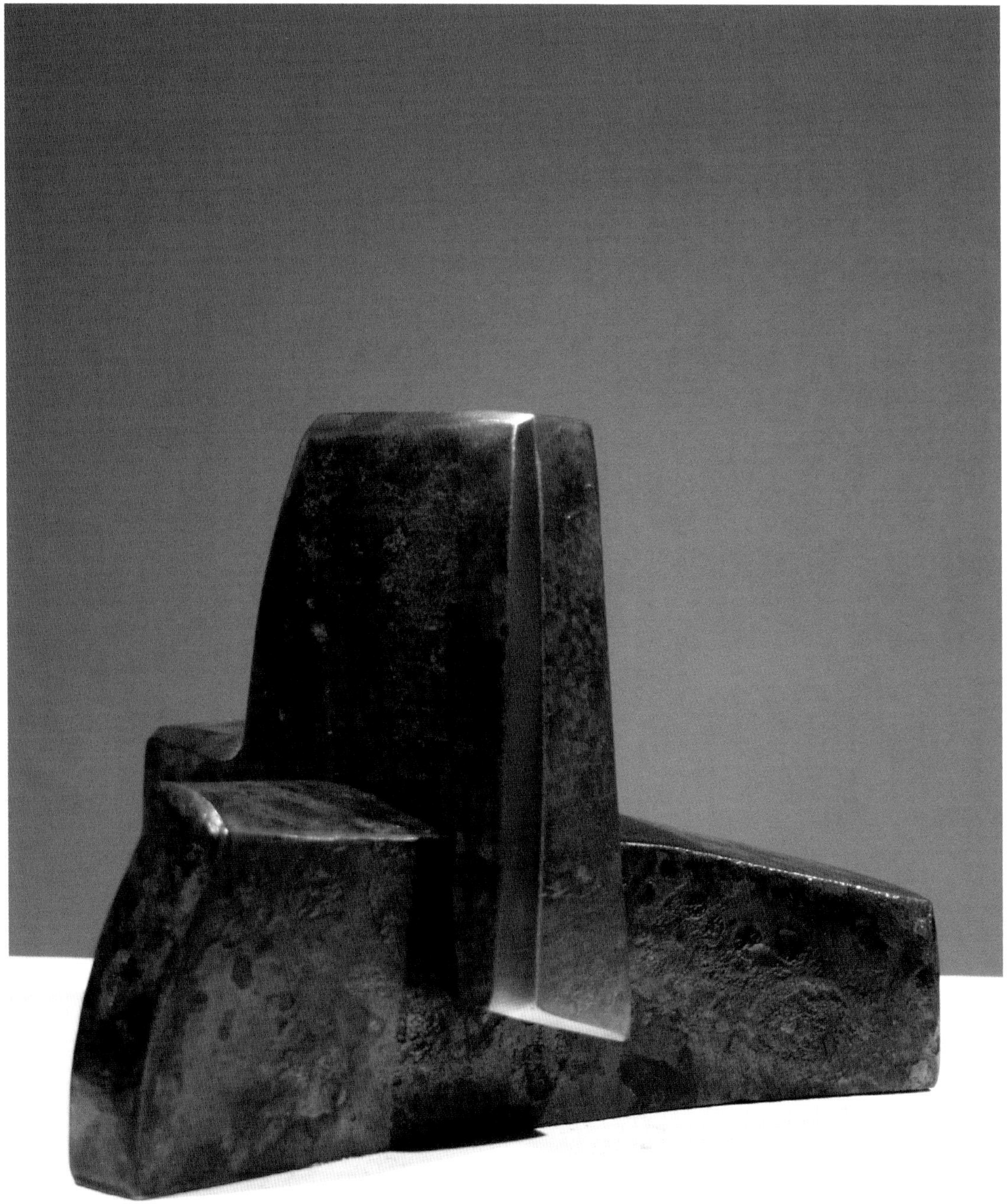

Matt Haugh. *Gary,* 2007. Forged iron. 10" h x 12" w x 10" l. *Photo, artist*

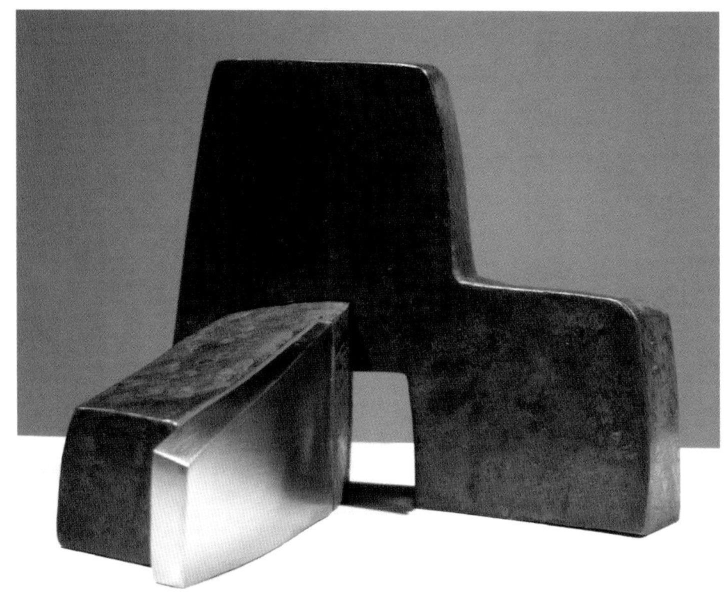

Matt Haugh. *Gary.* Second view. *Photo, artist*

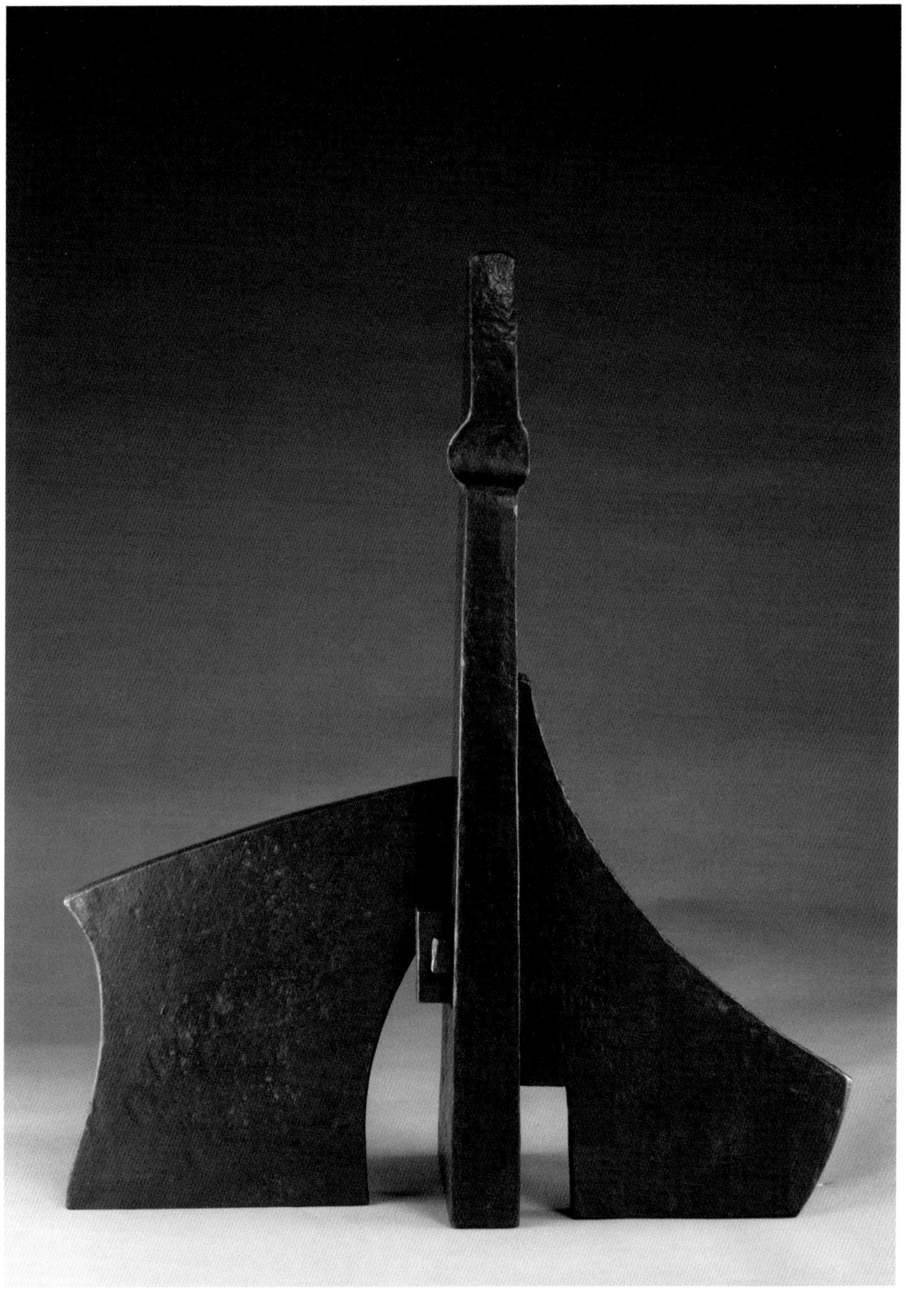

Matt Haugh. *Curly,* 2007. Forged iron. 15" h x 15" w x 7" l. *Photo, artist*

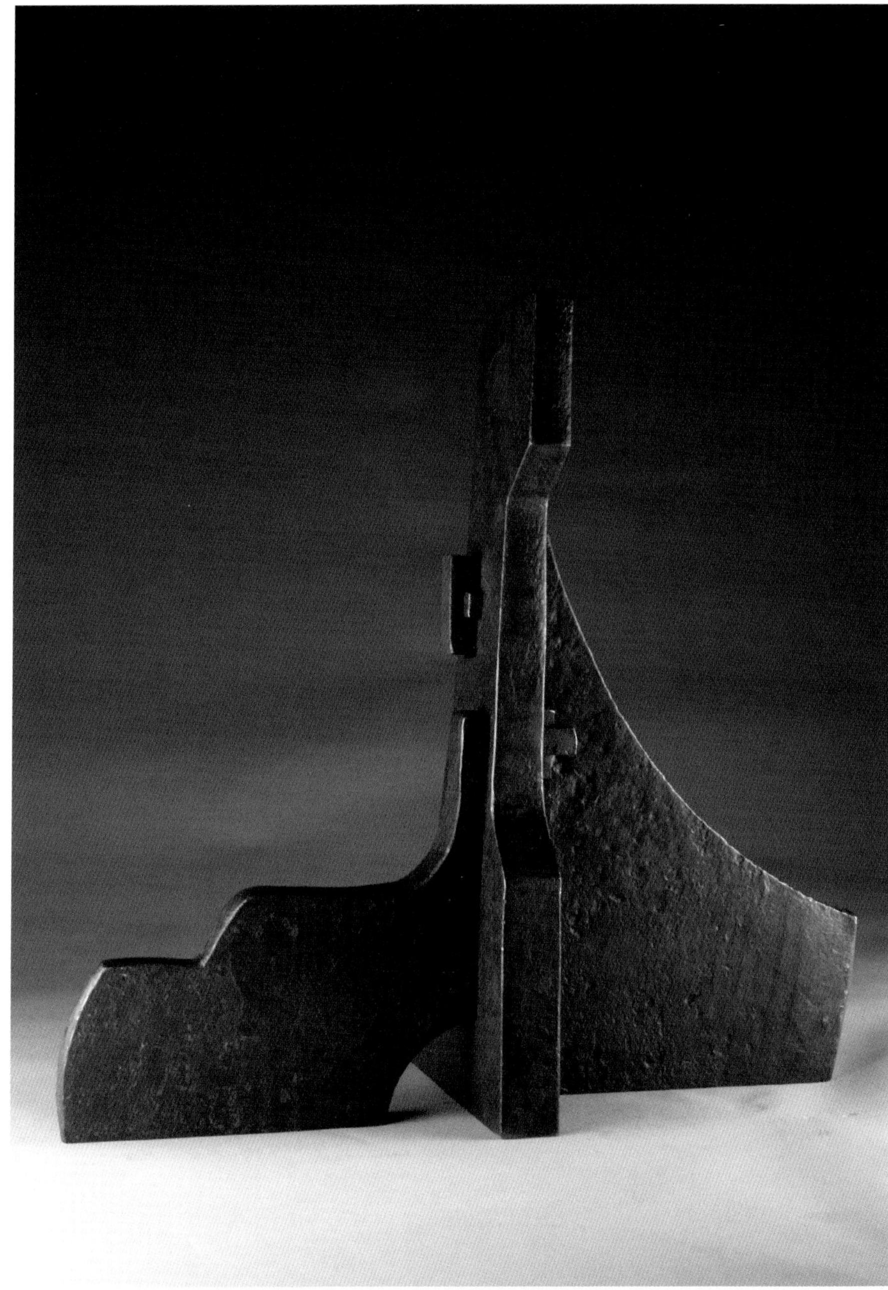

Matt Haugh. *Joe,* 2007. Forged iron. 15" h x 2" w x 5" l. *Photo, artist*

Matt Haugh. *Annie,* 2007. Forged iron.
13" h x 8" w x 3" l.

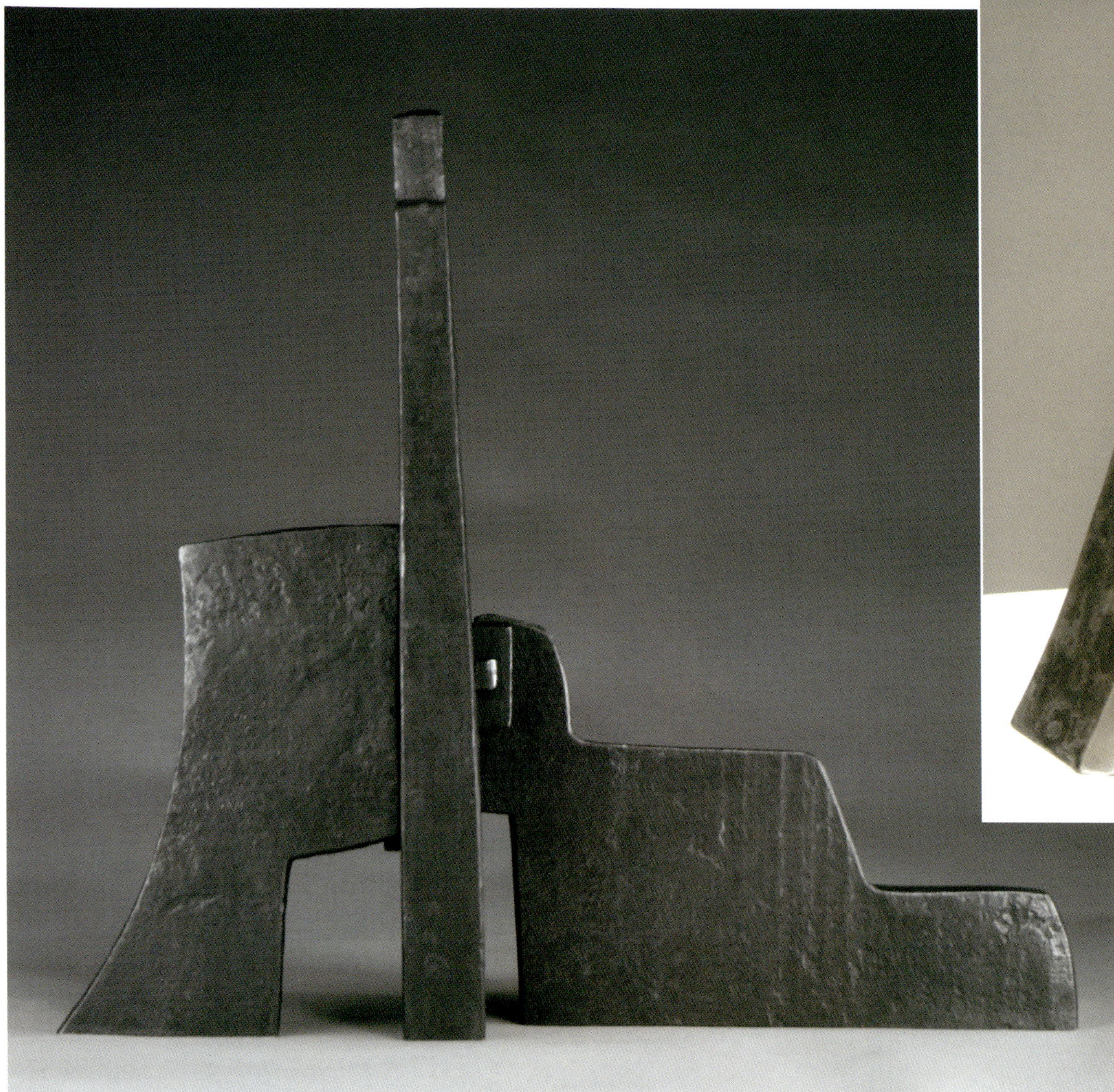

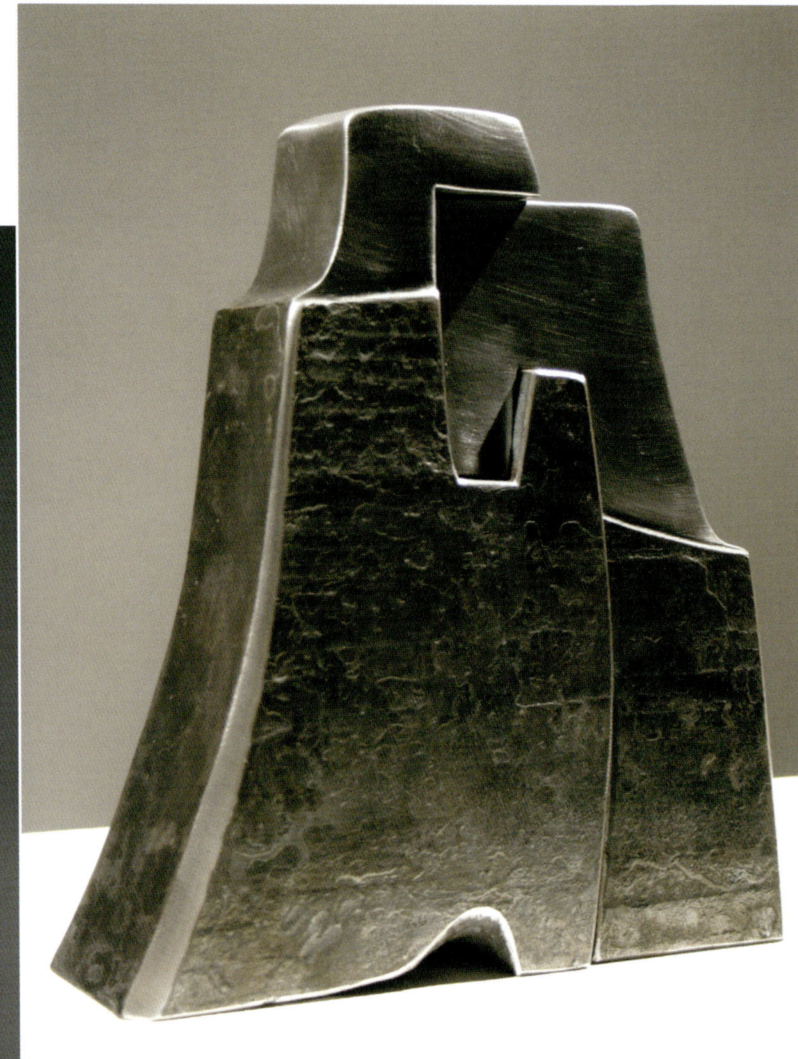

Matt Haugh. *Larry,* 2007. Forged iron.
10" h x 14" w x 5" l. *Photo, artist*

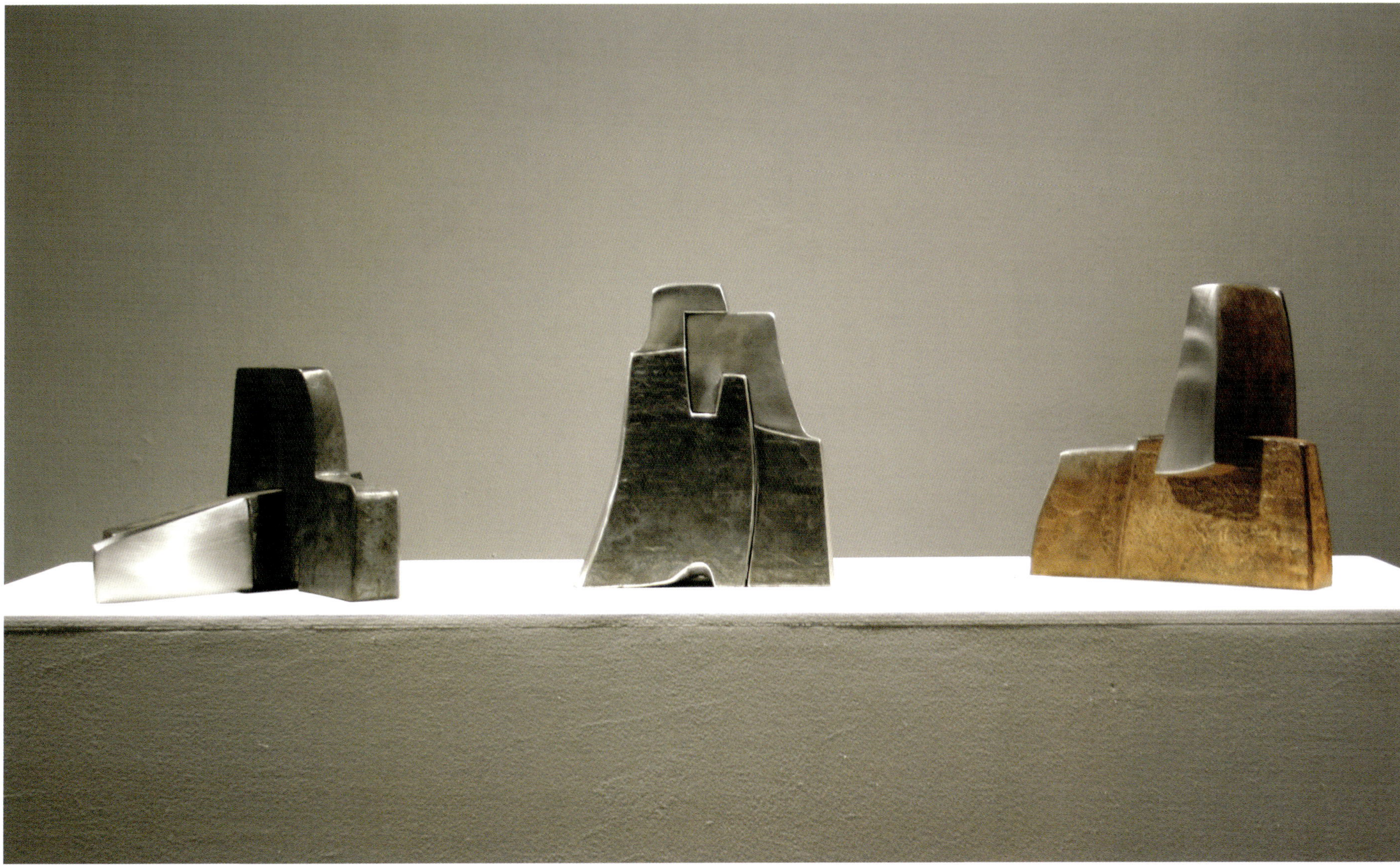

Matt Haugh. *Scrap Yard Series*, Group Photo. *Photo, artist*

The works that make up the Scrap Yard Series emerged from salvaged iron gleaned from scrap yards, and bear remnants of the industrial processes that produce them, Commonly parts of a circle or radius. I chose to preserve this attribute in the new form, a historical record of the distinct process and manufacturing methods of iron production. The materials range in size from 1" to 3" plate, and were forged in a Nazel 3B power hammer, and formed in a hydraulic press to create dimensional variance. By way of the arrangement of form on the horizontal and vertical plane these small format wrought iron sculptures recall figures in the landscape, and tend toward the mythic and architectonic. Out of reverence for the efforts of the individuals that work the mines, foundries, and mills, these works are given names like Curly and Joe and are fitted with traditional joinery that evokes the careful attention to detail associated with skilled handwork. – Matt Haugh

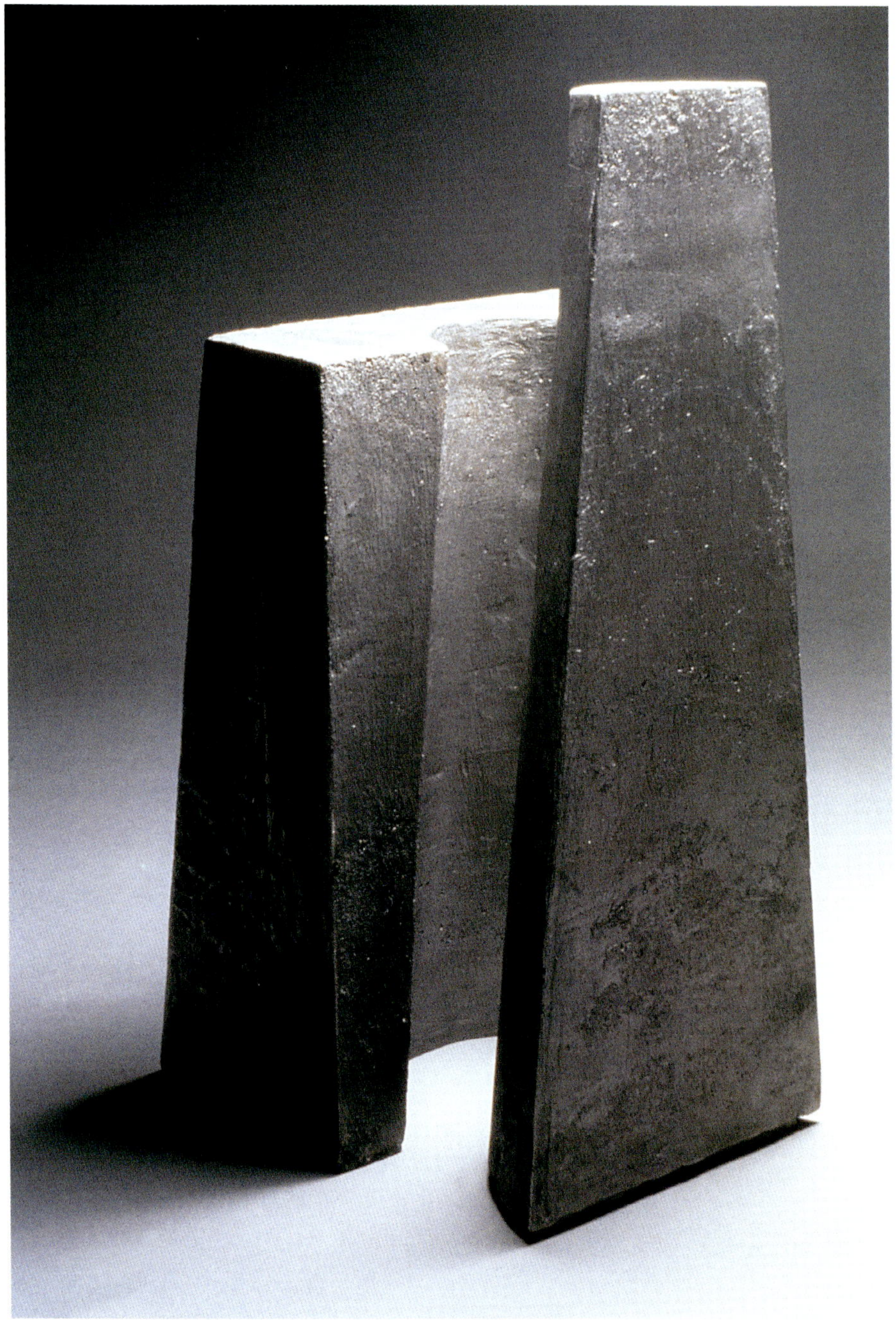

Michael J. Saari. *Untitled.* Formed and forged steel. 10" w x 20" h. *Photo, artist*

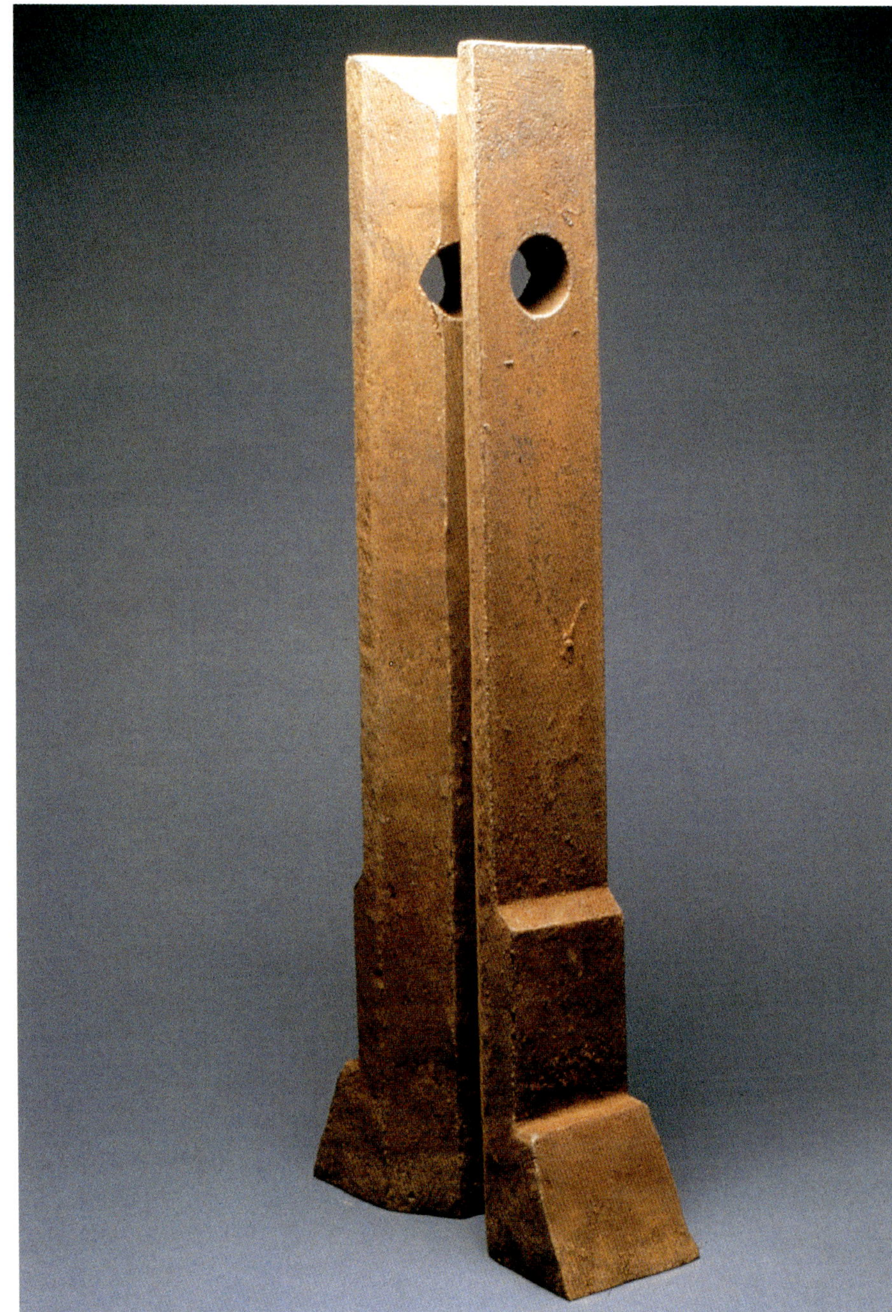

Michael J. Saari. *Untitled.* Formed and forged steel. 30" h x 9" w. *Photo, artist*

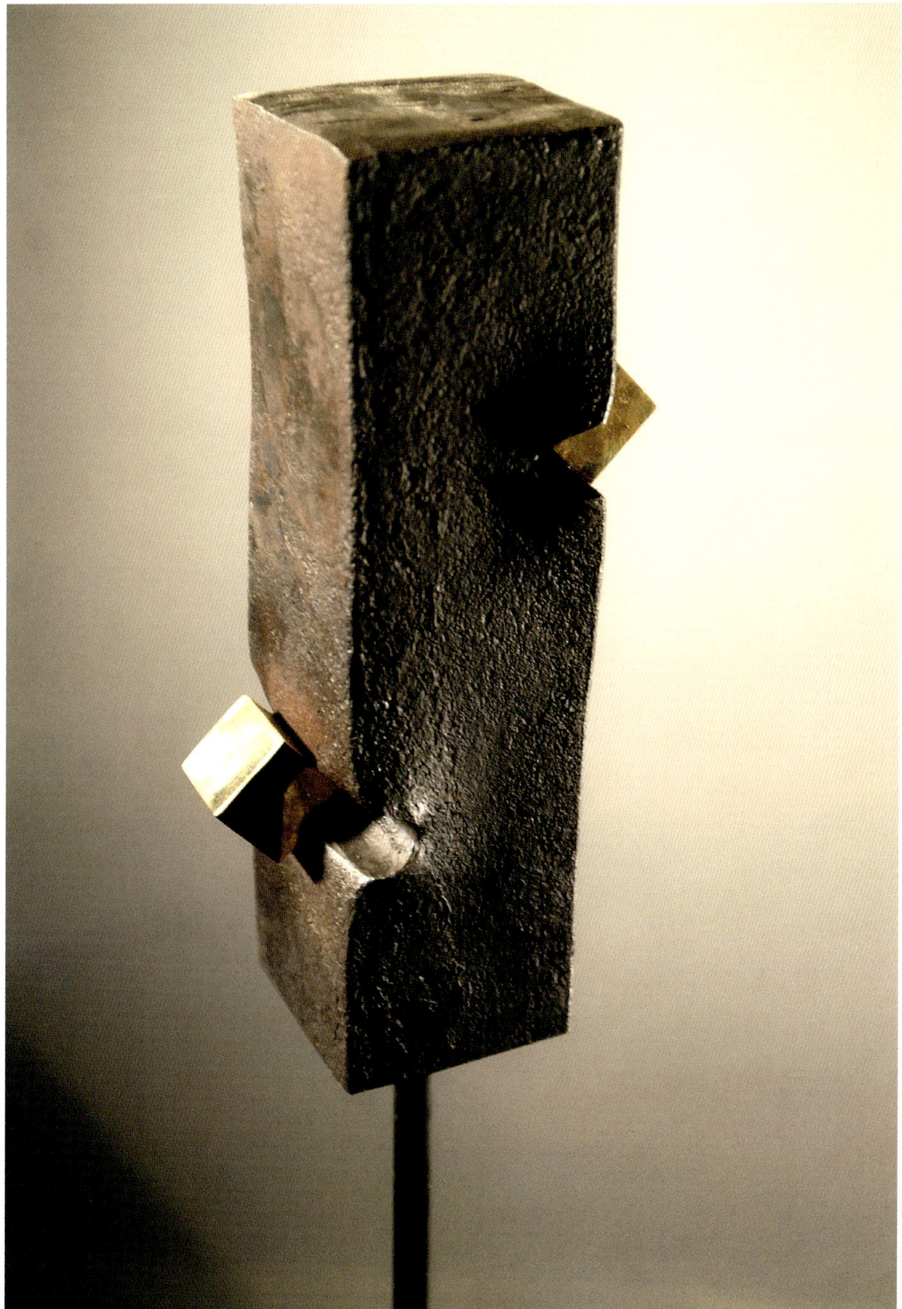

Latifa Sayadi. *En Deux* (In a Pair), 2007. Mild steel, polished brass, sawn and split and welded, 59" h. *Photo, Holger Ziefus*

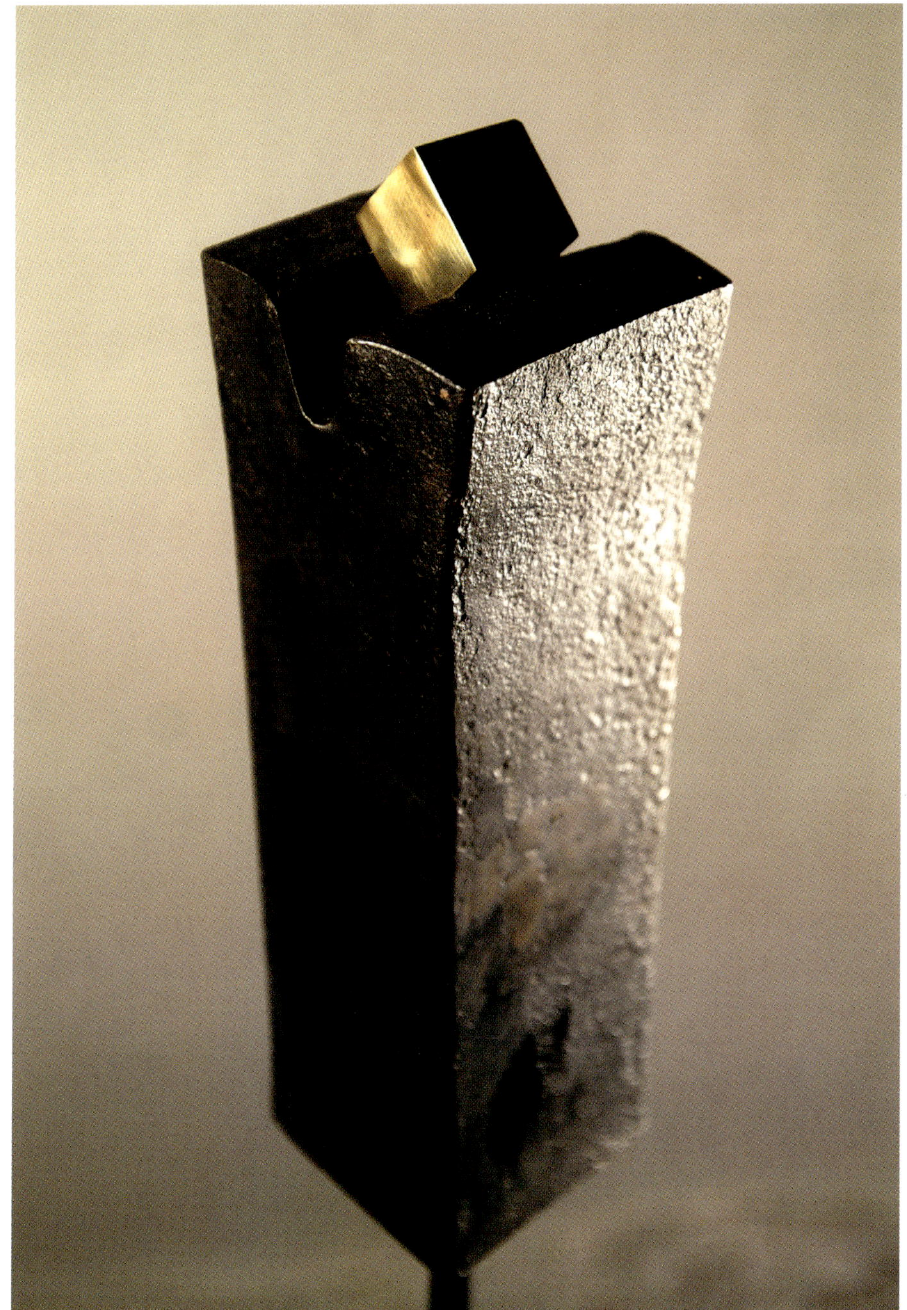

Latifa Sayadi. *Seul* (Alone), 2007. Mild steel, polished brass, sawn and split and welded, 59" h. *Photo, Holger Ziefus*

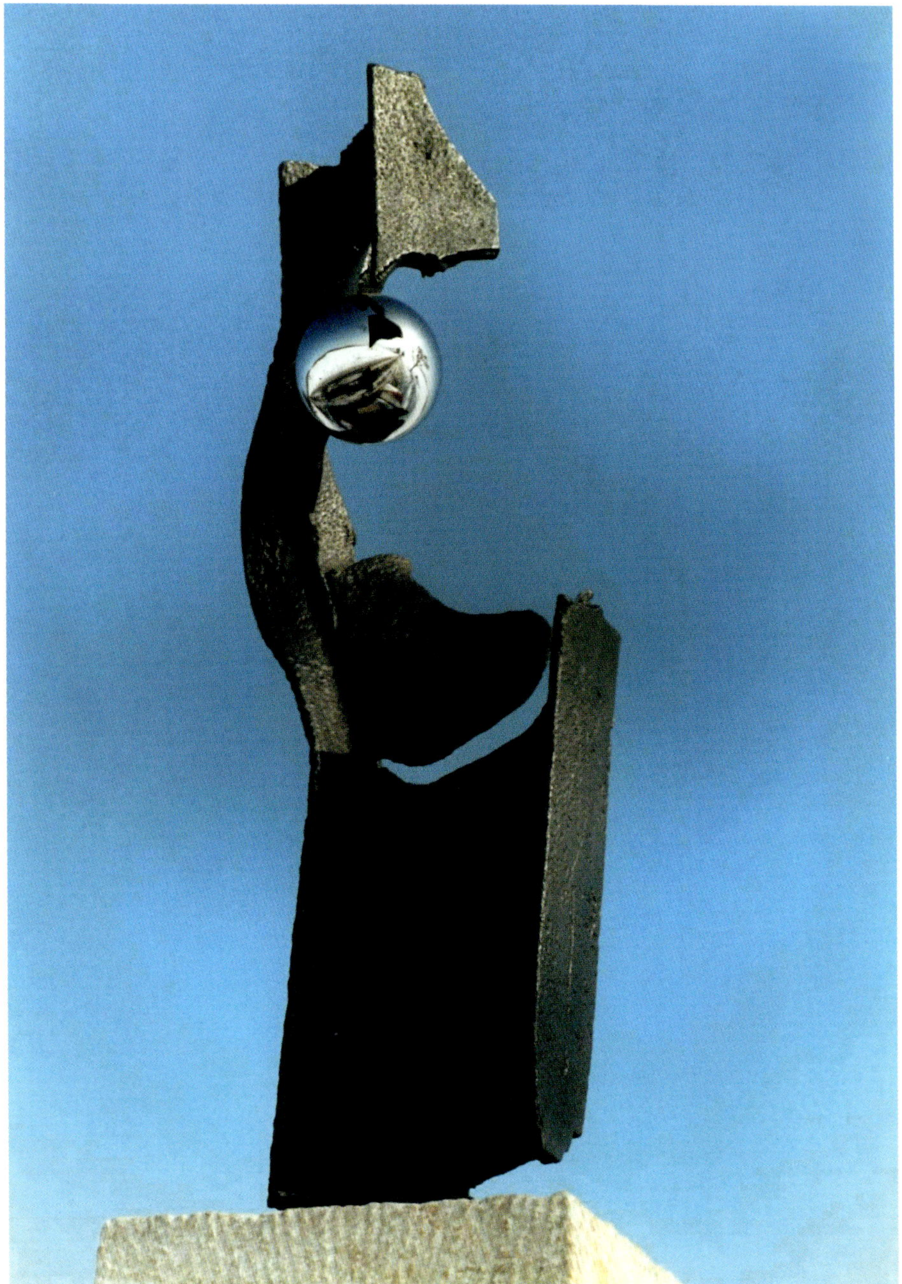

Karel Meloun. *Fighter II,* 1992. Steel, sandstone. 12" x 12" x 40.5". *Private collection. Photo, artist*

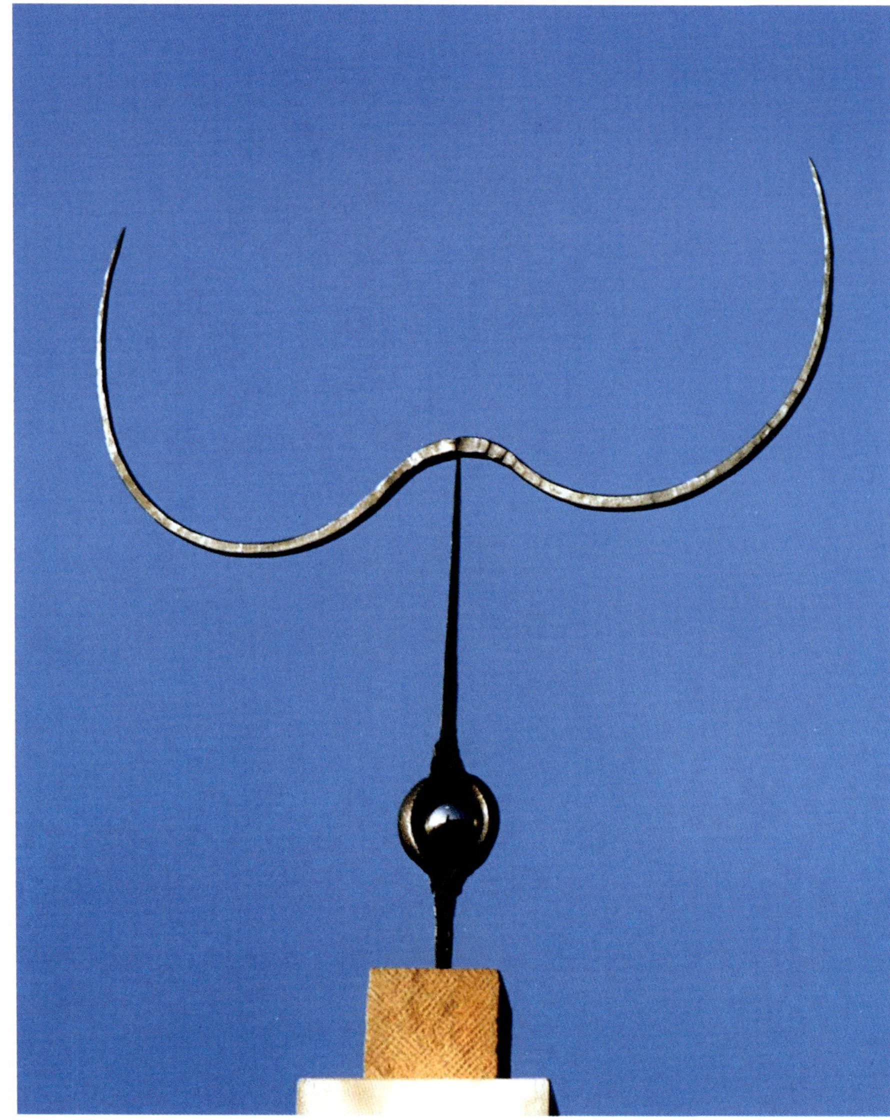

Karel Meloun. *Homage to Salvador Dali,* 1996. Kinetic, forged steel, anticorrosive steel and sand stone. 6" x 41" x 49". *Private collection. Photo, artist*

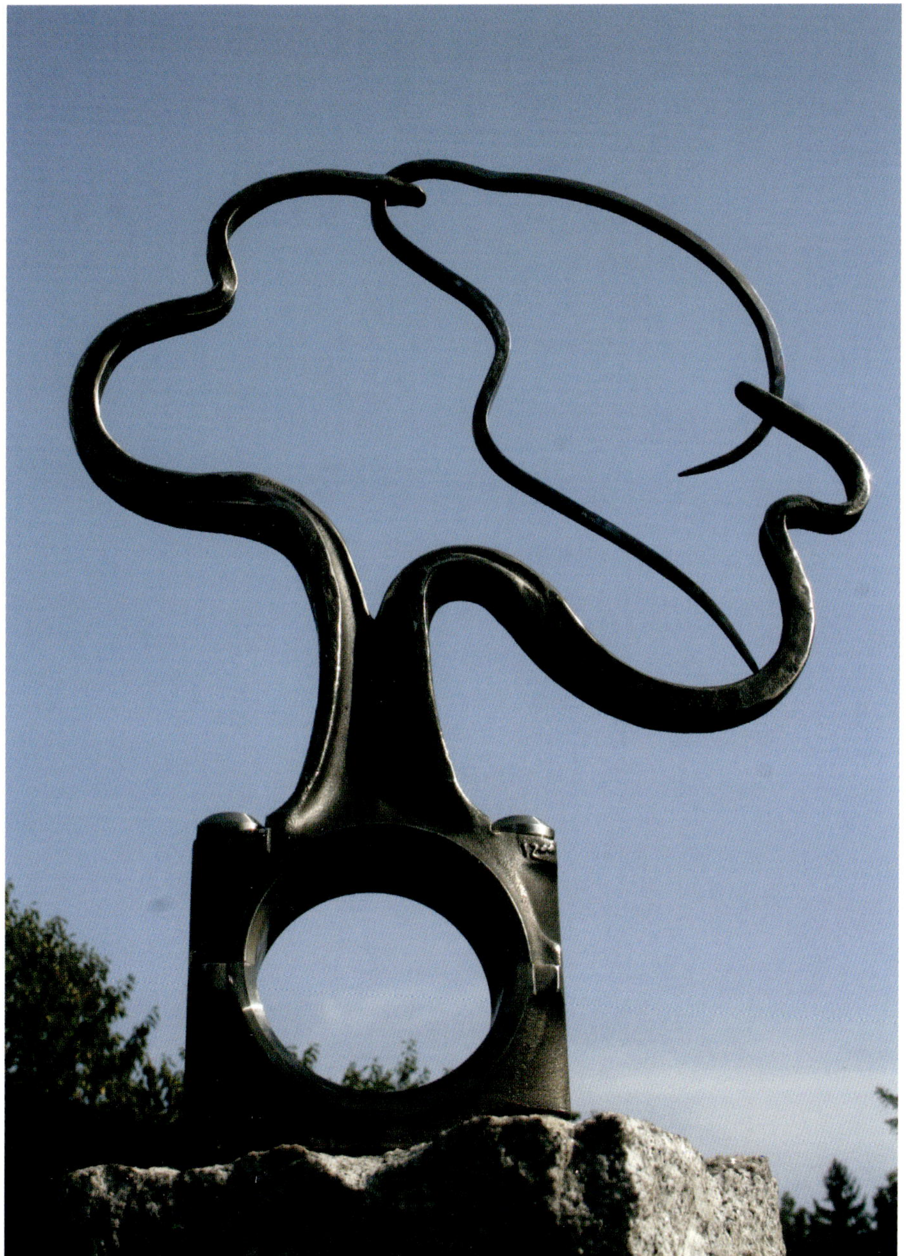

Roberto Giordani. *Connecting Rod in Motion*, 2007. Obtained from the connecting rod of a truck and the insertion of forged titanium. 16" h x 30" w. *Photo, artist*

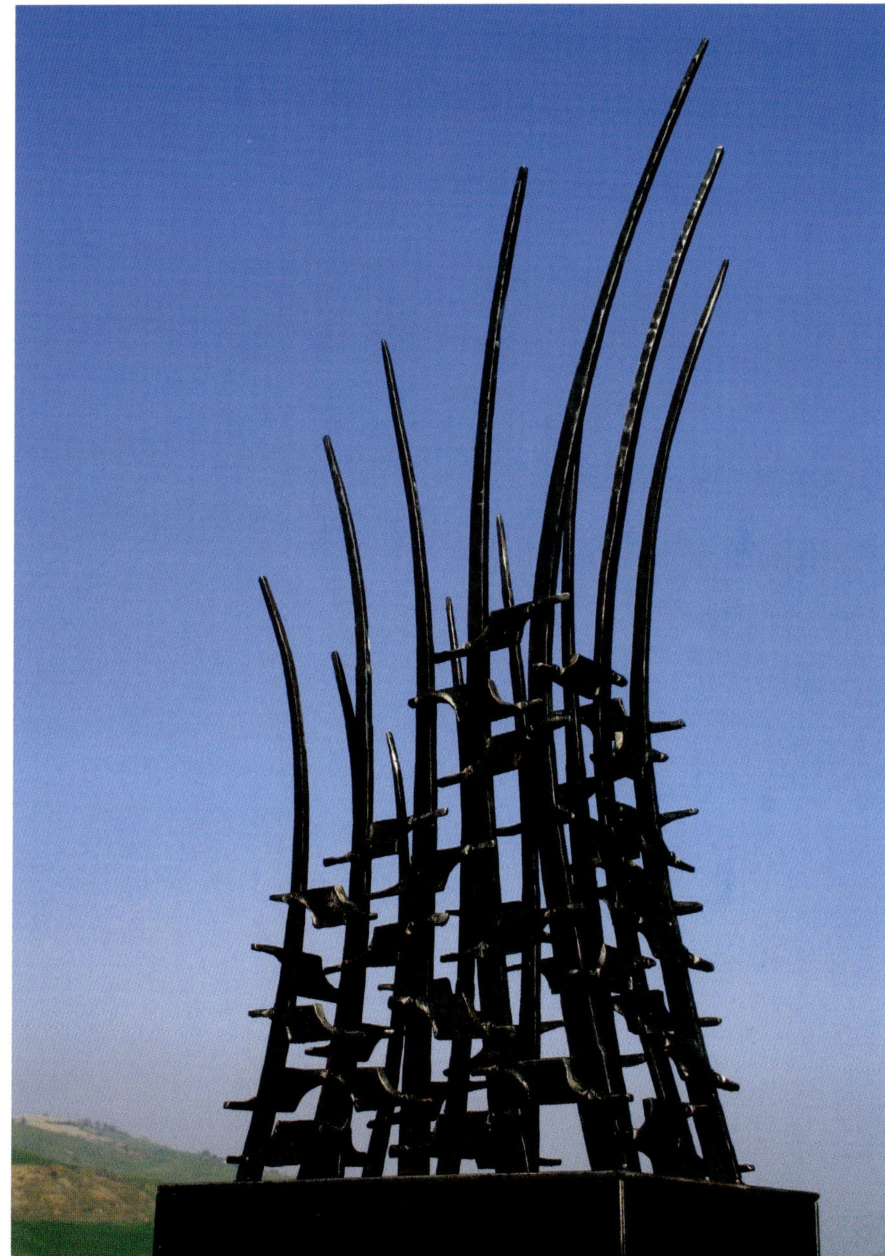

Roberto Giordani. *The Tower*, 2006. Forged steel. 295" x 177" x 71". This sculpture serves as a 1.10 scale model for a monumental sculpture to be placed in the urban center of Forlì, Italy. *Photo, artist*

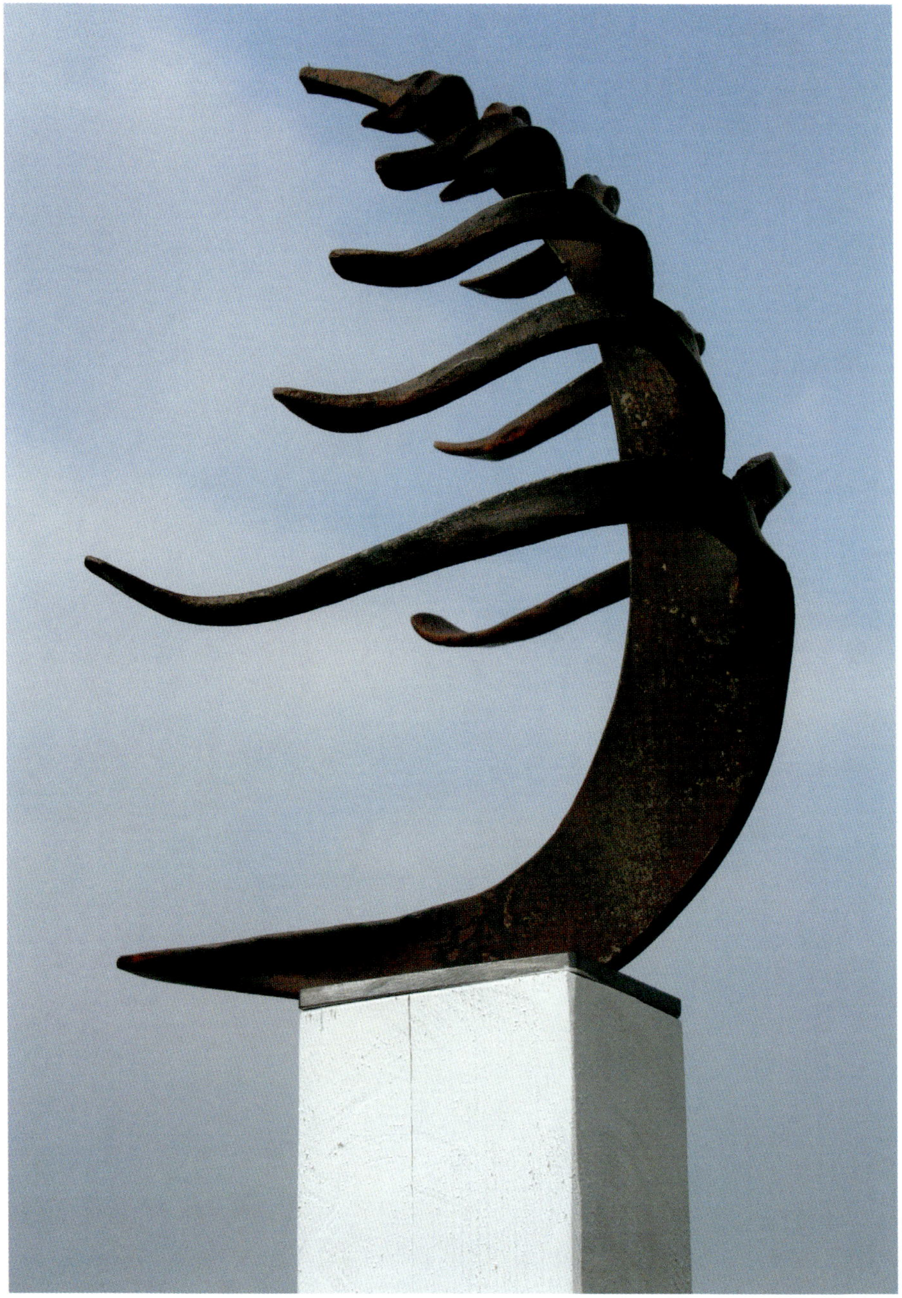

Roberto Giordani. *Marine Plant,* 2007. Created from 8mm thick slab. 12" h x 9" w x 6" d. *Photo, artist*

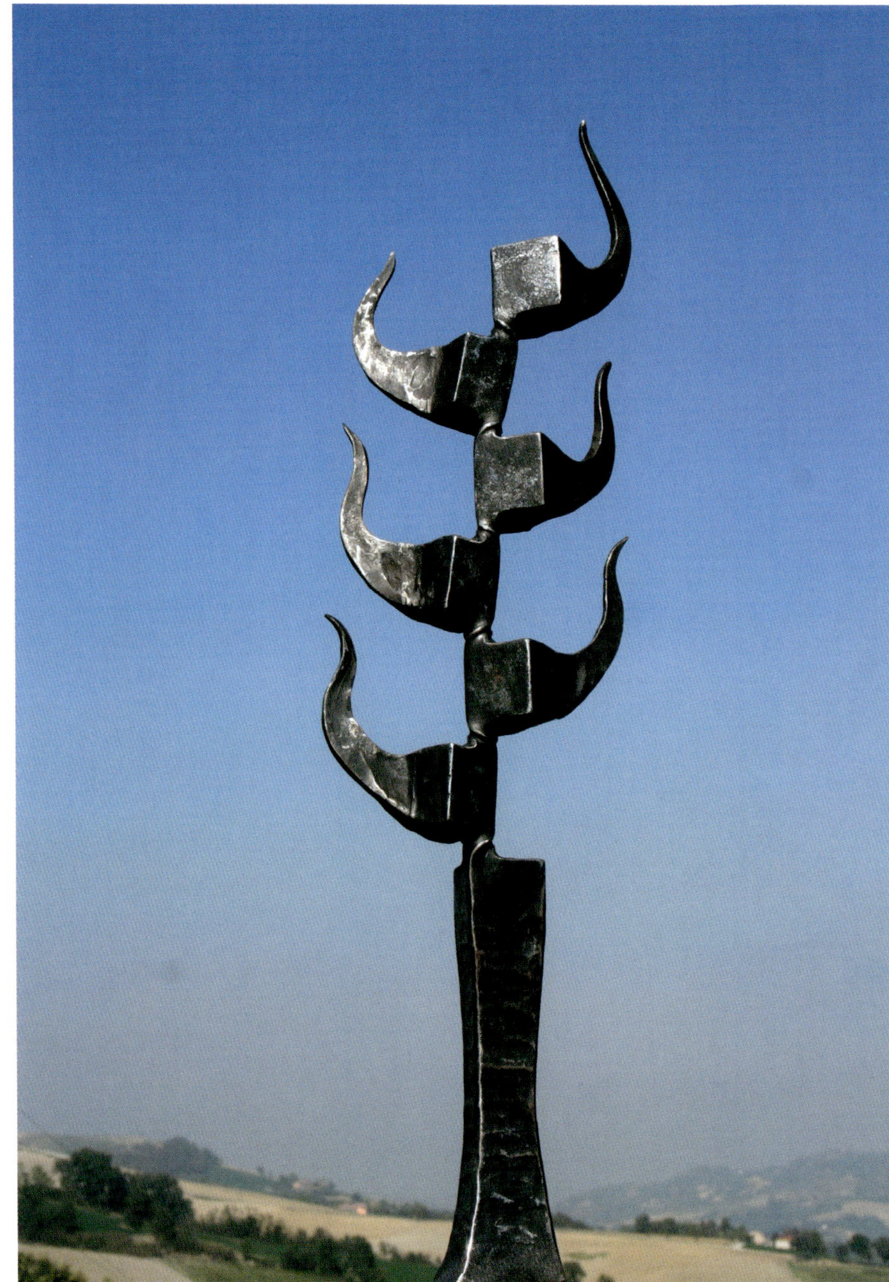

Roberto Giordani. *Ear of Corn,* 2007. Forged steel. *Photo, artist*

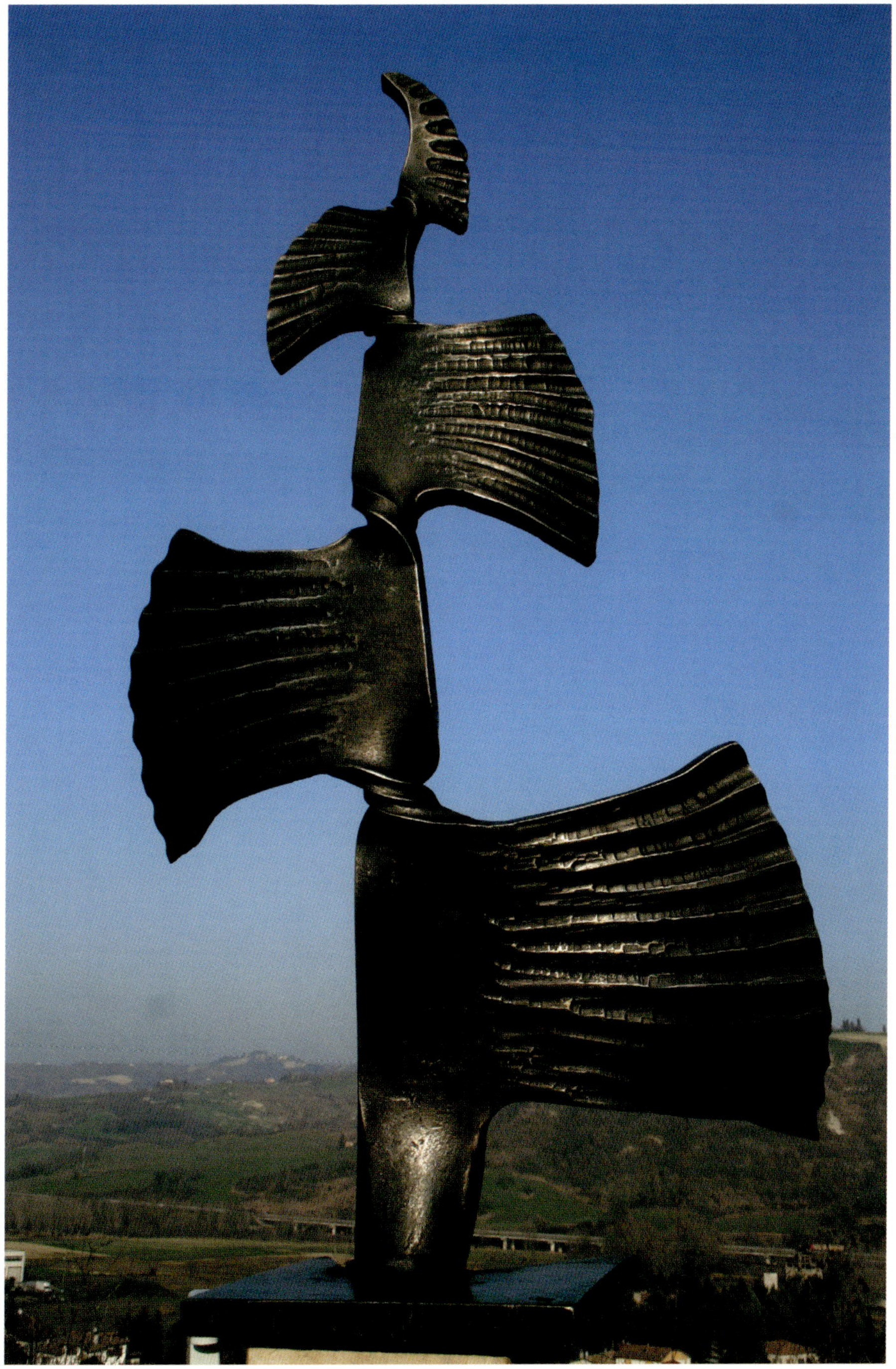

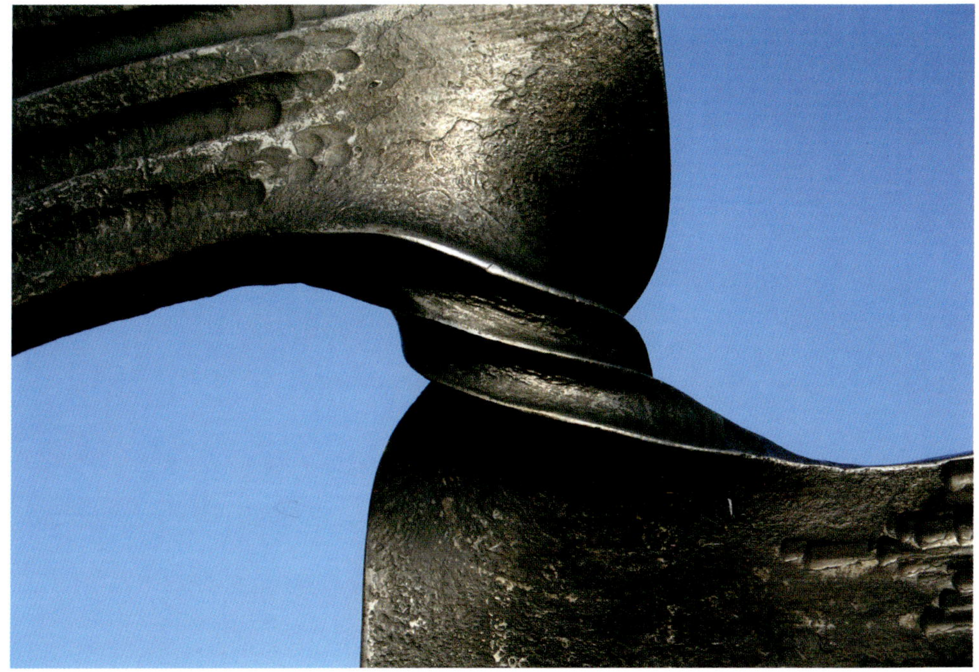

Roberto Giordani. *Sails,* 2004. Detail. *Photo, artist*

Roberto Giordani. *Sails,* 2004. Created from a single iron sheet. 43" h x 29.5" w. *Photo, artist*

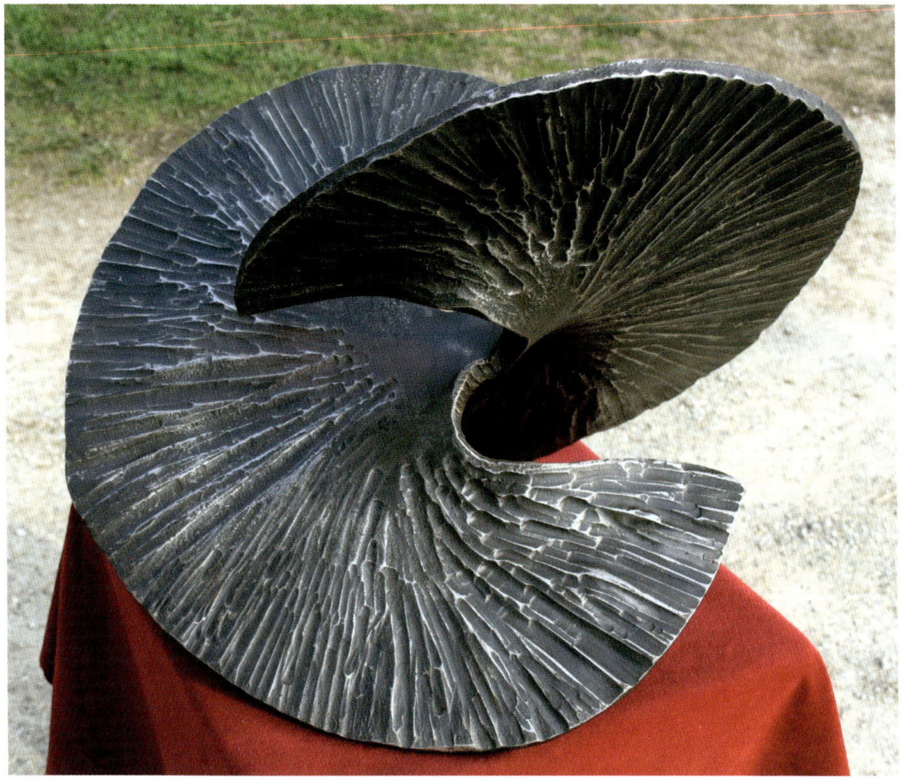

Roberto Giordani. *The Kiss*, 2005. Forged from sheet iron, 0.9" thick, 27.5" in diameter. *Photo, artist*

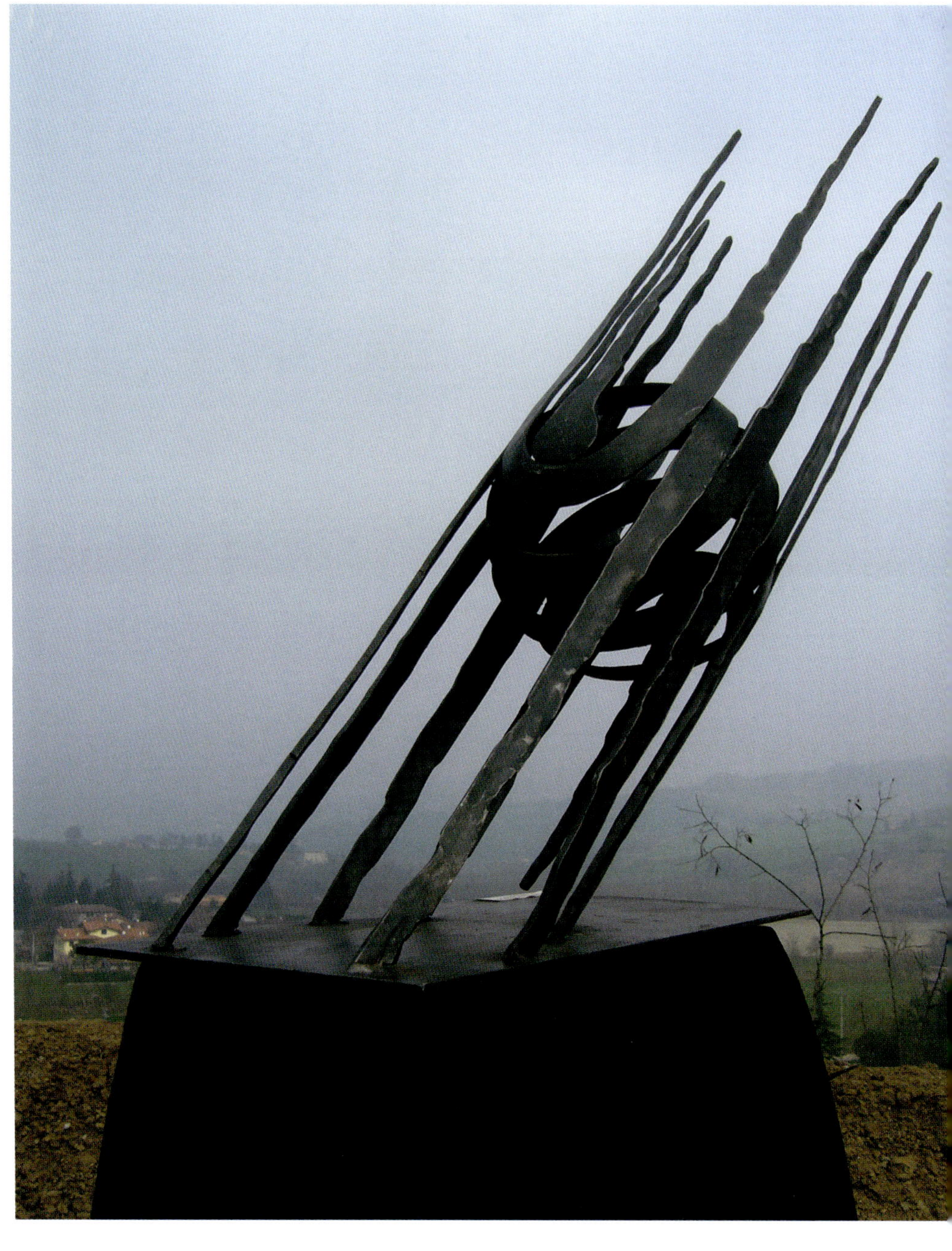

Roberto Giordani. *Meeting of Energy,* 2006. Forged plates, 118" h x 157" l x 31" d. Built with the help of colleagues: Jry Bat'a, Gianluca Volontario, and Pietrino Dettori, during the forum for Castle Helfstyn, Czech Republic. *Photo, artist*

Pavel Tasovský. *No*, 2005. Pendulum. 25" x 17" x 10". *Photo, artist*

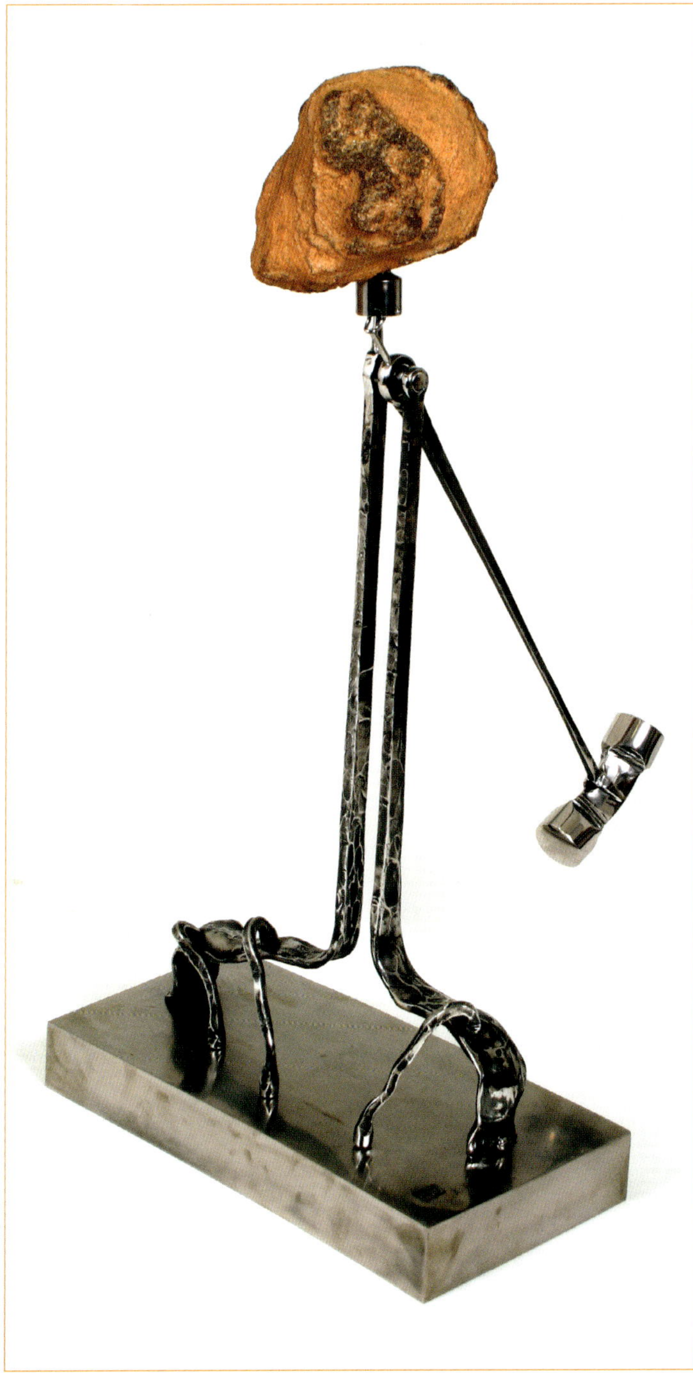

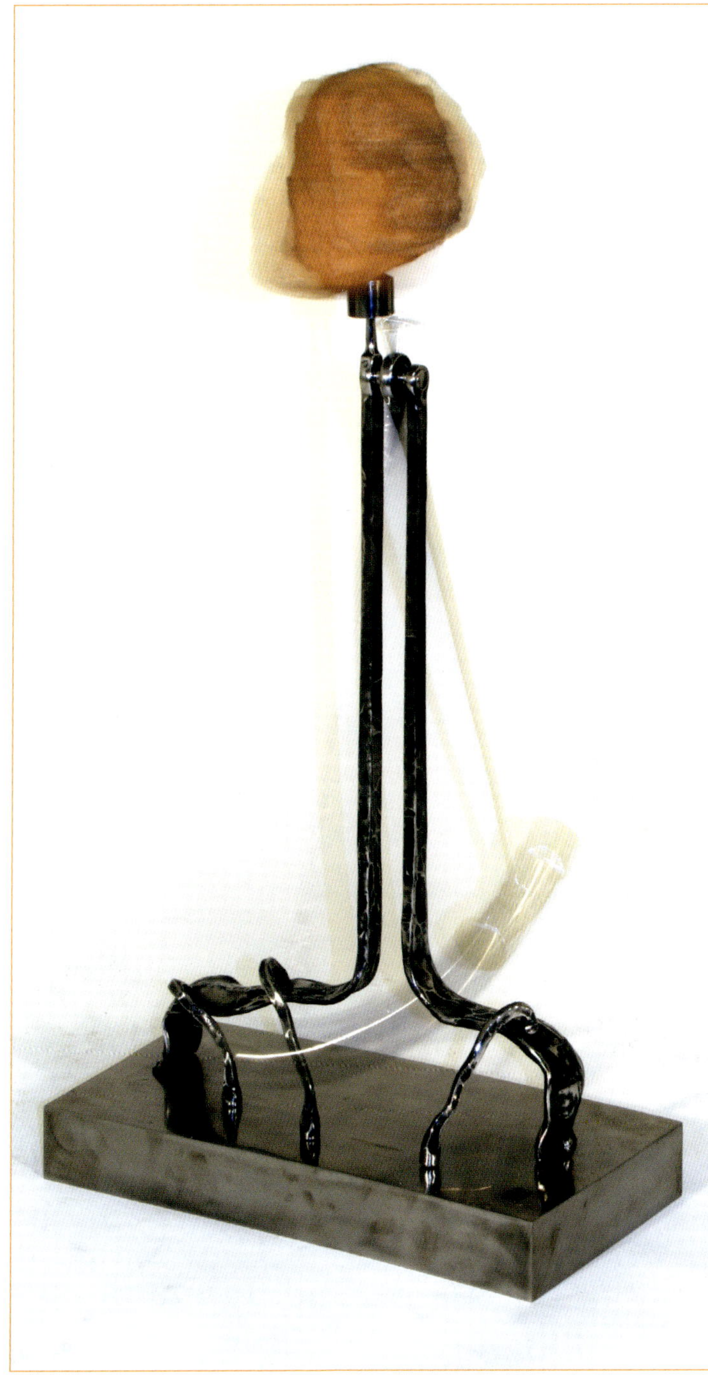

Pavel Tasovský. *No*, 2005. Pendulum in motion. *Photo, artist*

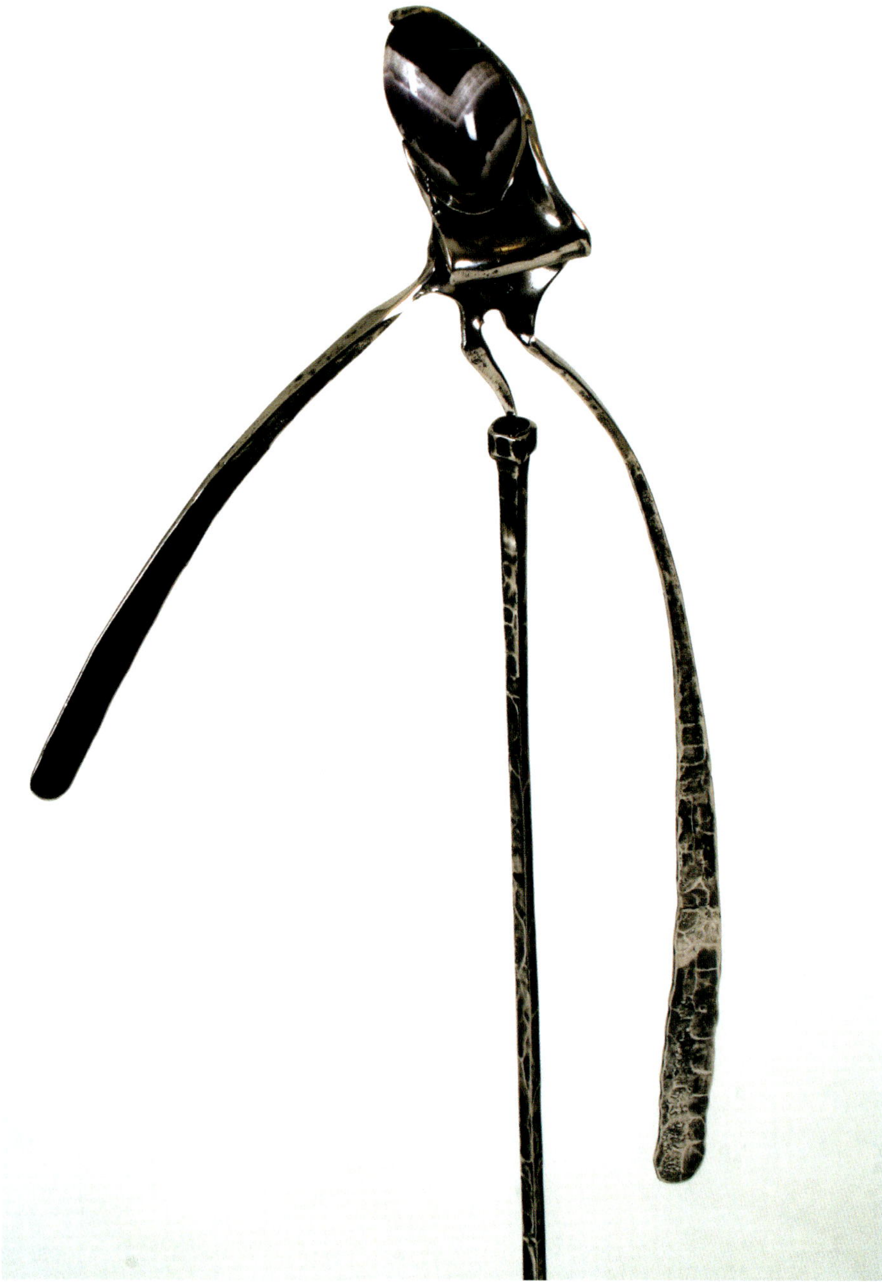

Pavel Tasovský. *Tvor,* 2005. 57" x 13.5" x 5.5". *Photo, artist*

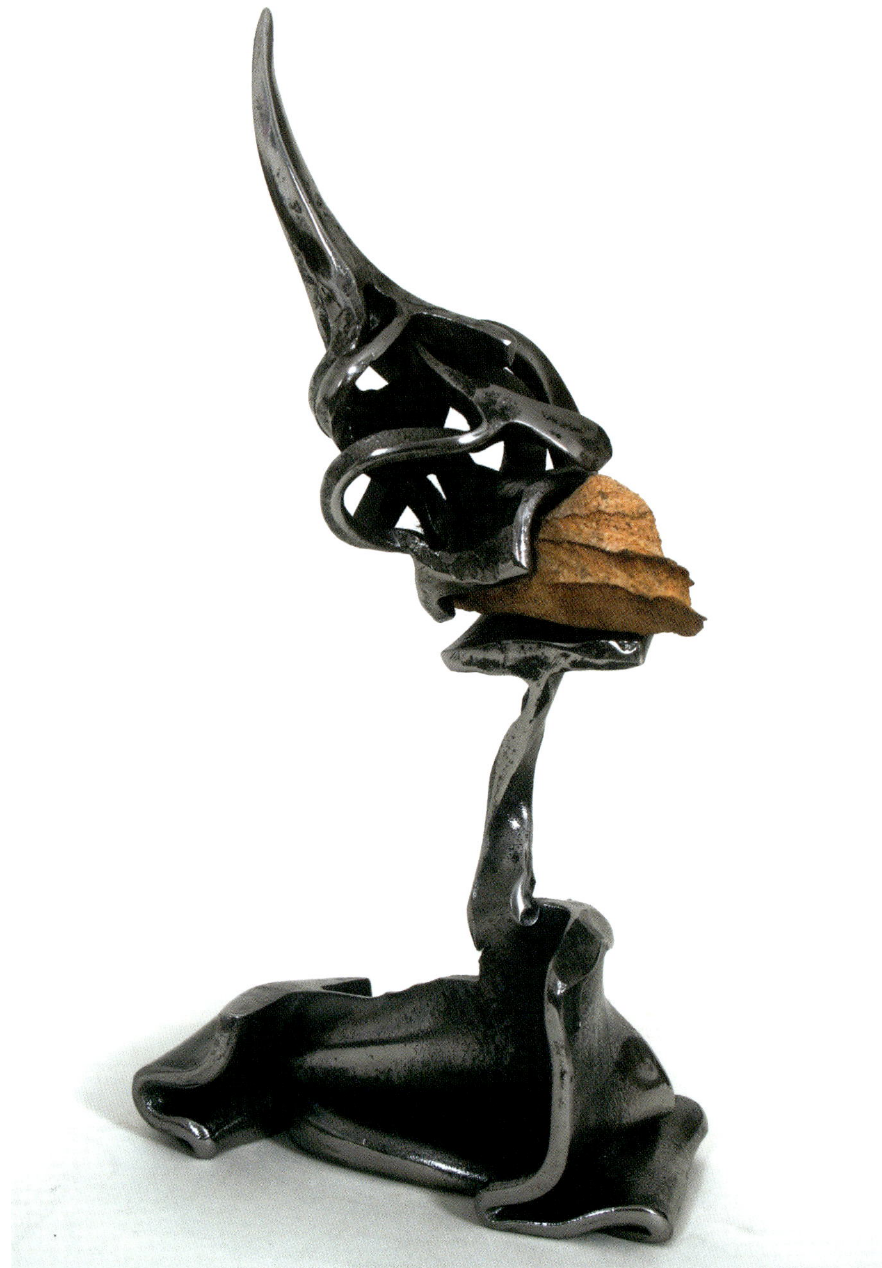

Pavel Tasovský. *Creature,* 2006. 9" x 5" x 3". *Photo, artist*

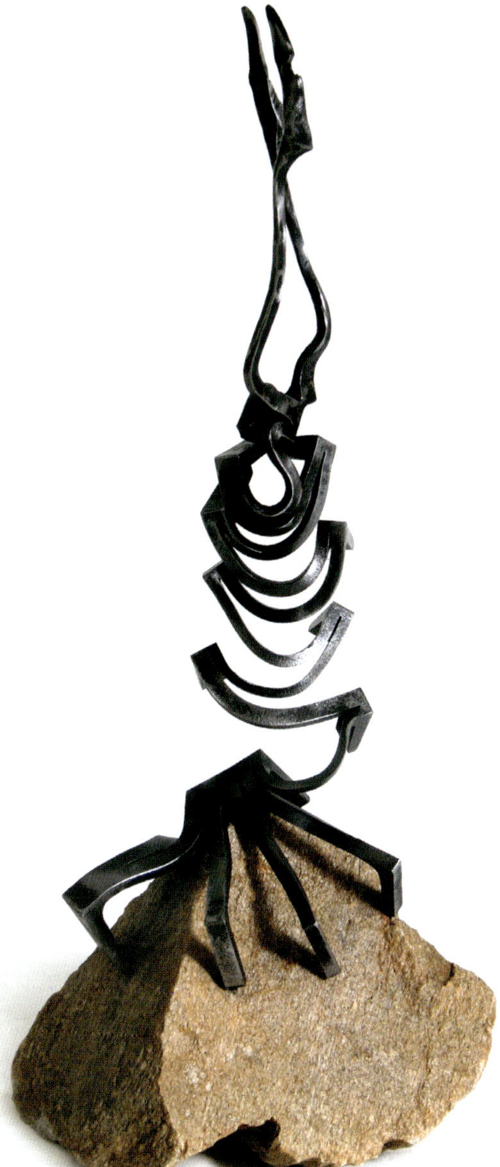

Pavel Tasovský. *Creature,* 2005. 27" x 11" x 10". *Photo, artist*

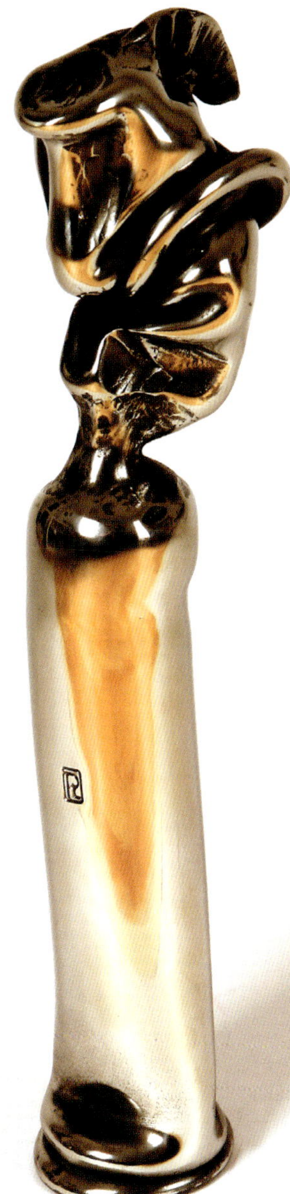

Pavel Tasovský. *Head,* 2007. 21" x 3" x 3". *Photo, artist*

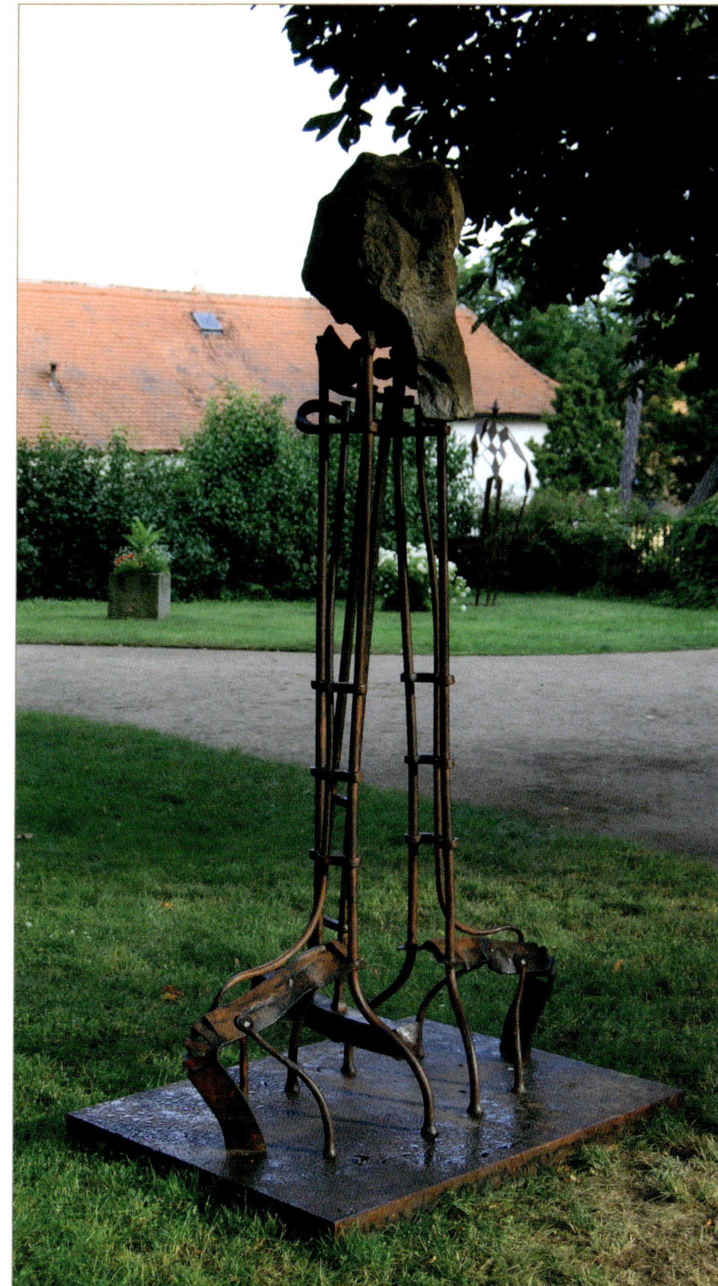

Pavel Tasovský. *Yes.* Interior kinetic sculpture. 28" x 17" x 10". *Photo, artist*

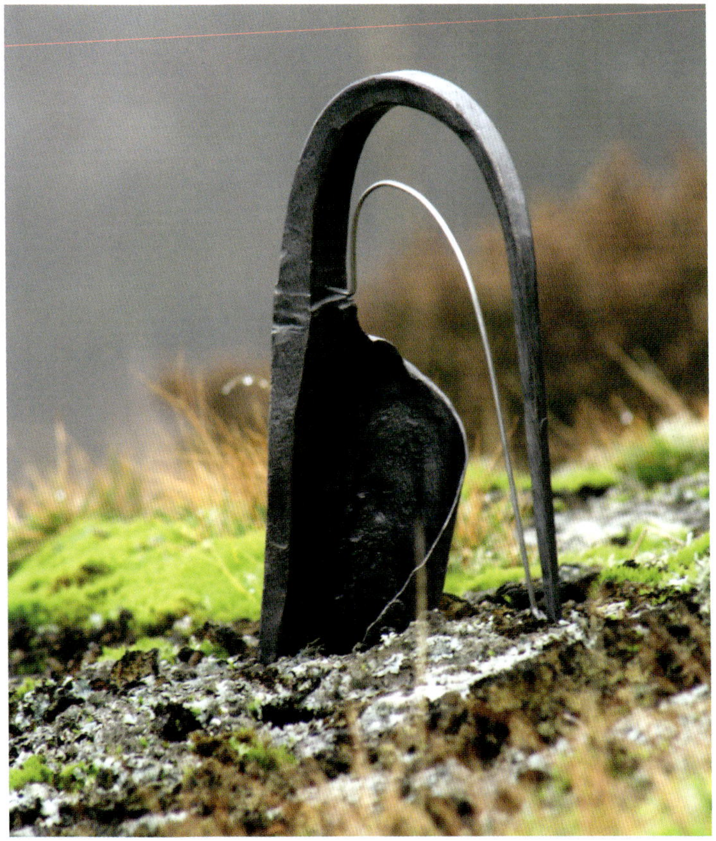

Johan Sangberg. *Vault.* Mild Steel and Stainless Steel. 5" x 3". *Photo, artist*

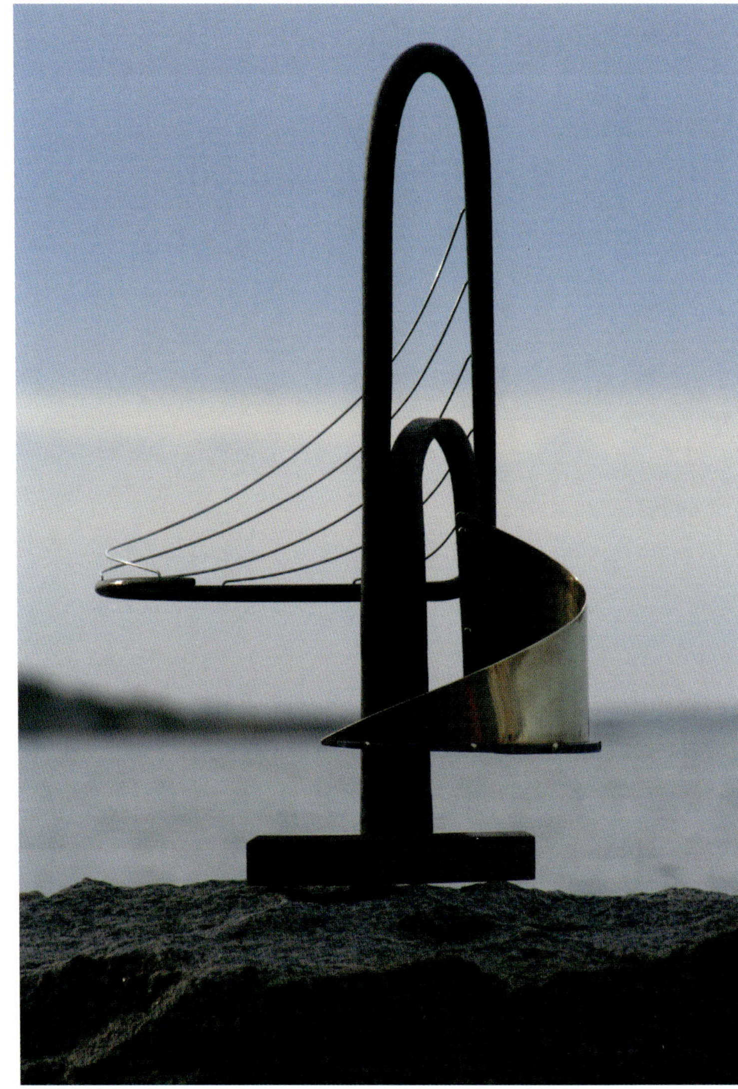

Johan Sangberg. *Ship.* Steel, Brass, and Stainless Steel, 24" x 16". *Photo, artist*

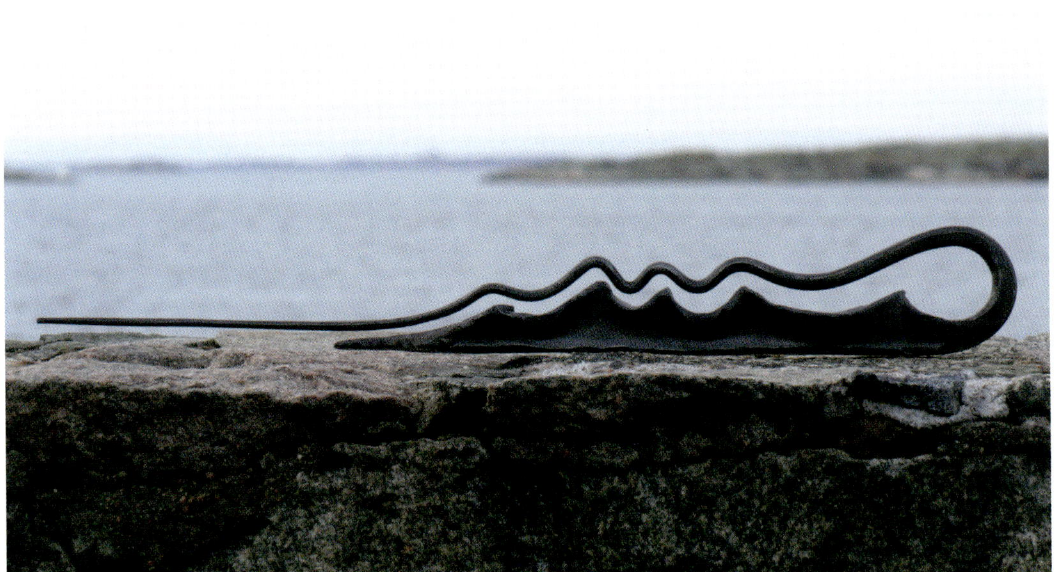

Johan Sangberg. *Wave.* Forged steel, 12" x 3". *Photo, artist*

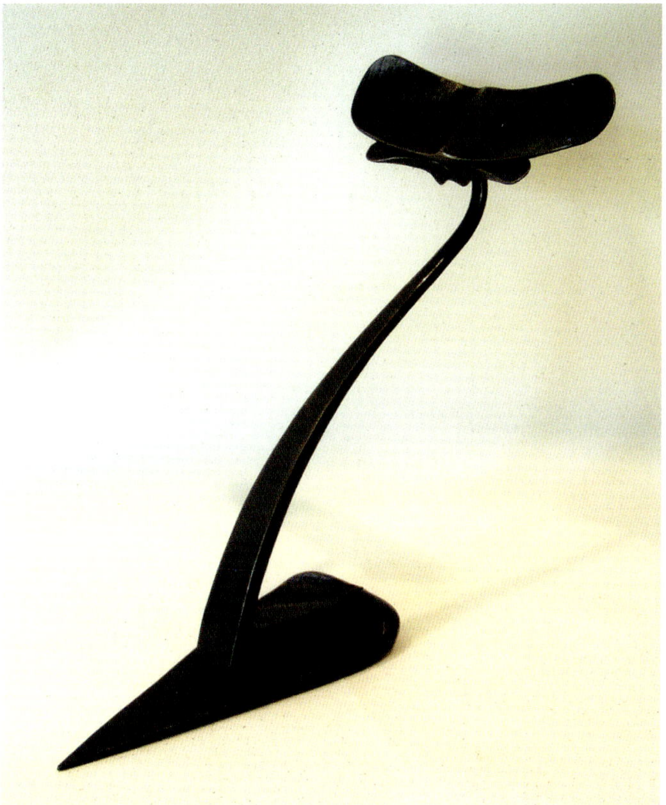

Dereck Glaser. *Fluke.* Forged steel, concealed welds, study in cross sectional changes 5" x 13" x 14", wax over forge scale finish. *Photo, artist*

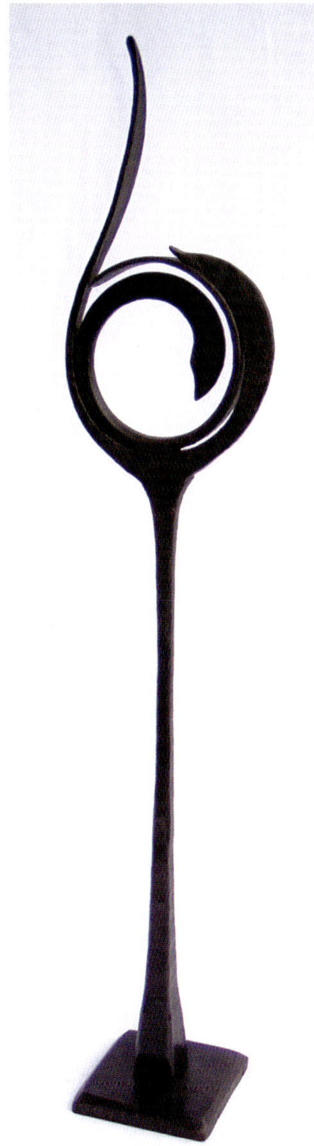

Dereck Glaser. *Tension II.* Forged and fire welded steel. 5" x 5" x 17". Wax over forge scale. *Photo, artist*

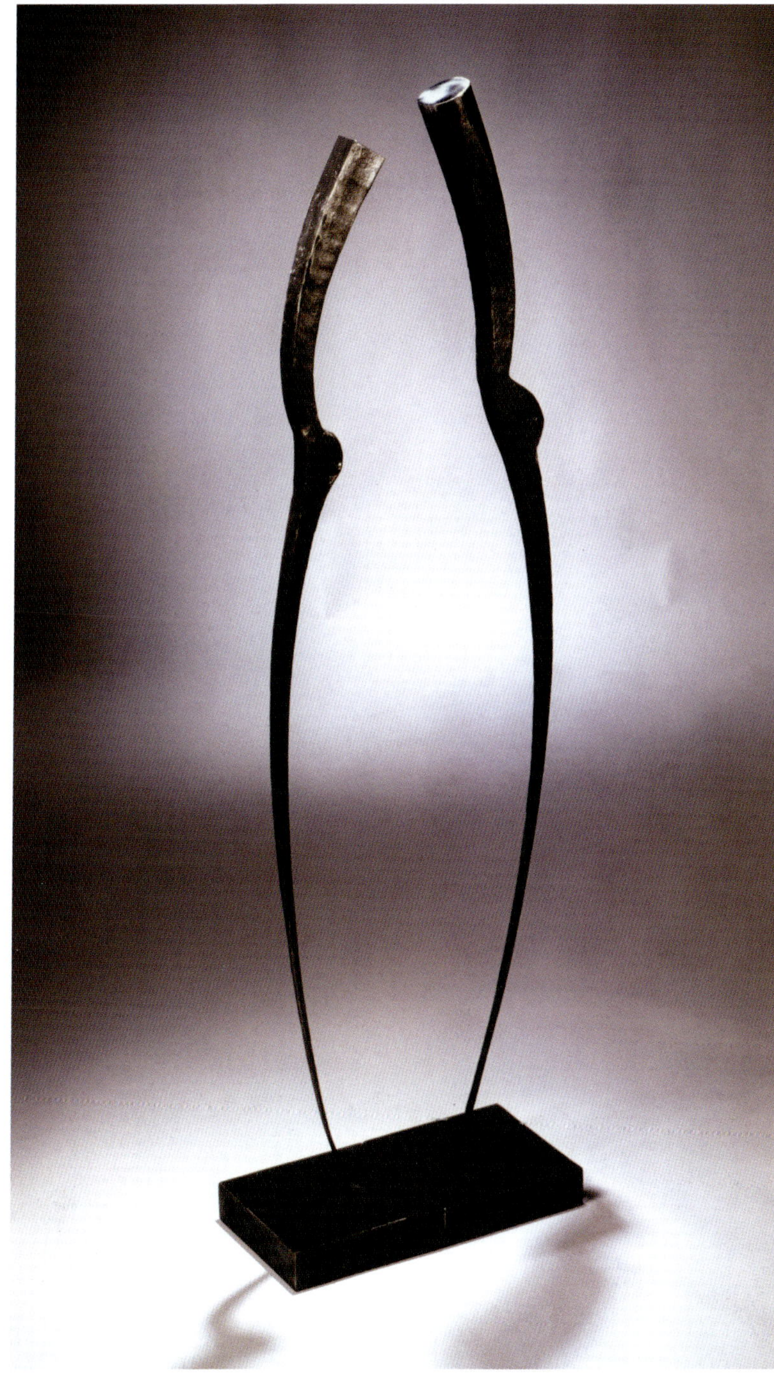

Alfred Bullermann. *Konkubinat.* Forged from 2" round bar and 2" x 2" steel, 49" in height. This sculpture swings or moves when touched. *Photo, Gerald Lampe*

Alfred Bullermann. *Touch-Me.* Forged from 5" x 5" steel. When touch the sculpture begins to move, revealing its meaning. *Photo, Gerald Lampe*

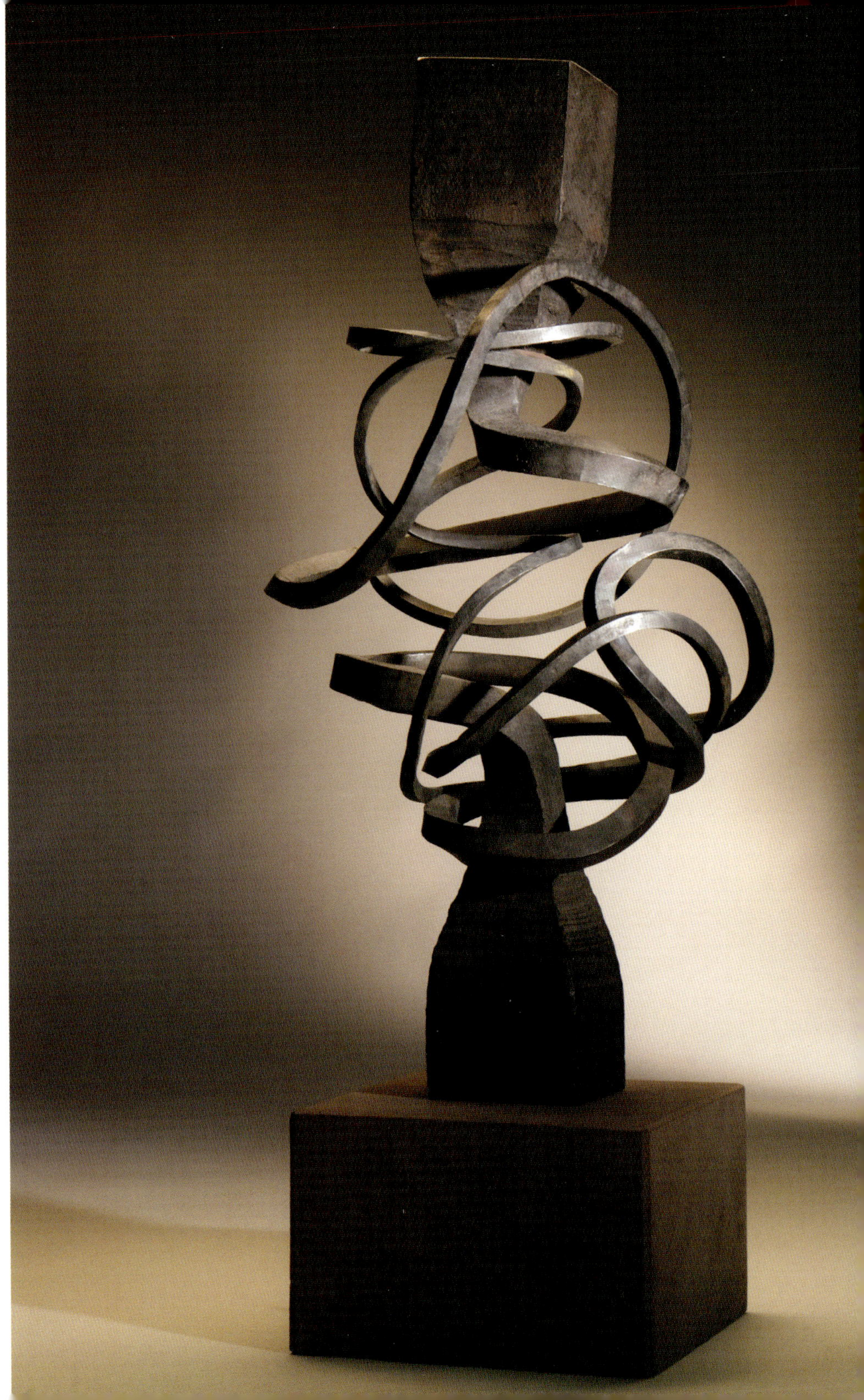

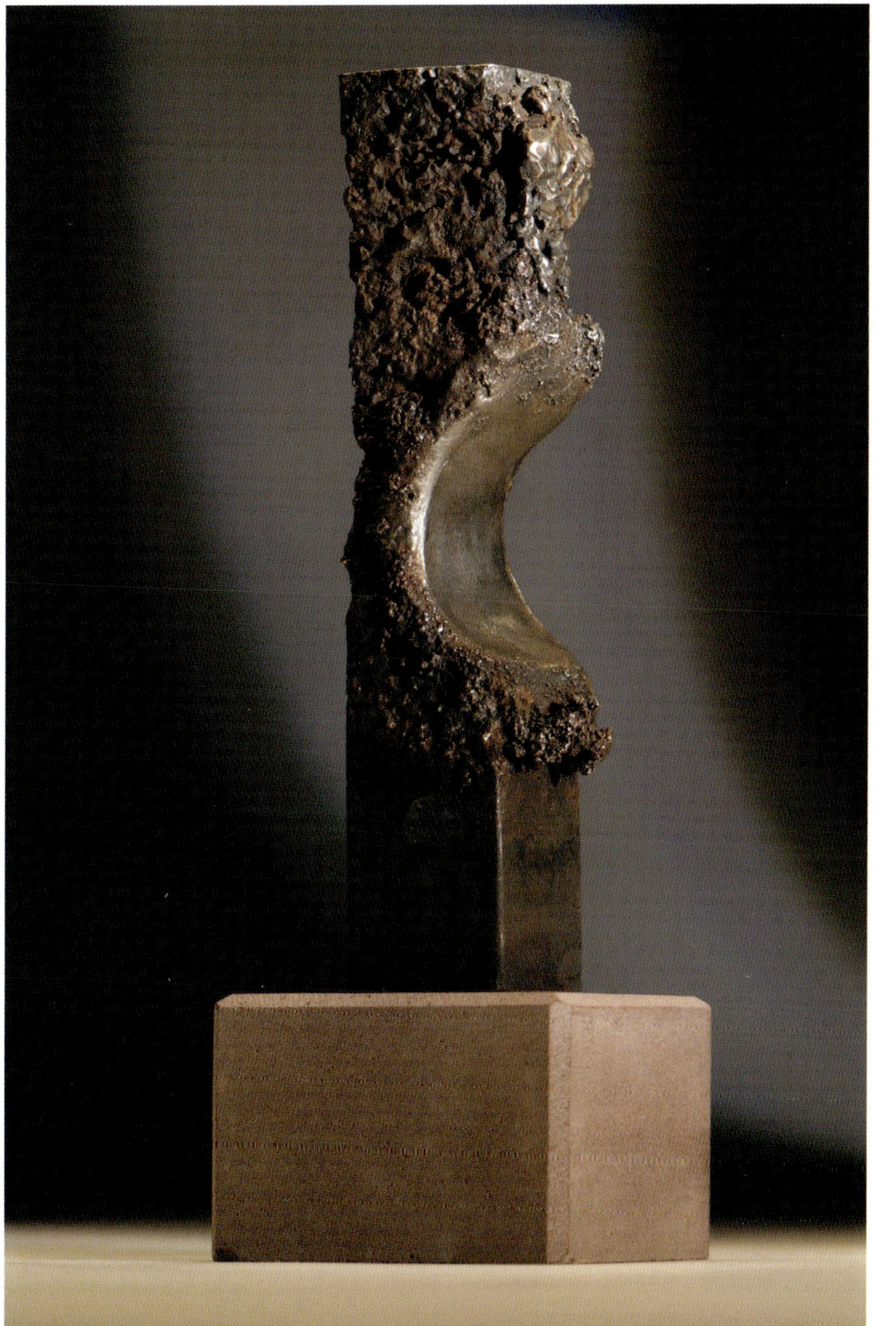

Alfred Bullermann. *Cry 1.* Burned and forged iron. 3" x 3". *Photo, Gerald Lampe*

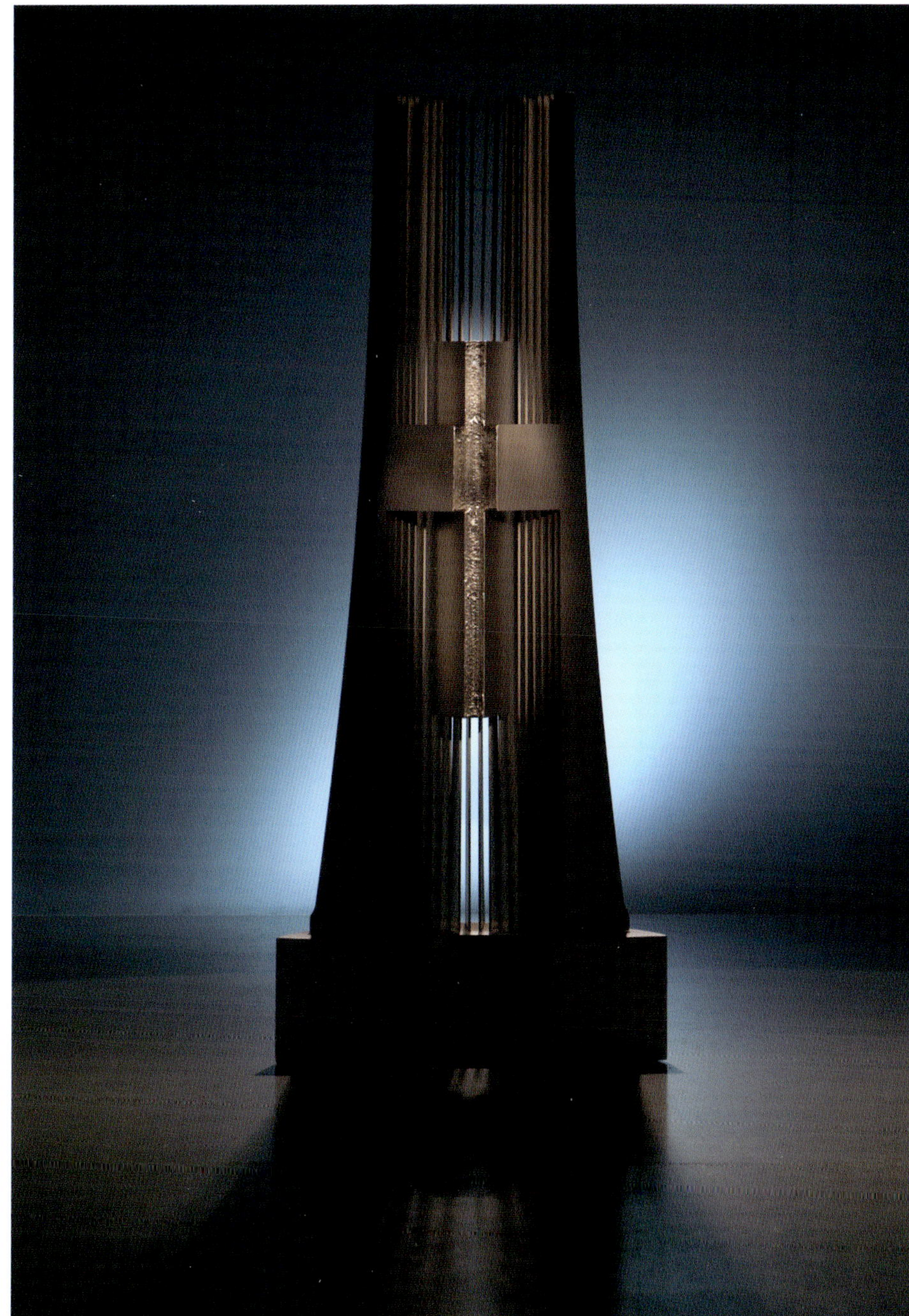

Alfred Bullermann. *Kreuz.* Forged steel. 20" x 11" x 45" h, 121 lbs. *Photo, Gerald Lampe*

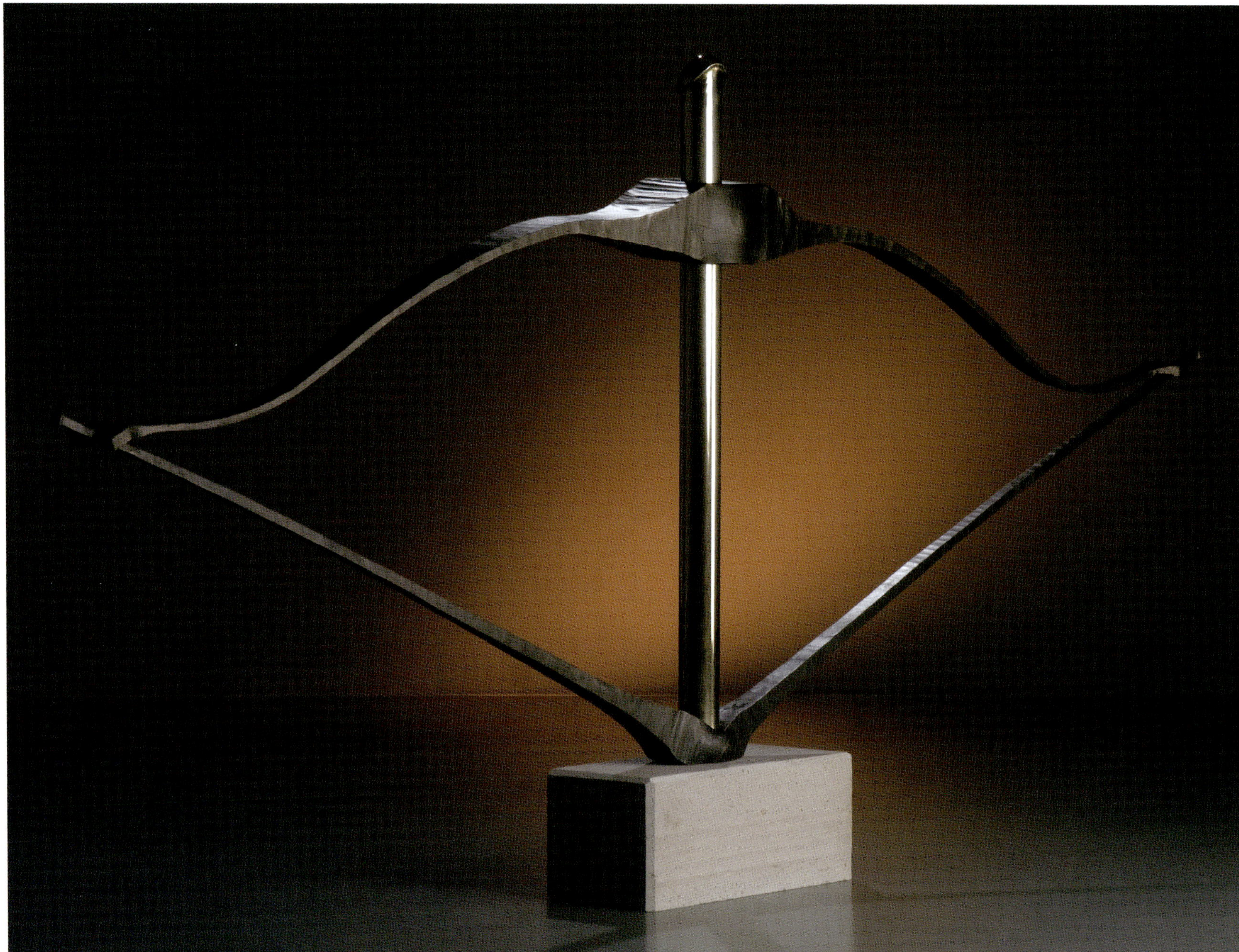

Alfred Bullermann. *Odysseus.* The bow is made of 5" x 5" steel, 67" wide. The arrow is 2" forged brass round bar.
The sculpture pays homage to an old story of a traveling man, far away from home, dreaming of his lovely wife. *Photo, Gerald Lampe*

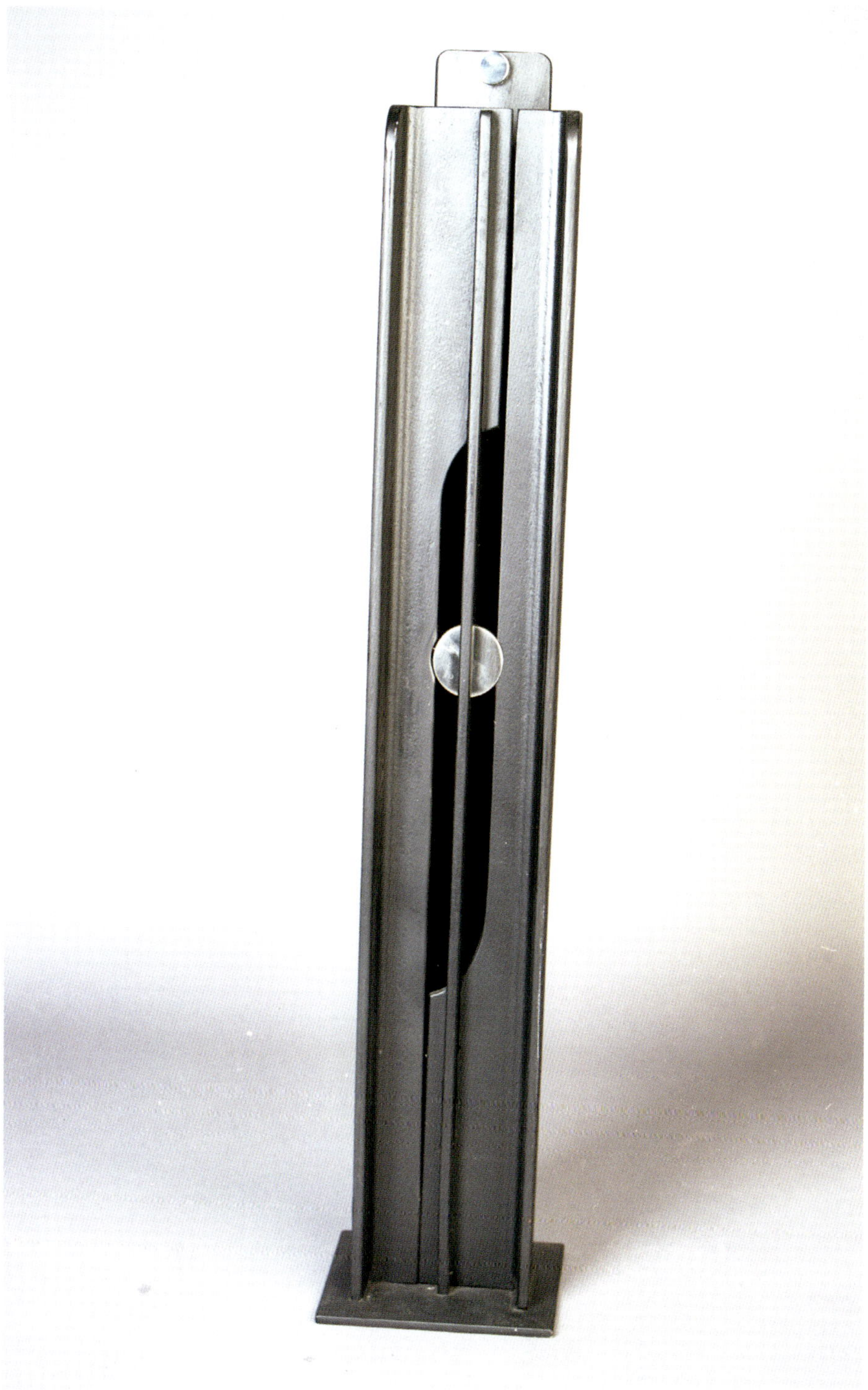

Maximilian Filleböck. *Stahl – Stele 1*, 2002. Consist of three girders, each 4" x 4". 42" h x 6' w. *Photo, Rolf Brecht*

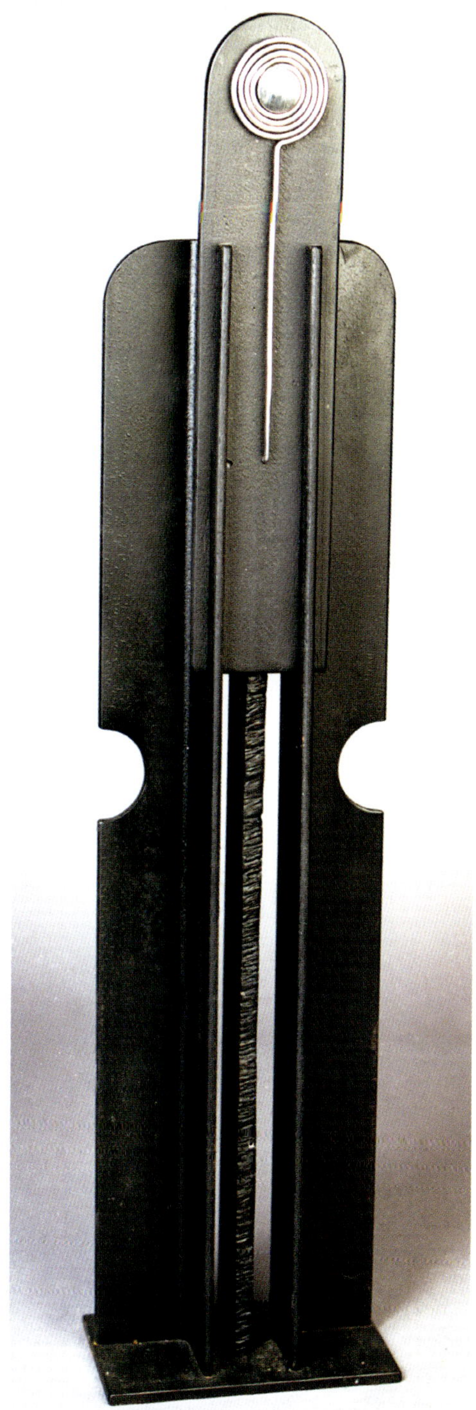

Maximilian Filleböck. *Stahl – Stele 2*, 2002. Consist of two girders, 4" x 4" and 3" x 3". 38" h x 9' w. *Photo, Rolf Brecht*

With these steles Maximilian Filleböck participated at the competition "Stahl-innovationspreis 2006" of the German Steel Information Center.

In the Greek culture steles were used as upright tombs, made of stone. Maximilian Filleböck copied this idea by using steel girders.

Raw steel was combined with polished Cr-Ni steel. The wrought girders give the impression of a firm and earthly stability whereas the noble Cr-Ni steel has given certain ease to the roughness of the steles.

The specialty about this piece of art is that all connections are stuck together without welding.

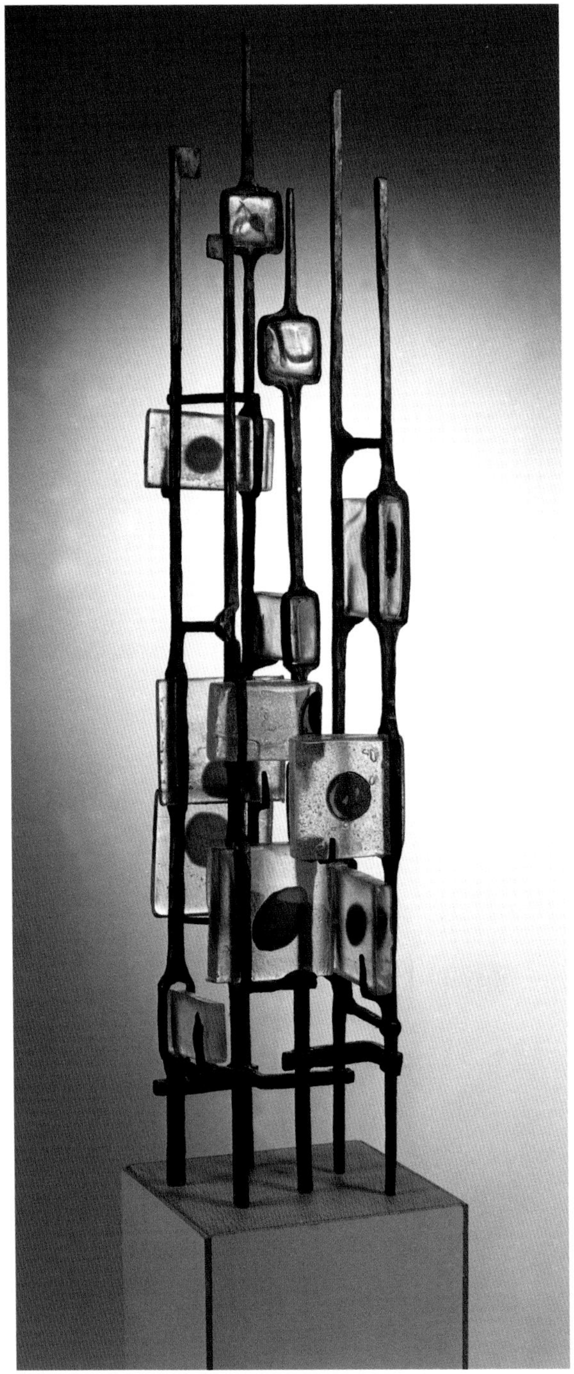

Maximilian Filleböck. *Herausforderung* (Challenge) 2005. *Photo, Rolf Brecht*

To combine elements that are opposites from their nature's origin was the desire of Maximilian Filleböck. Over the years working and experimenting with glass as a material he tried to connect this brittle substance with the ductile steel.

In the beginning of the object "Herausforderung" he melted different colored glass in a self-developed procedure without getting the colors mixed and having the glass diminished. Only after he finished the glasses did he start to think how they should be connected to the steel.

This work was a "Challenge" indeed, especially because the steel and glass parts are stuck together in a complex manner without welding or gluing.

It was his most intense work in 2005.

Chris Gavin. *Gateway*, 2007. Forged steel 7/8" square bar, 21" x 9" x 4". *Photo, Mark Lee*

The folding and squashing of bar stock happened much by chance one day while playing around with hammer die effects.

It grew into a bit of an obsession – wanting to explore all the different ways metal could be folded and arranged to create totemic-like sculptures. As the size of the bar stock increased, so did the difficulties of bending and controlling the organized results for symmetry. As the groupings of folded and squashed bars multiplied, so did the powerful effect of repetition of form. "Gateway" exemplified this outcome, creating a very interesting honeycombed effect across the mid-section of the piece. – Chris Gavin

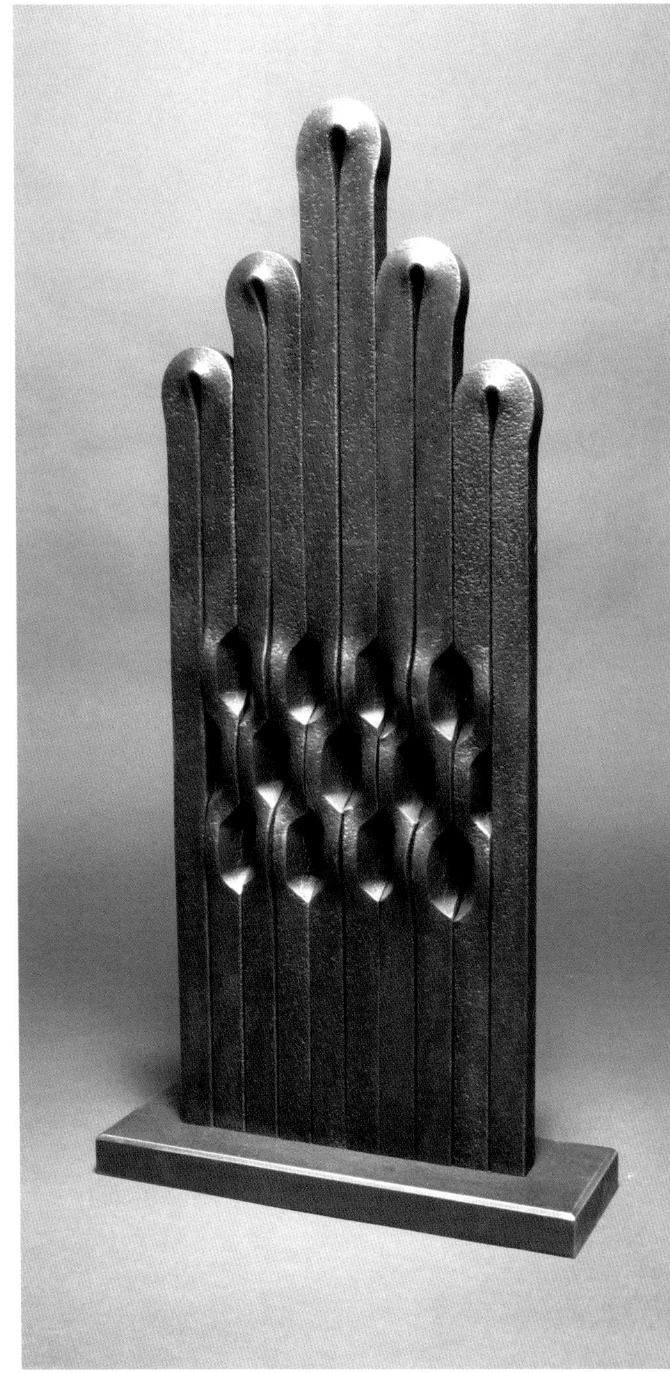

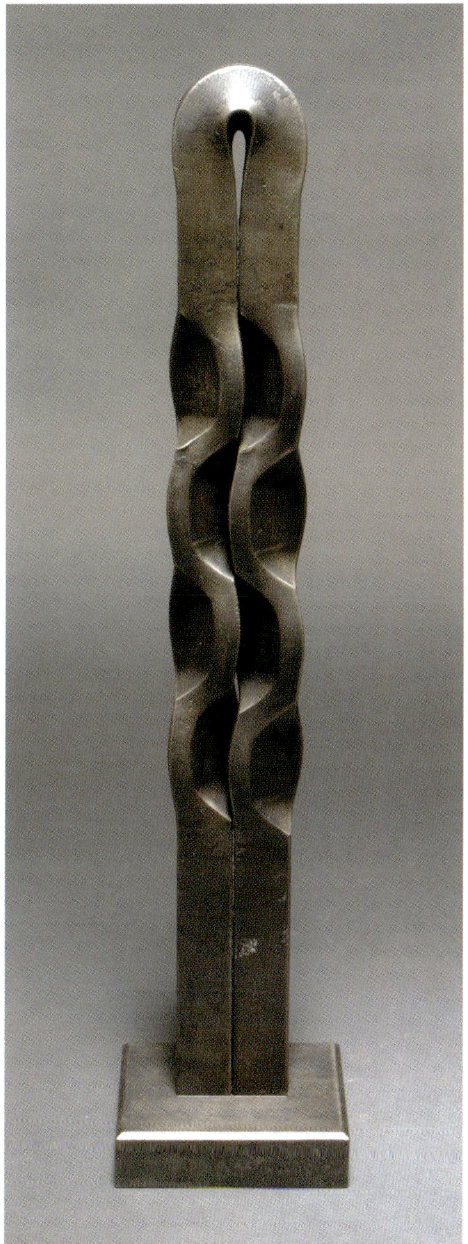

Chris Gavin. *Parallel Totem,* 2007. Forged steel 1" square bar with wax finish, 18" x 4" x 4". *Photo, Mark Lee*

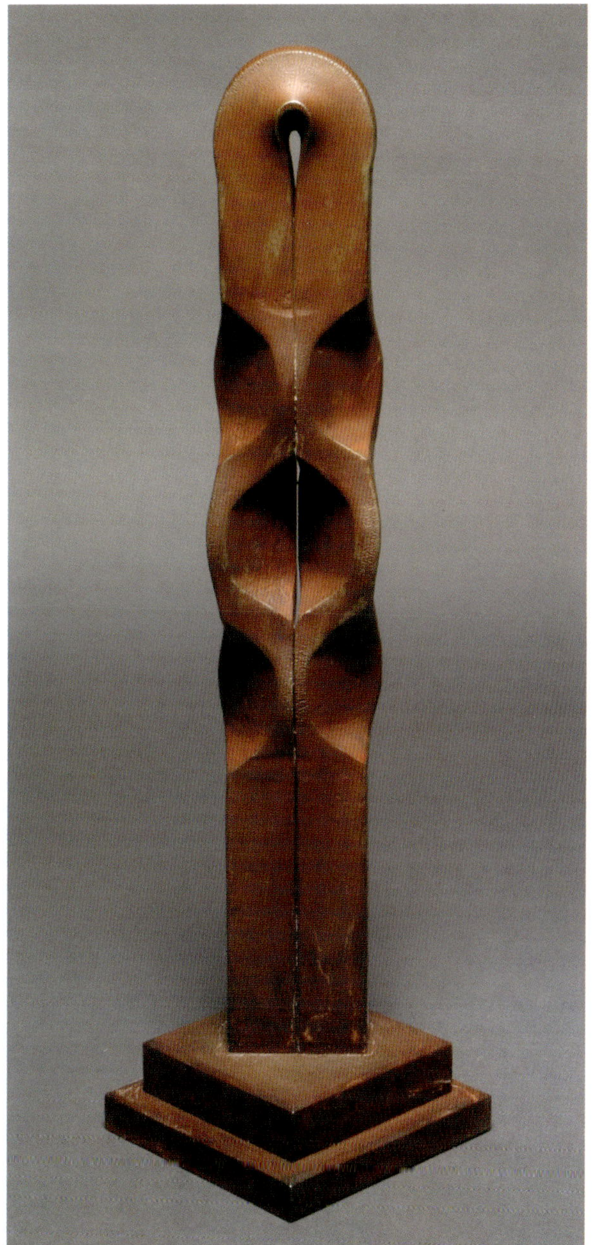

Chris Gavin. *Isis,* 2007. Forged steel 1.5" square bar with rust patina and wax finish, 19" x 5" x 5". *Photo, Mark Lee*

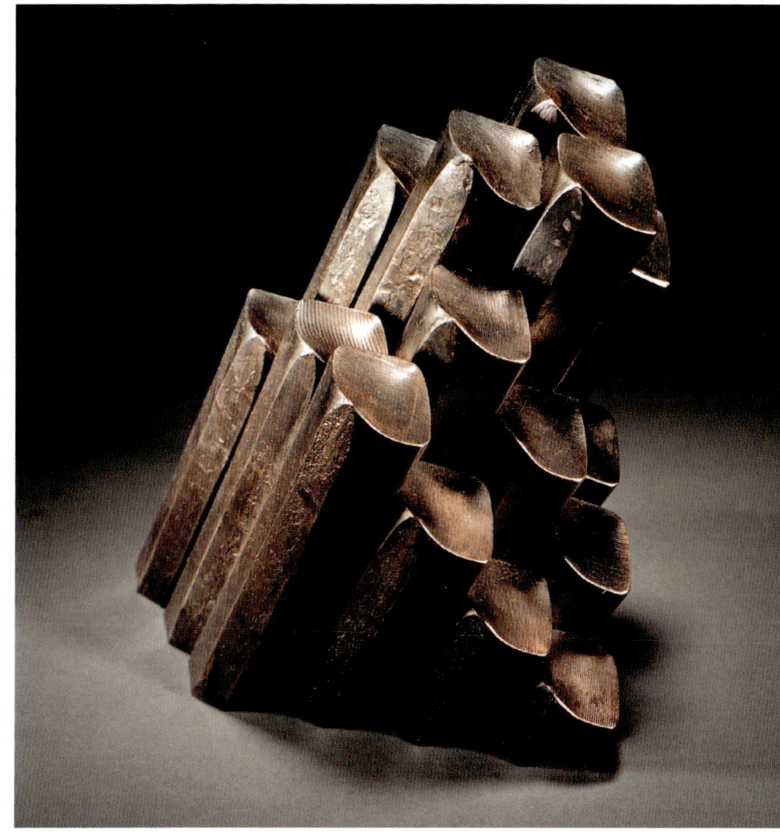

Chris Gavin. *Thrust,* 2004. Forged and fabricated 1.25" square bars, 10" x 9.5" x 5". *Photo, Mark Lee*

This particular sculpture was influenced by the columnar basalt rock formations I have seen in several countries around the world. Square stock was forged flat on the diamond, using a spacer block between the power hammer dies to create a uniformly even hexagonal bar. As the metal is flattened and extruded outward, the ends of the square cut bars curl forward, accentuating the upward "thrust" motion of the piece.

This sculpture was first created three years ago and not until recently did I have the commissioned opportunity to take the sculptural statement into the practical realm – "Thrust" table base. – Chris Gavin

George Rousis. *Comfort,* 2002. Hand forged steel, sterling silver, copper, rivets, and wax. *From the collection of Beatriz McAnany. Photo, Chris Dennis*

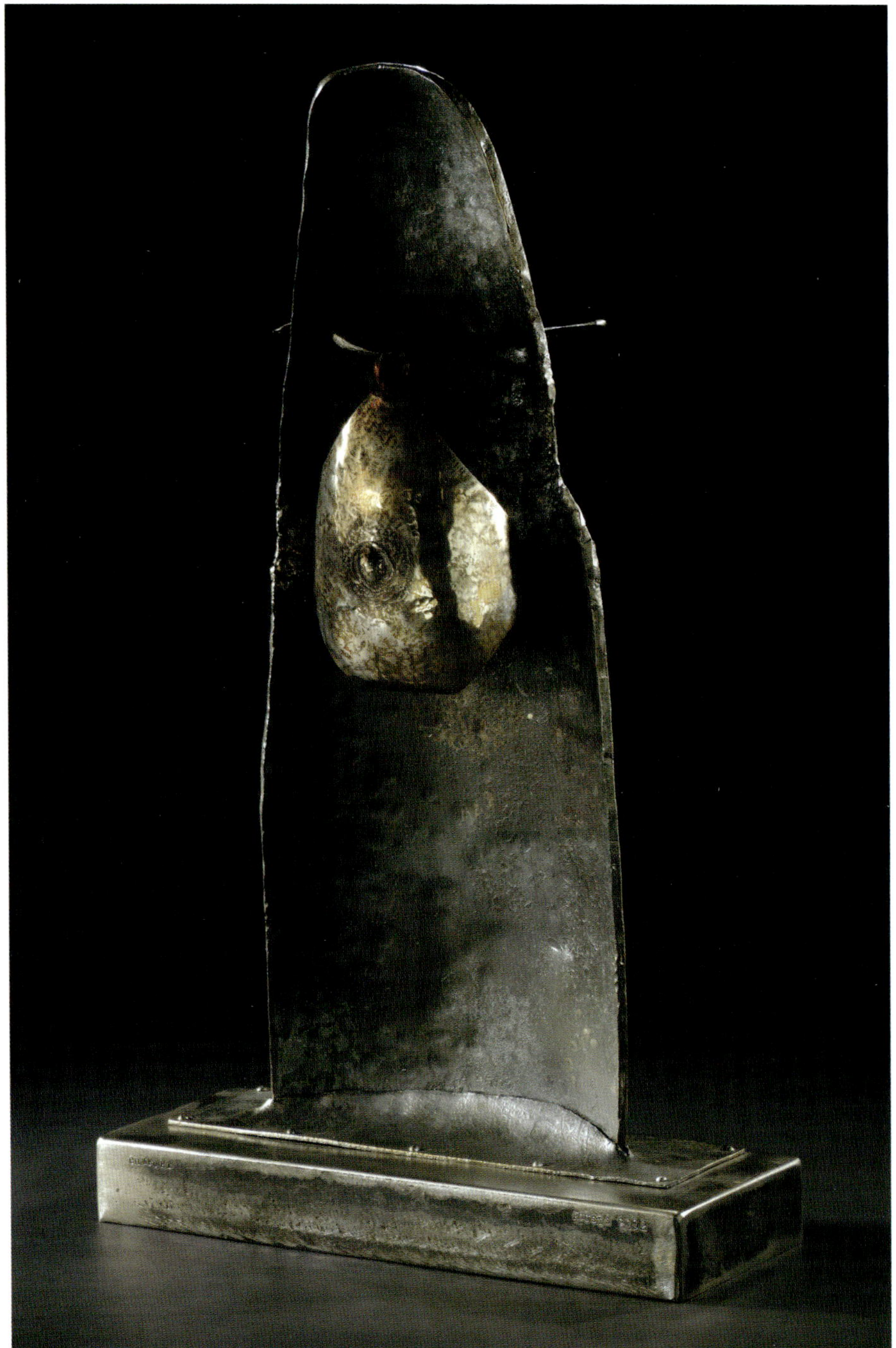

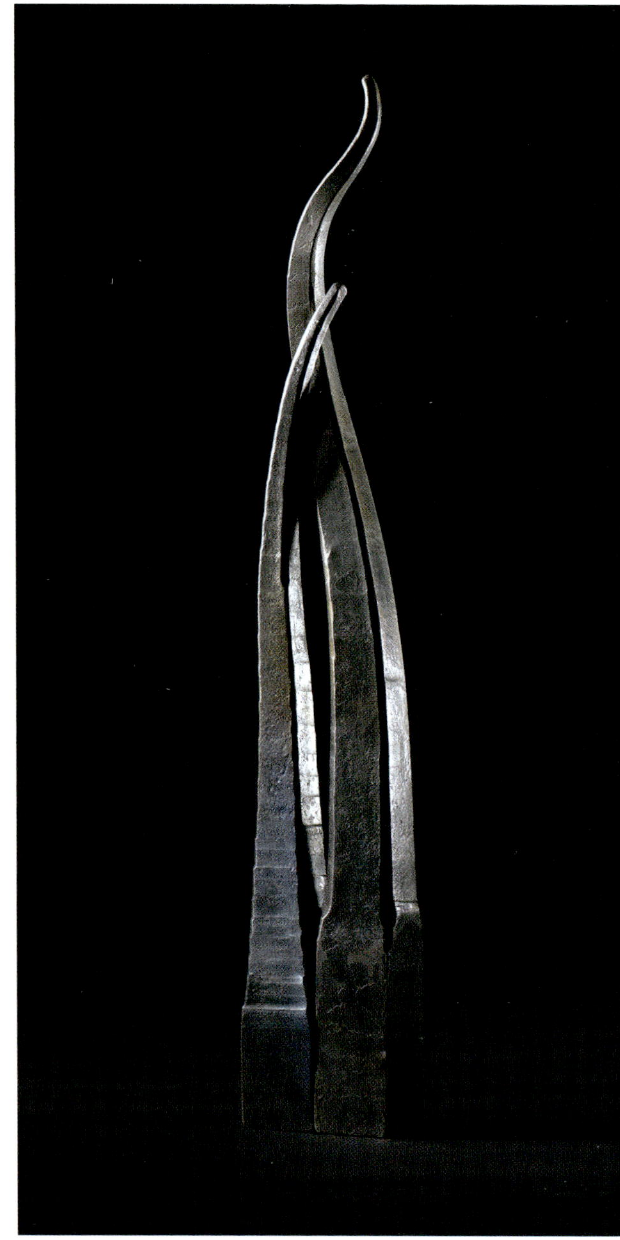

George Rousis. *Intimacy, Growth Series Numbers 5 and 26,* 2005/2008. Forged steel, oil. *From the collection of the artist. Photo, Chris Dennis*

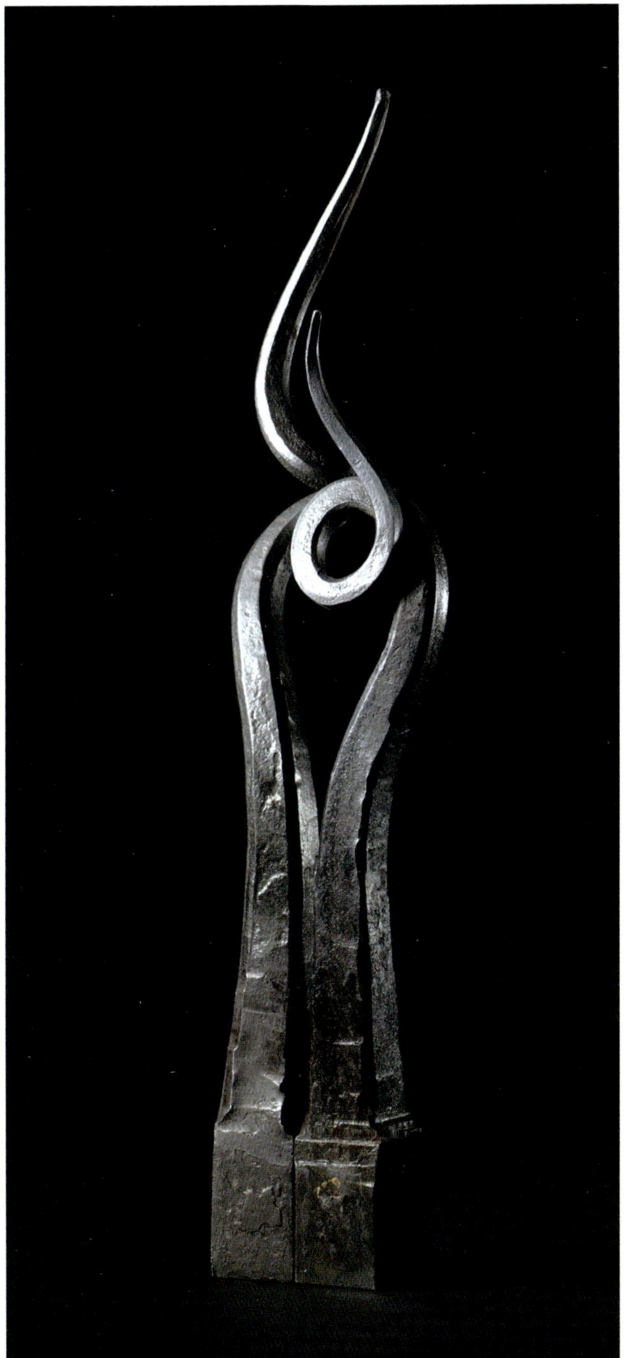

George Rousis. *Eternal Flame, Growth Series Numbers 7 and 18*. Forged steel, oil. *From the collection of the artist. Photo, Chris Dennis*

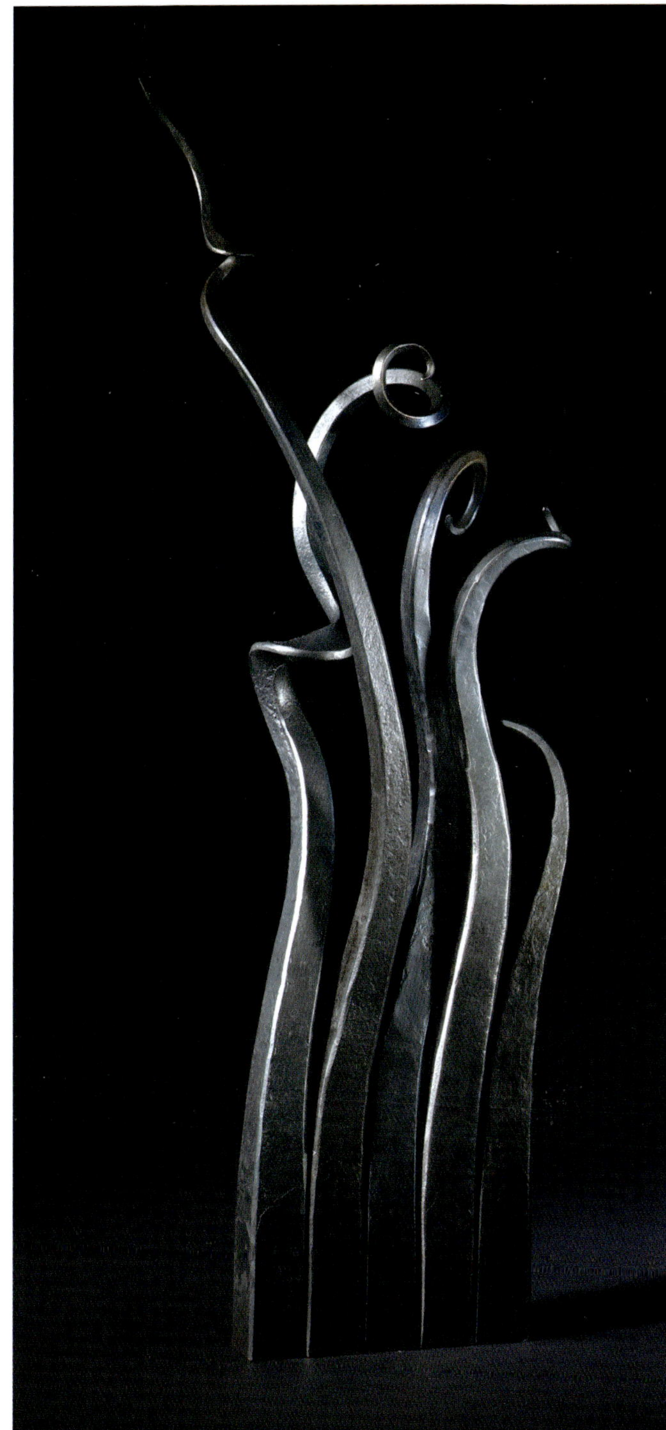

George Rousis. *An homage to Dadaist Marcel Duchamp's Nude Descending Staircase, Growth Series Numbers 18 and 22*, 2005/2008. Forged steel, oil. *From the collection of the artist. Photo, Chris Dennis*

The Growth Series began in 2000 when I would find a particular piece of drop that was too good to throw away. I established a set of criteria that had to be followed for a piece to belong in this series, including the shape and size of material. Another of the criteria is that the piece is not to be designed around another. These are individual pieces, forged to stand alone, that when given the chance to have a dialogue with others in the series take on lives and relationships beyond themselves. – George Rusis

George Rousis. *Pregnant With…*, 2008. Self Portrait Series Numbers 36 and 37. Forged steel, oil. *From the collection of the artist. Photo, Chris Dennis*

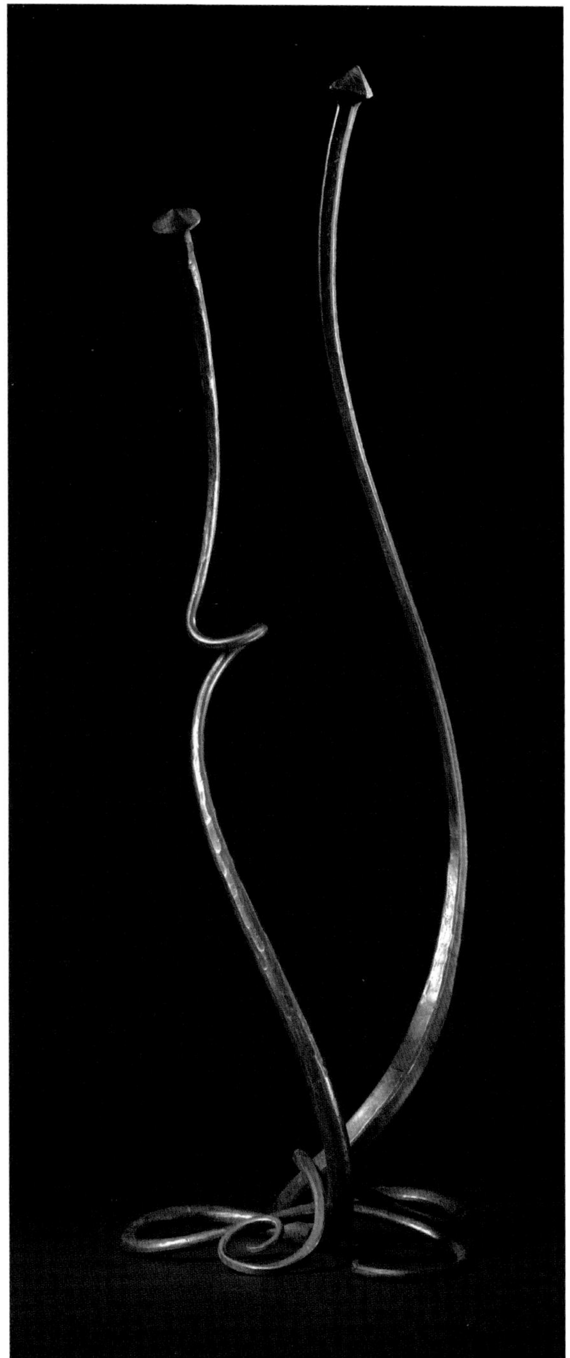

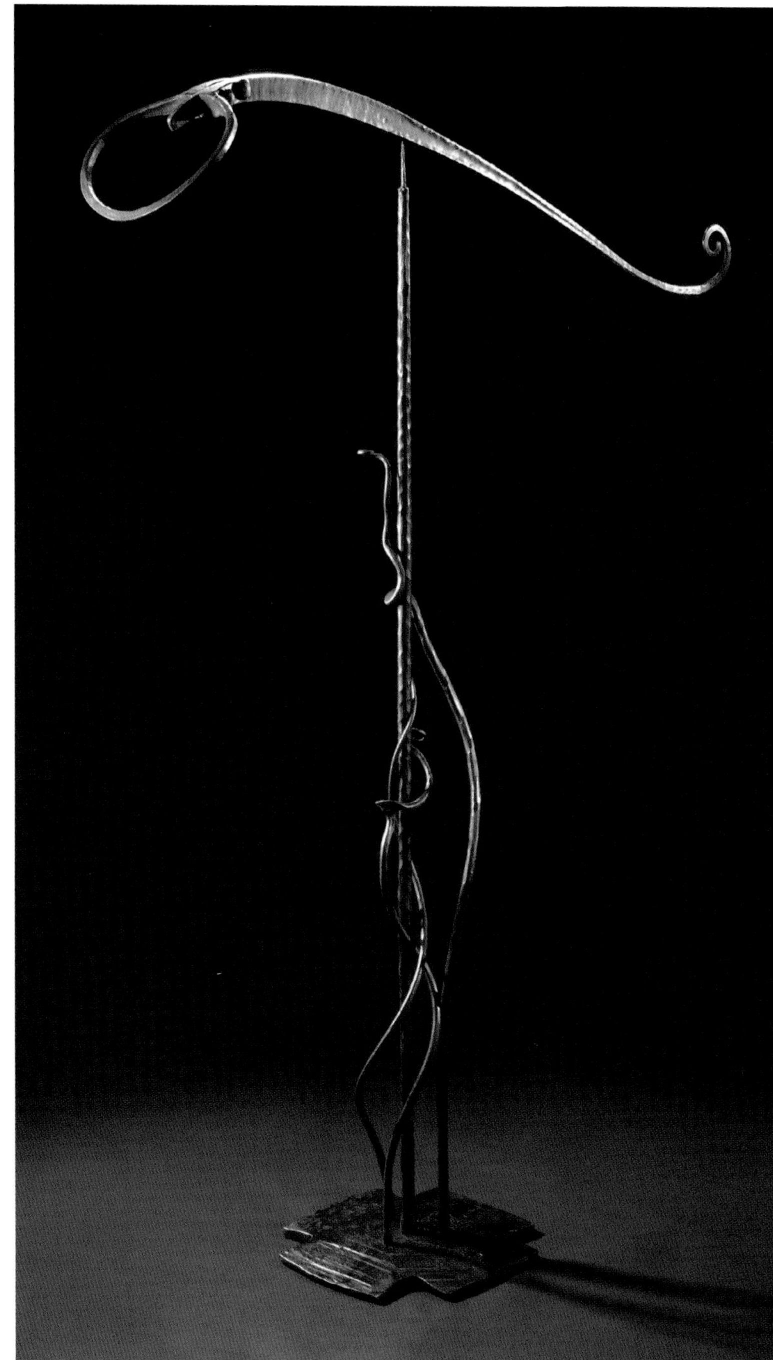

George Rousis. *Perched,* 2008. Forged steel and bronze, steel rivets, oil. *From the collection of Tracy Thomas. Photo, Chris Dennis*

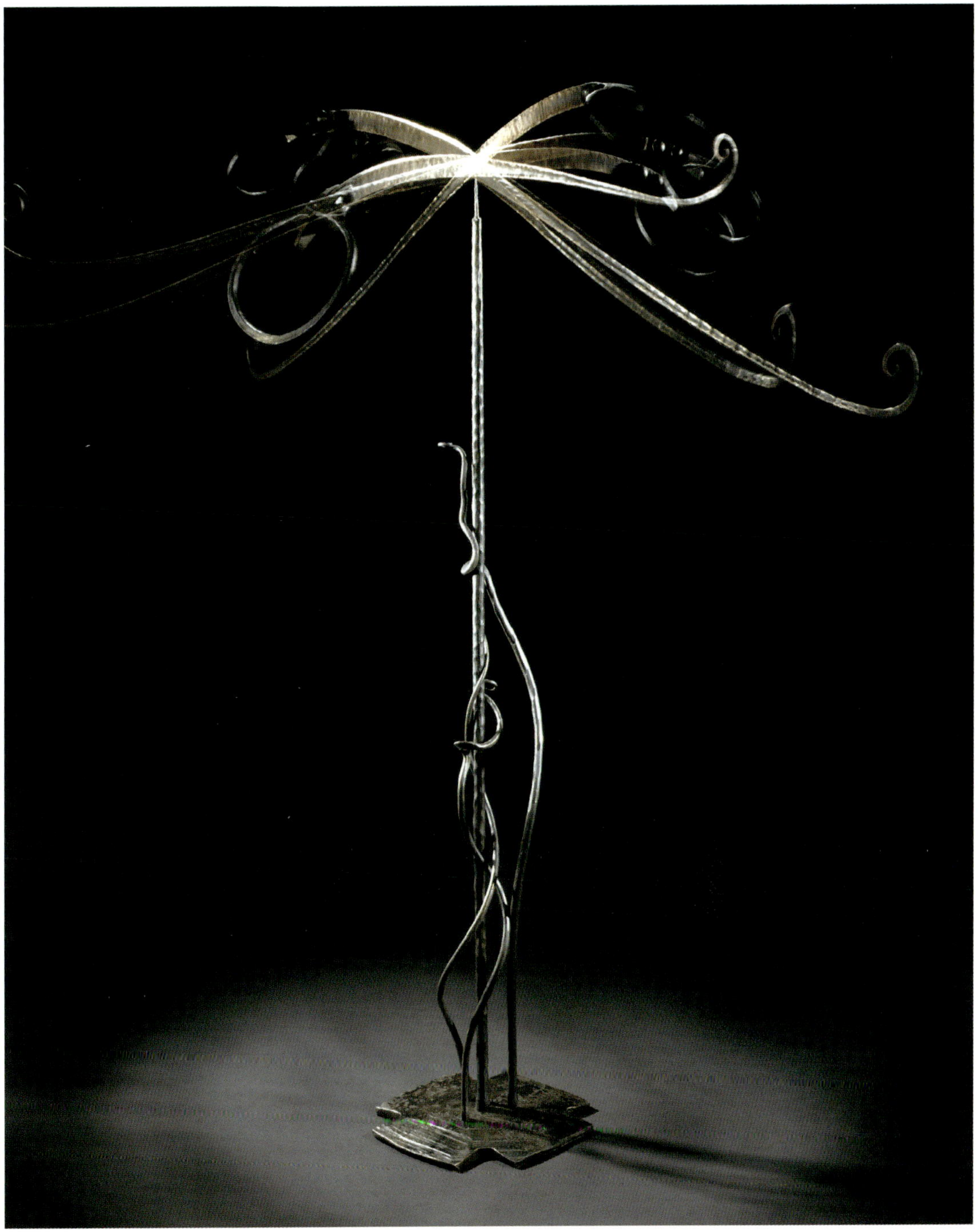

George Rousis. *Perched,* 2008. Perched in motion. *Photo, Chris Dennis*

George Rousis. *Phytomorphic,* 2002. Forged steel and bronze, wax. *From the collection of the artist. Photo, Chris Dennis*

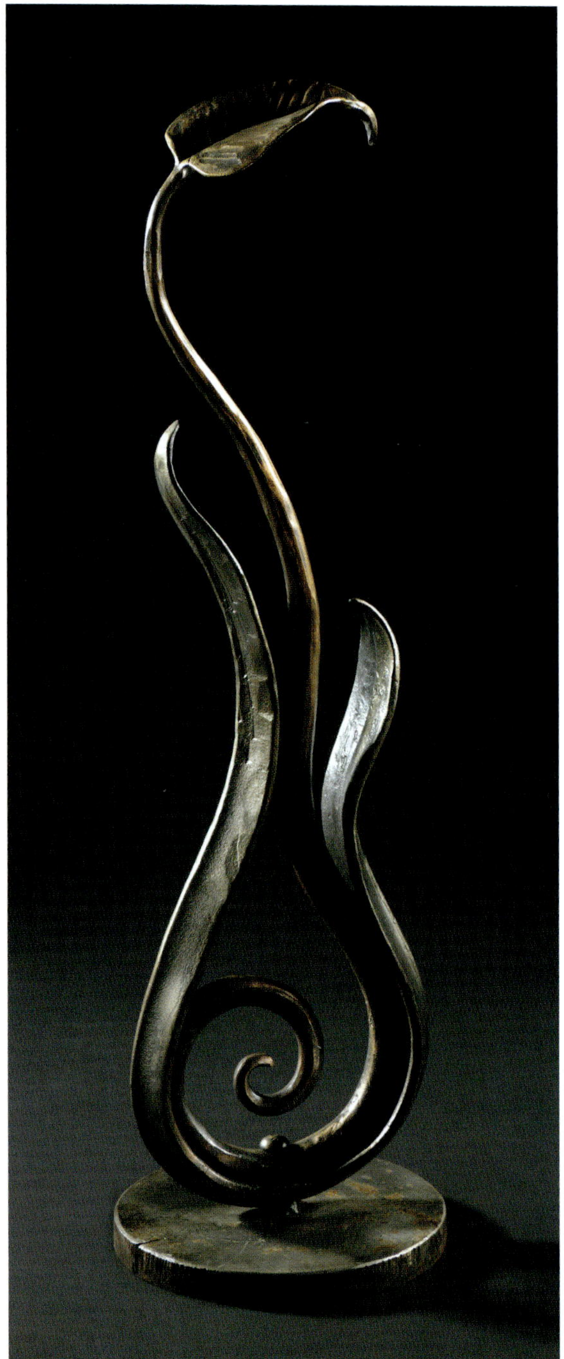

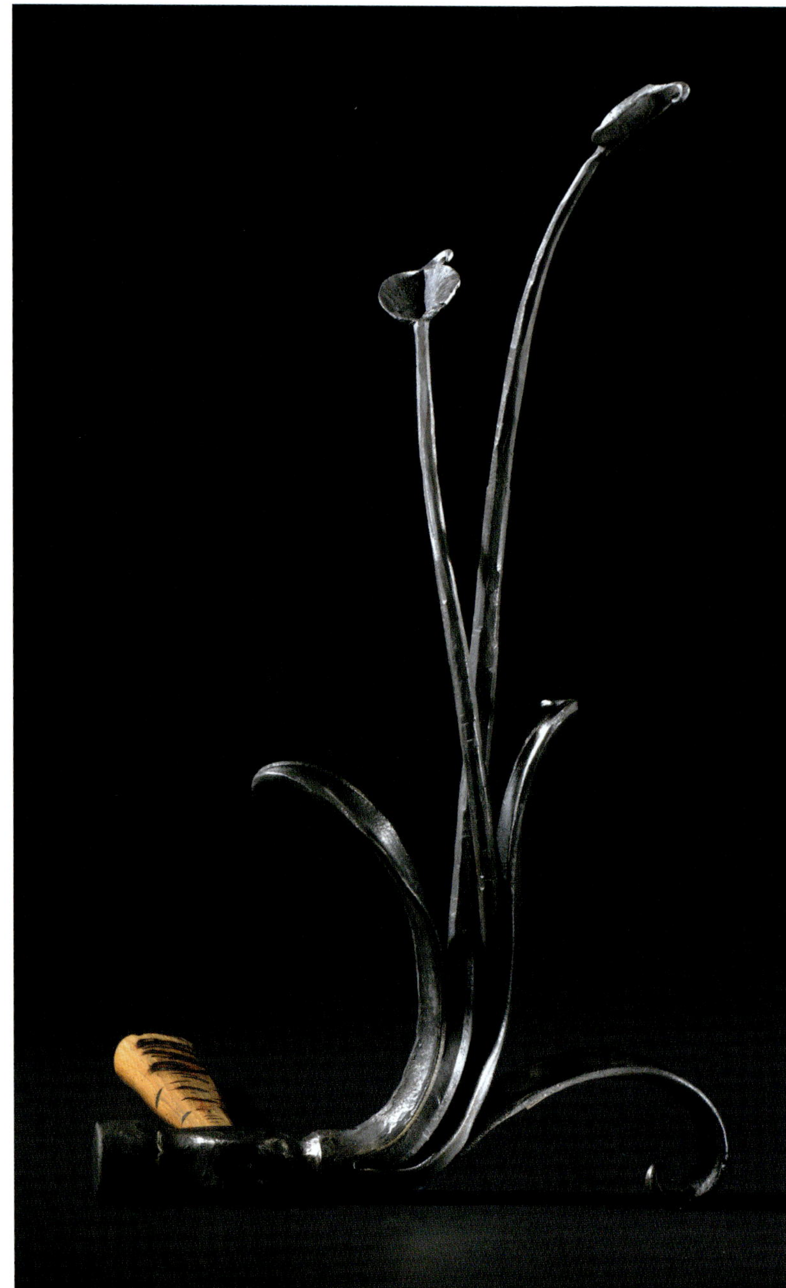

George Rousis. *Plantishing Hammer, Wordplay Series*, 2001/2008. Forged steel, wood, and oil. *From the collection of the artist. Photo, Chris Dennis*

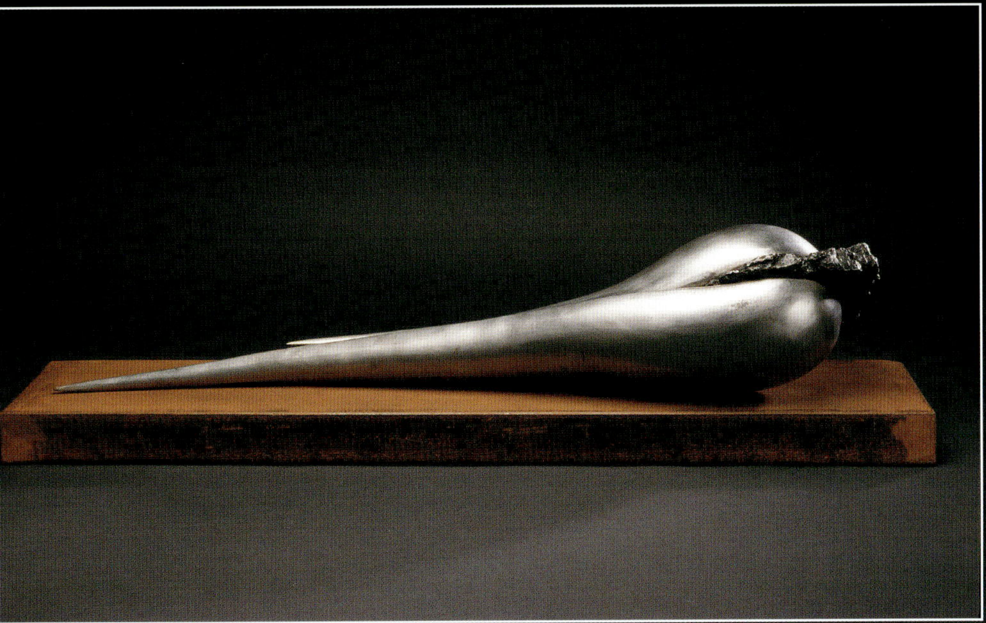

Lee Sauder. *Mollusca Voluptus 3,* 2004. Second view. *Photo, Ellen Martin*

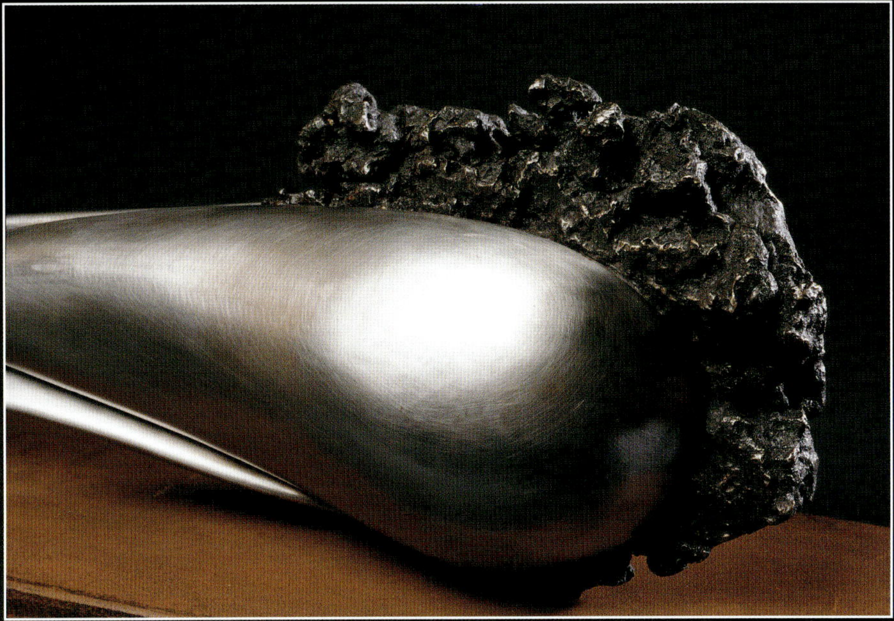

Lee Sauder. *Mollusca Voluptus 3,* 2004. Detail. *Photo, Ellen Martin*

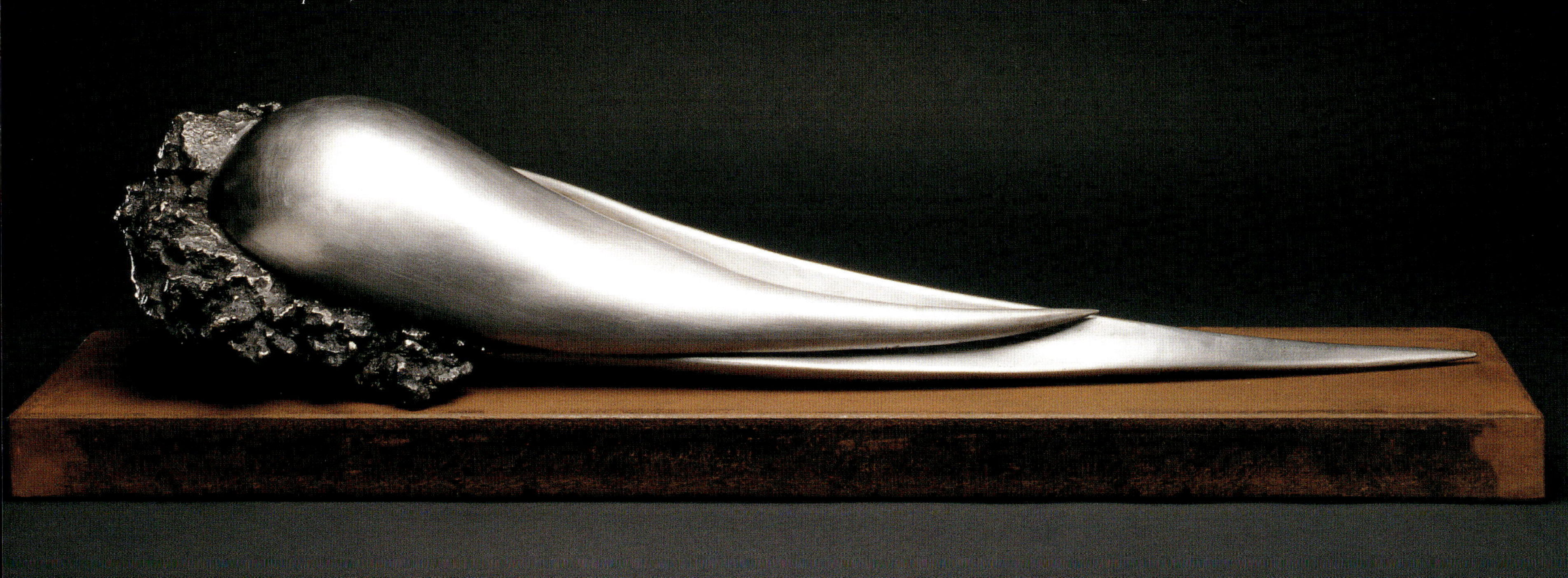

Lee Sauder. *Mollusca Voluptus 3,* 2004. Bloom iron, steel. 28" w x 8" h x 6" d. *Photo, Ellen Martin*

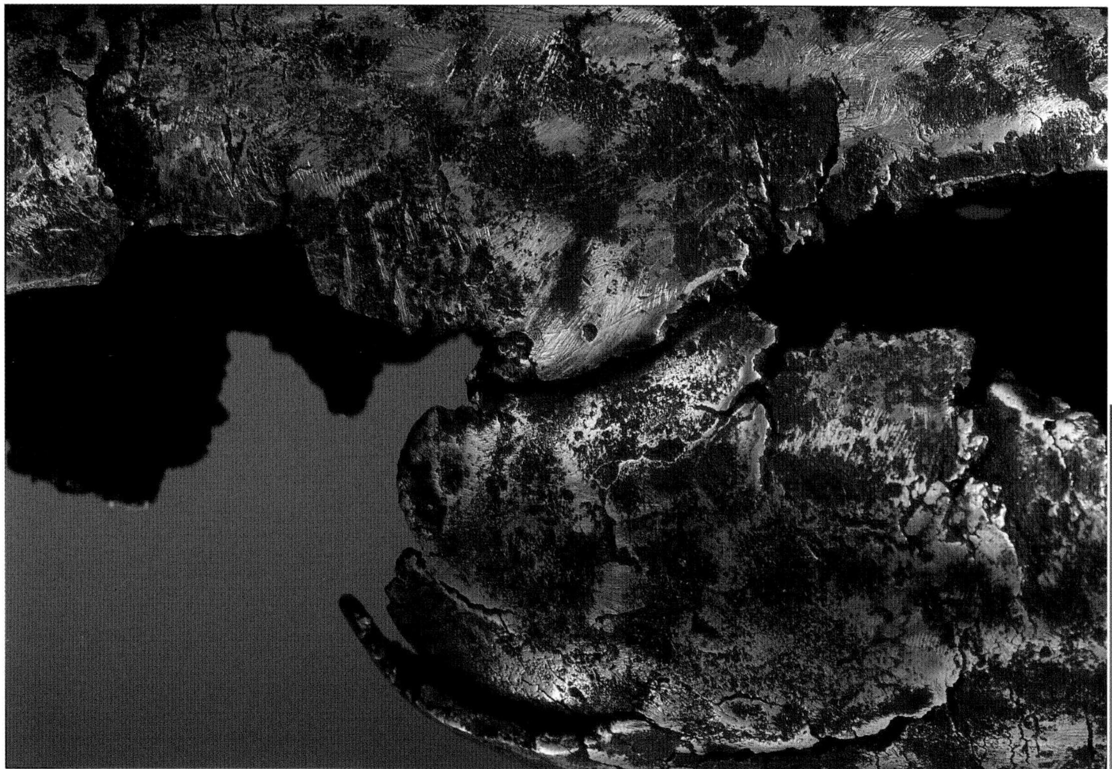

Lee Sauder. *Odalisque*. Detail.
Photo, Ellen Martin

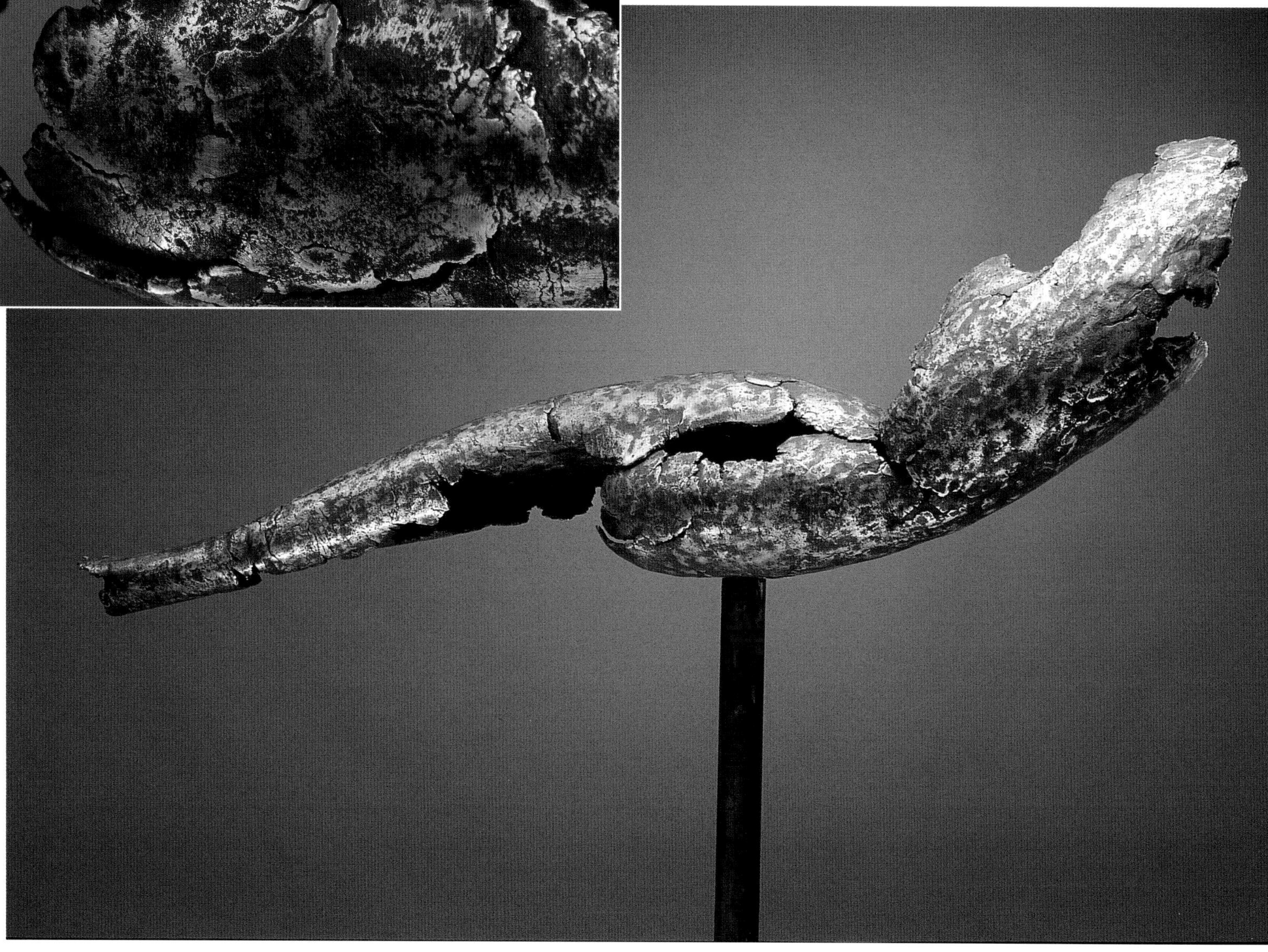

Lee Sauder. *Odalisque*. Bloom iron. 58" w x 48" h x 8" d.
Photo, Ellen Martin

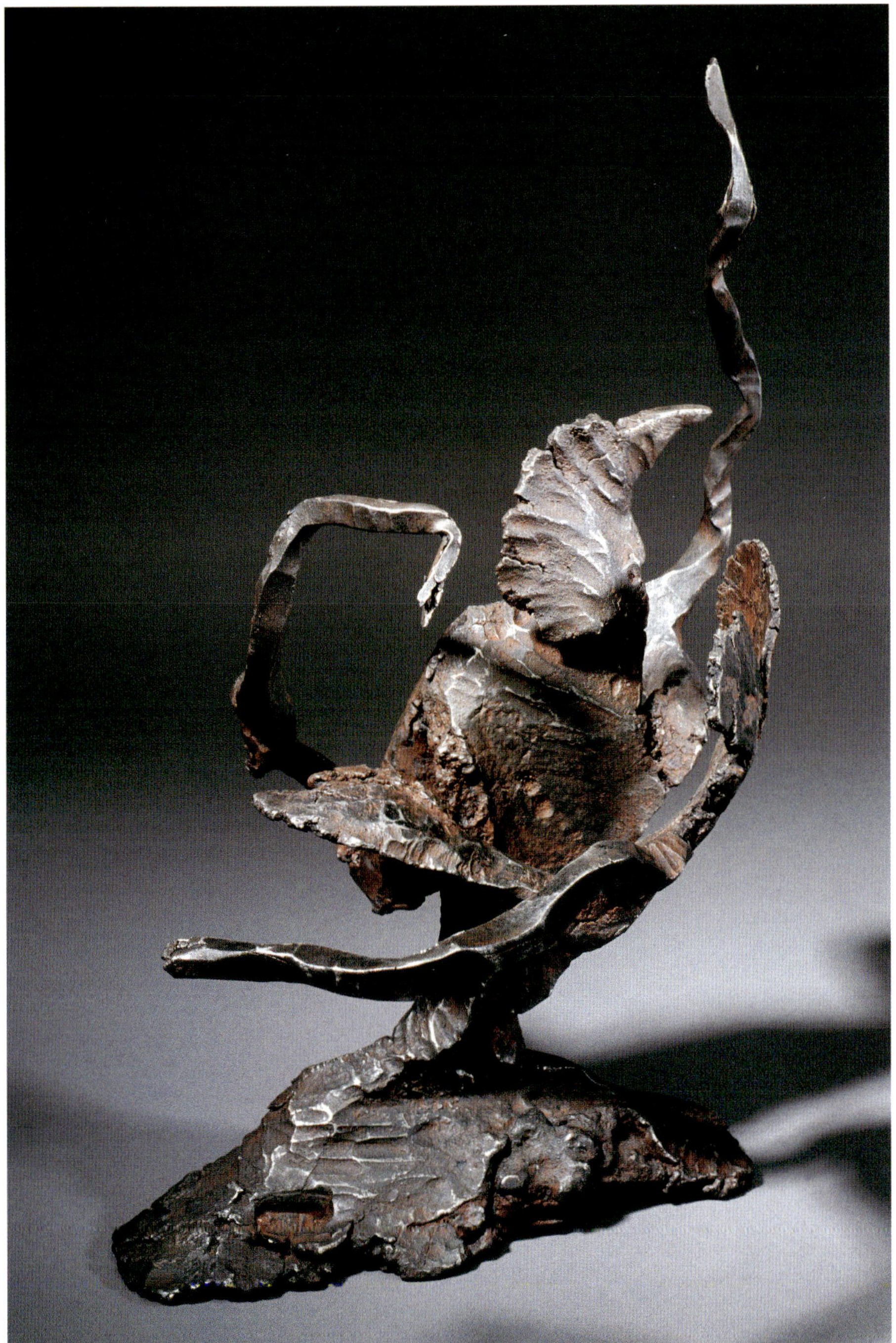

Lee Sauder. *Free Radical Raven*. Bloom iron. 12" w x 16" h x 10" d. *Photo, Ellen Martin*

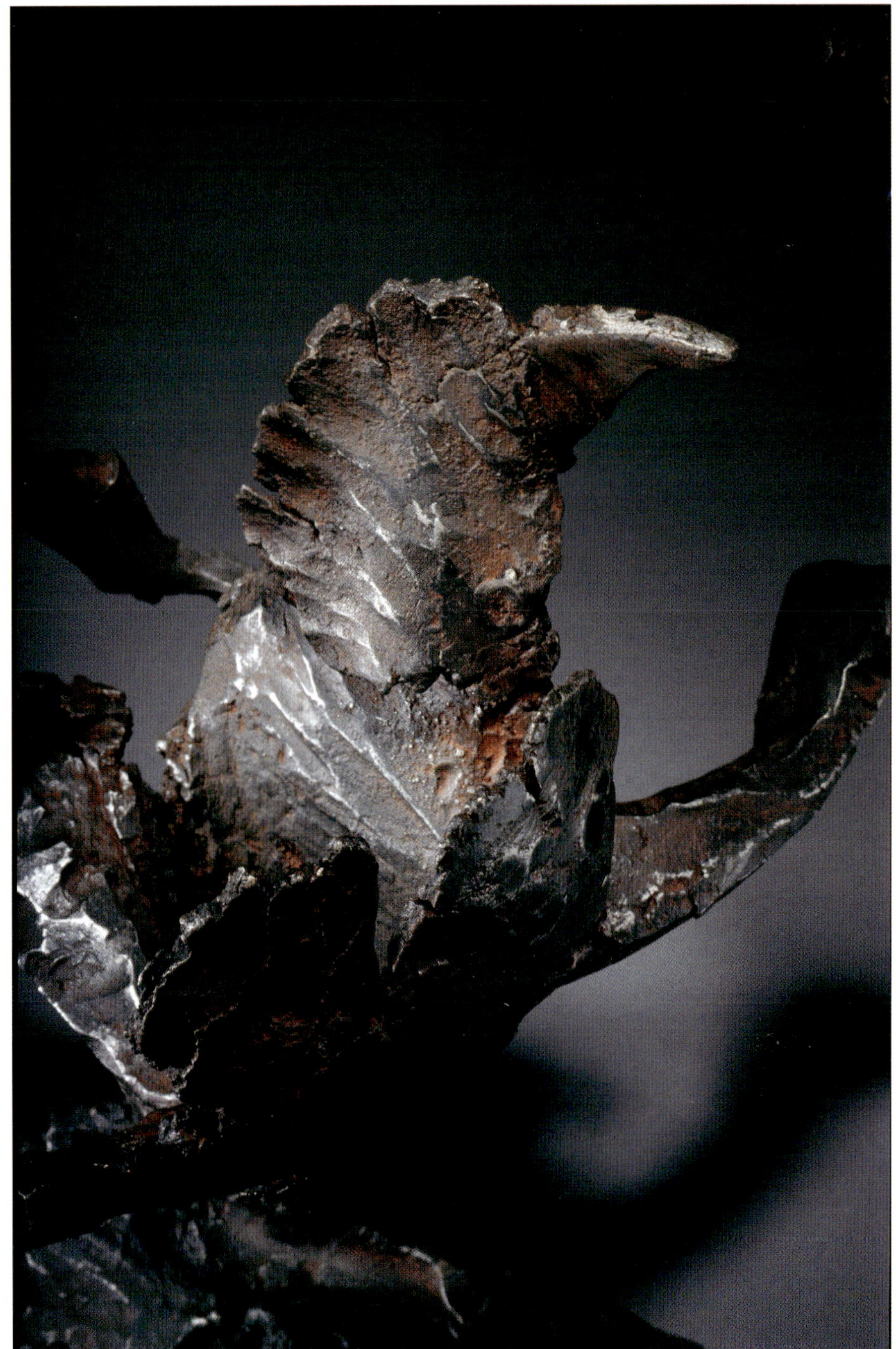

Lee Sauder. *Free Radical Raven*. Detail. *Photo, Ellen Martin*

Lee Sauder. *Orbicentricity.* Bloom iron and oak. 10" w x 24" h x 8" d. *Photo, Ellen Martin*

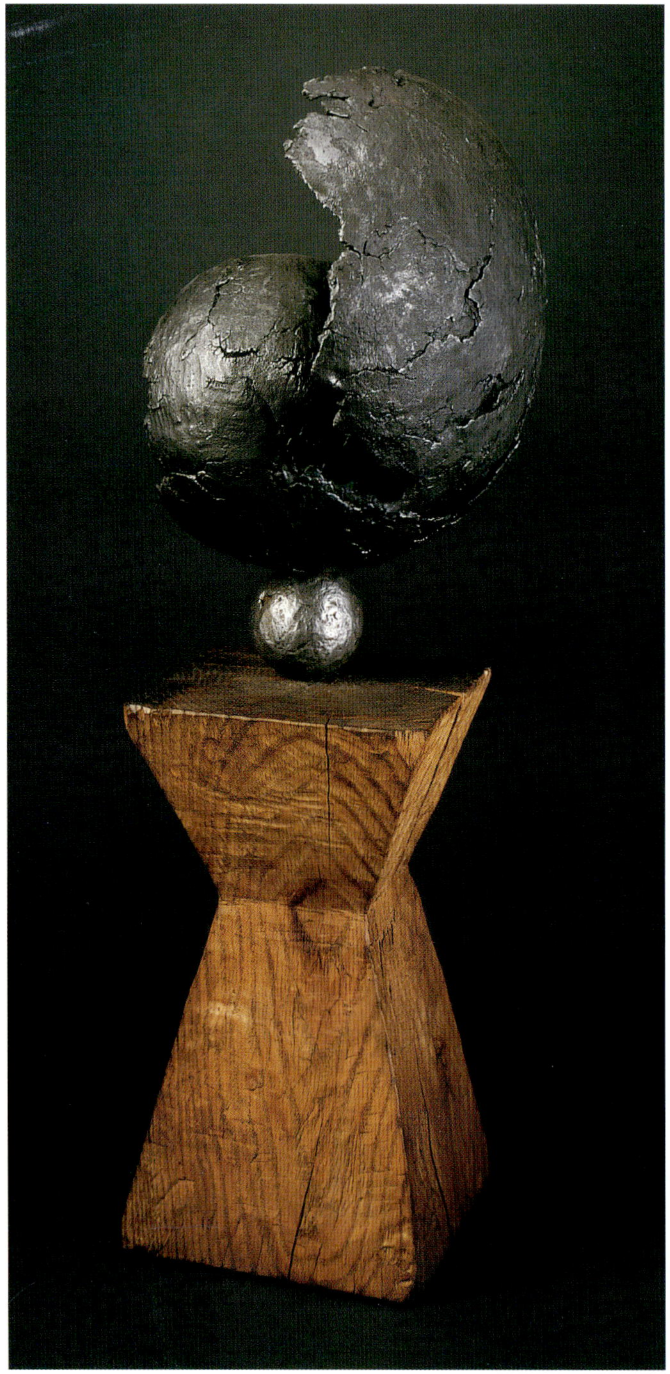

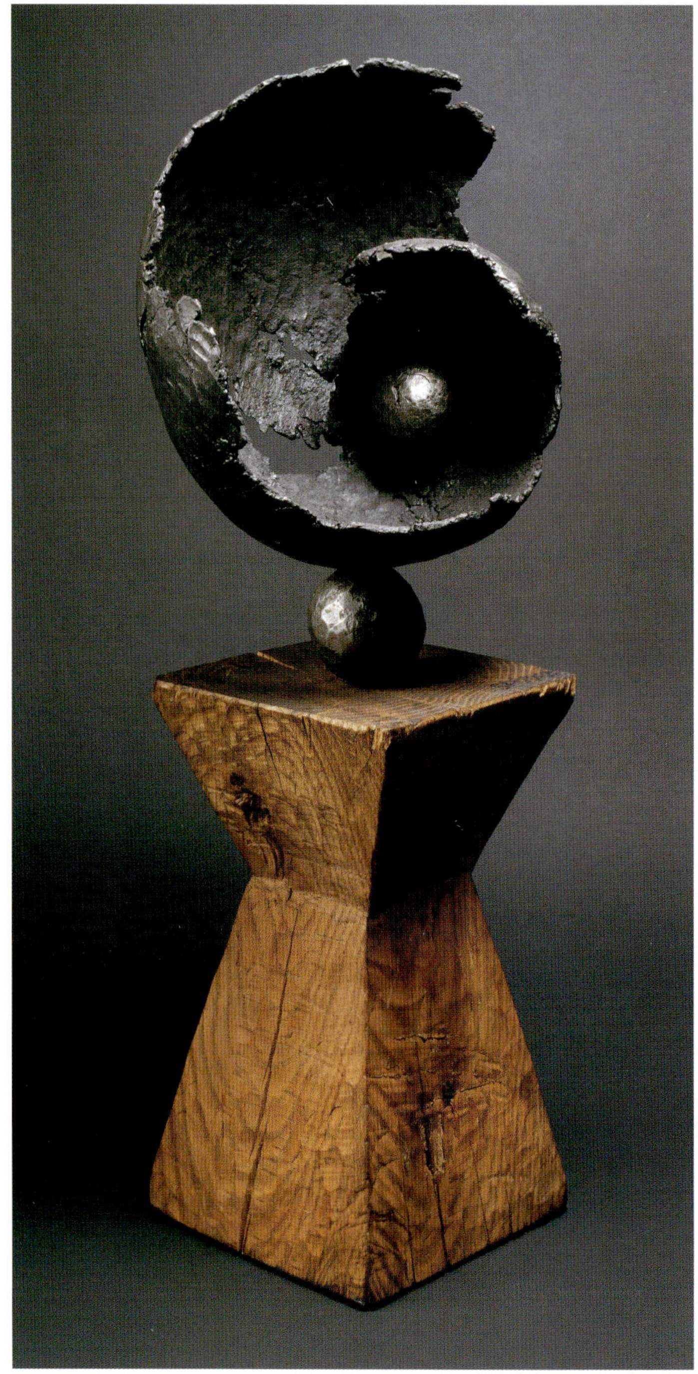

Lee Sauder. *Orbicentricity.* Second view. *Photo, Ellen Martin*

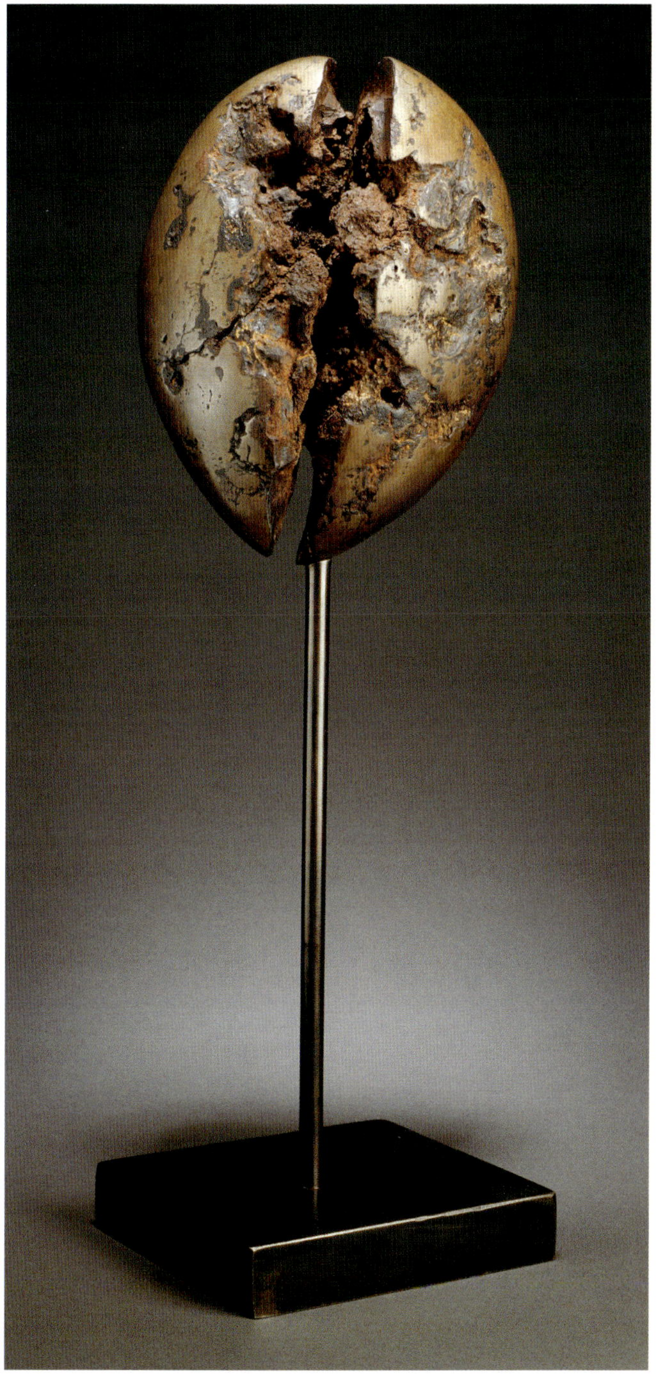

Lee Sauder. *Mollusca Voluptus 2*, 2003. Bloom iron, steel base. 6" w x 6" h x 18" d. *Photo, Ellen Martin*

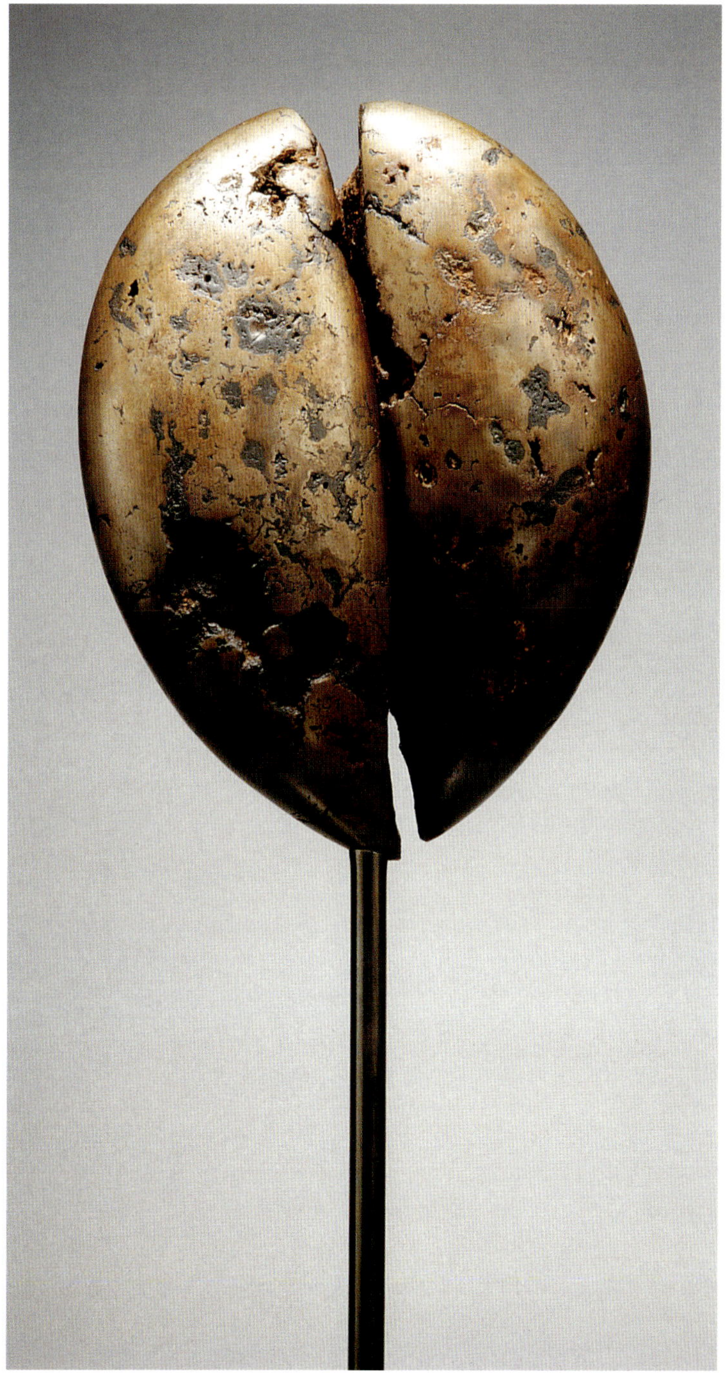

Lee Sauder. *Mollusca Voluptus 2*, 2003. Detail. *Photo, Ellen Martin*

These sculptures are forged from iron I've smelted from the raw ore. I gather ore near my home, and convert it to workable iron using the ancient "bloomery" process, the method people originally used to win iron from its ore.

My original impulse for exploring early smelting technology was a kind of moral curiosity about iron – my need to "kill what you eat" to properly appreciate the full value of what has sustained me in my thirty-odd years as a blacksmith and sculptor.

But my original curiosity was sustained by my aesthetic fascination with the material produced by this process. Each "bloom" of iron is unique both morphologically and metallurgically, leading to the same kind of dialogue with the material that a wood or stone carver experiences.

Most folks tend to think of iron as an "industrial" material, and begin their thinking with the bar and plate forms provided by modern industry, or the scrap forms cast off by industry. Working with iron I've smelted myself is helping me to view iron in its rightful place as a natural material, the very stuff the planet is built of. – Lee Sauder

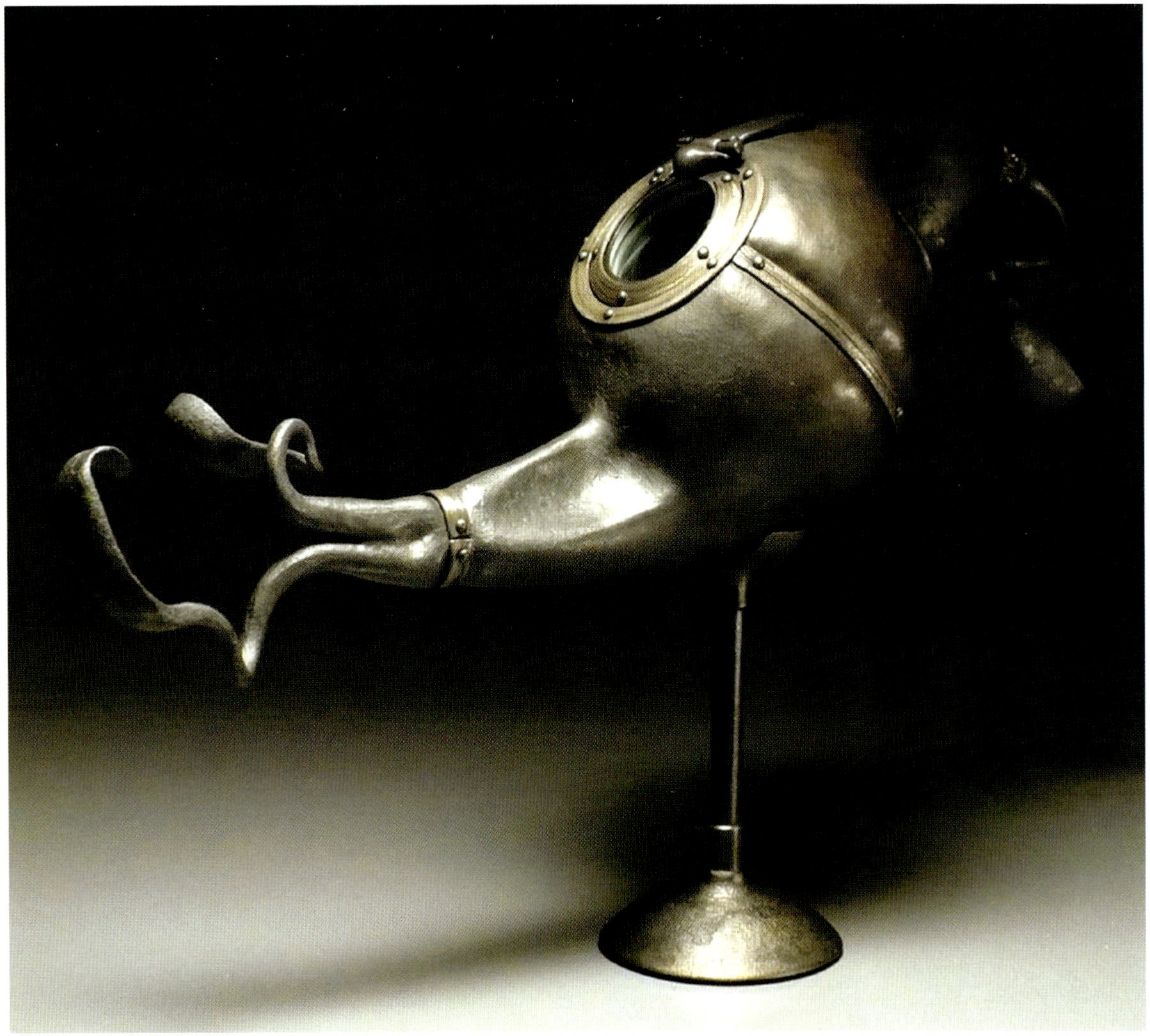

Jon Shearin. *Reliquary for the Iku-Turso*. Mild steel, wrought iron, Damascus steel, mica, and glass, 24" l x 7" w x 17" h. Forged, pattern welded, MIG and TIG welding, plasma cutting, and riveting. *Photo, Shane Darwent*

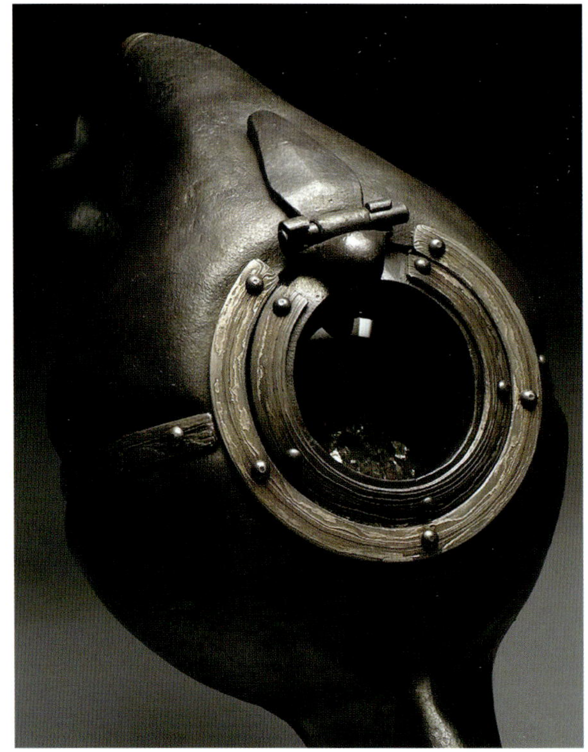

Jon Shearin. *Reliquary for the Iku-Turso*. Detail. *Photo, Shane Darwent*

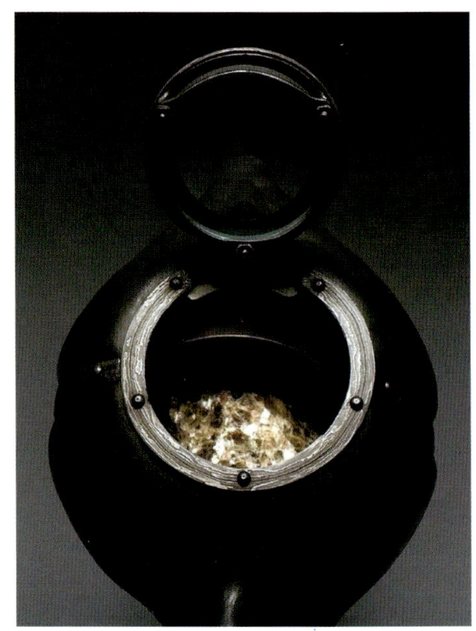

Jon Shearin. *Reliquary for the Iku-Turso*. Detail. *Photo, Shane Darwent*

I found a lot of inspiration for this piece through imagery of old diving bell helmets and submarines. This paired with the organic lines found in etchings of sea monsters produce an interesting combination. The title references this since Iku-Turso is the name of an ancient Finnish sea creature as well as the name of a modern day Finnish navy ship. – Jon Shearin

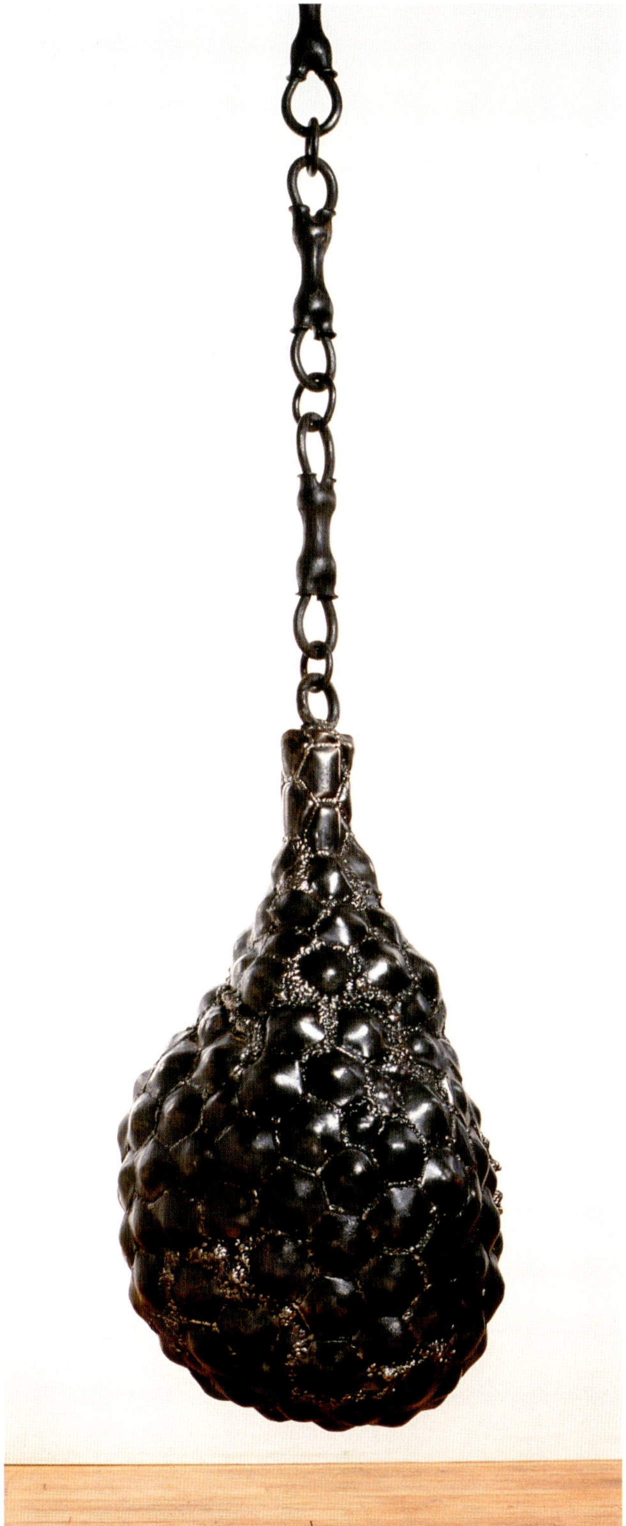

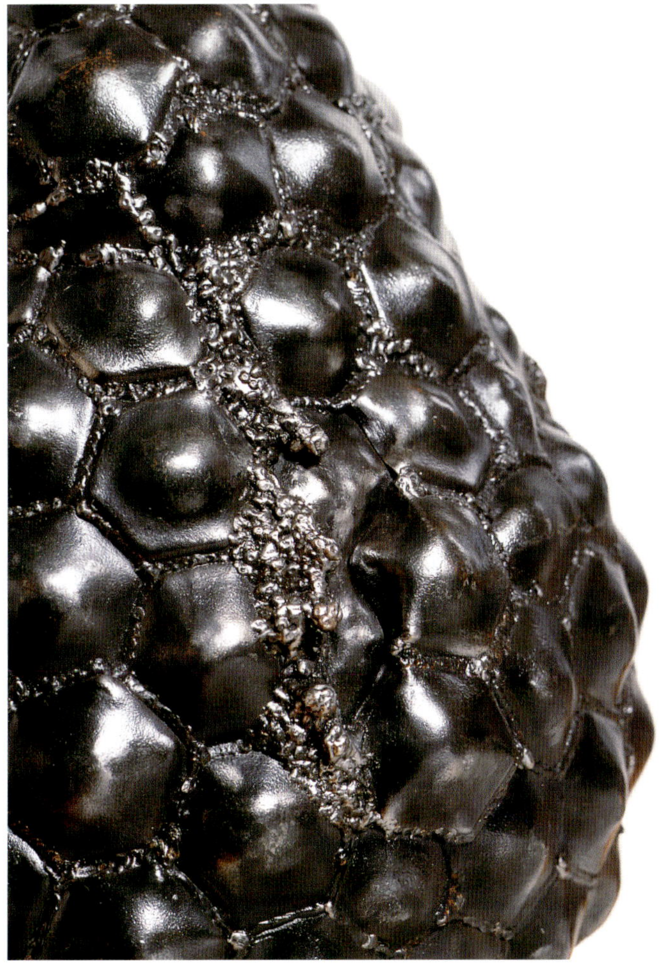

Maegan E. Crowley. *Wrecking Ball,* 2002. Detail. *Photo, Dominic Episcipo*

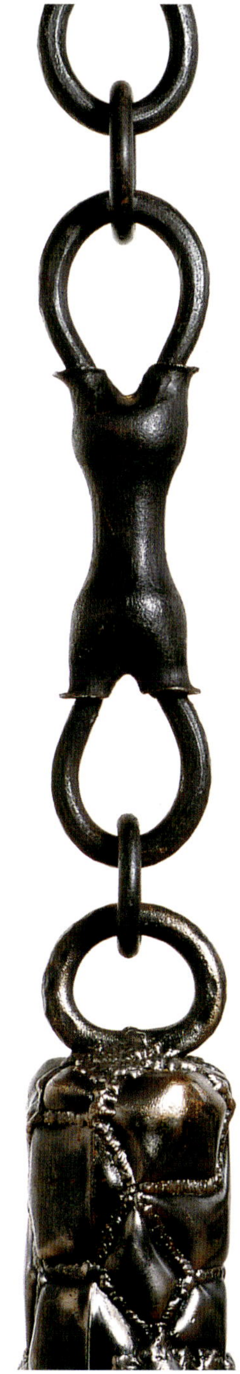

Maegan E. Crowley. *Wrecking Ball,* 2002. Chain detail. *Photo, Dominic Episcipo*

Maegan E. Crowley. *Wrecking Ball,* 2002. Forged and fabricated steel, 36" x 24" x 24", 96" chain. *Photo, Dominic Episcipo*

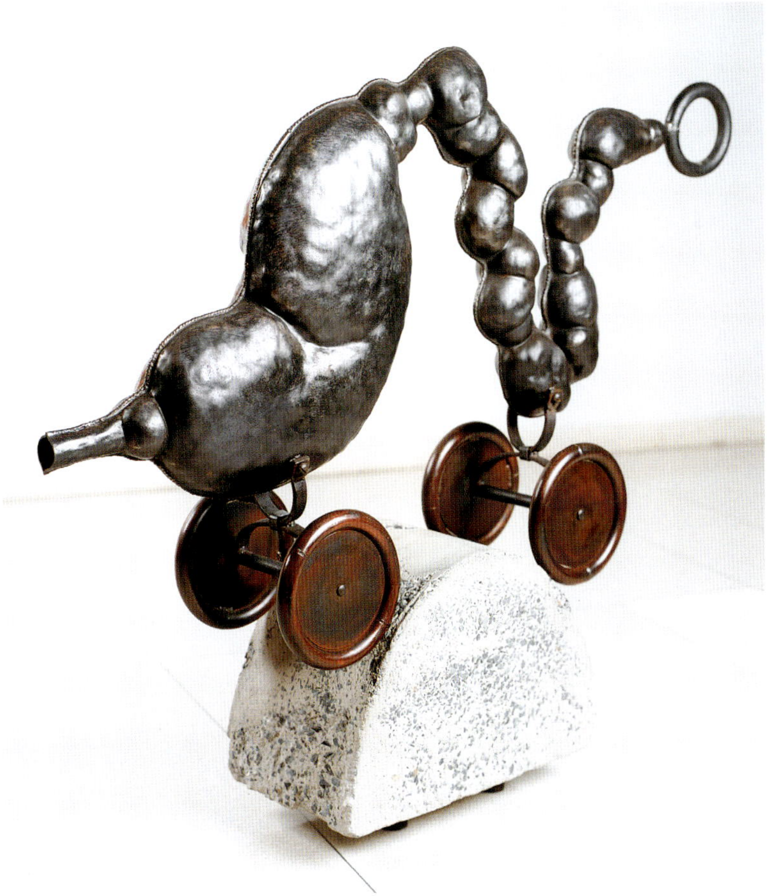

Warren Holzman. *Small Victory,* 2005. Inflated and fabricated steel, concrete, 34" x 12". *Photo, Domenic Episcopo*

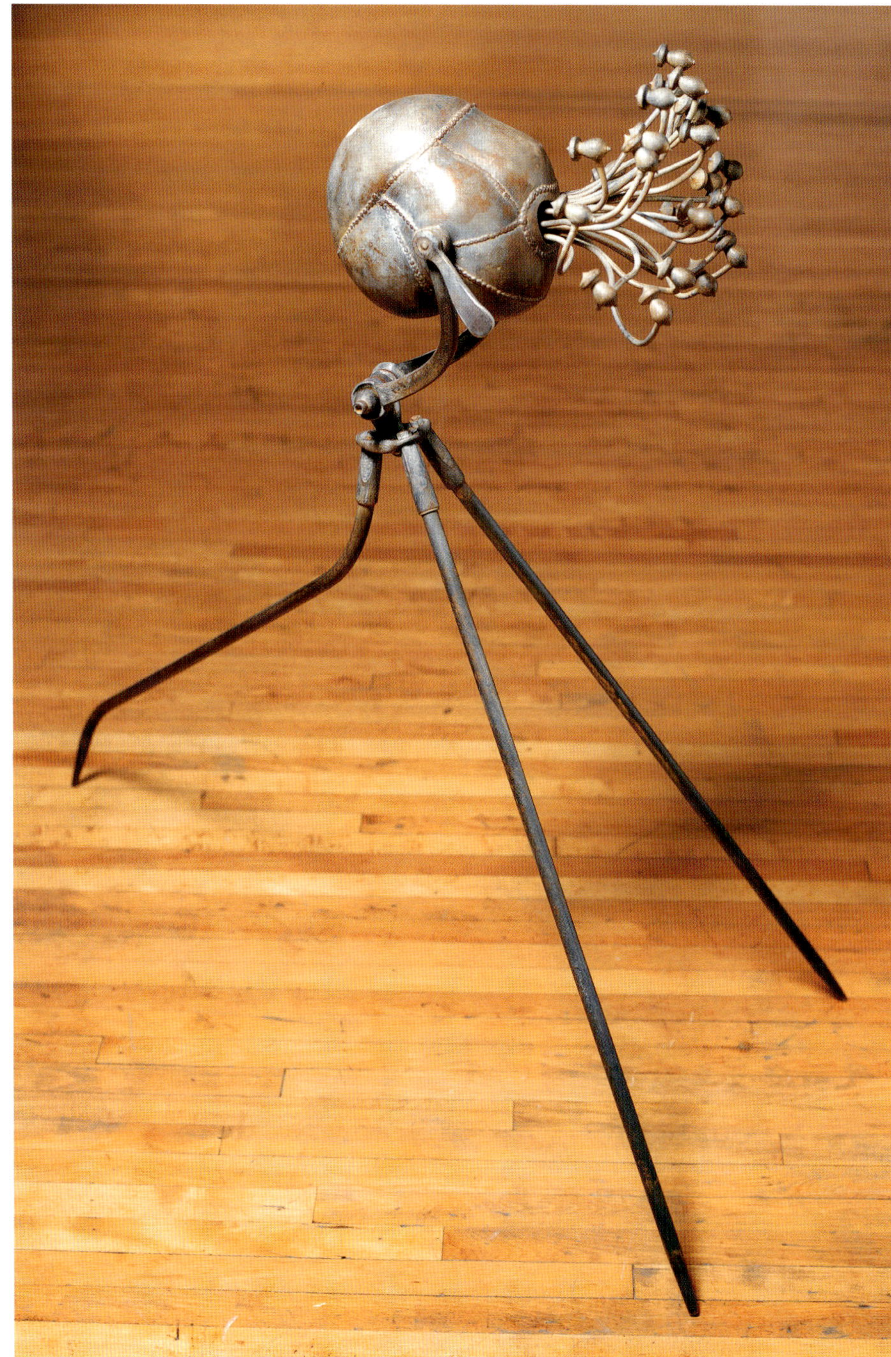

Warren Holzman. *Bad Breath,* 2005. Forged and fabricated steel. 74" x 60". *Photo, Domenic Episcopo*

My relationship to craft and sculpture has been an ongoing commitment for eighteen years, and I feel that the two disciplines have mutually informed each other in a way that reinforces a spirit of authenticity. This authenticity helps to carry the narrative themes in my work; often the process of the metalworking is evident to help illiterate content. Iron and steel have a specific material presence that can be more expressive, and therefore lend itself to a wider vocabulary, and its industrialized history has become part of our landscape. Adding to this landscape is an exciting prospect, the interplay of natural manmade objects and forms can inspire and inform the richness of our lives. – Warren Holzman

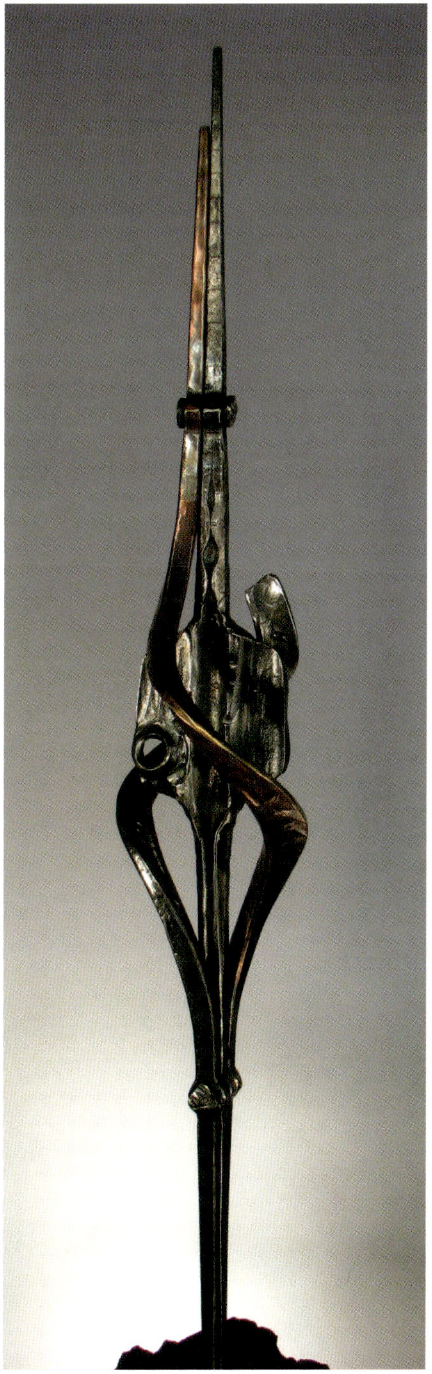

Tim Cisneros. *Helios.* Silicon Bronze, mild steel. *Photo, Svetomir Jurcan*

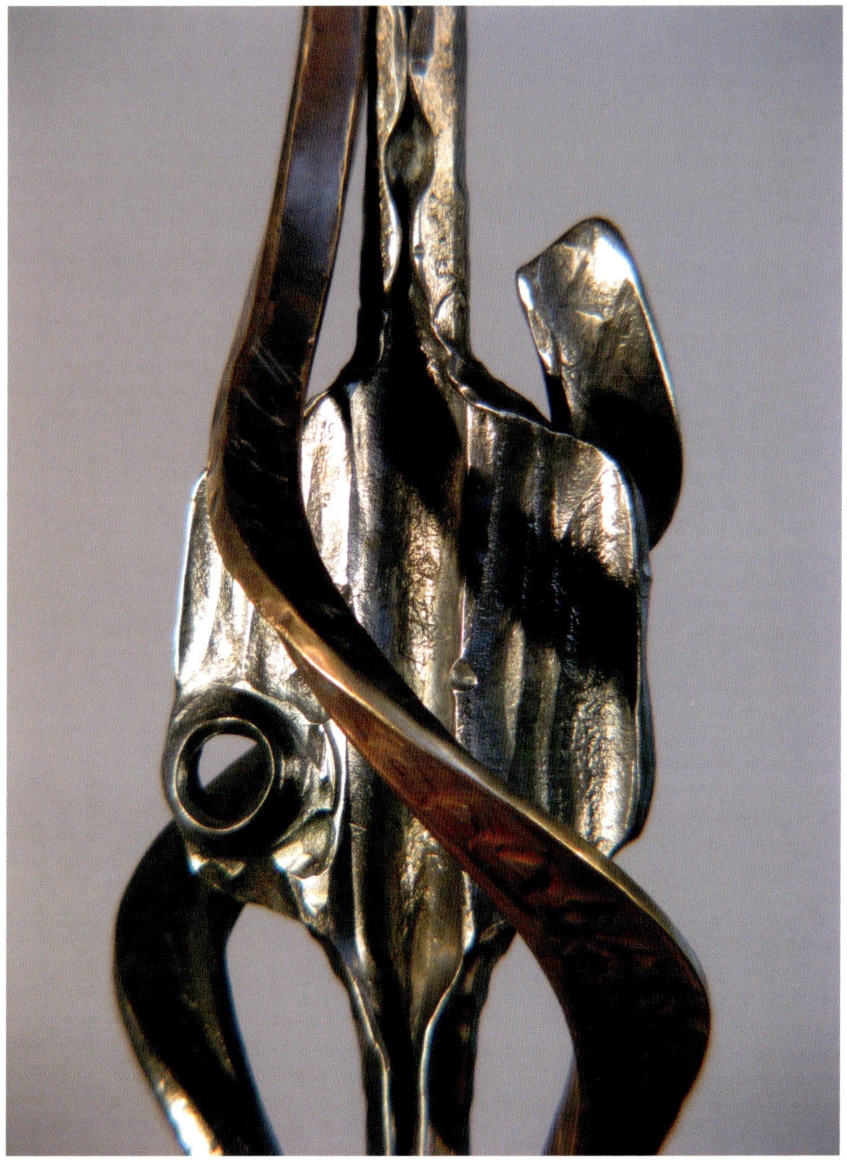

Tim Cisneros. *Helios.* Detail. *Photo, Svetomir Jurcan*

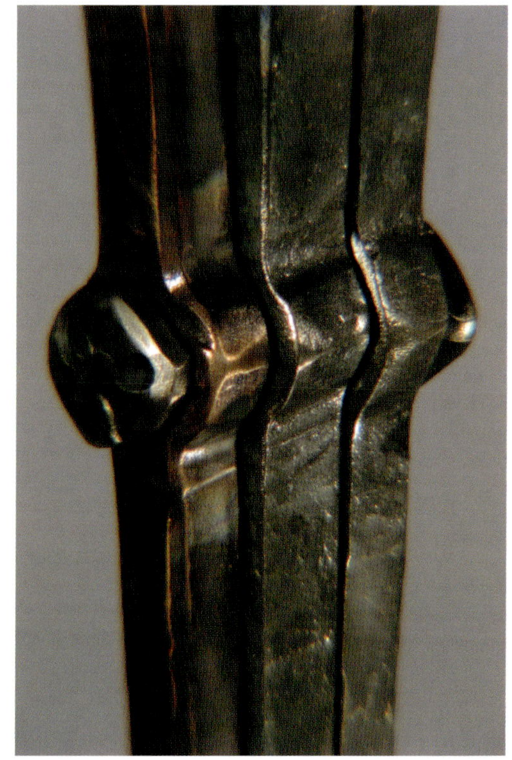

Tim Cisneros. *Helios*. Detail. *Photo, Svetomir Jurcan*

Helios was the Greek God of the sun. He rode a golden chariot across the sky from sunup to sundown and possessed an "All-seeing eye" It was believed that Helios had a golden cup, The work of the God of fire "Hephaistos," the blacksmith's God, in which he would sail all night back to the east, so that in the morning he could start his journey again. – Tim Cisneros

Tim Cisneros. *Ode to Alfred.* Mild steel. In honor of Alfred Habremann. *Photo, Svetomir Jurcan*

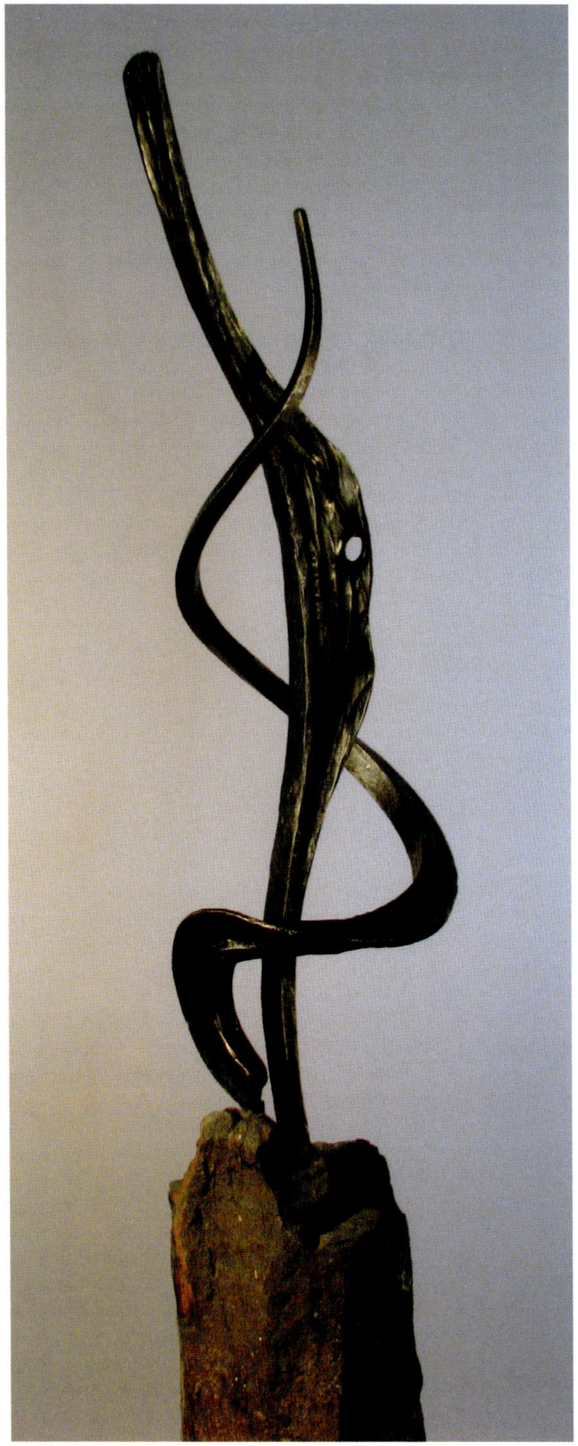

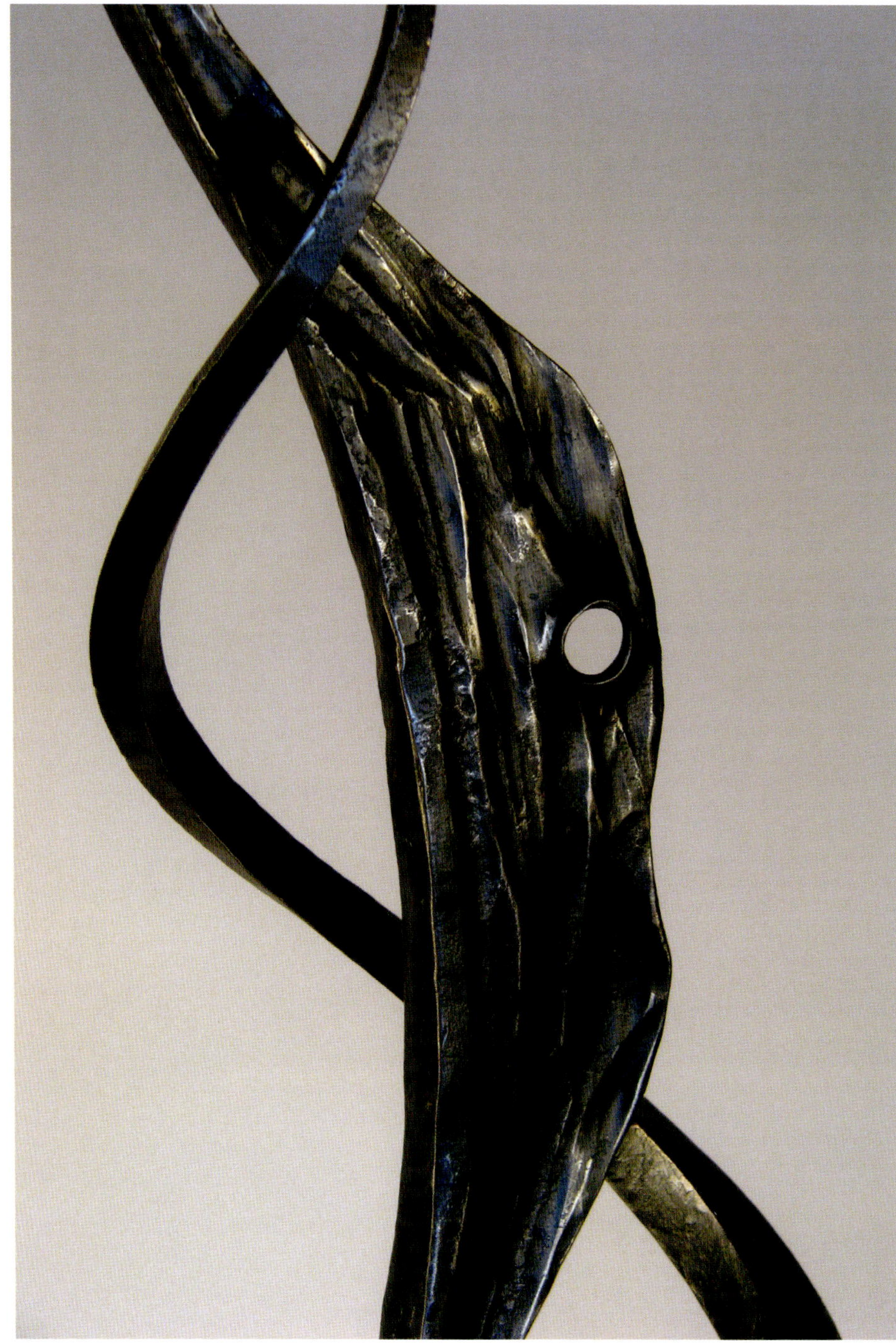

Tim Cisneros. *Ode to Alfred.* Detail. *Photo, Svetomir Jurcan*

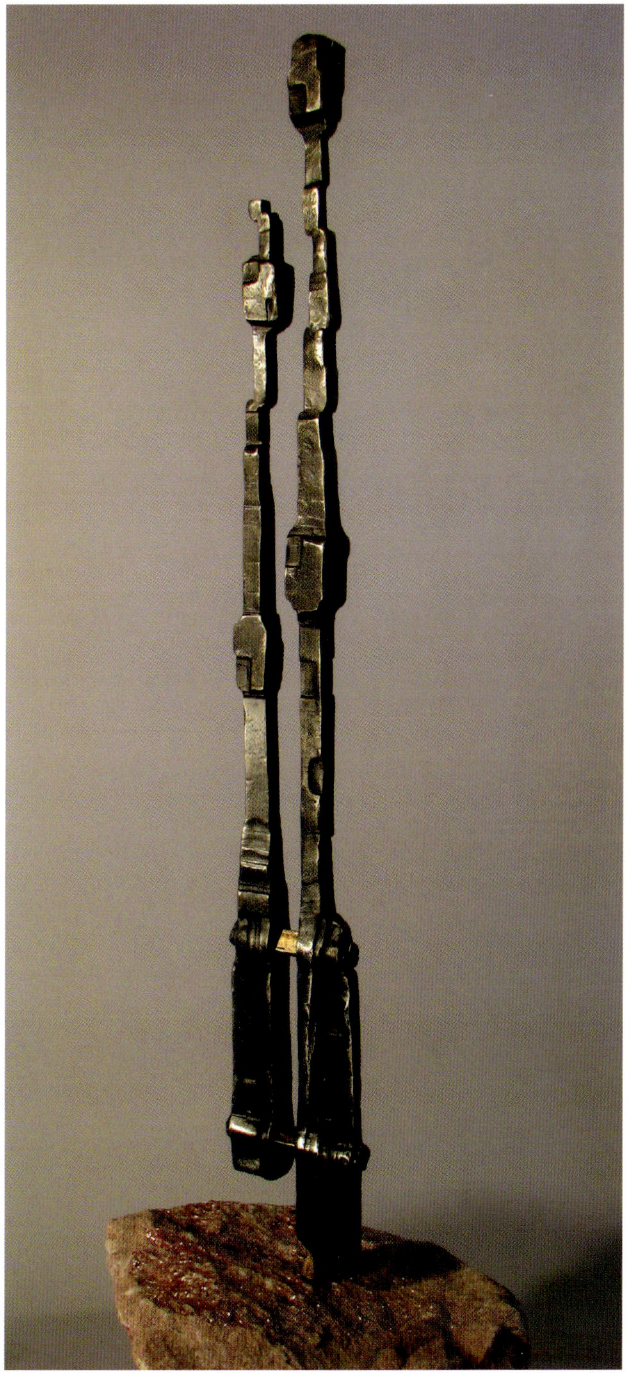

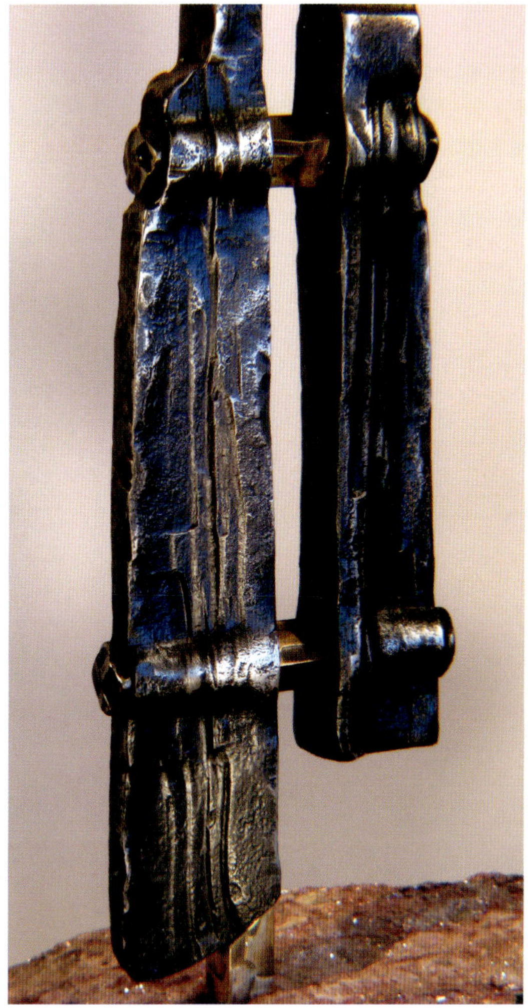

Tim Cisneros. *Levitation.* Detail.
Photo, Svetomir Jurcan

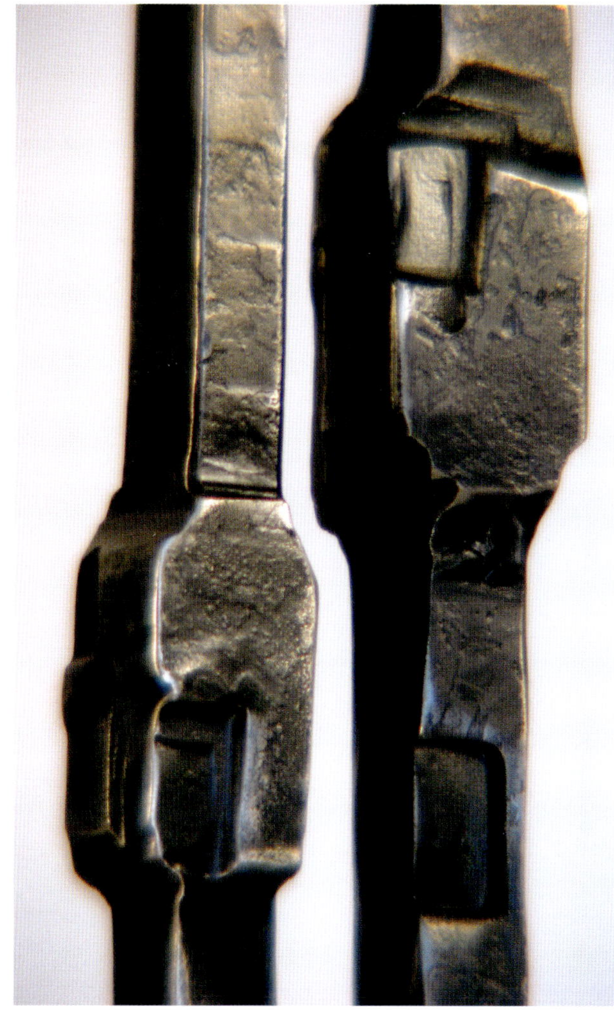

Tim Cisneros. *Levitation.* Detail.
Photo, Svetomir Jurcan

Tim Cisneros. *Levitation.* Mild steel.
Photo, Svetomir Jurcan

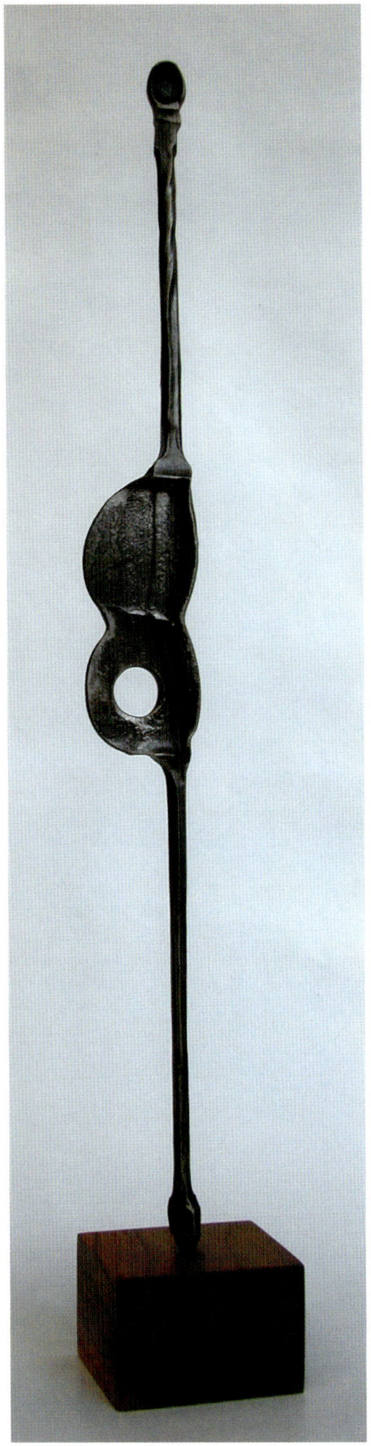

Andy Leritz. *Forged Figure #7*. Forged steel and walnut, 18" h. *Photo, artist*

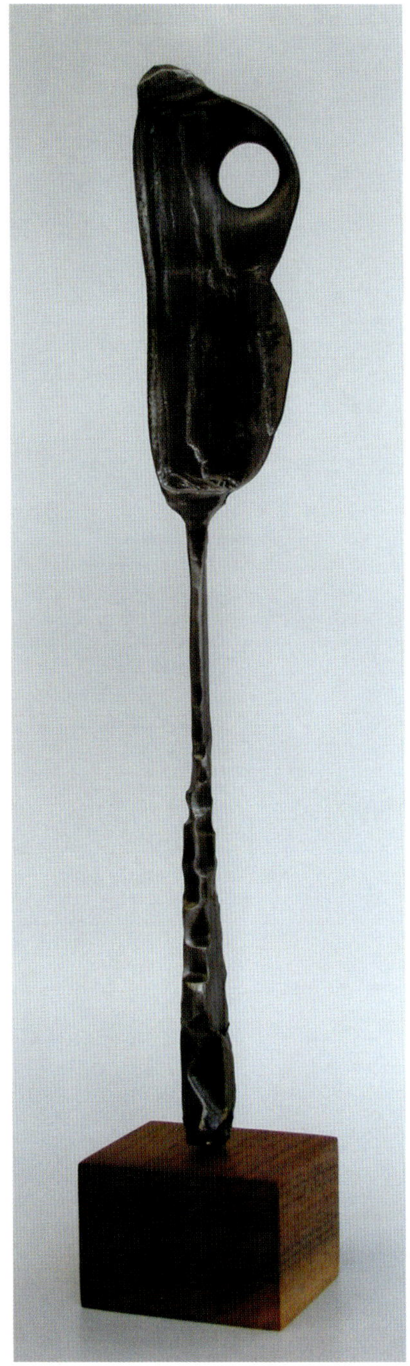

Andy Leritz. *Forged Figure #3*. Forged steel and walnut, 15" h. *Photo, artist*

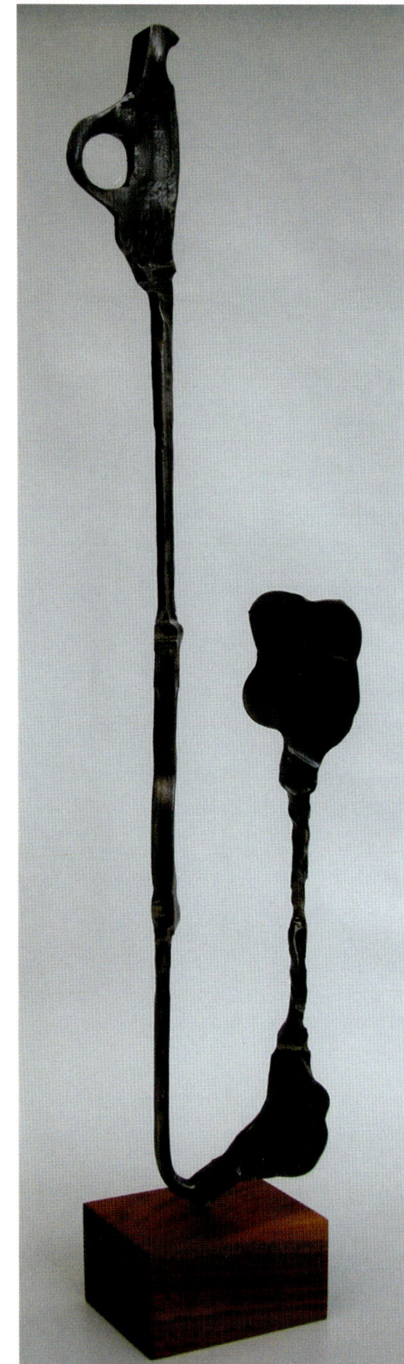

Andy Leritz. *Forged Figure #11*. Forged steel and walnut, 21" h. *Photo, artist*

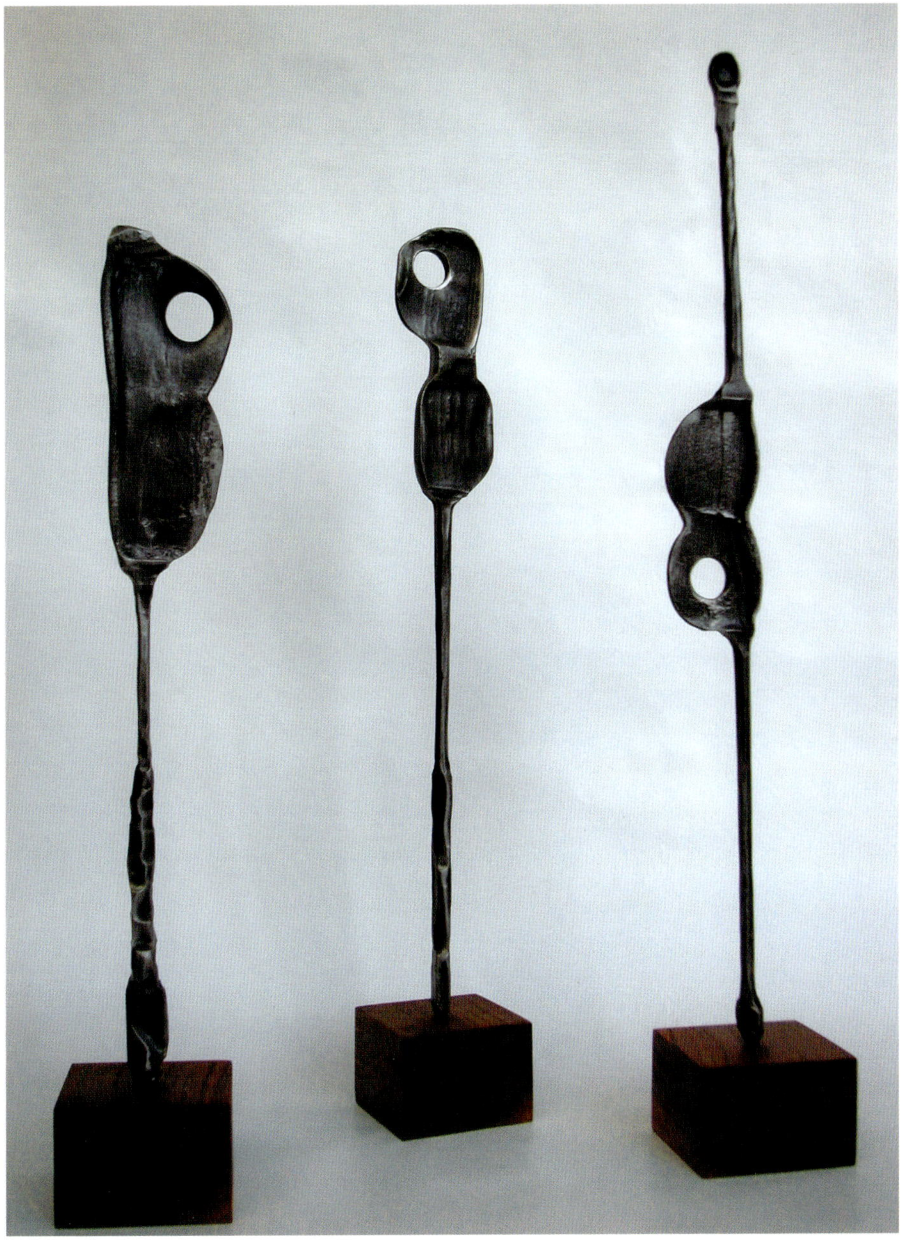

Andy Leritz. *Forged Figures #3, #4, #7*. Forged steel and walnut, 15"-18". *Photo, artist*

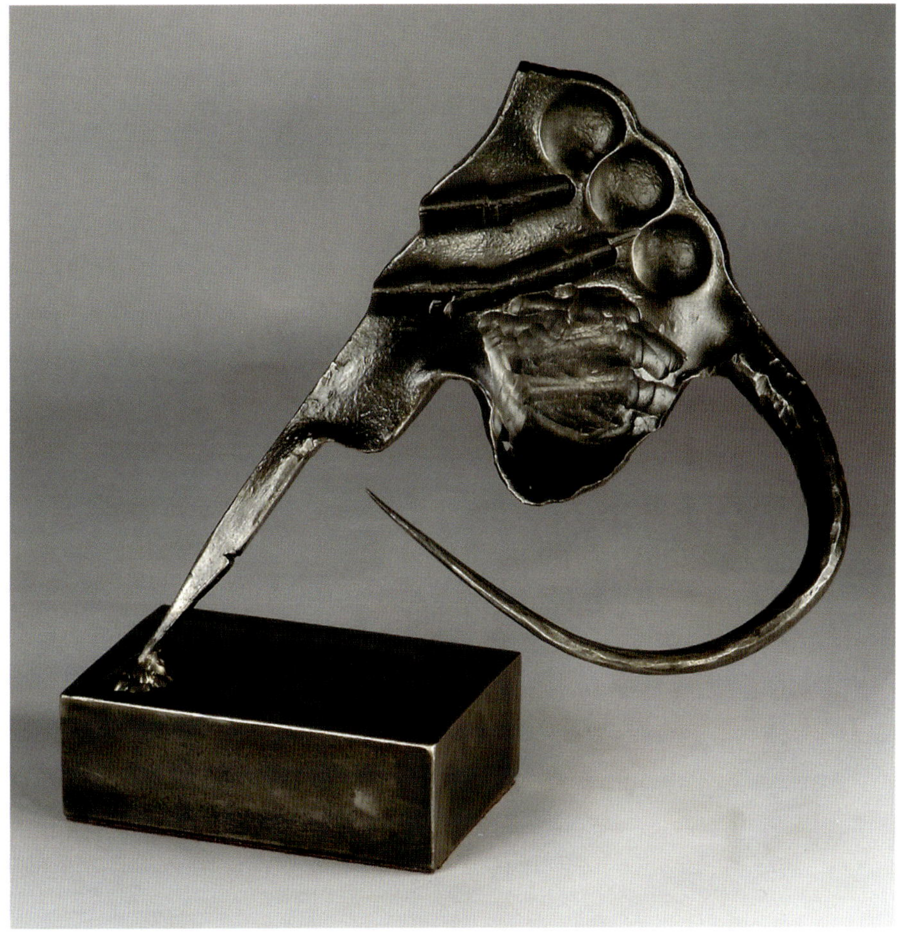

M. Craig Campbell. *Free Form*, 2007. Forged and fabricated steel, past wax. 17" h x 17" w x 8" d. *Photo, Trent Watts*

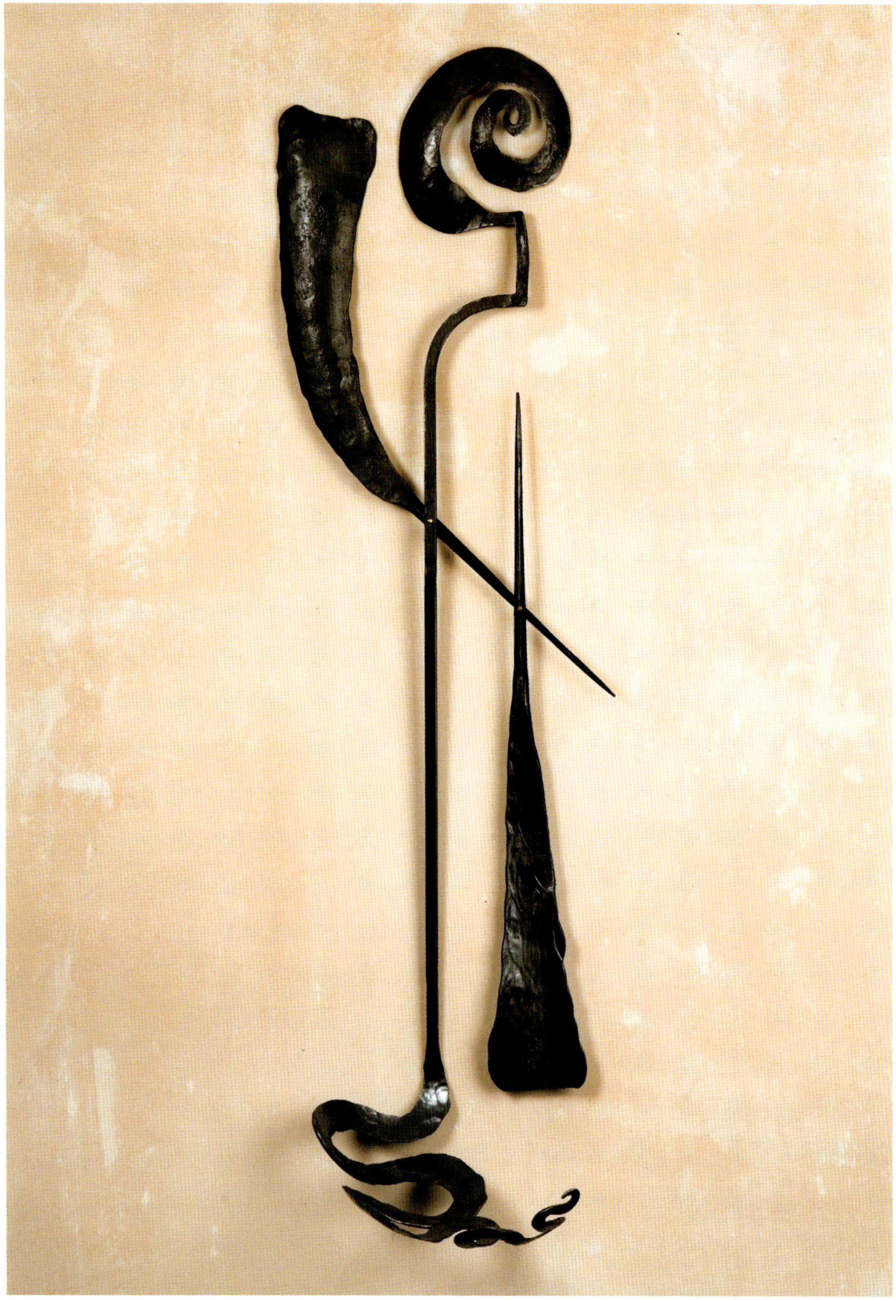

Christopher Thomson. *Primordial Improvisation #6*. Forged steel. 48" h x 17" w x 12" d. *Photo, Robert Miller*

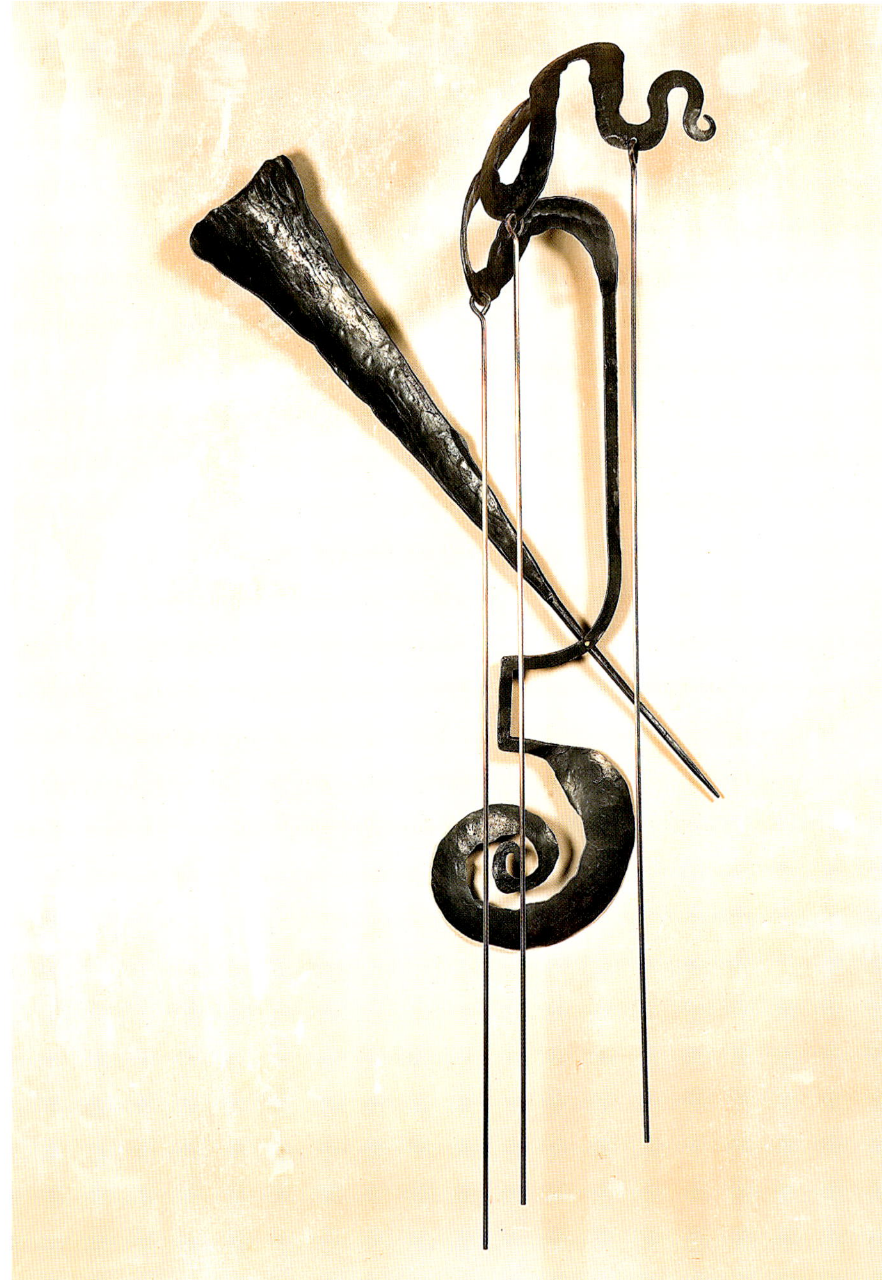

Christopher Thomson. *Primordial Improvisation #1*. Forged steel and bronze, 43" h x 19" w x 10" d. *Photo, Robert Miller*

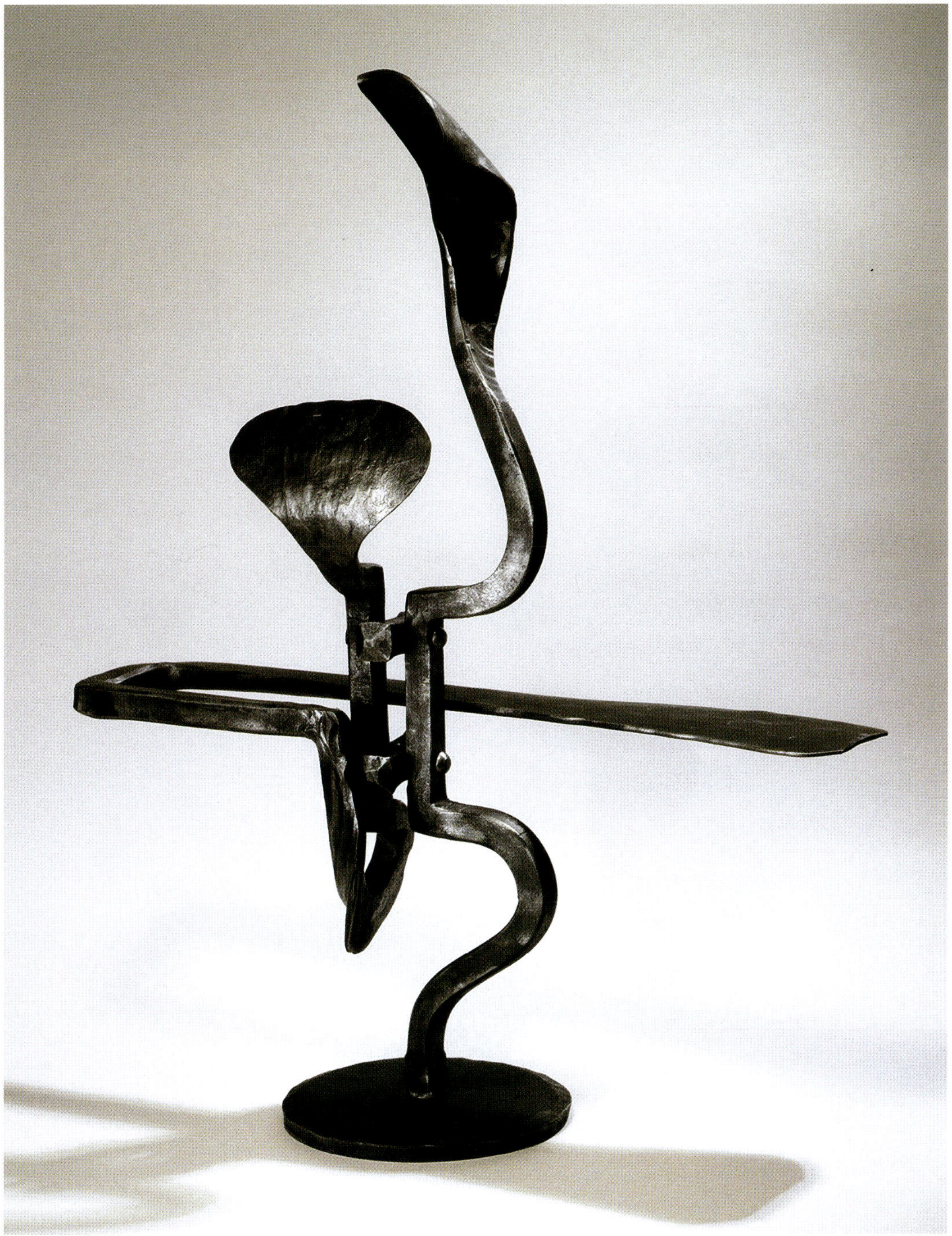

Christopher Thomson. *Interface.*
Forged steel. 29" h x 11" w x 8.5" d.
Photo, Herb Lotz

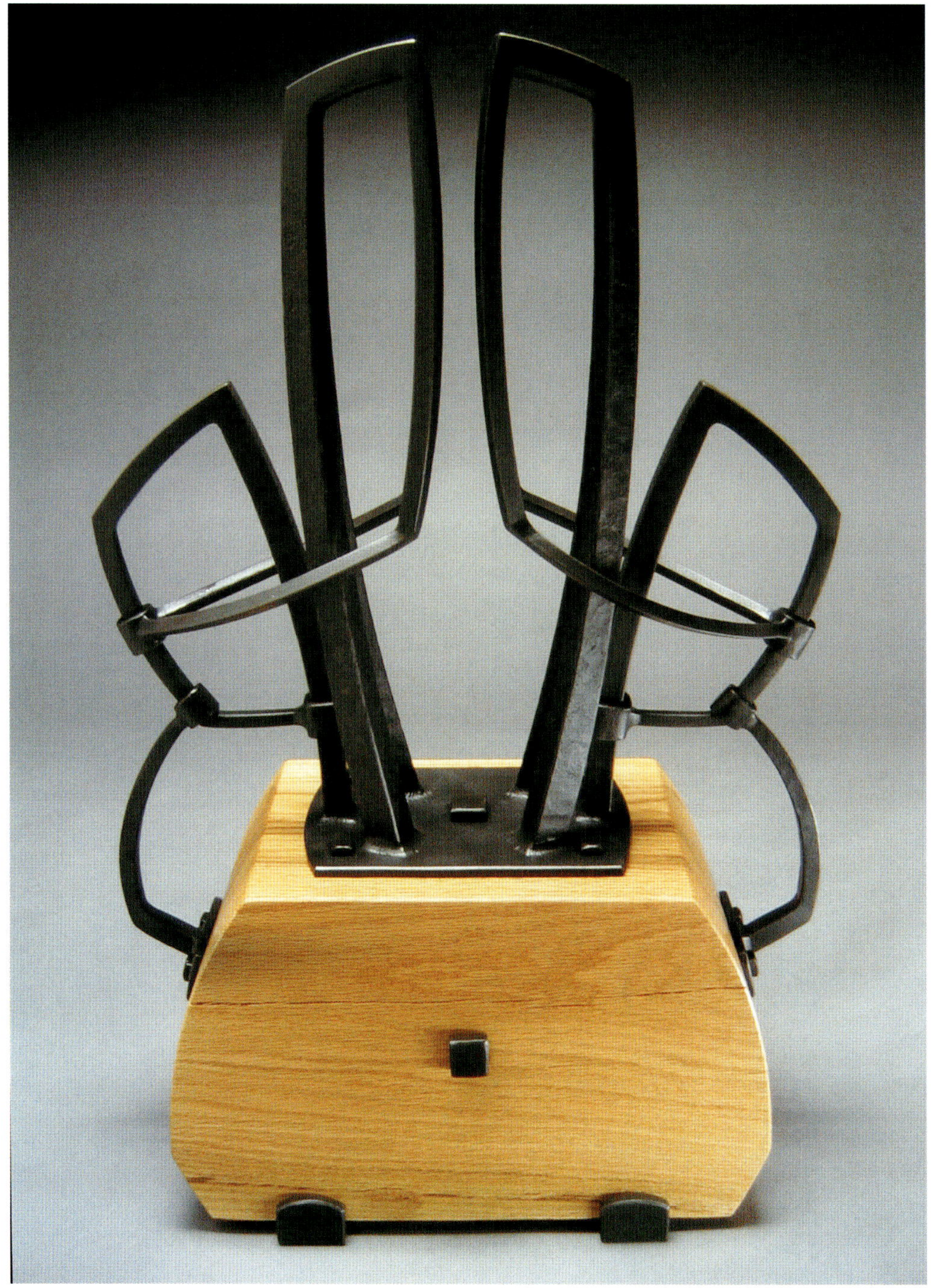

Greg Gehner. *Equiponderant* (D60), 2007.
Steel and oak. 29" x 19" x 12". *Photo, artist*

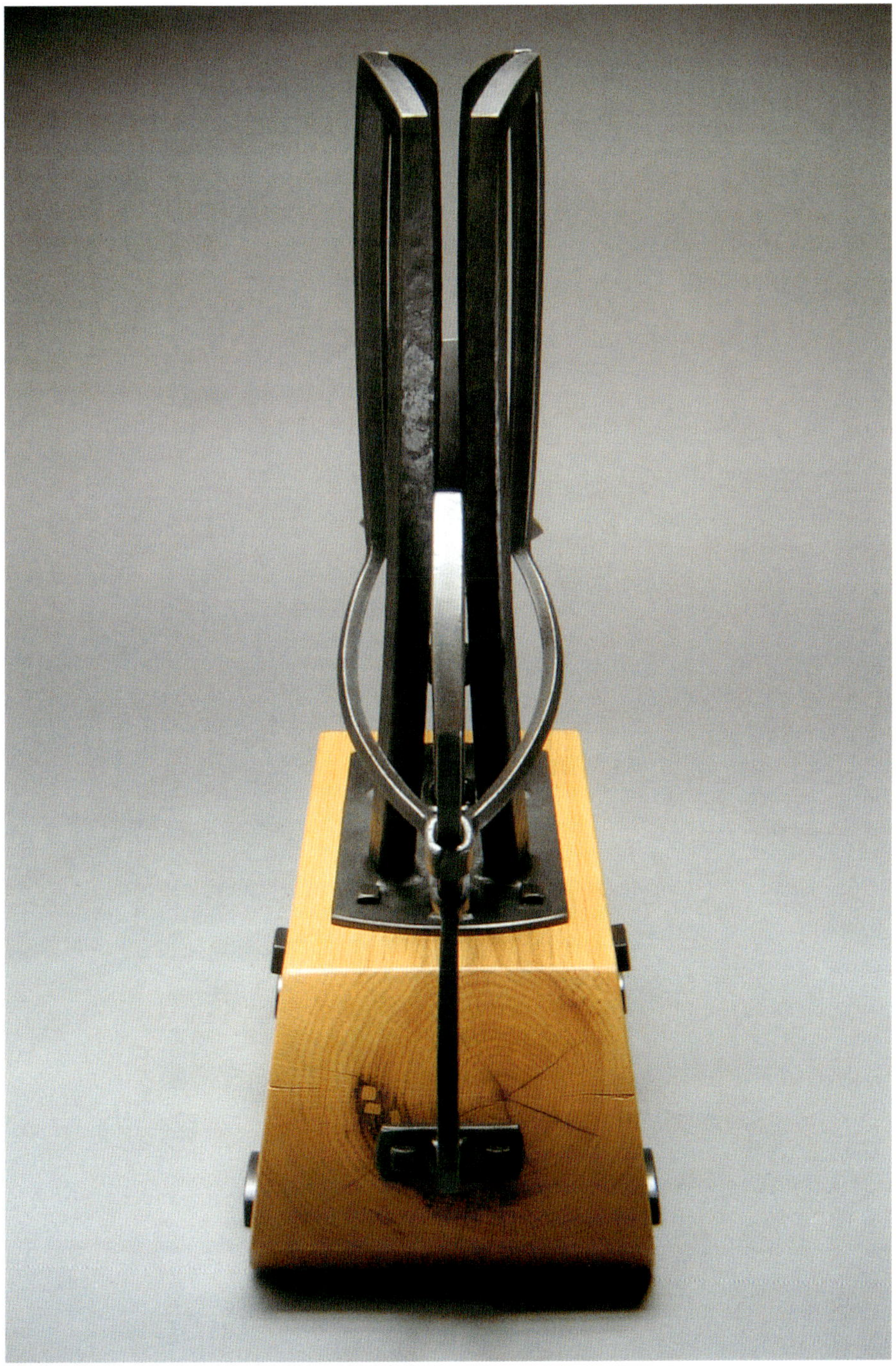

Greg Gehner. *Equiponderant* (D60), 2007. Detail. *Photo, artist*

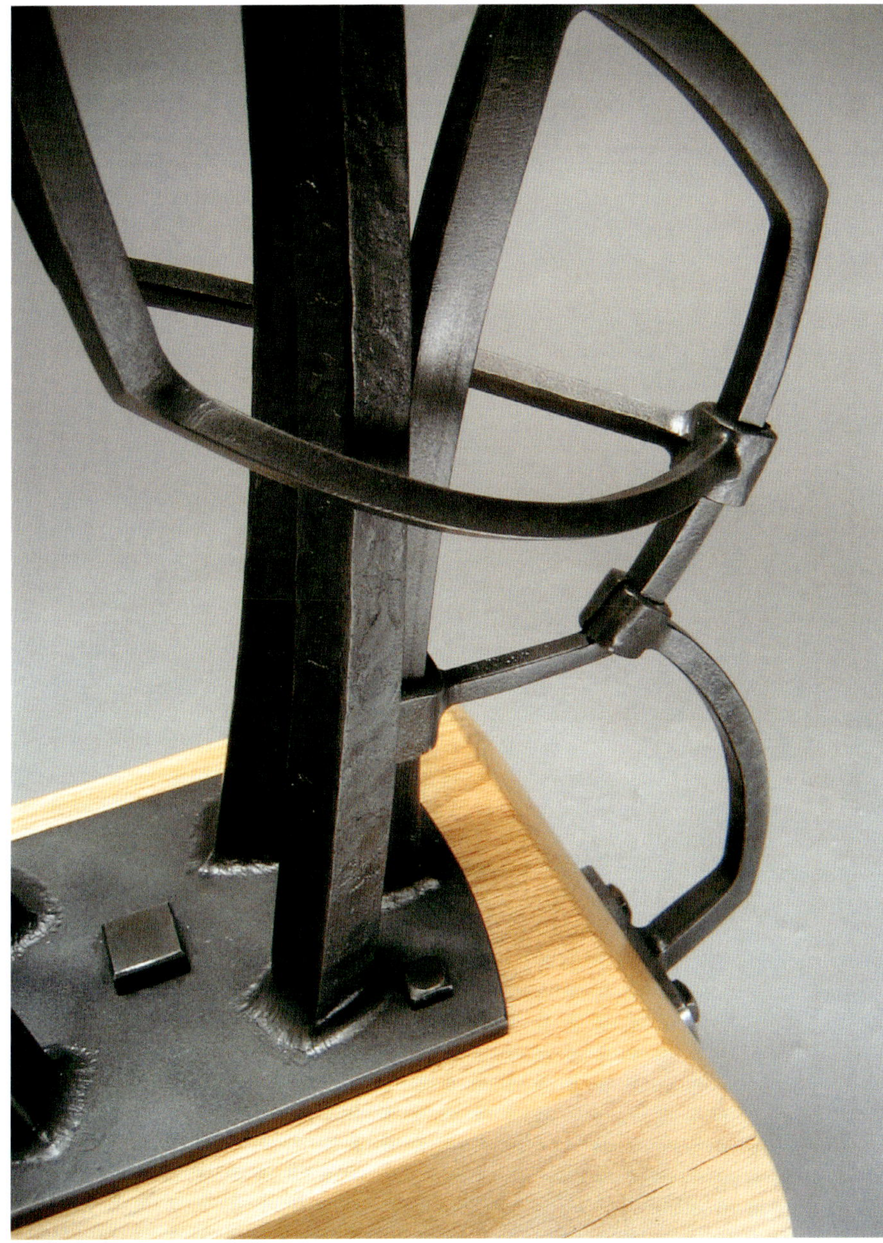

Greg Gehner. *Equiponderant* (D60), 2007. Detail. *Photo, artist*

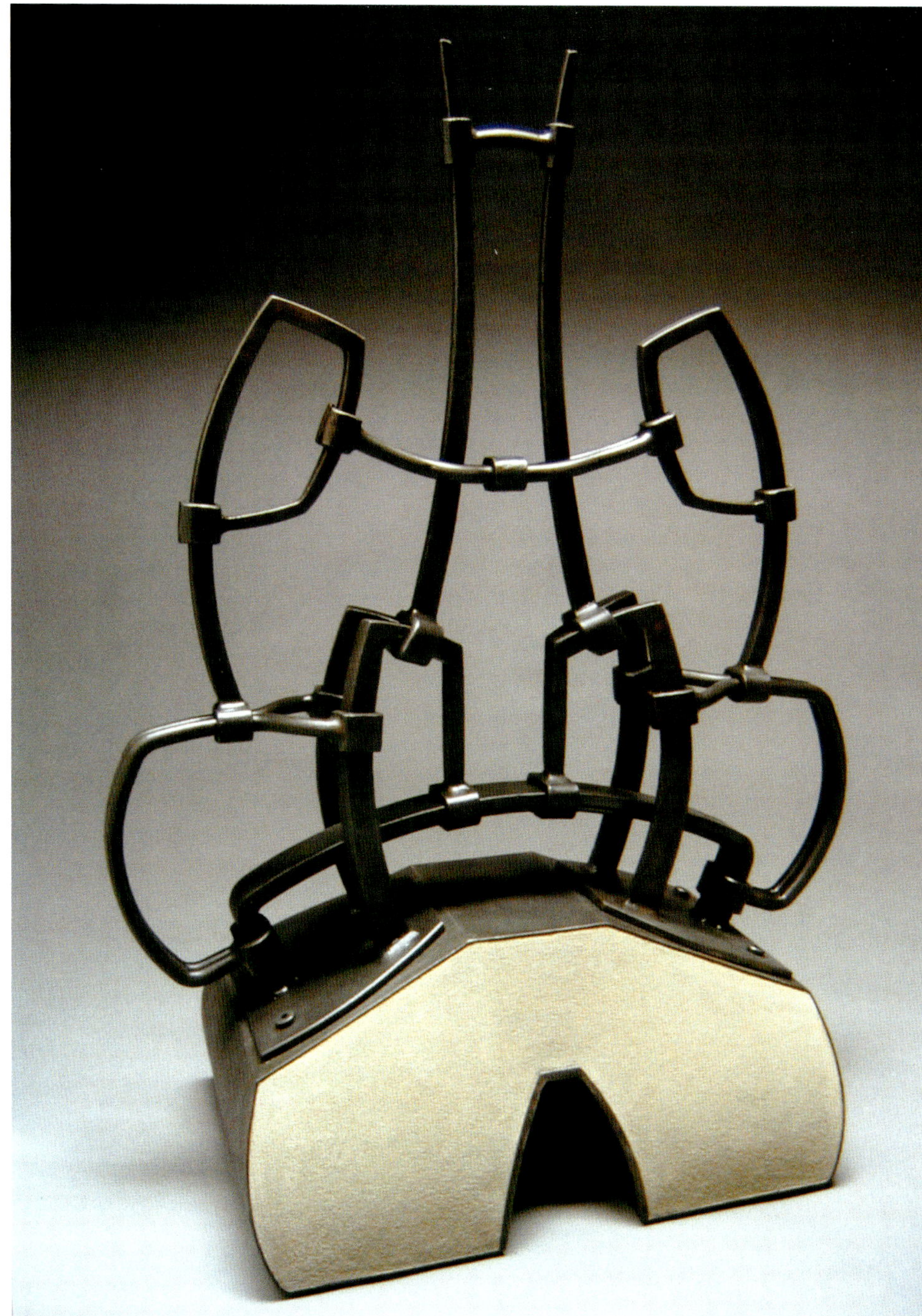

Greg Gehner. *Concinnus* (D66), 2007.
Steel and cement. 31" x 23" x 12".
Photo, artist

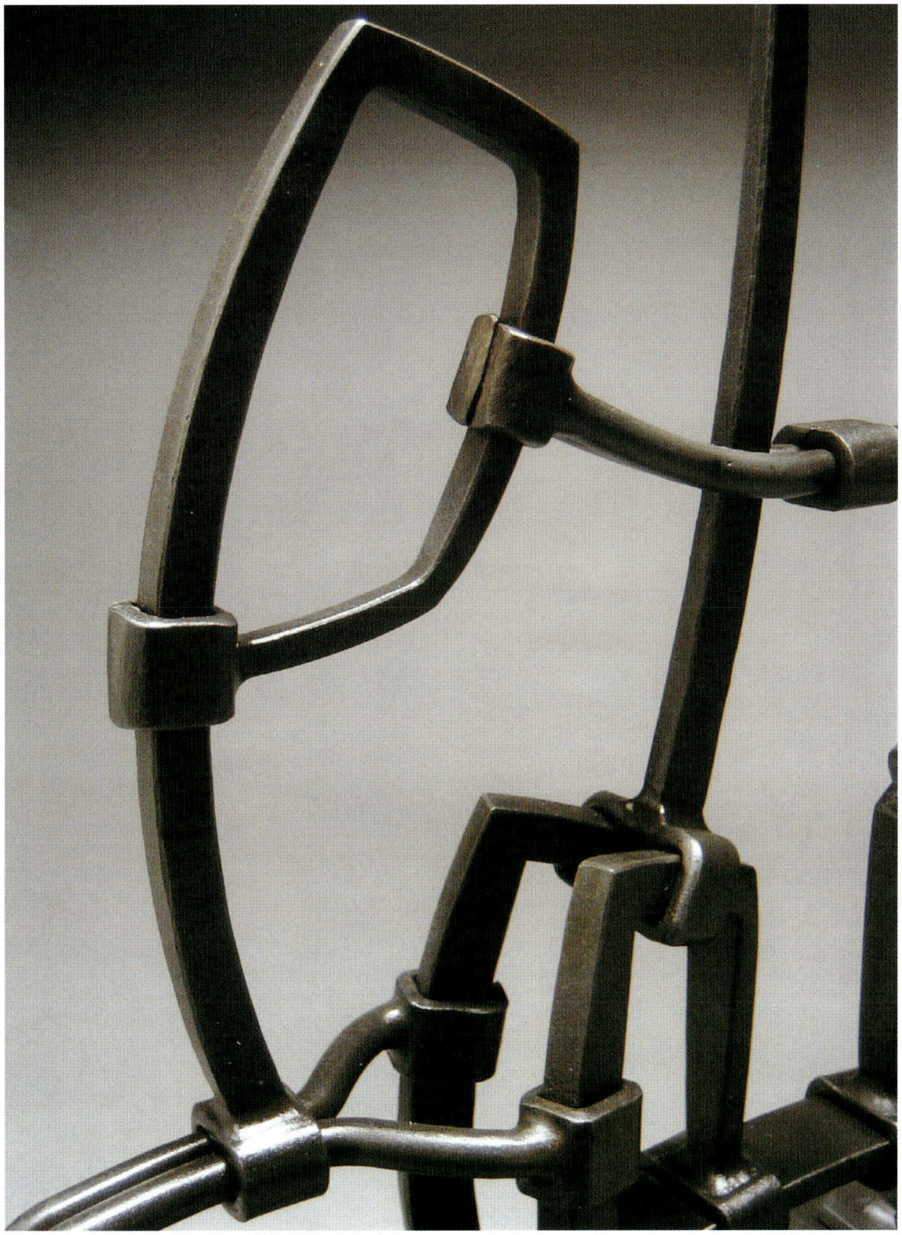

Greg Gehner. *Concinnus* (D66), 2007. Detail. *Photo, artist*

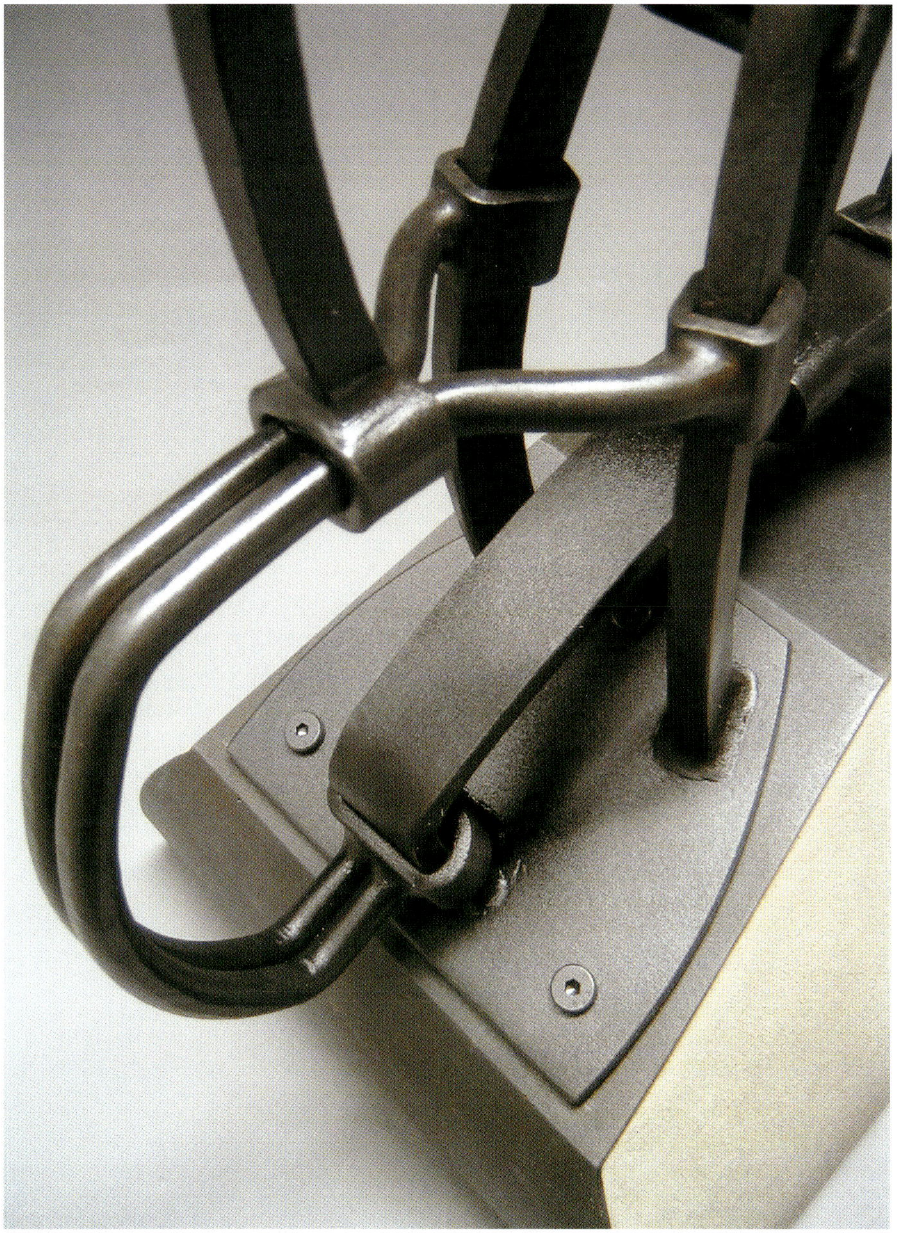

Greg Gehner. *Concinnus* (D66), 2007. Detail. *Photo, artist*

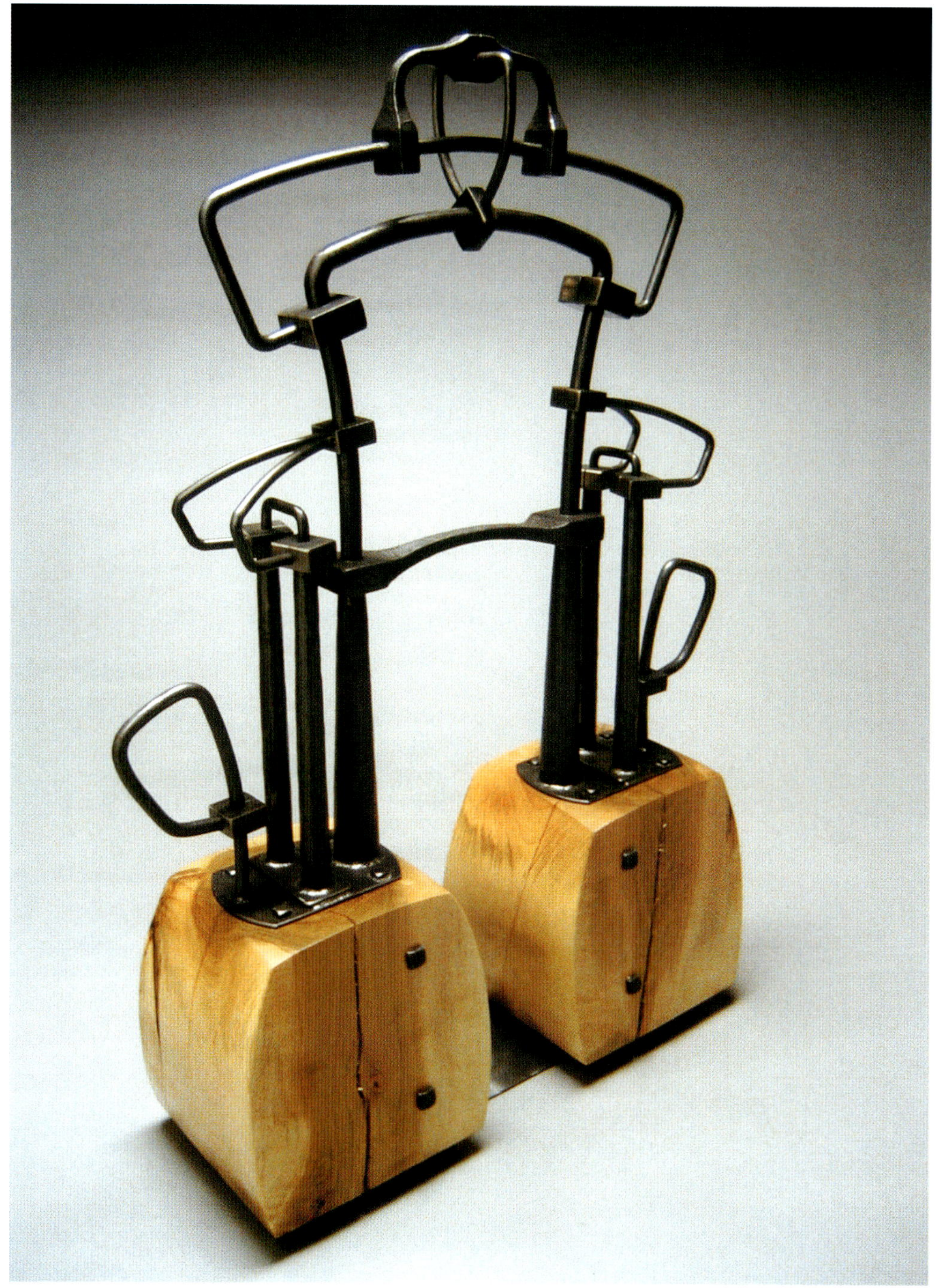

Greg Gehner. *Ponderous* (D75), 2006.
Steel and maple. 38" x 28" x 9".
Photo, artist

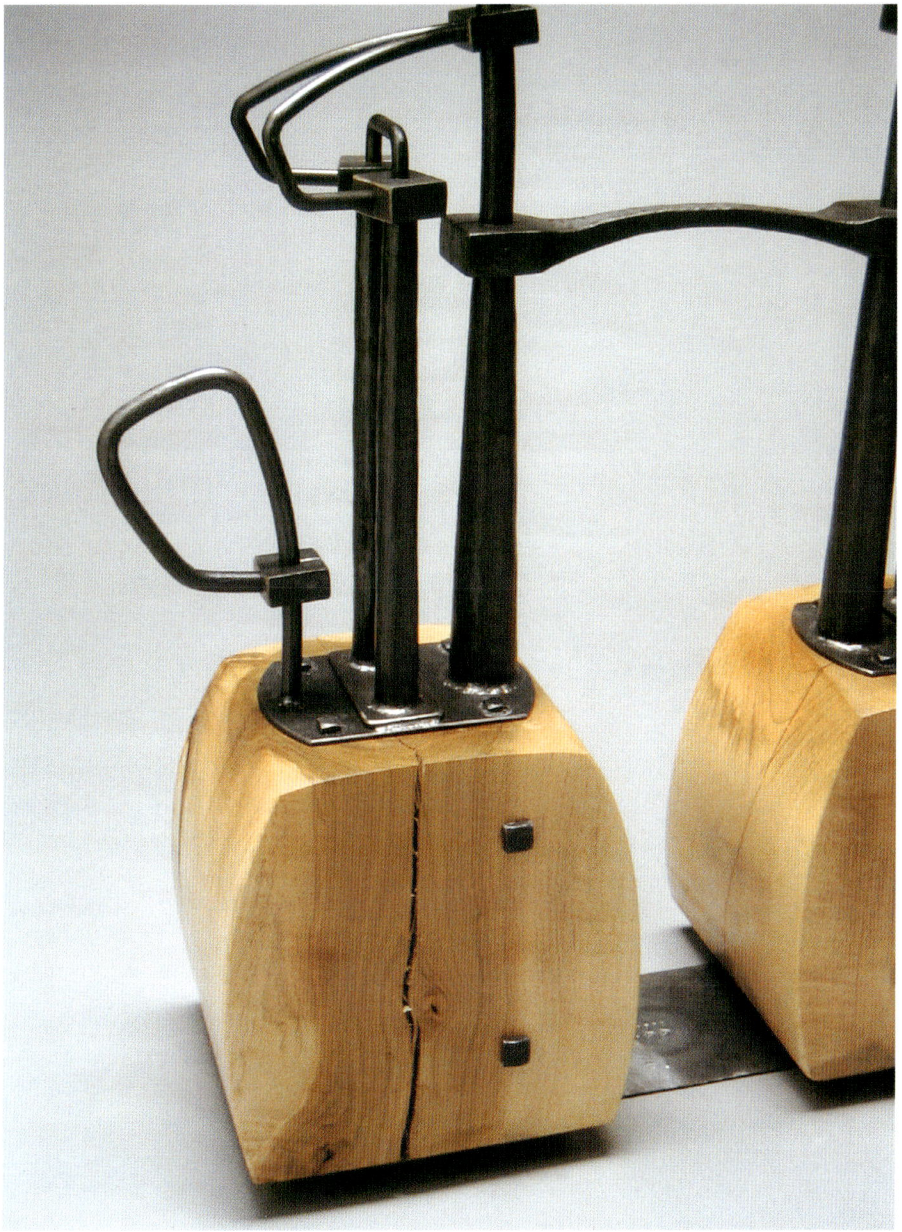

Greg Gehner. *Ponderous* (D75), 2006. Detail. *Photo, artist*

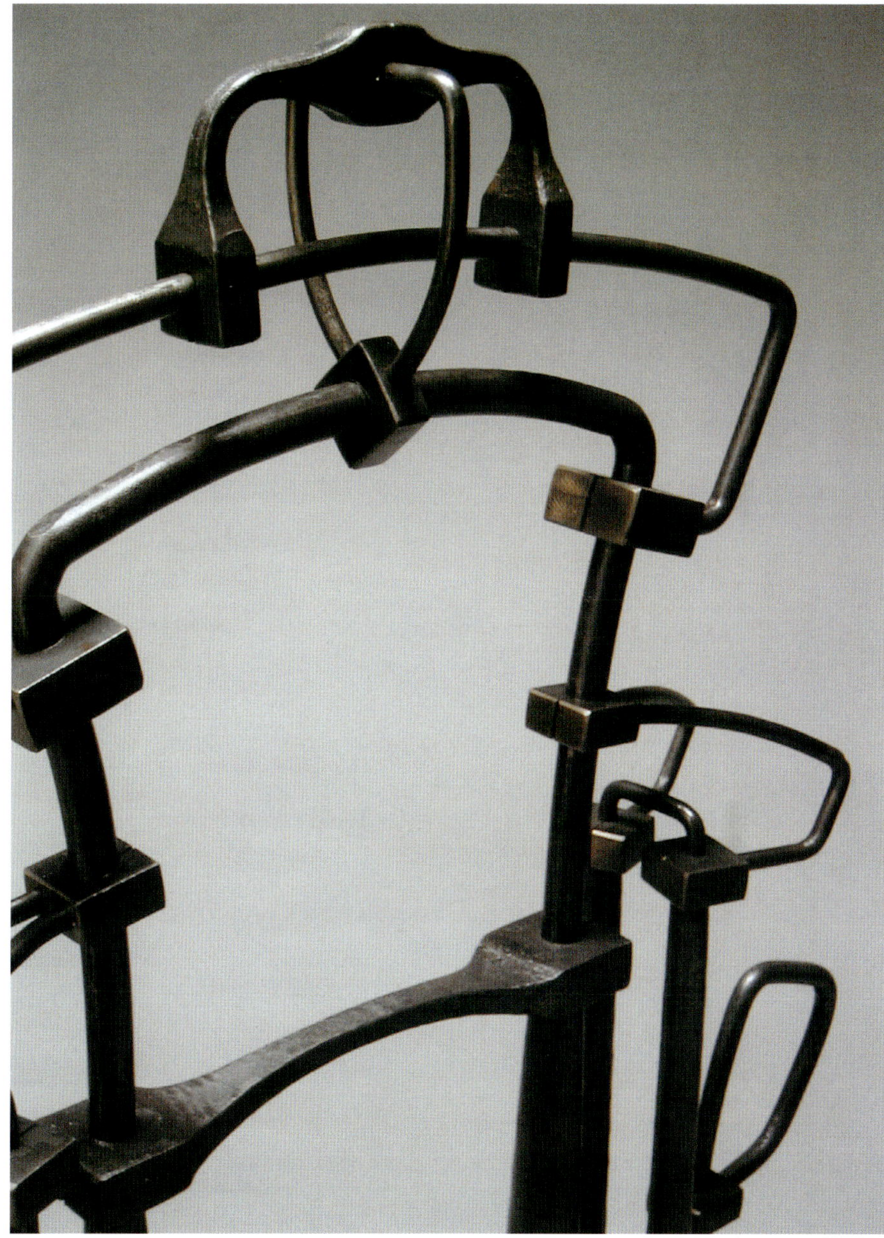

Greg Gehner. *Ponderous* (D75), 2006. Detail. *Photo, artist*

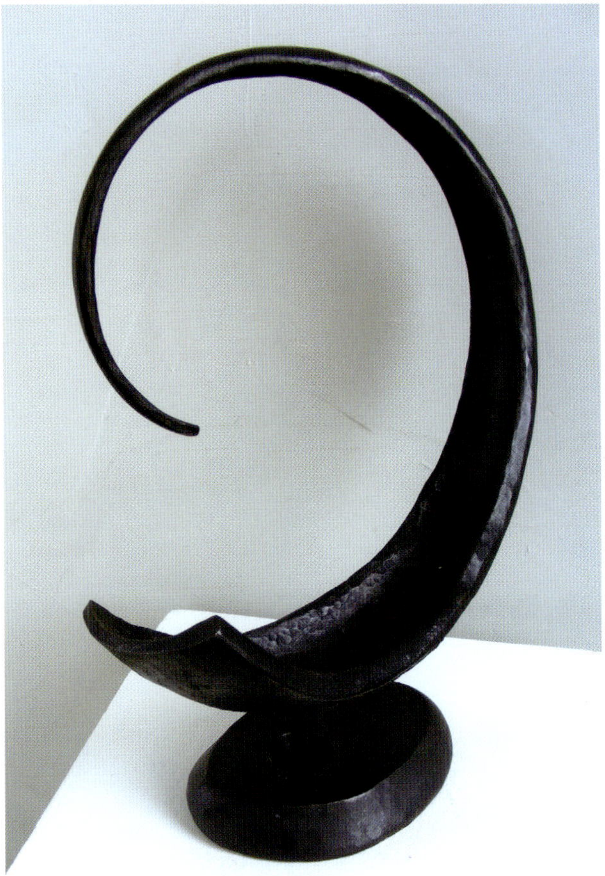

John Little. *Eclipsing Moon,* 2004. Forged steel.
12" h x 8" w x 8" d. *Photo, artist*

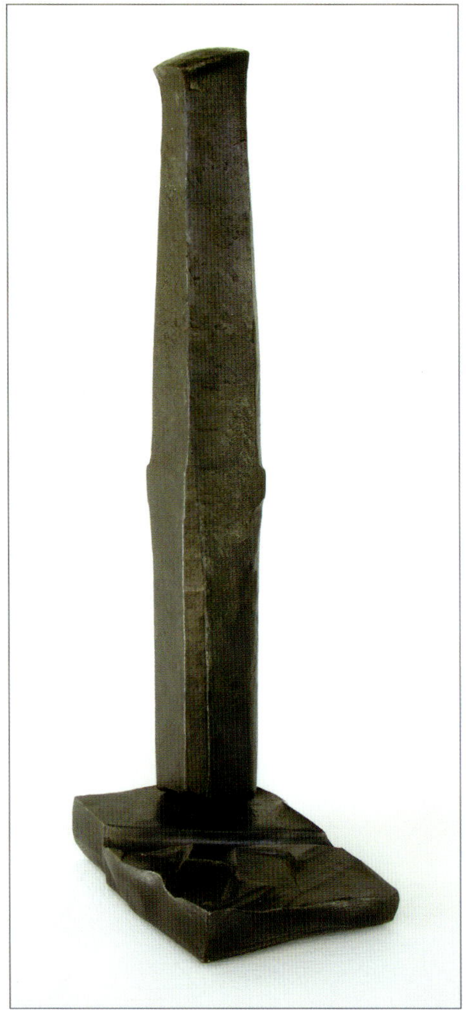

John Little. *Obelisk*, 2005. Forged steel.
19" h x 8" w x 7" d. *Photo, artist*

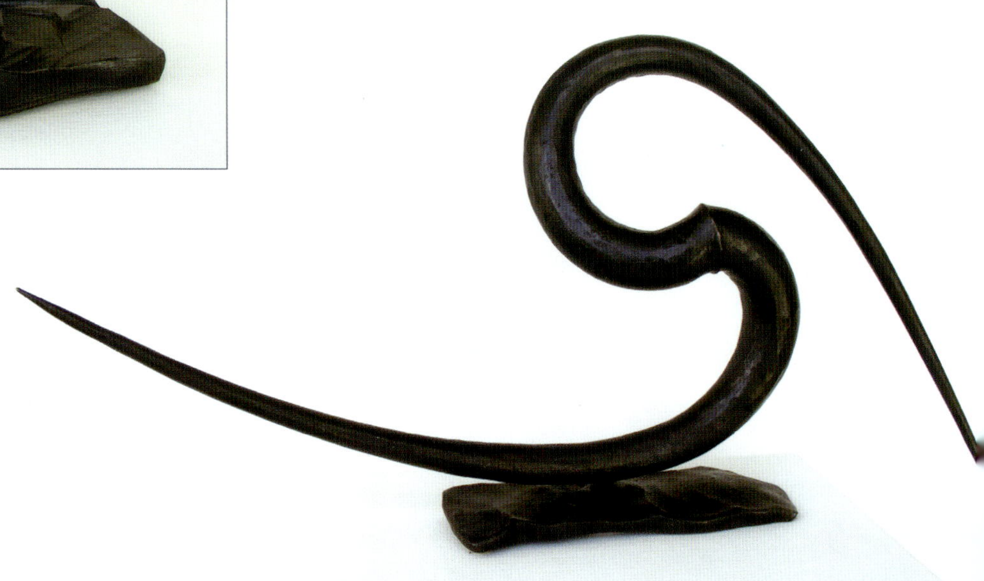

John Little. *Su Asti 4*, 2005. Forged steel.
15" h x 29" w x 5" d. *Photo, artist*

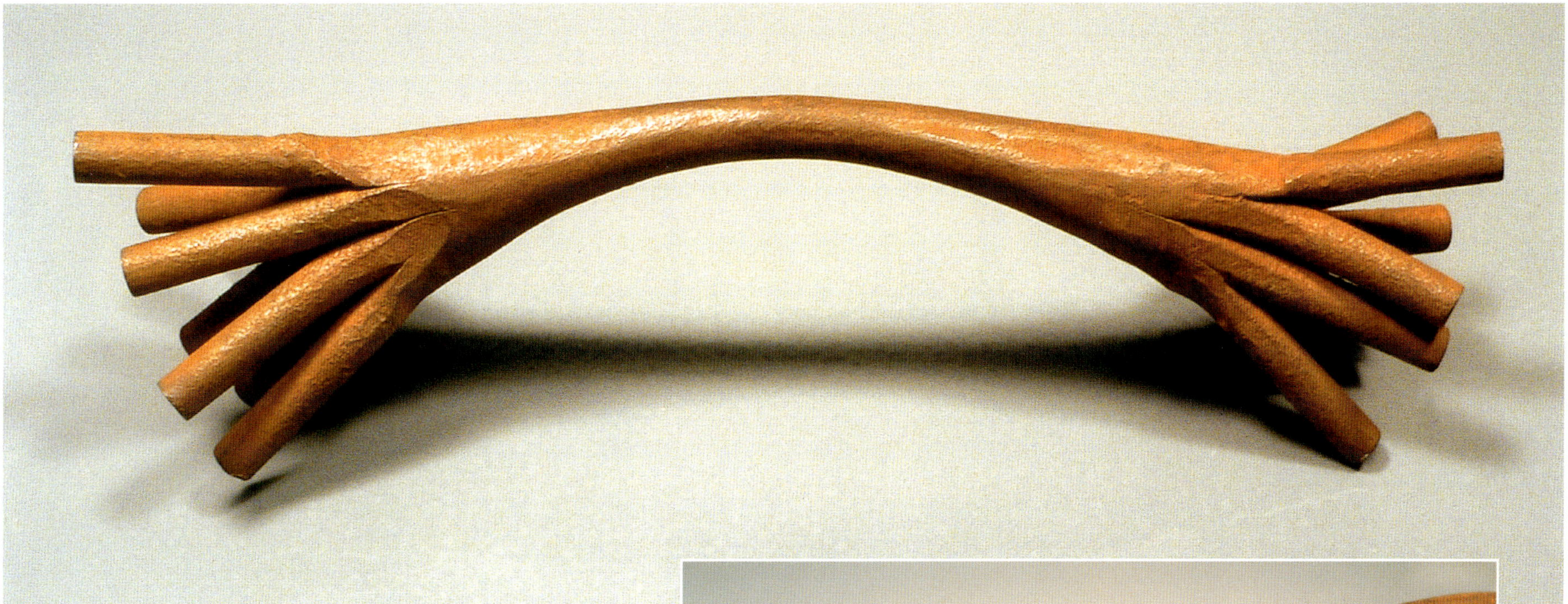

Mike Rossi. *Self Portrait,* 2006. Forged mild steel. 13" x 4". *Photo, artist*

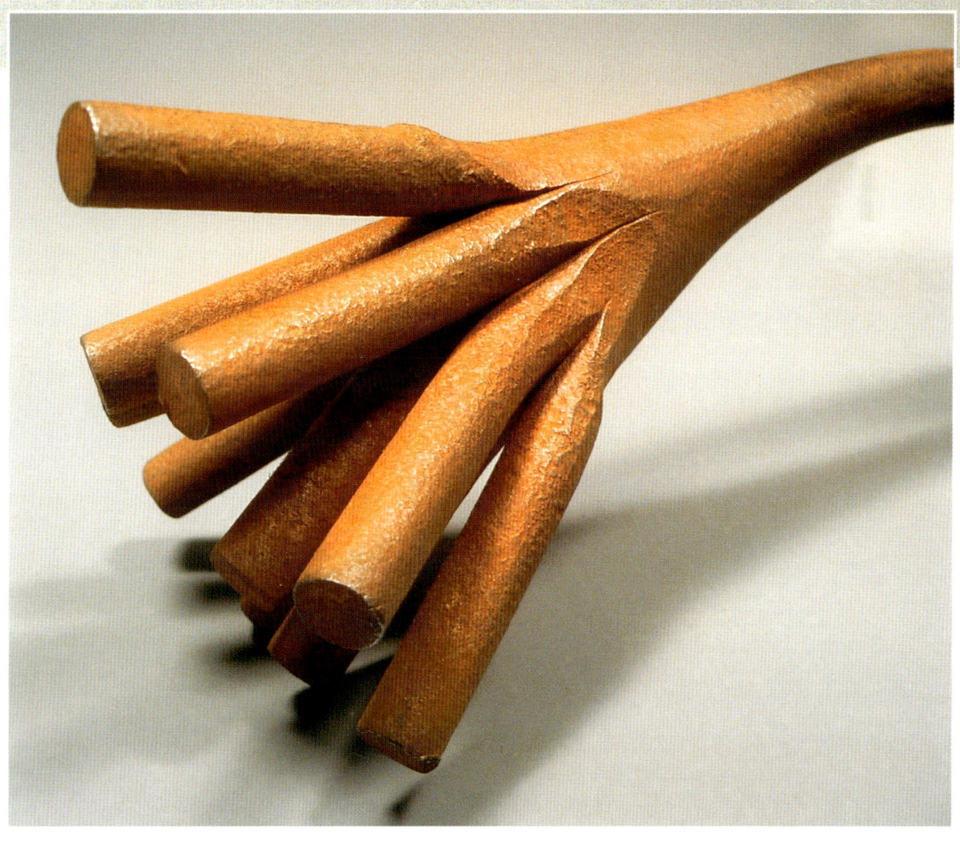

Mike Rossi. *Self Portrait,* 2006. Detail. *Photo, artist*

I am a first generation Italian-American. This did not really register until I spent some time in Italy in 2002. I was immersed in an incredibly different, but weirdly familiar, cultural structure. All the idiosyncrasies I had thought unique to my family suddenly became "social signifiers," our focus on food as a sensual experience, our obsession with physical contact, shouting while talking, etc.

When my Italian grandfather died, it made me question how people come to define themselves, especially in a country composed of separate culture, familial, and social elements. It is possible to isolate the pieces, but ultimately they are unified.

This piece was constructed through a process called forge welding. The individual pieces were heated to an exceptionally high temperature and struck with a hammer until they fuse on a molecular level. So, you can see the history of the piece on the ends, but it is absolutely cohesive. – Mike Rossi

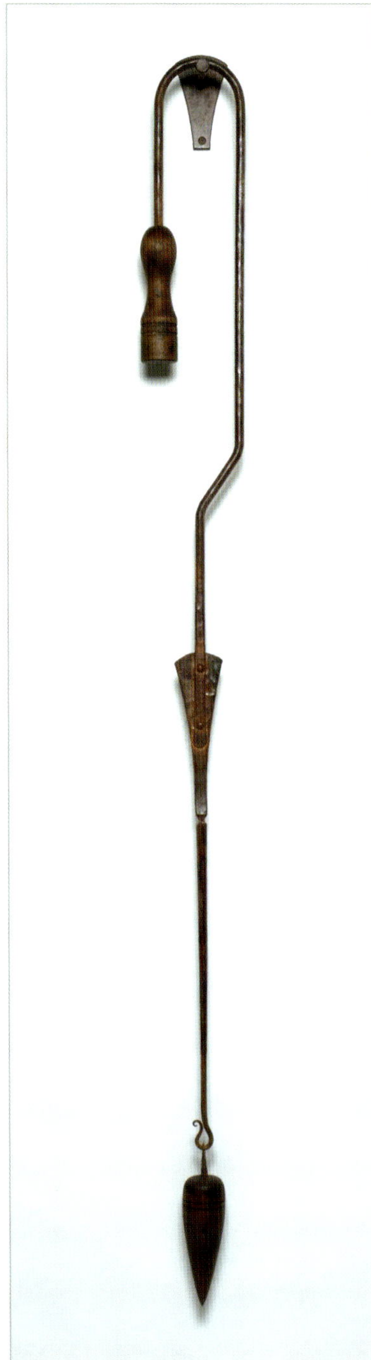

Tony Higdon. *Yizzer Y'aint*, 2007. Forged steel, turned wood. 5" x 60". *Private collection. Photo, artist*

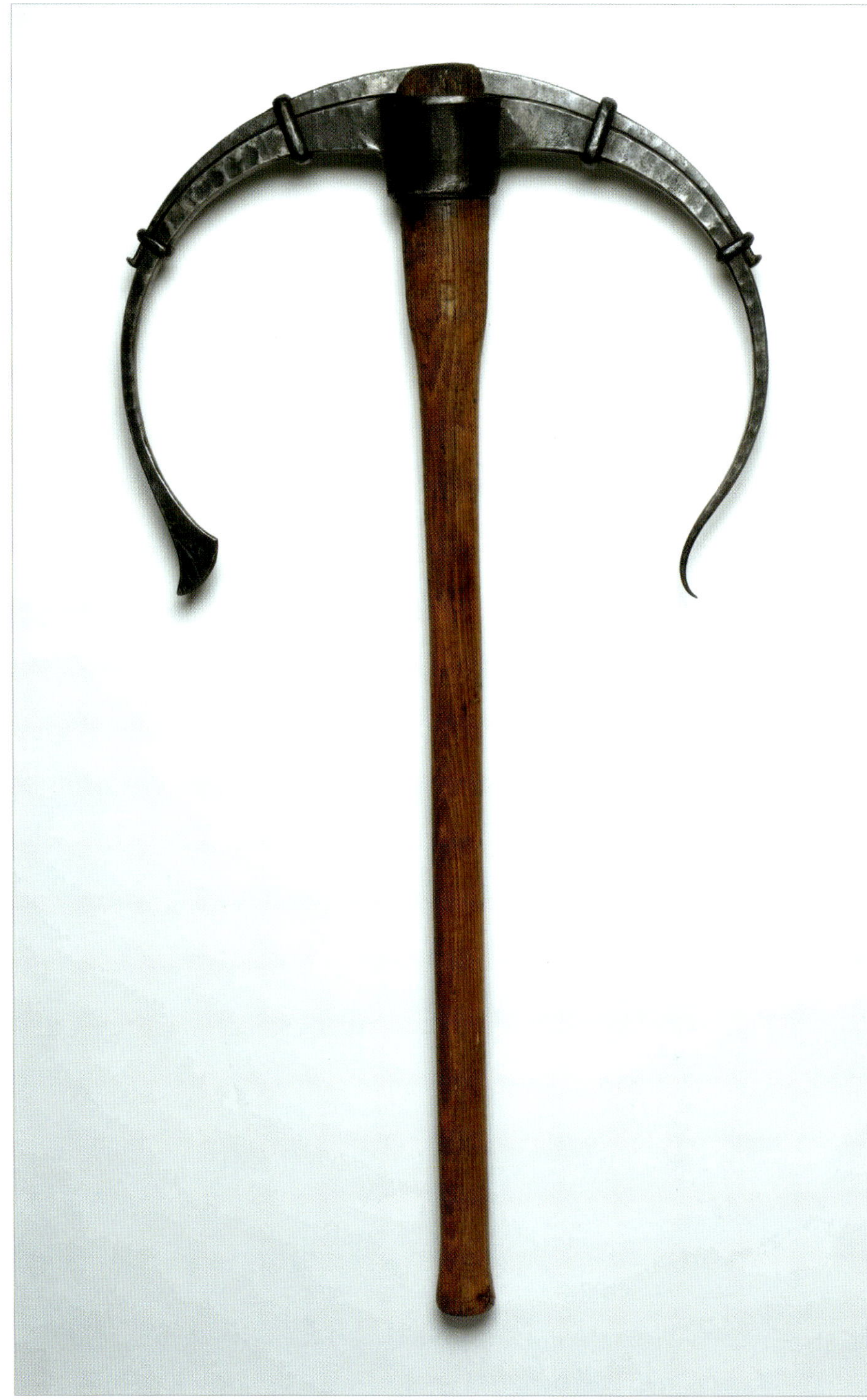

Tony Higdon. *Like a Beau Does*, 2006. Forged steel, wood. 24" x 42". *Private collection. Photo, Mary Resny*

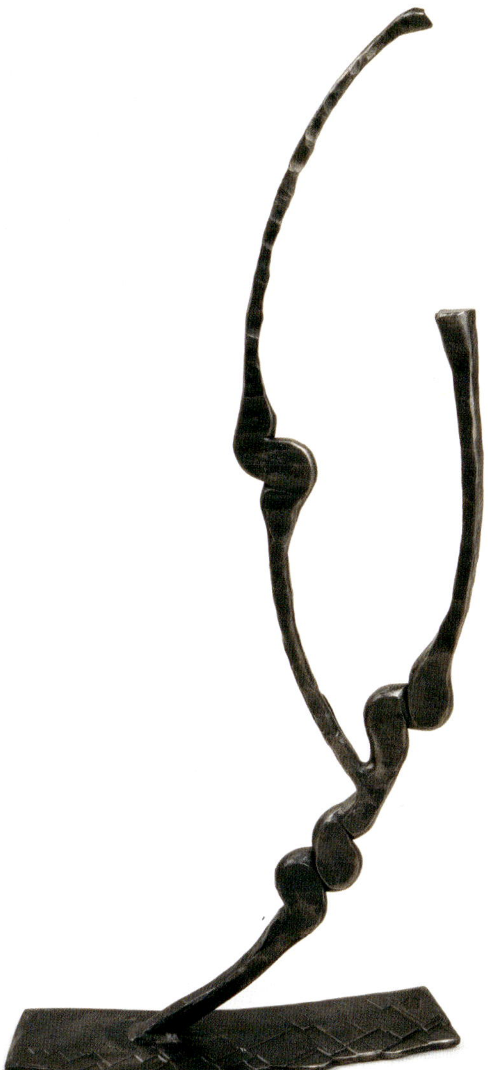

Jeff Fetty. *Samson and Delilah*. 23" h x 10" w x 4" d. Reflecting on the ultimate dominance of the feminine. *Photo, Gefeti*

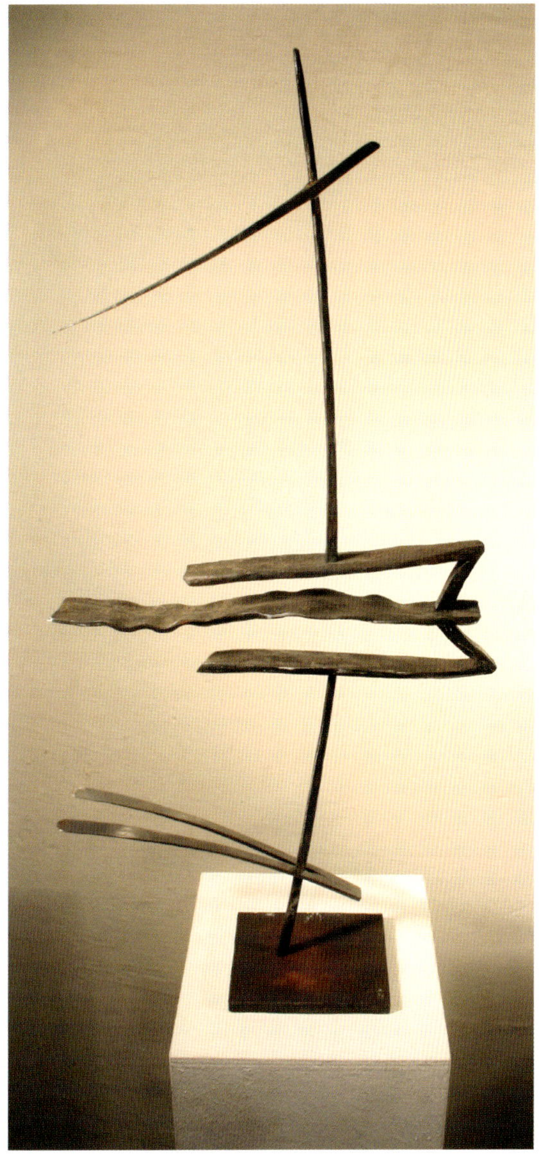

Achim Kühn. *Masts and Lines*. Forged steel, stainless steel wire. *Photo, artist*

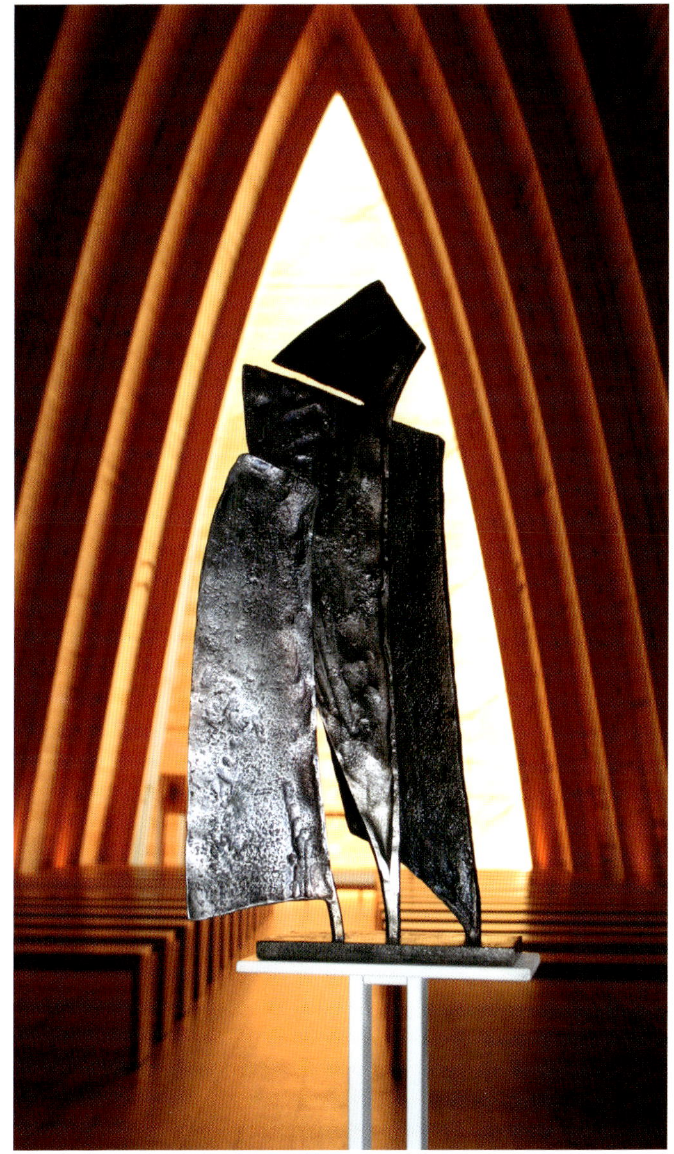

Achim Kühn. *Reflections*. Forged steel, 24" h. *Photo, artist*

James R. Johnson. *Meniscus*. 28" h x 18" w x 6" d. *Photo, Eye Photography*

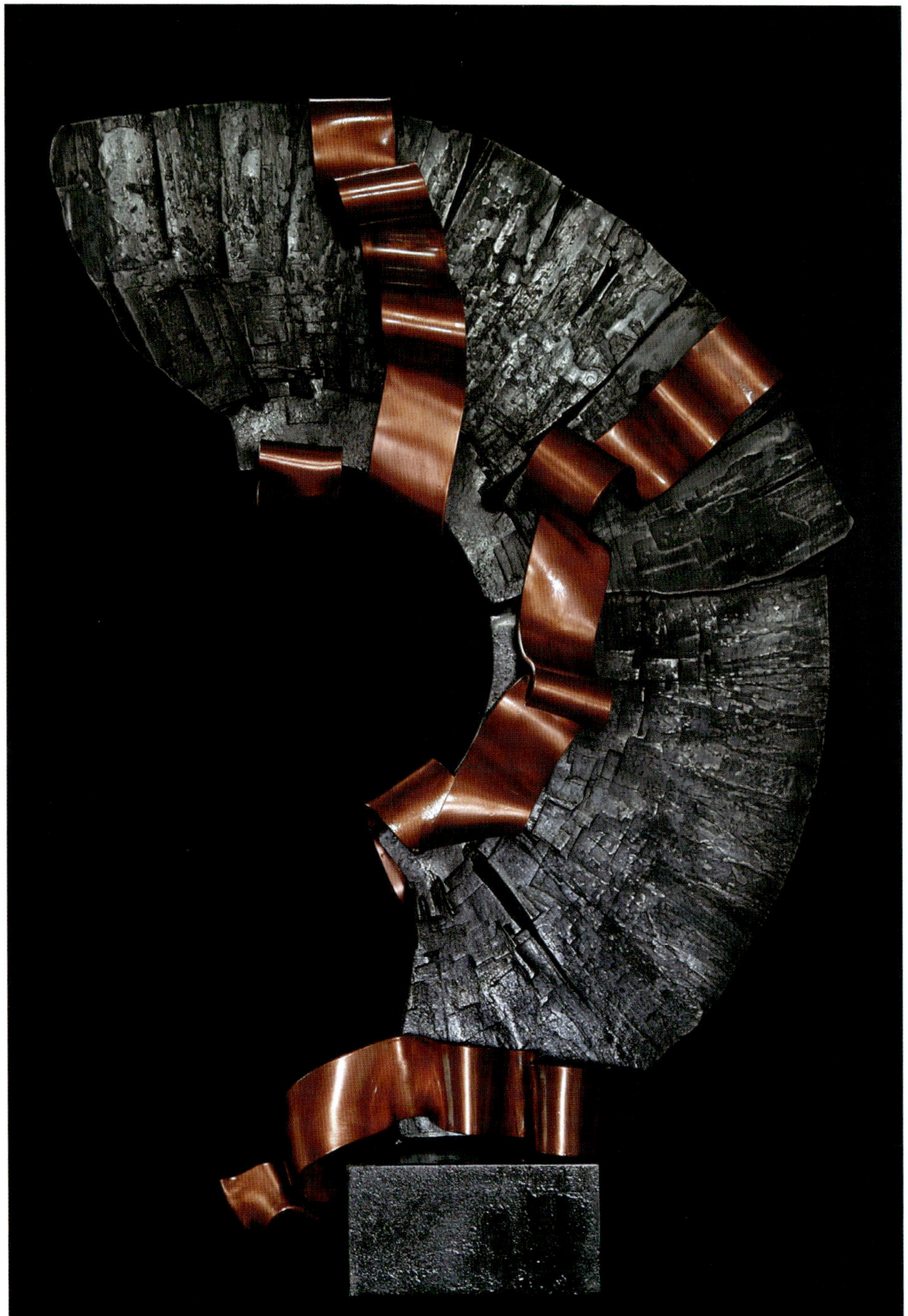

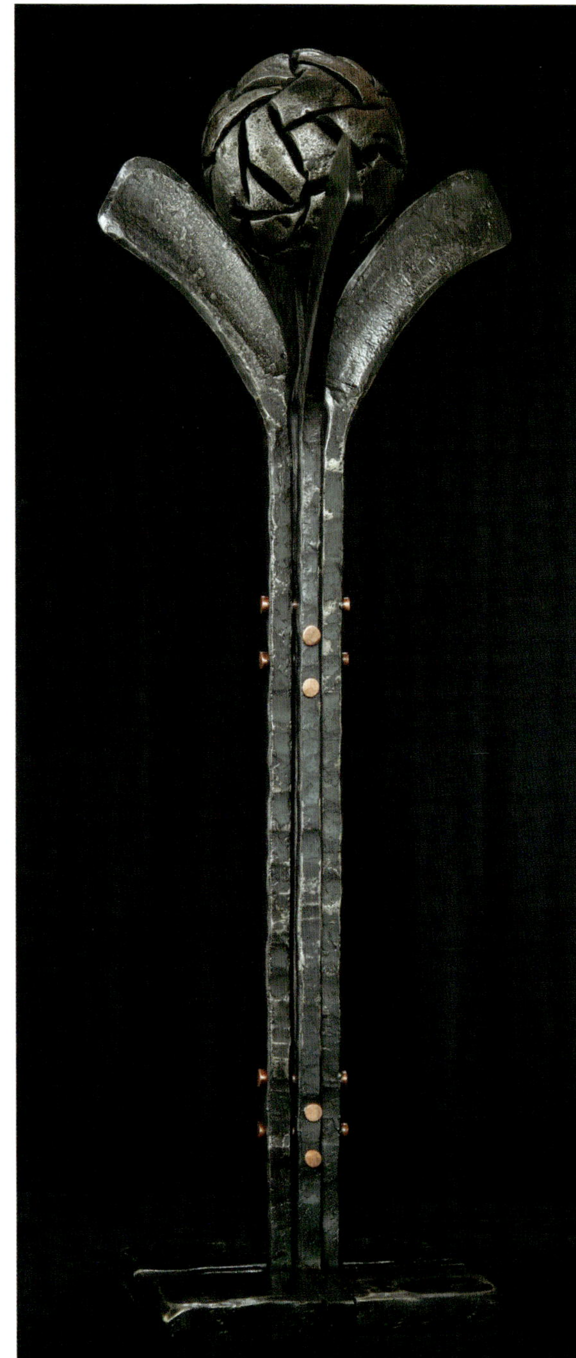

James R. Johnson. *Pursuing Balance*. 25" h x 9" w. *Photo, Eye Photography*

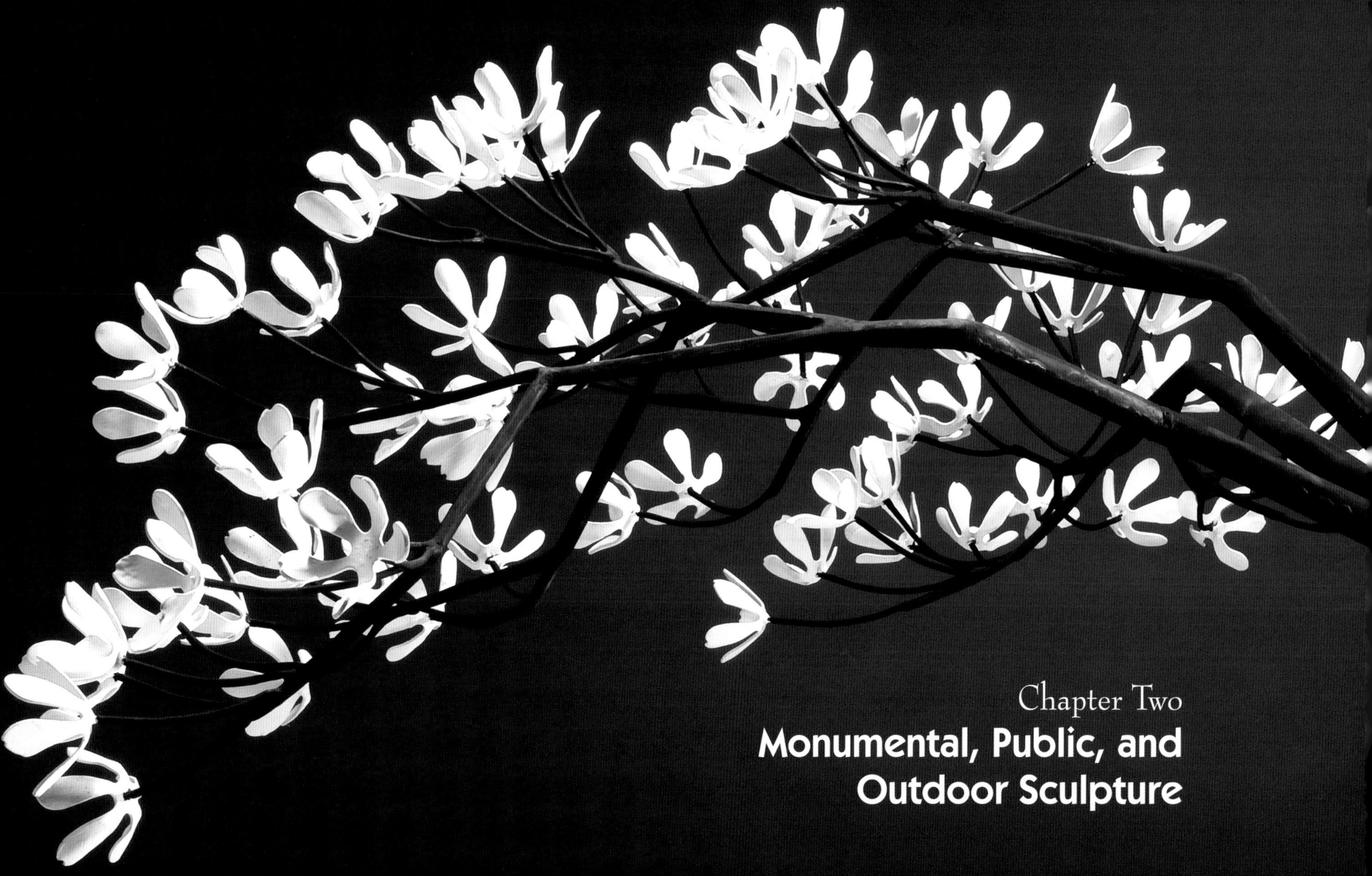

Chapter Two

Monumental, Public, and Outdoor Sculpture

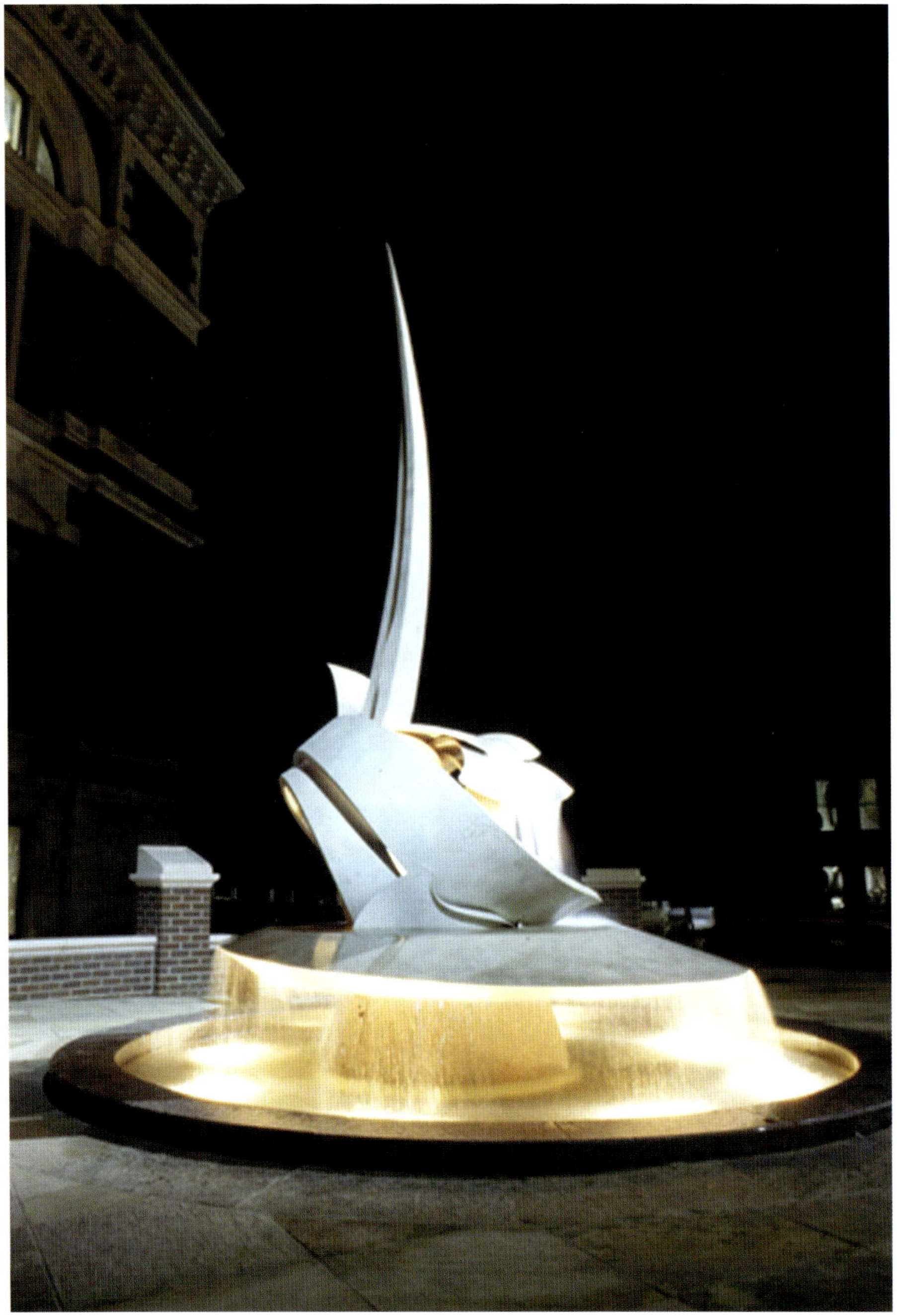

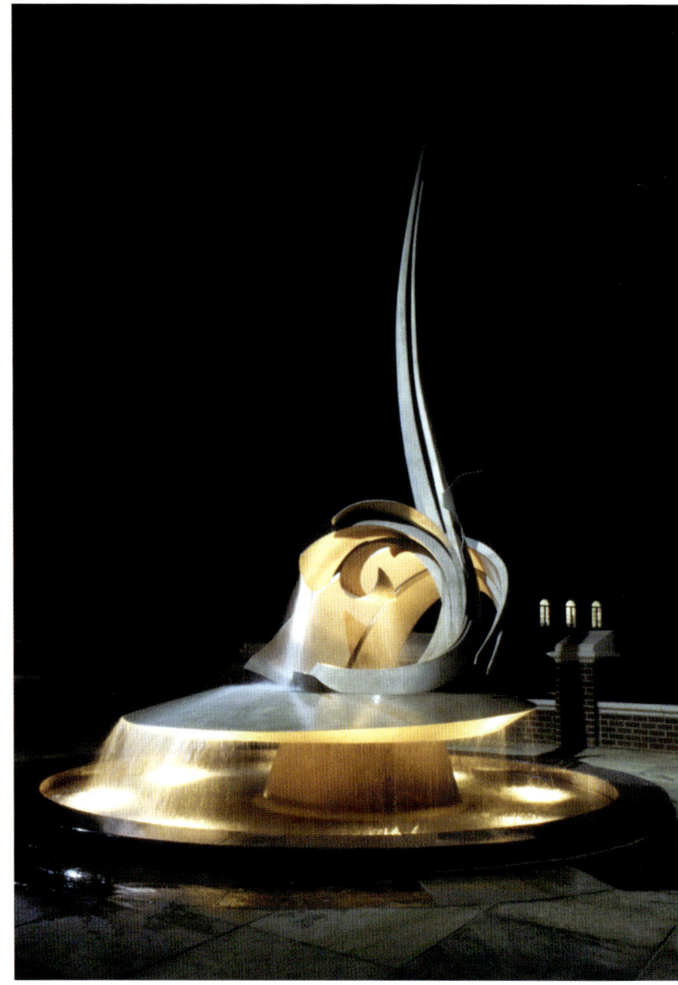

John Medwedeff. *Millennium Plaza Fountain*, 2002. East view. *Photo, Susan Bryant*

John Medwedeff. *Millennium Plaza Fountain*, 2002. Forged and fabricated bronze, 16' 2" x 8' 9" diameter. Commissioned by Montgomery County, Tennessee, for the Courthouse Square by national competition, Clarksville, Tennessee. *Photo, Susan Bryant*

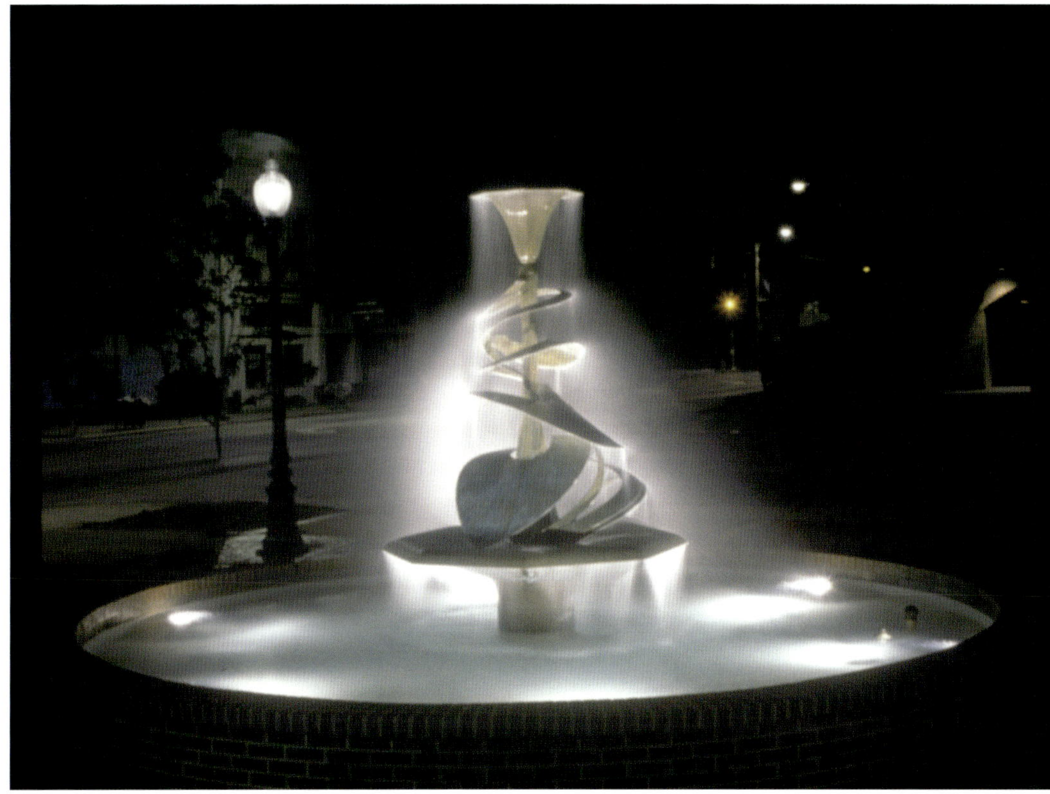

John Medwedeff. *Smysor Fountain*, 1999. Forged and fabricated bronze. 10' x 6' x 6'. *Commissioned by the Elizabeth A. Smysor Trust for the Smysor Plaza, Murphysboro, Illinois. Photo, Jeffrey M. Bruce*

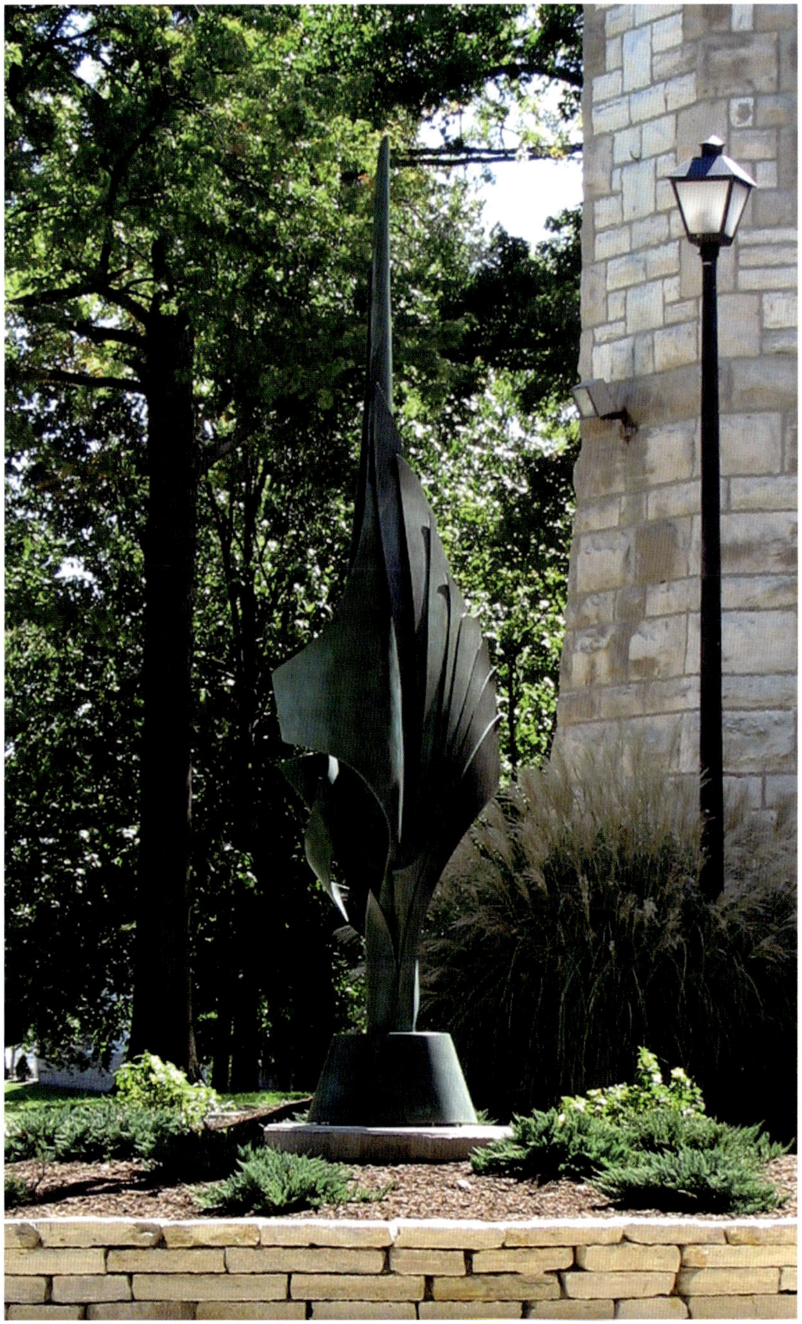

John Medwedeff. *Bloom*, 2006. Forged and fabricated bronze. 12' x 4' x 2.5'. *Commissioned by private donors for Lewis & Clark College, Godfrey, Illinois. Photo, artist*

John Medwedeff. *Ava*, 1999.
Forged bronze. 8' 8" x 34" x 27".
Private collection. Photo, artist

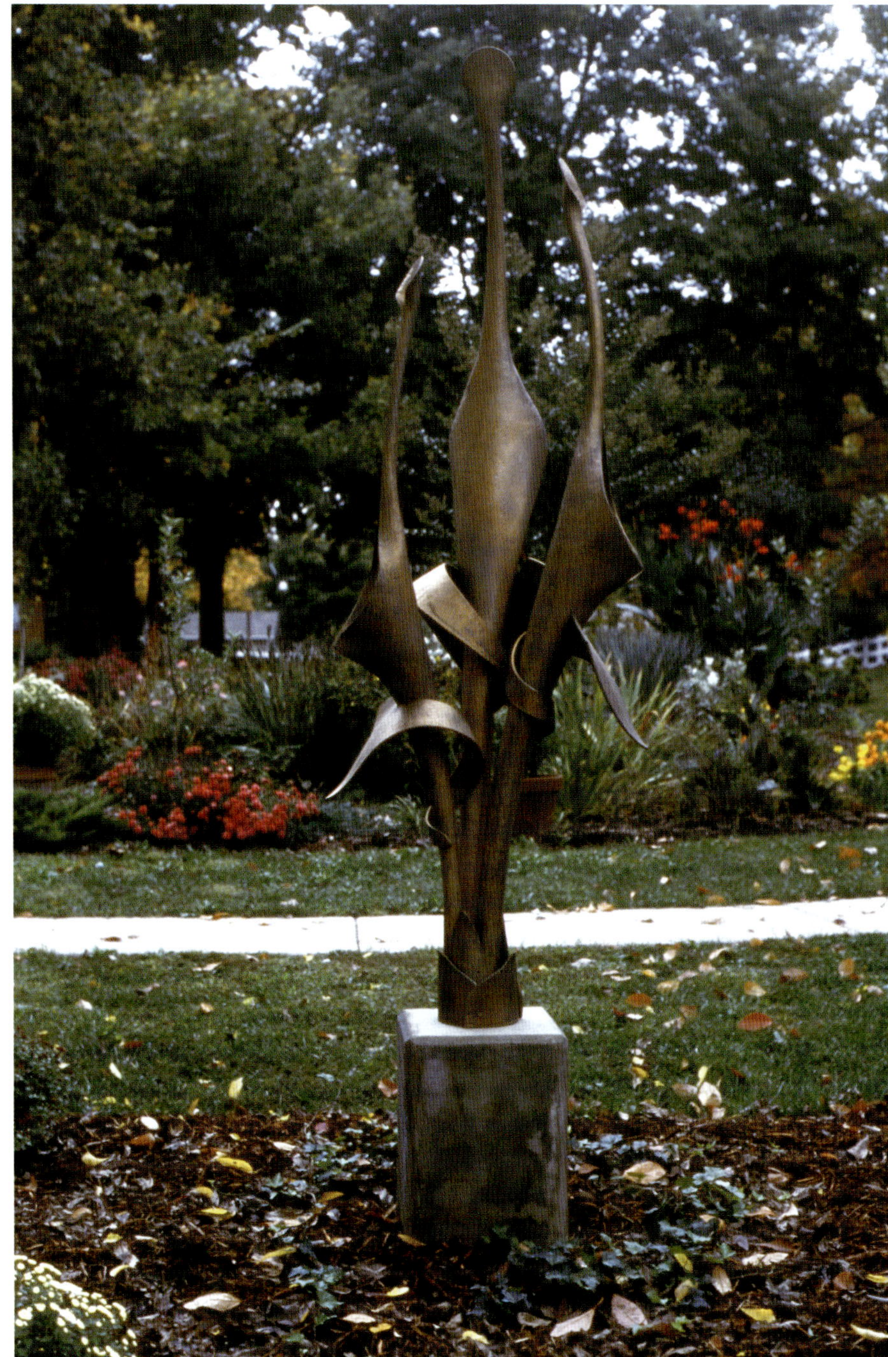

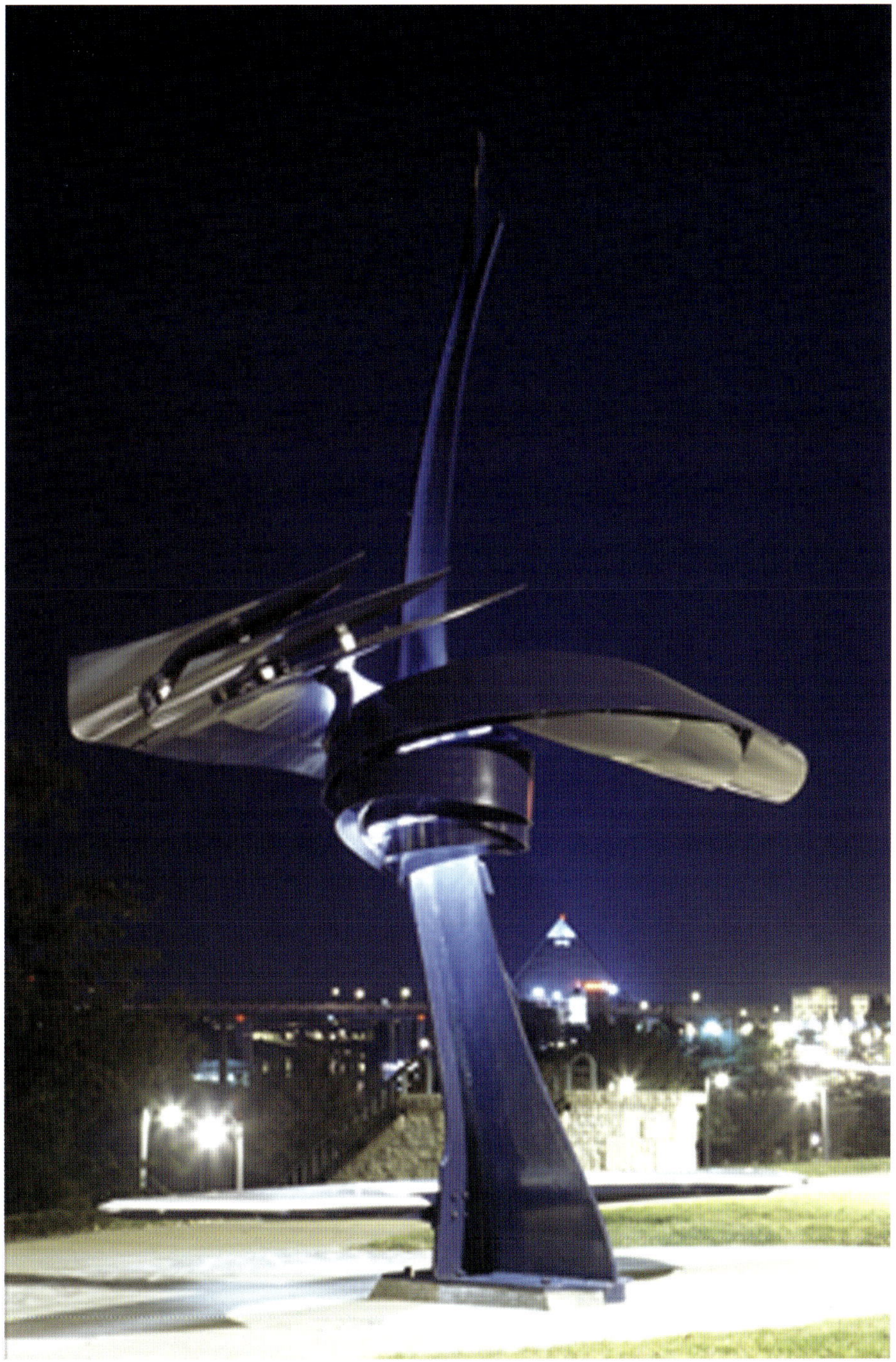

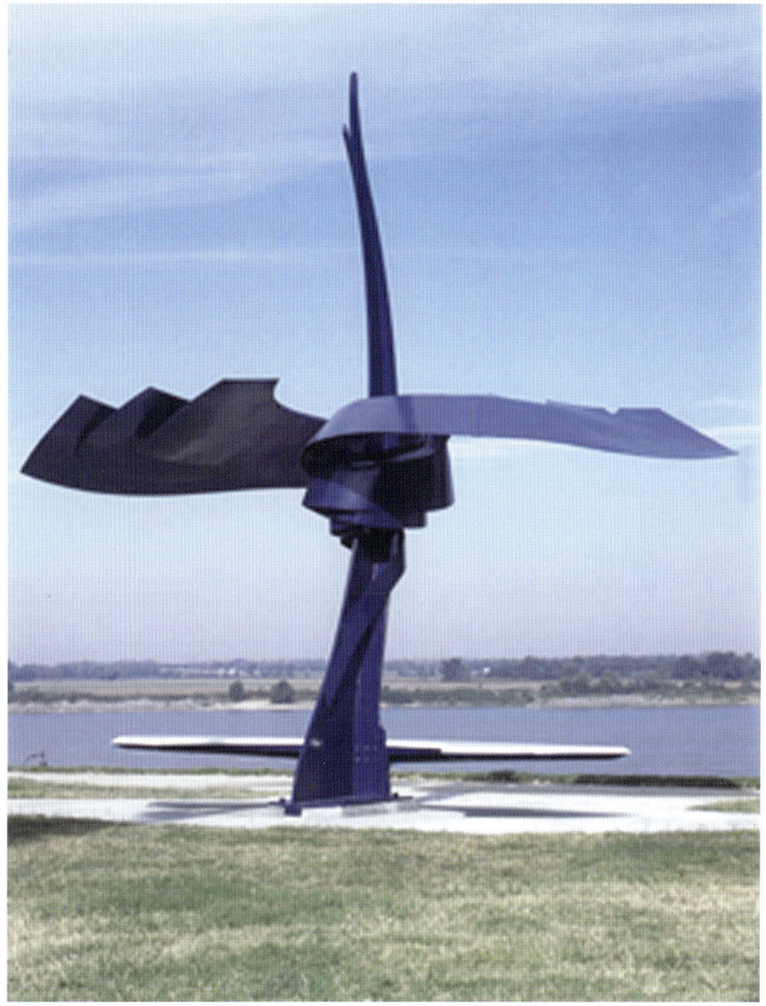

John Medwedeff. *Whirl*, 2001. Second view. *Photo, Jeffrey M. Bruce*

John Medwedeff. *Whirl*, 2001. Forged and fabricated steel and aluminum sculptural shade shelter. 18' x 21' x 8'. *Commissioned by Urban Art (a division of the Greater Memphis Arts Council) by national competition. Photo, Jeffrey M. Bruce*

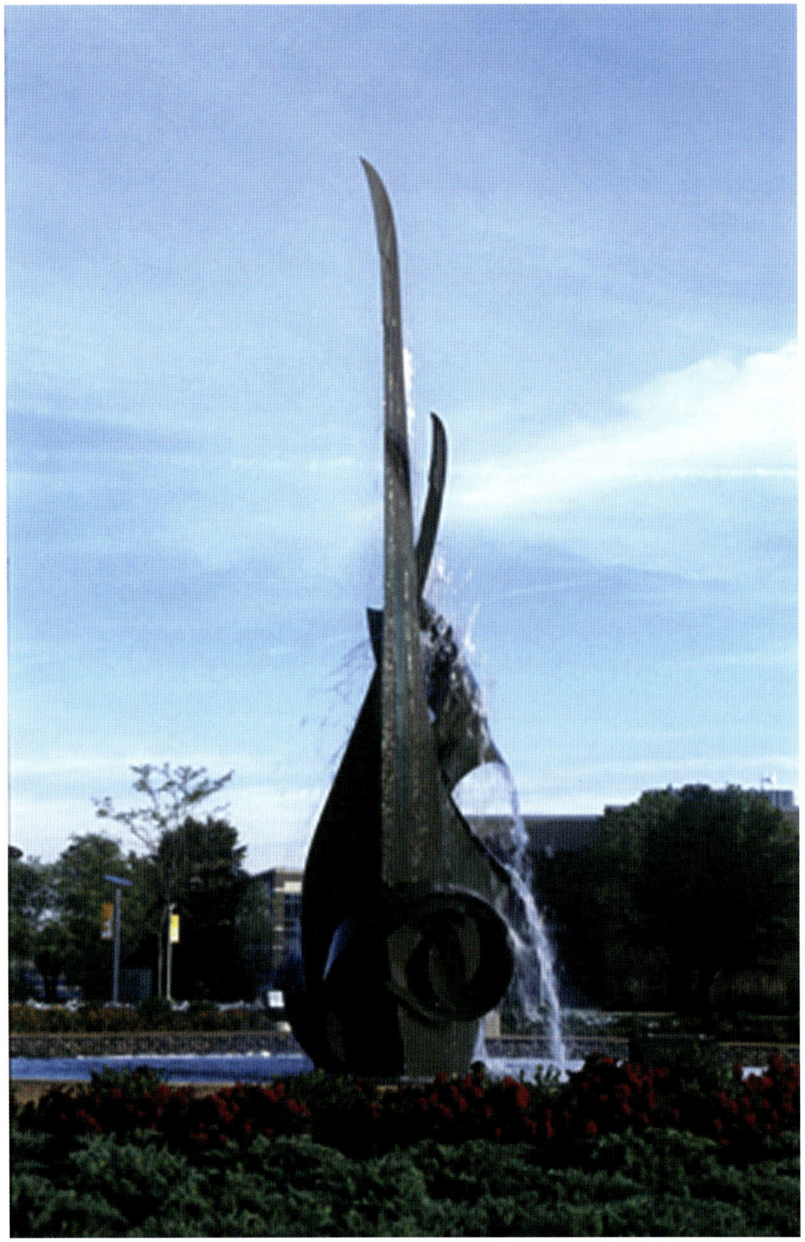

John Medwedeff. *Oasis*, 2002. Forged and fabricated bronze. 27' x 7' x 9'. *Commissioned by the State of Illinois for William Rainey Harper College, Palatine, Illinois. Photo, Jeffrey M. Bruce*

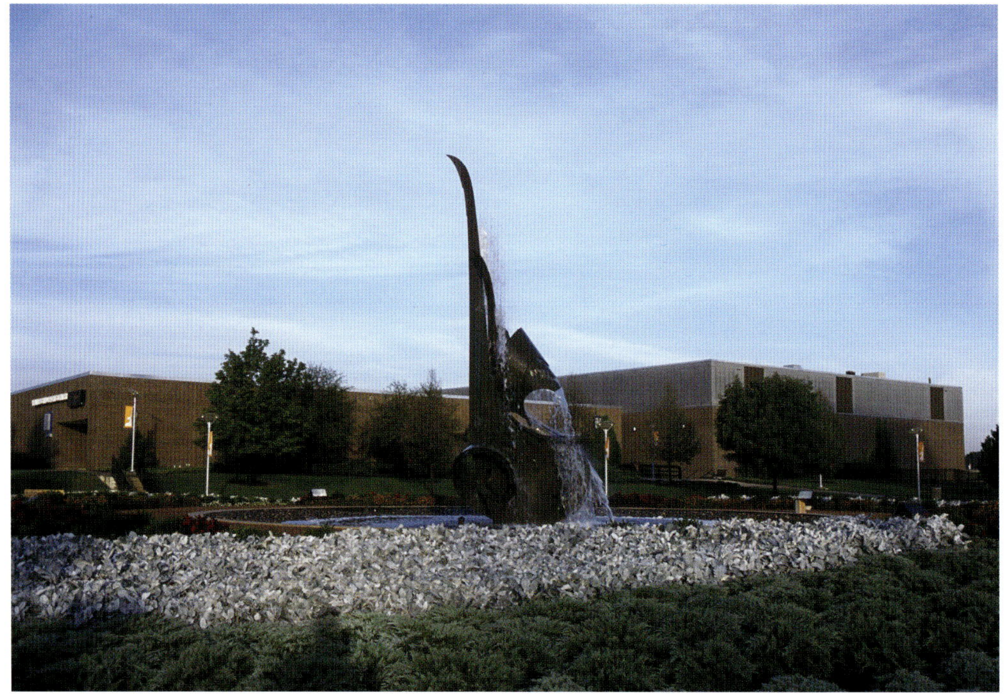

John Medwedeff. *Oasis*, 2002. Second view. *Photo, Jeffrey M. Bruce*

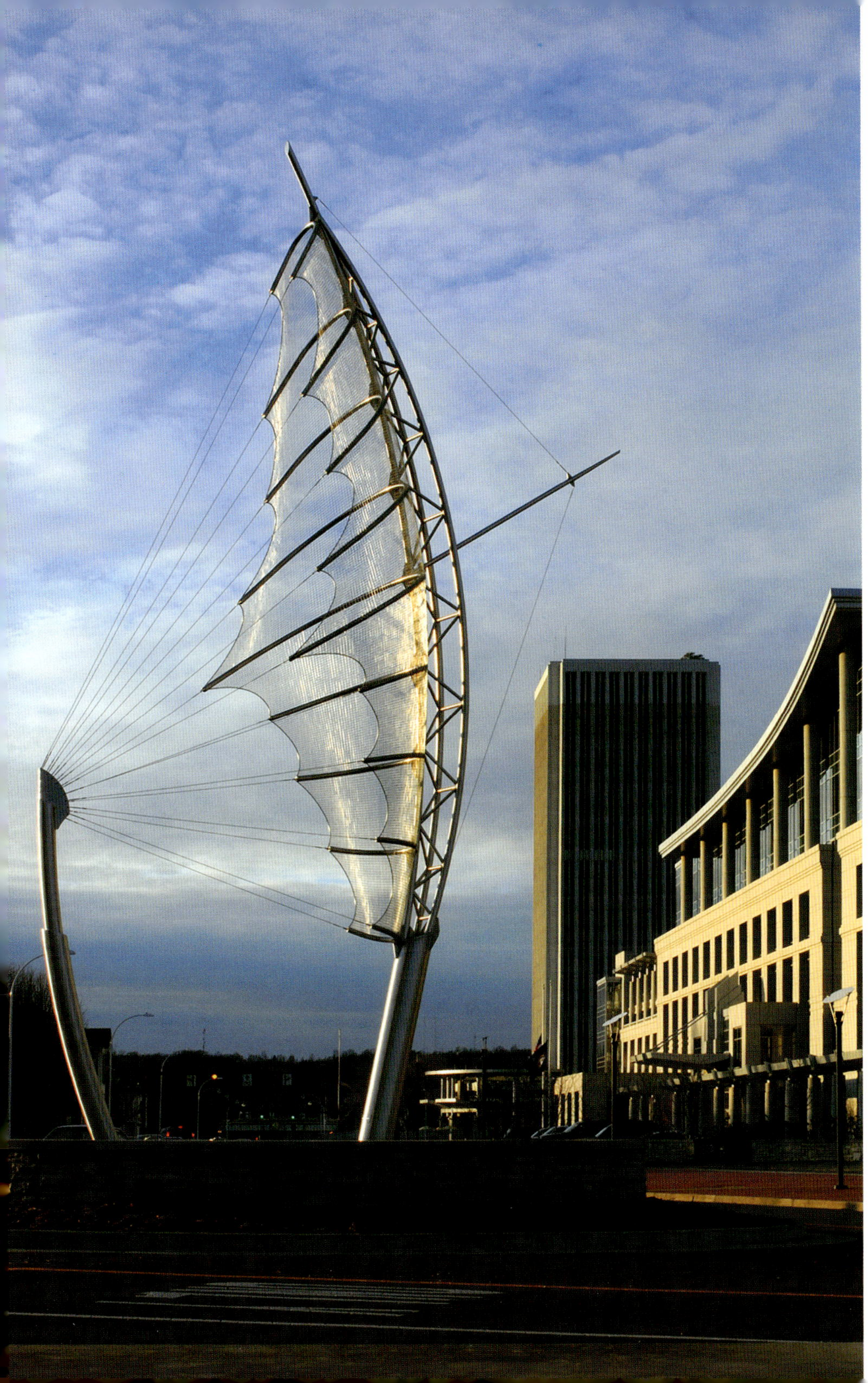

Tony Higdon and Erika Strecker, (Higdon-Strecker Studio, Inc.) *Nexus*, 2006. Stainless steel, stainless cable and turnbuckles. 600" h x 144" w x 324" d. Commissioned by the State of Kentucky for placement in front of the Transportation Cabinet Building, Frankfort, Kentucky. Photo, Lee Thomas Photography.

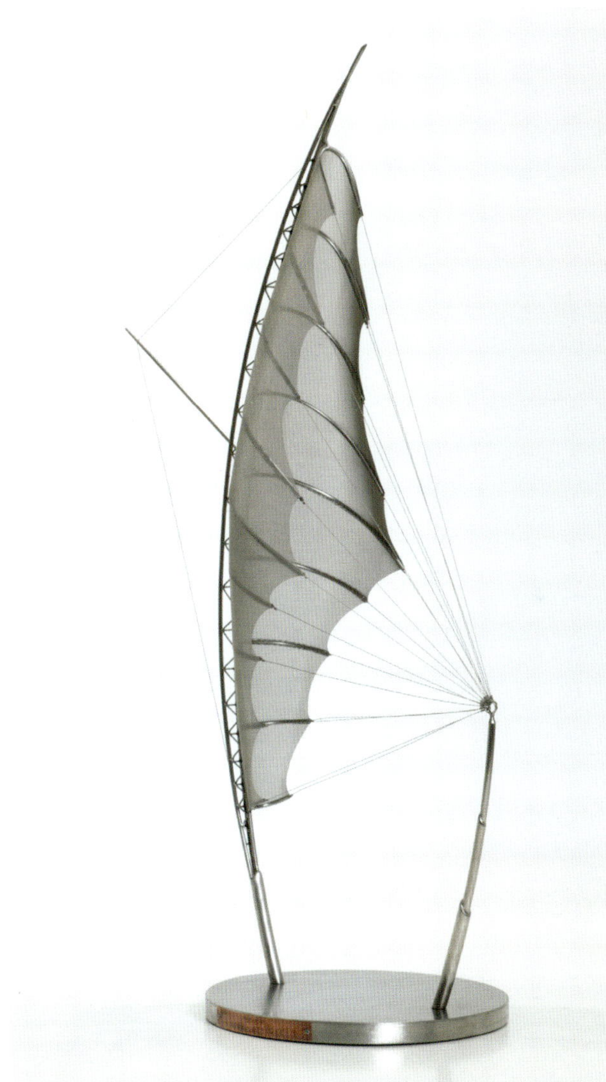

Tony Higdon and Erika Strecker, (Higdon-Strecker Studio, Inc.) *Nexus*. Scale model 18" diameter x 48"h. Photo by LeeAnn Greer.

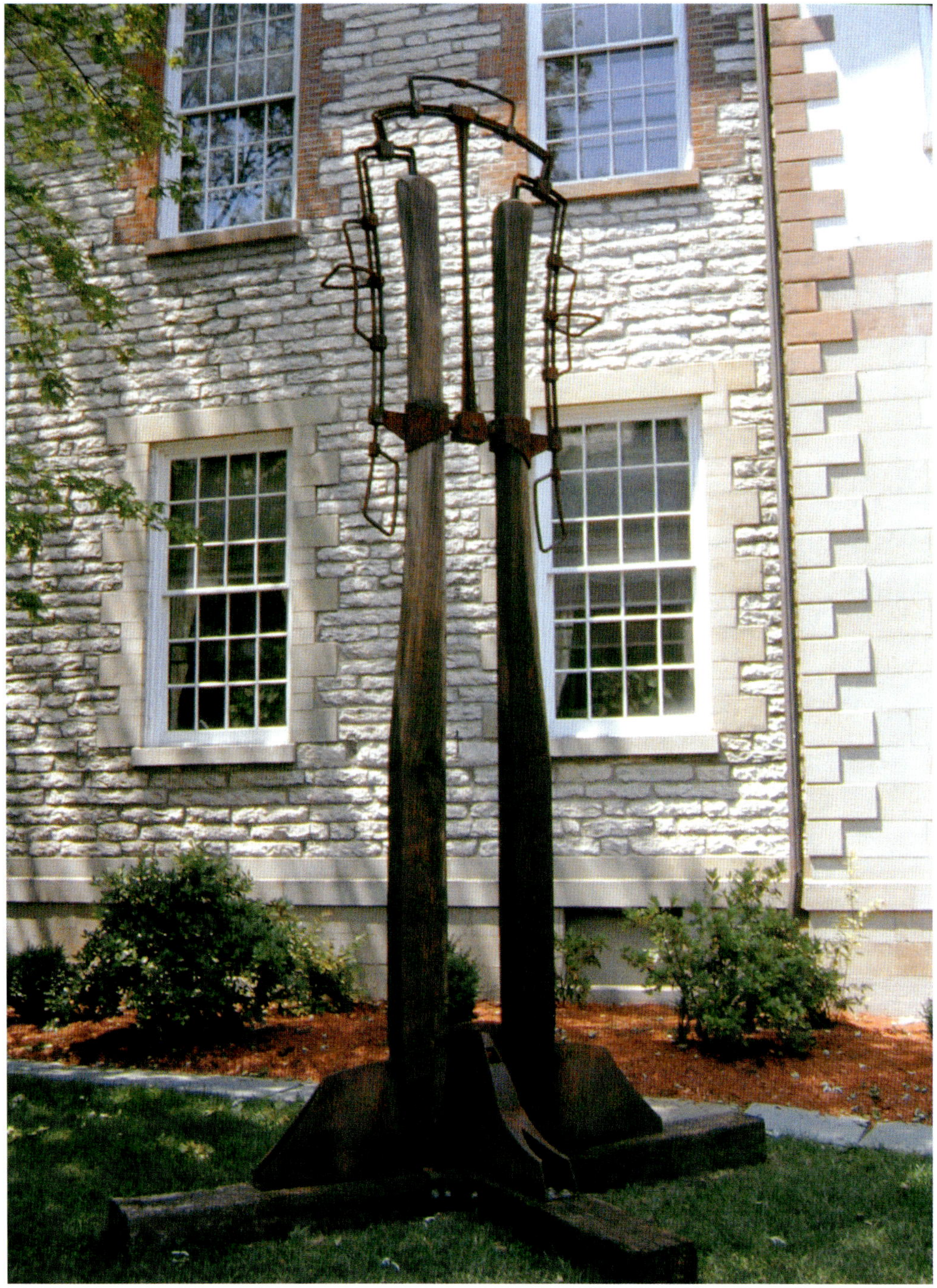

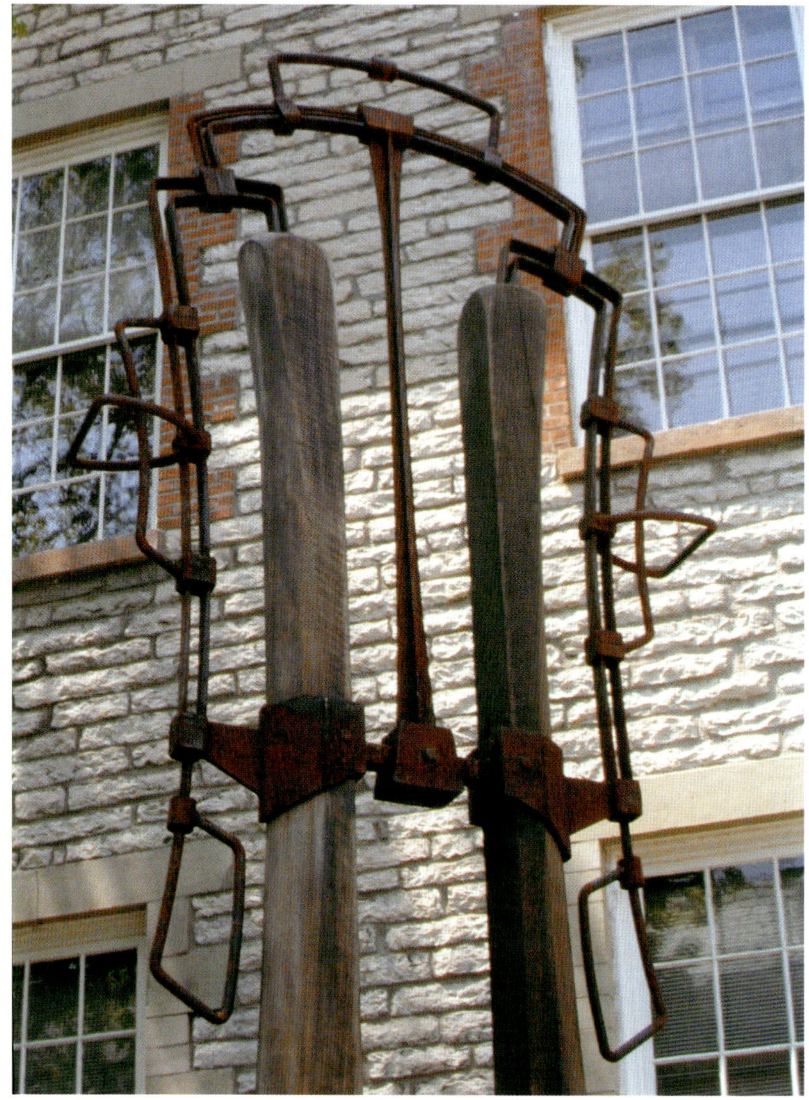

Greg Gehner. *Primary Standard* (OX24-7), 2006. Detail. 175" x 72" x 48". *Photo, artist*

Greg Gehner. *Primary Standard* (OX24-7), 2006. Steel and tulipwood. 175" x 72" x 48". *Photo, artist*

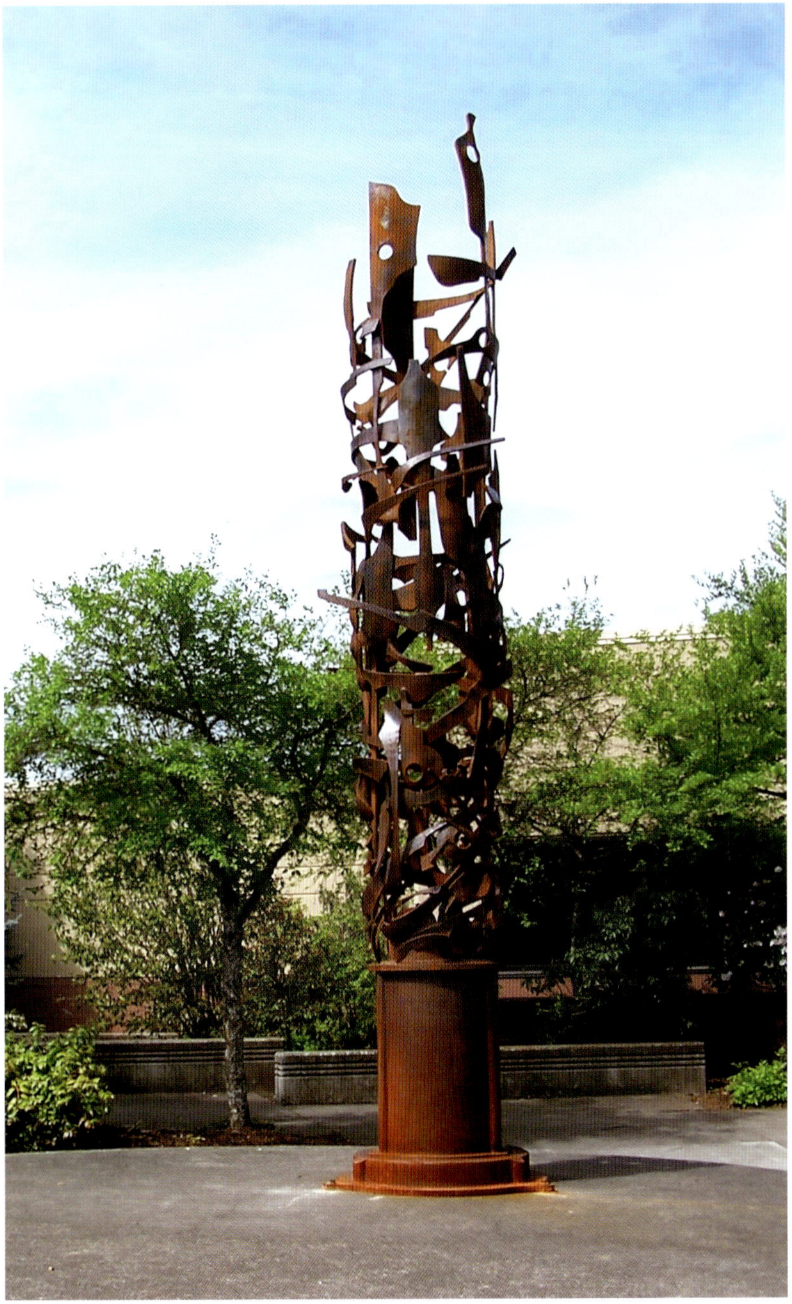

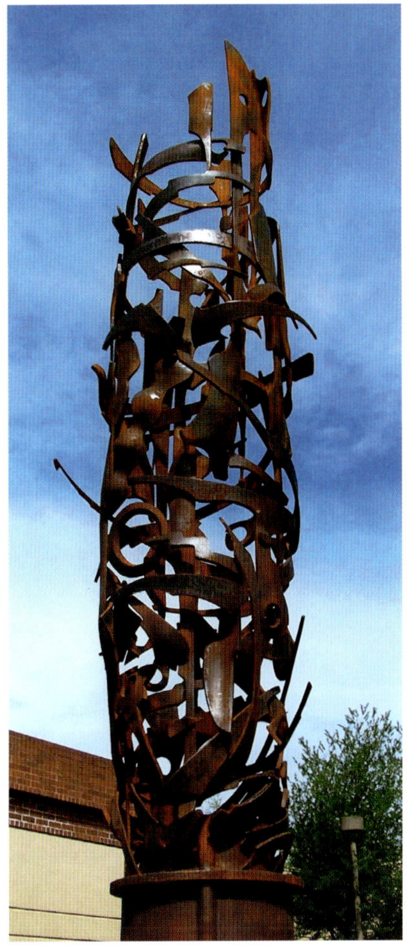

Mike Suri. *Gather.* Detail 1. *Photo, artist*

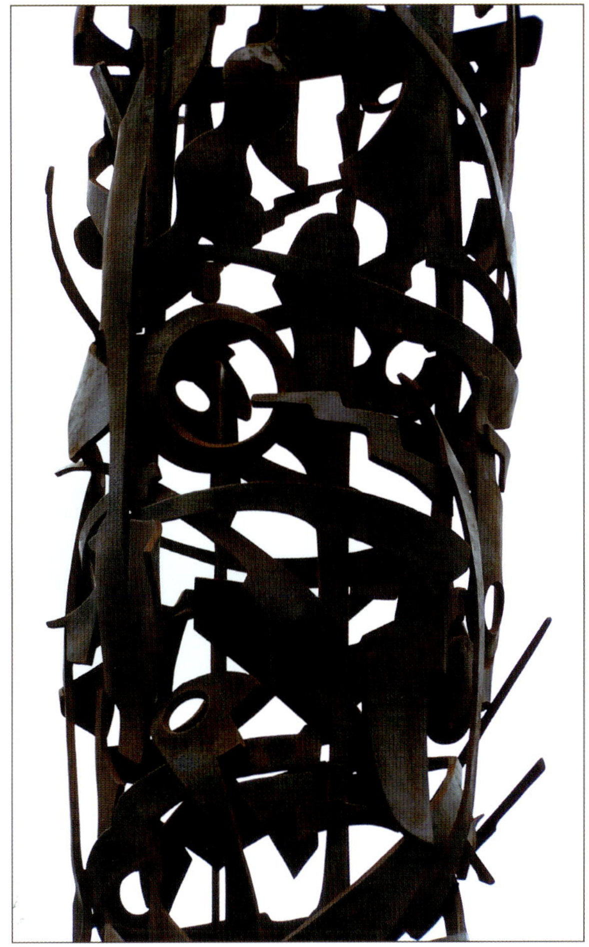

Mike Suri. *Gather.* Detail 2. *Photo, artist*

Mike Suri. *Gather.* Forged and formed steel. 38" x 38" x 192". *Photo, artist*

Roberto Giordani. *Spine,* Forged steel, 216" high without base, 106" w x 51" d. The sculpture was commissioned by the CNA Market Saraceno to be placed in a roundabout in an urban center. It depicts a stylized spine, formed by five rings of different material, the foundation stone then wood, terra cotta, steel, plastic, and iron structure, all to represent the raw materials of local handicrafts. *Photo, artist*

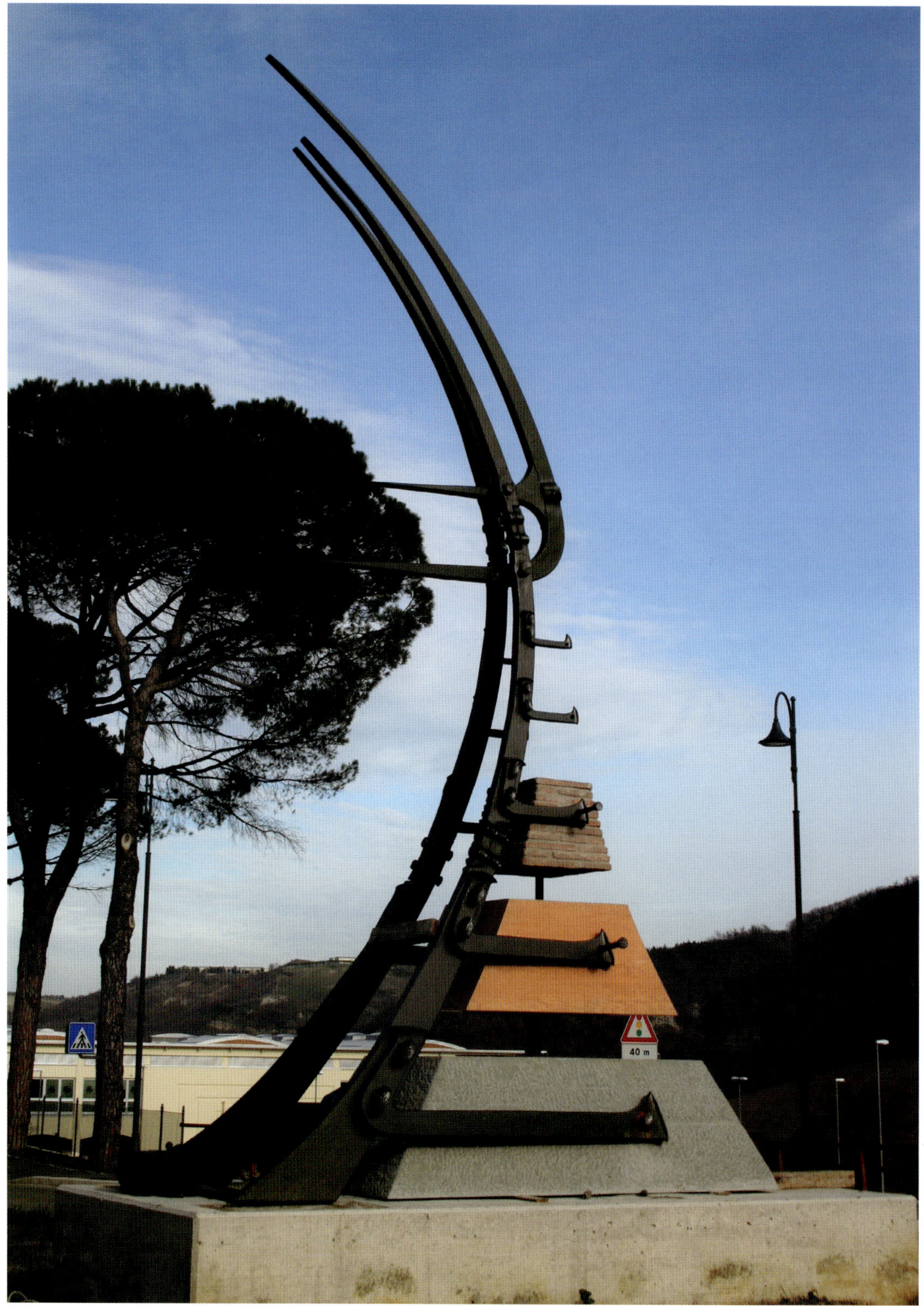

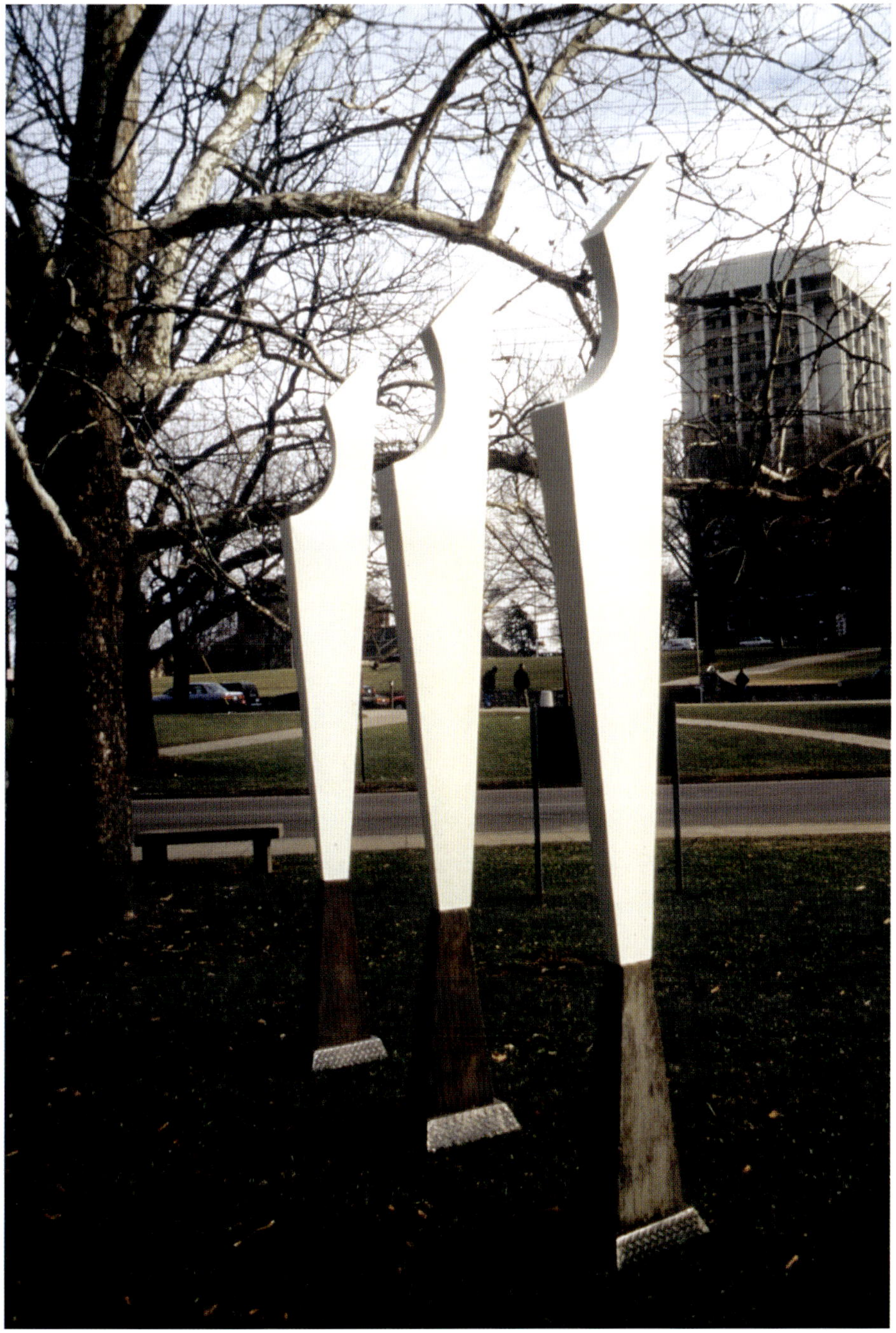

Tony Higdon. *Architectural Remnant*, 1999. Fabricated steel and concrete, Three pieces, 180" x 24" x 12" each. *Private Outdoor Collection, Gray Construction Company, Lexington, Kentucky. Photo, artist*

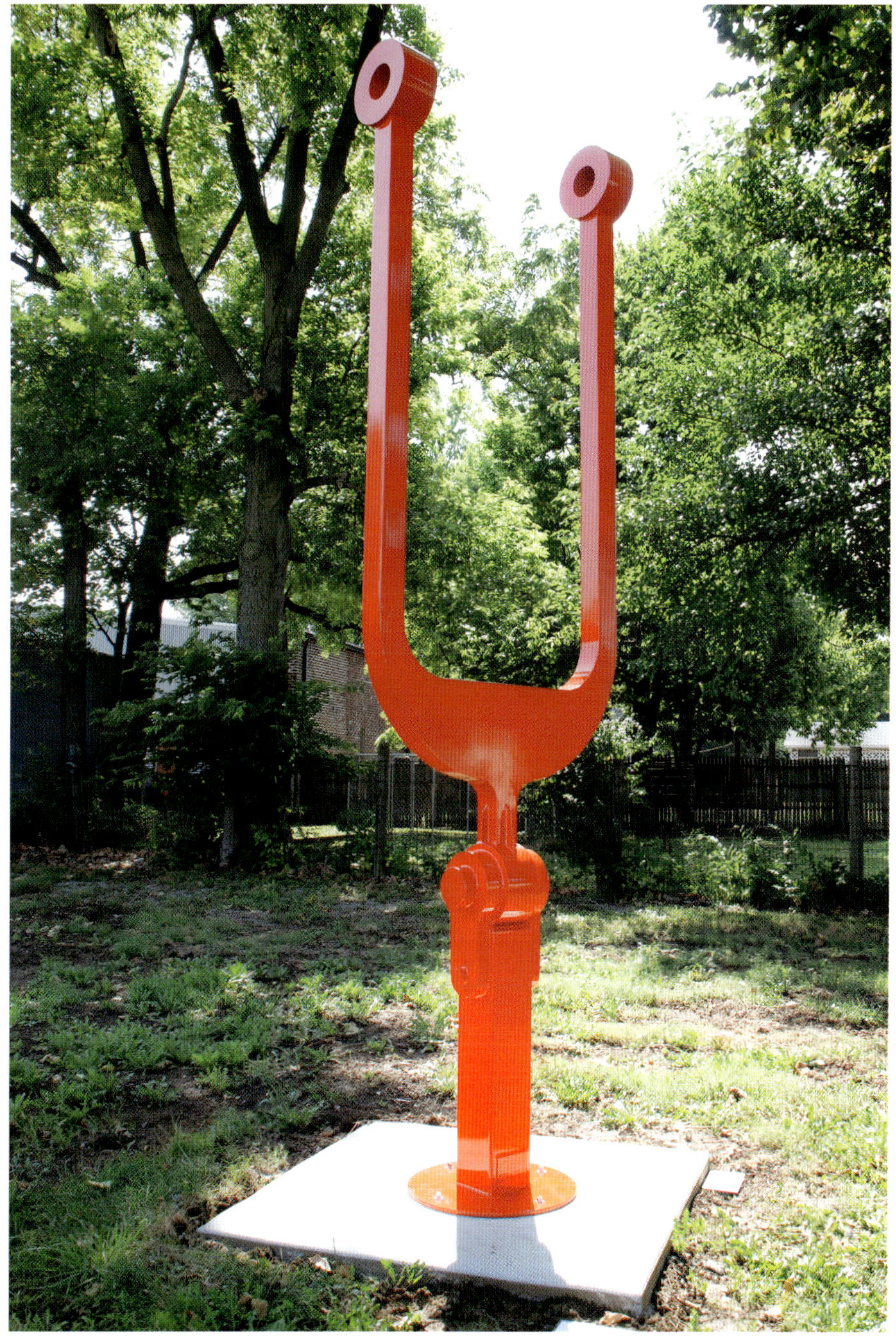

Erika Strecker. *Connect,* 2007. Fabricated steel, painted. 28" x 10" x 180". *Photo, artist*

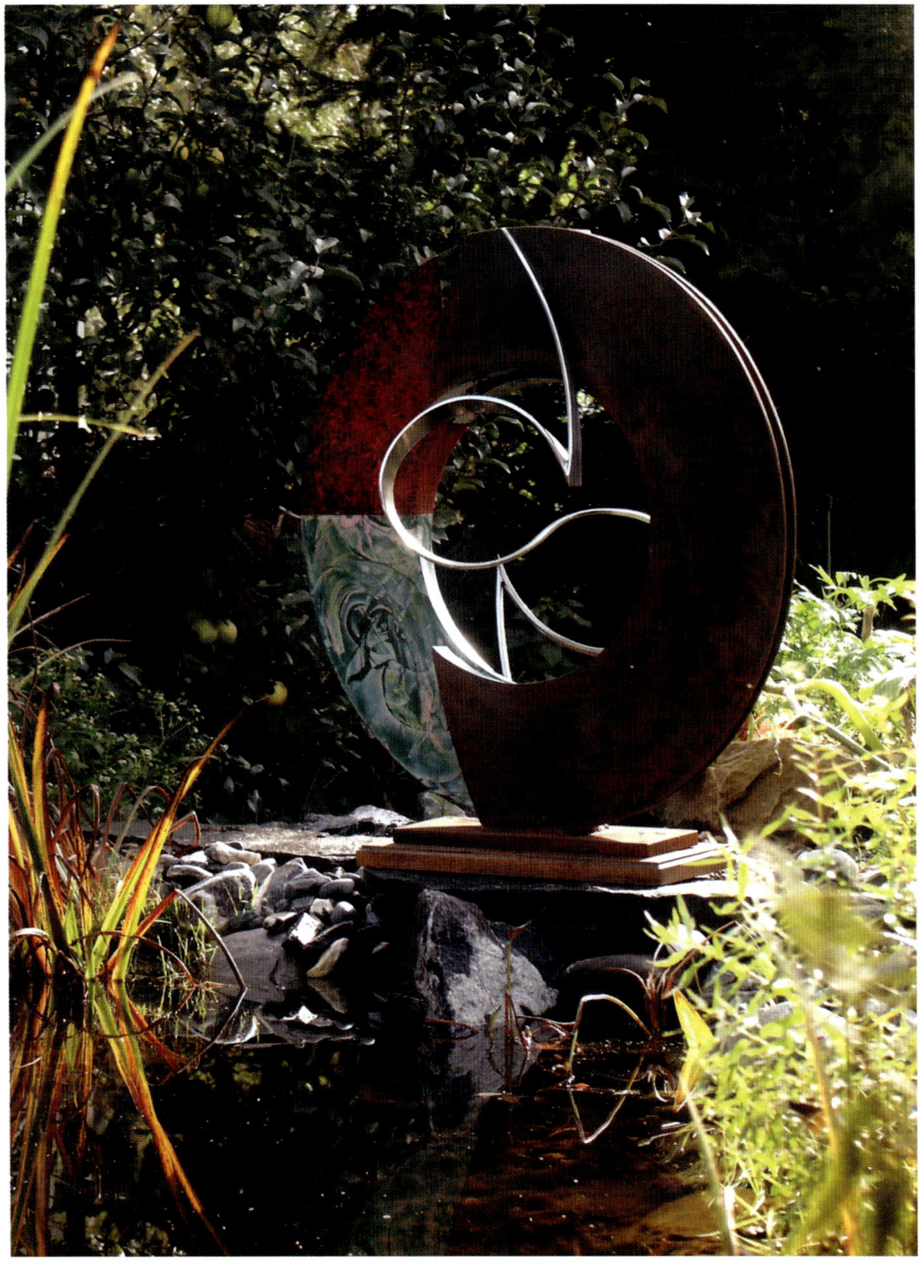

Beat Kriemler. *Tunnel Through the Mind Sphere*, 2003. Forged and polished stainless steel. Rolled, fabricated, rusted, and painted steel plate. 33" x 33" x 16.5". *Photo, artist*

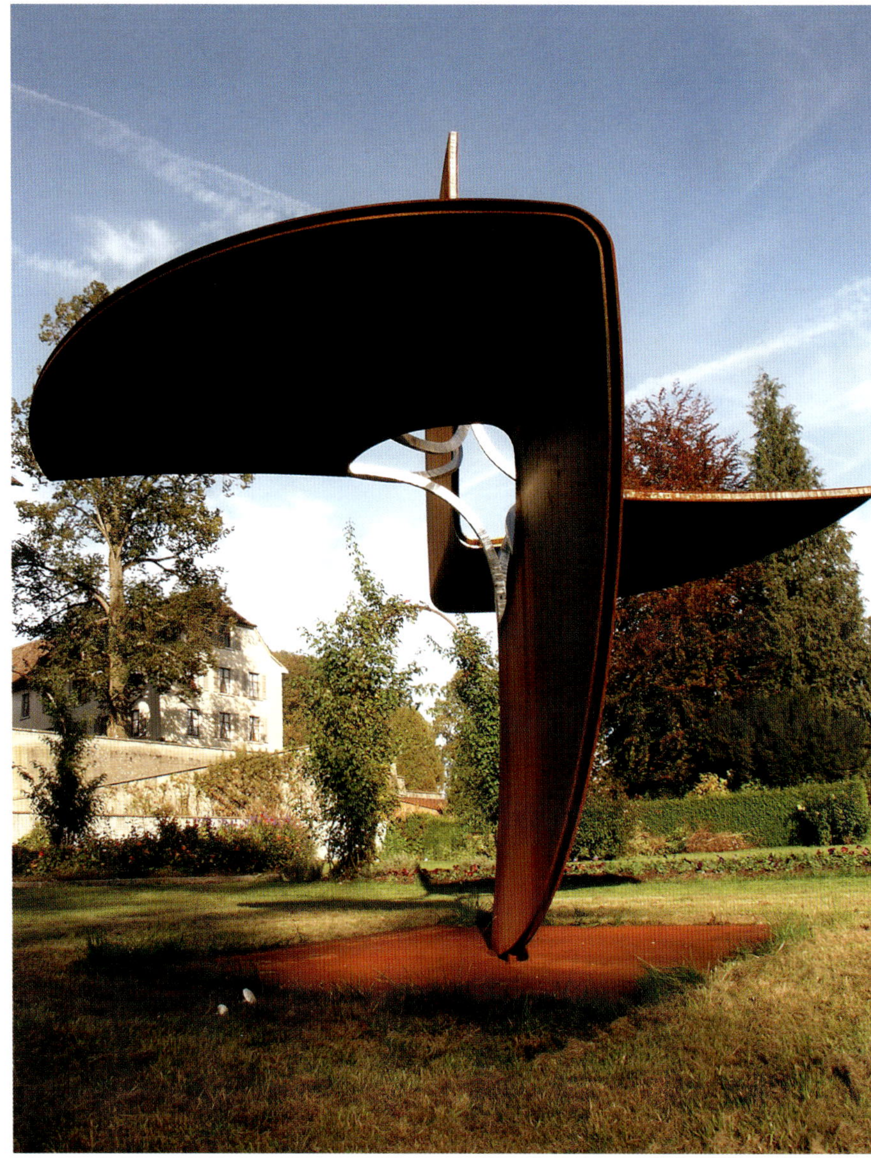

Beat Kriemler. *The Very Essence of Love Bridges the Deepest Gaps of our Separation*, 2003. Forged and polished stainless steel bar. Rolled and bent steel plate, 142" x 142" x 142". *Photo, artist*

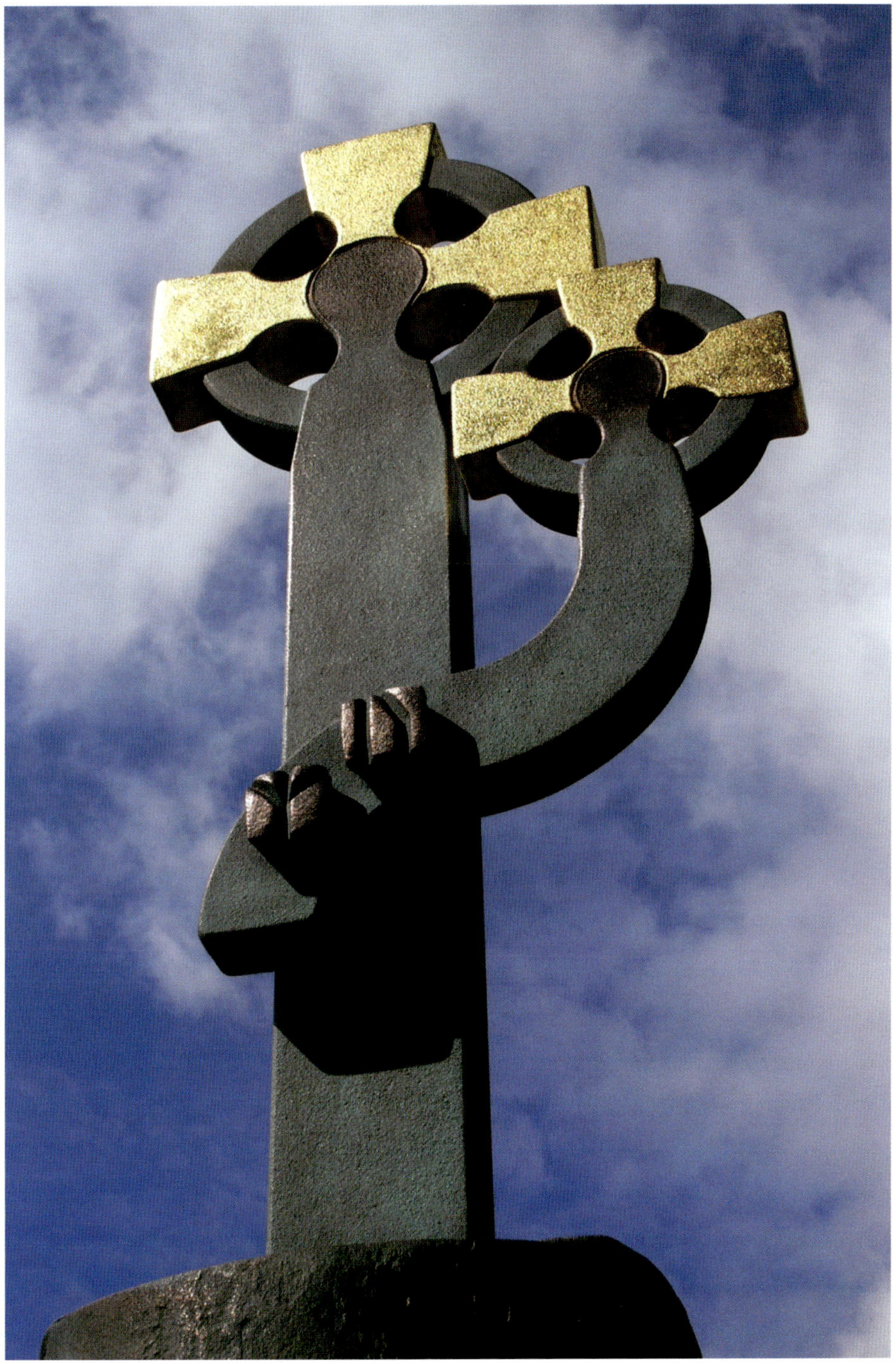

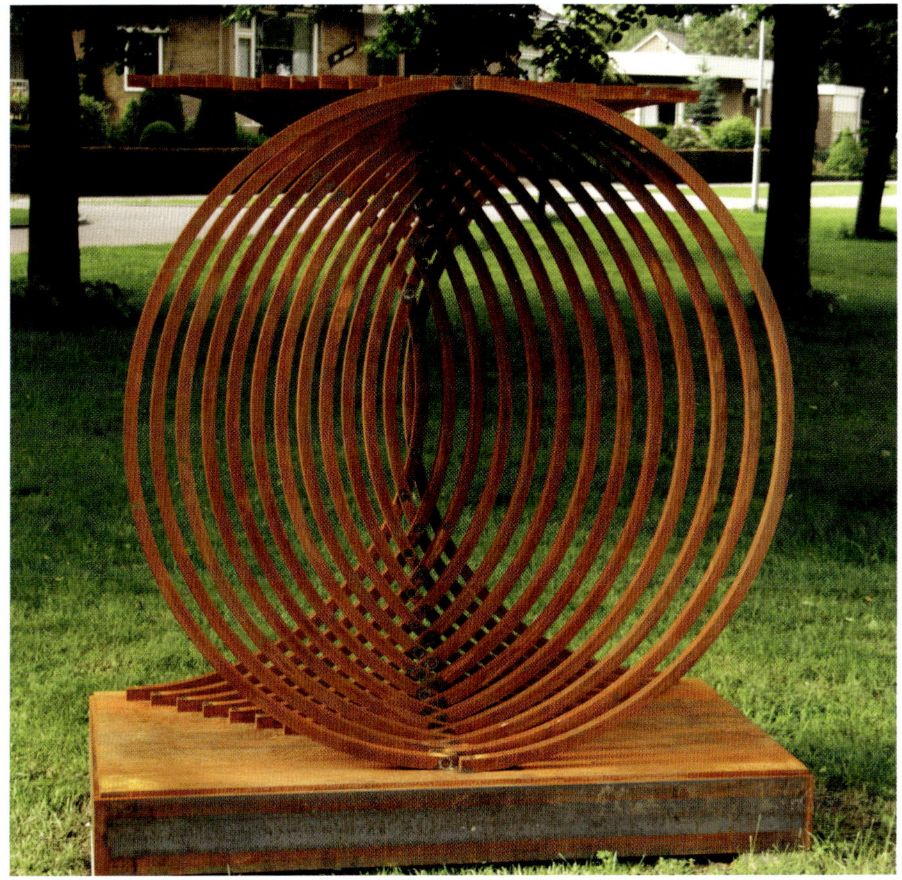

Michael Kaczmar. *Moon*, 2007. 1" x 1" square steel bar. 79" x 79" x 39". *Photo, artist*

Karel Meloun. *St. Patrick's Madonna*, 2007.
Forged steel, cast iron, gold, chemical patina.
16" x 12" x 35". *In private collection. Photo, artist*

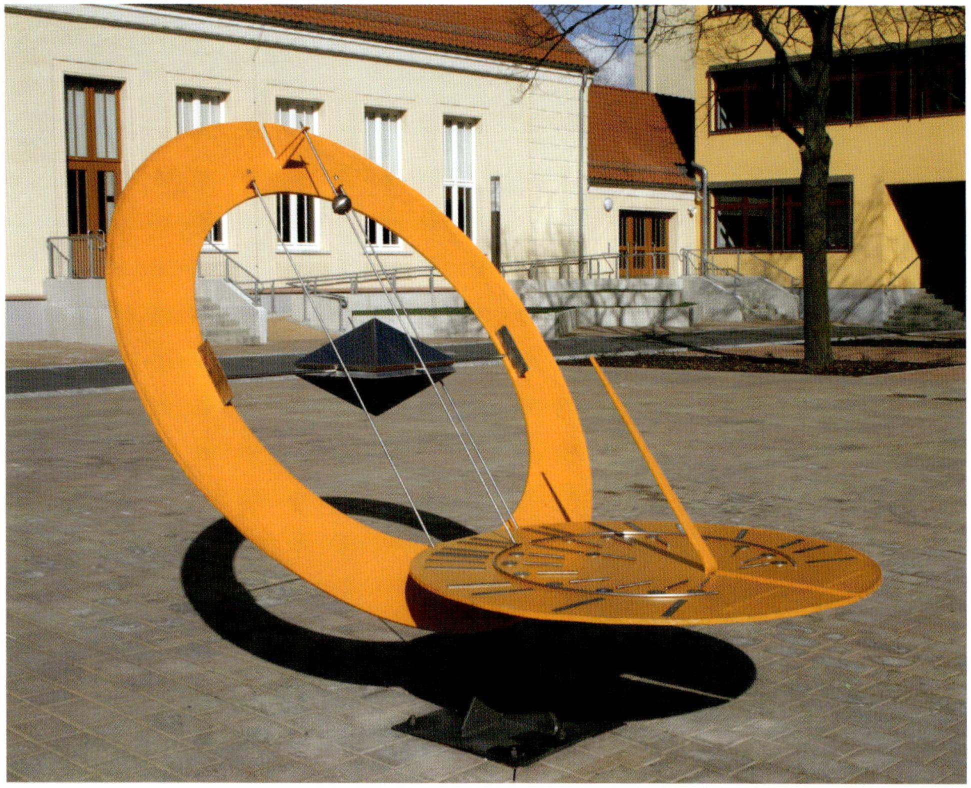

Achim Kühn. *Sundial.* Forged steel, stainless steel, 79" diameter. The sundial is set to the exact calculations for the location of Neubrandenburg, 8 different points of time to read for 24 cities of the world. *Photo, artist*

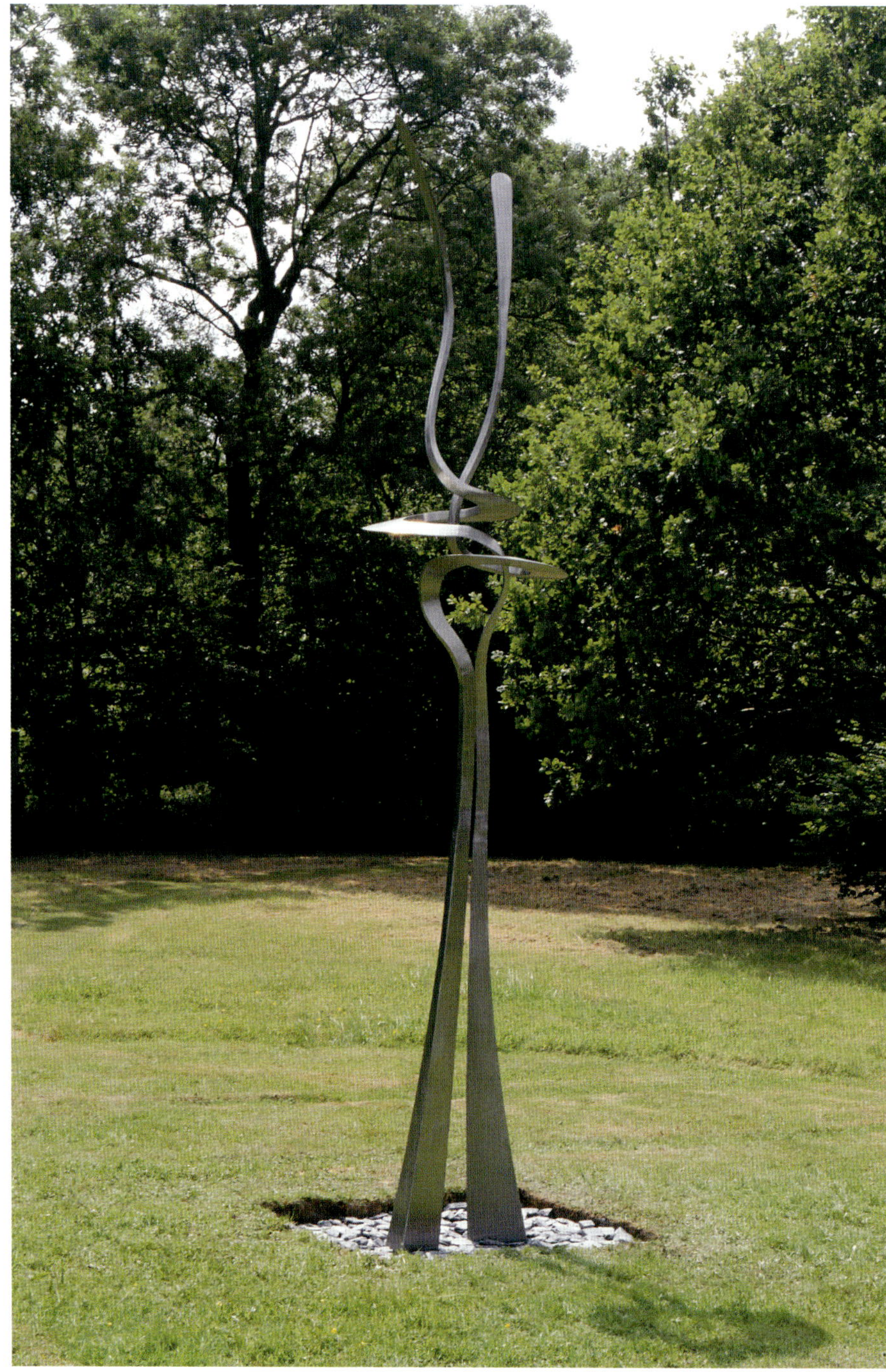

Melissa Cole. *Jubilation*, 2002. Forged and fabricated stainless steel. 165". *Photo, artist*

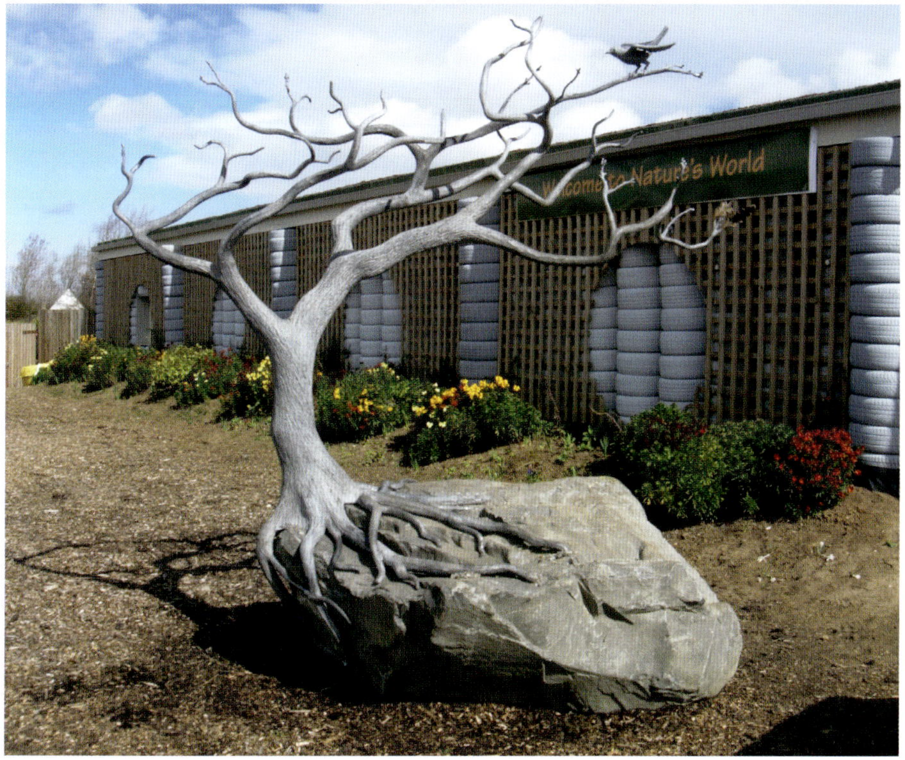

Brian Russell. *Tenacity* – Tree sculpture at "Nature's World." This piece depicts an apparently dead, windswept tree grimly hanging on to a massive lump of basalt. However, two of last year's leaves are still in place, and buds are forming on one of the limbs. The bird is struggling with the wind as well, but is managing to hold on. This project was a combination of forging and fabrication. The stem and thicker limbs are tubular, formed in two halves from steel plate; the smaller branches are forged down from 3" solid steel. Finish, galvanized, etched, and waxed. *Photo, artist*

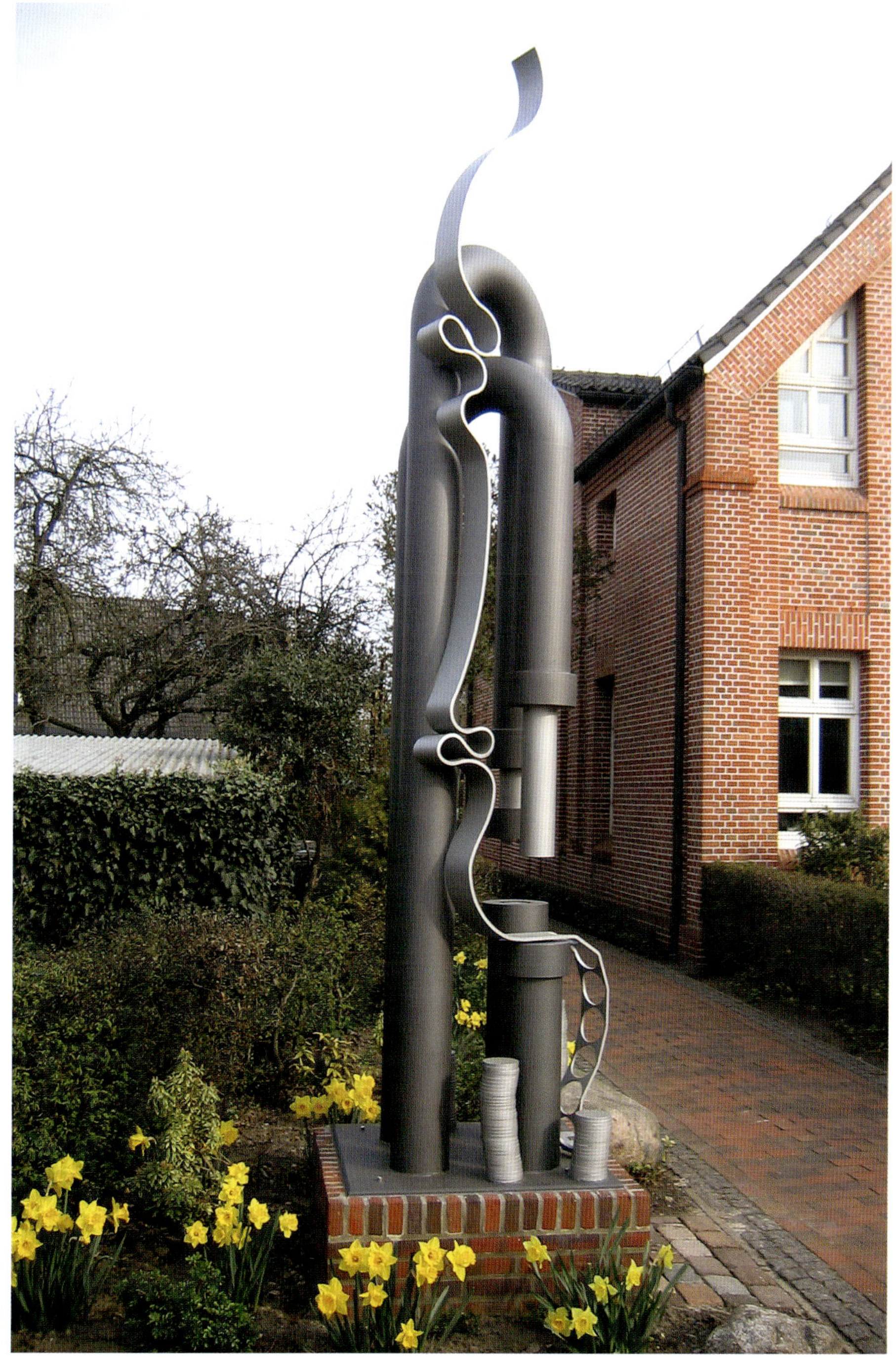

Alfred Bullermann. *Moneymaker.* Made from steel tubing. The section being stamped into coins is aluminum. 236" in height. Galvanized and colored. *Photo, artist*

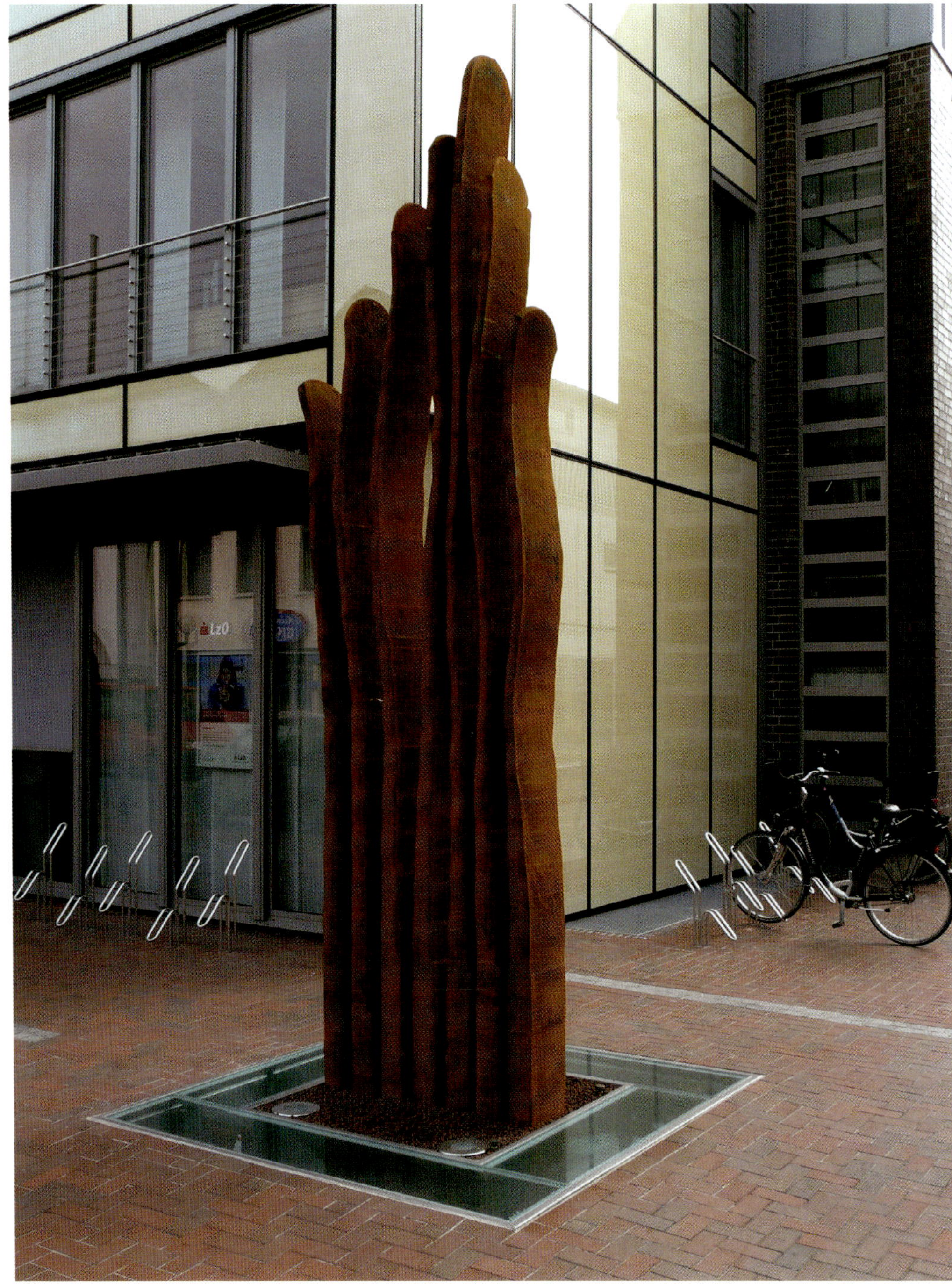

Alfred Bullermann. *Eisen.* Forged from cor-ten steel, 197" in height, weighing 7.5 tons. In the city of Friesoythe, Germany, there is an old history of blacksmithing. When digging in the ground, one often finds old remnants of this. At the base of this sculpture there is a space where some of these found items have been placed as remembrance of the town's history. *Photo, artist*

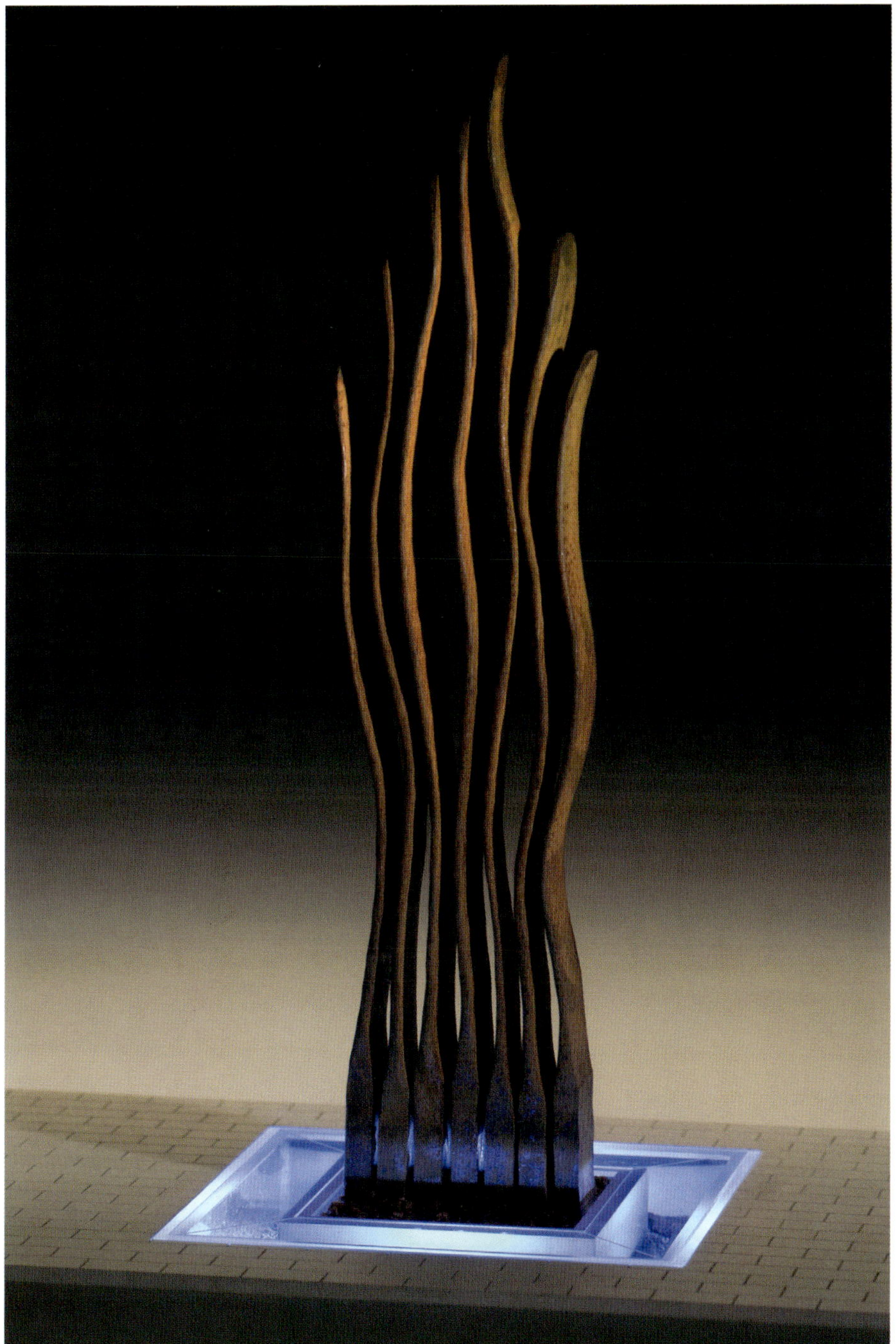

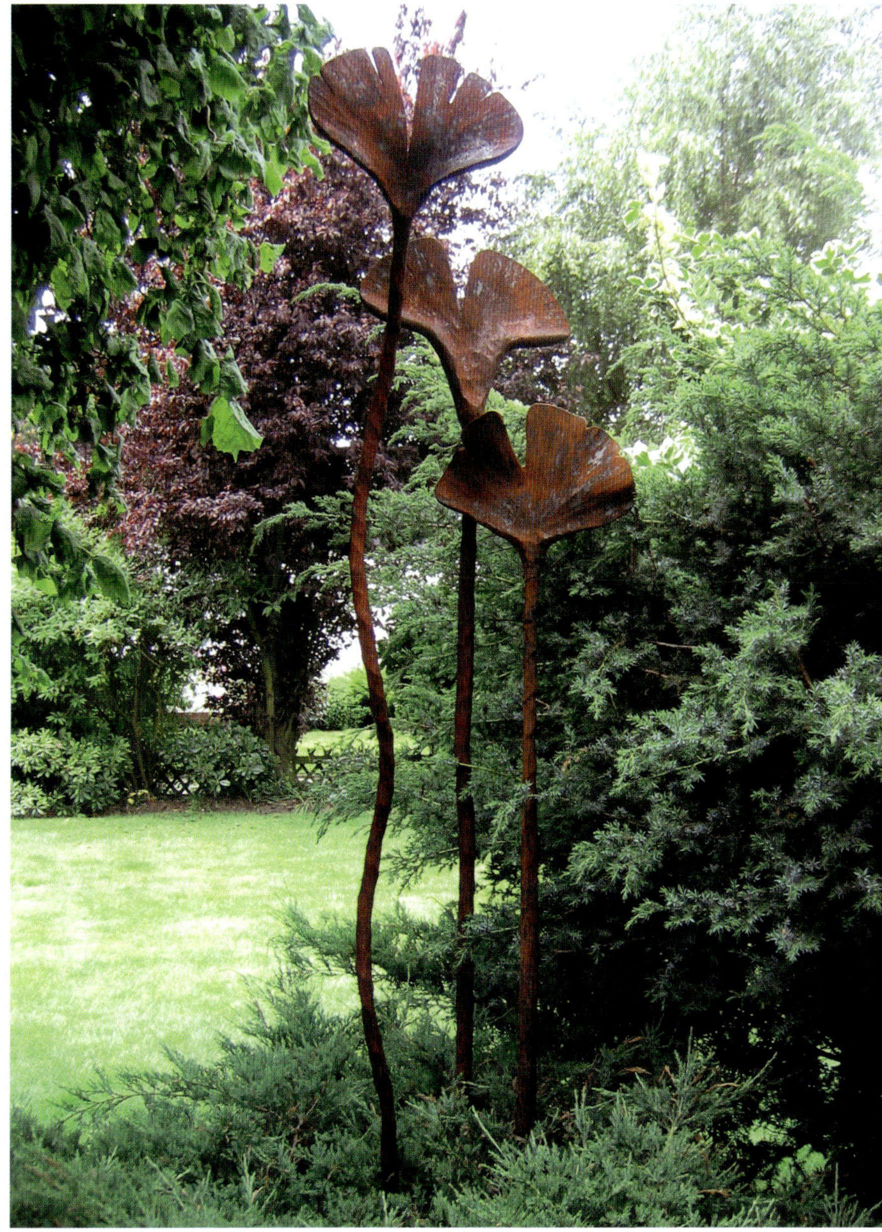

Alfred Bullermann. *Ginho*, Forged iron sheet, colored, 197" in height. *Photo, artist*

Alfred Bullermann. Model of *Eisen*. *Photo, Gerald Lampe*

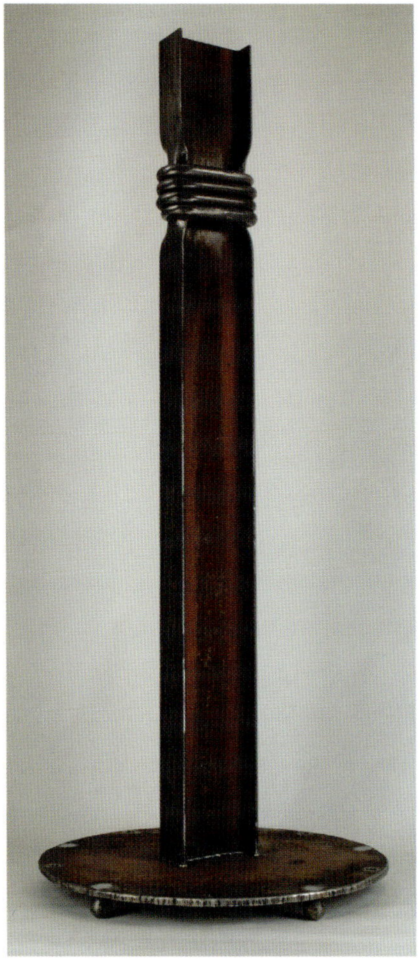

M. Craig Campbell. *Wrap (8by78)*, 2007. Forged and fabricated steel. 78" h x 31" w x 31" d. *Wrap (8by78)* is the fifth such experiment, each one progressively larger than the last. This piece was installed as a public sculpture with the base buried so that the I-beam seems to grow from the earth itself. *Photo, Trent Watts*

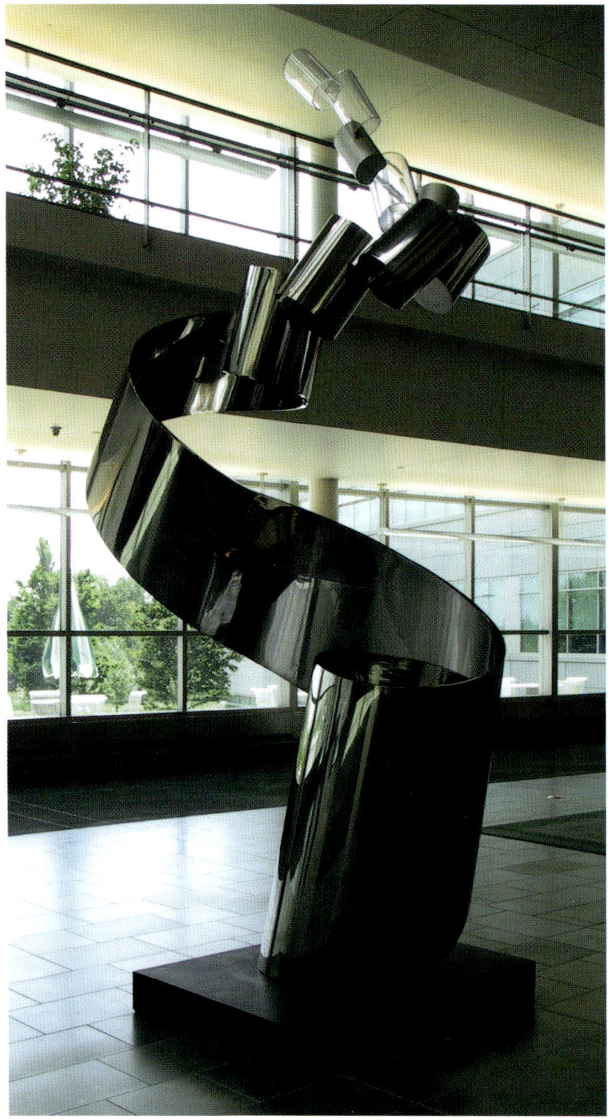

Harold Kimmelman. *Ascension,* Stainless steel, polycarbonate, 108" h x 48" w x 42" d. For the lobby of the corporate headquarters of Crown Cork and Seal (Crown Holdings), Philadelphia, Pennsylvania.

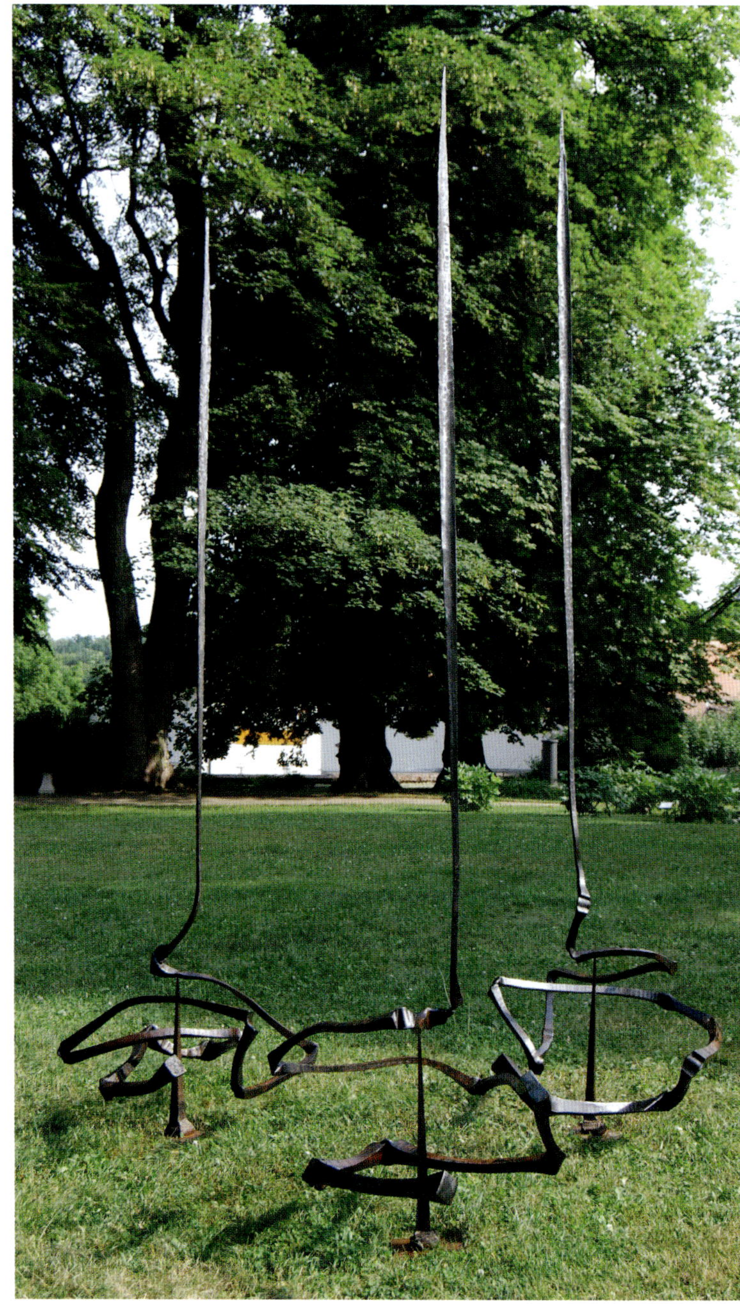

Pavel Tasovský. *Blades.* External kinetic sculpture. 118" x 49" x 49". *Photo, artist*

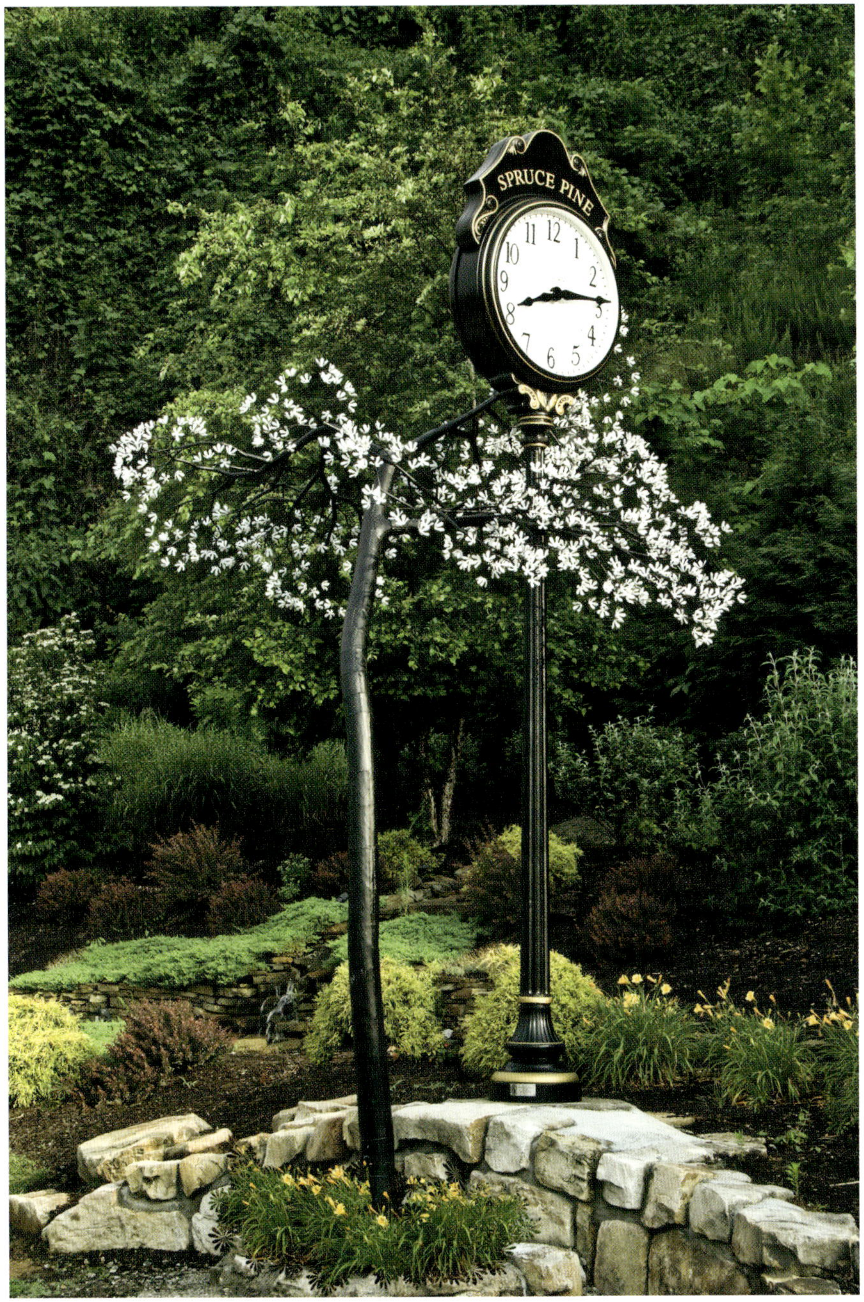

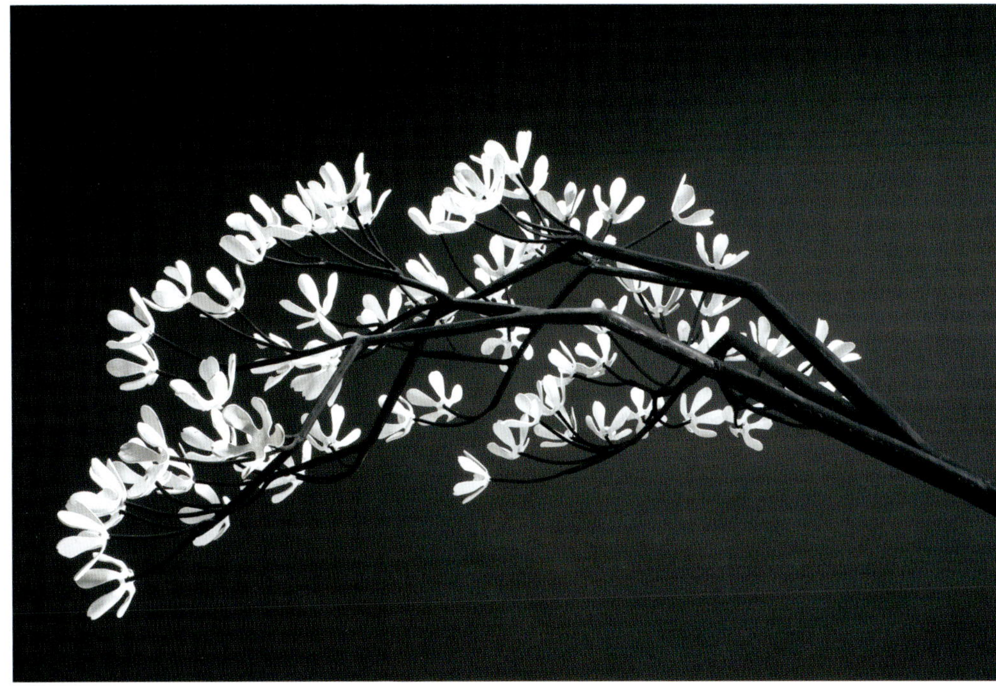

Elizabeth Brim and Jeff McDowell. *Sarviceberry,* 2008. Detail. *Photo, Tom Mills*

Elizabeth Brim and Jeff McDowell. *Sarviceberry,* 2008. The blossoms were plasma cut and shaped by community members. The branches are tapered tubes, gas welded. The trunk was made of rings that decrease in size toward the top of the tree. They are welded to a central core and are covered in 14-gauge sheet steel. The tree is painted with enamel paint, 204" h x 108" d at the top. *Photo, Mary Vogel*

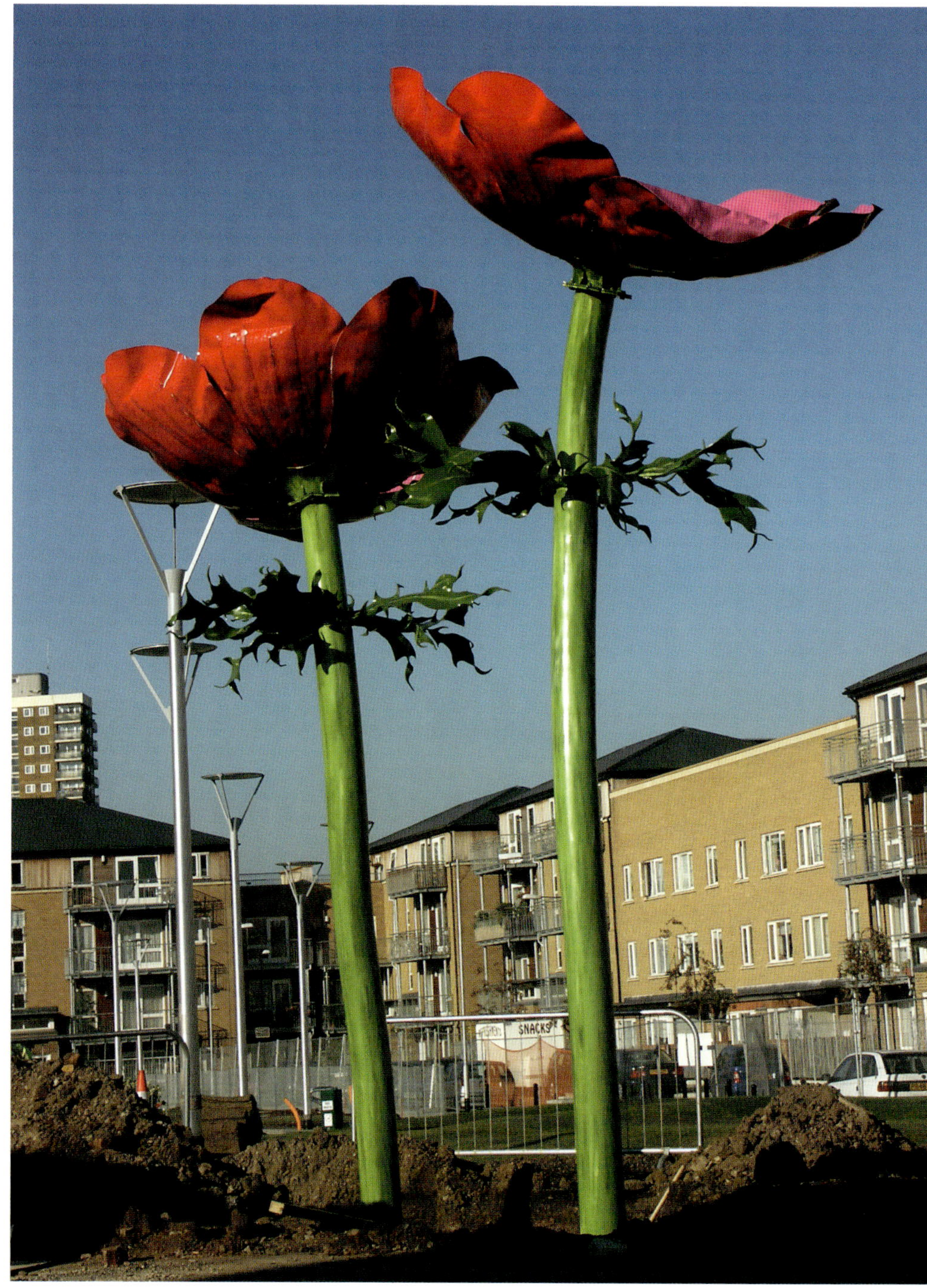

Gideon Petersen. *Flower Sculpture*, 2005. Bow, East London. The flowers are made from mild steel and stand at 236" in height, all hand forged, galvanized, and hand painted. *Photo, artist*

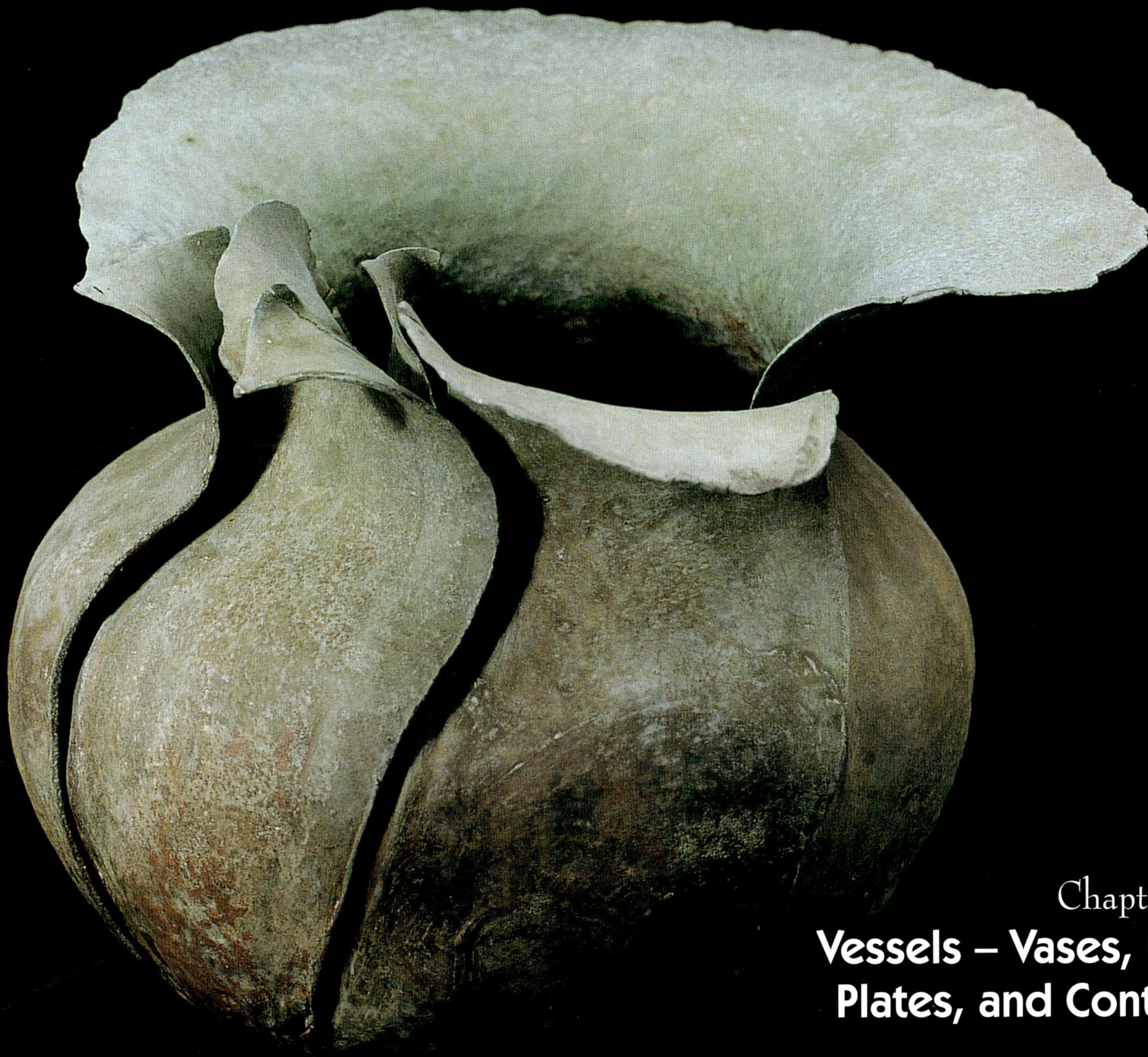

Chapter Three

Vessels – Vases, Bowls, Plates, and Containers

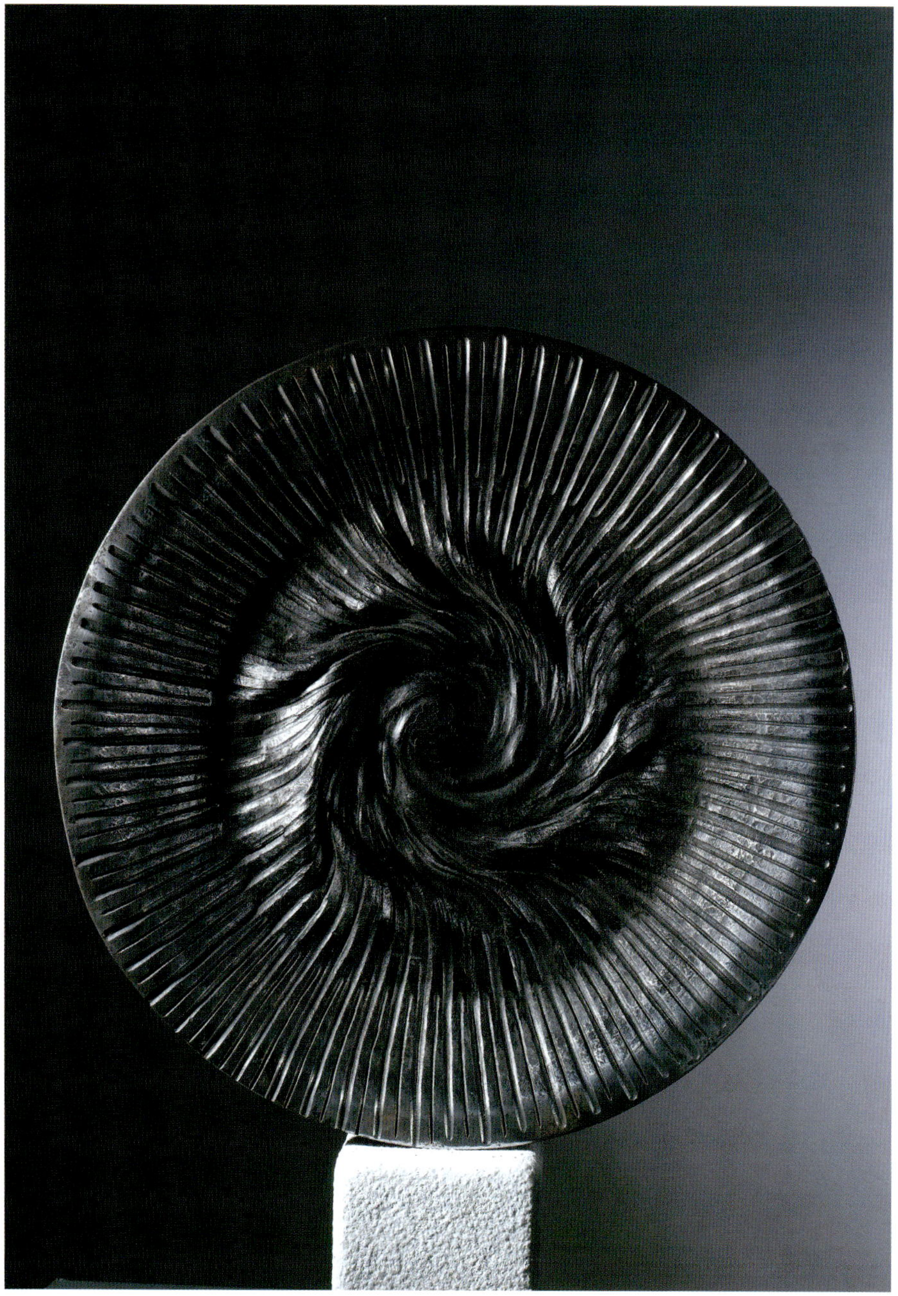

Claudio Bottero. Dish. 22". *Photo, artist*

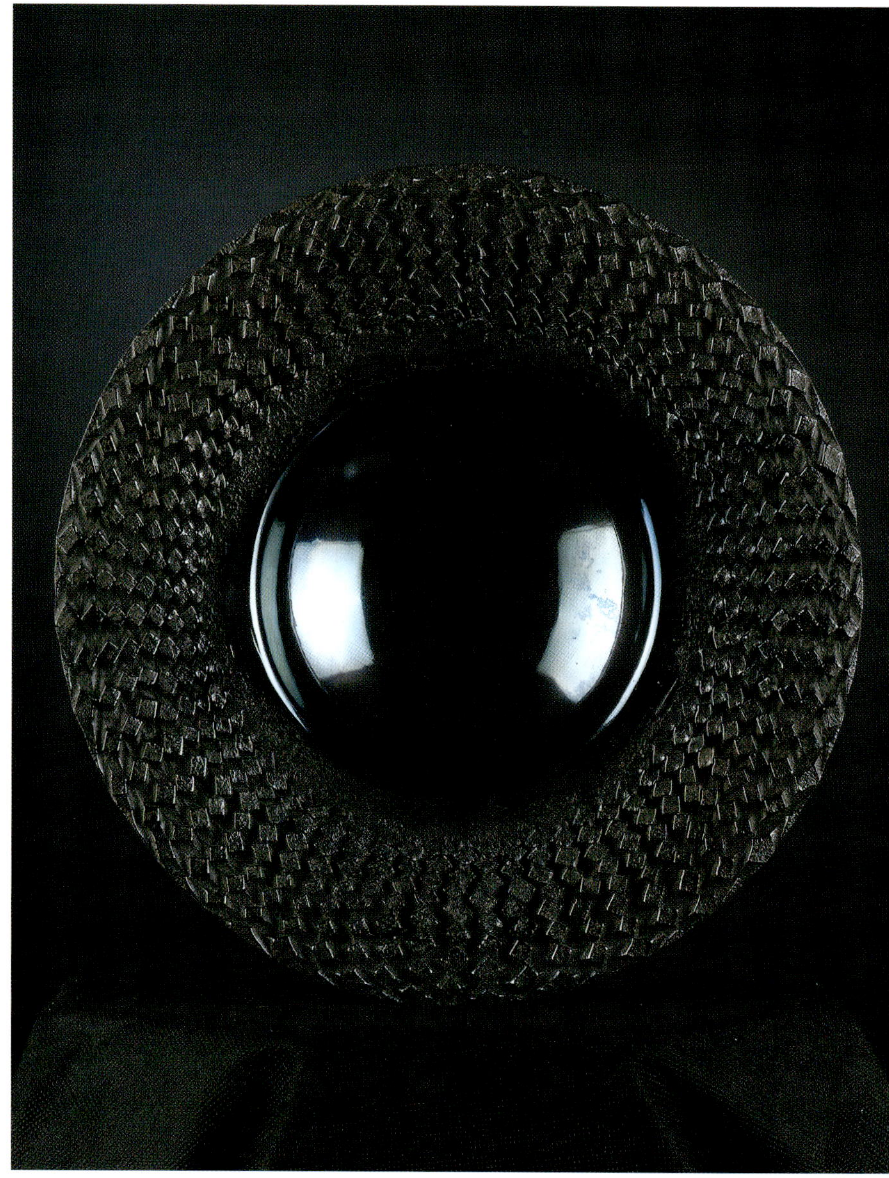

Claudio Bottero. Dish. 11". *Photo, artist*

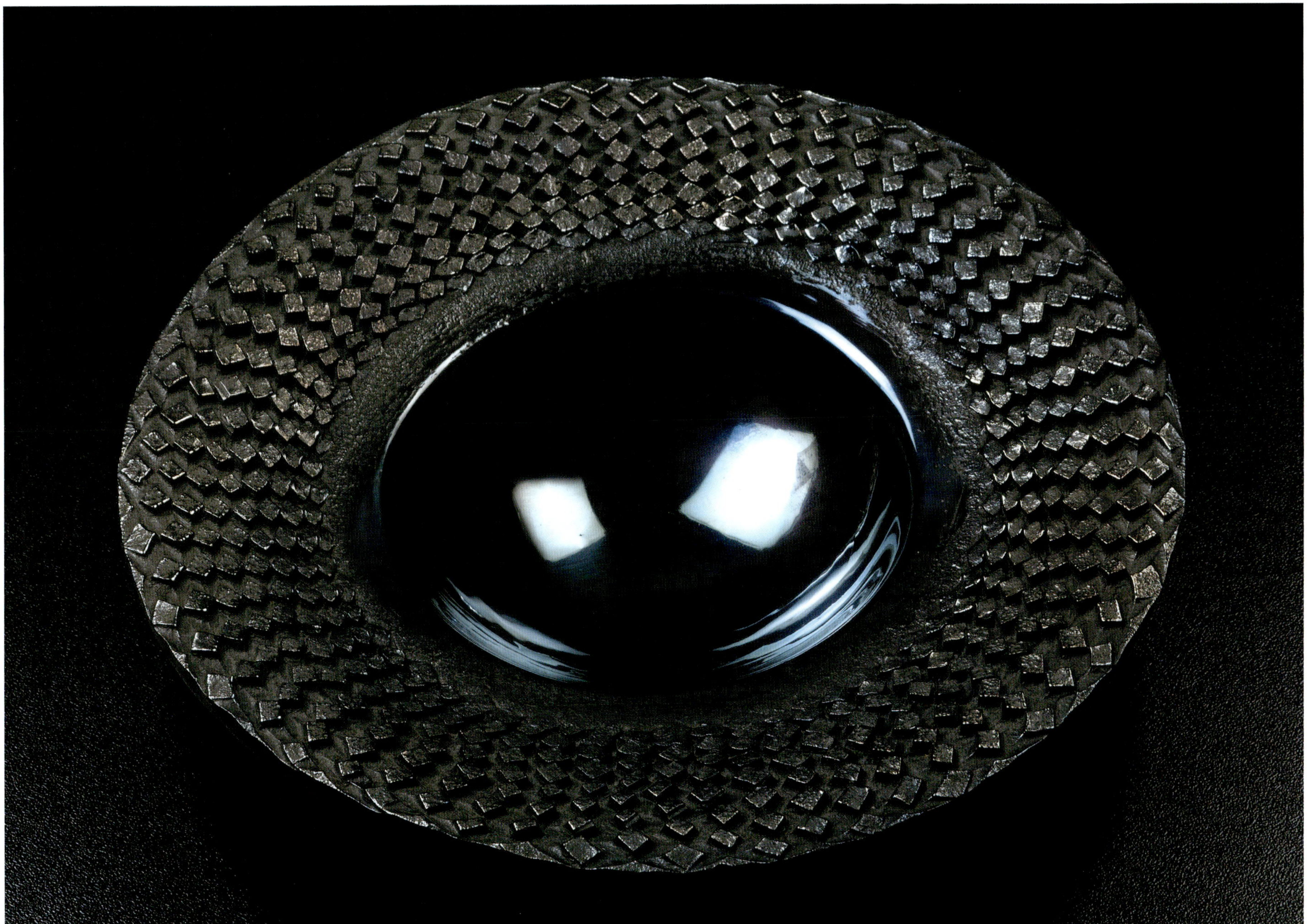

Claudio Bottero. Dish. 11". Second view. *Photo, artist*

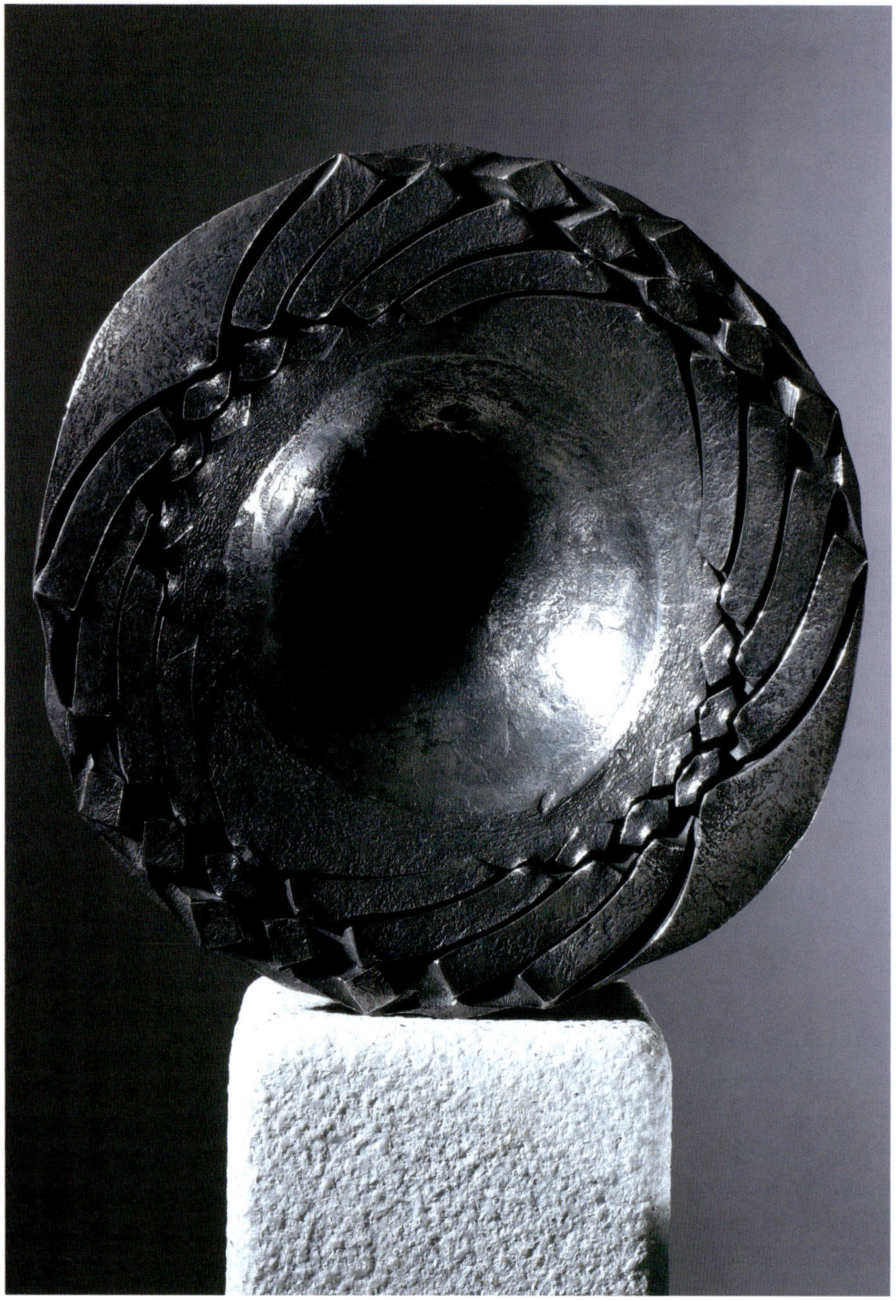

Claudio Bottero. Dish. 11". *Photo, artist*

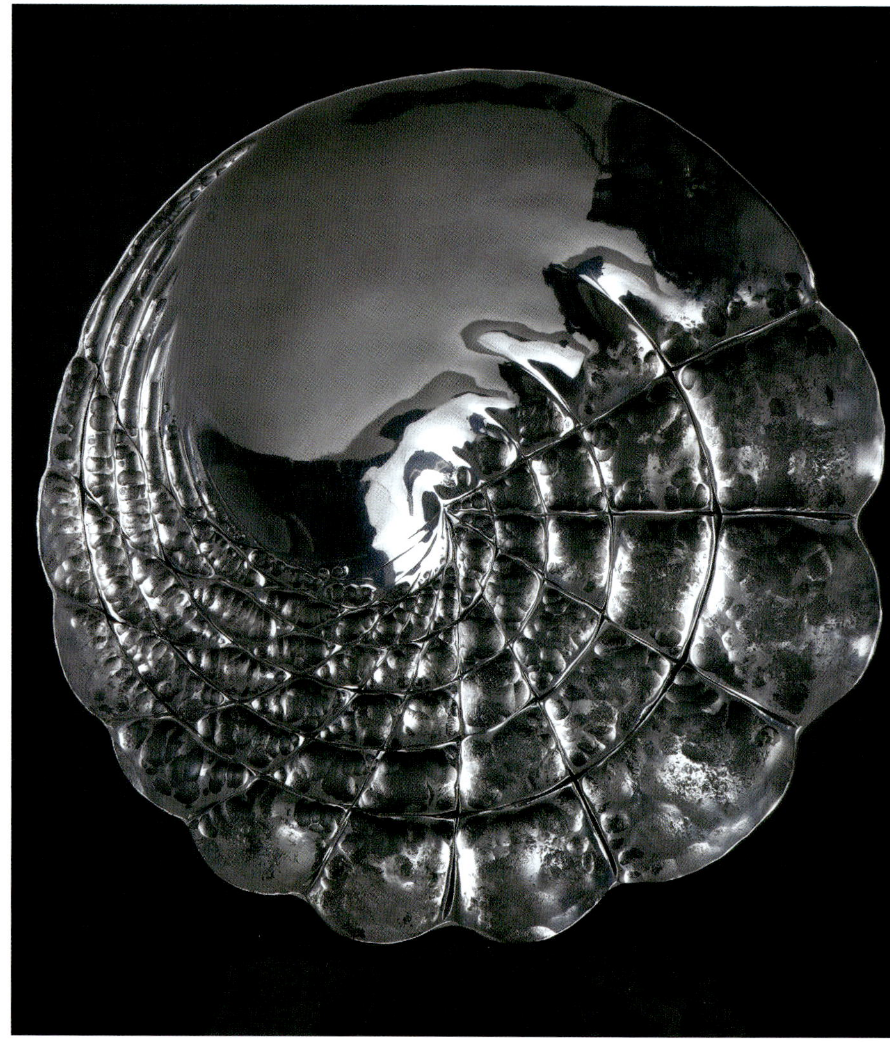

Claudio Bottero. Dish. 24". *Photo, artist*

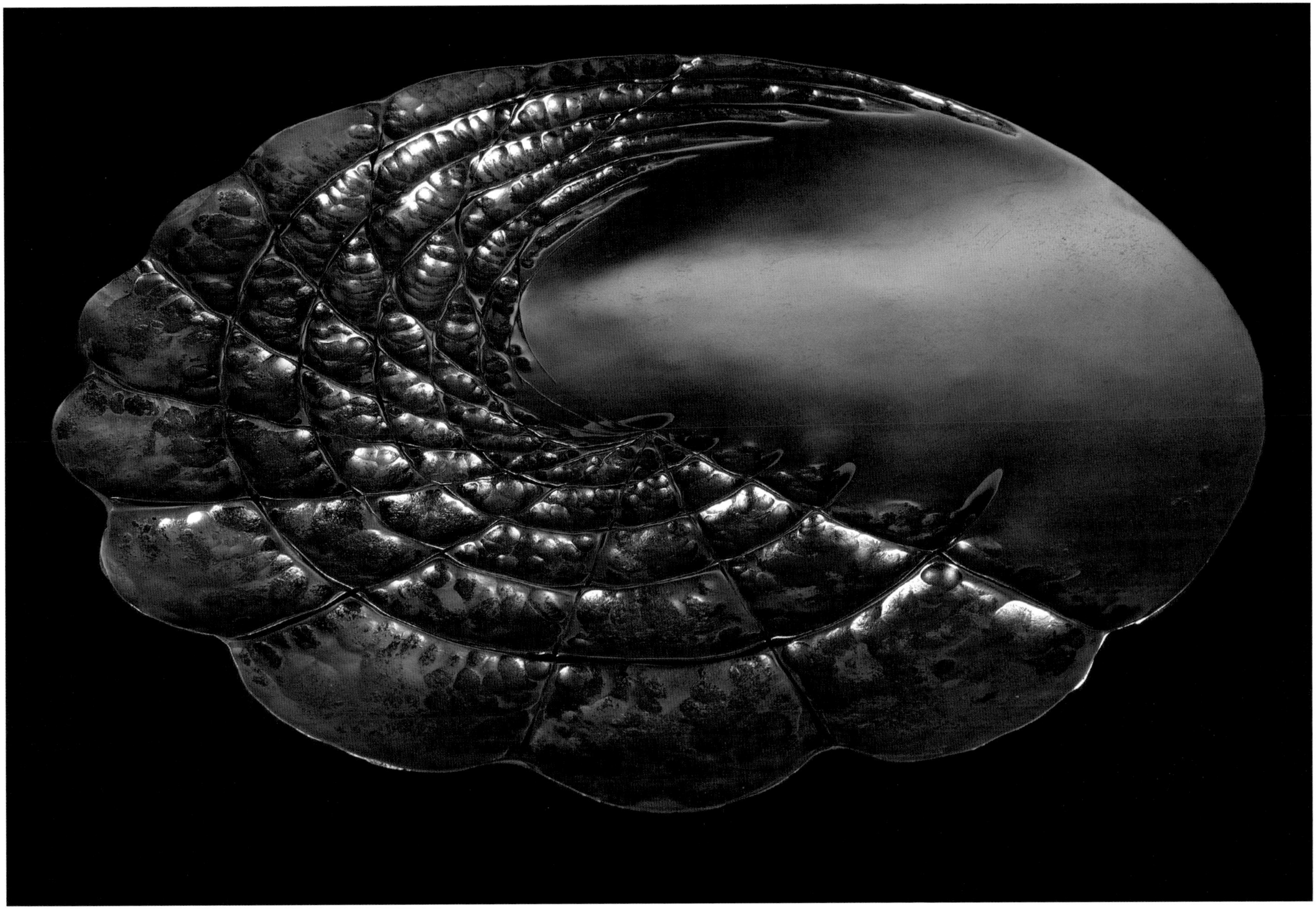

Claudio Bottero. Dish. 24". Second view. *Photo, artist*

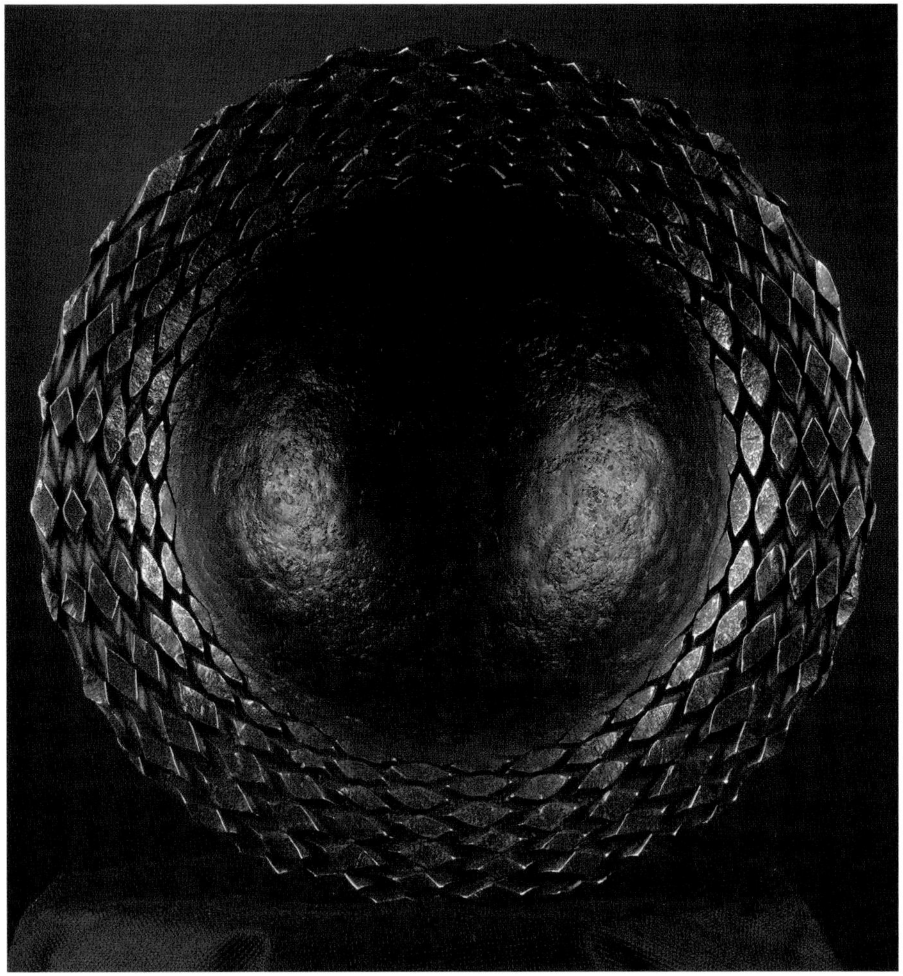

Claudio Bottero. Dish. 11". *Photo, artist*

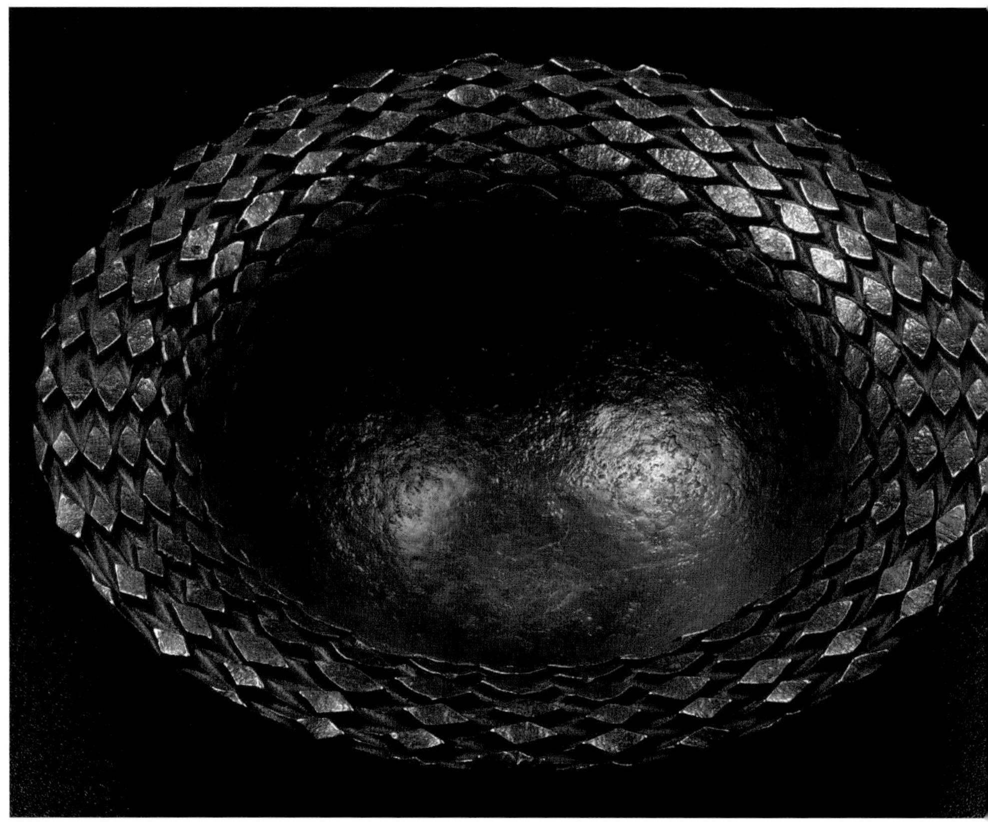

Claudio Bottero. Dish. 11". Second view. *Photo, artist*

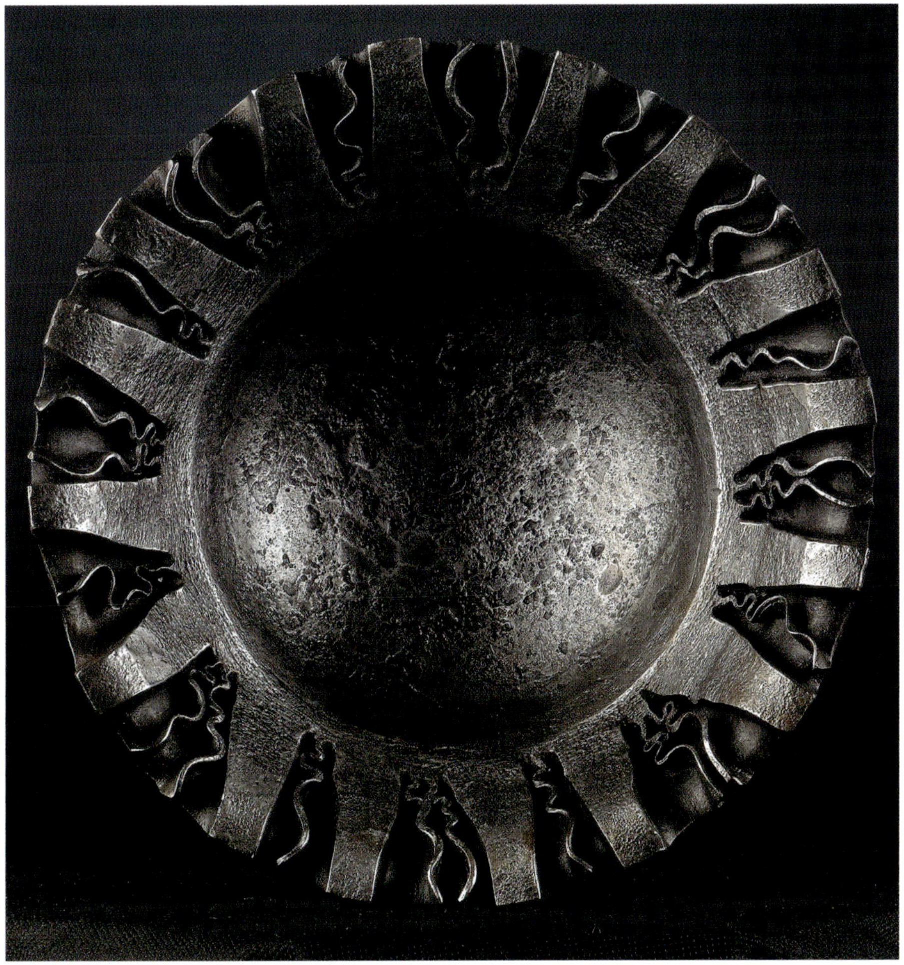

Claudio Bottero. Dish. 10". *Photo, artist*

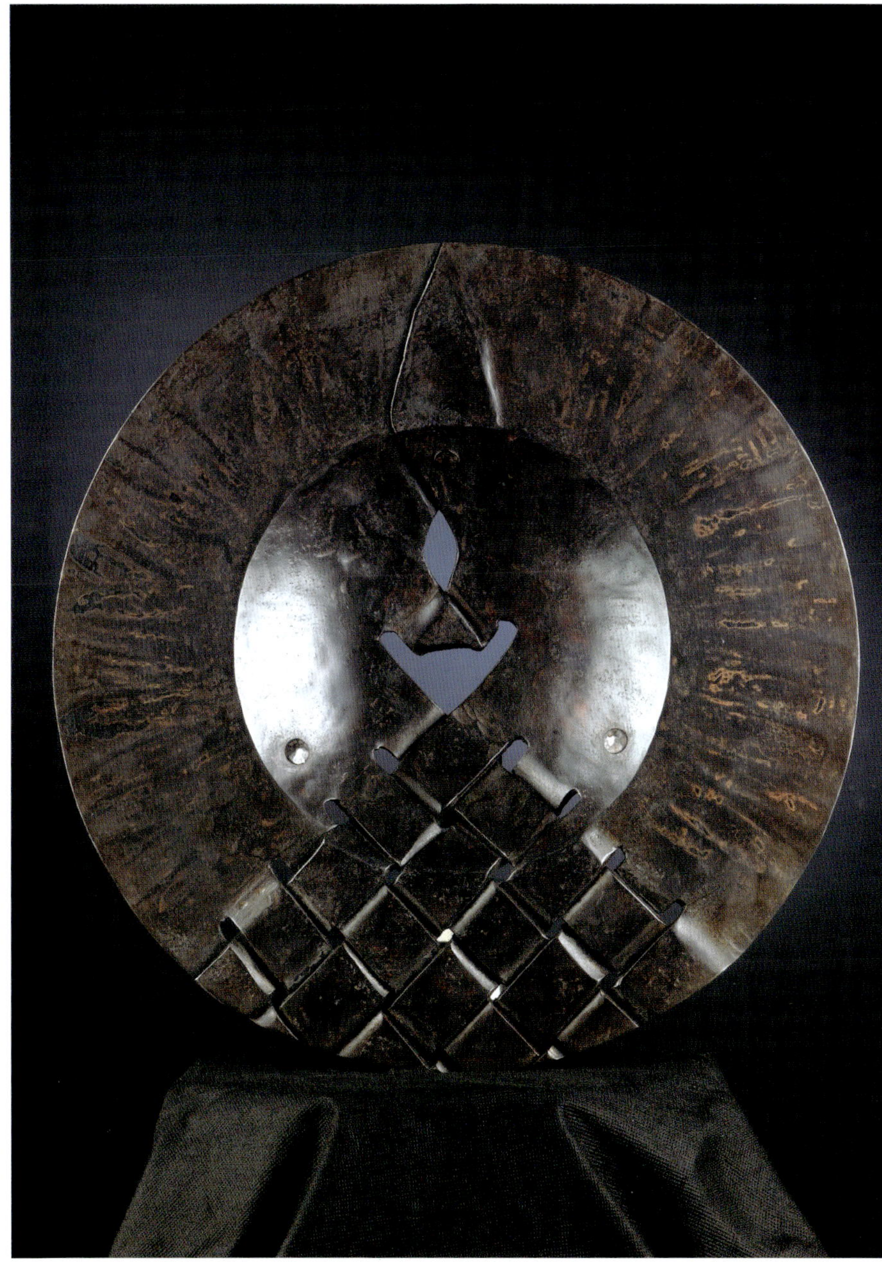

Claudio Bottero. Dish. *Photo, artist*

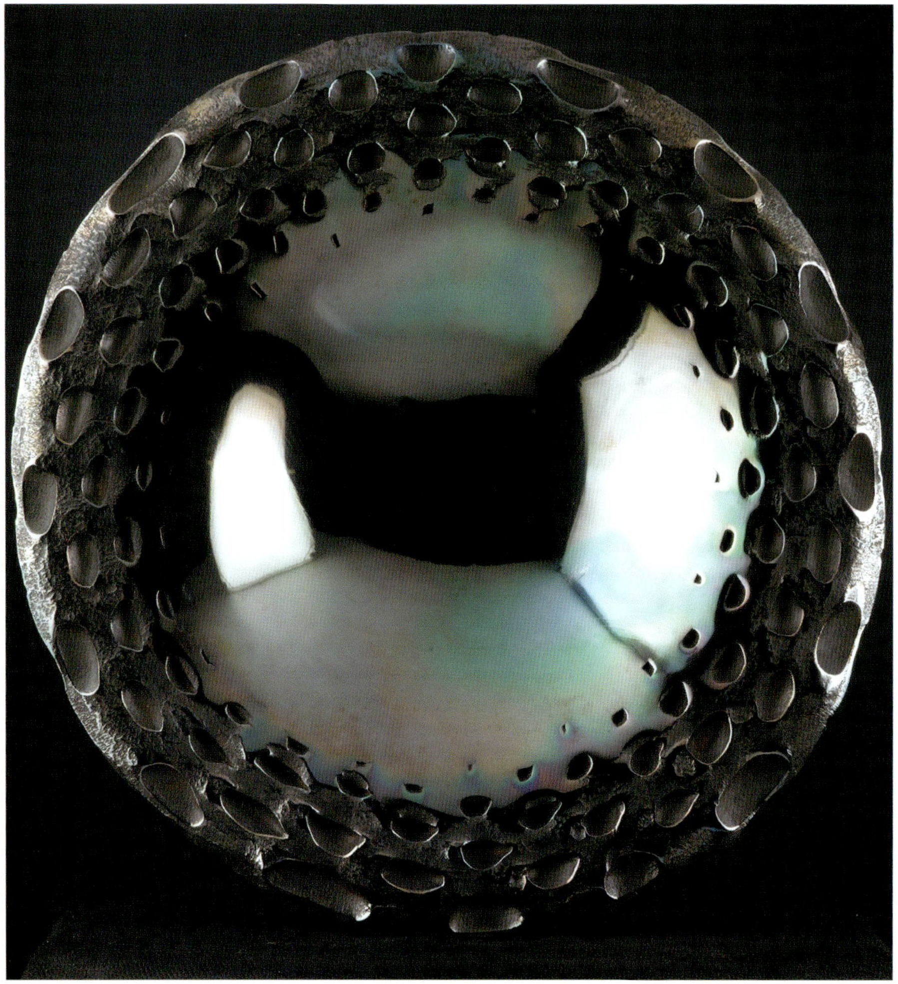

Claudio Bottero. Dish. 11". *Photo, artist*

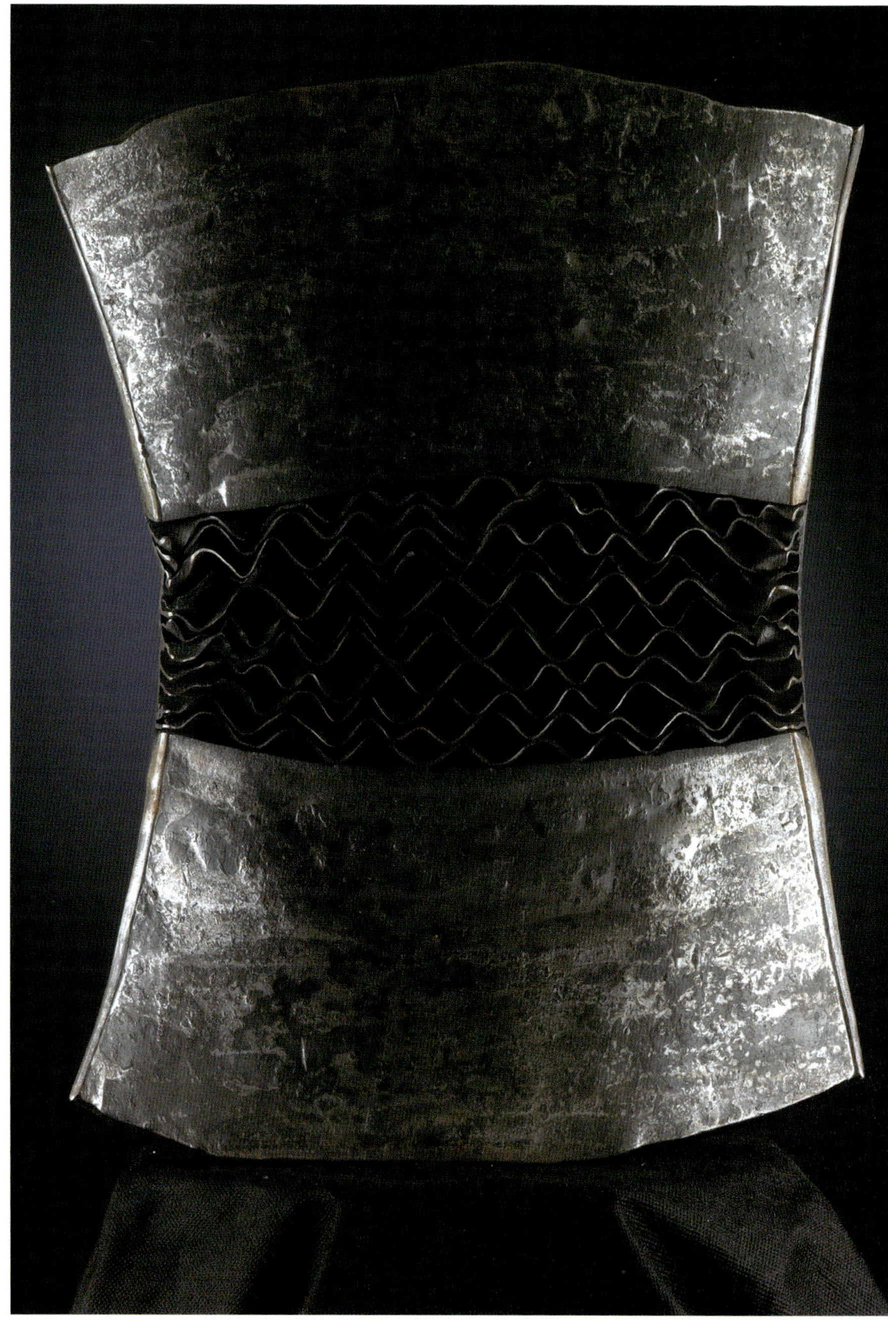

Claudio Bottero. Dish. 15" x 10". *Photo, artist*

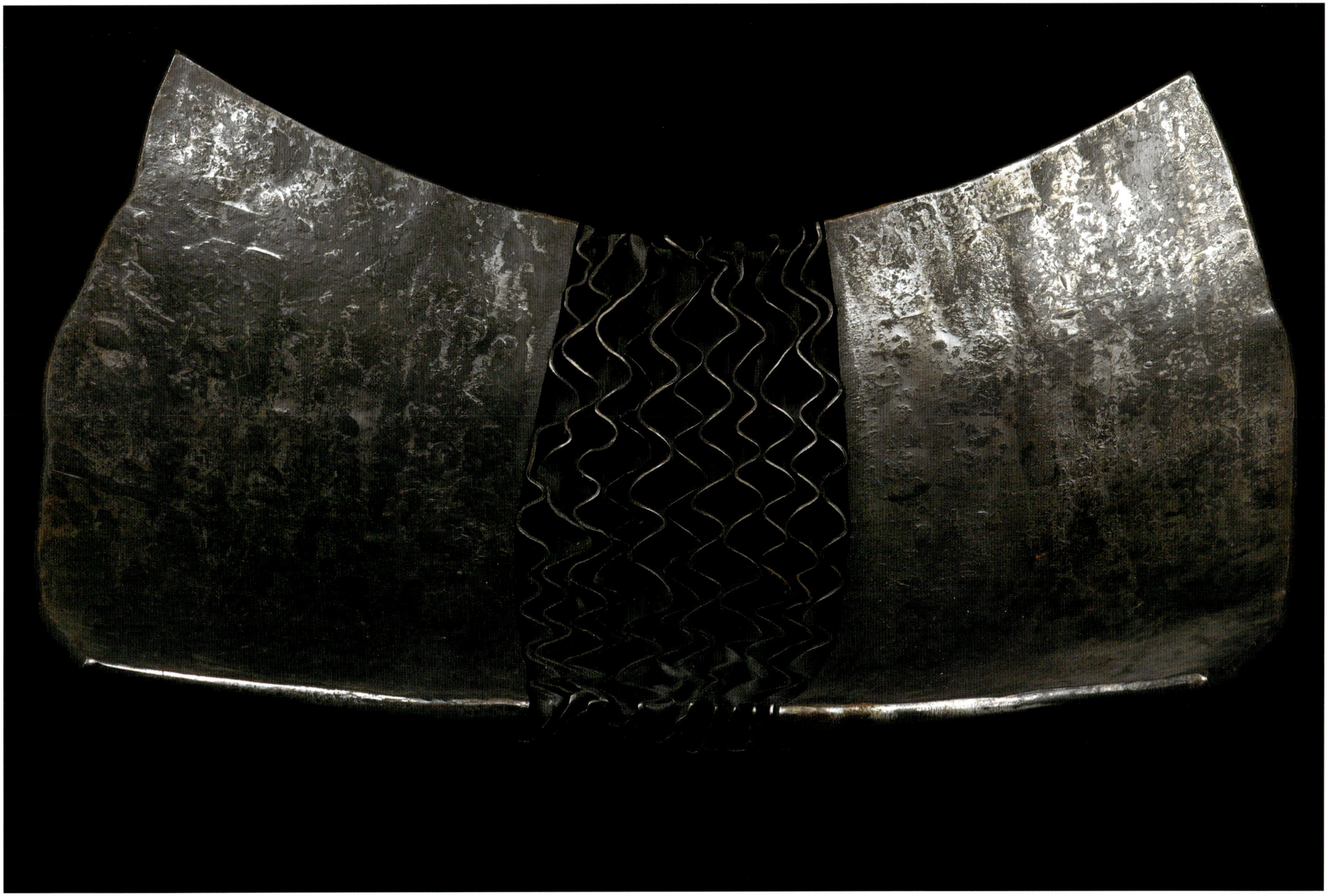

Claudio Bottero. Dish. Second view. *Photo, artist*

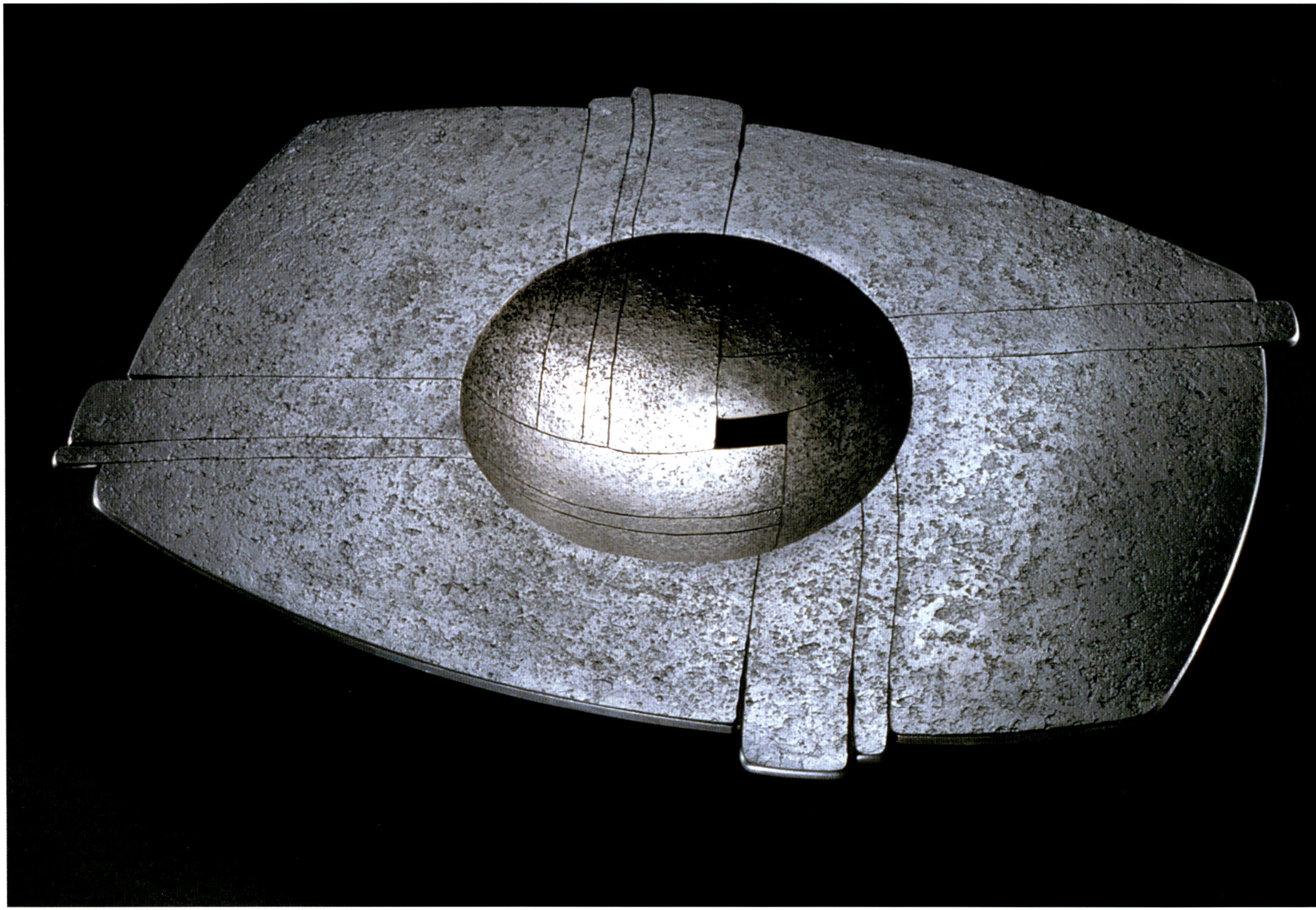

Tom Joyce. Pieced Plate Bowl. Forged iron. 3.25" h x 23.25" w x 18" d. *Photo, Nick Merrick*

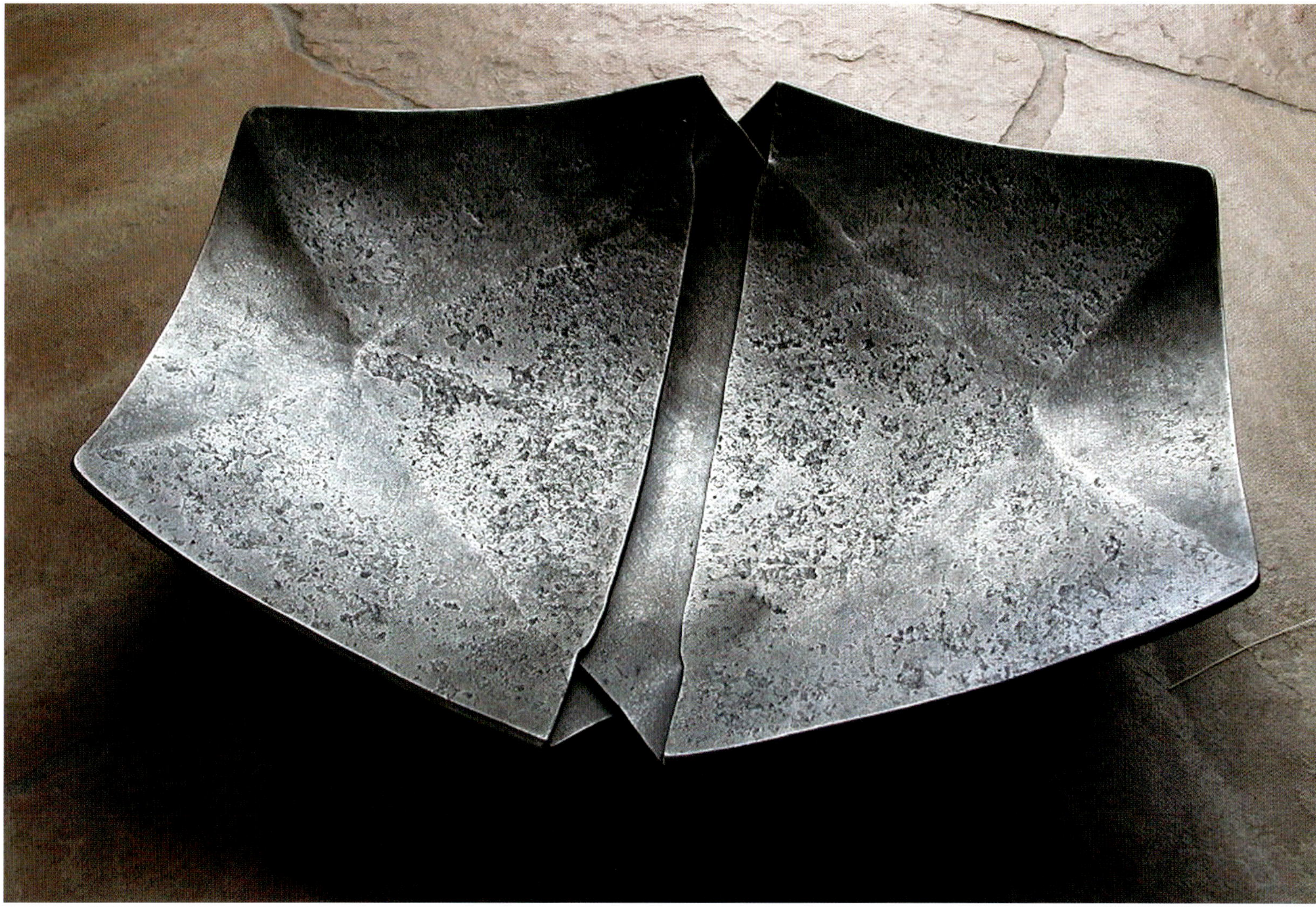

Tom Joyce. Double Spiral Compressed Bowl. Forged iron. 2.5" h x 17.75" w x 14" d. *Photo, artist*

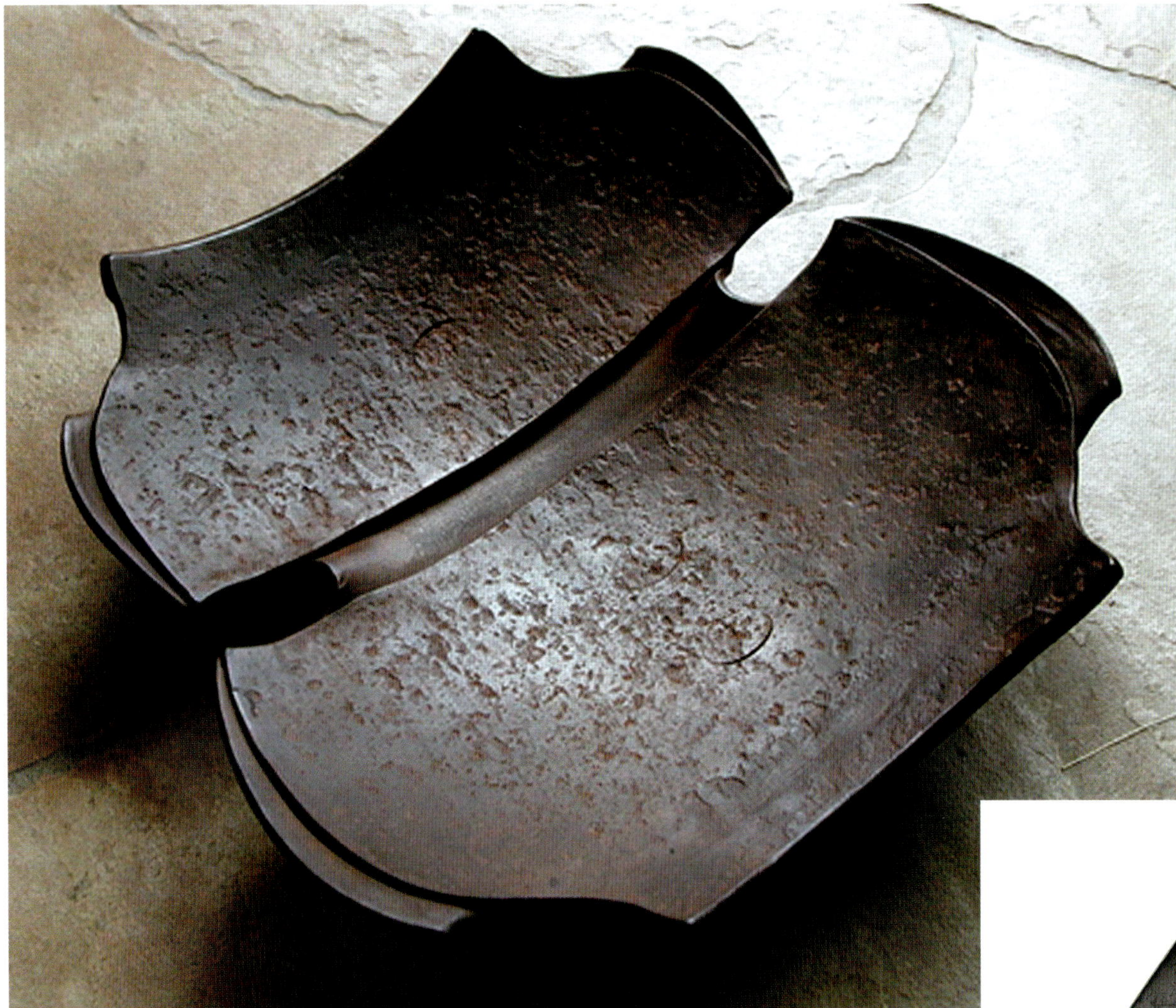

Tom Joyce. Fibonacci Bowl. Forged iron, 4" h x 15" w x 14" d. *Photo, artist*

The folds in this bowl are dimensioned in a numerical order that relate to a discovery by the thirteenth century Italian mathematician, Leonardo of Pisa, nicknamed Fibonacci. He observed a numerical relationship found in the growth patterns of living structures that approximated the proportion of the golden ratio. Egyptian, Greek, Roman, European, and Islamic artists and architects used this formulaic root to arrive at pleasing shapes for everything from pots to palaces. This relationship illustrates the growth patterns in nature and these proportions are inherent in most everything from seashells to sunflowers and pineapples to pinecones.

My experiment here was to take Fibonacci's theorem and apply it to a folded vessel. The folded formula resulted in a parallel-sided iron plate. Beginning with the shortest fold, the next longest would relate to it as the sum of the two would relate to the next longest and so on until six folds were completed. The piece was heated and forged to a uniform thickness. The triple and double-layered folds being reduced nearly to the original single layer thickness. The thicker section stretched out more than the thinner, resulting in the irregular shape of the bowl. By likening the process of forging to any other organic growth medium, the bowl grew in a proportional manner to the original formula, taking it a step further than mathematics alone. – Tom Joyce

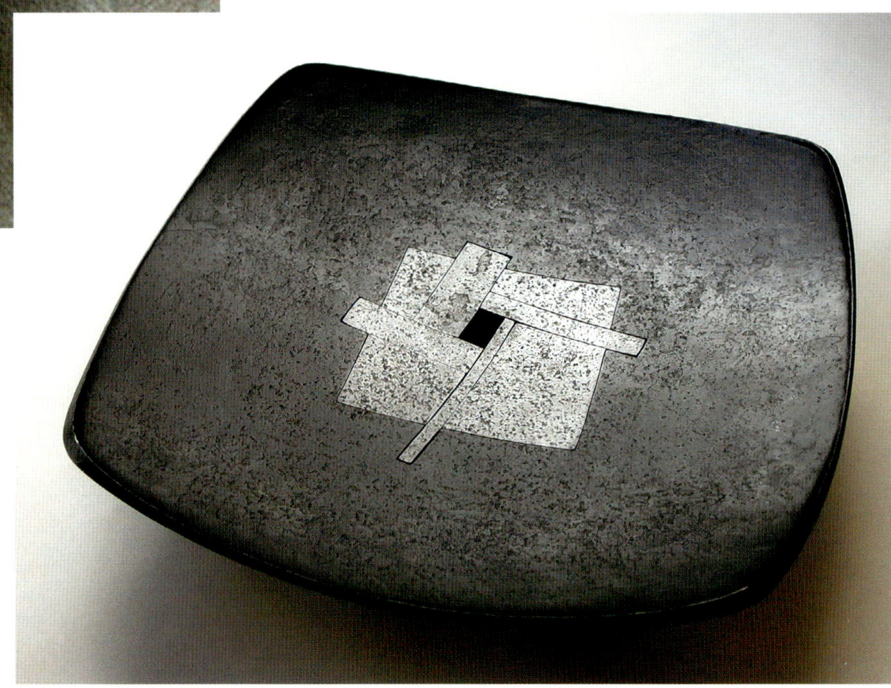

Tom Joyce. Inlaid Bowl. Forged iron, 4" h x 14.5" w x 14.5" d. *Photo, artist*

Pavel Tasovský. Dish, 2003.
3" x 26" x 17". *Photo, artist*

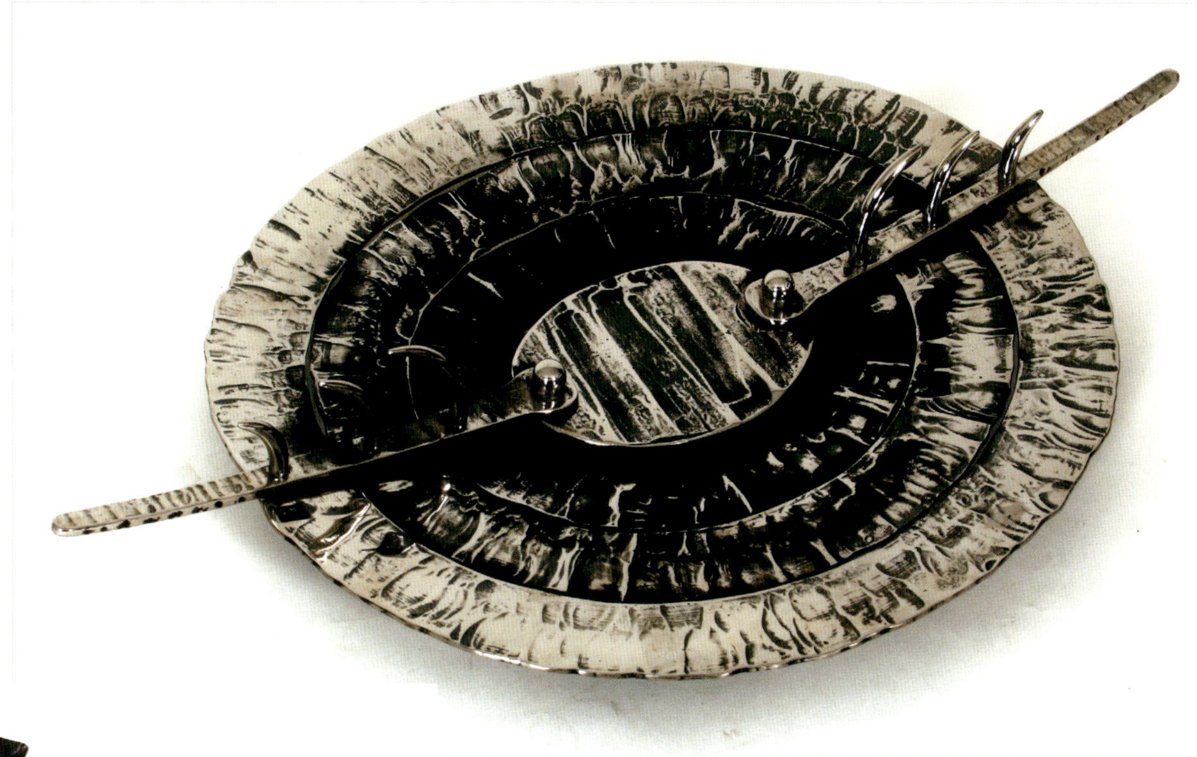

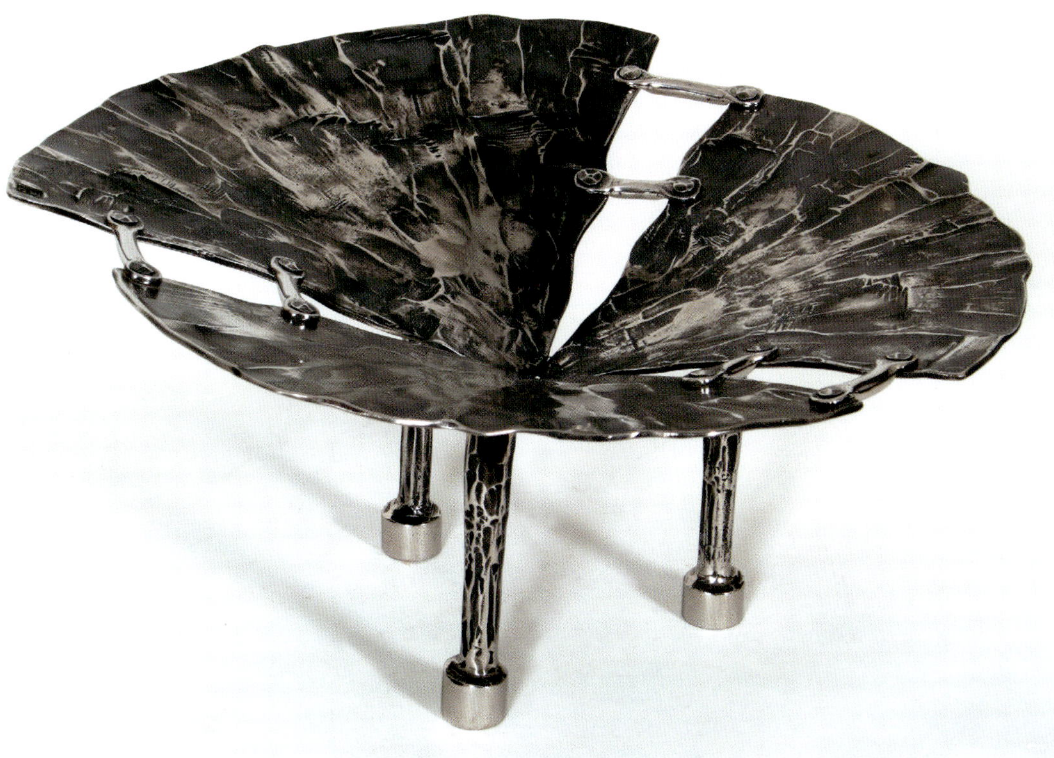

Pavel Tasovský. Dish, 2003.
10" x 18" x 18". *Photo, artist*

Pavel Tasovský. Dish, 2006. 5" x 14" x 14". *Photo, artist*

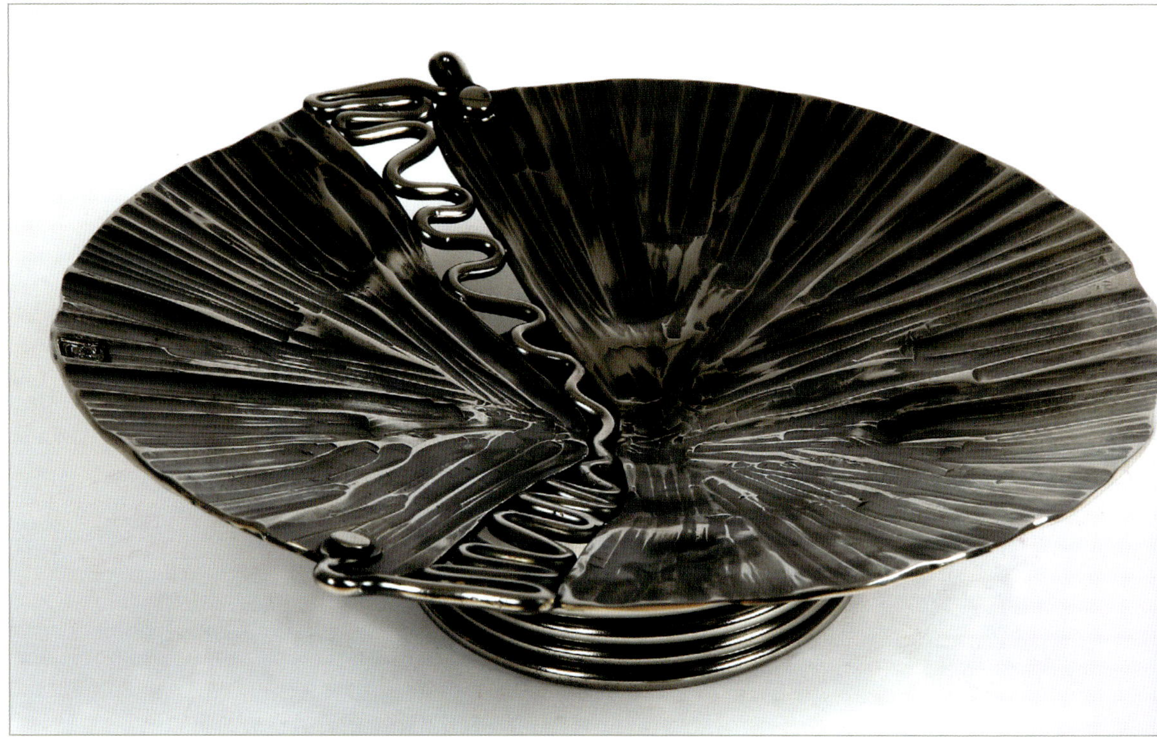

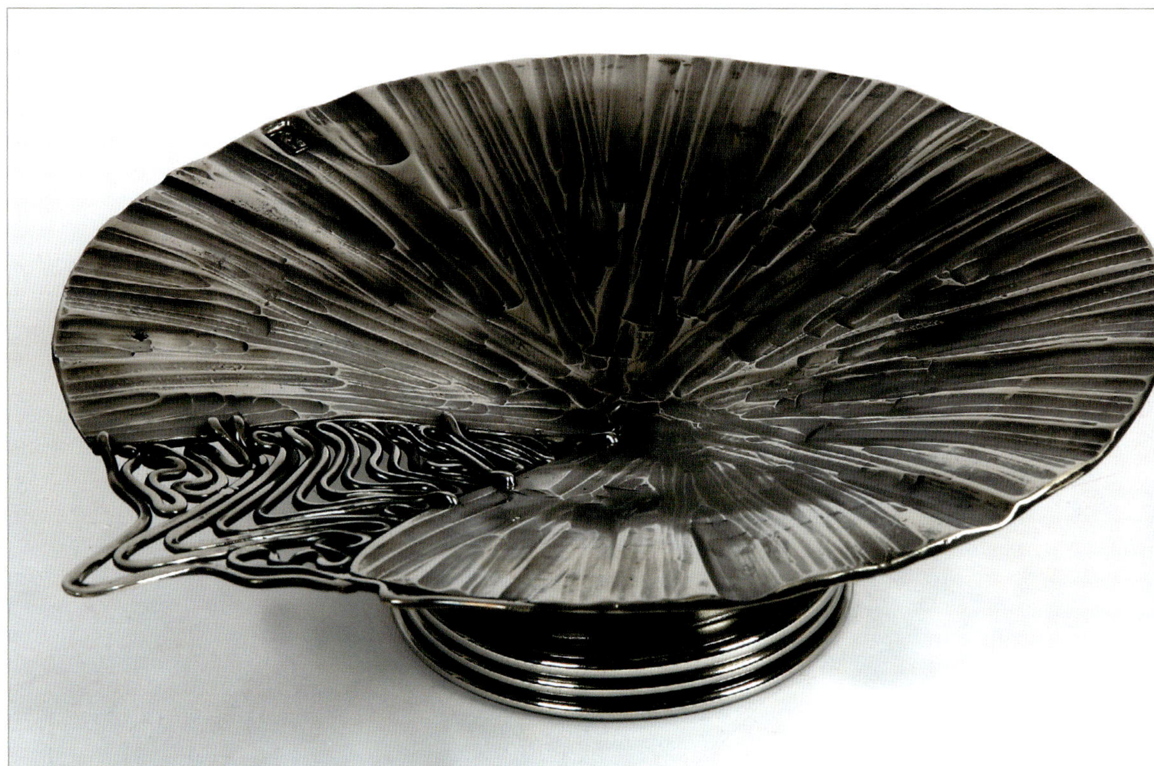

Pavel Tasovský. Dish, 2006. 5" x 15" x 16.5". *Photo, artist*

Pavel Tasovský. Dish, 2006.
25" x 17" x 11". *Photo, artist*

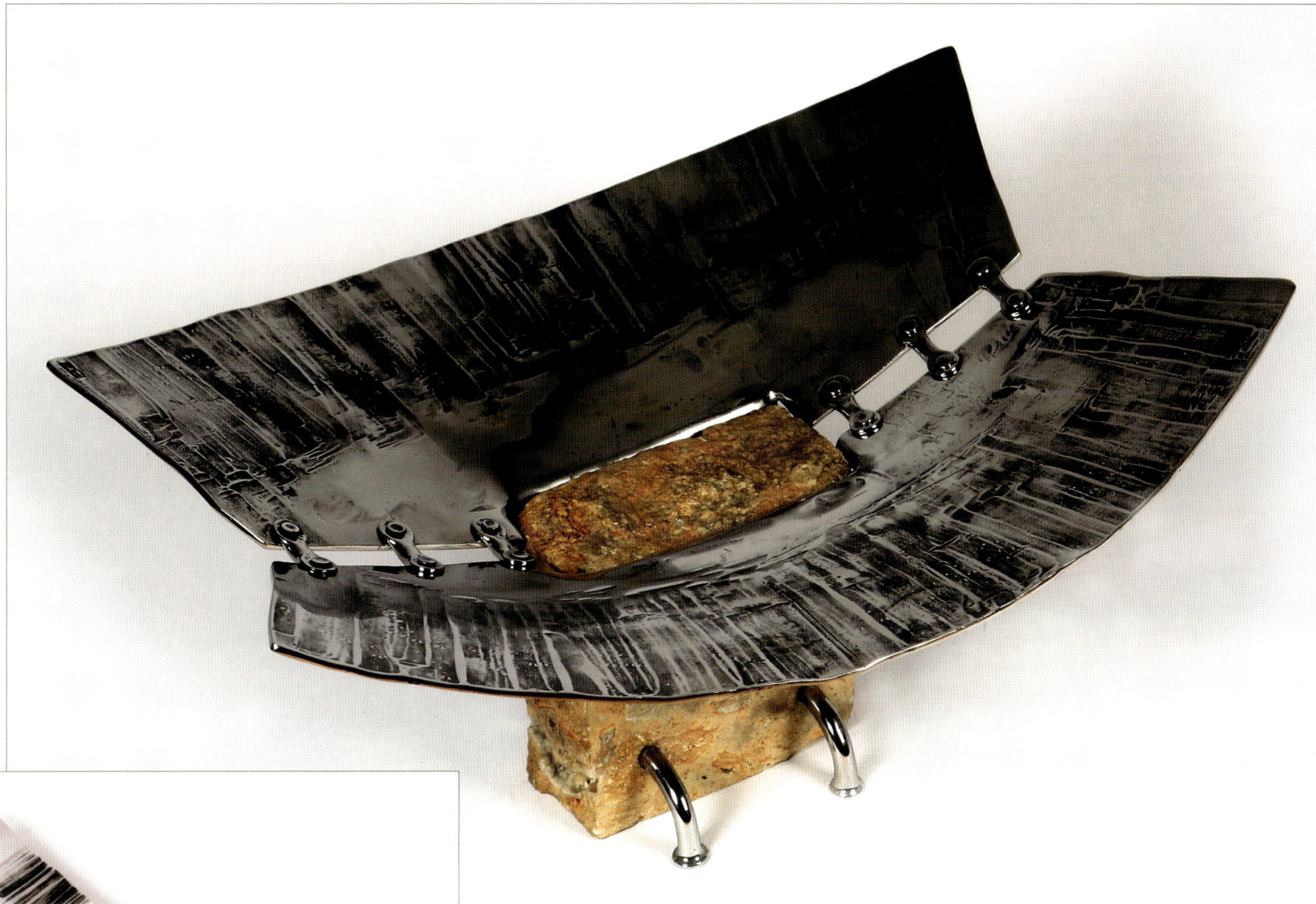

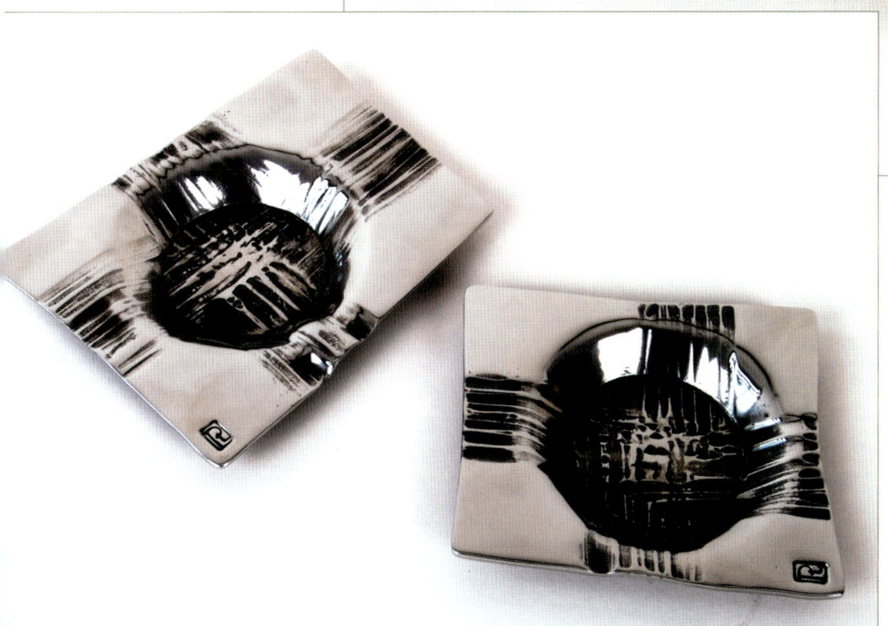

Pavel Tasovský. Dish, 2007.
Photo, artist

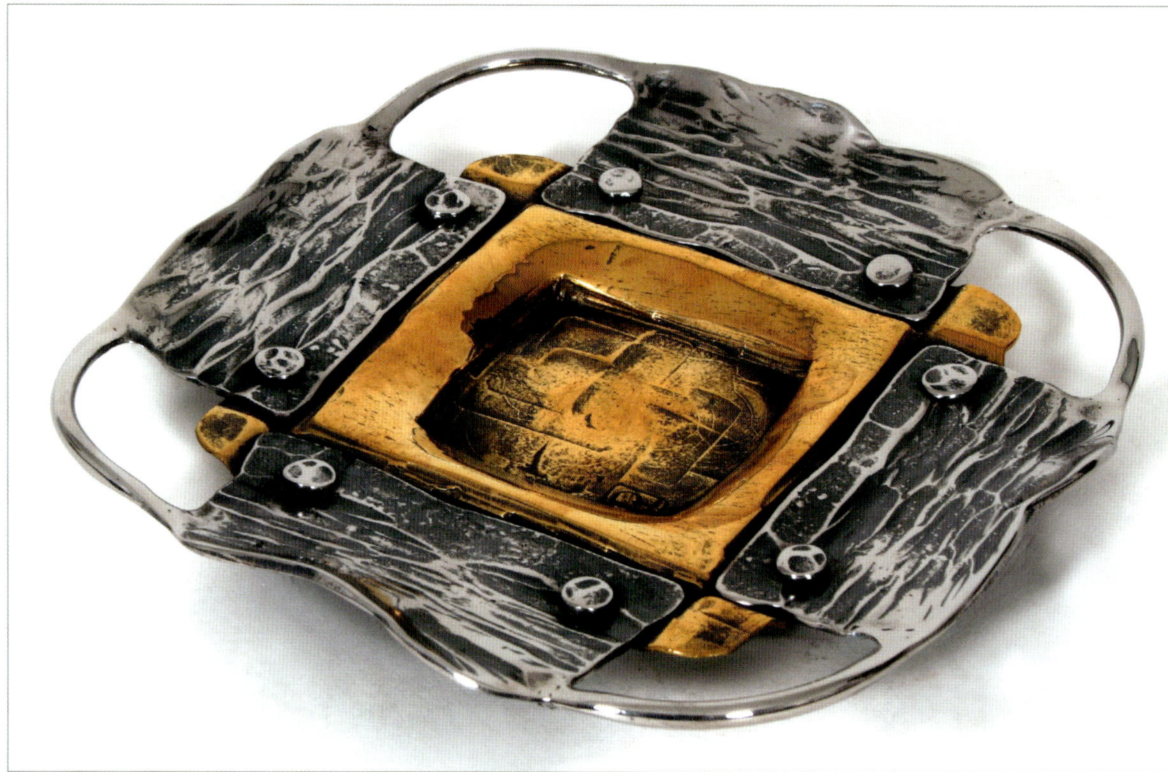

Pavel Tasovský. Tray, 2004.
Photo, artist

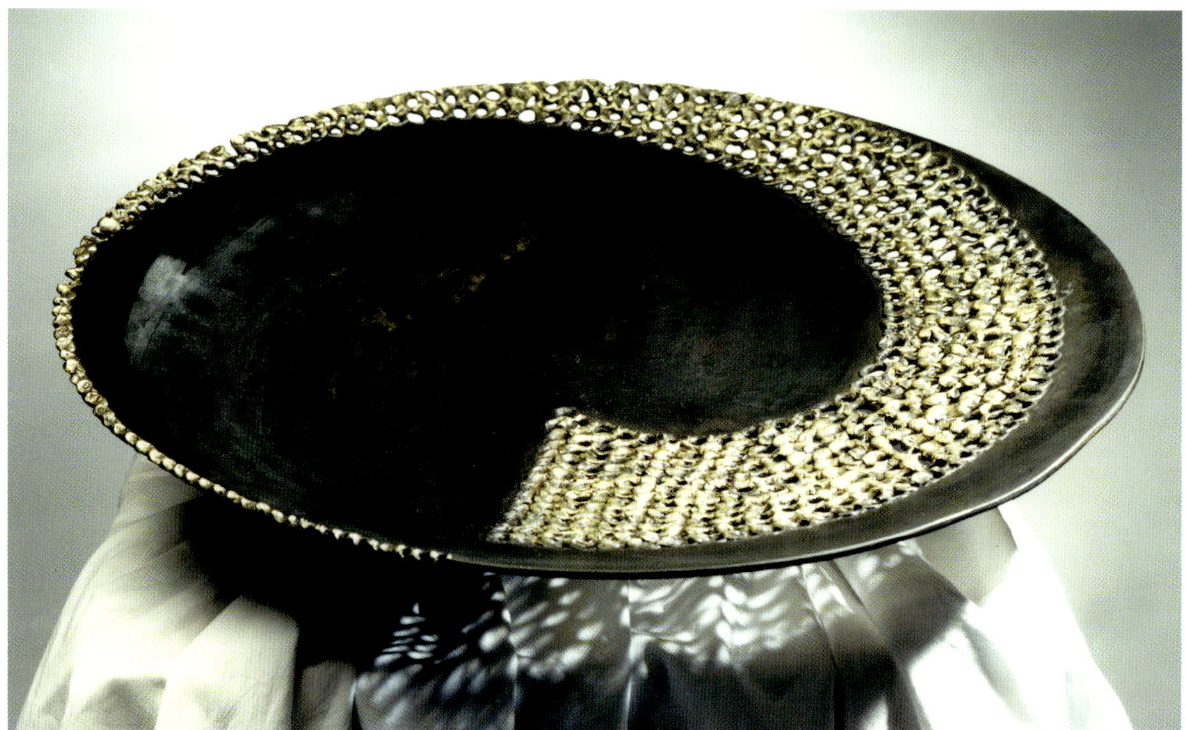

Alfred Bullermann. *Bole.* Made from iron sheet and smelted by brass and polished. *Photo, Gerald Lampe*

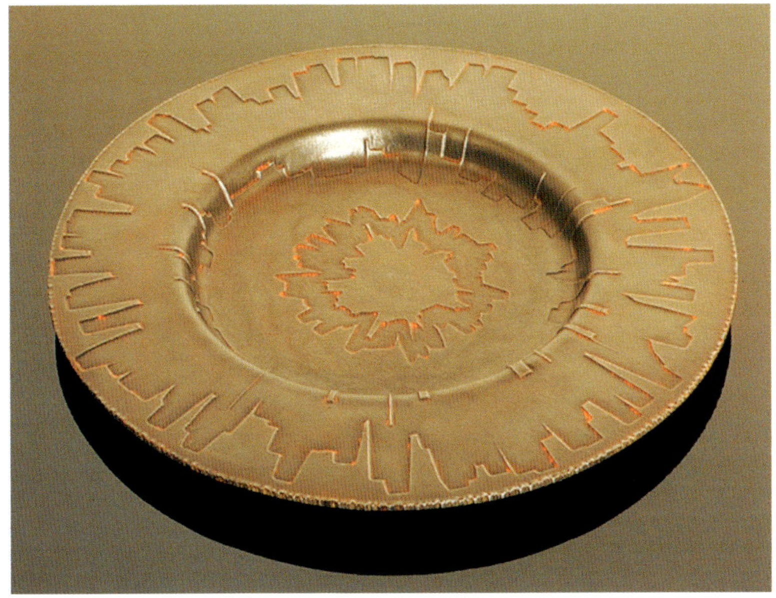

Eric A. Ryser. *Cities Plate #24*, 2008.
Forged mild steel, acid etched. 13" x 1".
Photo, Chris Bendet

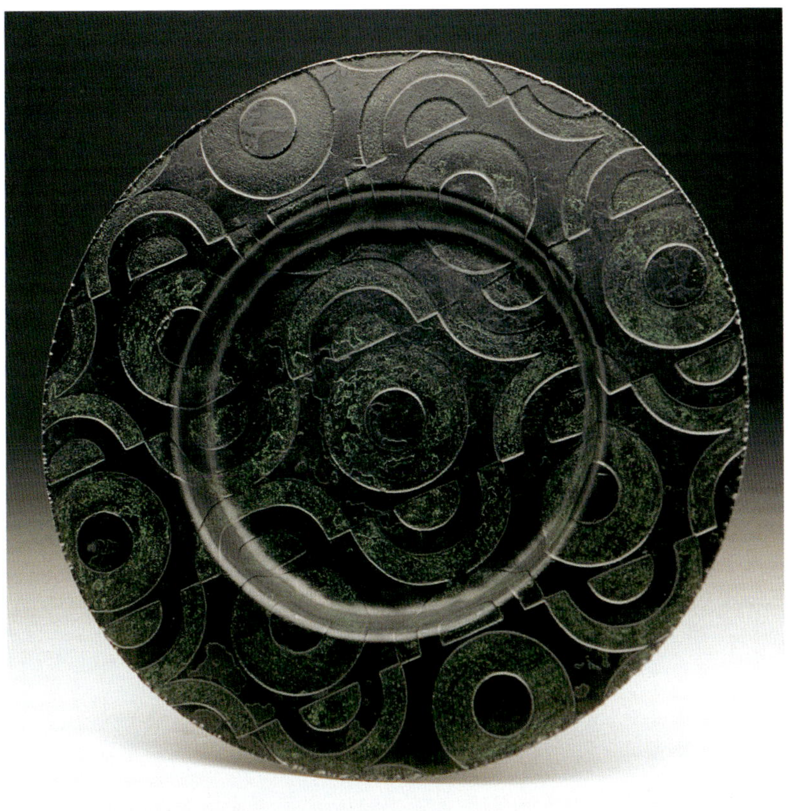

Eric A. Ryser. *Pattern Plate #5*, 2007. Forged mild steel, acid etched. 13" x 1". *Photo, Chris Bendet*

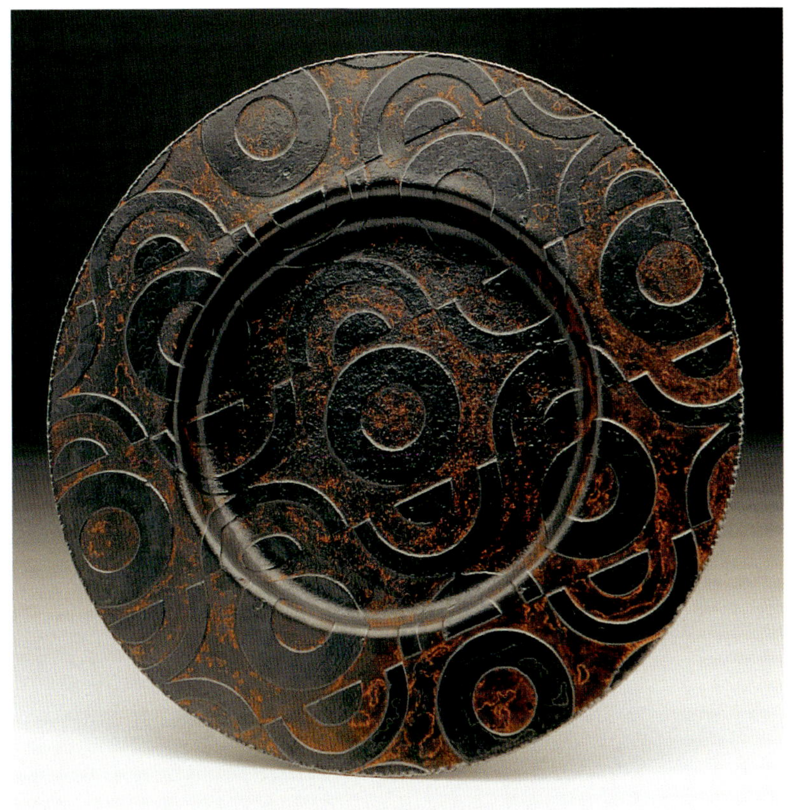

Eric A. Ryser. *Pattern Plate #6*, 2007. Forged mild steel, acid etched. 13" x 1". *Photo, Chris Bendet*

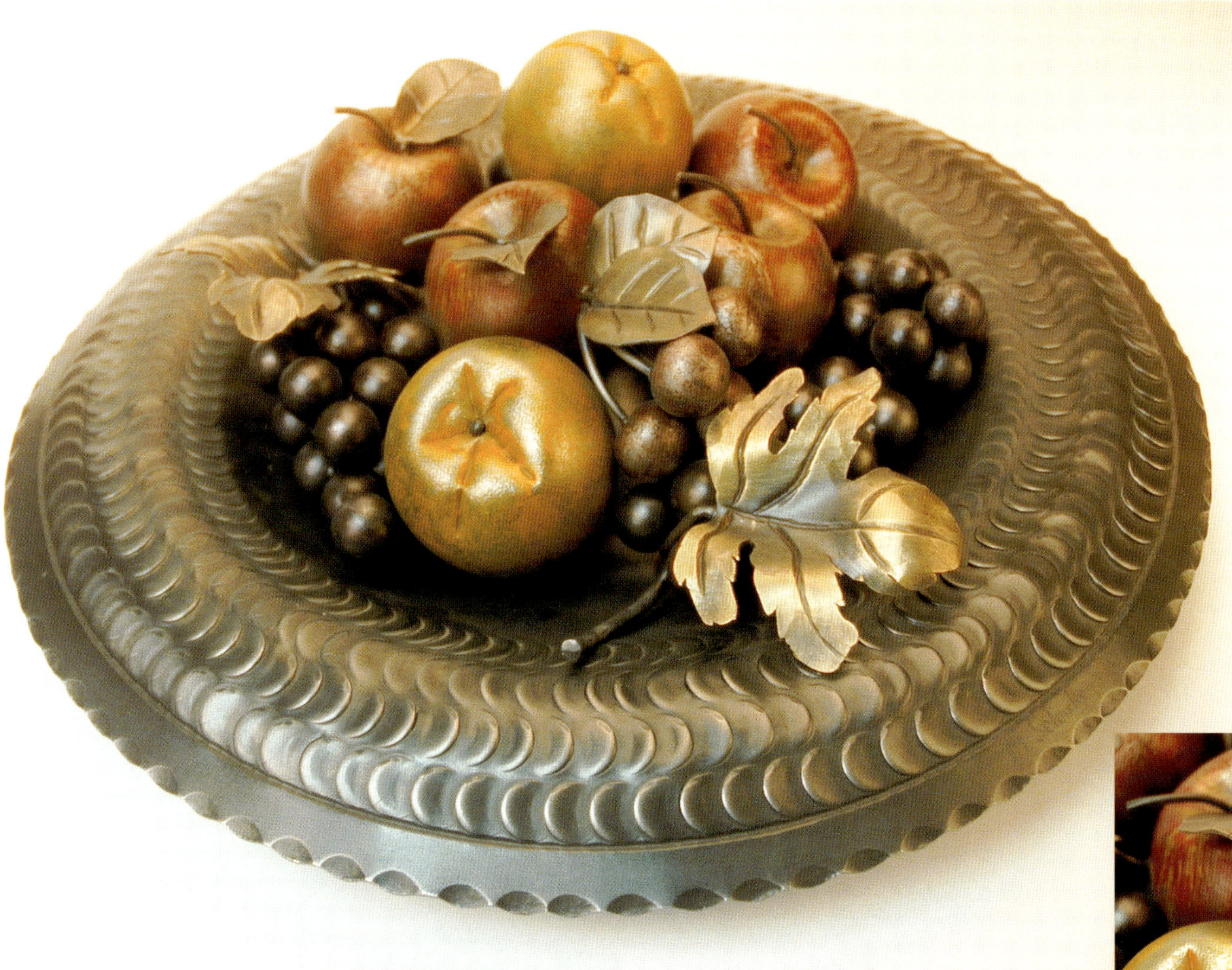

Mike Selinsky. *Fruit Bowl*. Forged mild steel with pigmented wax finishes, 18" diameter. Everything is made from raw materials. The bowl itself was formed on a fly press. The textures of the fruit were made as realistic as possible by using various forging techniques. *Photo, artist*

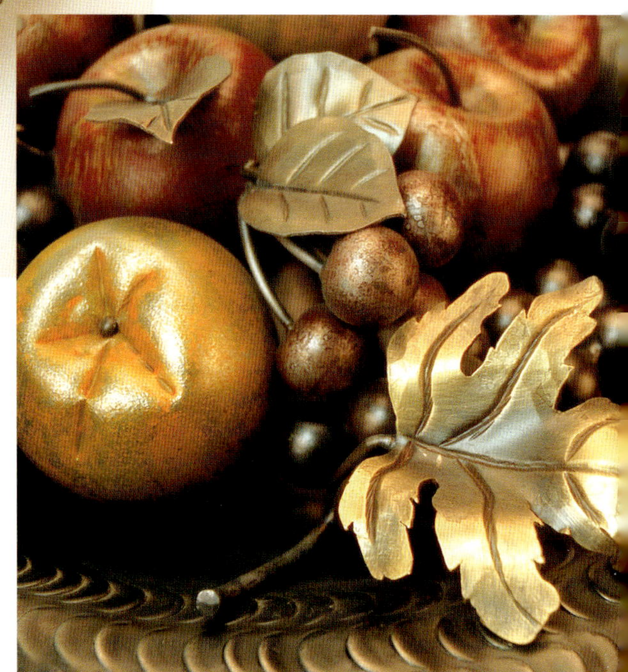

Mike Selinsky. *Fruit Bowl*. Detail. *Photo, artist*

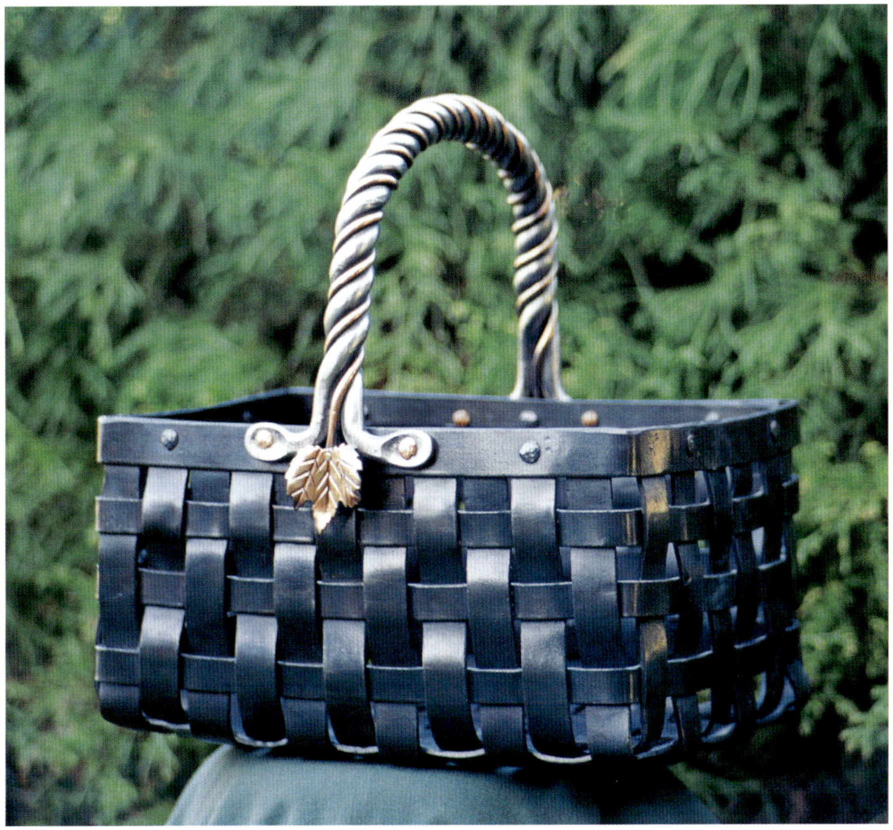

Ky Green. *Zero Calorie Basket*. Forged steel, stainless steel, copper. 13" x 10" x 7.5", 15" to the top of the handle. Woven from one inch by one-eighth steel mild steel. The handle consists of two twisted half inch diameter 316 stainless steel round bars with two quarter inch copper rods following the helix of the twist. Forged copper leaves complete the handle. The handle is held in place with copper rivets. The weight is 21.5 lbs. The basket is flame blackened and waxed; the handle is buffed to a satin finish. Titled, *Zero Calorie Basket*; "You can't put more in it than you work off carrying." *Photo, artist*

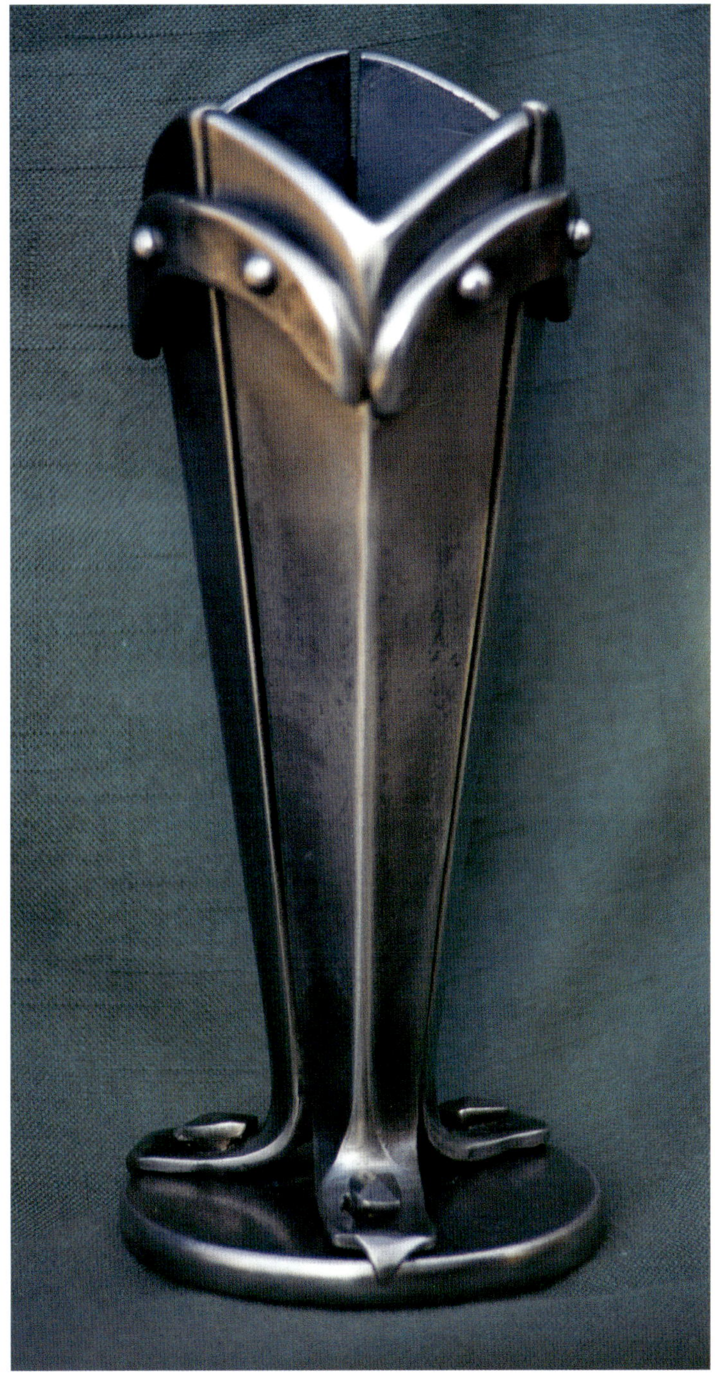

Ky Green. *Missy's Peace*. Forged steel, 4" x 9". Forged angle iron uprights, hand forged steel disks for the base, three four faced square head rivets fasten the uprights to the base, round rivets hold the top straps to the uprights. Brushed and waxed. *Photo, artist*

Maegan E. Crowley. *Alien Pod*, 2003. Forged and fabricated steel. 24" x 24" x 42". *Photo, Dominic Episcipo*

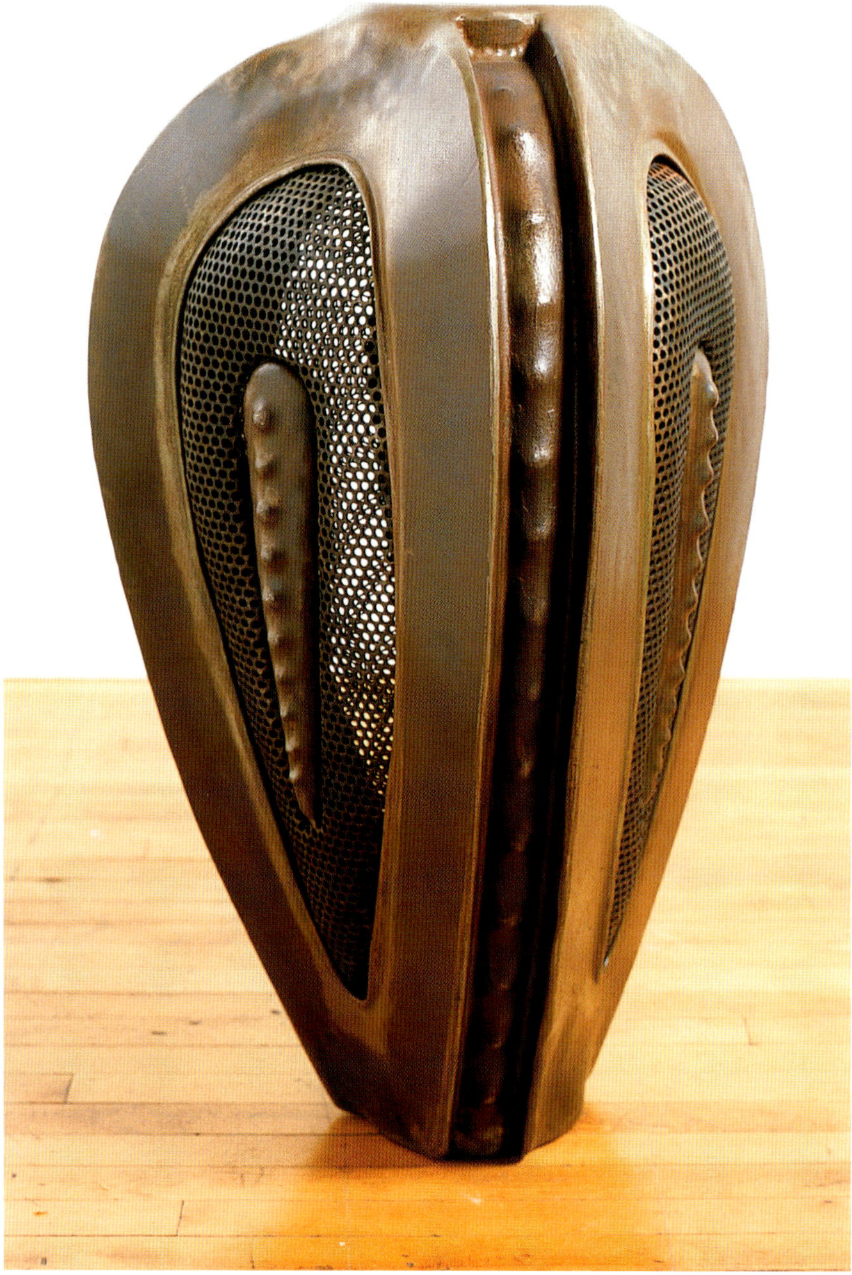

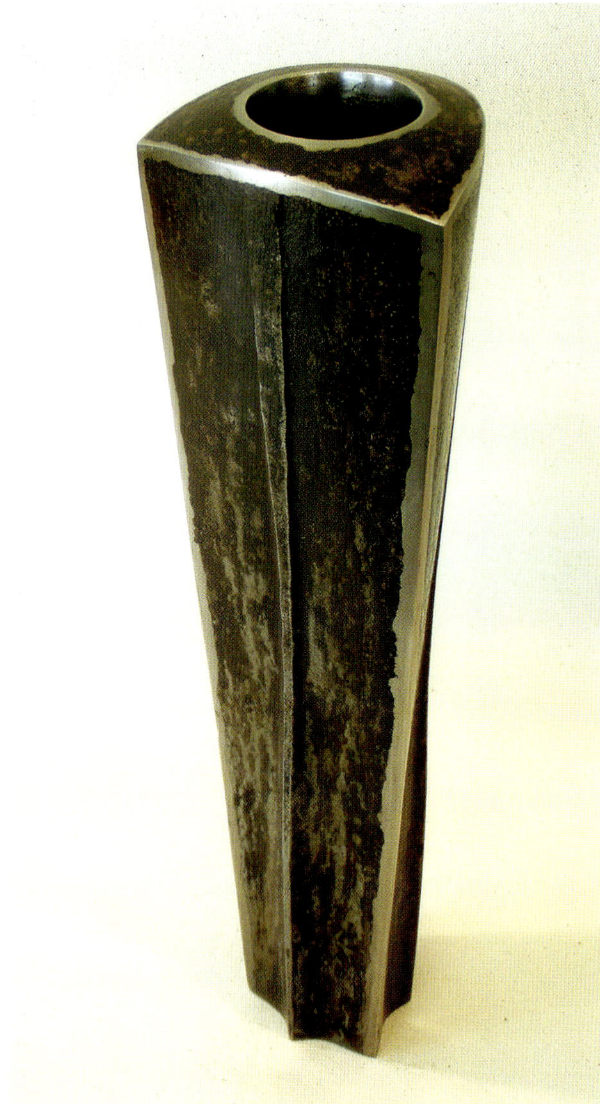

Dereck Glaser. *Austier.* Forged steel, fabricated with stainless steel. 3" x 3" x 13" inches, rust patina. *Photo, artist*

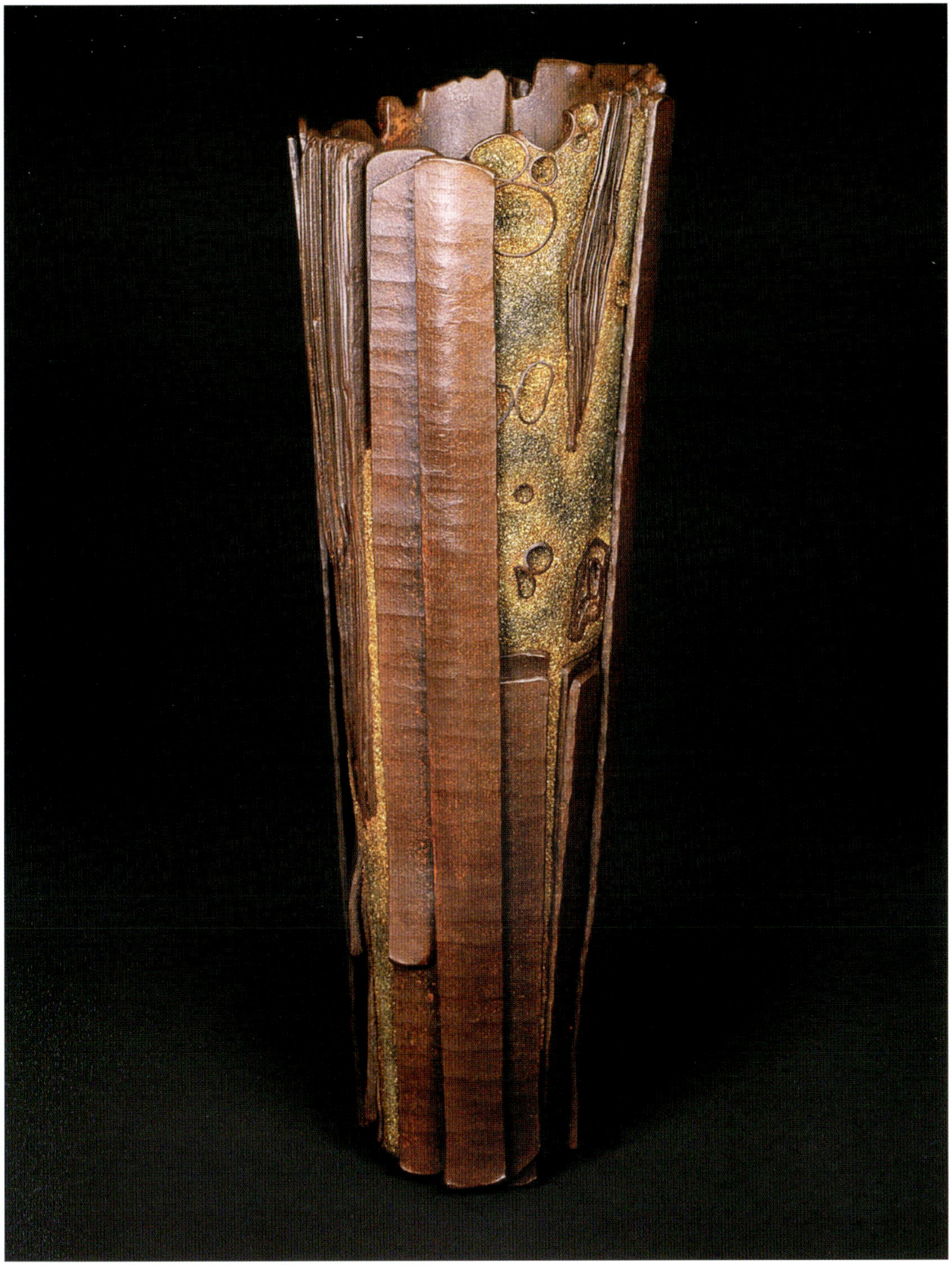

Nathan Blank. *Untitled.* Sculptural vessel. Steel and concrete. 35" x 11" x 11". Forged steel with concrete, colored with patinas and masonry dyes. *Photo, artist*

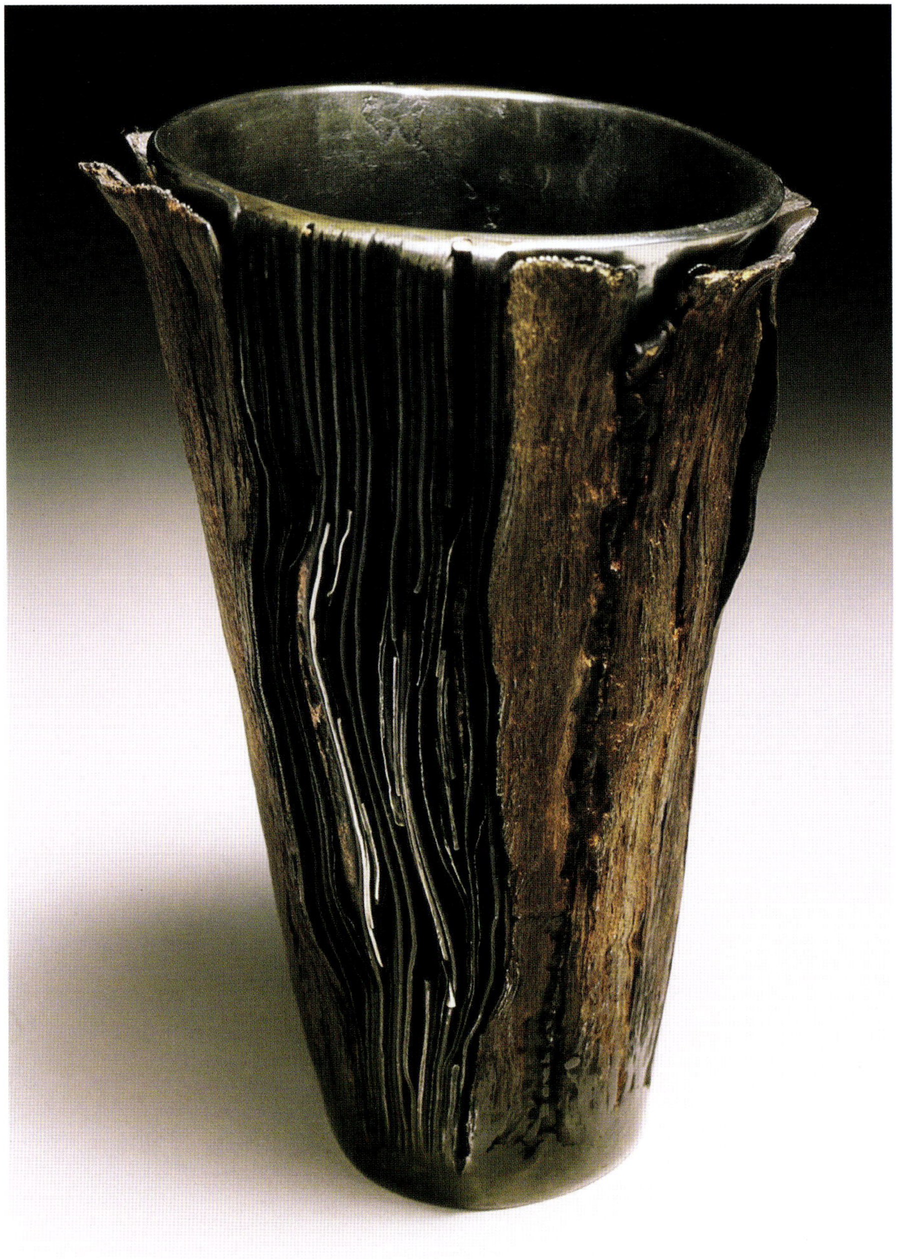

Nathan Blank. *Growth through Decay*. Sculptural vessel. Steel, wrought iron, sterling silver, and copper, 8" x 4" x 4". Forged and fabricated with forge welded details, finished with patinas. *Photo, artist*

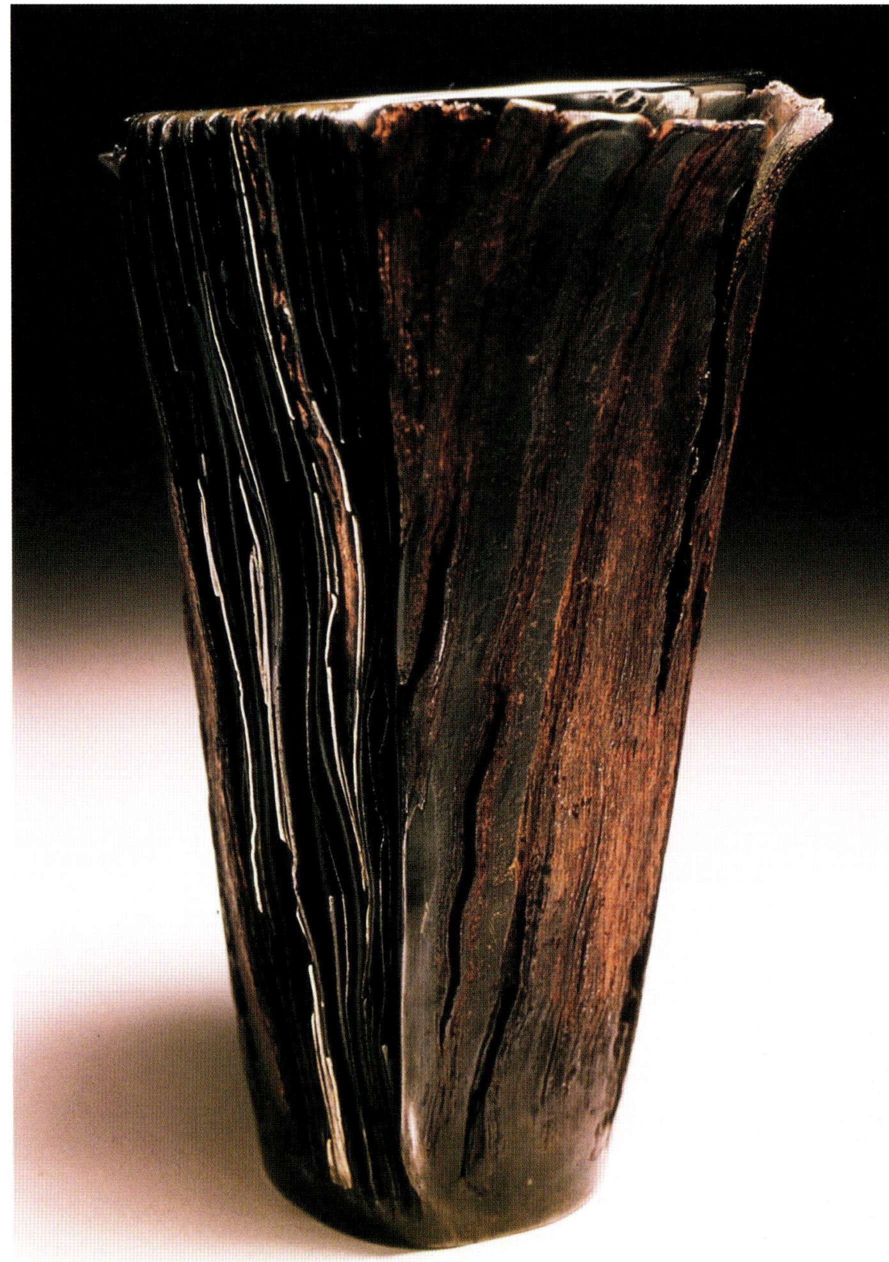

Nathan Blank. *Growth through Decay.* Back view. *Photo, artist*

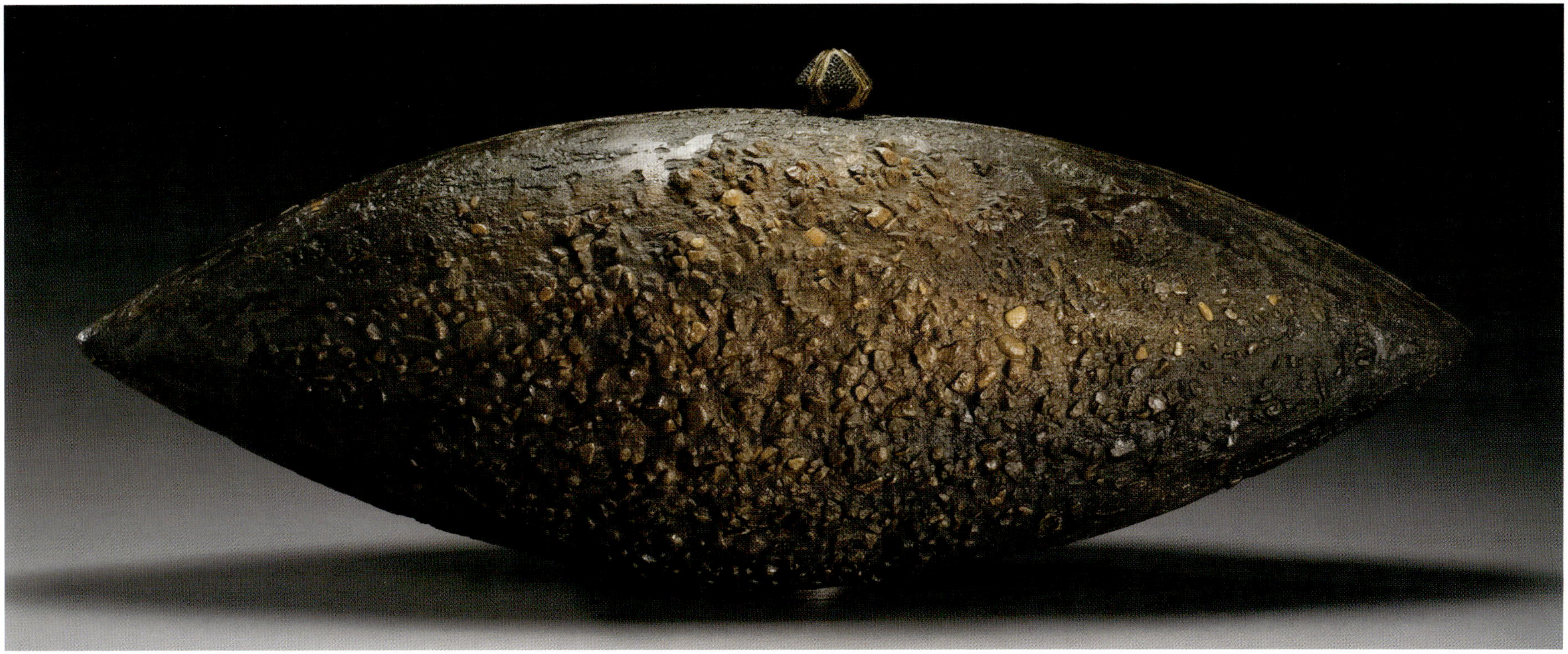

Nathan Blank. *Petraea.* Steel, wrought iron, and concrete. 38" x 12" x 12". Forge welded and fabricated steel details, hollow constructed concrete, colored with patinas and masonry dyes. *Photo, Tom Mills*

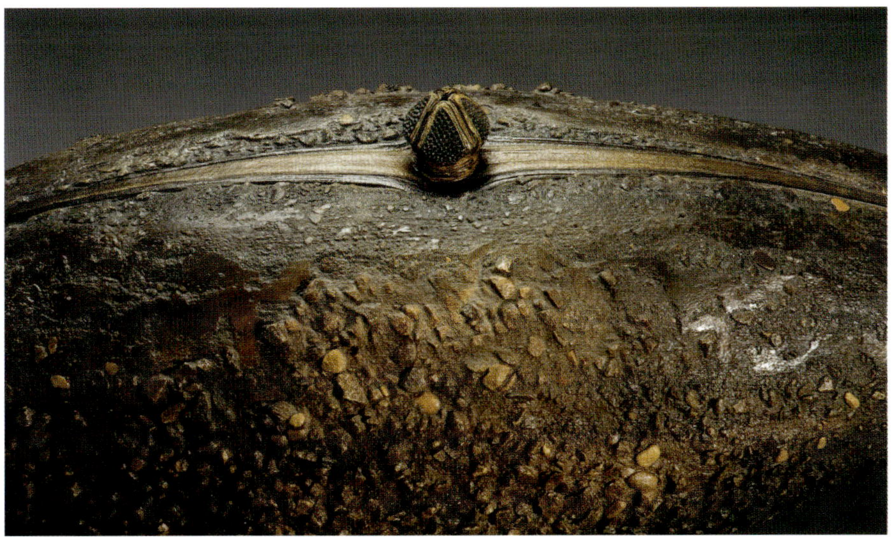

Nathan Blank. *Petraea.* Detail of lid. The lid was forged, chiseled, and chased. *Photo, Tom Mills*

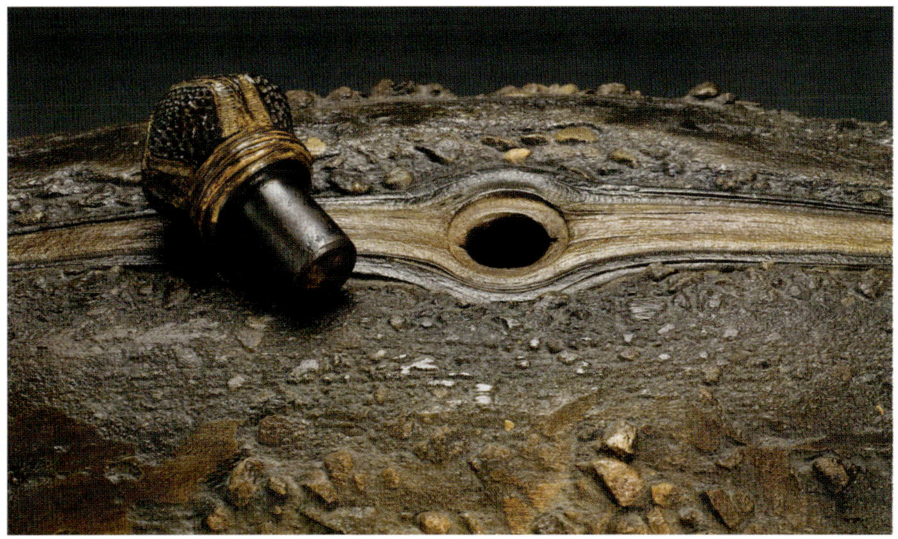

Nathan Blank. *Petraea*. Detail of lid opened. *Photo, Tom Mills*

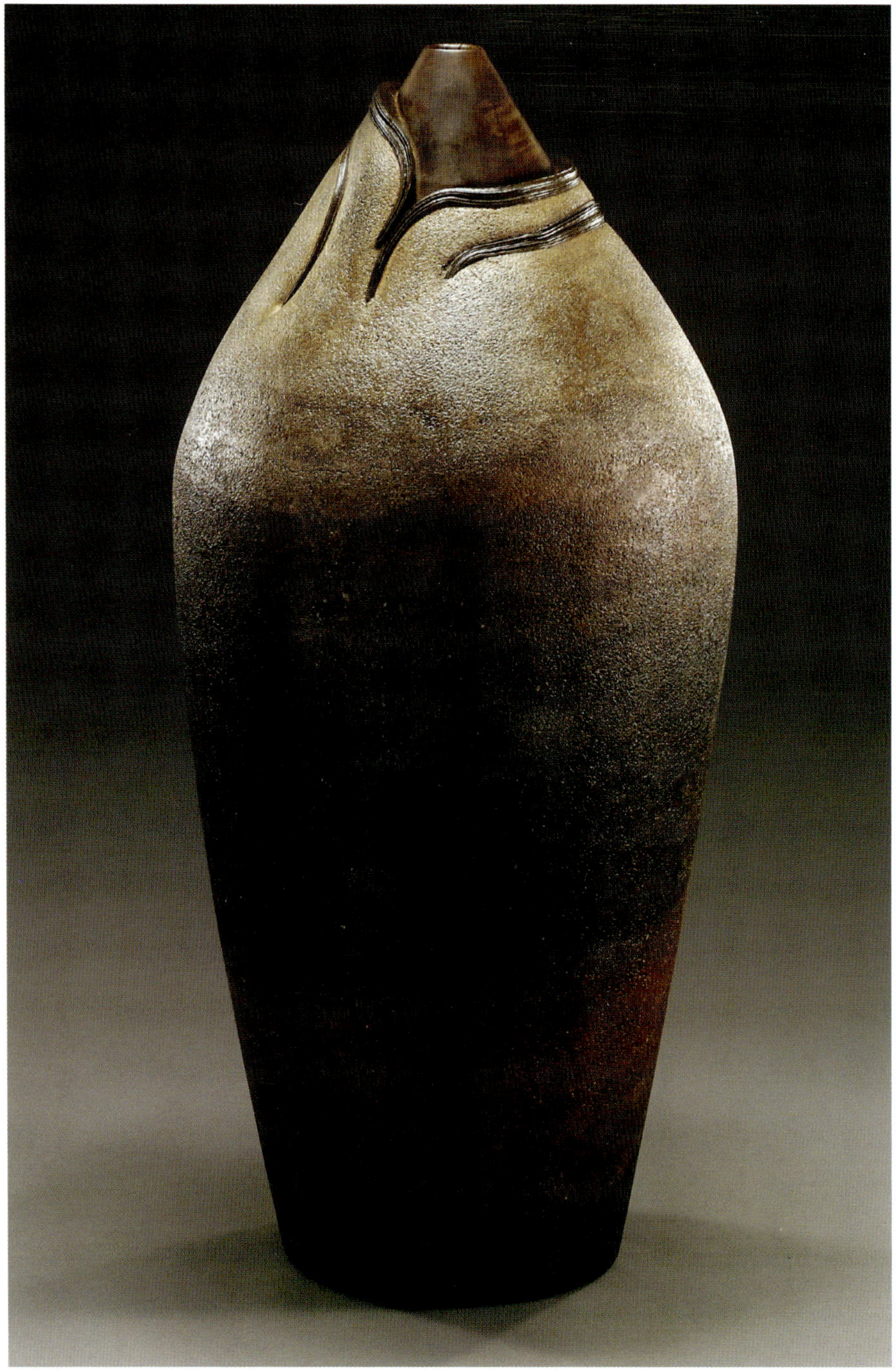

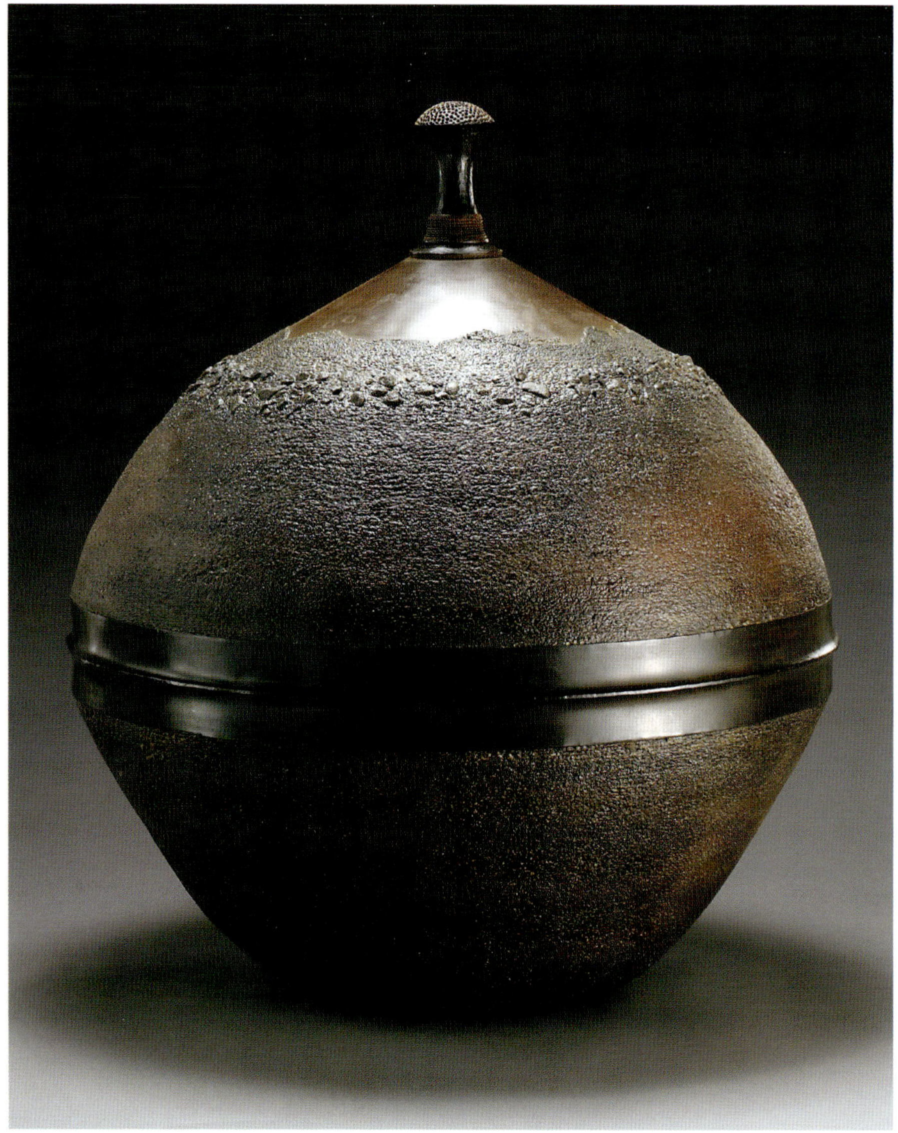

Nathan Blank. *Terra.* Sculptural vessel. Steel and concrete. 36" x 32" x 32". Forged and fabricated steel details, hollow constructed concrete, colored with patinas and masonry dyes. *Photo, Tom Mills*

Nathan Blank. *Lithos.* Sculptural vessel. Steel and concrete. 39" x 18" x 18". Forge welded and fabricated steel details, hollow constructed concrete, colored with patinas and masonry dyes. *Photo, Tom Mills*

John Rais. *Propped up7*, 2005. Forged steel, patina paint. 12" x 11" x 8". *Photo, D. James Dee*

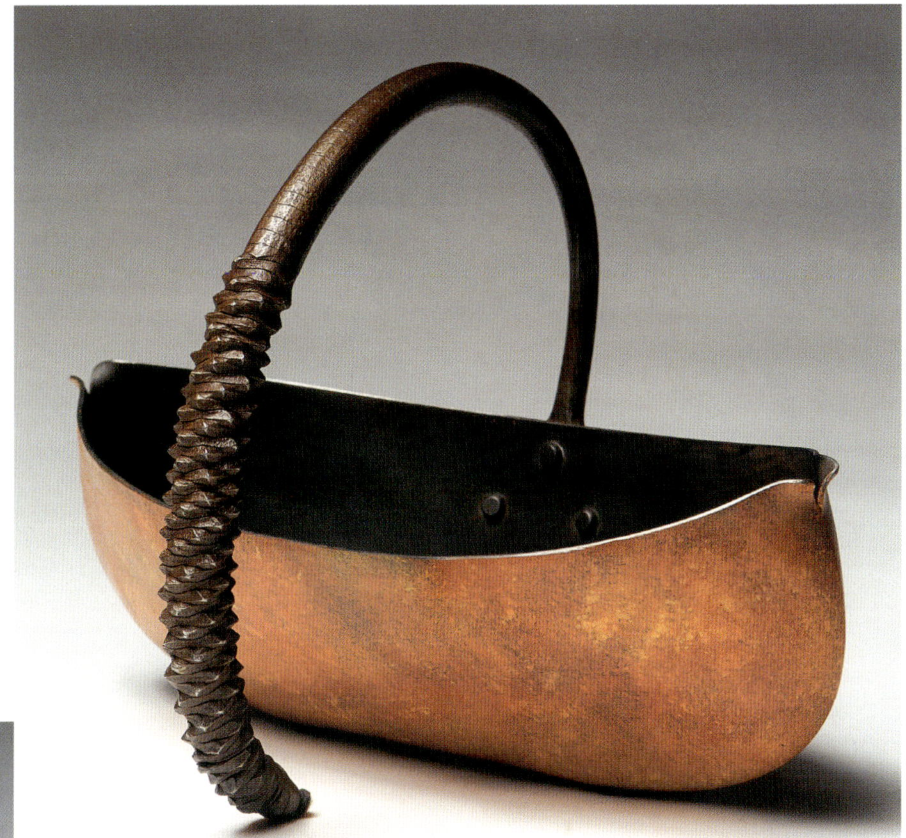

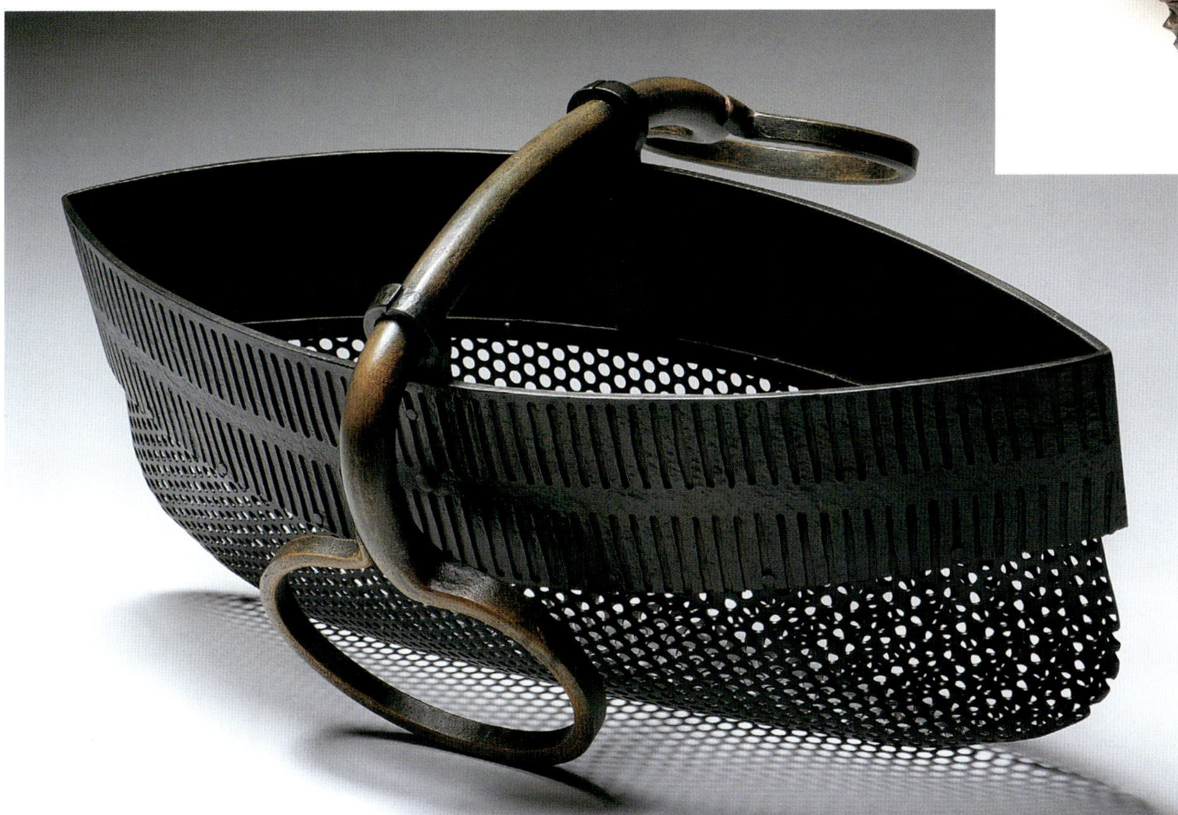

John Rais. *Sifting Sunlight,* 2003. Forged steel, patina paint. 16" x 21" x 18". *Photo, D. James Dee*

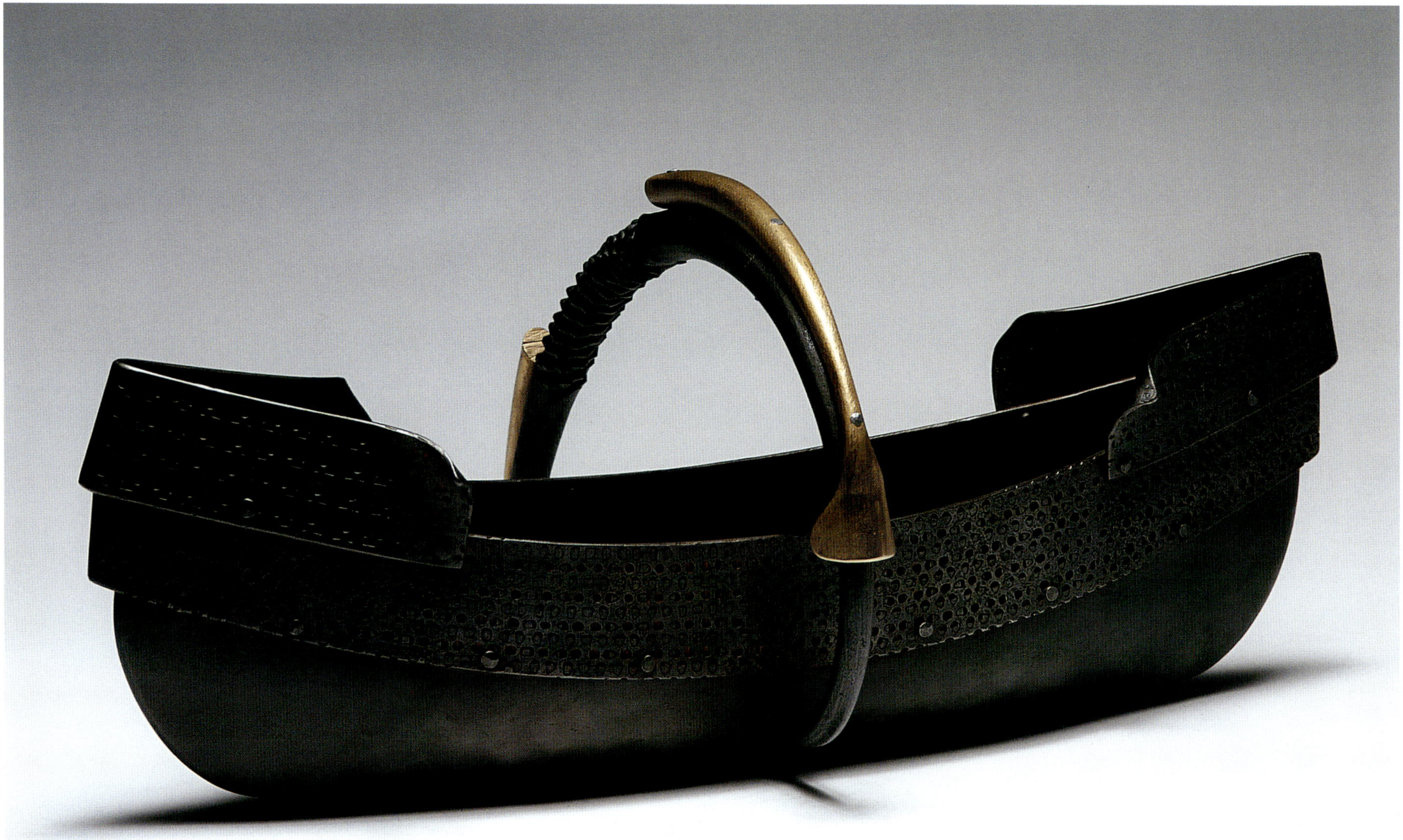

John Rais. *Water Mark*, 2004. Forged steel and brass. 10" x 22" x 14". *Photo, D. James Dee*

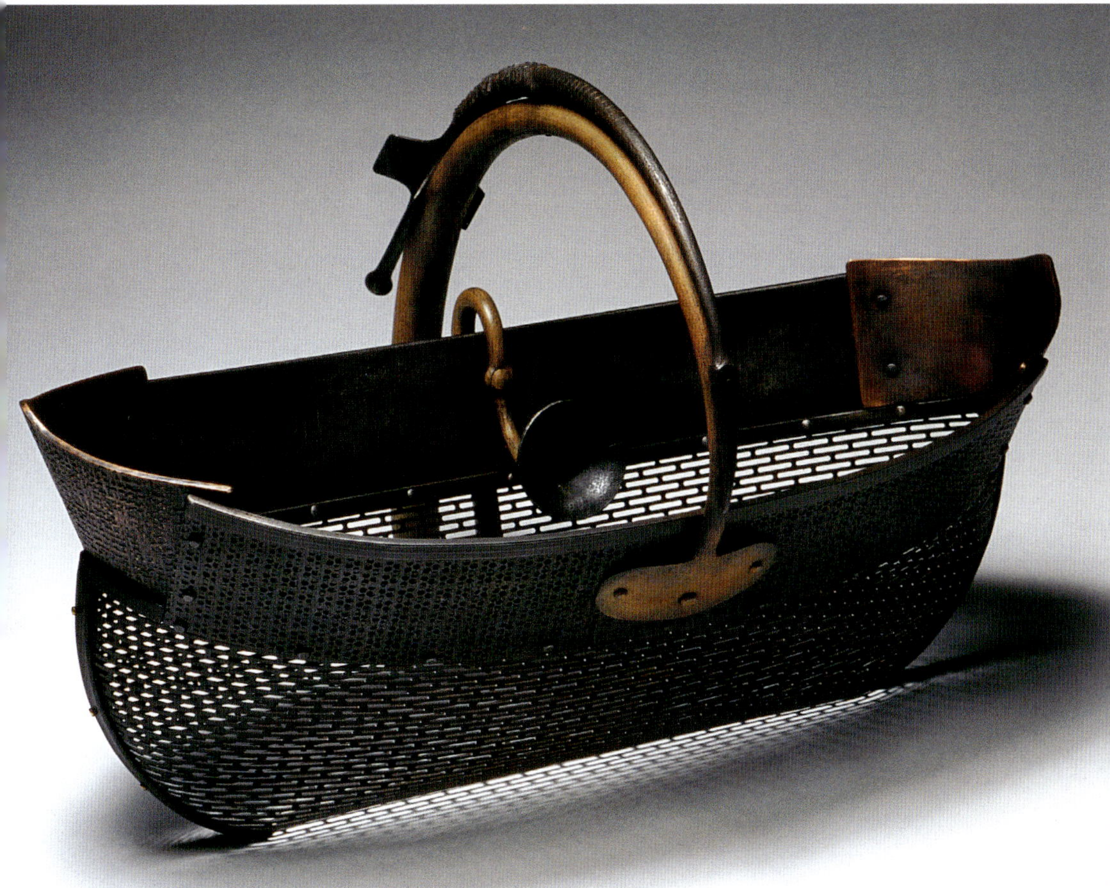

John Rais. *Hard Leisure*, 2004. Steel, copper, paint patina. 22" x 30" x 18". *Photo, D. James Dee*

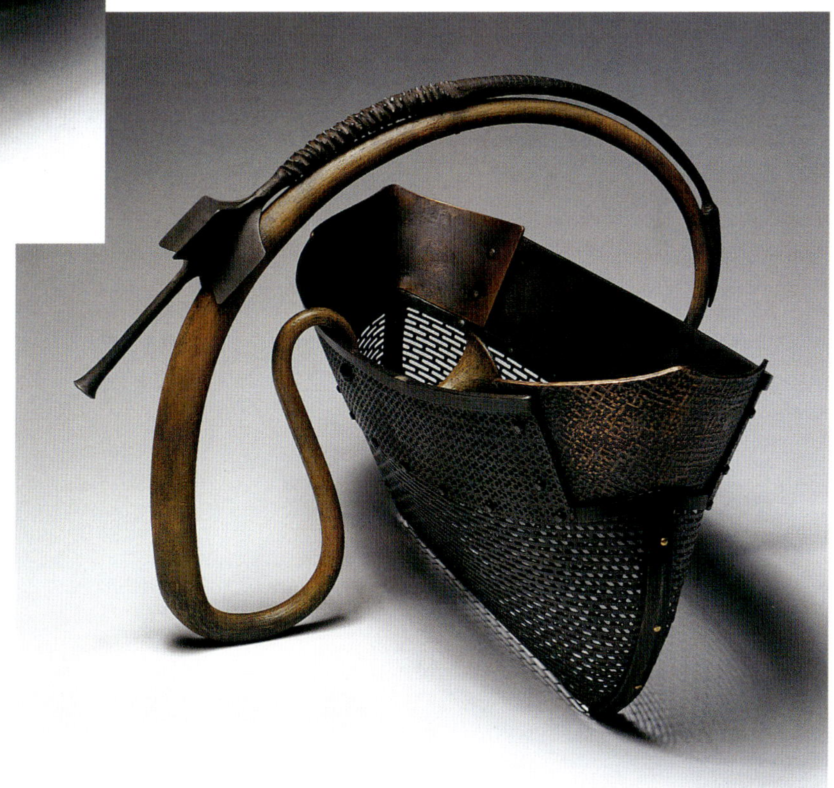

John Rais. *Hard Leisure*, 2004. Second view. *Photo, D. James Dee*

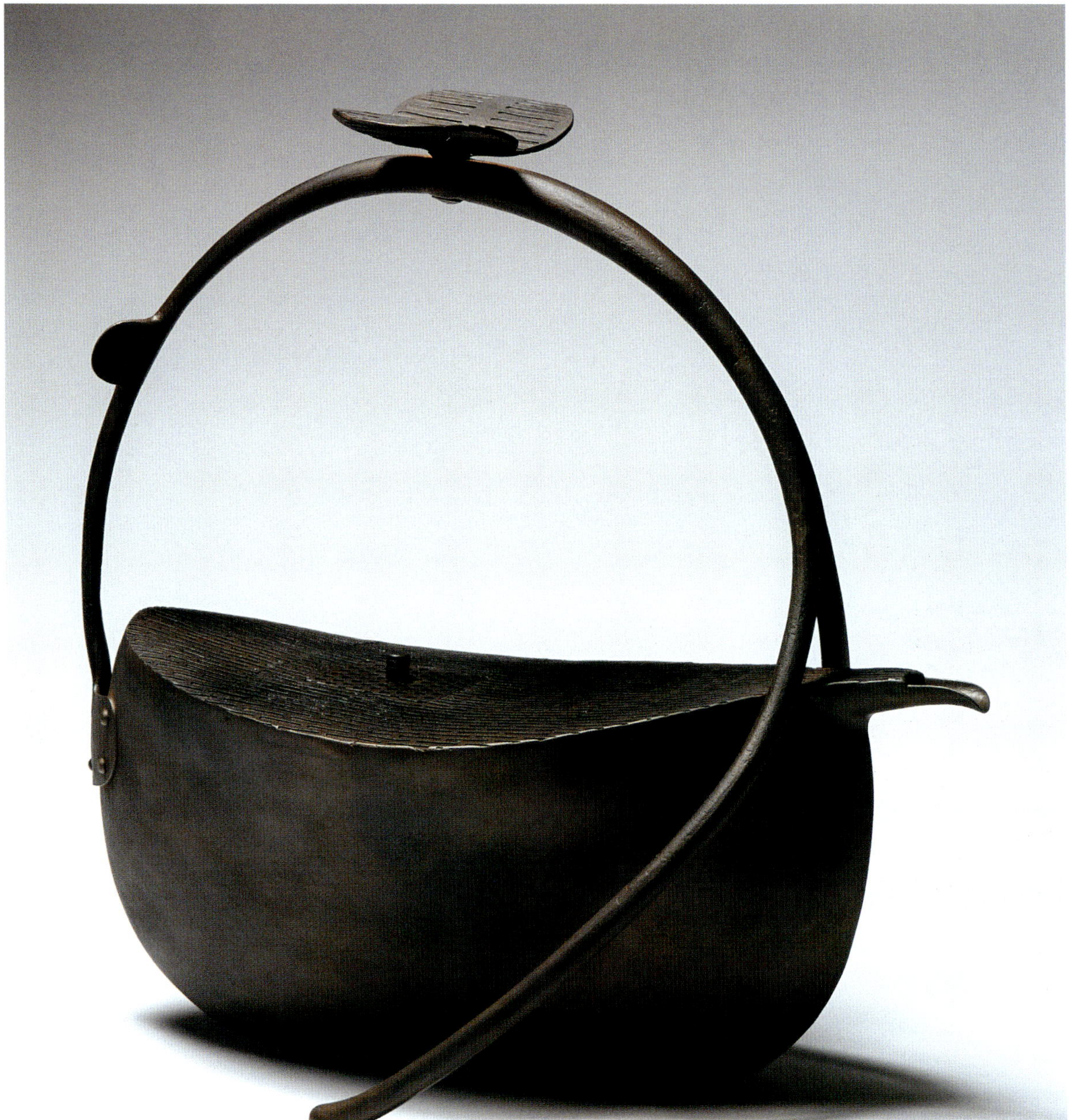

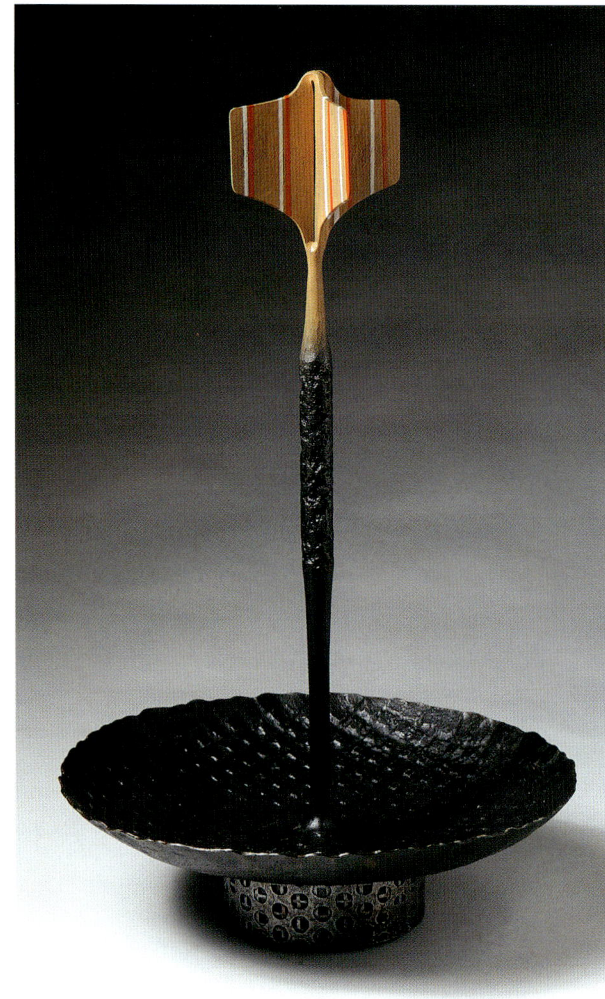

John Rais. *Sand Dart,* 2006. Forged steel, patina paint. 22" x 16" x 12". *Photo, D. James Dee*

John Rais. *Swollen Chamber*, 2003. Forged steel, patina. 24" x 22" x 10". *Photo, D. James Dee*

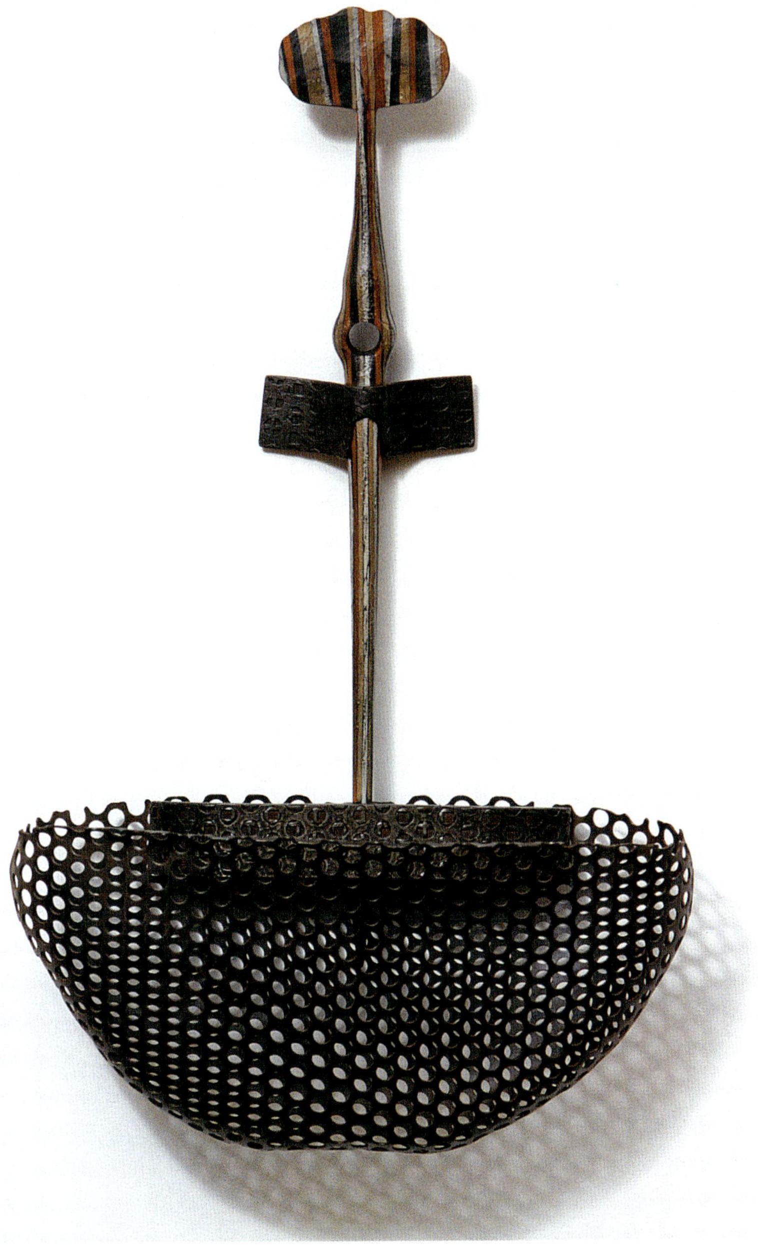

John Rais. *Piercing Sunlight*, 2007. Forged steel, patina paint. 33" x 22" x 7". *Photo, D. James Dee*

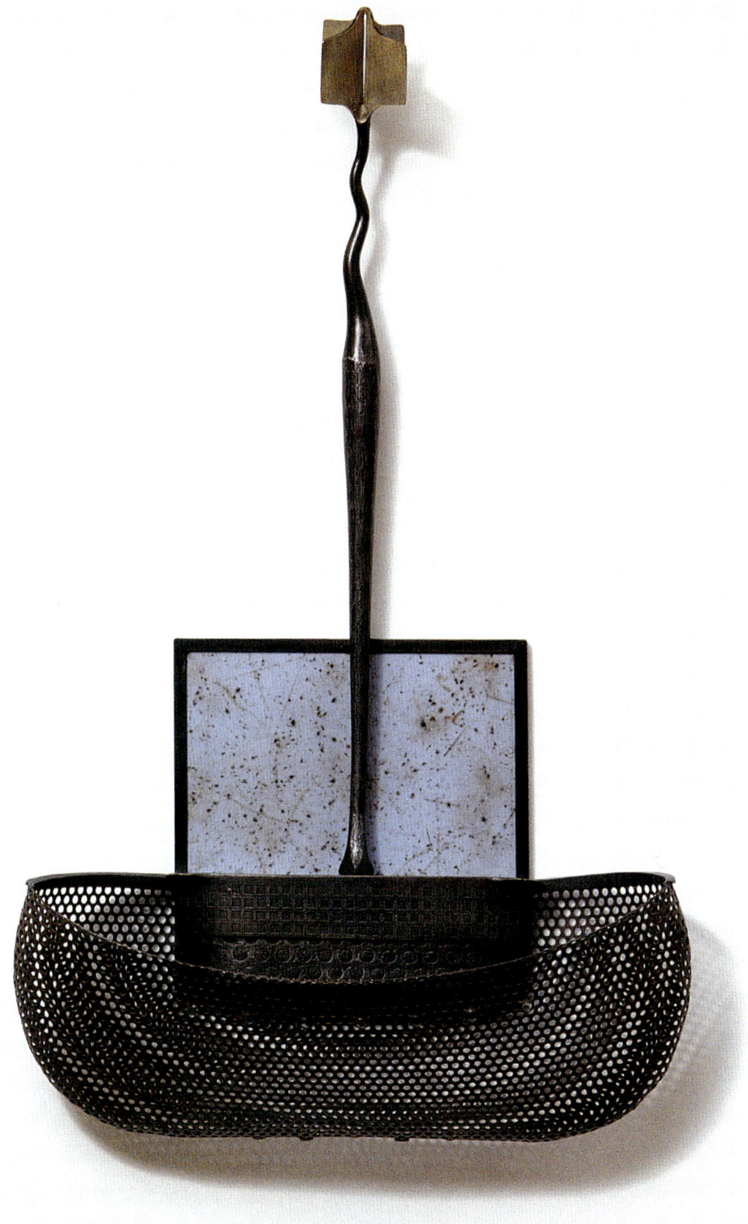

John Rais. *Disruptive Sky*, 2006. Forged and fabricated steel, patina, paint, scorched paint. 34" x 23" x 11". *Photo, D. James Dee*

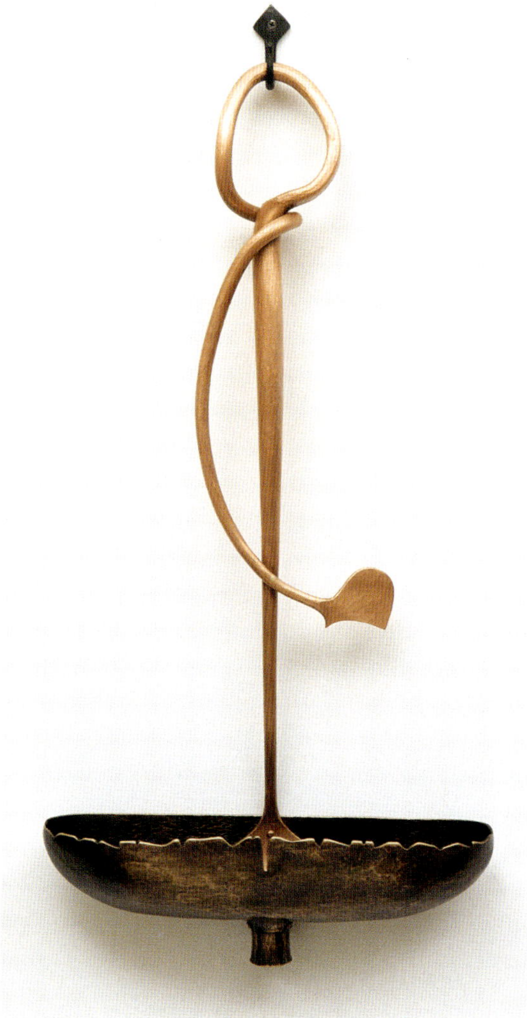

John Rais. *Drydock,* 2002. Forged copper, bronze, patina. 29" x 16" x 5". *Photo, D. James Dee*

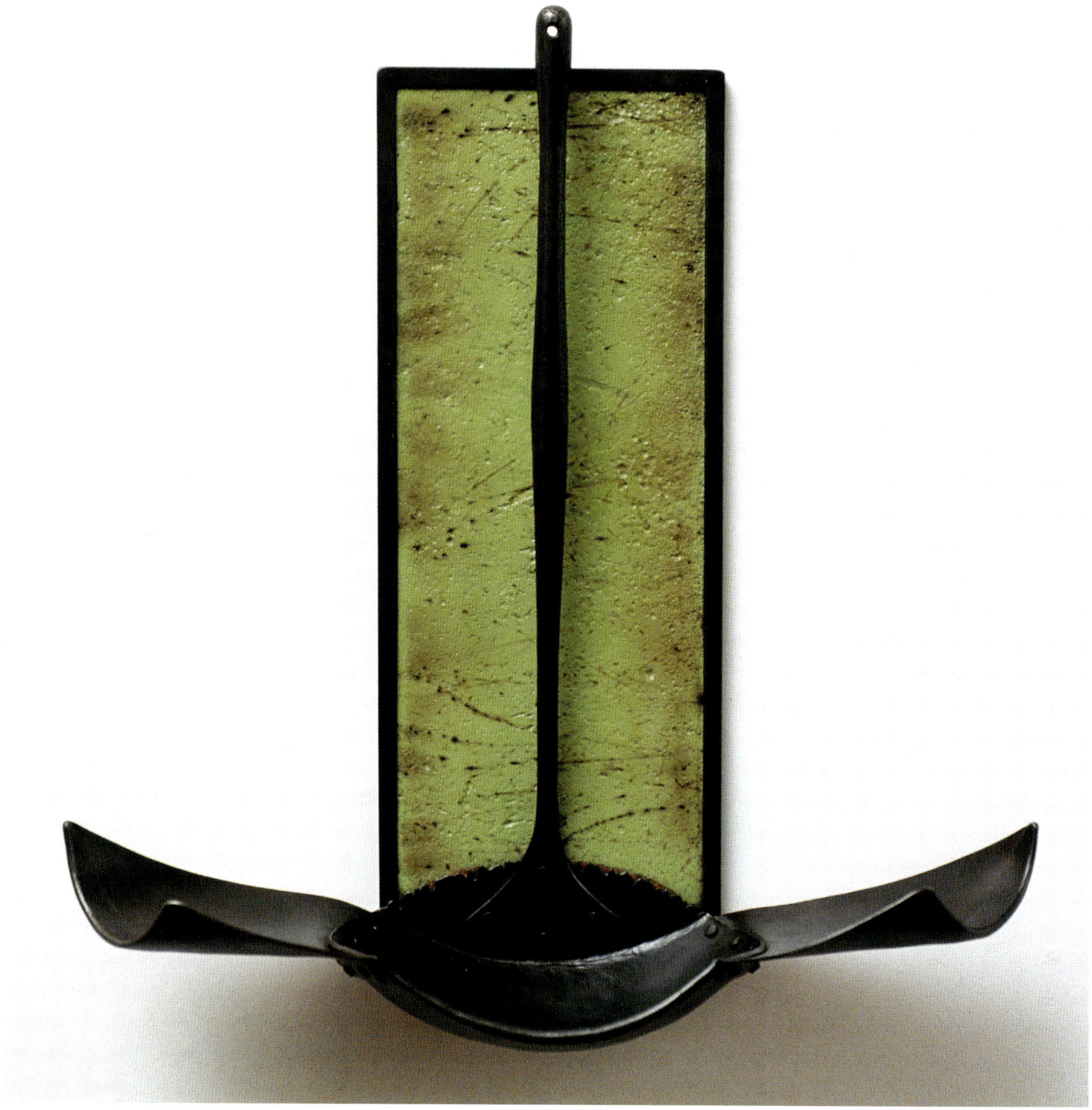

John Rais. *Scorched Field,* 2005. Steel, scorched paint. 34" x 26" x 9". *Photo, D. James Dee*

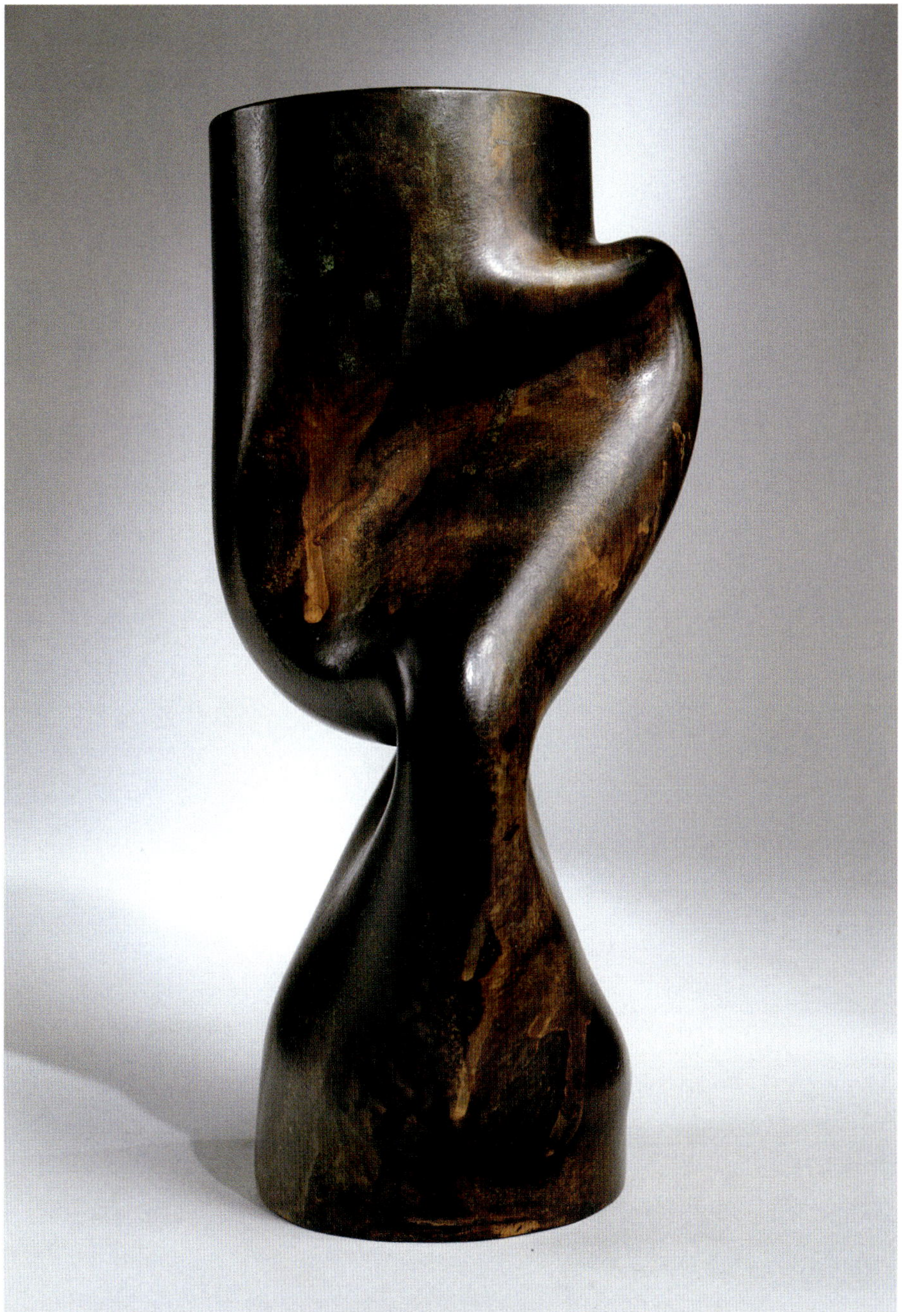

Bill Hornaday. *Steel Dancer.* Forged steel. 12.5" x 5" x 4.5". *Photo, artist*

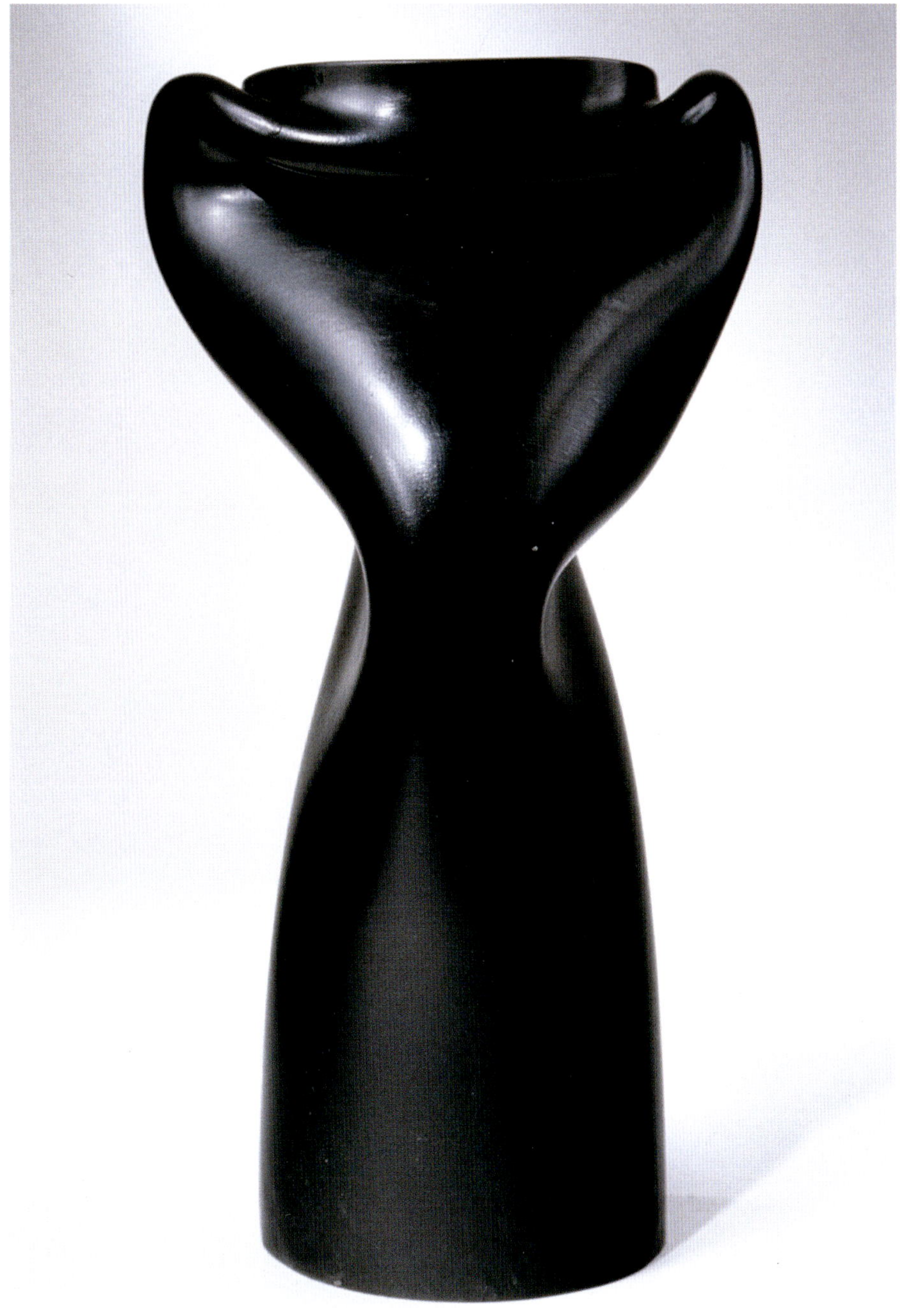

Bill Hornaday. *Black Dancer.* Forged steel, patina. 11" x 5.5" x 5.5". *Photo, artist*

Bill Hornaday. *Asian Torso.* Forged steel, patina. 6" x 2.5" x 2.5". *Photo, artist*

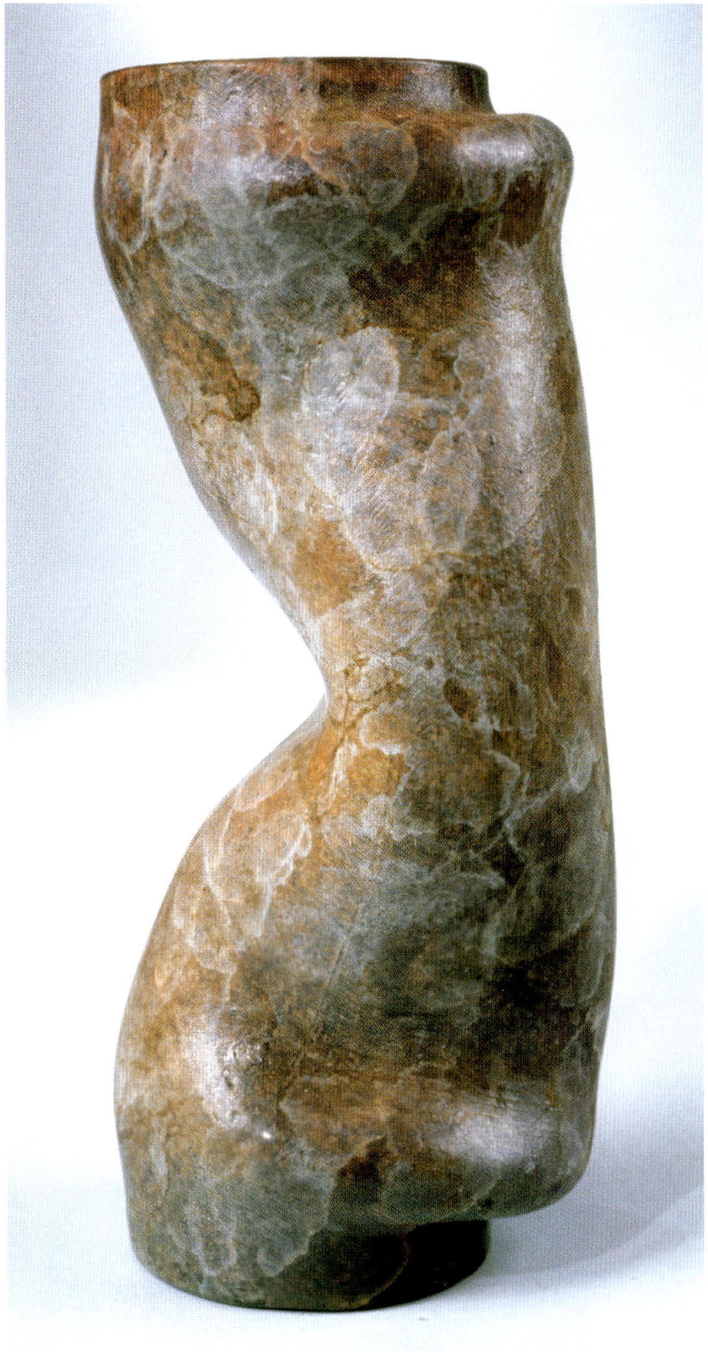

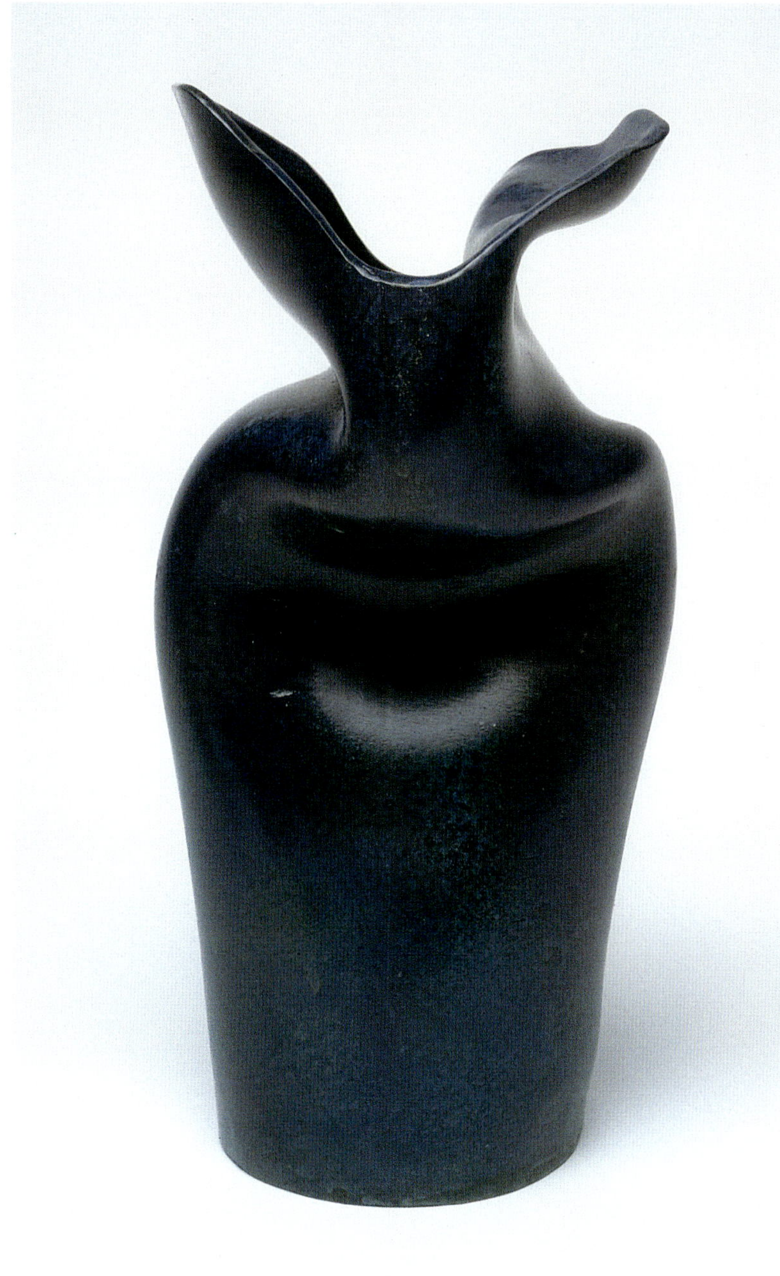

Bill Hornaday. *Blue Vessel 3.* Forged steel, patina. 12" x 4.5" x 4.5". *Photo, artist*

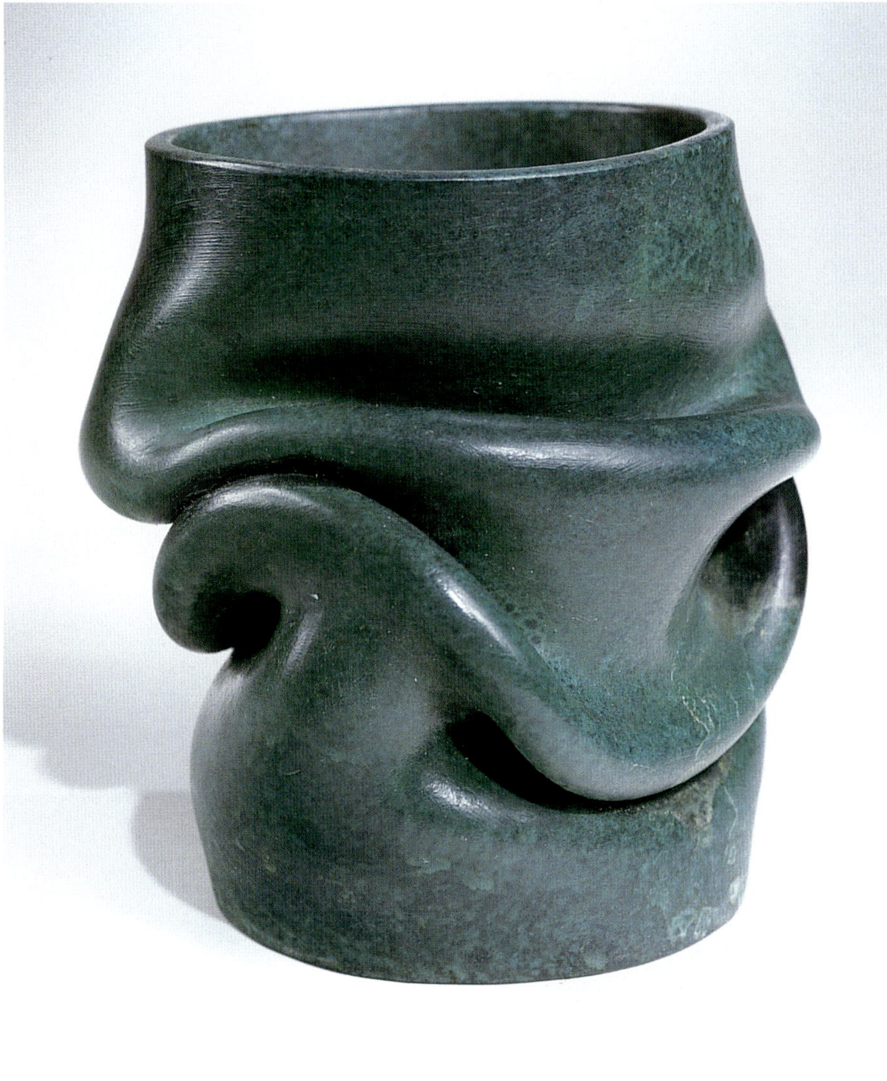

Bill Hornaday. *Forest Flower.* Forged steel, patina. 7" x 4.5" x 4.5". *Photo, artist*

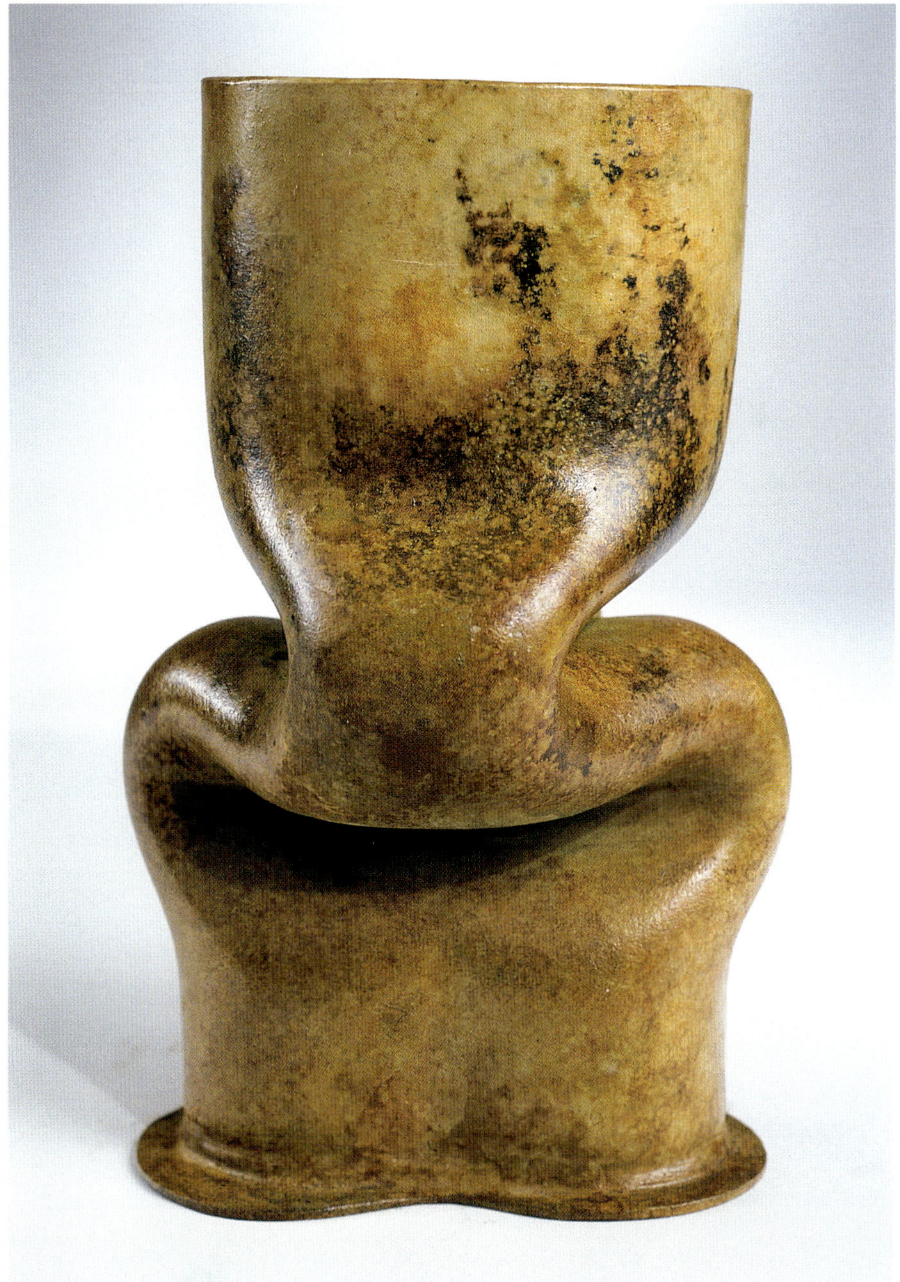

Bill Hornaday. *Mayan Vessel.* Forged steel, patina. 7.5" x 4.5" x 4.5". *Photo, artist*

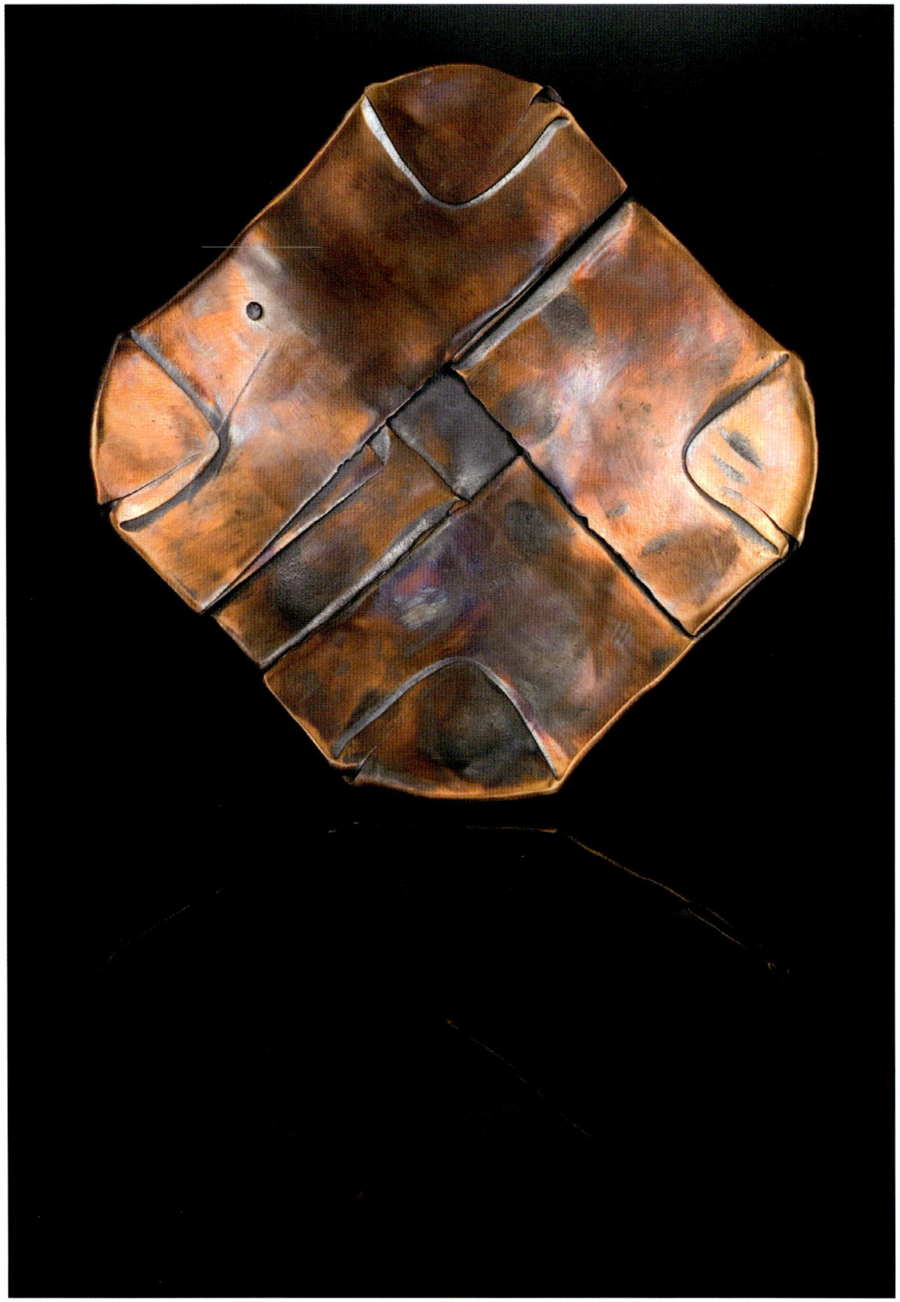

Paul Thorn. Plate. Folded stainless steel wall plate, 8" x 8". Flame patina. *Photo, Peter Kuhnlein*

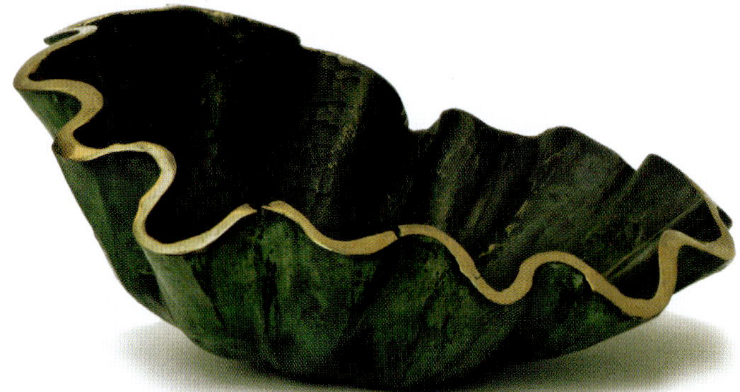

Michael Kacz-
mar. Bowl, 2000.
Forged bronze. 1
x 6". *Photo, artist*

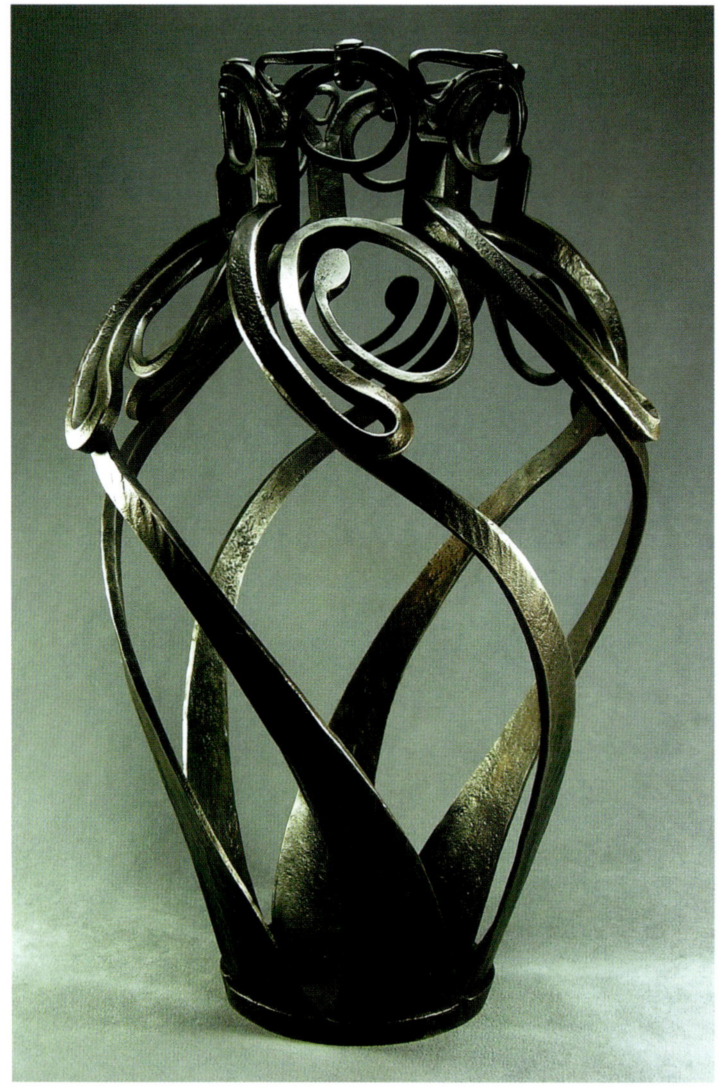

Michael Glennor
Vessel, 2008. Mil
steel. 9" d x 15"
Hand forged, pa
na, flame colorin
copper plating, a
bees wax. A study
of spatial relatior
ships, inspired
by the pottery of
George E. Ohr a
Artus Van Briggl
Photo, artist

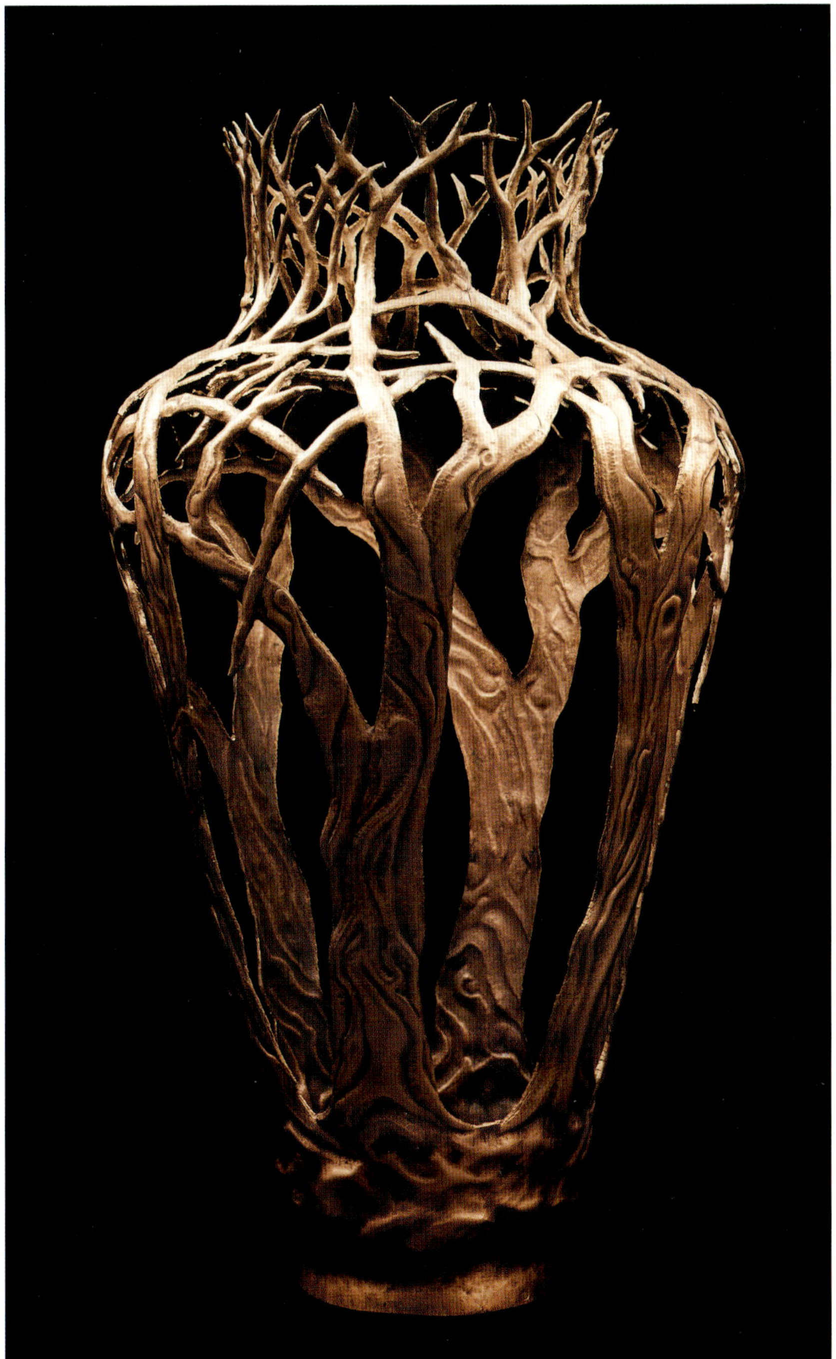

Travis Conn. *Ghost Trees,* 2006. Raised and reposed copper. 24" x 10" x 10". *Photo, artist*

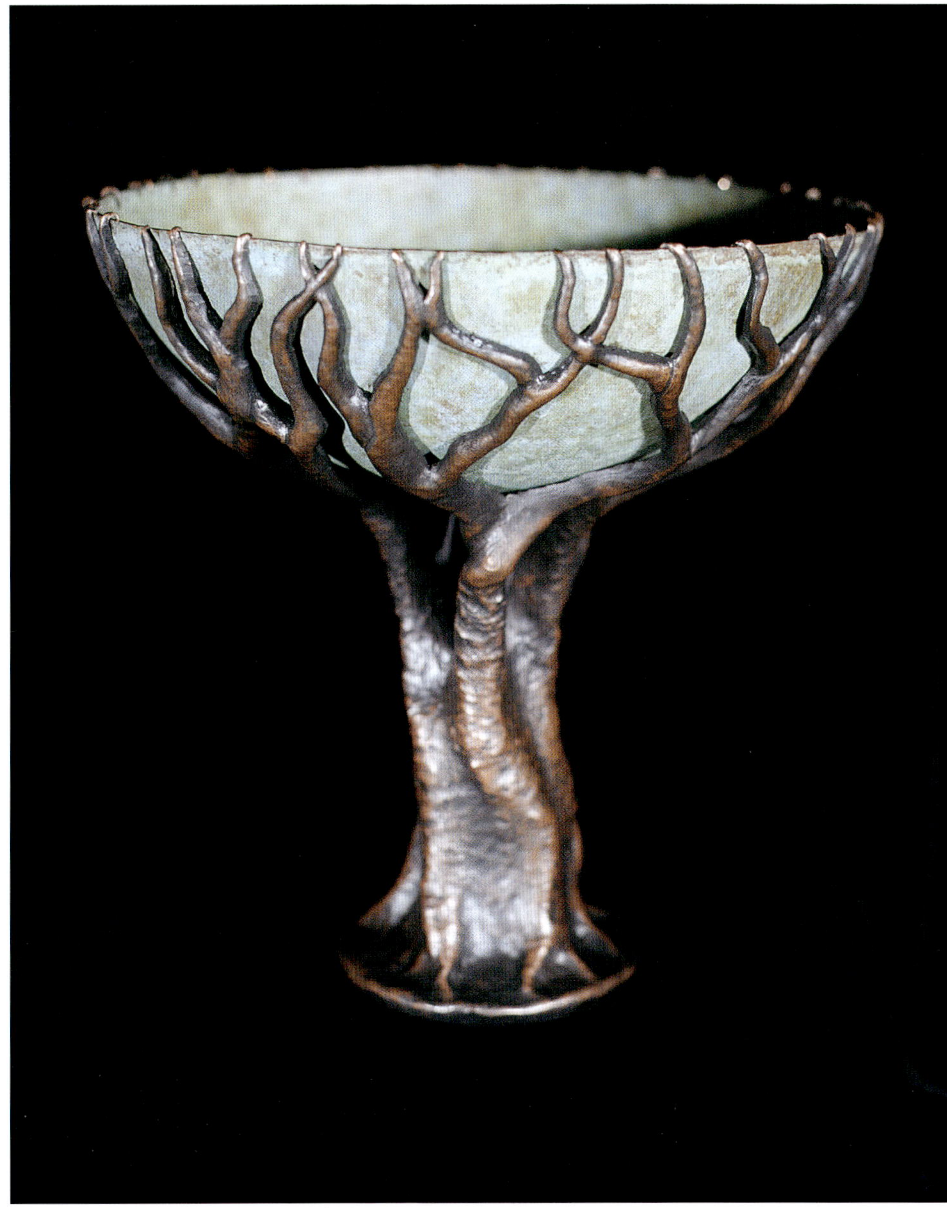

Travis Conn. *Deciduous Grail,* 2004. Raised and reposed copper. 14" x 12" x 12". *Photo, artist*

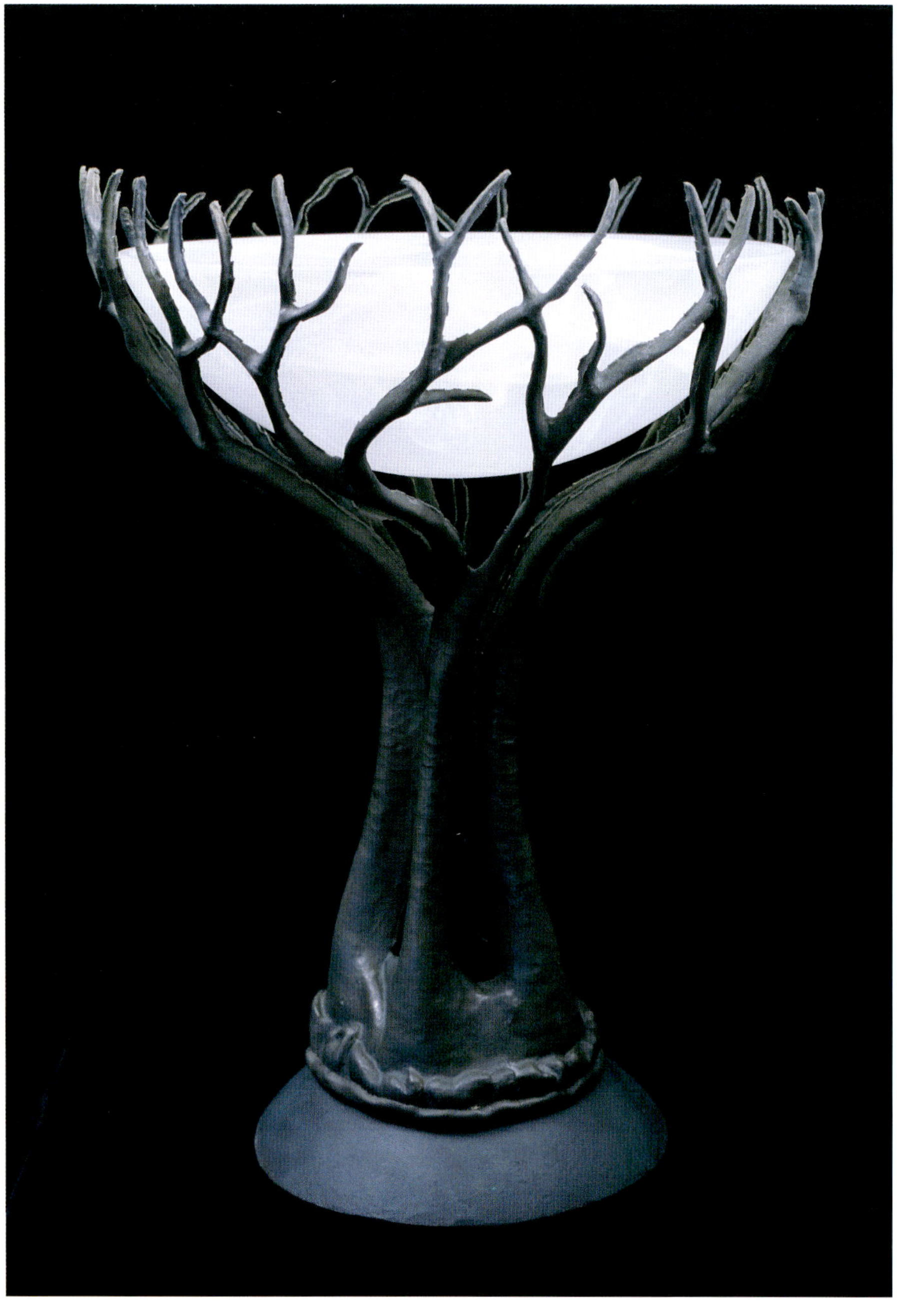

Travis Conn. *Forbidden,* 2007. Raised and reposed copper, found glass. 15" x 10" x 10". *Photo, artist*

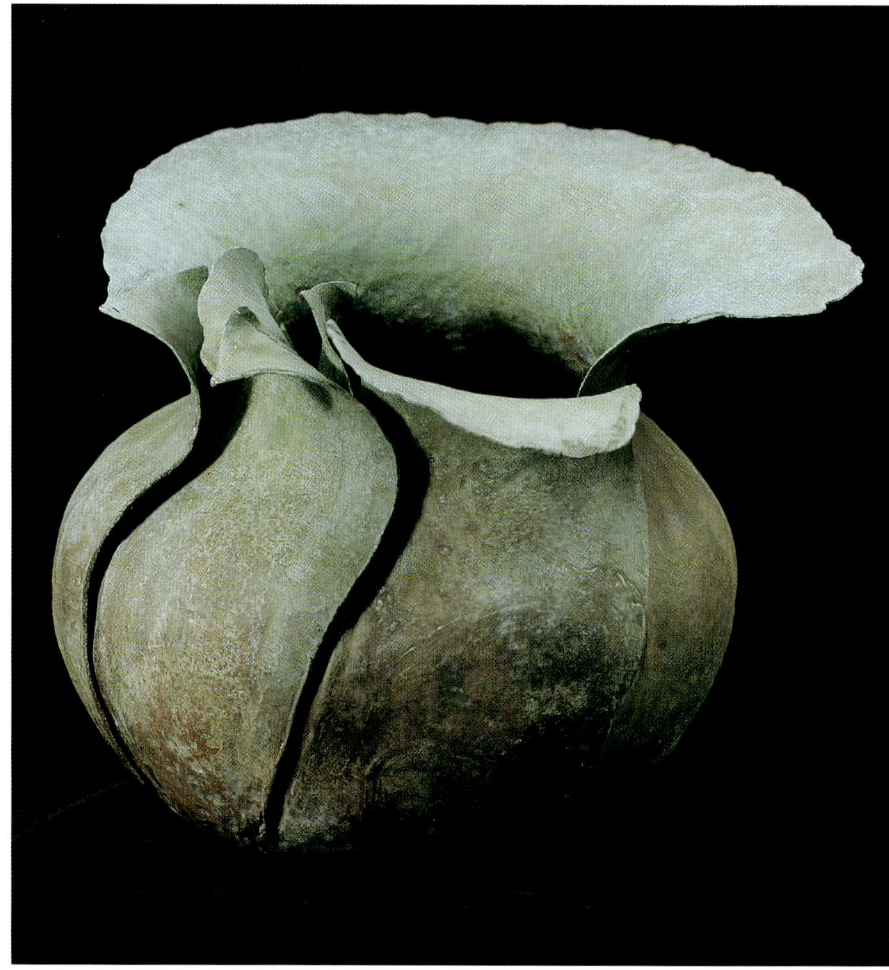

Travis Conn. *Folded Vase*, 2004. Raised copper. 15" x 10" x 10". *Photo, artist*

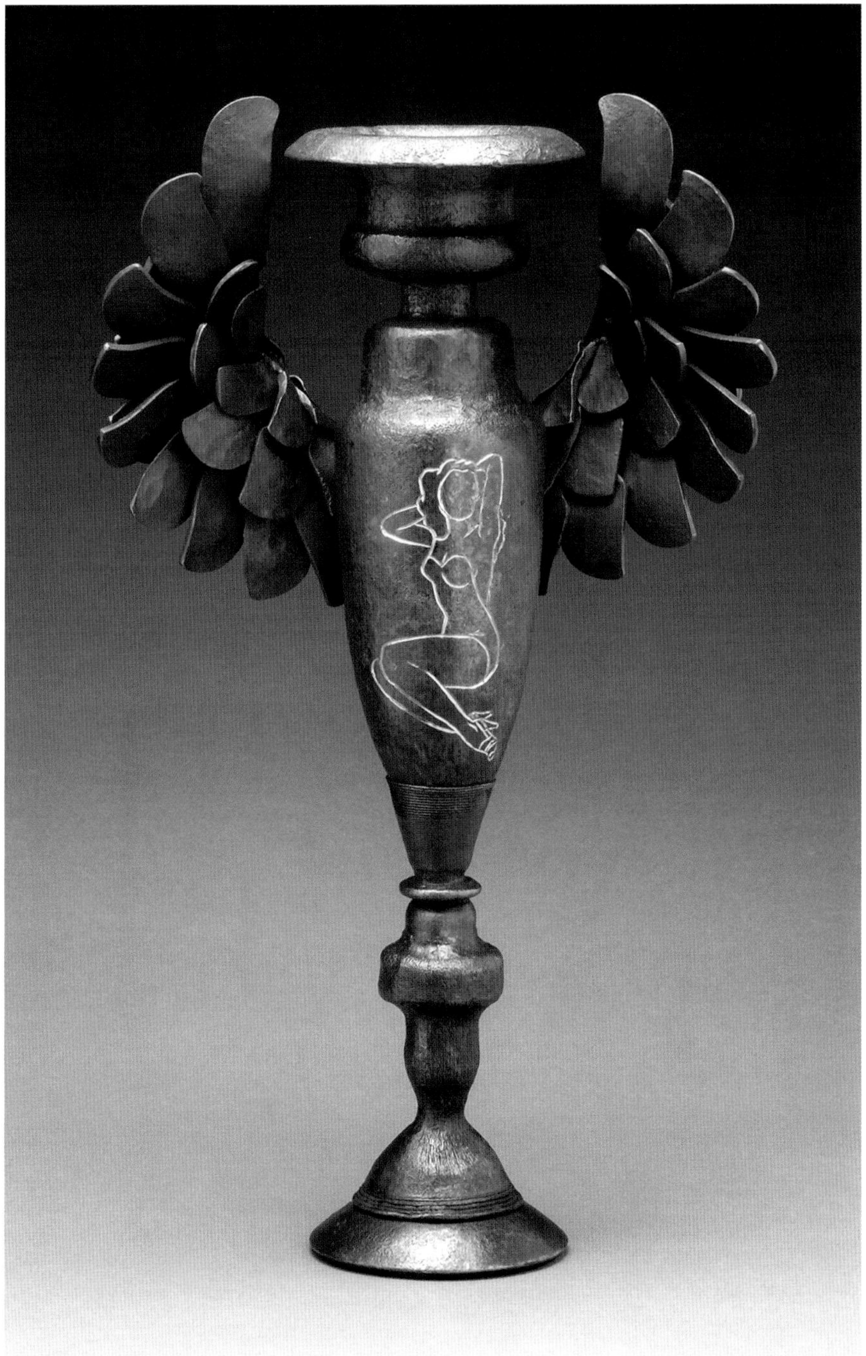

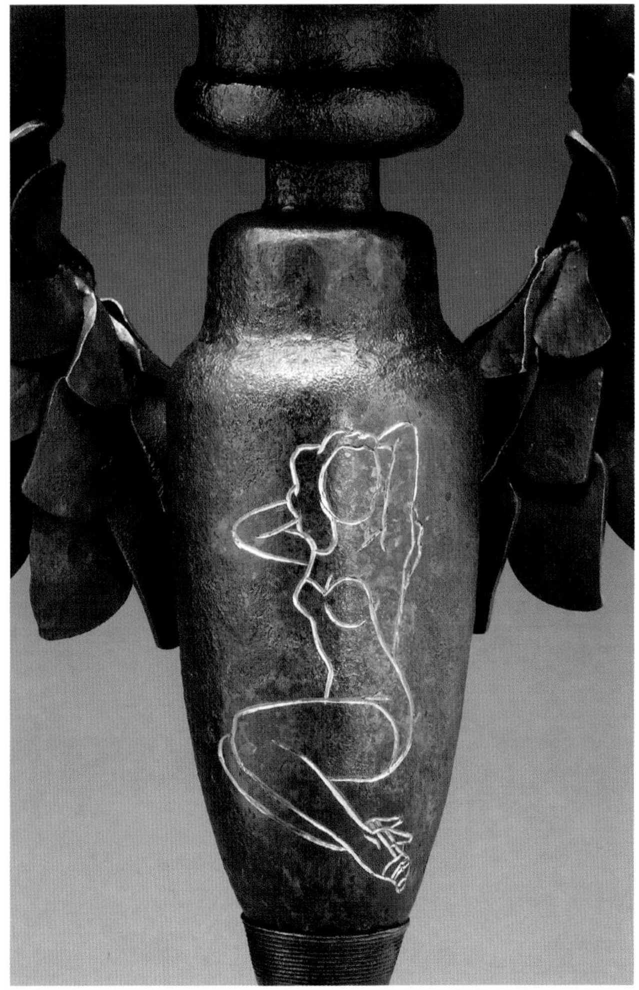

Jon Shearin. *Tribute to the Great American Pin-up.* Detail. *Photo, Tom Mills*

Jon Shearin. *Tribute to the Great American Pin-up.* Forged mild steel, pipe and solid stock, MIG and TIG welding, and engraving, 4" l x 12" w x 20" h. *Photo, Tom Mills*

I use a lot of pin-up imagery from the vintage era of such artists throughout my work. I made this as a trophy for the pin-up and her place in history. The vessel and its stand are made from multiple pieces of pipe that have been necked down, rolled over, and upset to achieve a classical Greek shape. The feathers of the wings were individually forges and welded together and then onto the vessel. Finally the pin-up was engraved. – Jon Shearin

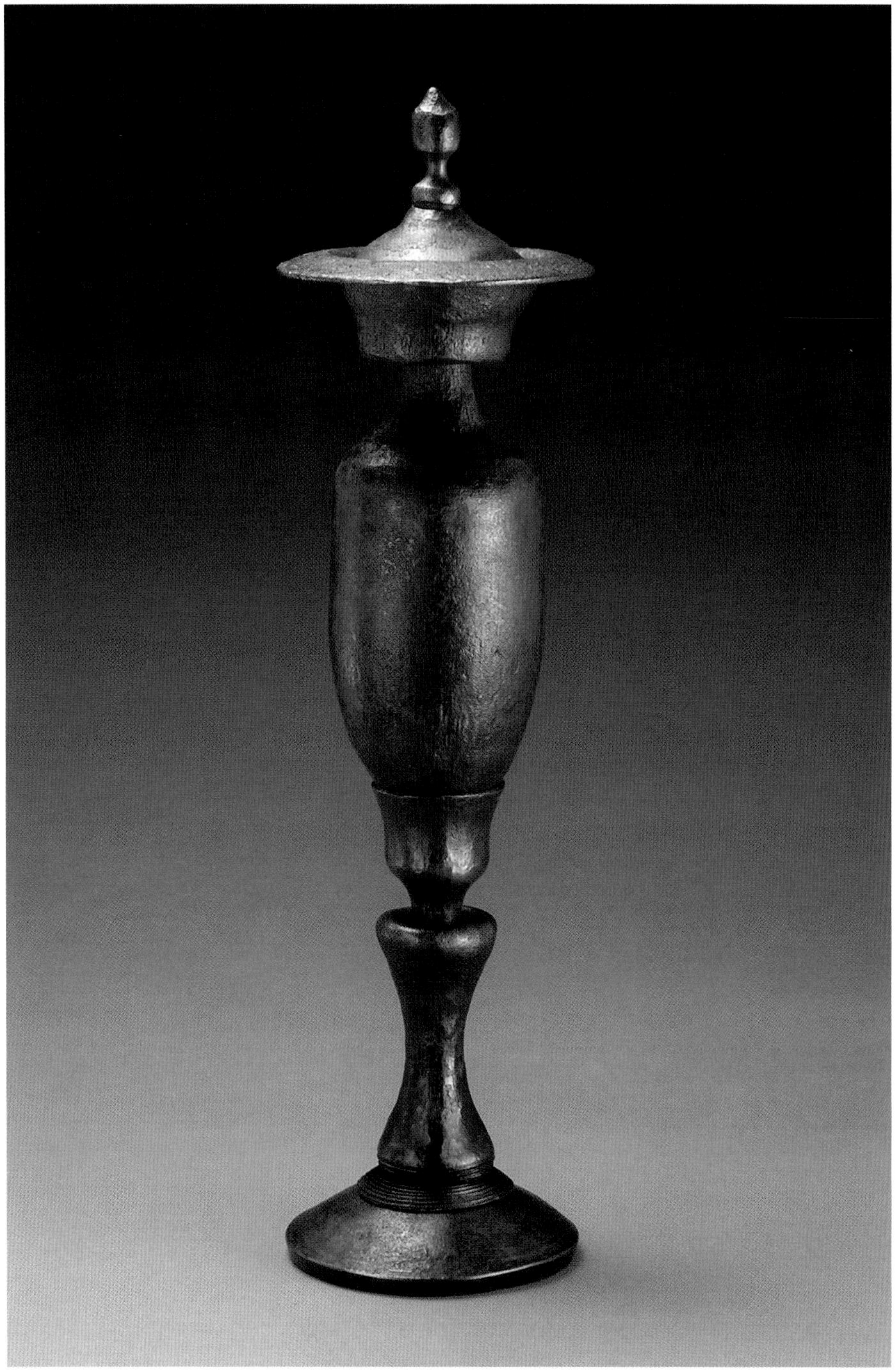

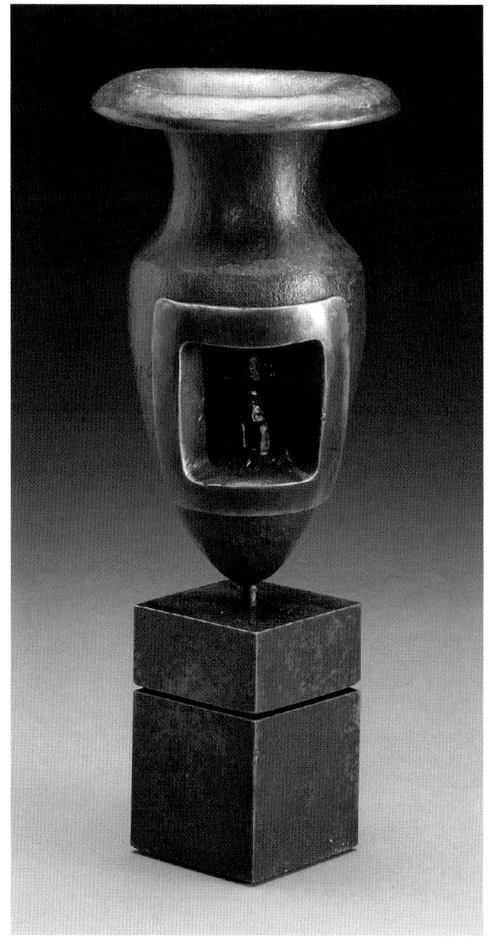

Jon Shearin. *Vessel Series #1.* Forged mild steel, stainless steel, pipe and solid stock, MIG and TIG welding, glass. 4" l x 4" w x 10" h. *Photo, Tom Mills*

This sculpture features the first piece of pipe I ever forged. This inspired me to start a series that I continue to explore. I am attracted to the window and the relationship created between inside and outside surfaces. The interior of the vessel is lined with a mosaic of red glass. – Jon Shearin

Jon Shearin. *Veronese Series #1.* Forged mild steel, pipe and solid stock, MIG and TIG welding, 5" l x 5" w x 24" h. *Photo, Tom Mills*

This vessel is made of multiple pieces of pipe that have been necked down, rolled over, and upset. I started this series as a way to incorporate all the shapes and methods I have been experimenting with. Veronese is a style of vessel that is most often used in glasswork. – Jon Shearin

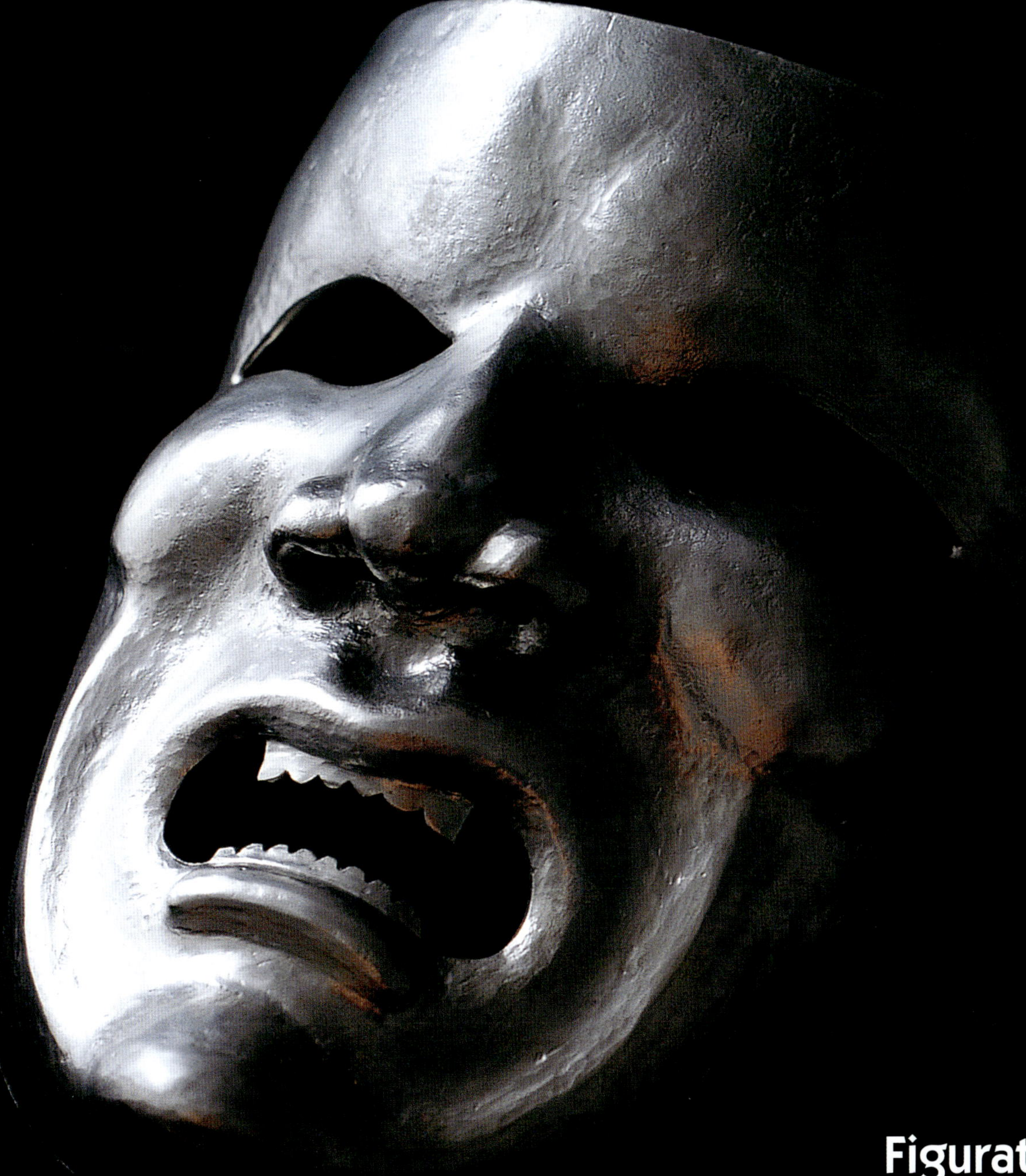

Chapter Four

Figurative Sculpture – Humans, Animals, and Objects

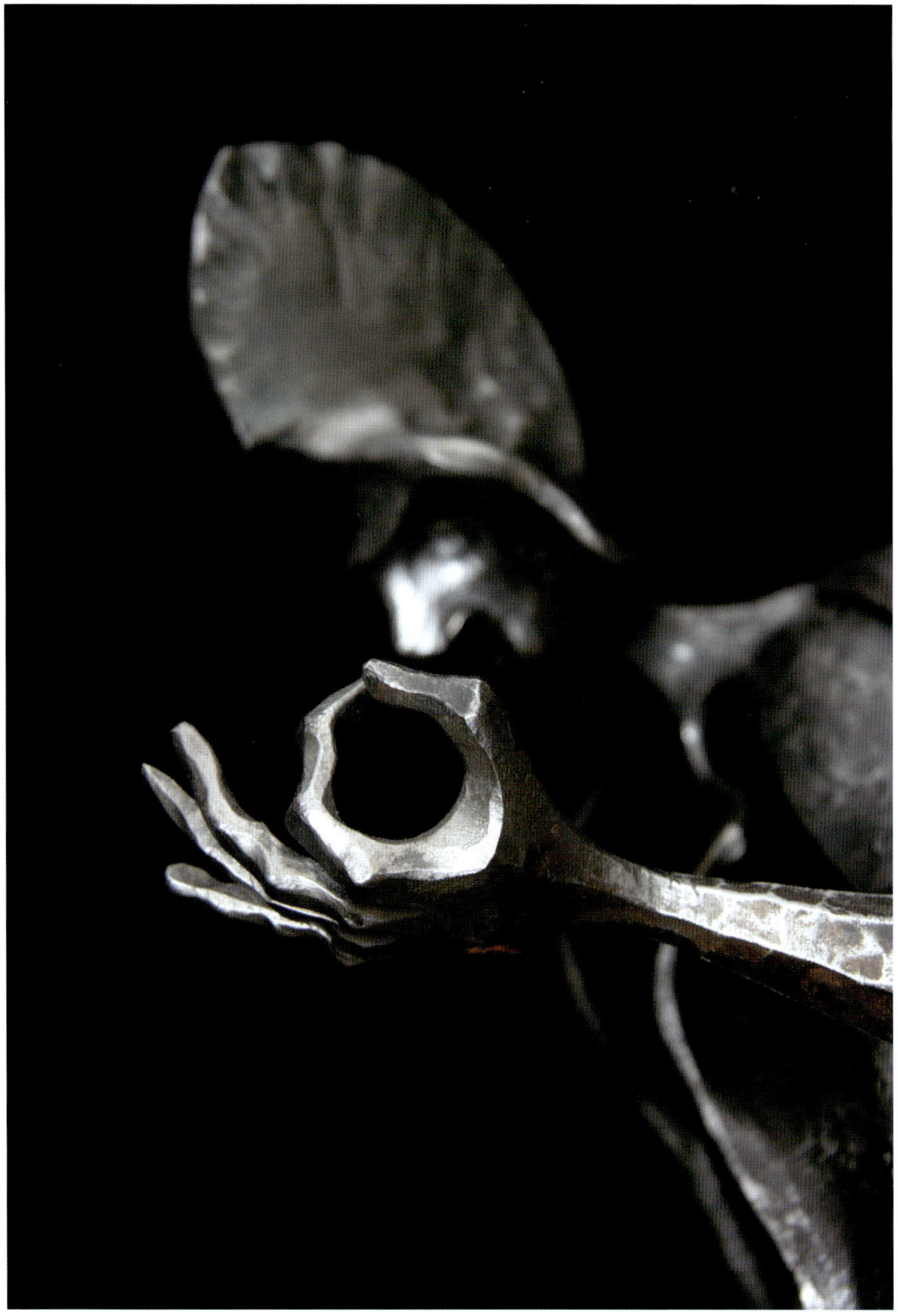

Claudio Bottero, *Figura anatomica 1*, Detail. *Photo, artist*

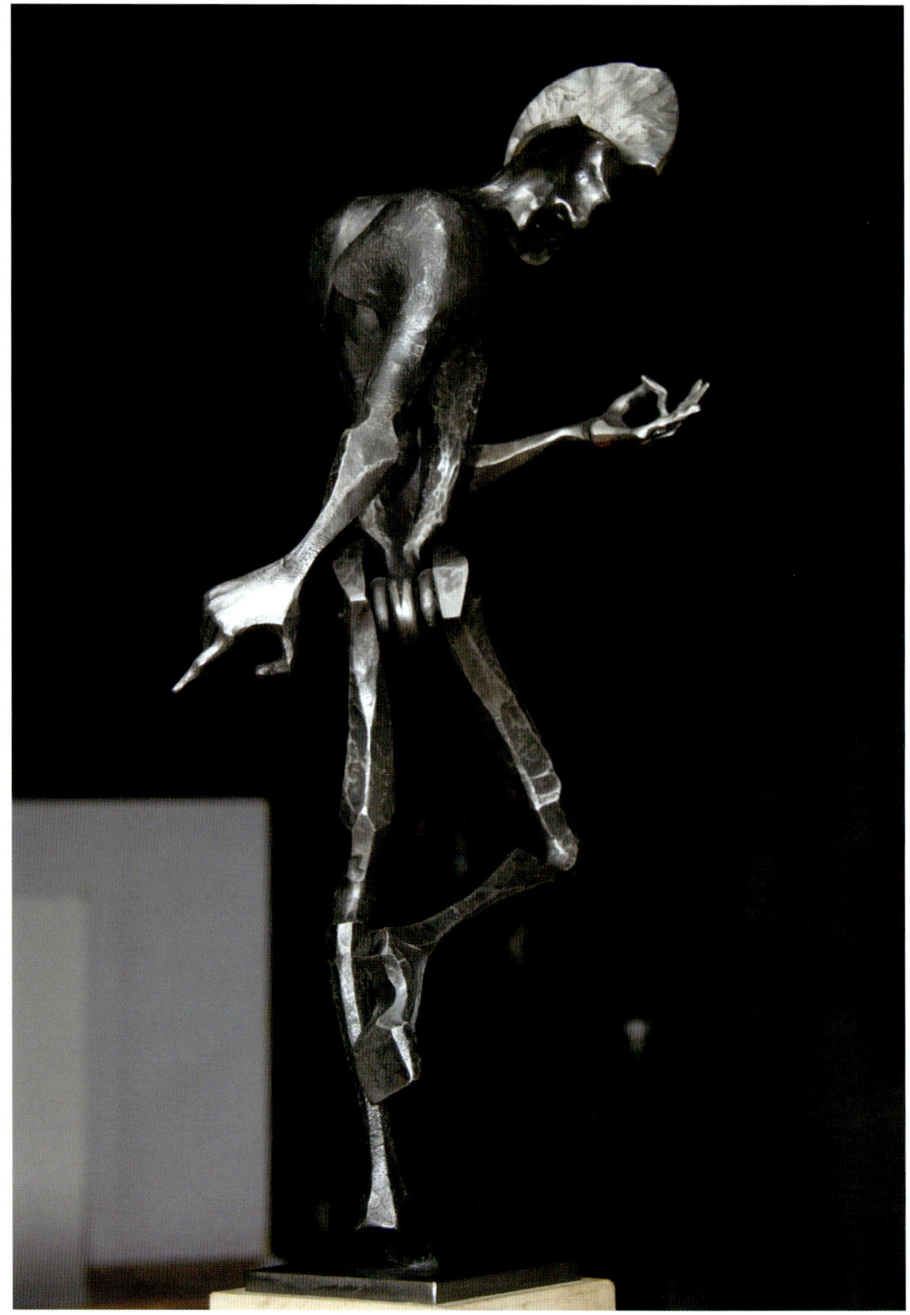

Claudio Bottero, *Figura anatomica 1.* Back view. *Photo, artist*

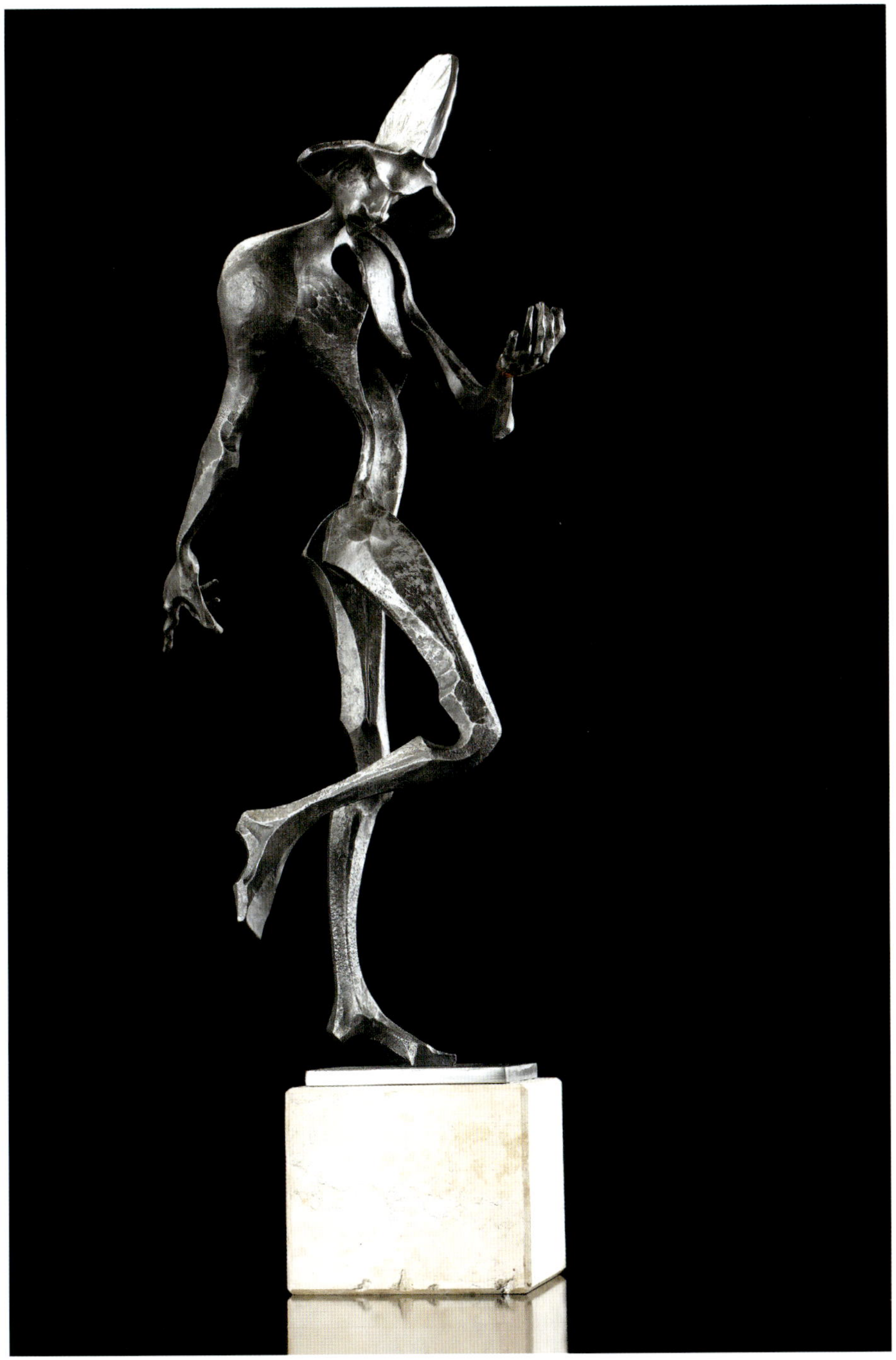

Claudio Bottero, *Figura anatomica 1*. Forged steel. 25.5". *Photo, artist*

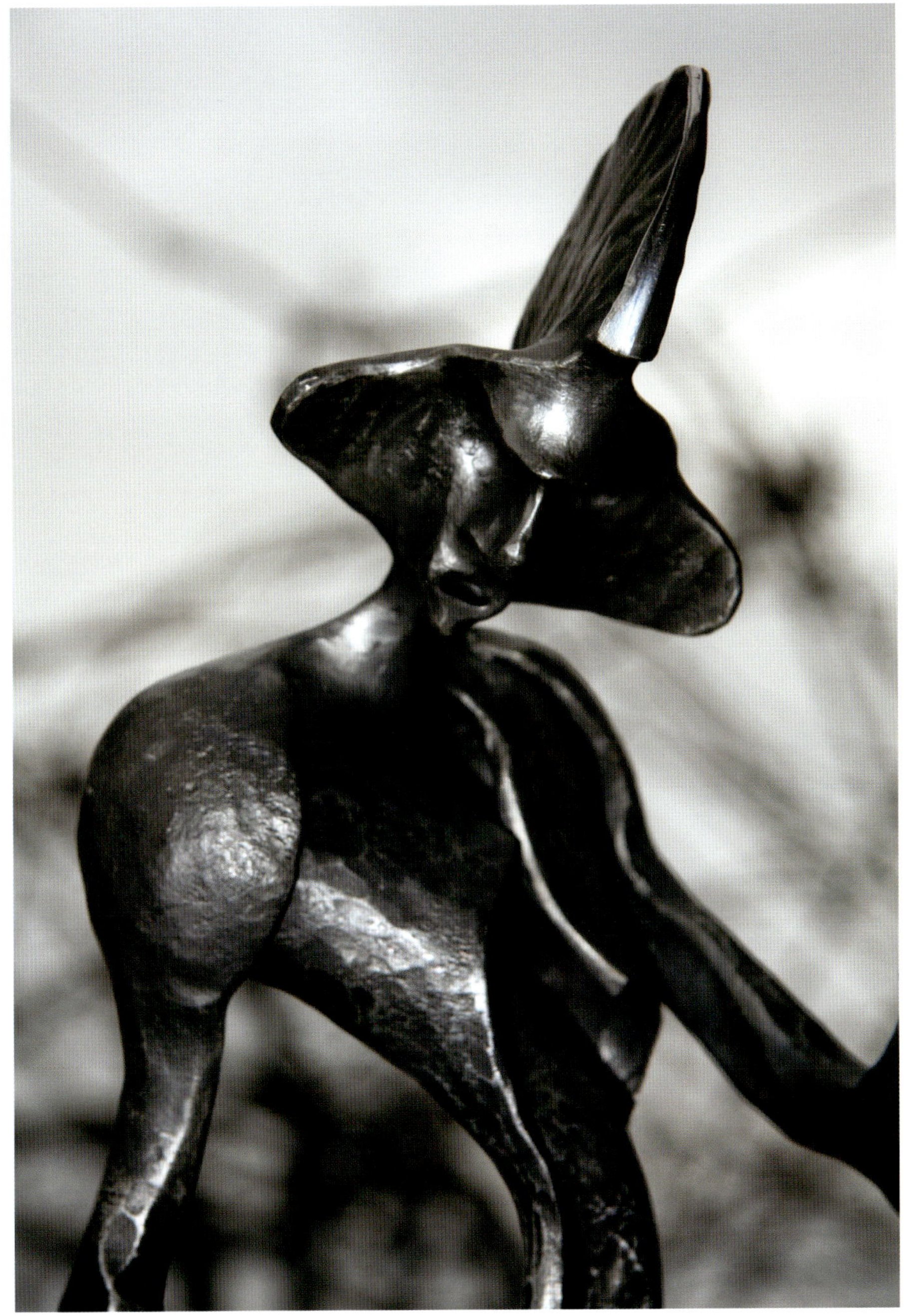

Claudio Bottero, *Figura anatomica 1*. Detail. *Photo, artist*

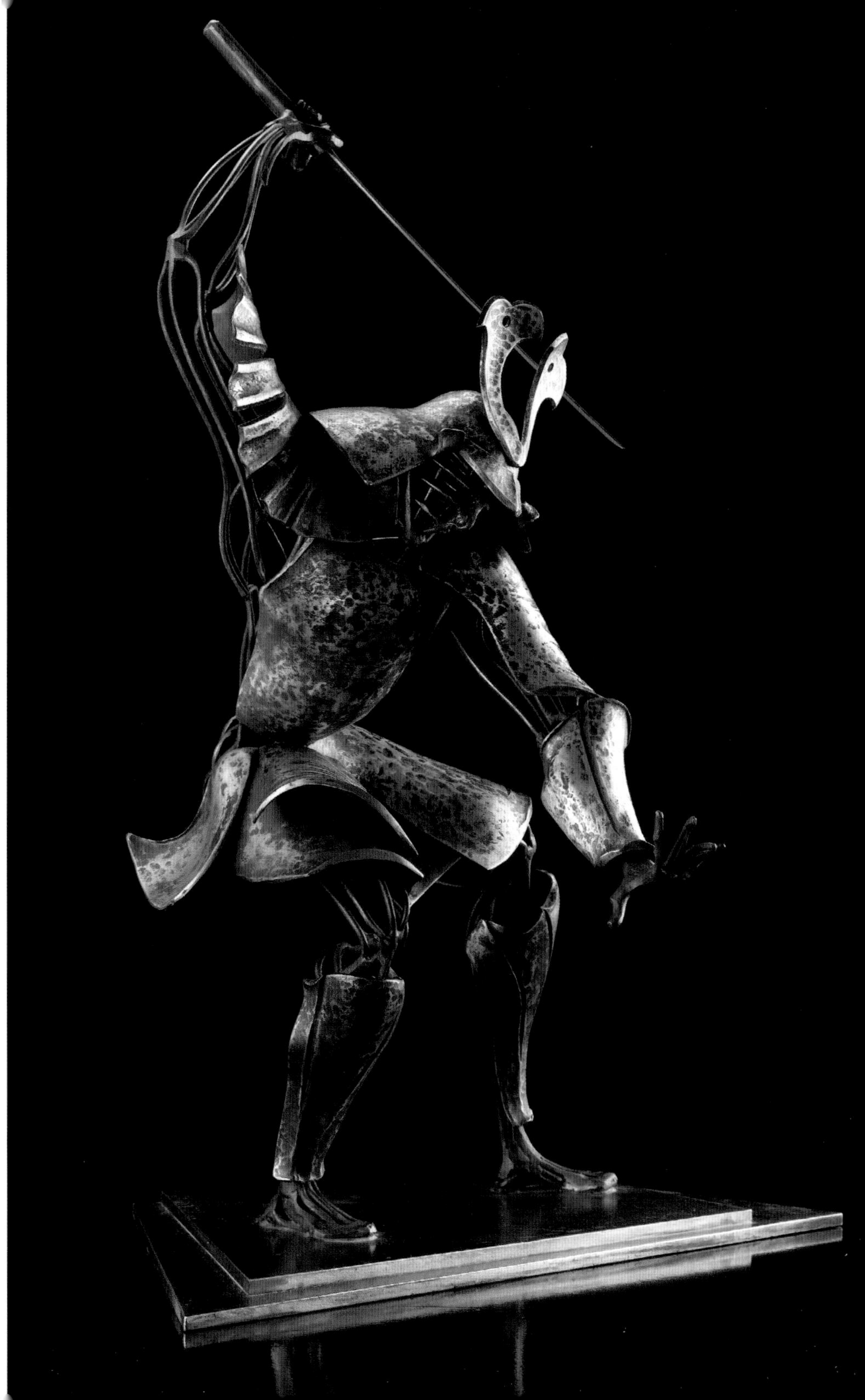

Claudio Bottero. *Samurai.*
Forged steel, 24". *Photo, artist*

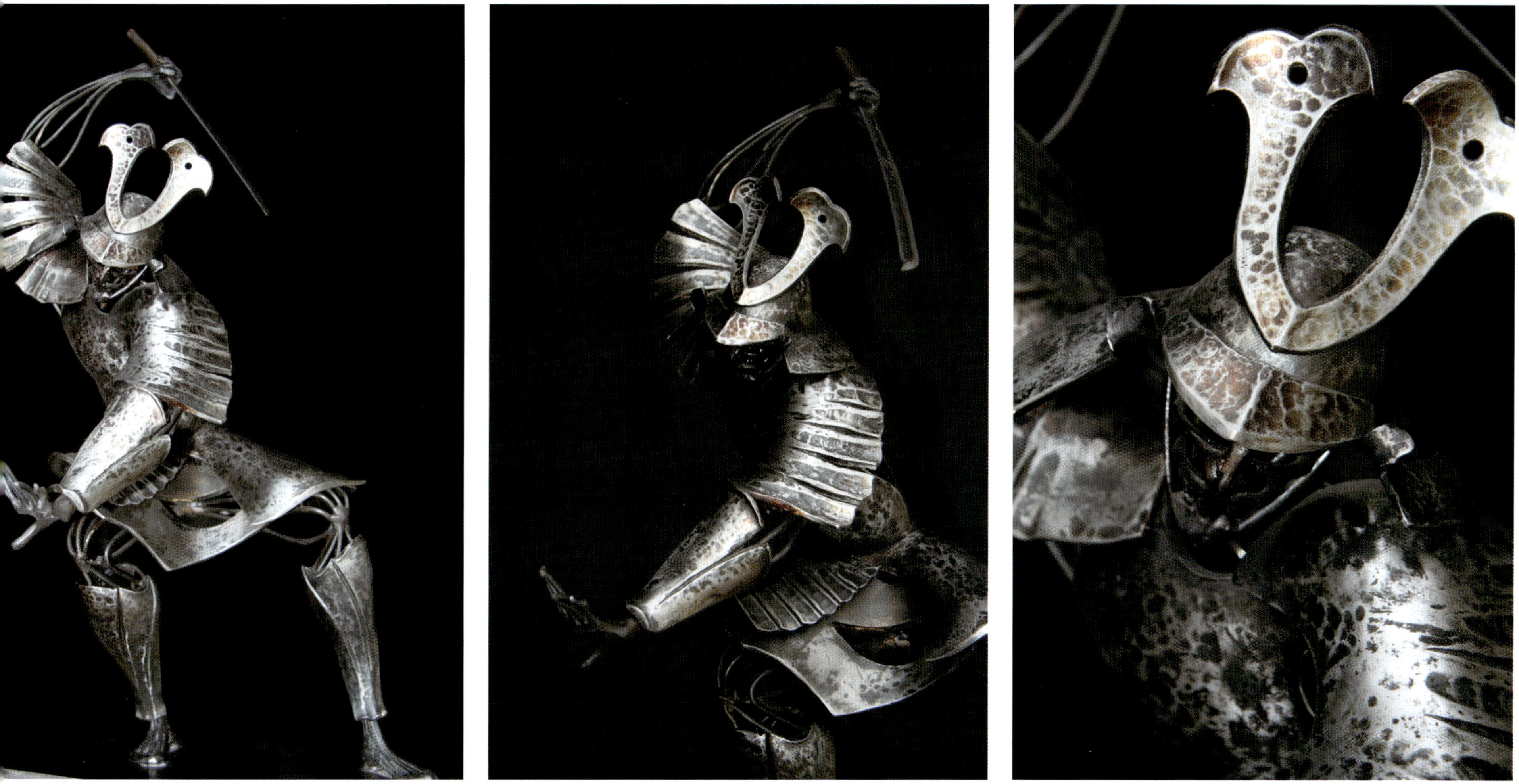

Claudio Bottero. *Samurai.* Details. *Photo, artist*

Claudio Bottero. *Figura anatomica 2.* Forged steel, 24". *Photo, artist*

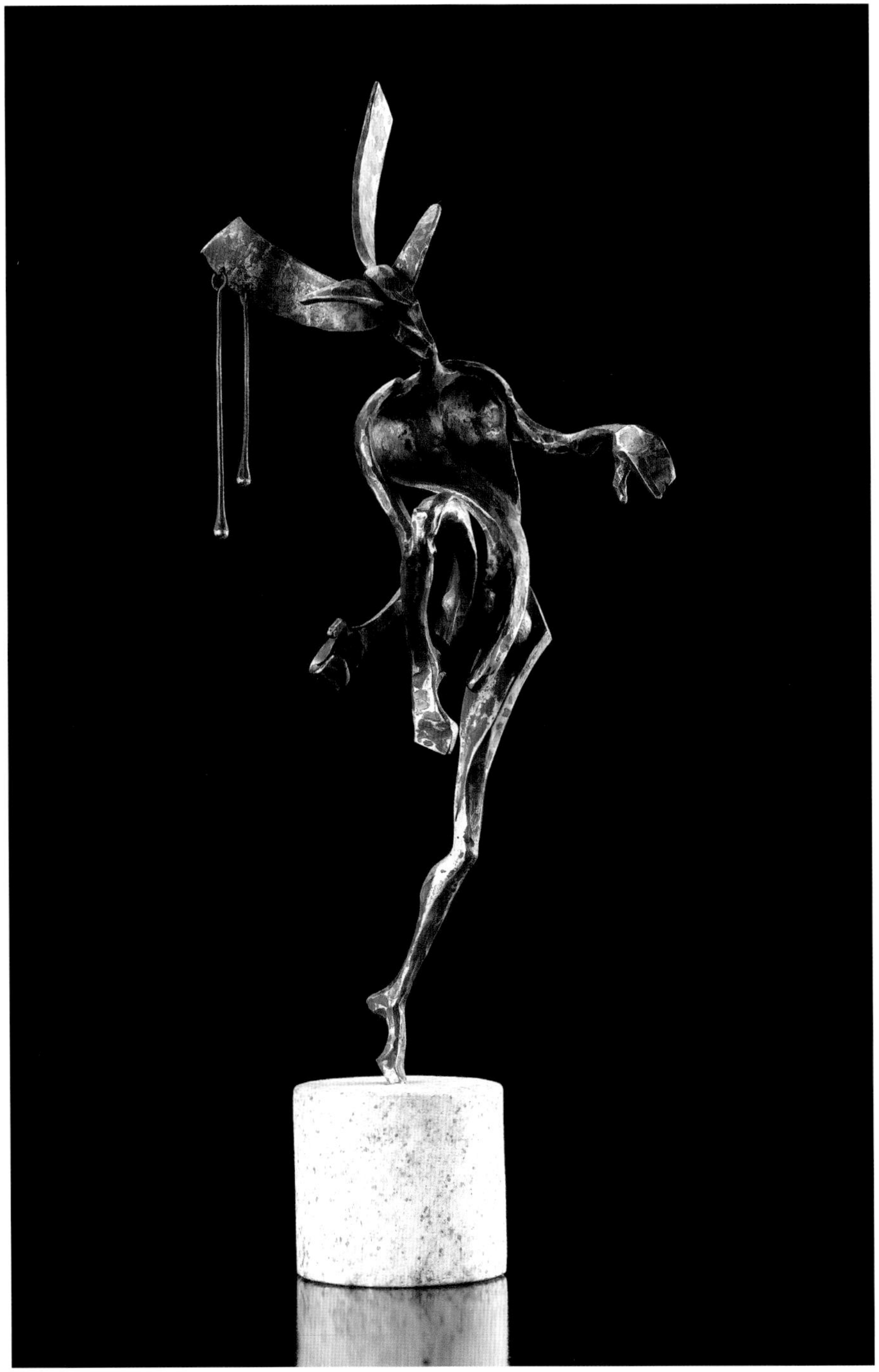

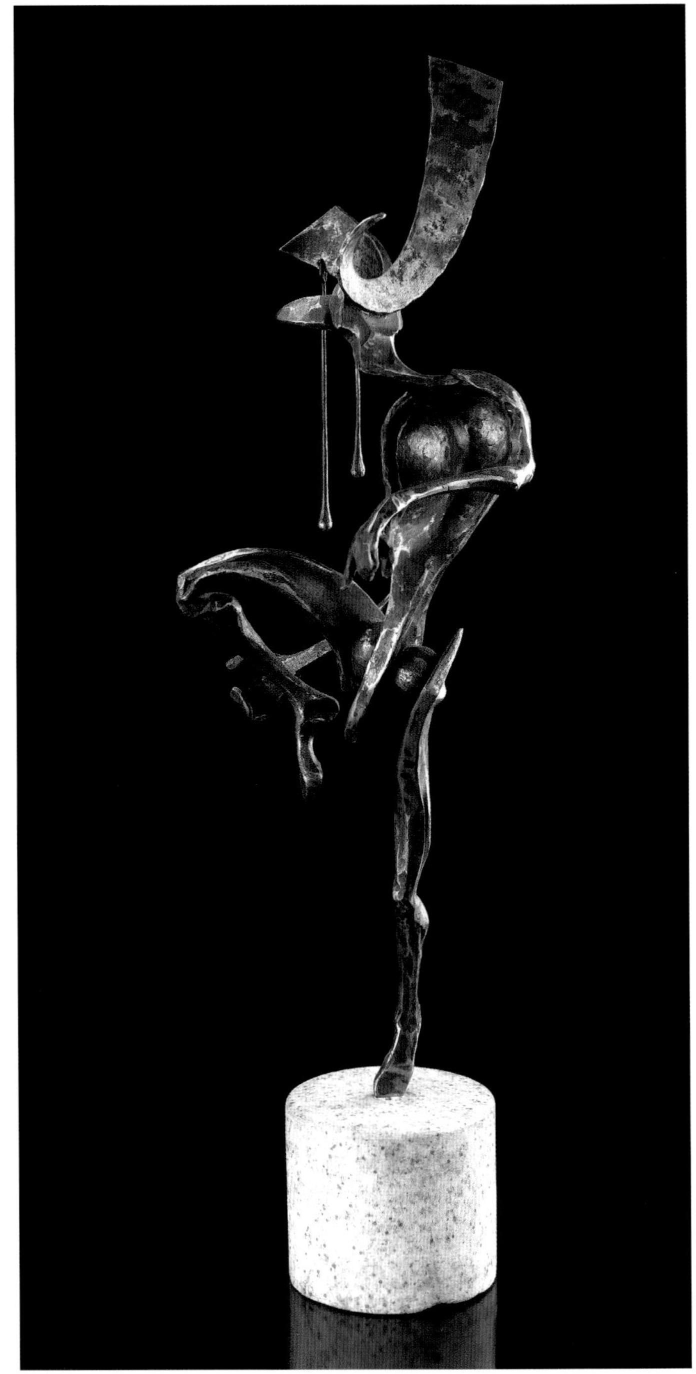

Claudio Bottero. *Figura anatomica 2.* Second view. *Photo, artist*

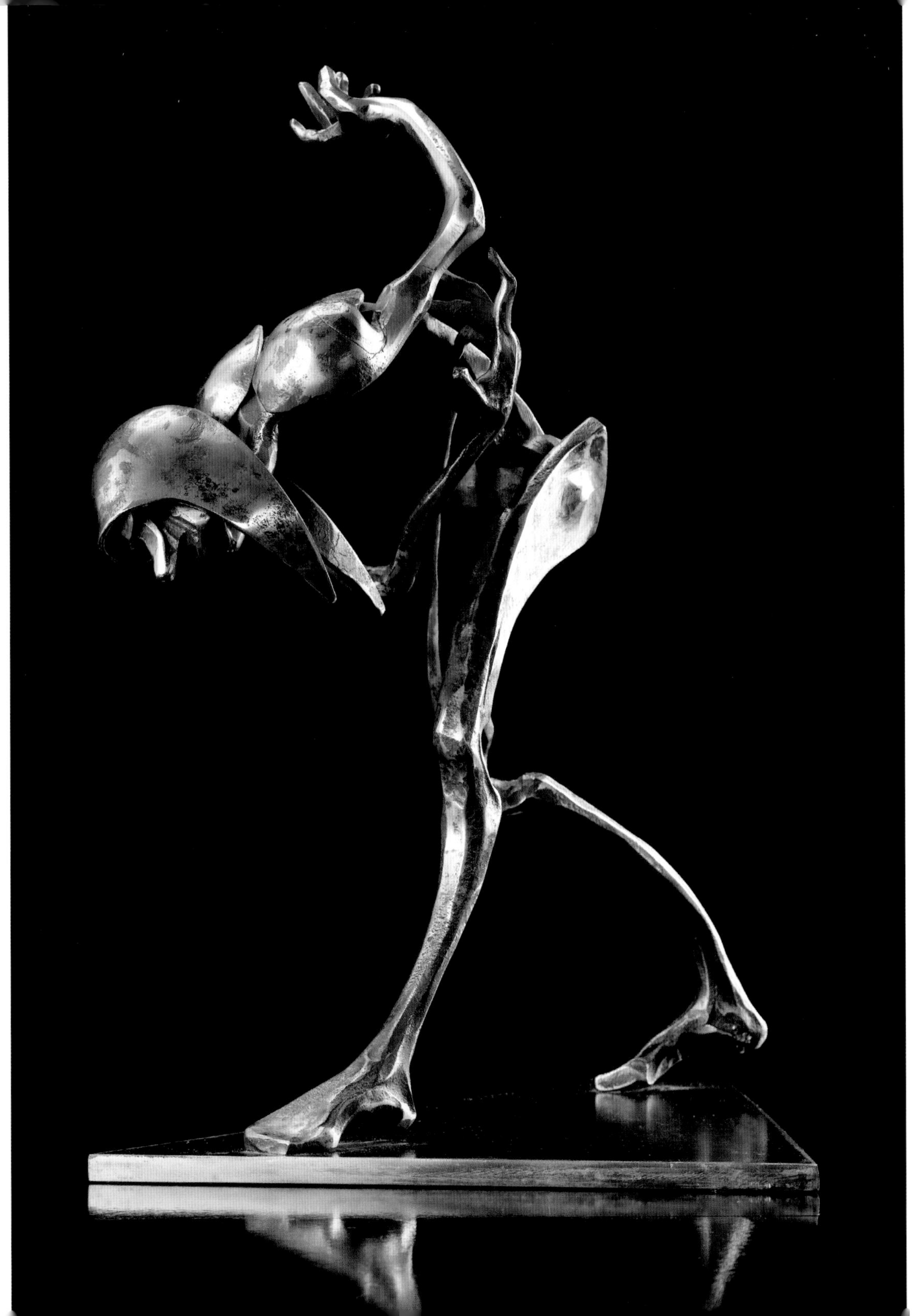

Claudio Bottero. *Figura anatomica 3*. Forged steel, 12". *Photo, artist*

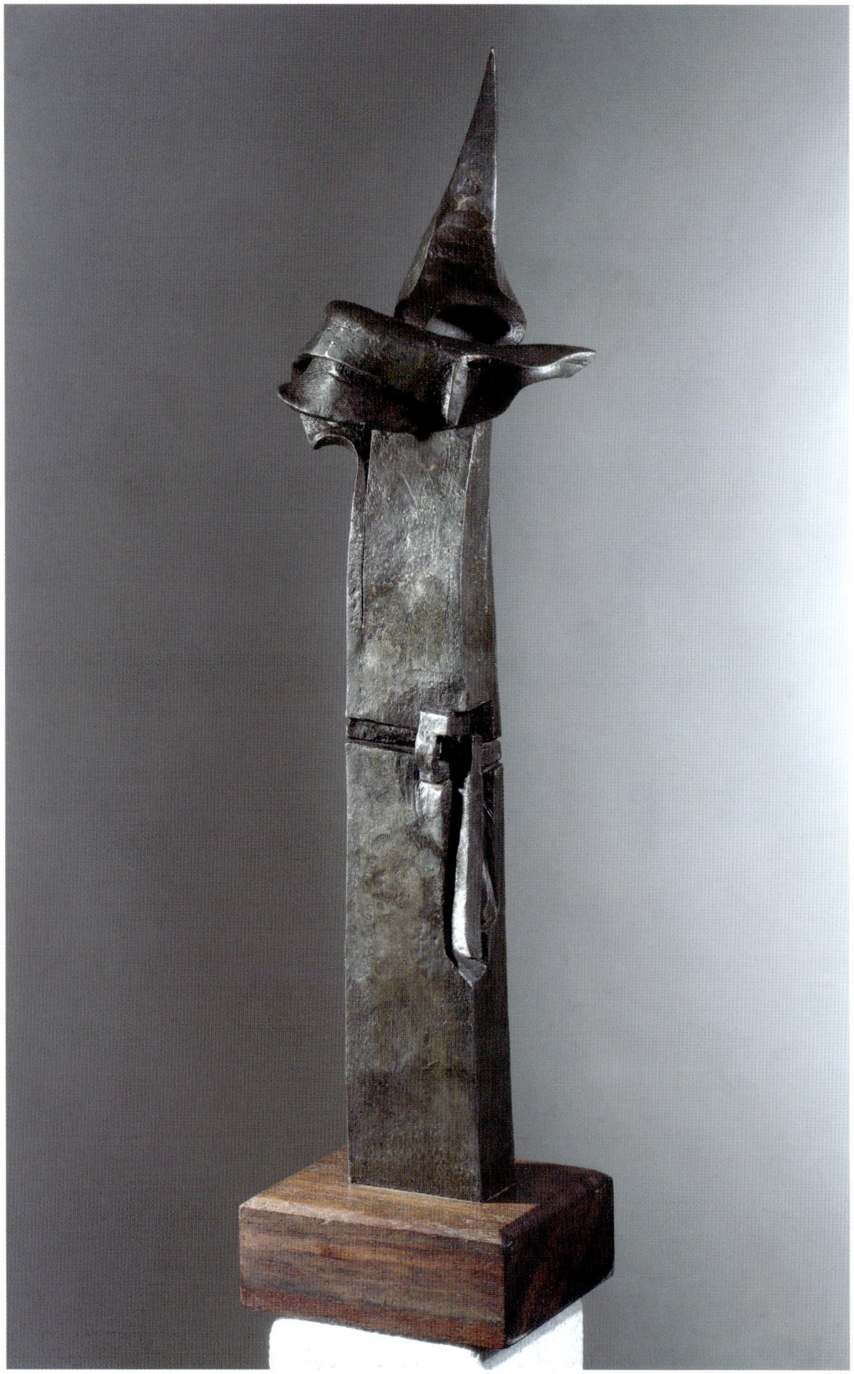

Claudio Bottero. *Monk*. Wrought forged iron, 19". *In private collection. Photo, artist*

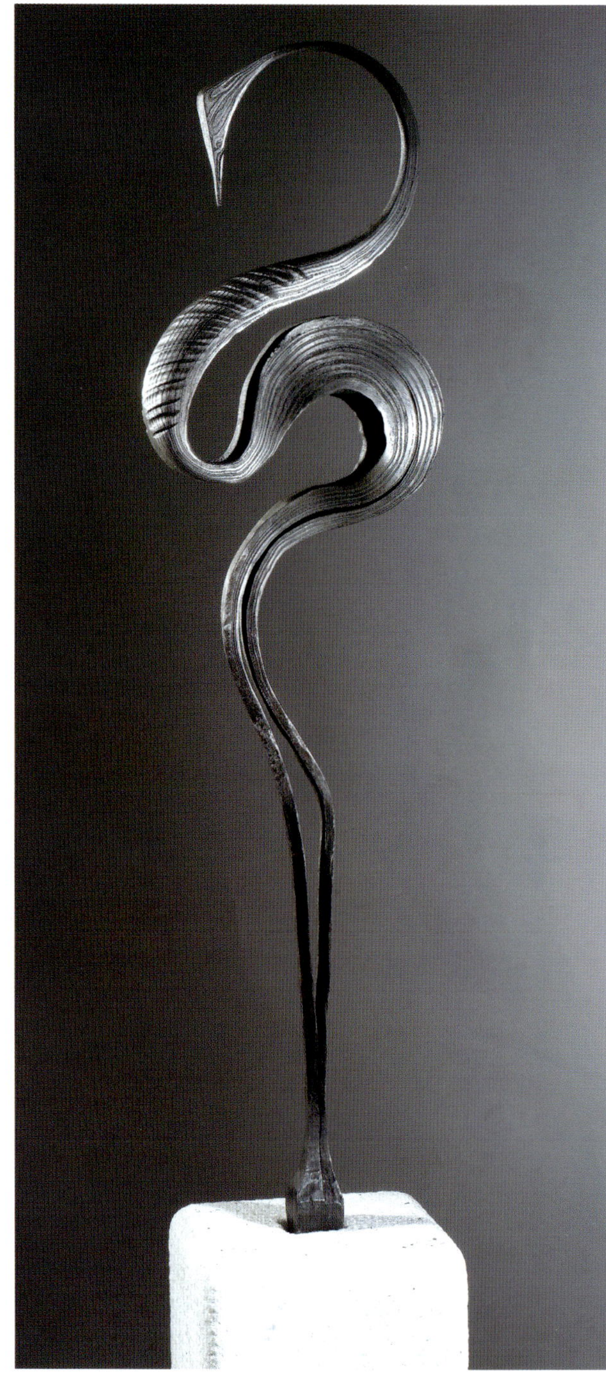

Claudio Bottero. *Heron*. Damascus, 19". *In private collection. Photo, artist*

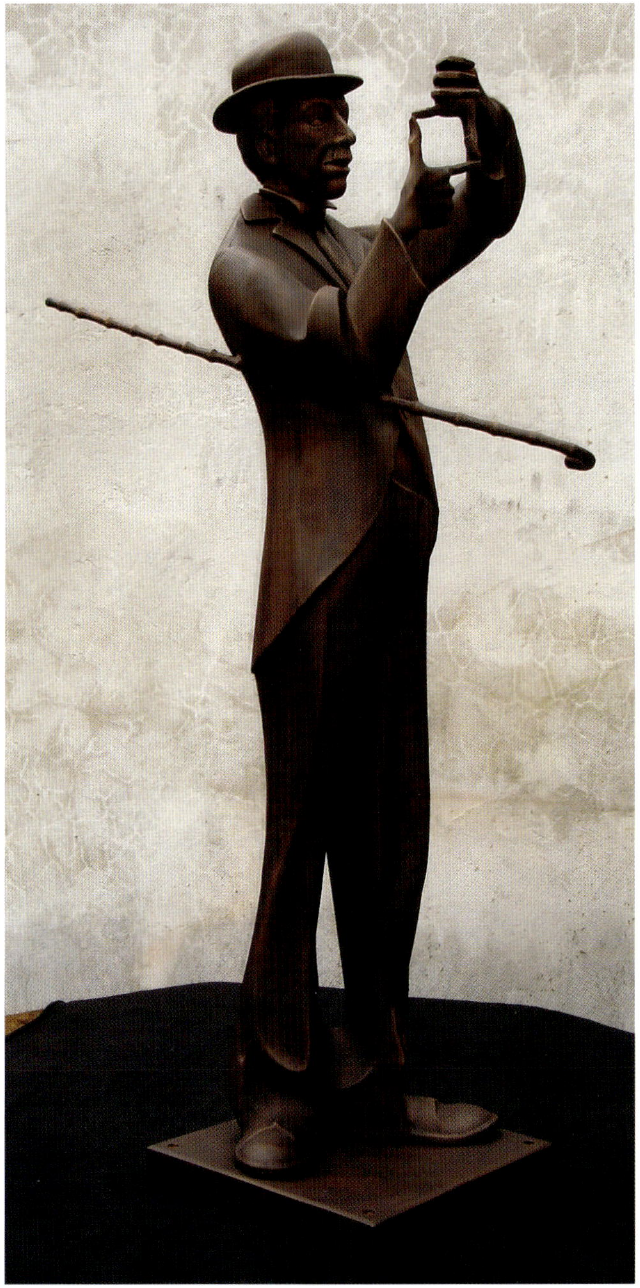

Libor Hurda. *Charlie*. Mild steel, bronzing, life-sized. *Photo, artist*

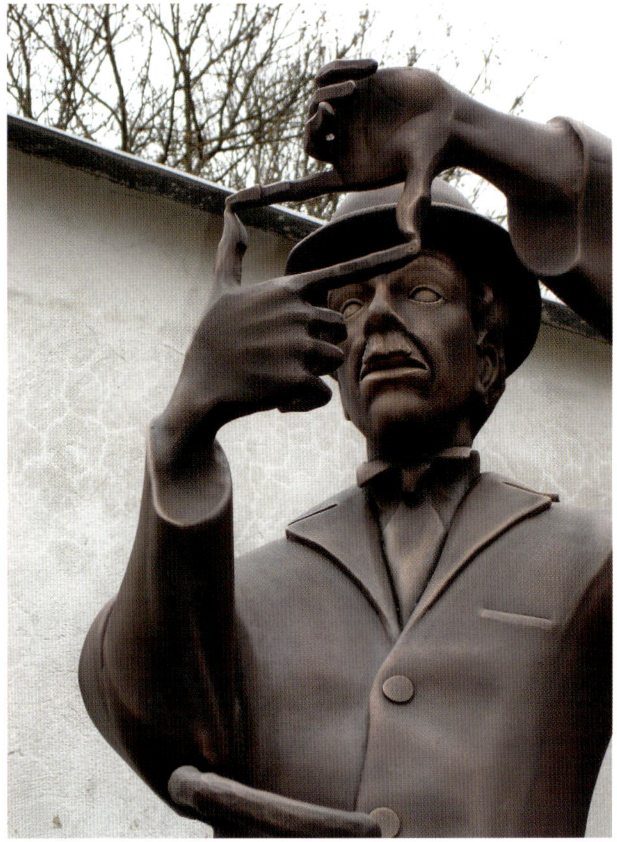

Libor Hurda. *Charlie*. Detail. *Photo, artist*

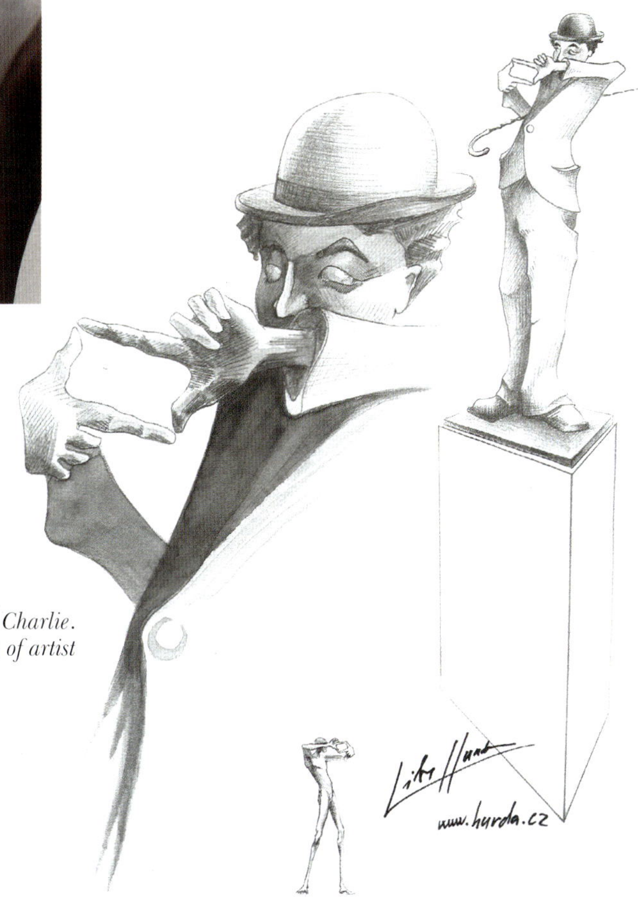

Libor Hurda. *Charlie*. Sketch. *Courtesy of artist*

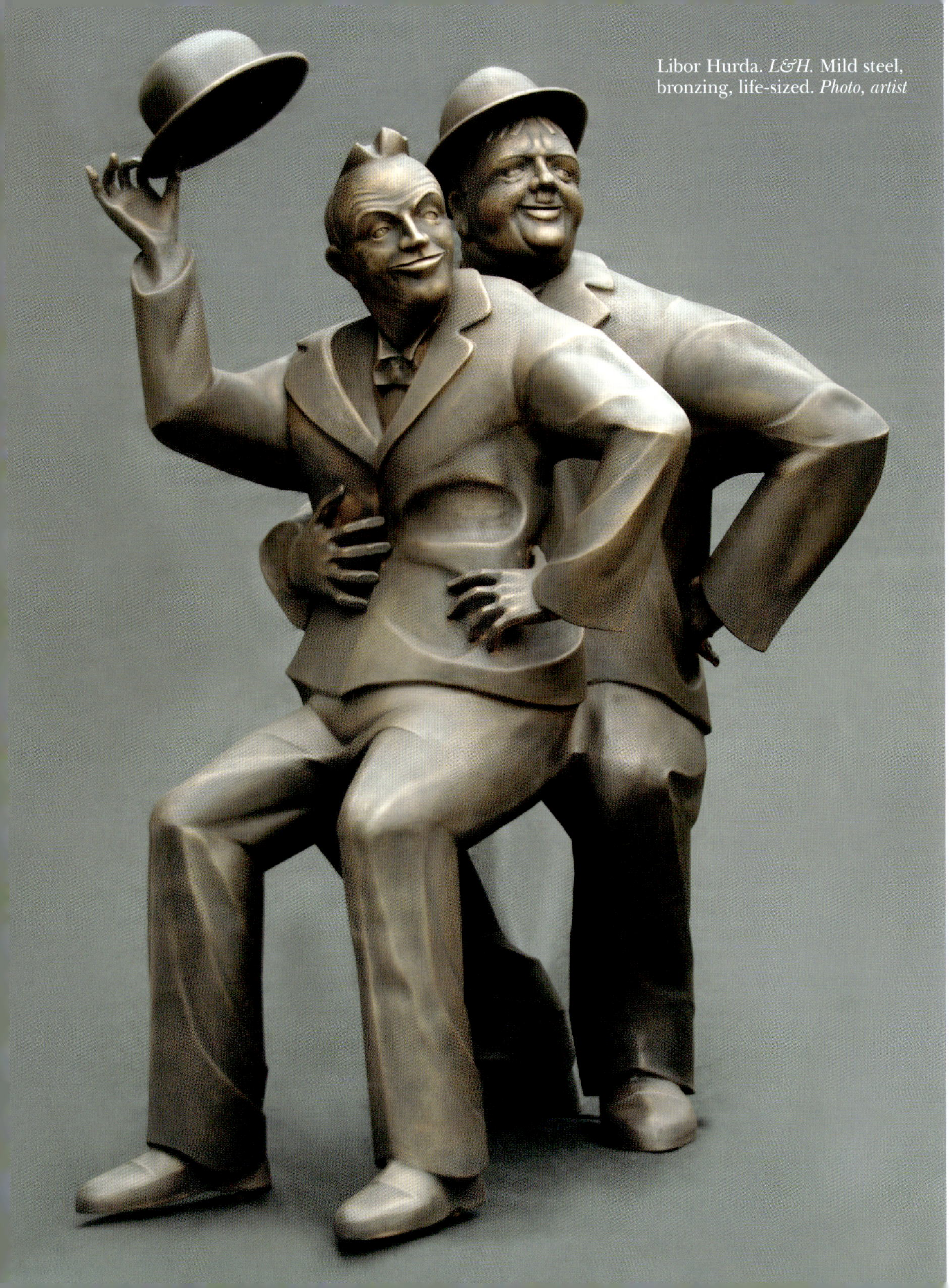
Libor Hurda. *L&H.* Mild steel, bronzing, life-sized. *Photo, artist*

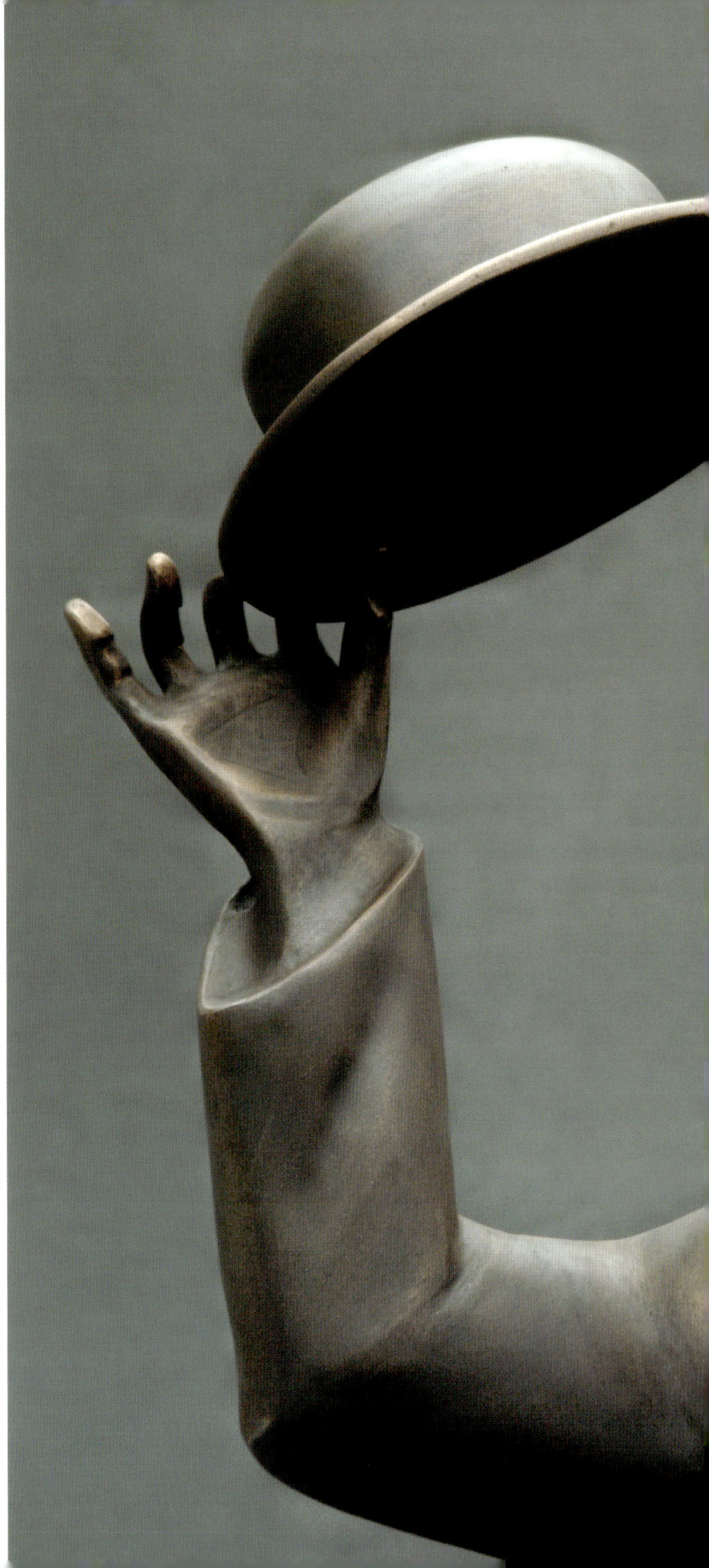

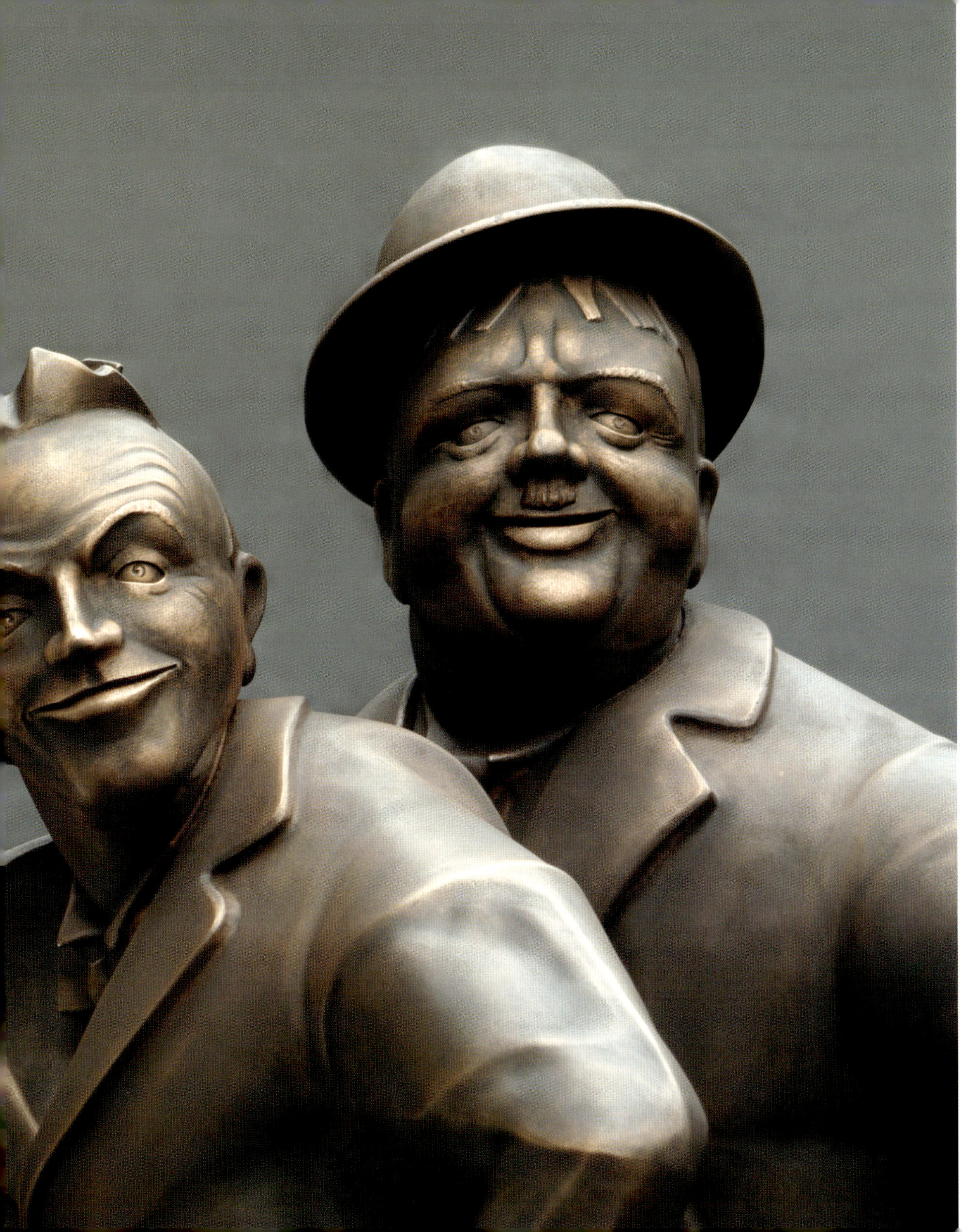

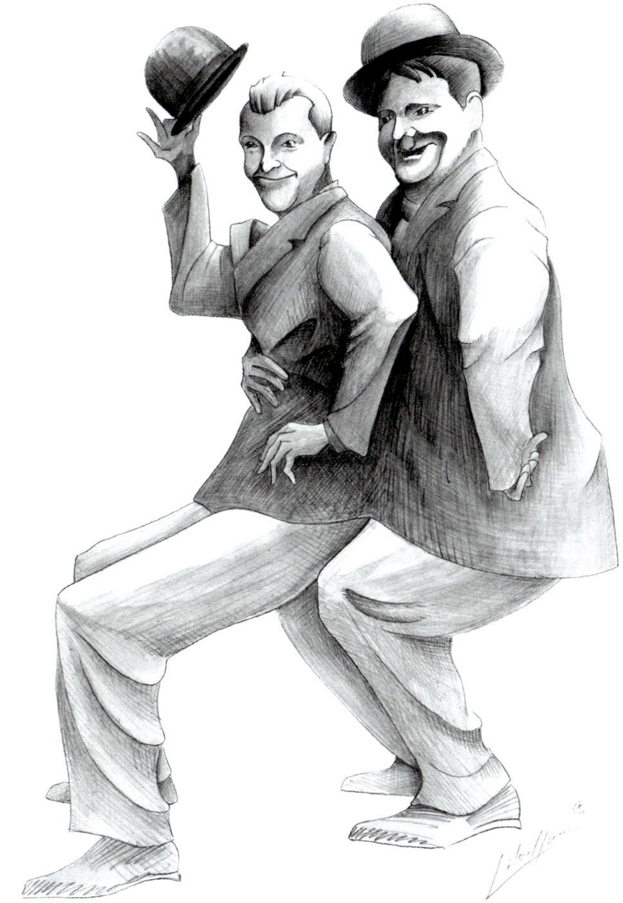

Libor Hurda. *L&H.* Sketch. *Courtesy of artist*

Libor Hurda. *L&H.*
Detail. *Photo, artist*

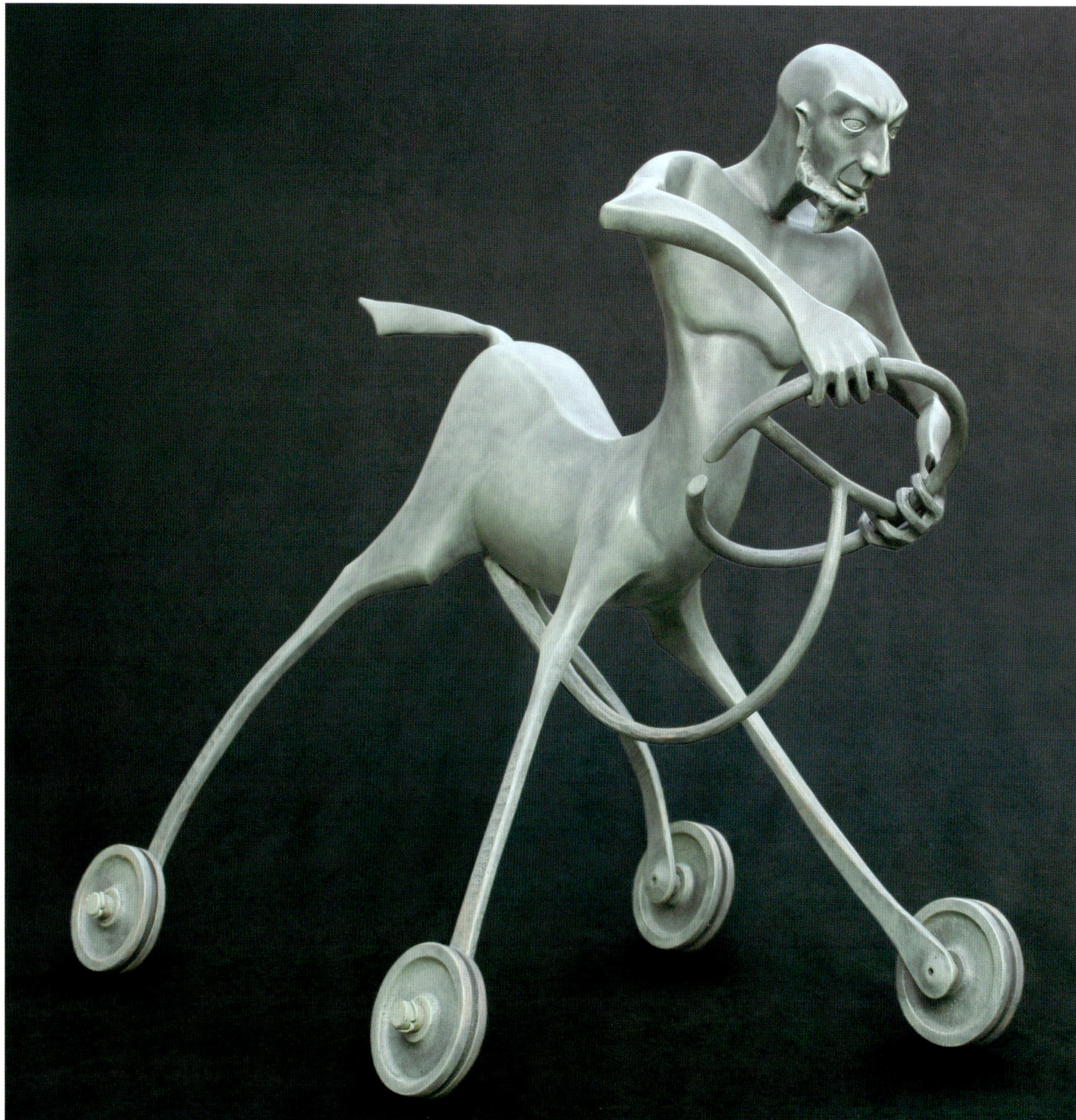

Libor Hurda. *Kentaur Enzo.* Mild steel, zincing, and patination, 45" h. *Photo, artist*

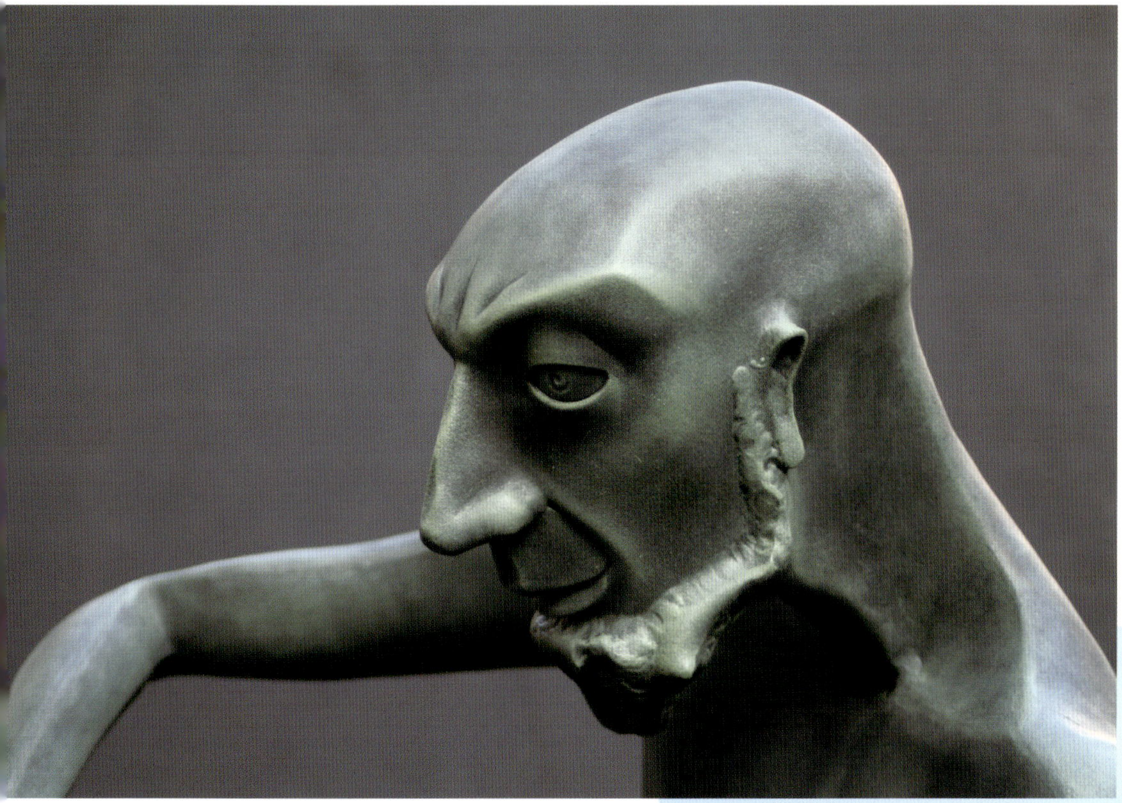

Libor Hurda. *Kentaur Enzo.* Detail. *Photo, artist*

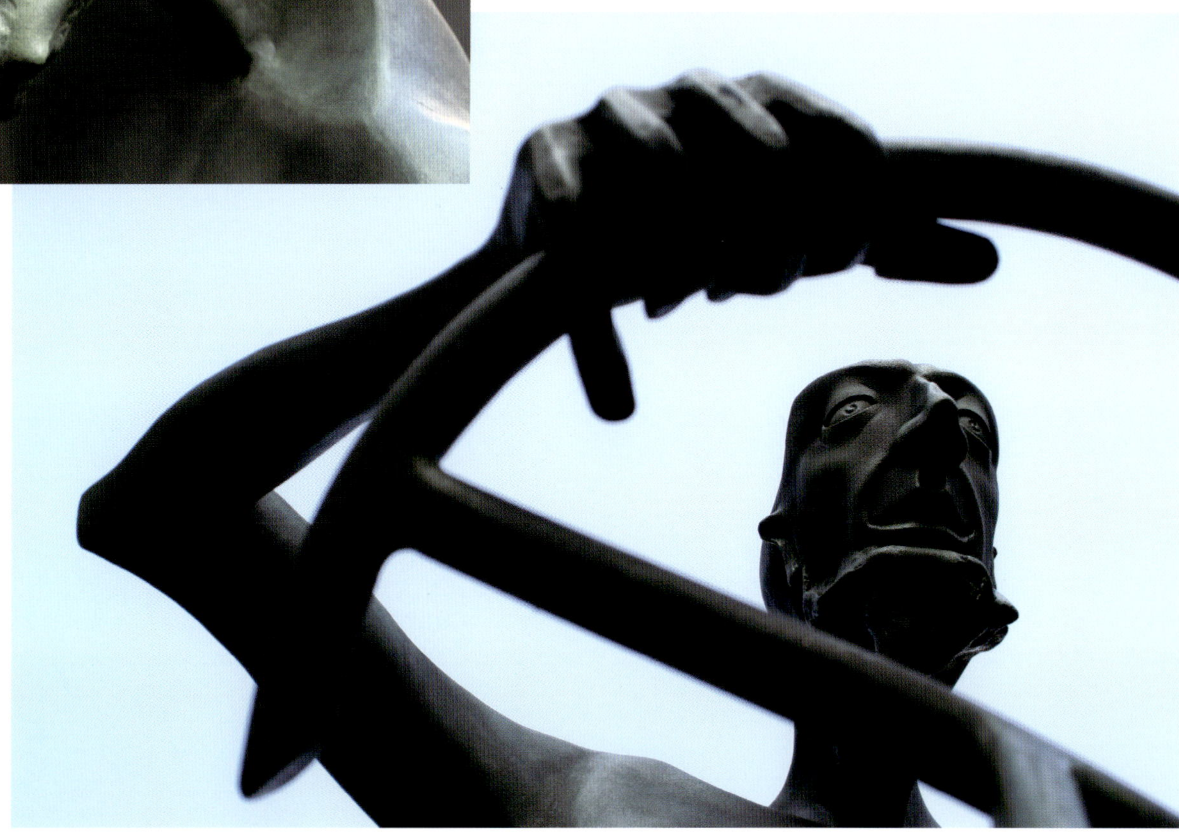

Libor Hurda. *Kentaur Enzo.* Detail. *Photo, artist*

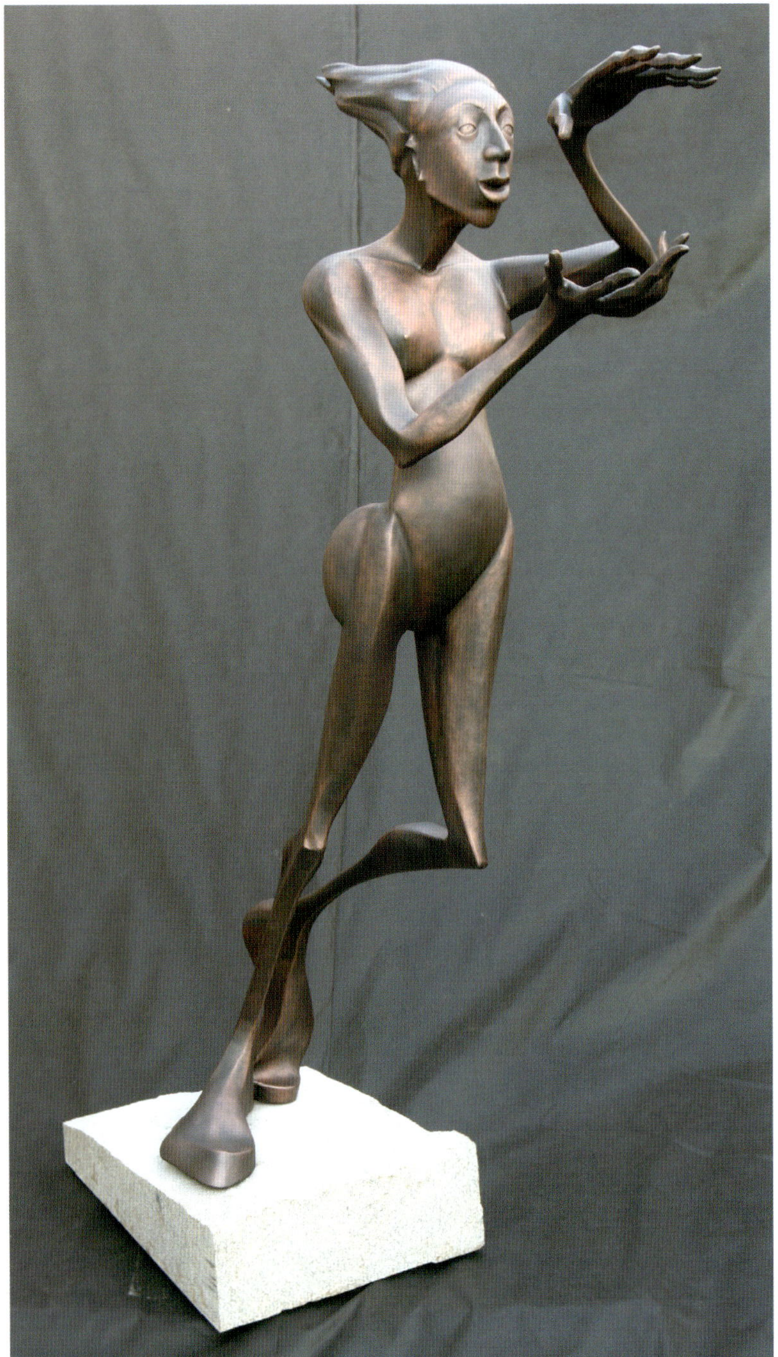

Libor Hurda. *Windy.* Mild steel, zincing, patination, and granite, 43" h. *Photo, artist*

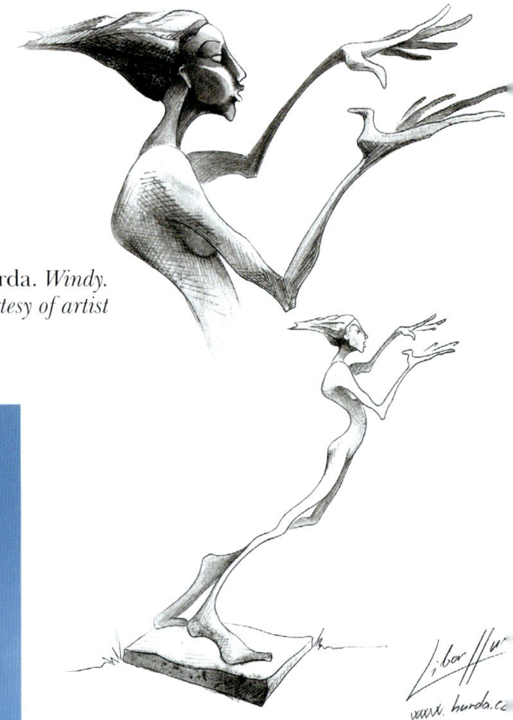

Libor Hurda. *Windy.* Sketch. *Courtesy of artist*

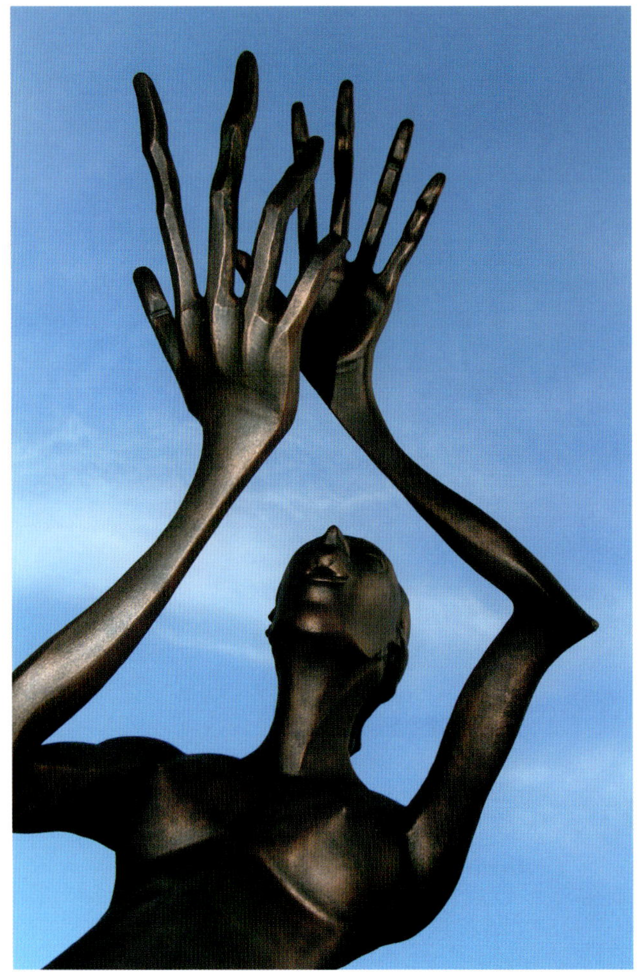

Libor Hurda. *Windy.* Detail. *Photo, artist*

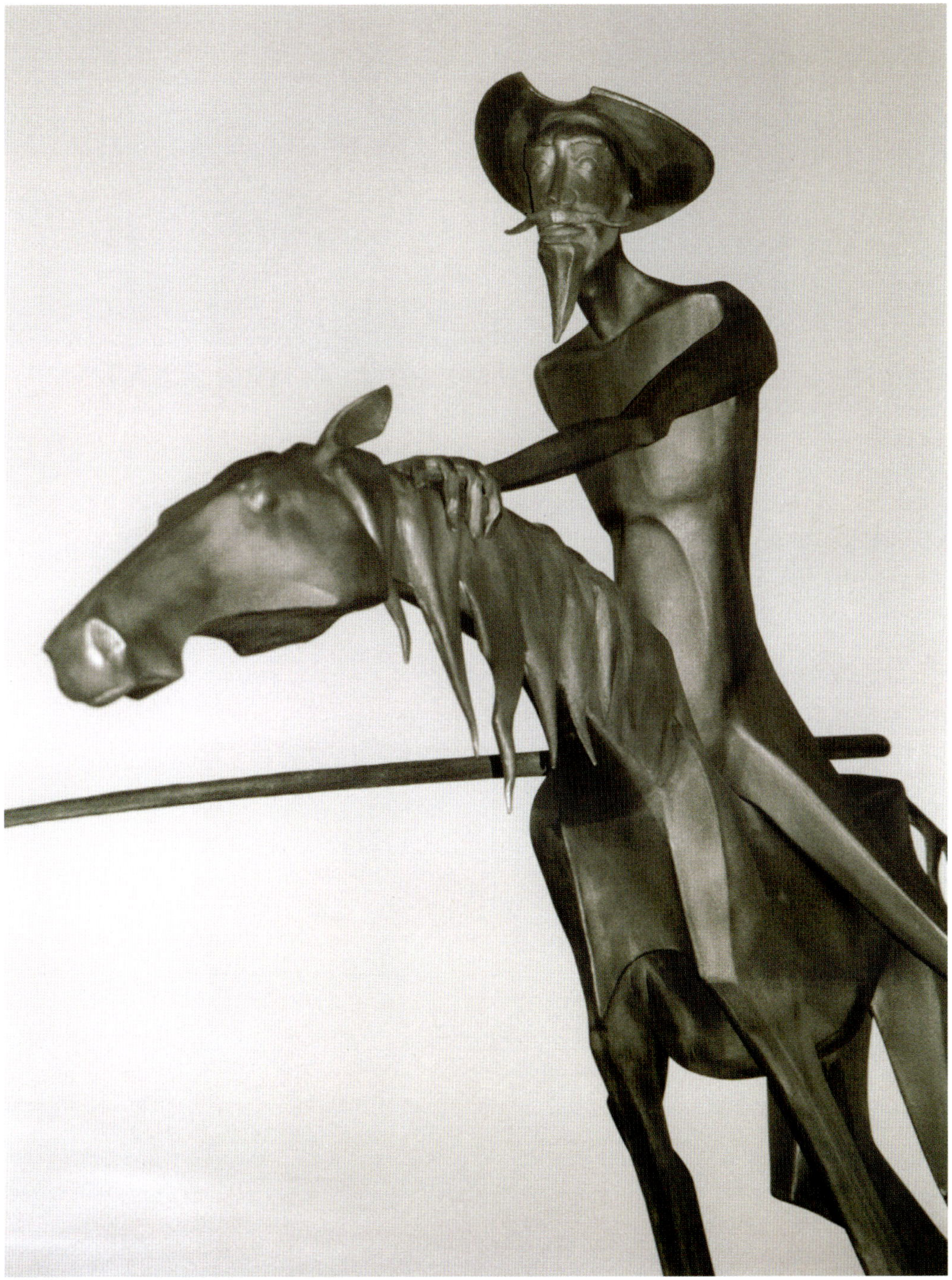

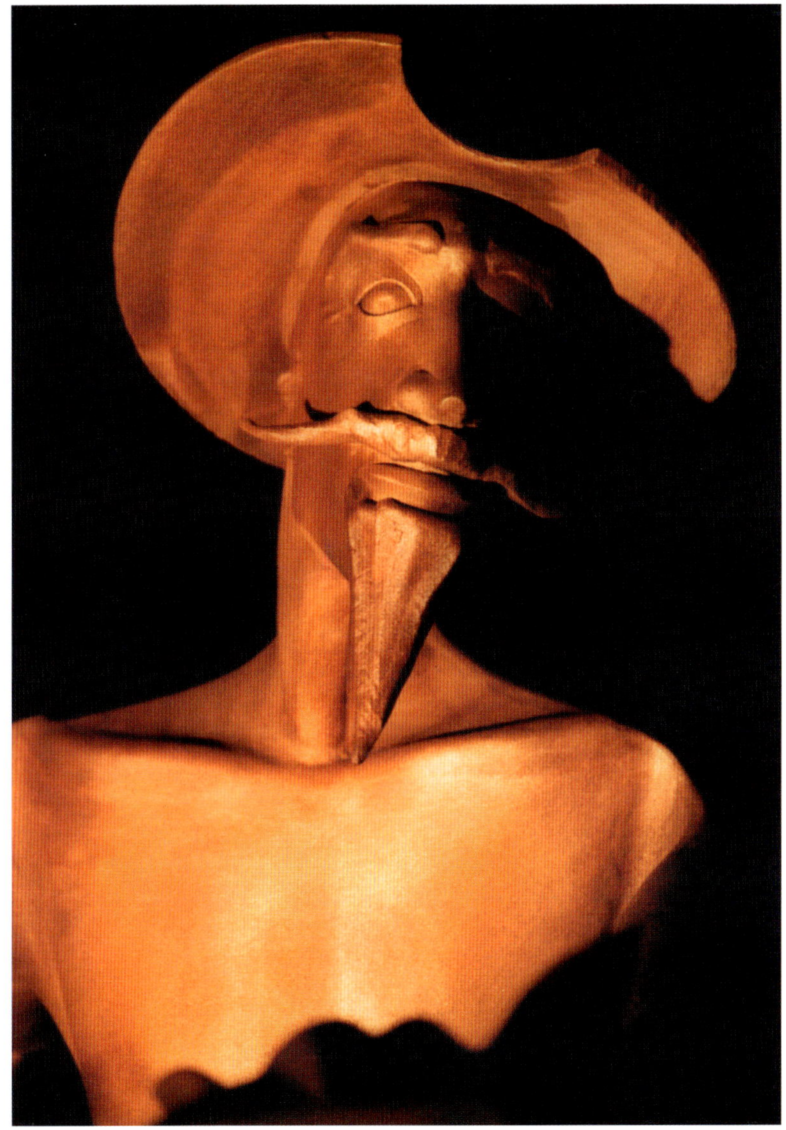

Libor Hurda. *Don "Q"*. Detail. *Photo, artist*

Libor Hurda. *Don "Q"*. Mild steel, bronzing. 90" h. *Photo, artist*

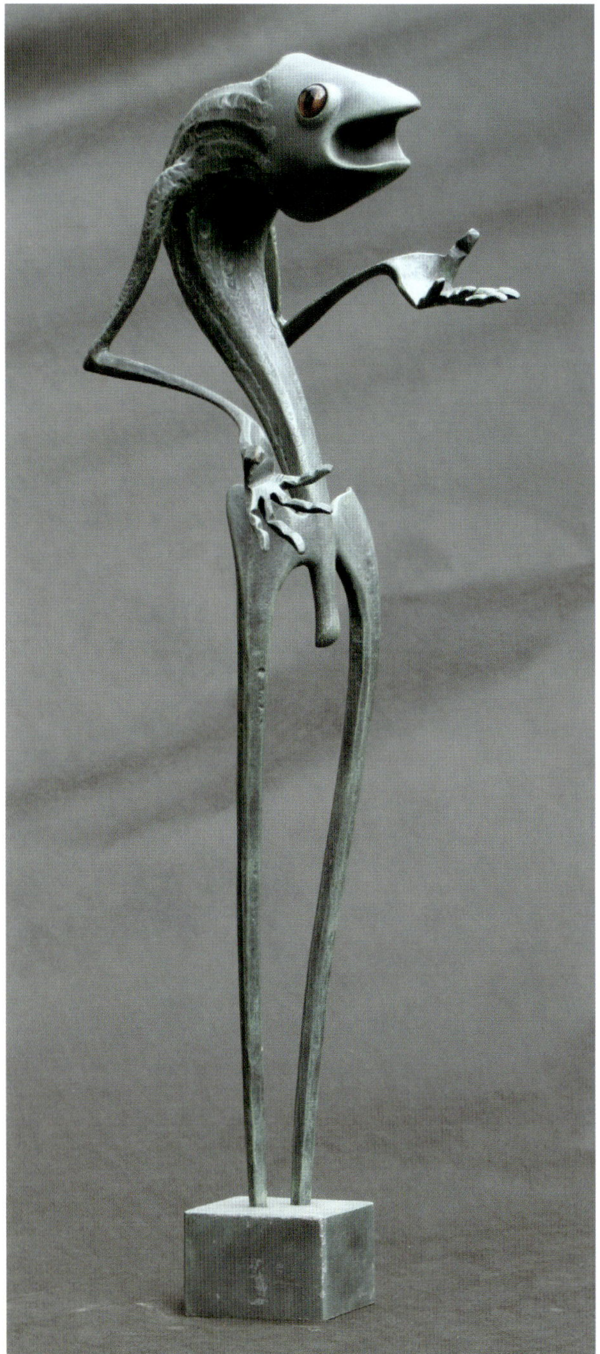

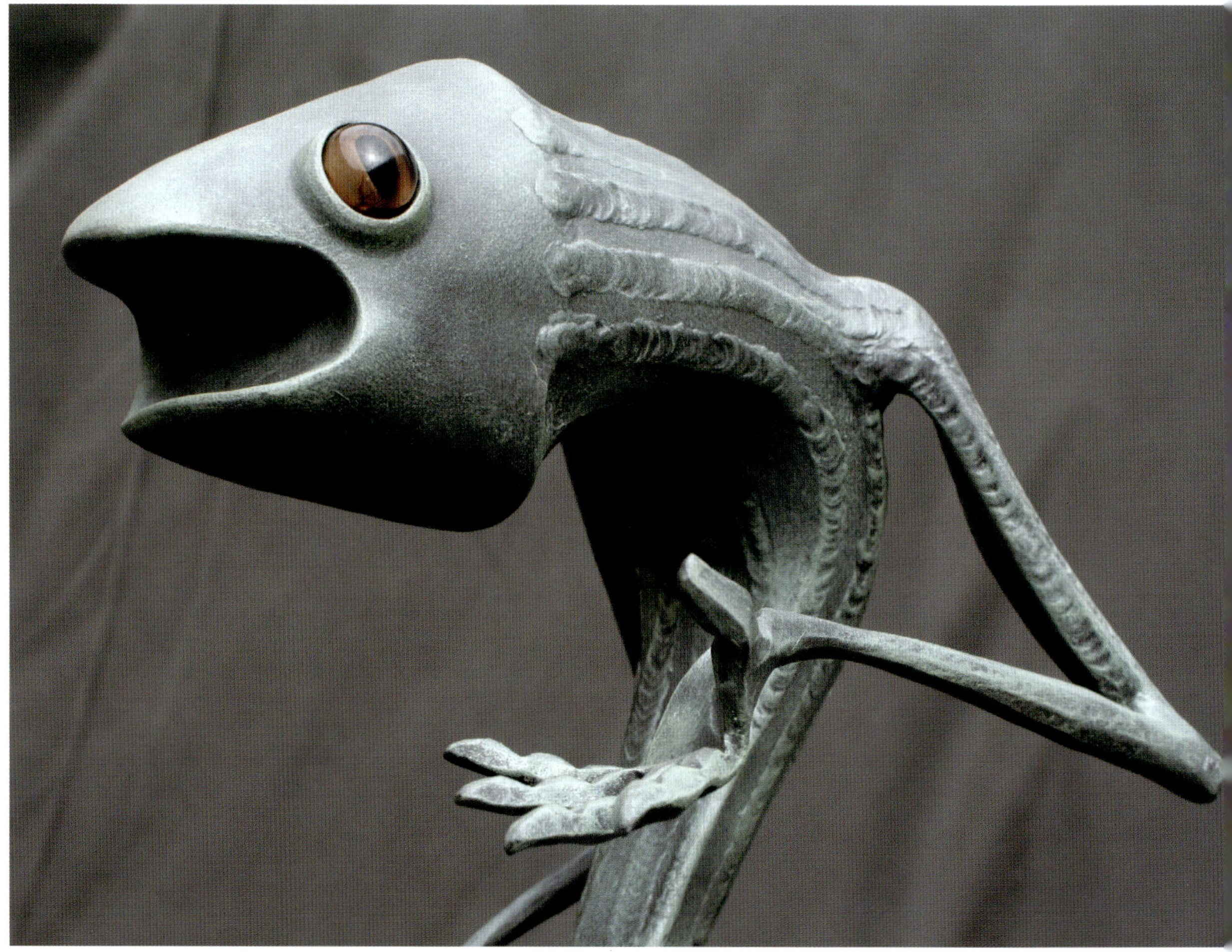

Libor Hurda. *Fischman.* Detail. *Photo, artist*

Libor Hurda. *Fischman.* Mild steel, zincing, and patination, glass. 32" h. *Photo, artist*

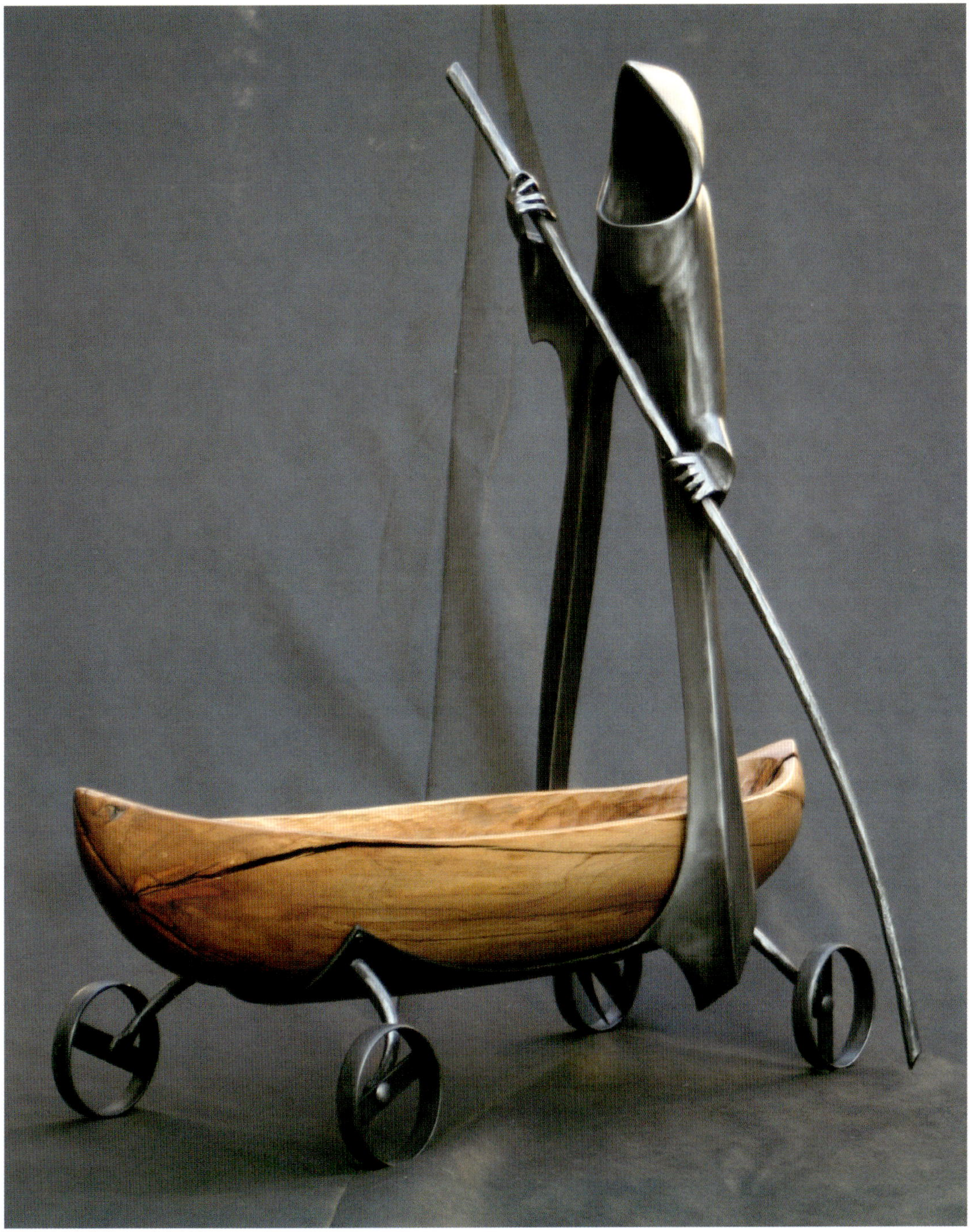

Libor Hurda. *Charon.* Mild steel and wood, 43" h. *Photo, artist*

Danielle Miller. *In Wind, We Woven, Weave*, 2000. Silicon bronze and marble. 112" h x 50" w x 24" d. *Photo, Steven Keull*

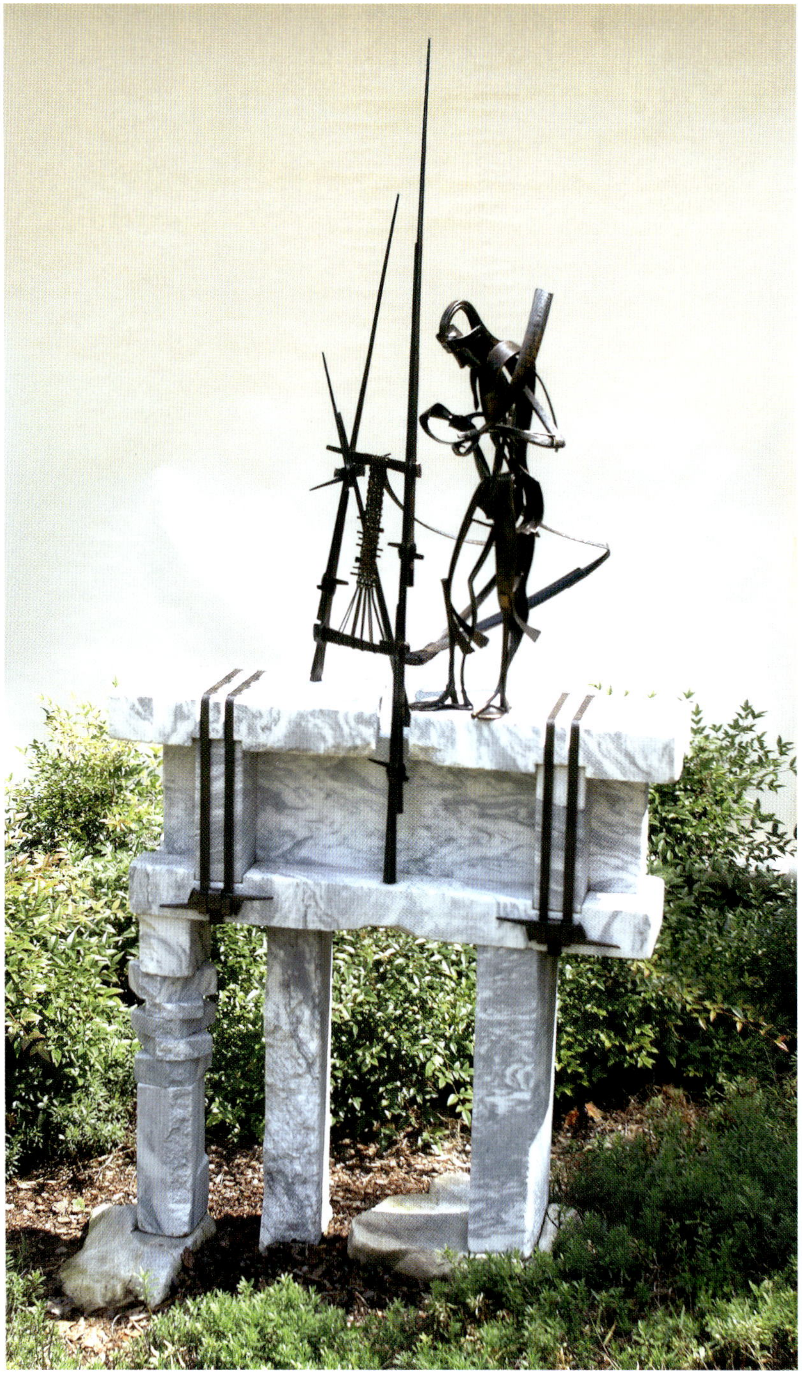

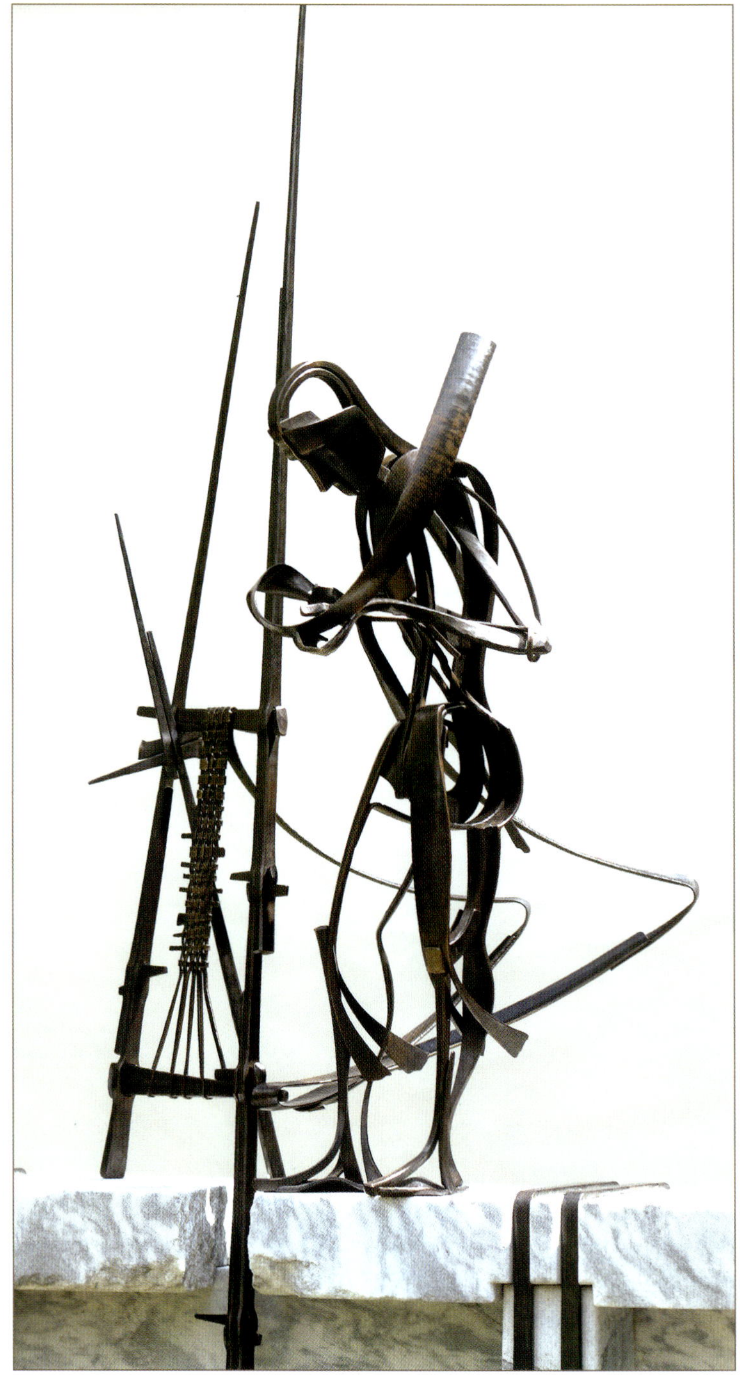

Danielle Miller. *In Wind, We Woven, Weave*, 2000. Detail. *Photo, Steven Keull*

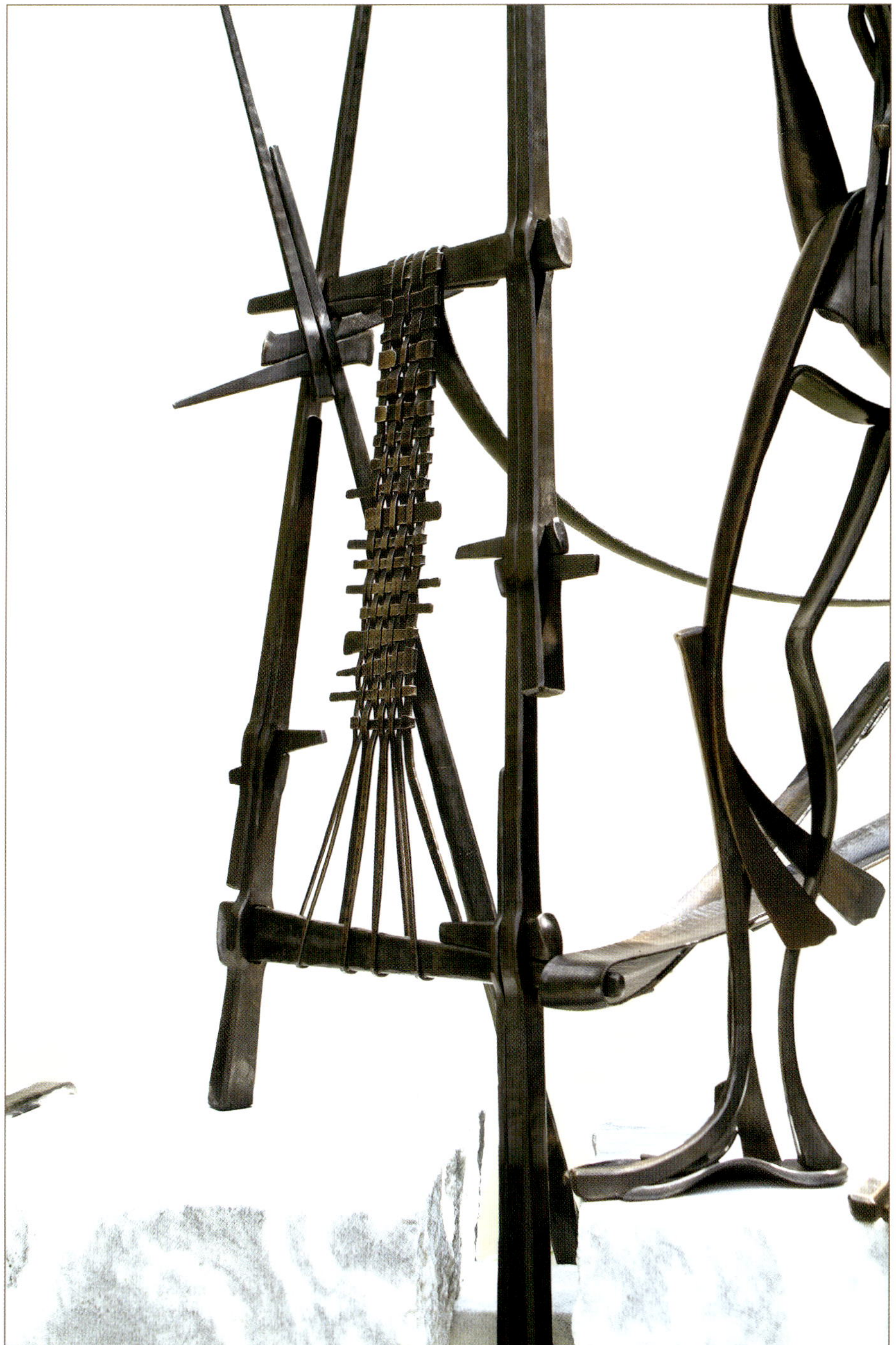

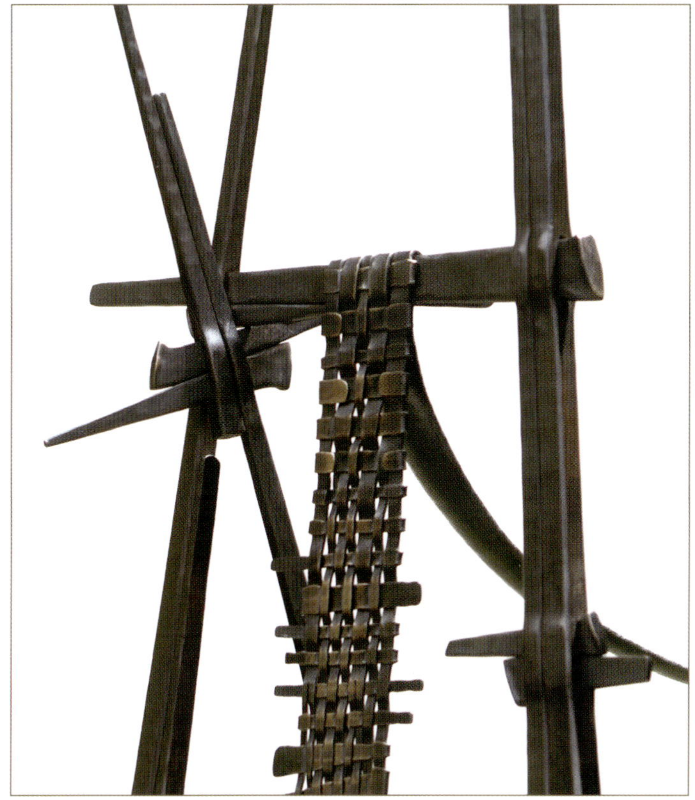

Danielle Miller. *In Wind, We Woven, Weave*, 2000. Detail. *Photo, Steven Keull*

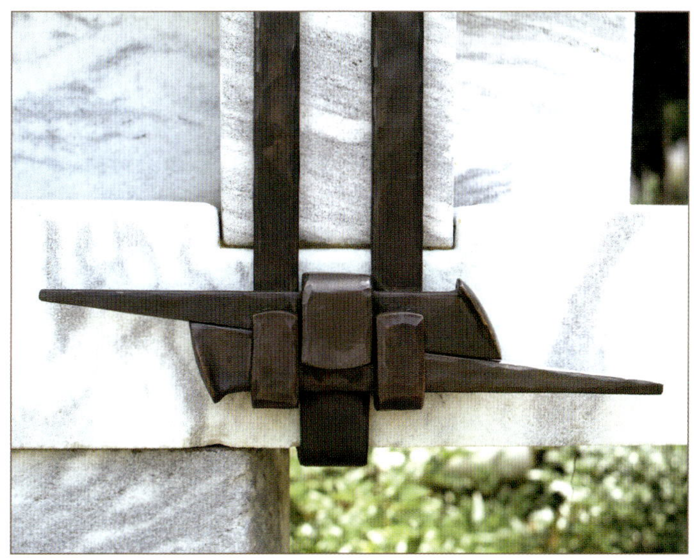

Danielle Miller. *In Wind, We Woven, Weave*, 2000. Joinery detail. *Photo, Steven Keull*

Danielle Miller. *In Wind, We Woven, Weave*, 2000. Detail. *Photo, Steven Keull*

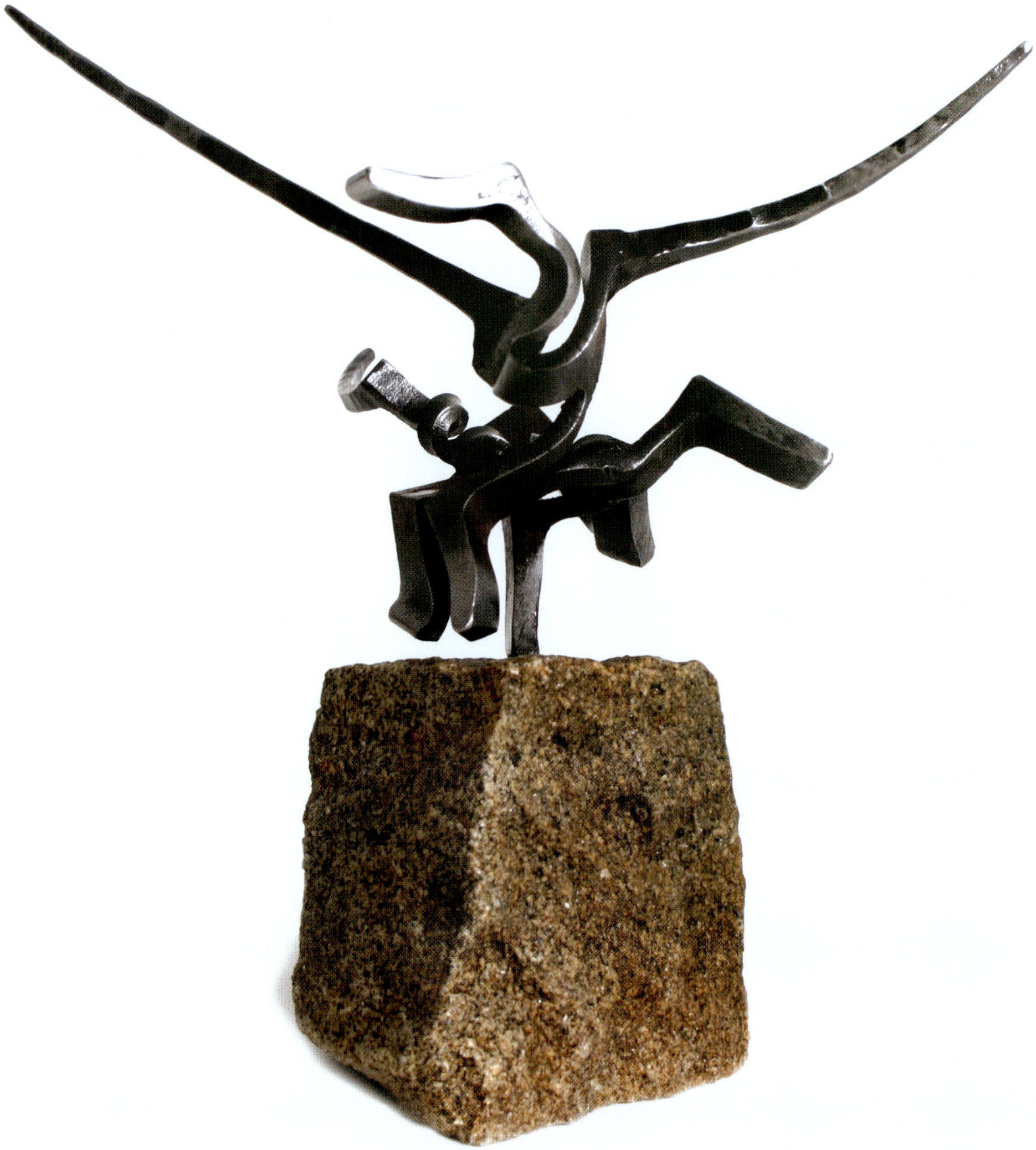

Pavel Tasovský. *Creature,* 2005. 10" x 15" x 9". *Photo, artist*

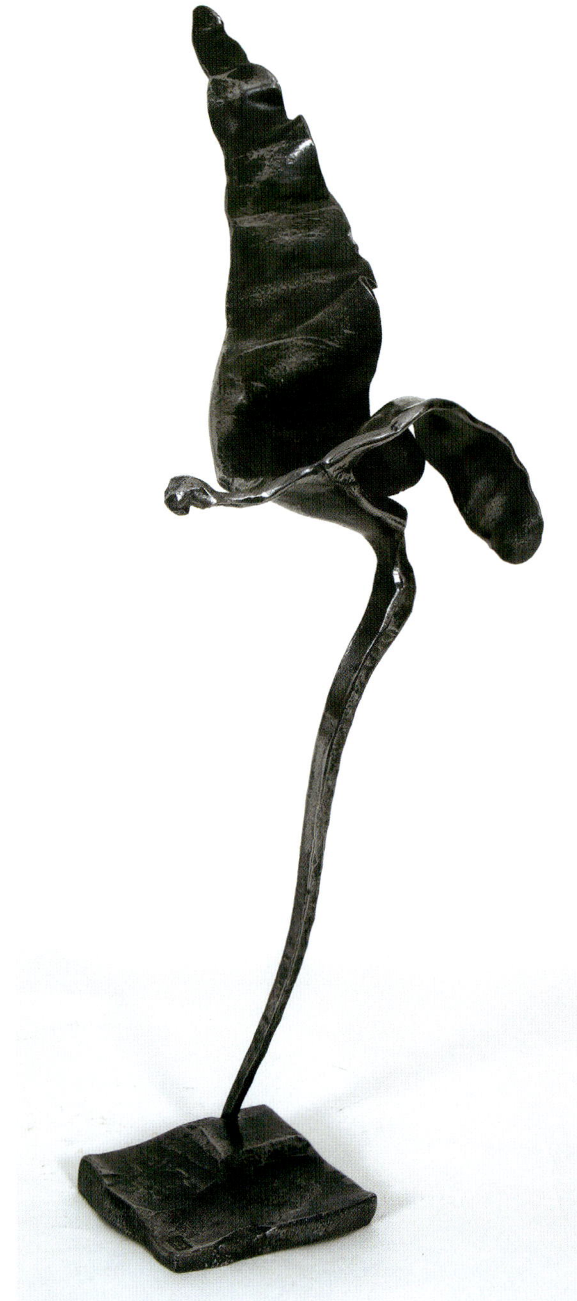

Pavel Tasovský. *Angel,* 1999. 20" x 19" x 8". *Photo, artist*

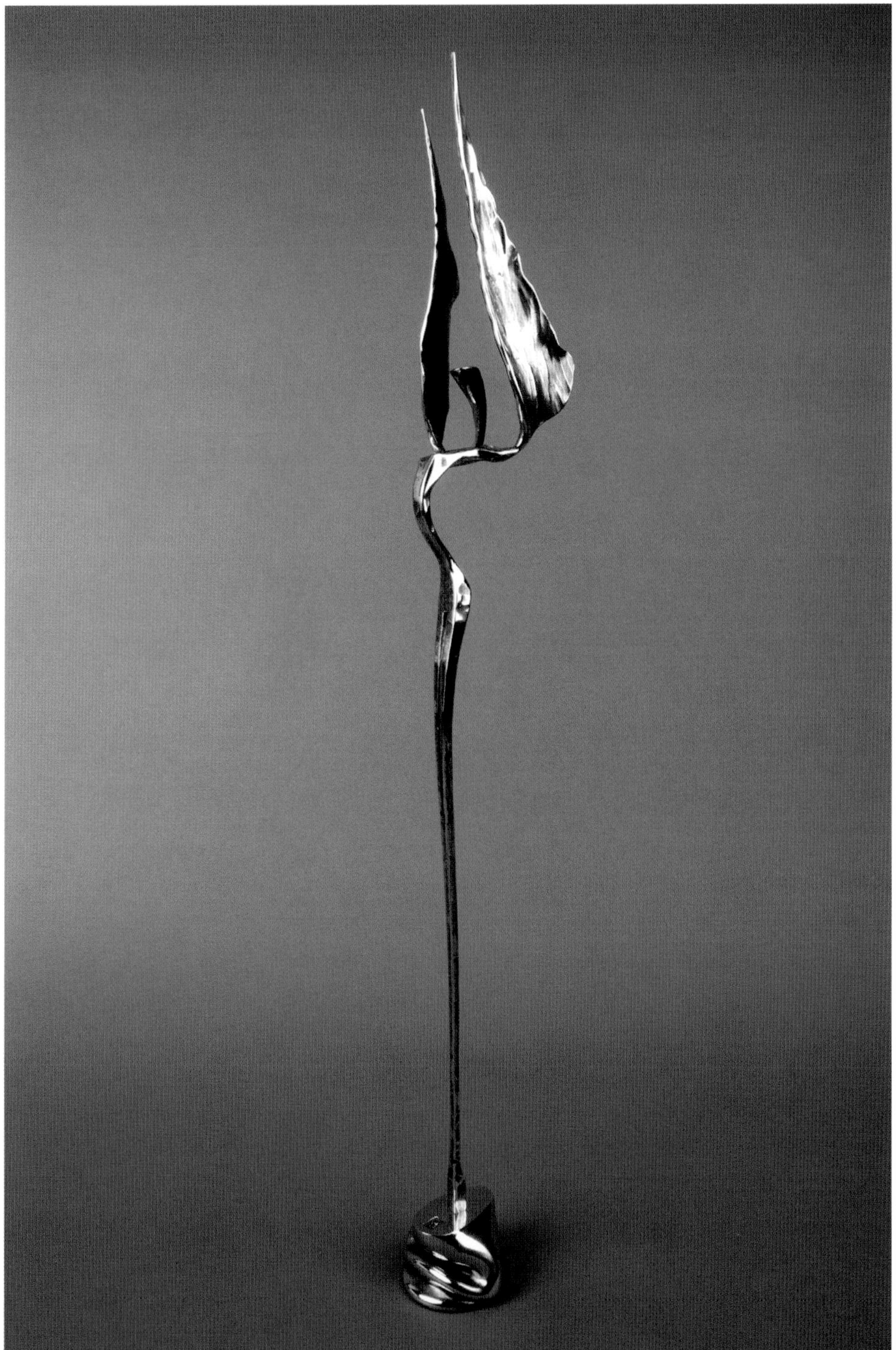

Pavel Tasovský. *Nike,* 2007. 31" x 5" x 3". *Photo, artist*

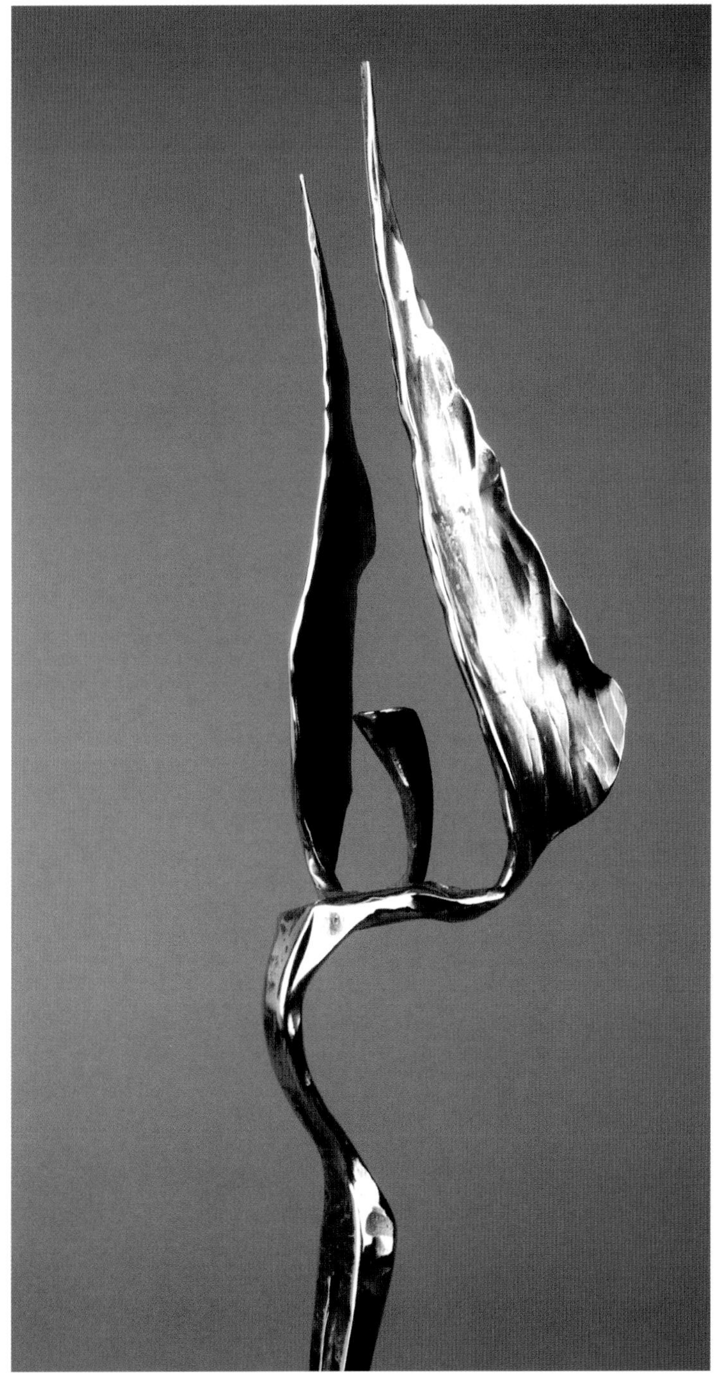

Pavel Tasovský. *Nike,* 2007. Detail. *Photo, artist*

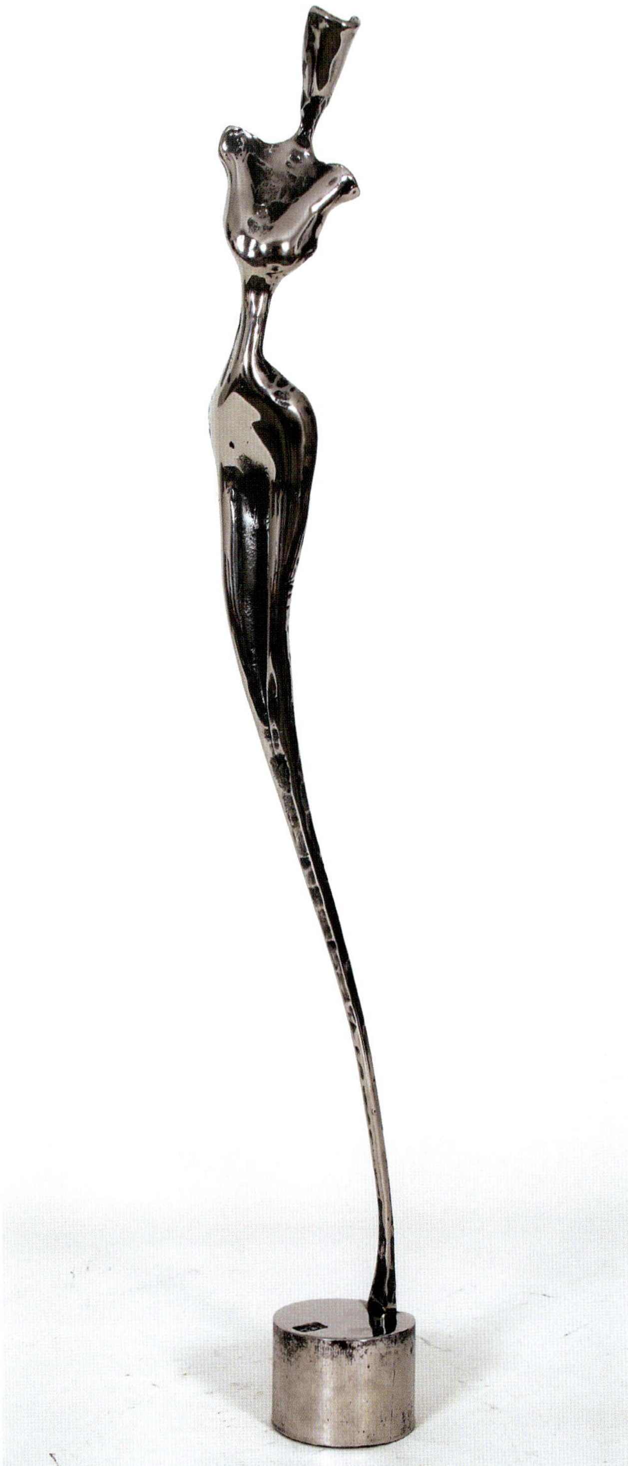

Pavel Tasovský. *Torso*, 2004. 21" x 2.5" x 2". *Photo, artist*

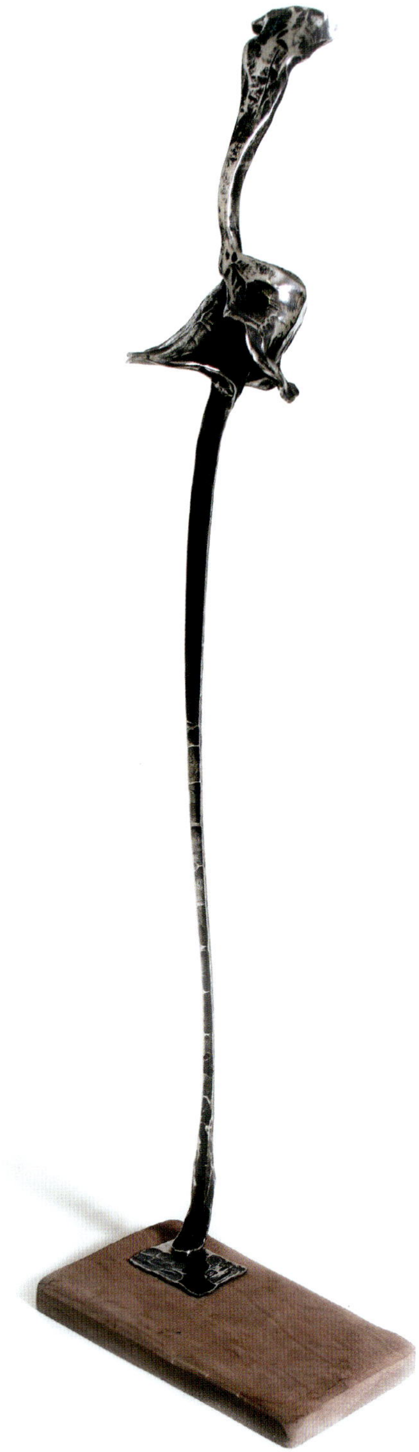

Pavel Tasovský. *Torso*, 2004. 61" x 13" x 10". *Photo, artist*

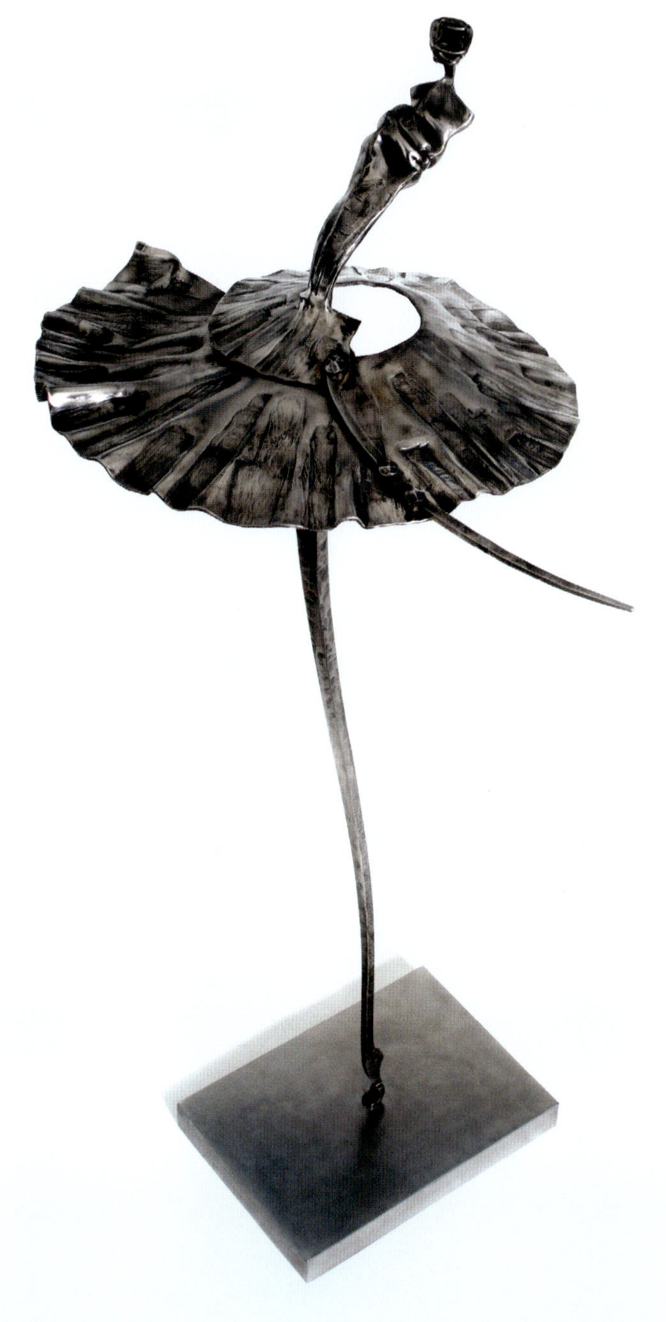

Pavel Tasovský. *Danser,* 2005. 57" x 209" x 18". *Photo, artist*

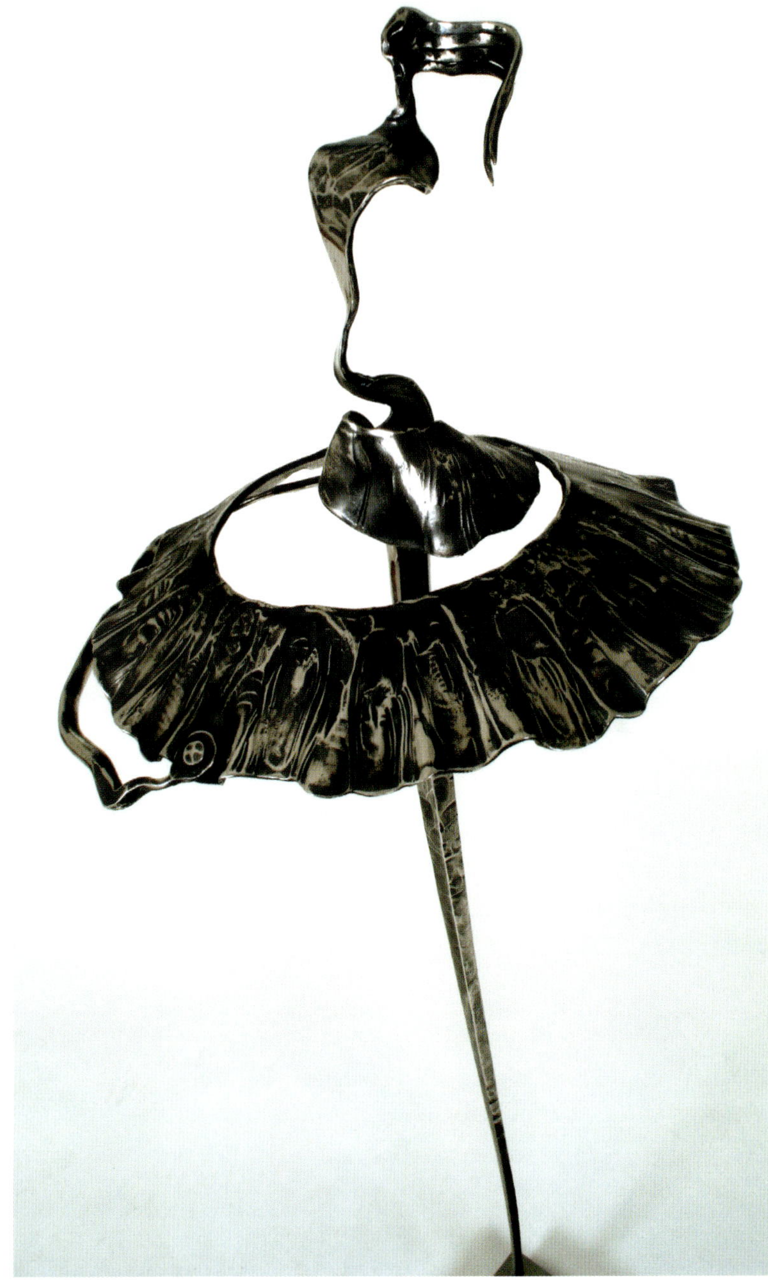

Pavel Tasovský. *Dancer,* 2005. 54" x 20" x 20". *Photo, artist*

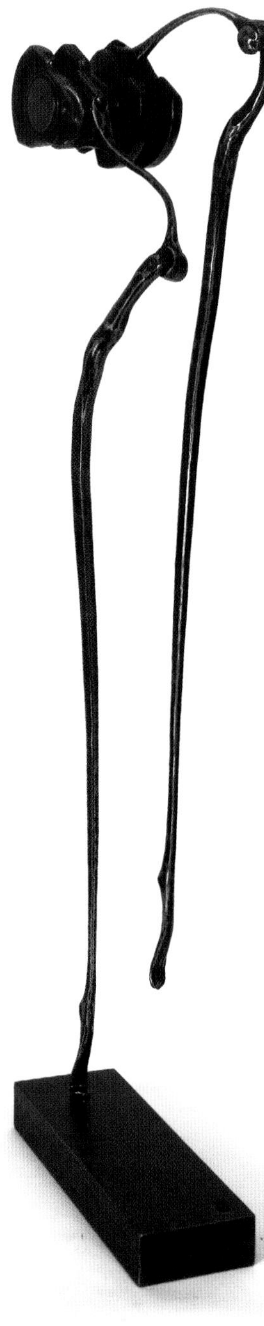

Pavel Tasovský. *Runner,* 2005. 56" x 15" x 19". *Photo, artist*

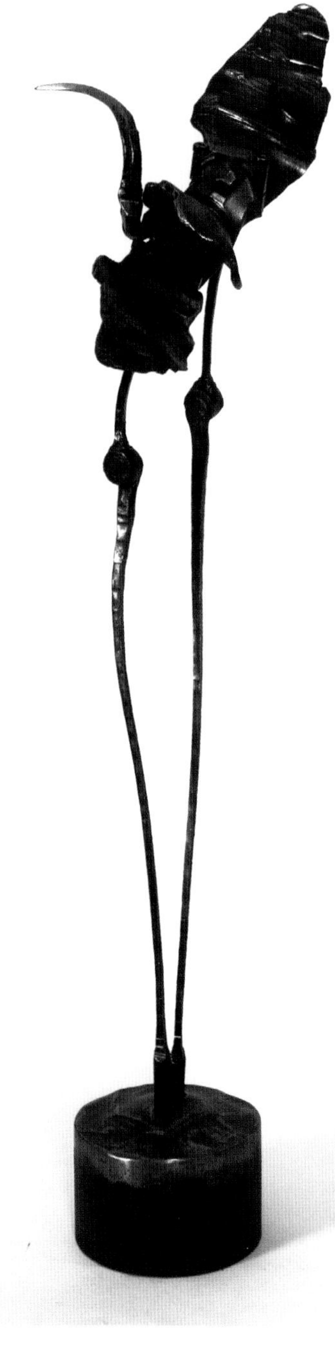

Pavel Tasovský. *Crank,* 2003. 41" x 22" x 9". *Photo, artist*

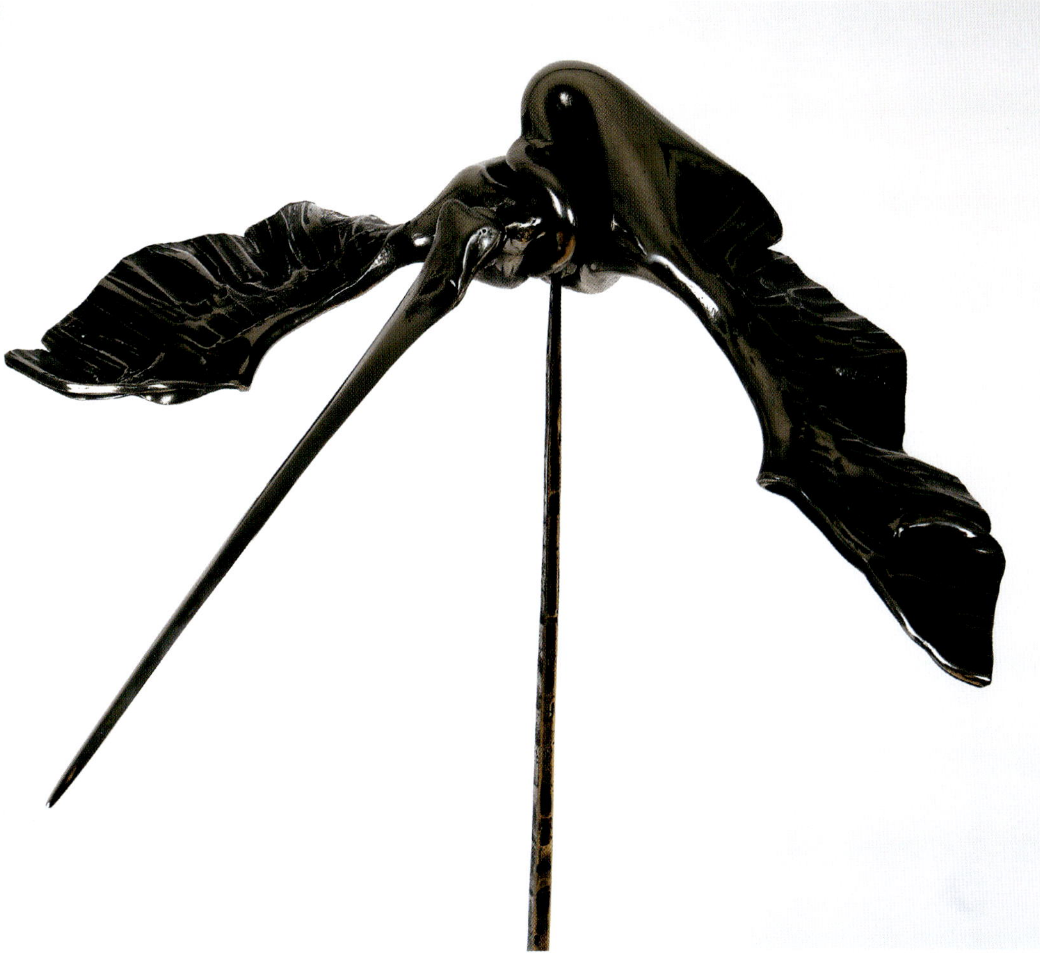

Pavel Tasovský. *Bird Fly,* 2006.
44" x 16.5" x 20". *Photo, artist*

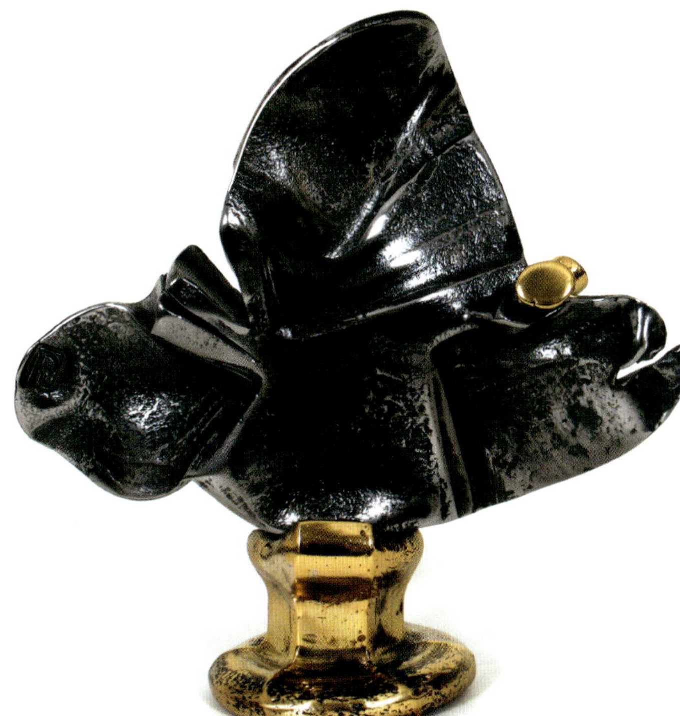

Pavel Tasovský. *Fisch,* 2004.
8" x 7" x 3". *Photo, artist*

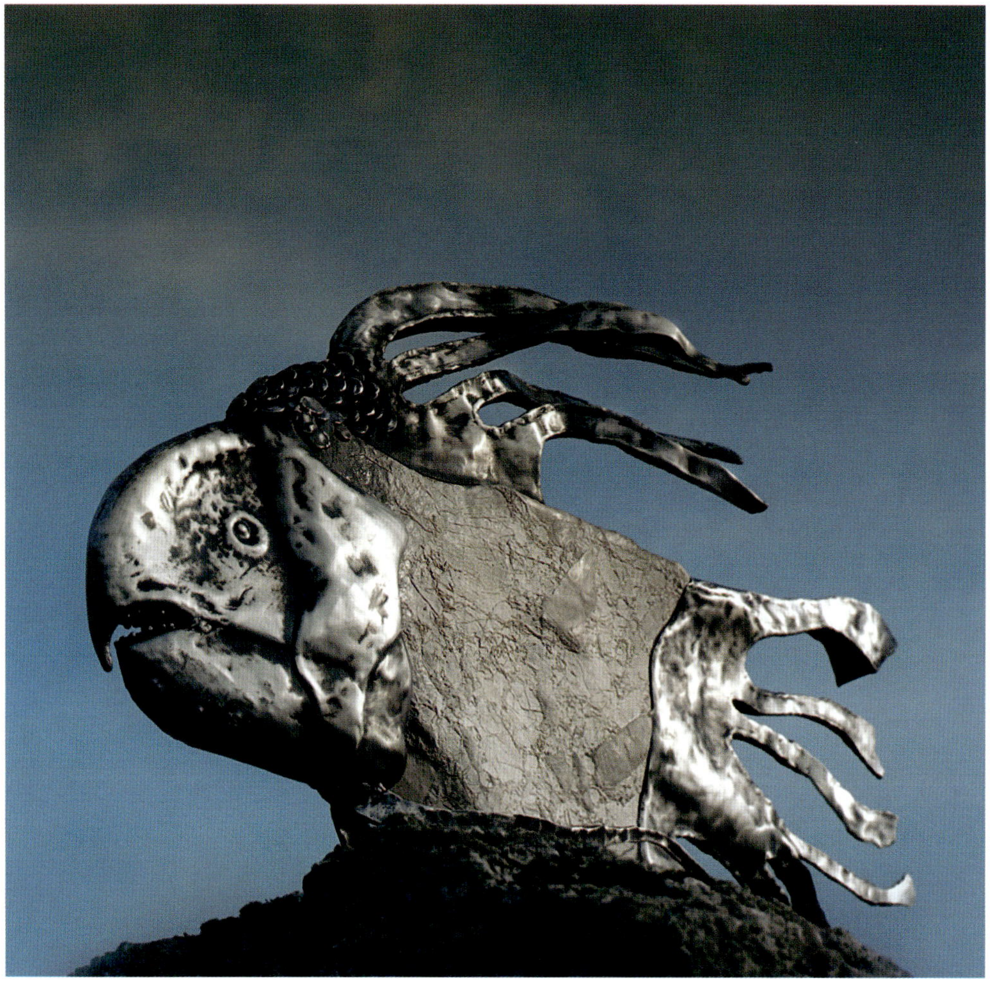

Radomír Bárta. *Fish,* Natural form. Stainless steel and marble. 24" h x 35" l. *Photo, Pavel Smékal*

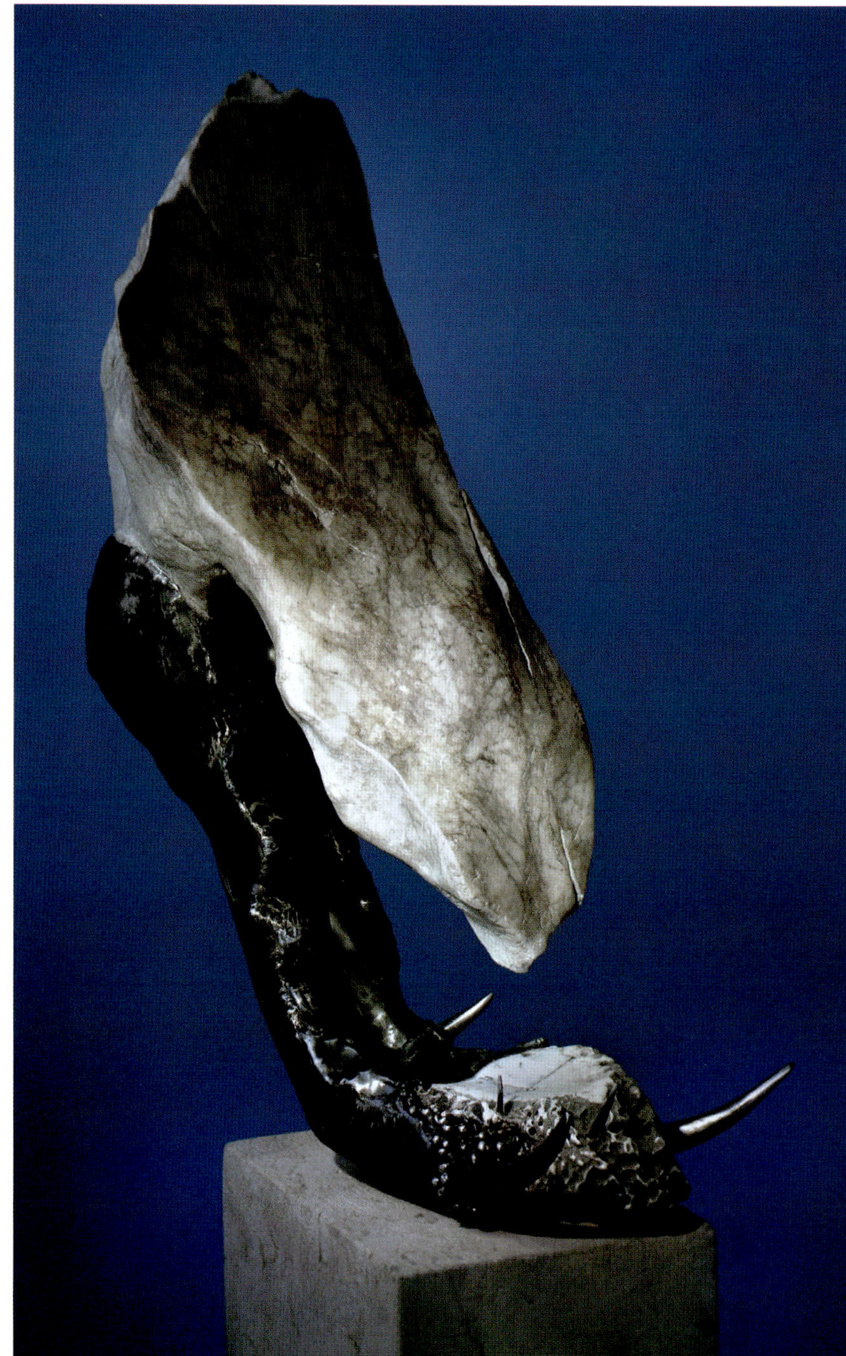

Radomír Bárta. *Boar Head.* Stainless steel and marble. 39" h x 20" l. *Photo, Pavel Smékal*

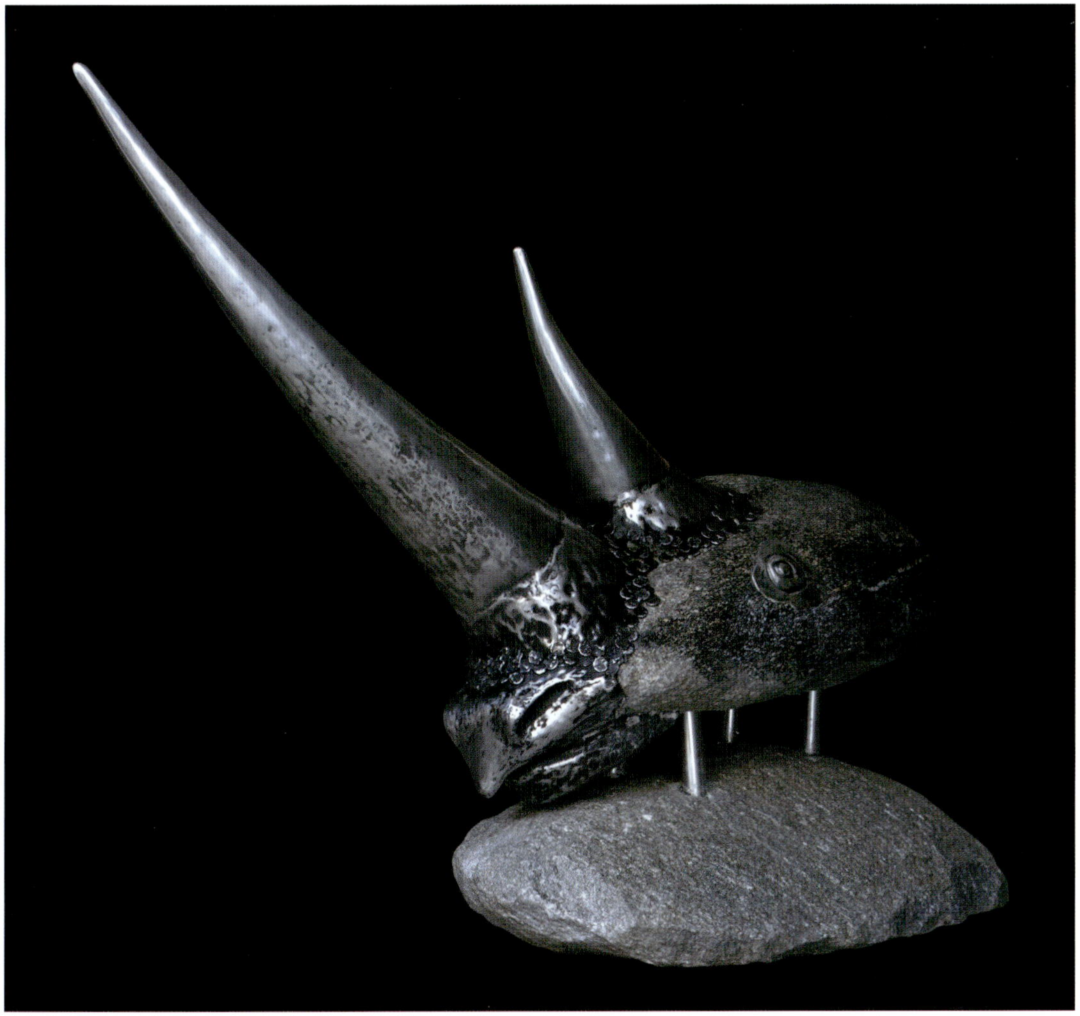

Radomír Bárta. *Rhinoceros.* Stainless steel, granite boulder. *Photo, Pavel Smékal*

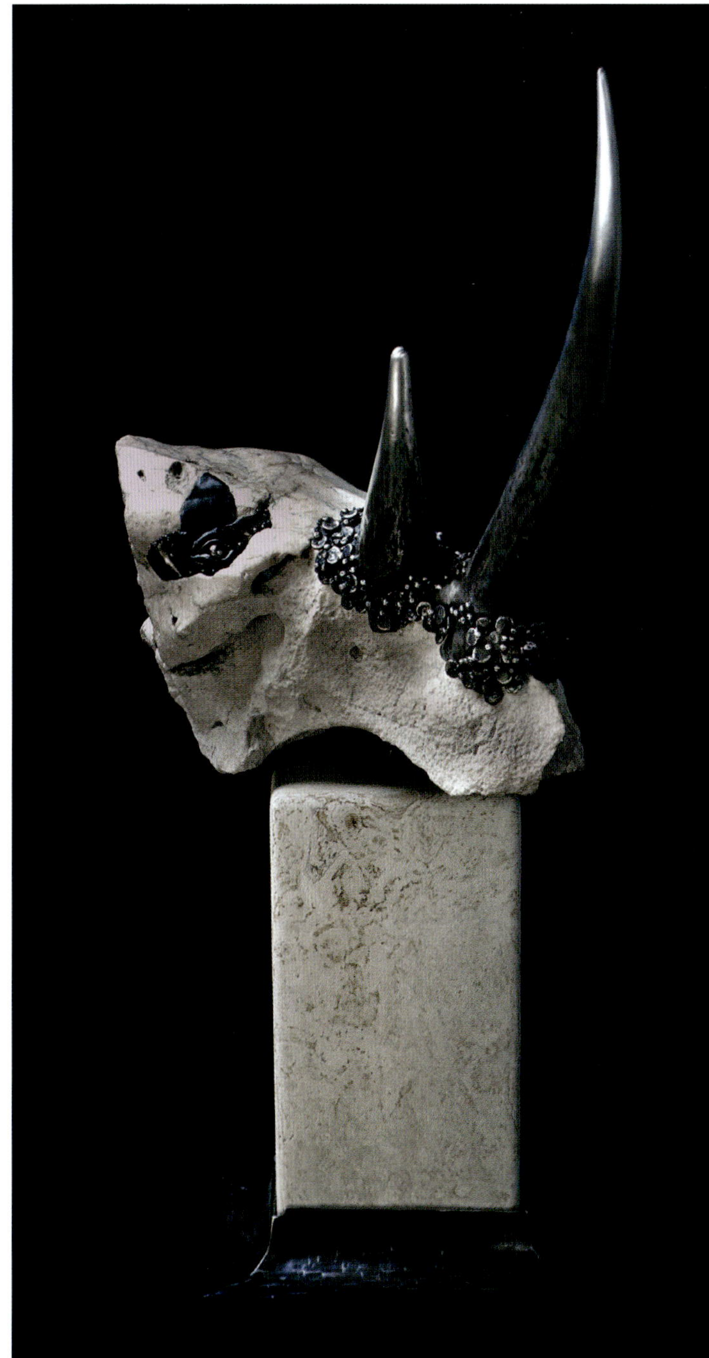

Radomír Bárta. *Rhinoceros.* Stainless steel and natural marble. 47" h, 24" horn length. *Photo, Pavel Smékal*

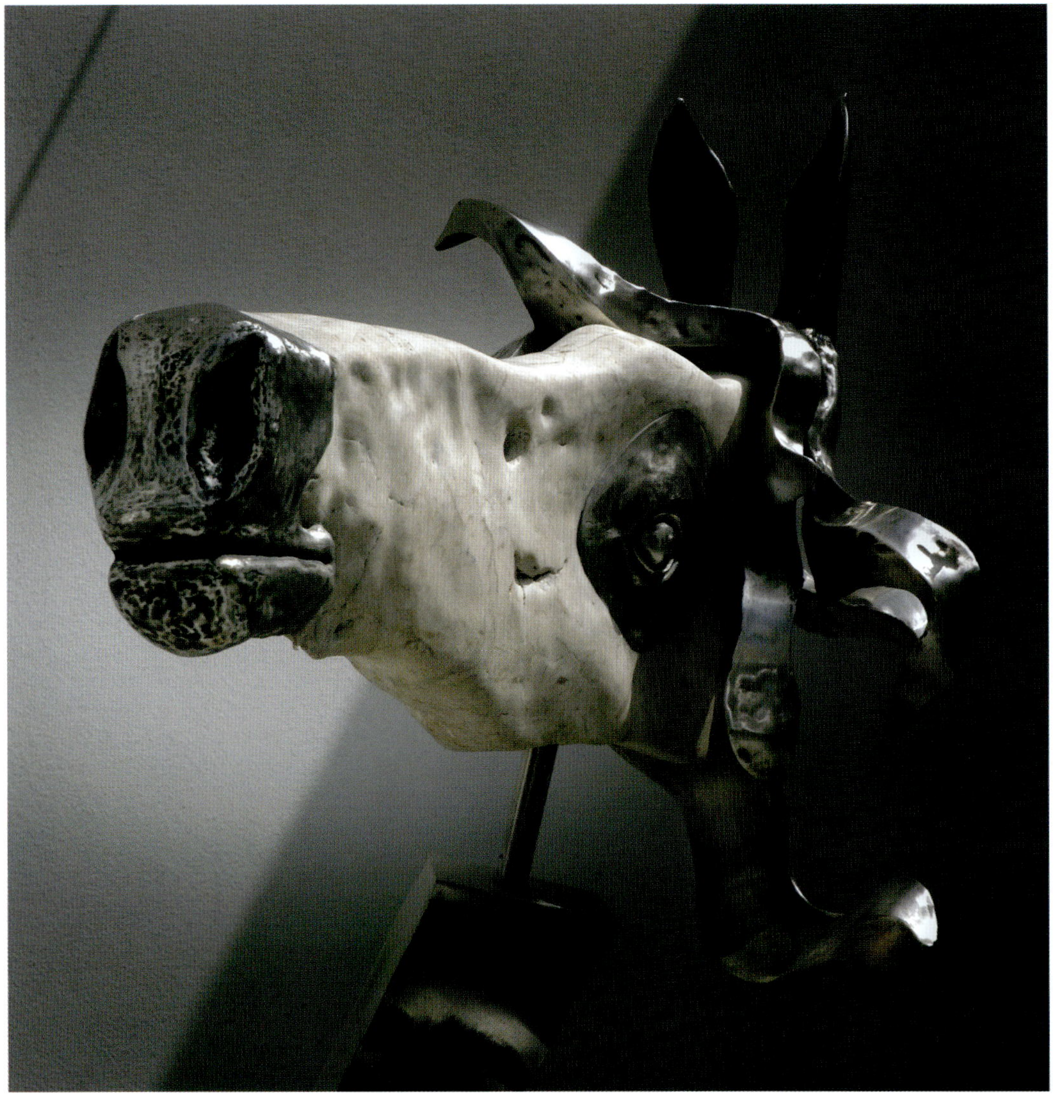

Radomír Bárta. *Horse Head.* Stainless steel and marble. 47" h. Head, 31" x 20". *Photo, Pavel Smékal*

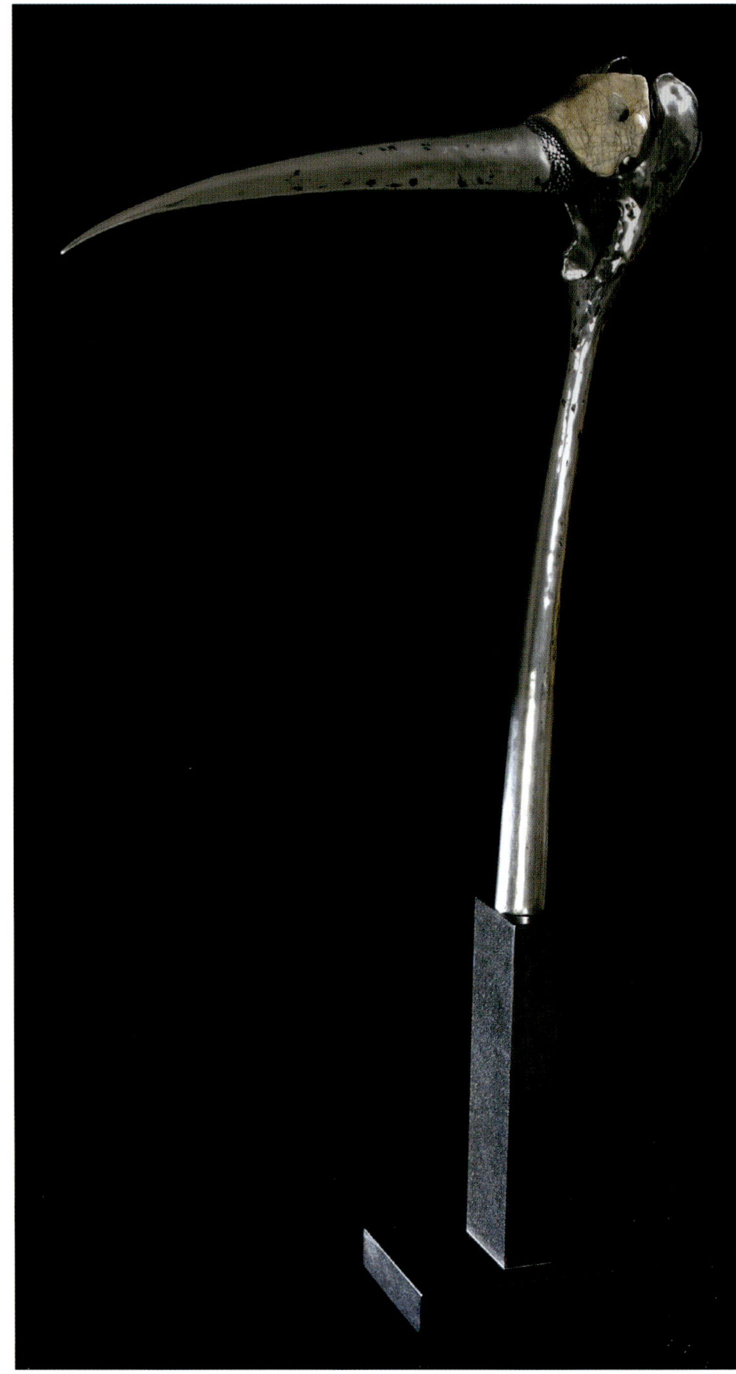

Radomír Bárta. *Marabou.* Stainless steel and marble, stand is from Swedish black granite. *Photo, Pavel Smékal*

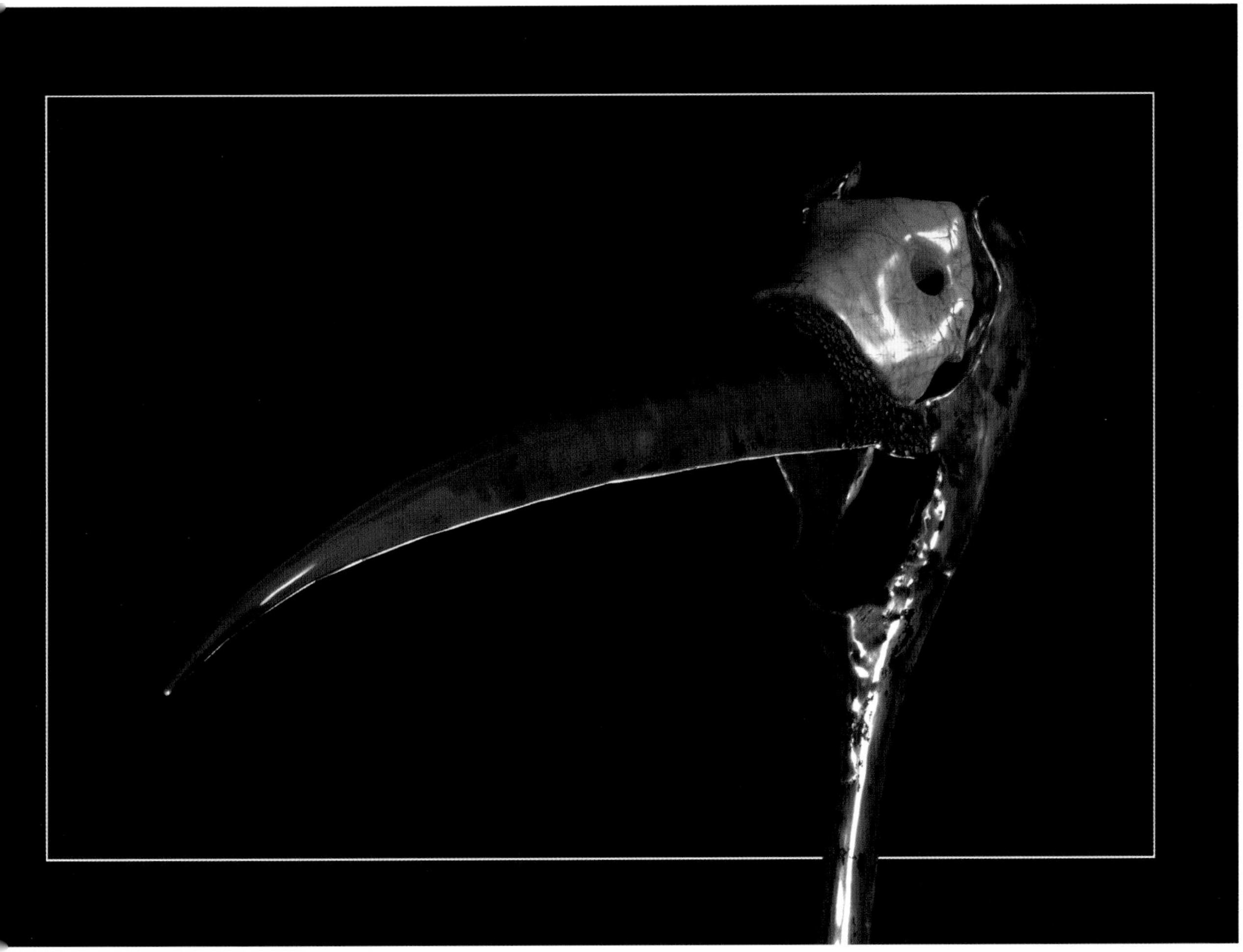

Radomír Bárta. *Marabou.* Detail. *Photo, Pavel Smékal*

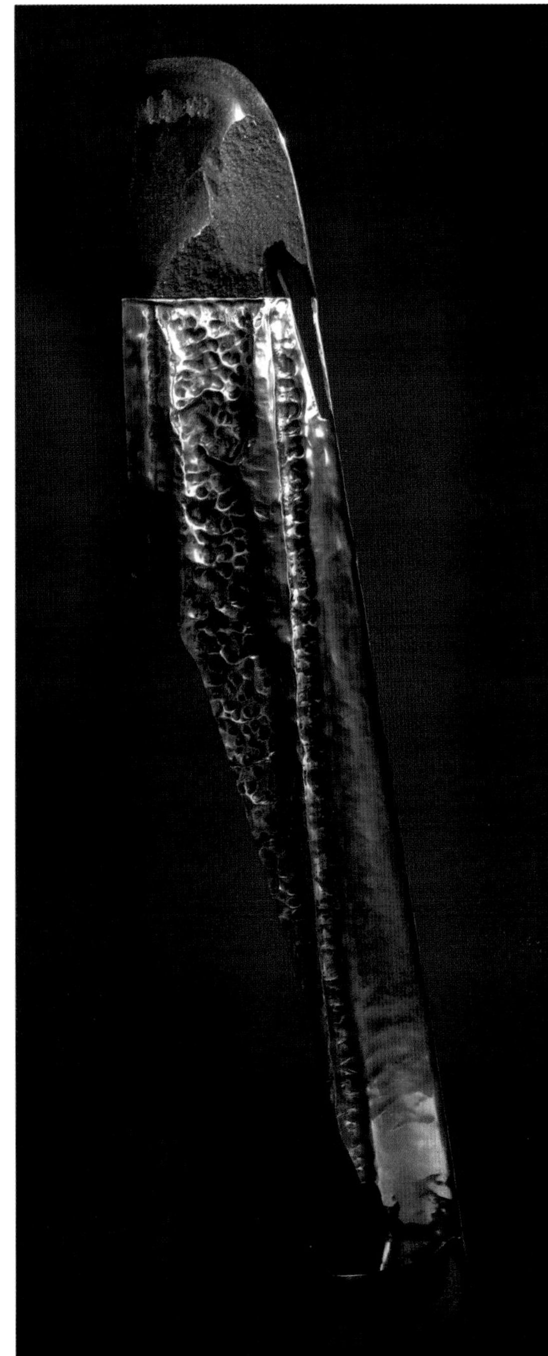

Radomír Bárta. *Falcon.* Stainless steel and Swedish black granite. *Photo, Pavel Smékal*

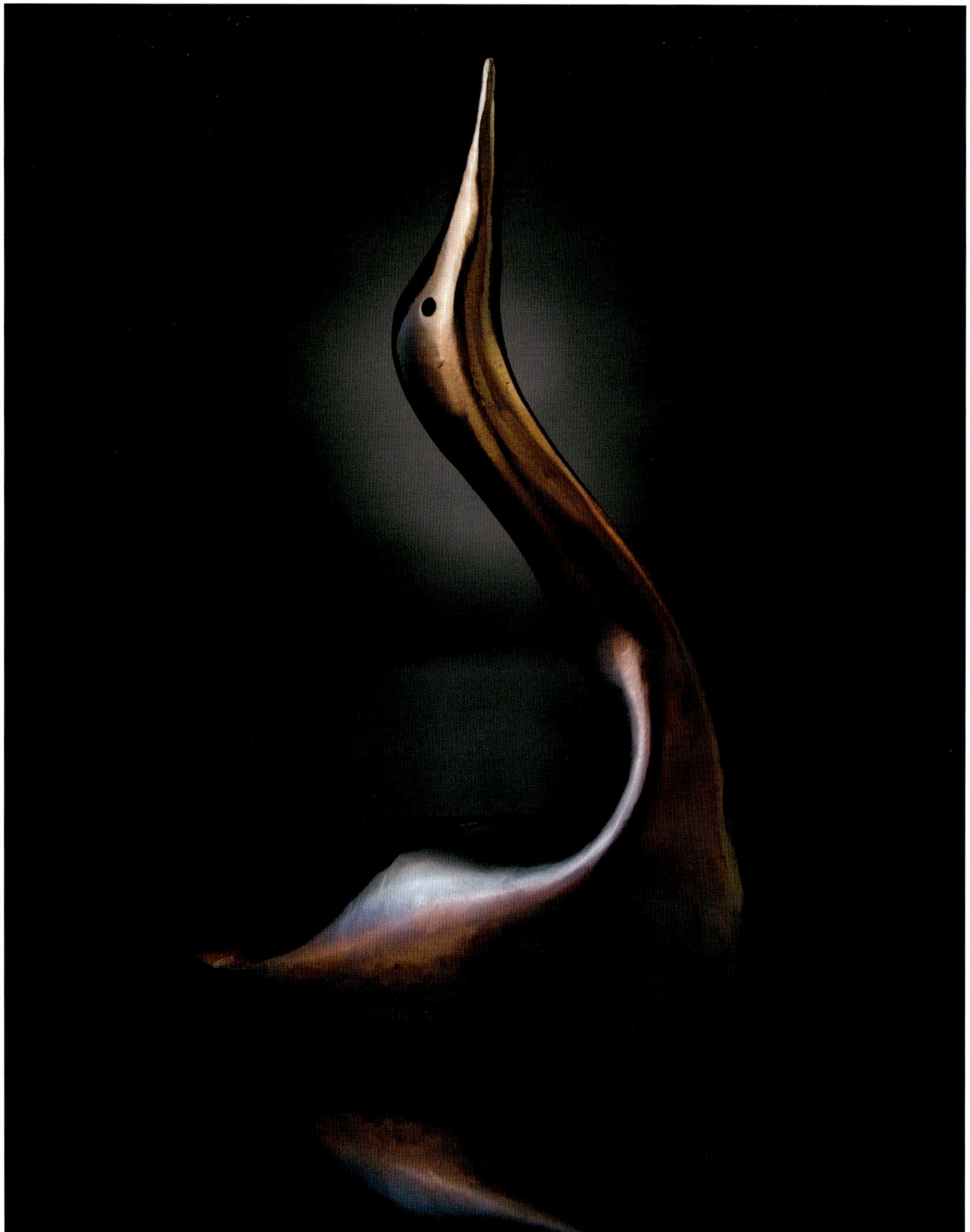

Paul M. Thorne. *Cormorant.* Forged iron hollow form, flame patina. 10" x 4" x 14" h. *Photo, Peter Kuhnlein*

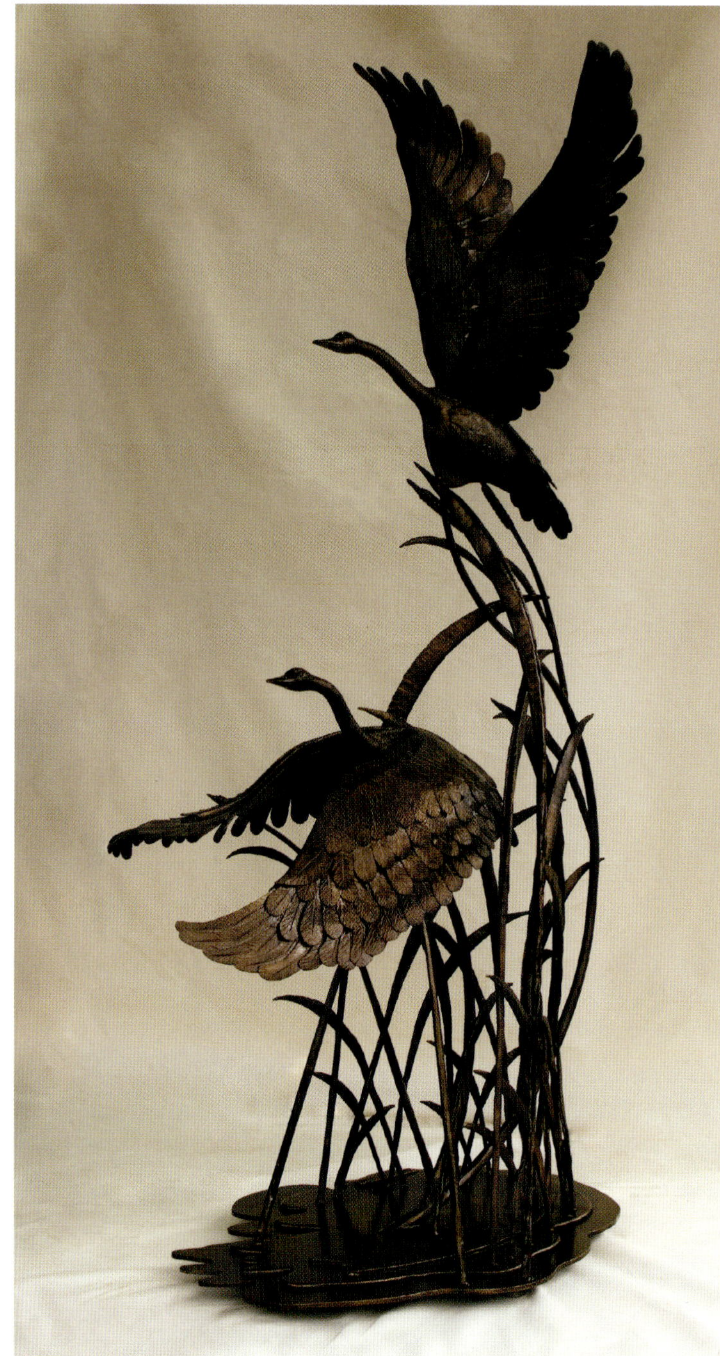

John Boyd Smith. *Wild Geese*. Mild steel, 96" h, 800 lbs., depicts two realistic and life-sized Canadian geese in flight. This piece was exhibited at the National Craft Gallery of Ireland in Kilkenny, Ireland. *Photo, Paul Nurnberg*

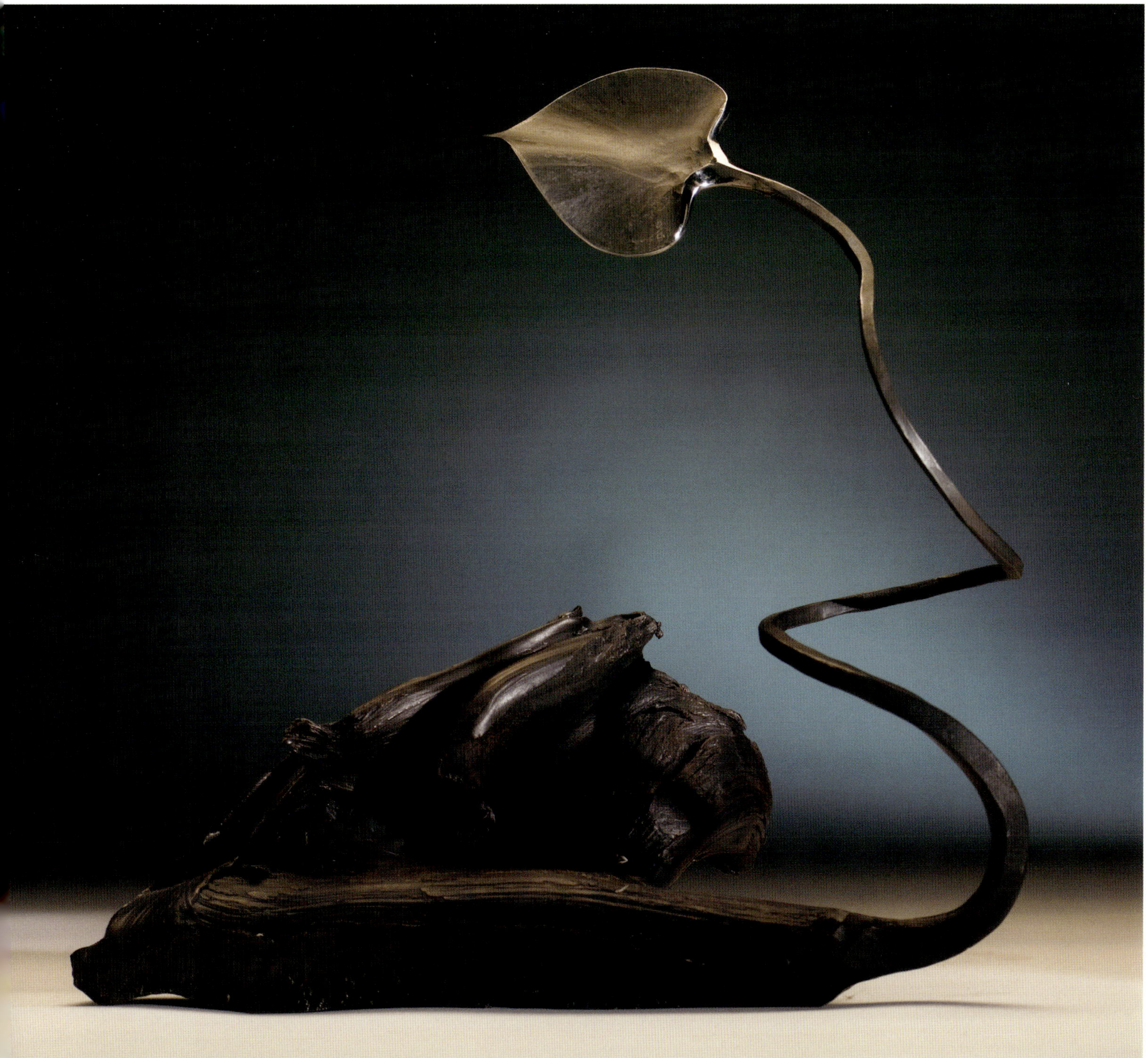

Alfred Bullermann. *Nature.* Forged from an industrial cast-off. 24" h, 28.6 lbs. The skin is made to resemble wood. *Photo, artist*

Maximilian Filleböck. *Stier* (Bull), 1984. Copper wrought out of only one piece. *Photo, Rolf Brecht*
For Maximilian Filleböck, this bull has always been his best-liked example of how to show nature's complexity in reduced abstract sculptures.

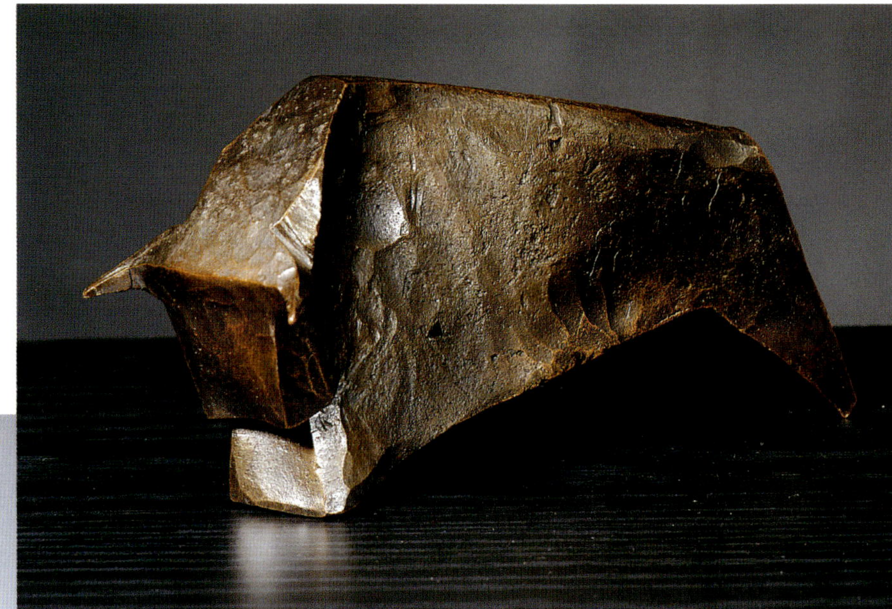

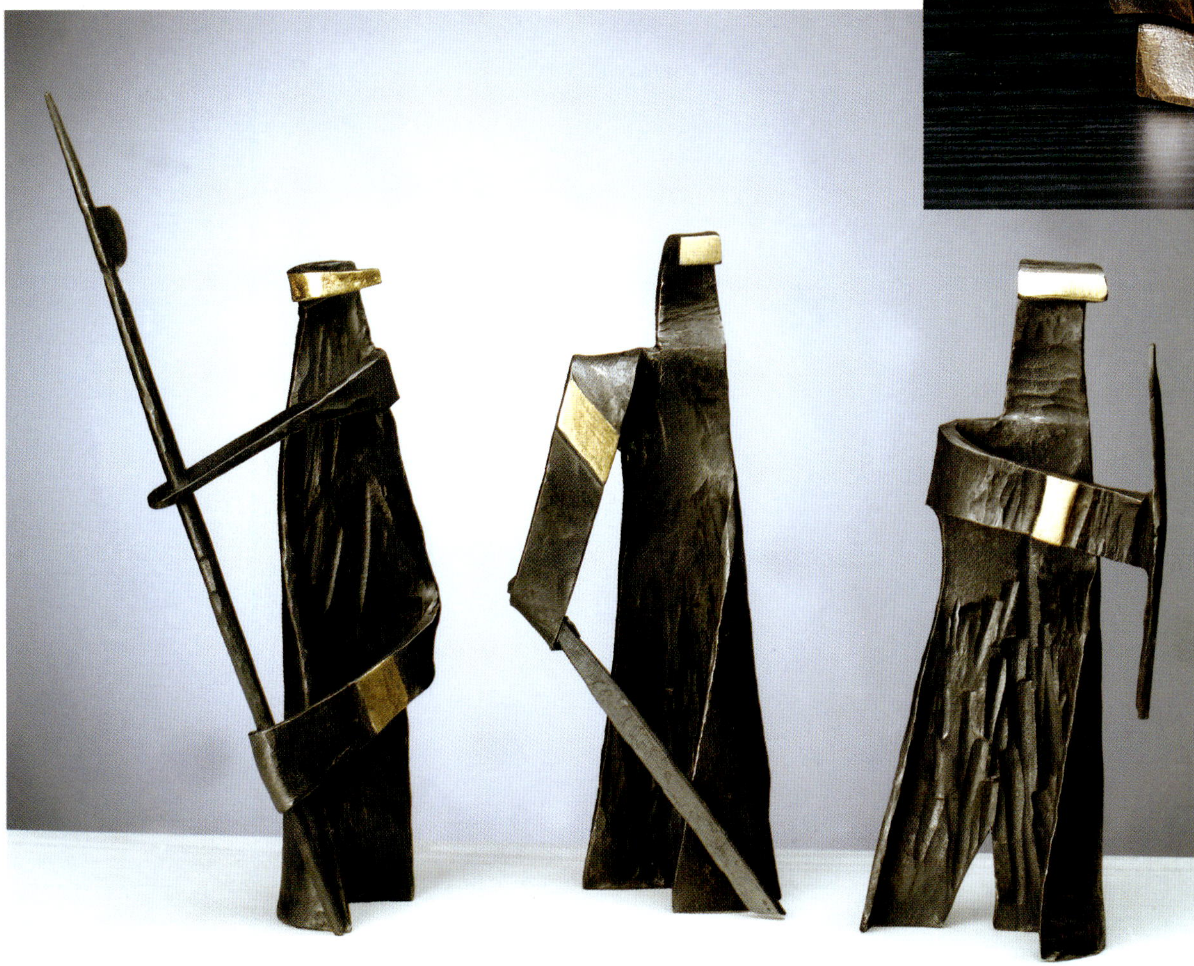

Maximilian Filleböck. *Nibelungen,* 1999. *Photo, Rolf Brecht*

Maximilian Filleböck was a great admirer of Richard Wagner and his music. The idea to create Wagner's heroes, i.e. King Gunther, Hagen, and Siegfried, out of martial steel and shiny gold was born while listening to "Der Ring des Nibelungen" (Wagner's Ring Cycle) on the radio.

King Gunther, with his protective shield, signifies absolute power. He has tolerated the murder on Siegfried but later on denies having anything to do with it.

Hagen shows the vassal's loyalty towards King Gunther. As the new owner of "Balmung," Siegfried's sword, Hagen gives no doubt about raising the sword to defend his King Gunther by any means.

Siegfried is symbolized with two left arms as the supposed hero. These two left arms hold a lance, which is the weapon he is to be killed with later.

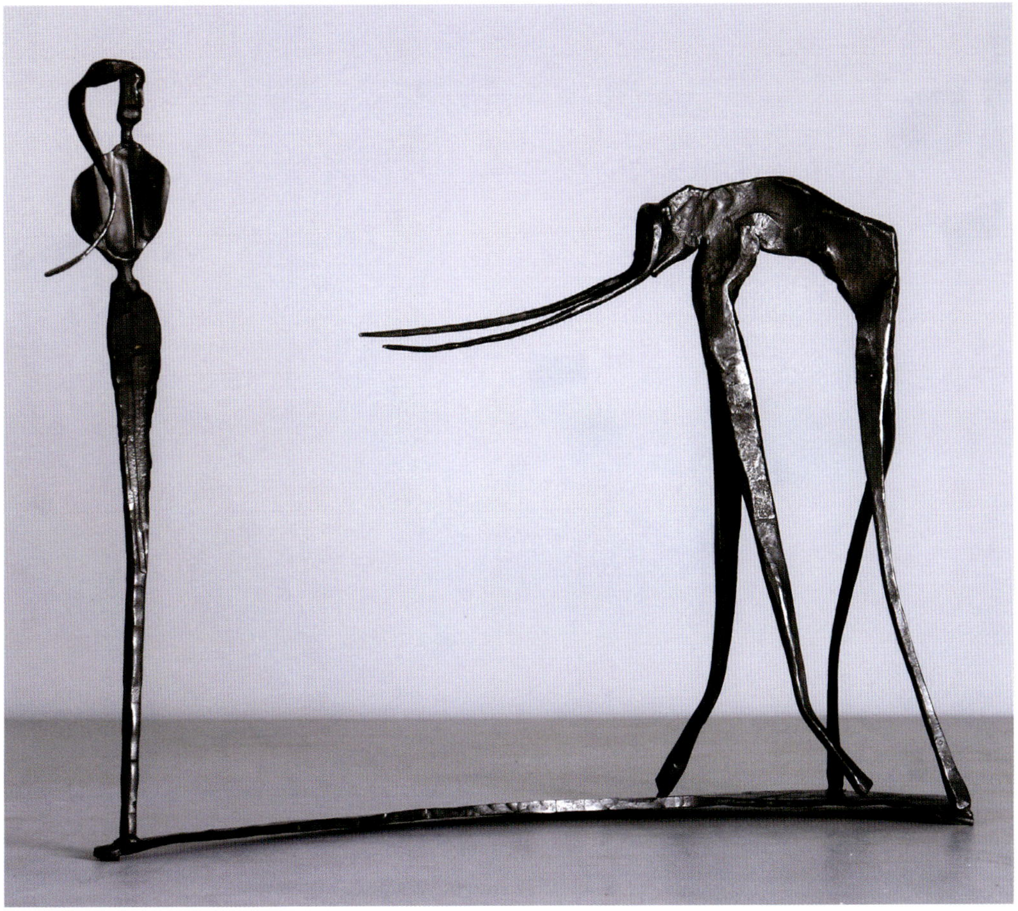

Jake James. *The Bullfight*. Forged steel. *Photo, Doug Gilbert*

This piece came about because a figurine I was making for another project didn't fit what I had in mind for it. Instead it looked very much like a matador, so I felt obliged to make a bull to partner it. The bull was all stretched from a single piece, with the exception of the horns, which given their exaggerated length I added afterwards. – Jake James

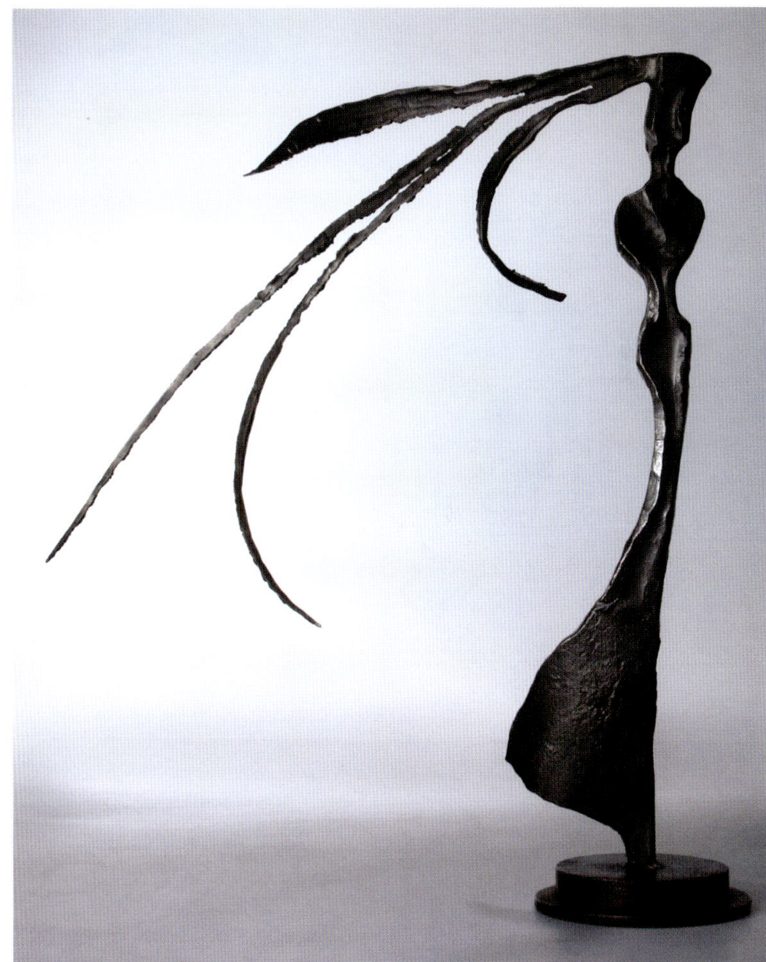

Jake James. *Freya*. Forged from 1" x 6" steel bar. *Photo, Doug Gilbert*

The Nordic Goddess of love and fertility. This is one of my favourite pieces. She is full of the movement, grace, and beauty that are so much in evidence when the steel is white hot and moving under the hammer! – Jake James

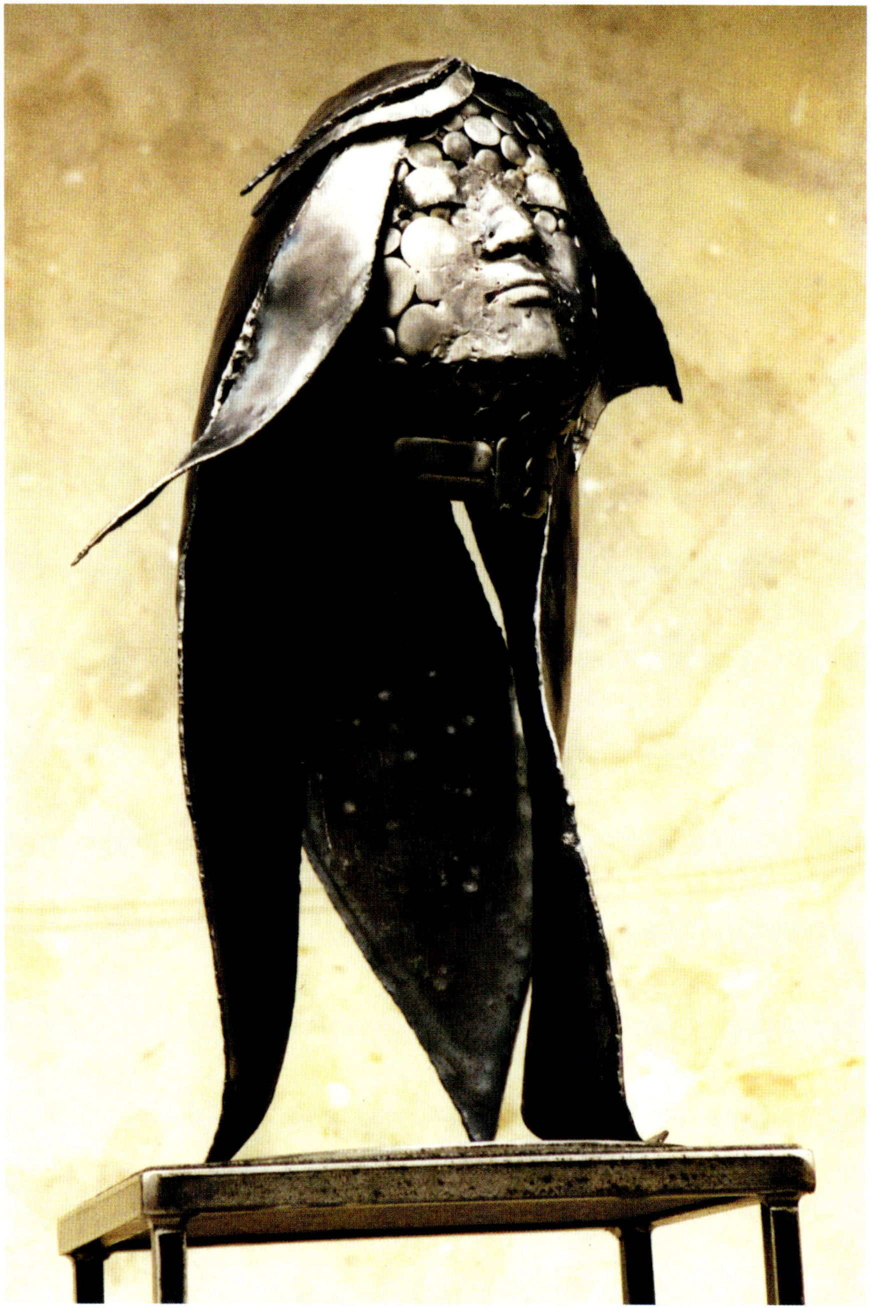

Stephen Fitz-Gerald. *Asia.* Steel, life-size. *Photo, artist*

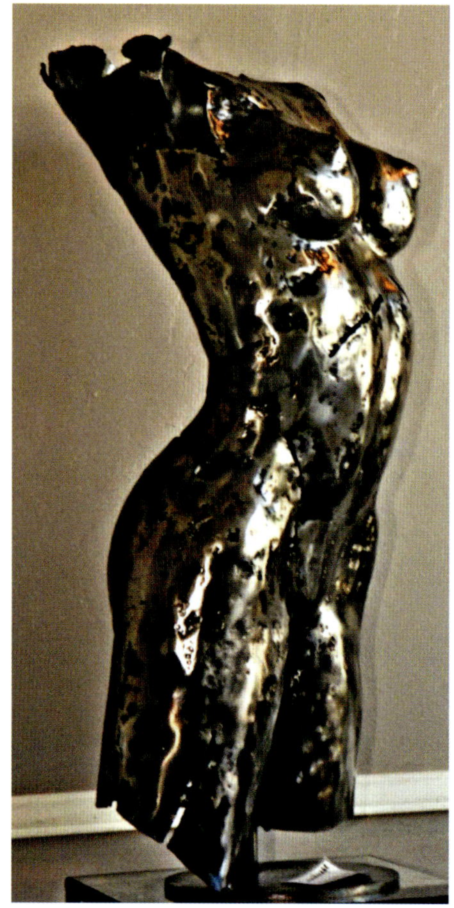

Stephen Fitz-Gerald. *Form Follows Function*. Life size figure in forged and welded steel plate. *Photo, artist*

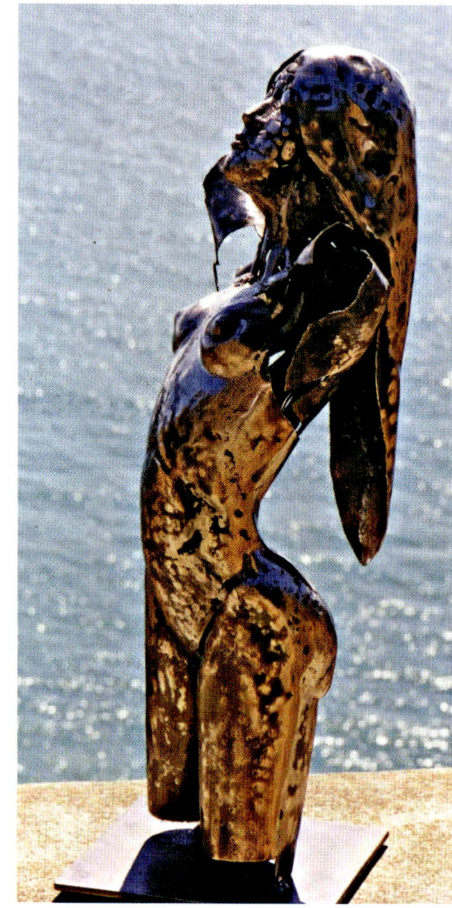

Stephen Fitz-Gerald. *Galatea.* Life-sized figure in forged and welded steel, inspired by the Greek myth of Pygmalion and Galatea. *Photo, artist*

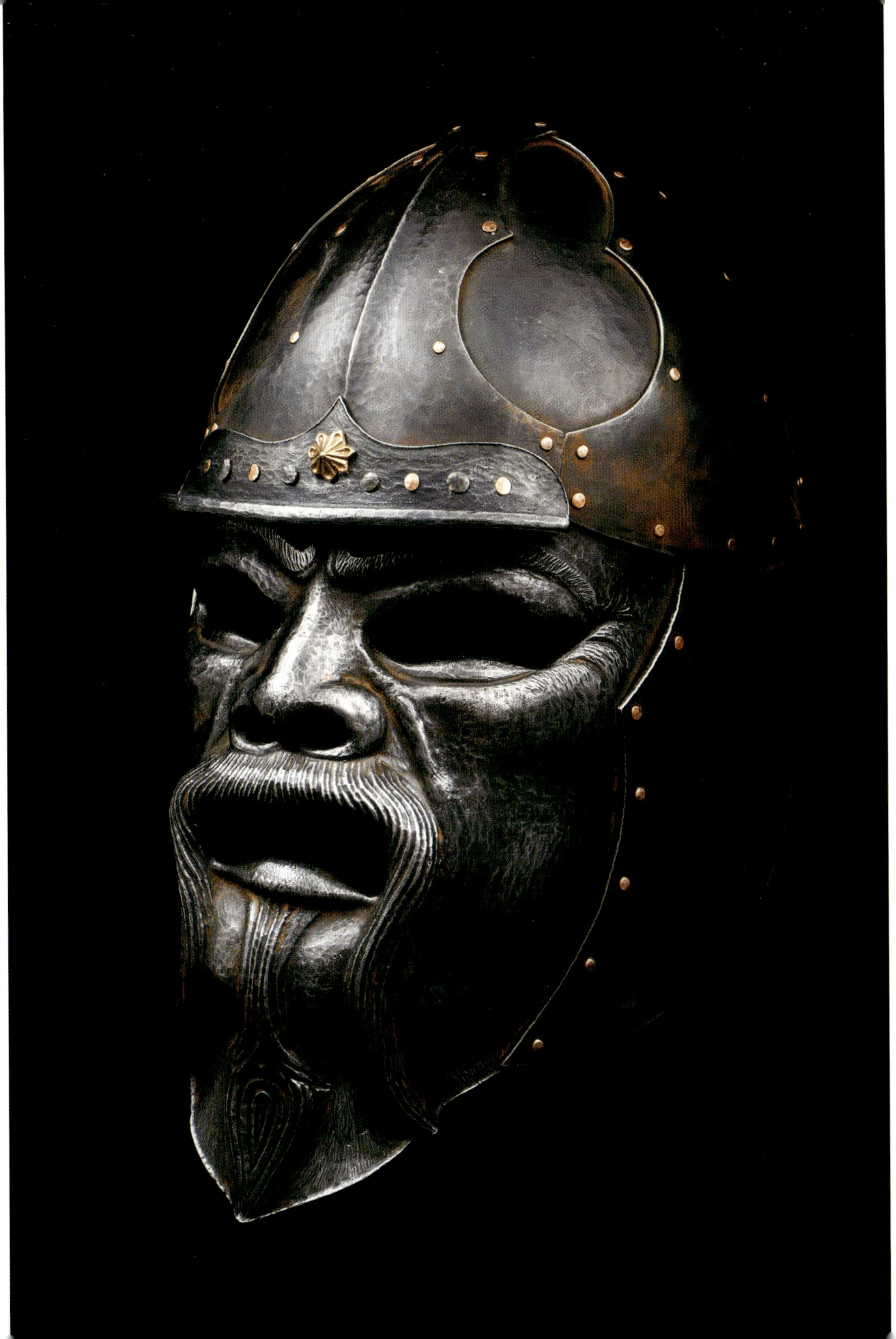

Travis Conn. *Mongol Helm*, 2006. Raised, reposed, and fabricated steel. 13" x 12" x 12". *Photo, artist*

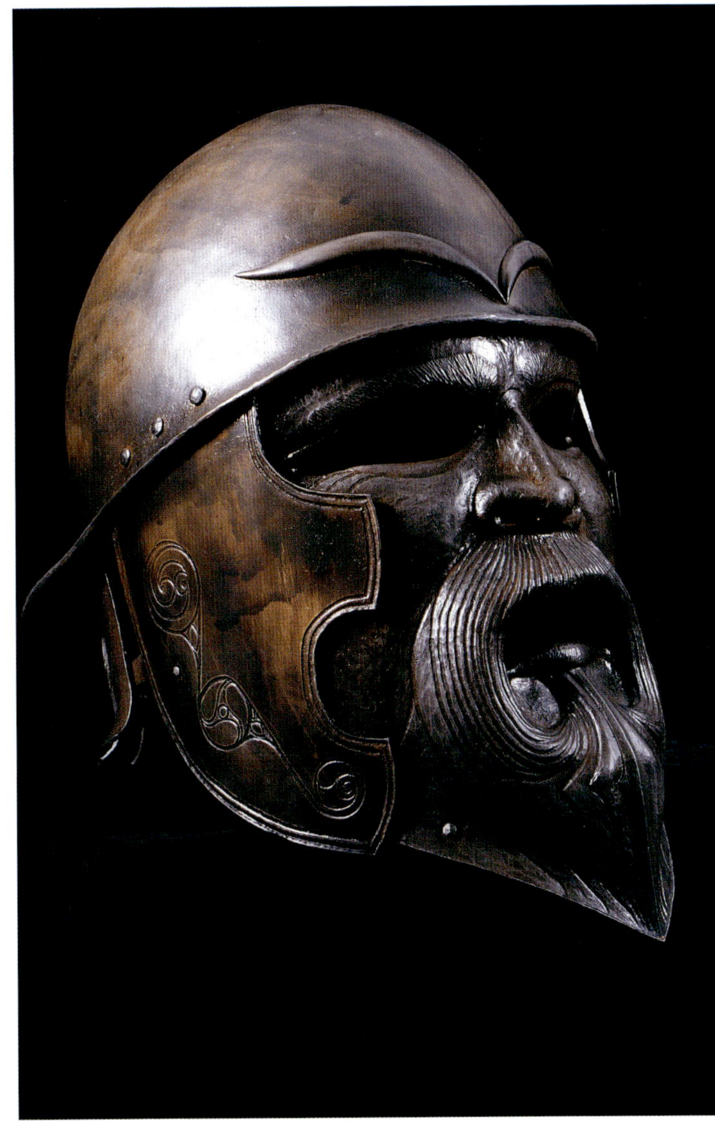

Travis Conn. *Olcan's Agen/Port*, 2007. Raised, reposed, and fabricated steel. 13" x 12" x 13". *Photo, artist*

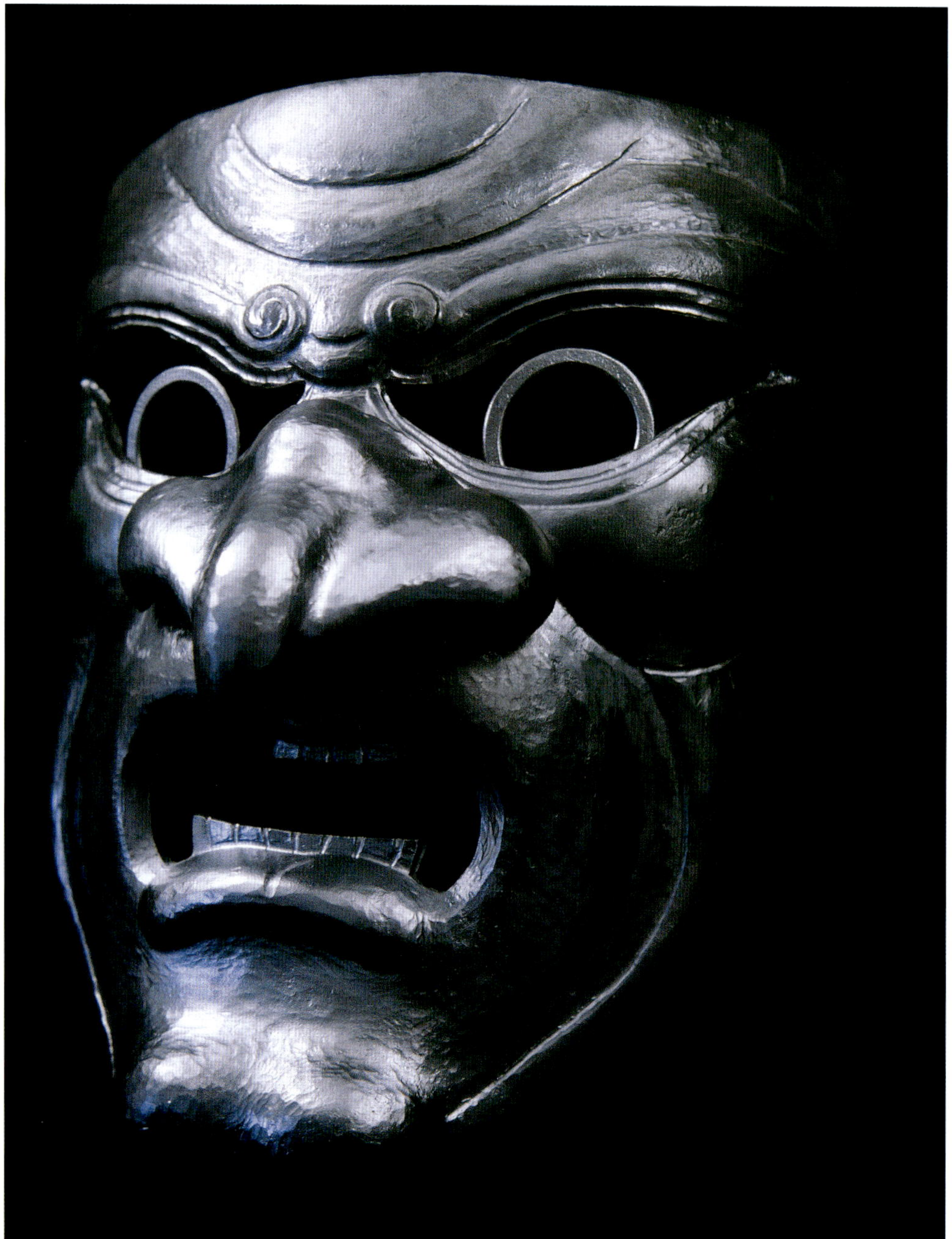

Travis Conn. *Rage,* 2008. Raised, reposed, and fabricated steel. 9" x 10" x 3". *Photo, artist*

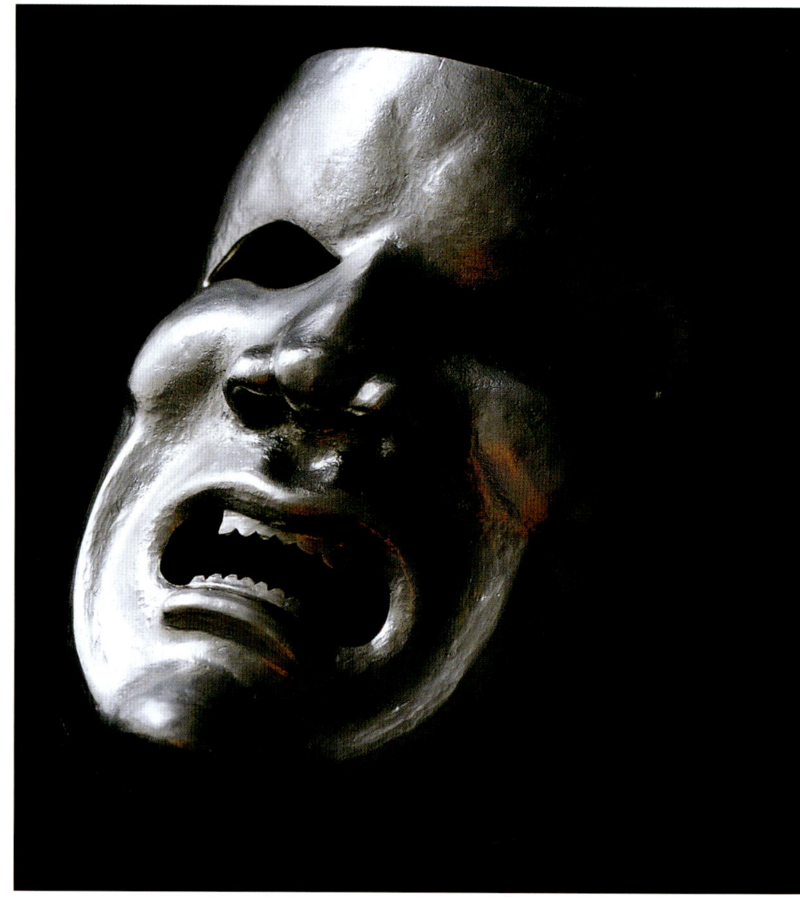

Travis Conn. *My War Face*, 2005. Raised and reposed steel. 9" x 10" x 3". *Photo, artist*

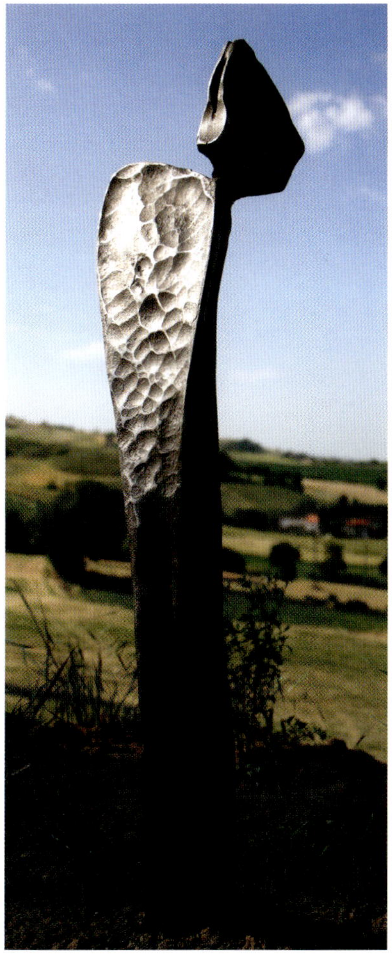

Roberto Giordani. *Bodyline*, 2005. Forged from a single piece of square iron. 31" h. *Photo, artist*

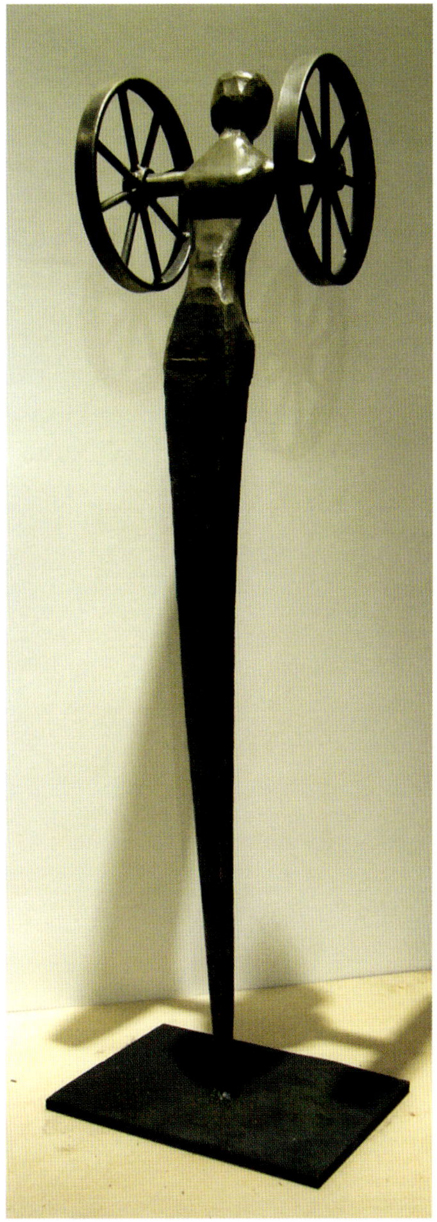

Nick Moran. *Spirit and Destiny 2*, 2006. Forged mild steel with brushed finish, 31" h. *Photo, artist*

This is one of my sculptures that mark a transition from my functional and architectural work into pure sculpture.

By using the industrial forging methods on a power hammer, the sculpture has an industrial quality with its heavily forged tapering form and engine-like arms. – Nick Moran

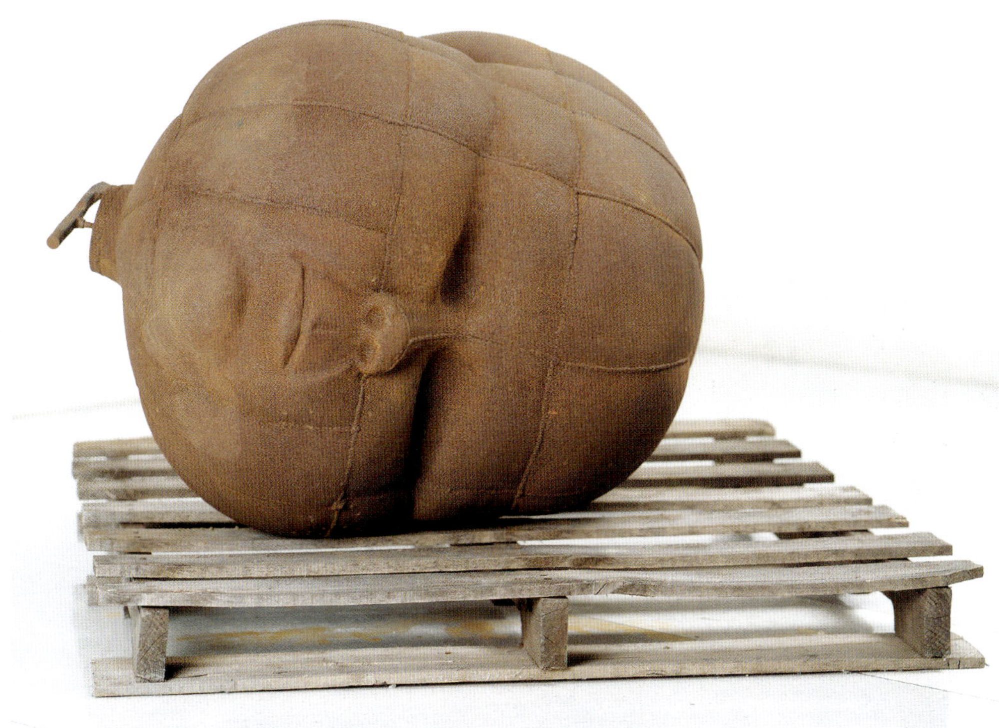

Warren Holzman. *Hard Labor*, 2003. Forged and fabricated steel. 60" x 60" x 30" h. *Photo, Dominic Episcopo*

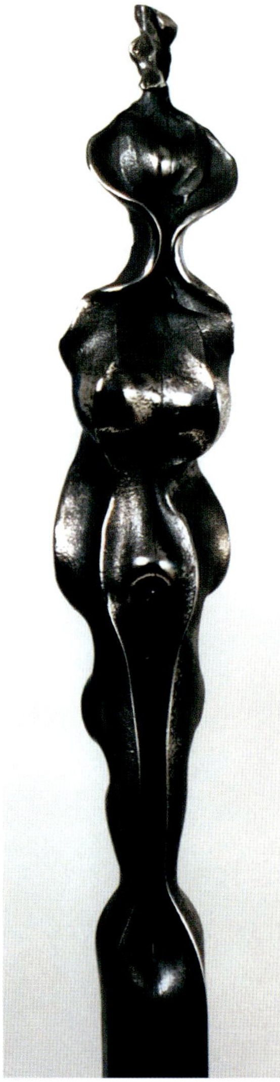

Karel Meloun. *The Venus of Klášterec*, 1996. Forged steel ("U" profile). 5.5" x 5.5" x 37". *Private collection. Photo, artist*

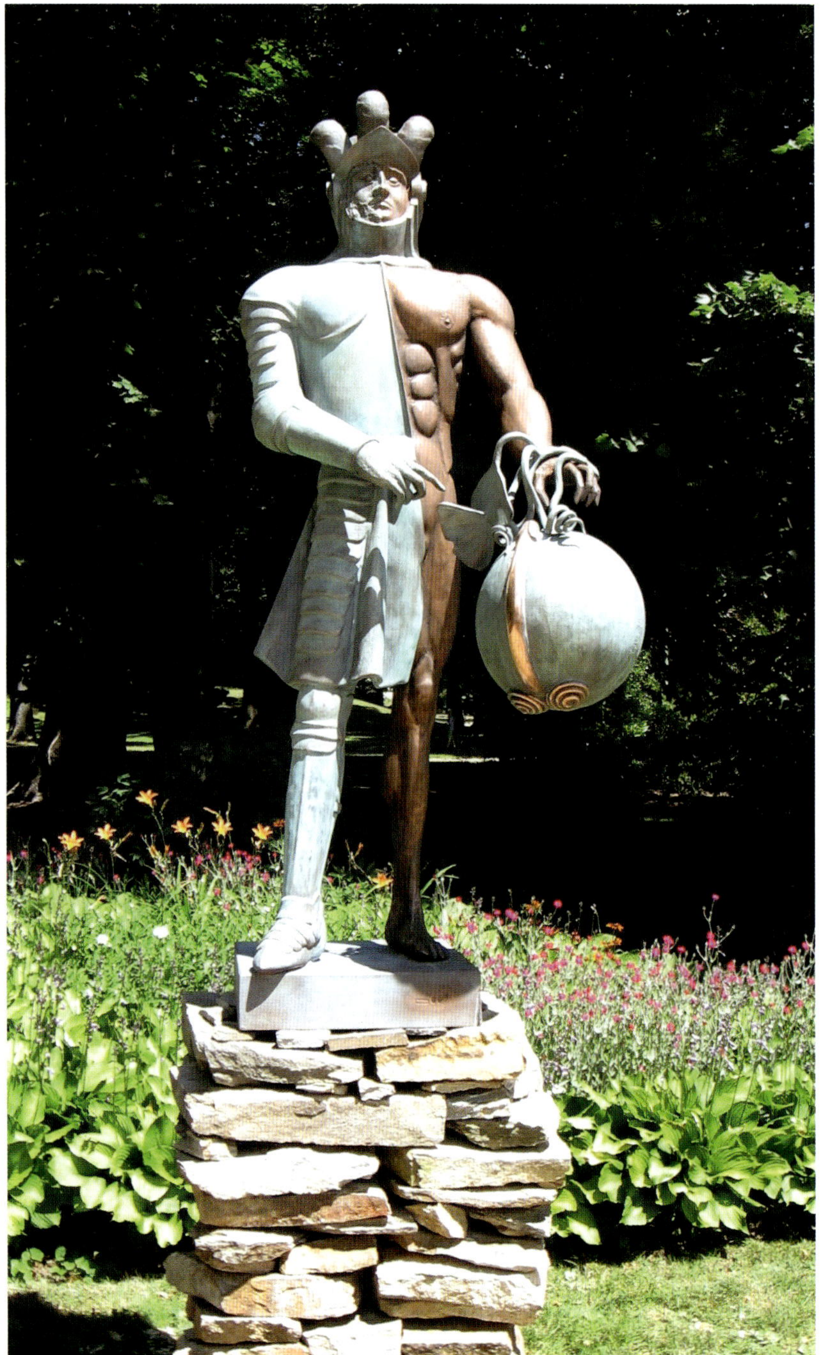

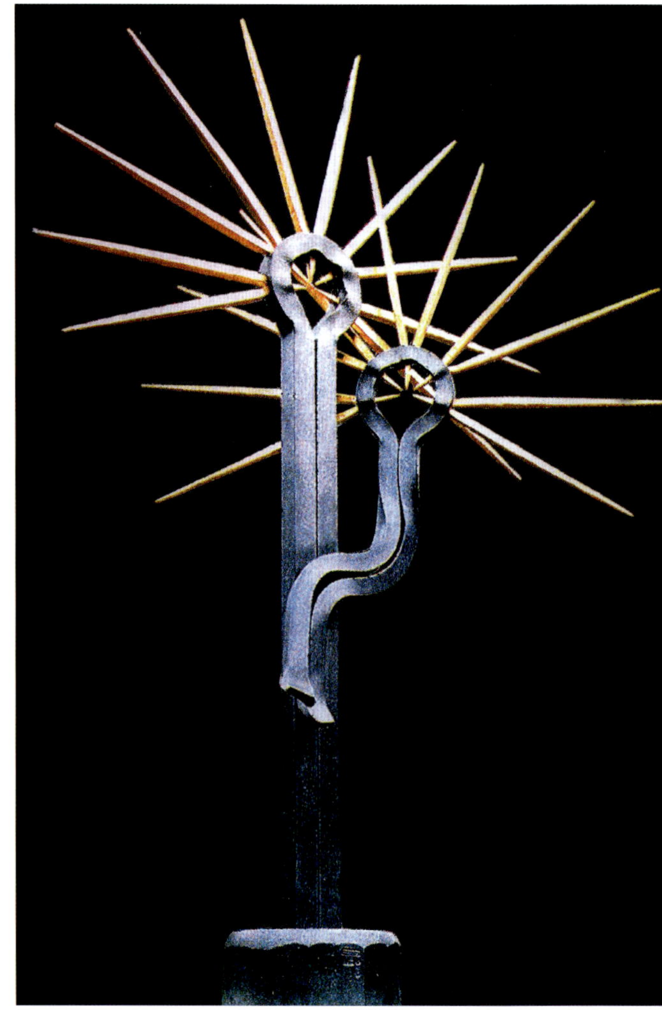

Karel Meloun. *The Madonna of Helfštýn*, 1999. Forged steel, gold. 64.5" x 43". *Permanent exhibition, Helfštýn castle. Photo, artist*

Karel Meloun. *Homage to My Fathers*, 2007. Beaten steel, forged steel, forged copper, chemical patina, copper. 33" x 28" x 83". *In private collection. Photo, Borek Nasadil*

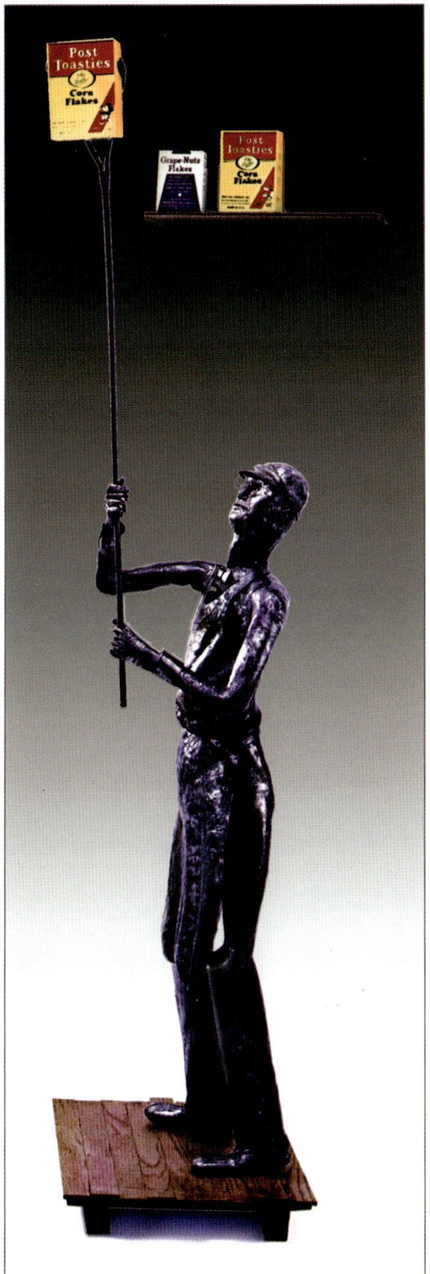

Harold Kimmelman. *Old Time Grocer*. Repousse steel, polychrome steel. 98" h x 36" w x 30" d. *Exhibited at Woodmere Art Museum, 9201 Germantown Avenue, Philadelphia. Photo, artist*

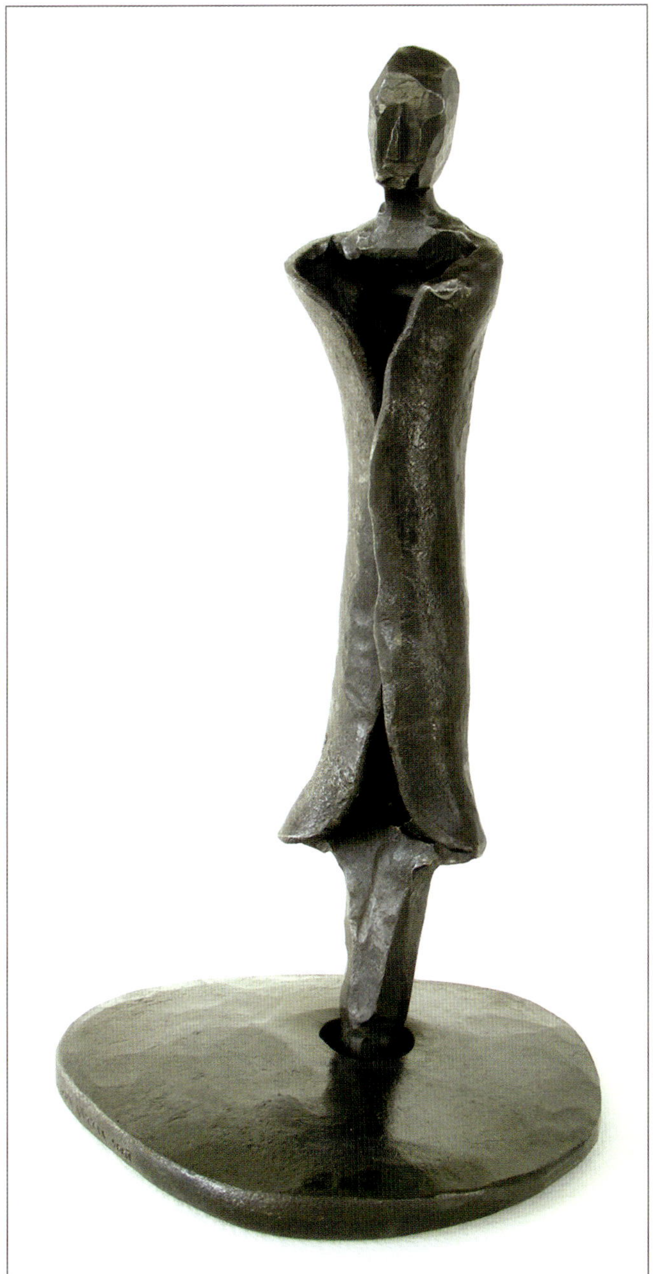

John Little. *The Coat*, 2007. Forged steel. 10" h x 5" w x 5" d. *Photo, artist*

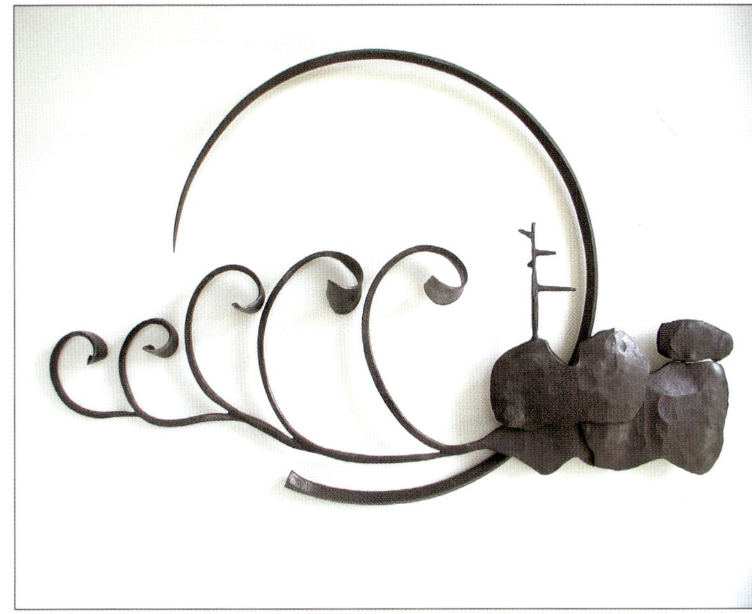

John Little. *Kingsburg*, 2007. Wall sculpture, stylized interpretation of the rocky shoreline of Nova Scotia near the town of Kingsburg. 30" h x 45" w x 4" d. *Photo, artist*

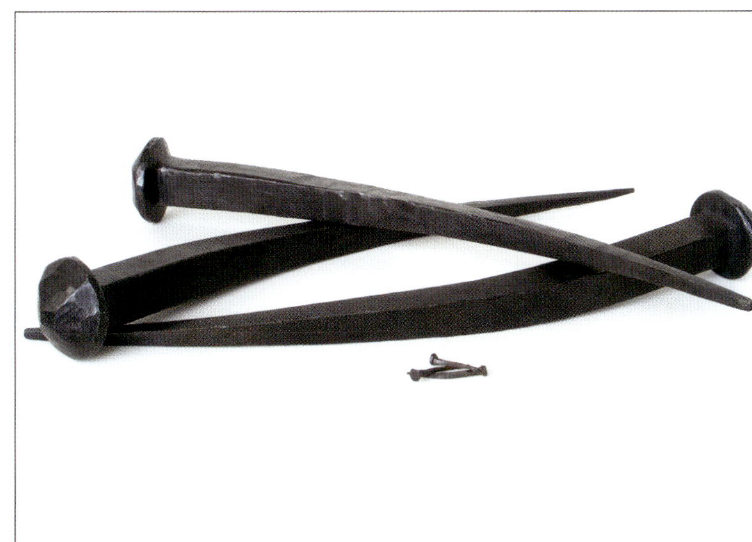

John Little. *Three Big Nails*, 2004. Forged from 2" square material. 14" h (in the image), 25" w x 3" d. *Photo, artist*

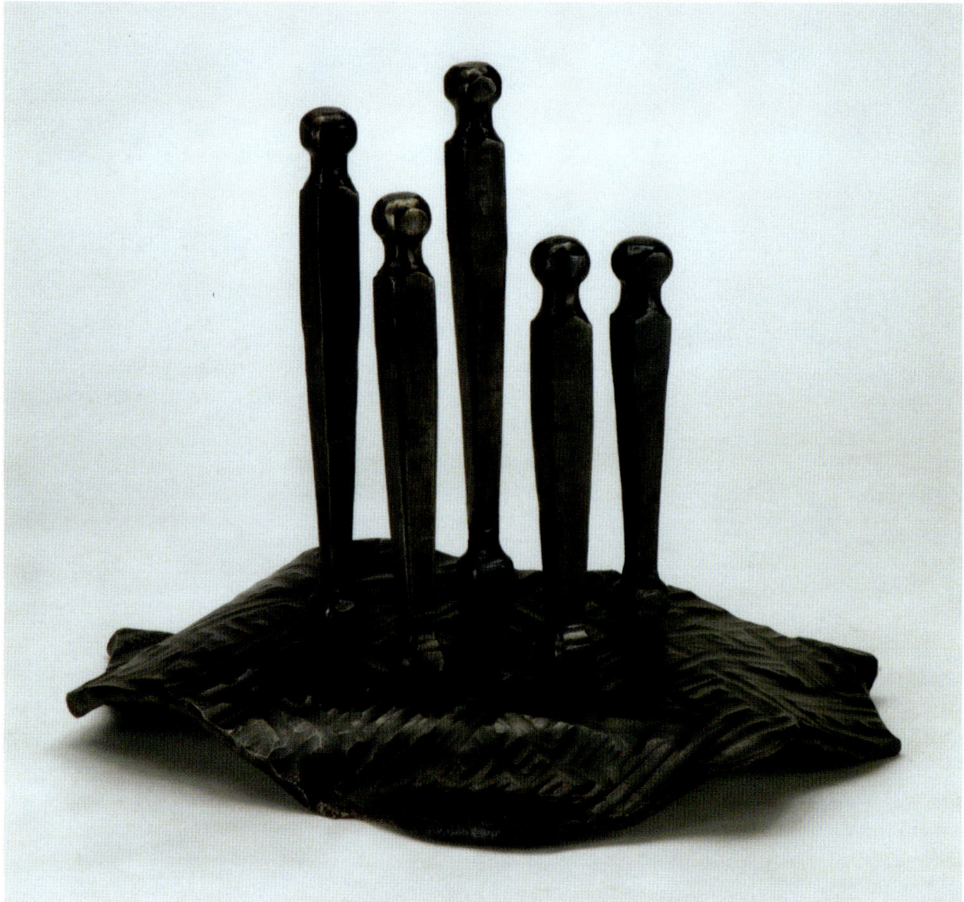

M. Craig Campbell. *Family of Five,* 2005. Forged and fabricated steel, paste wax. 14" h x 20" w x 10" d, 25 lbs. The human figures in this sculpture were the result of playful experimentation and Family of Five is the story of dear friends. *Private collection. Photo, Trent Watts*

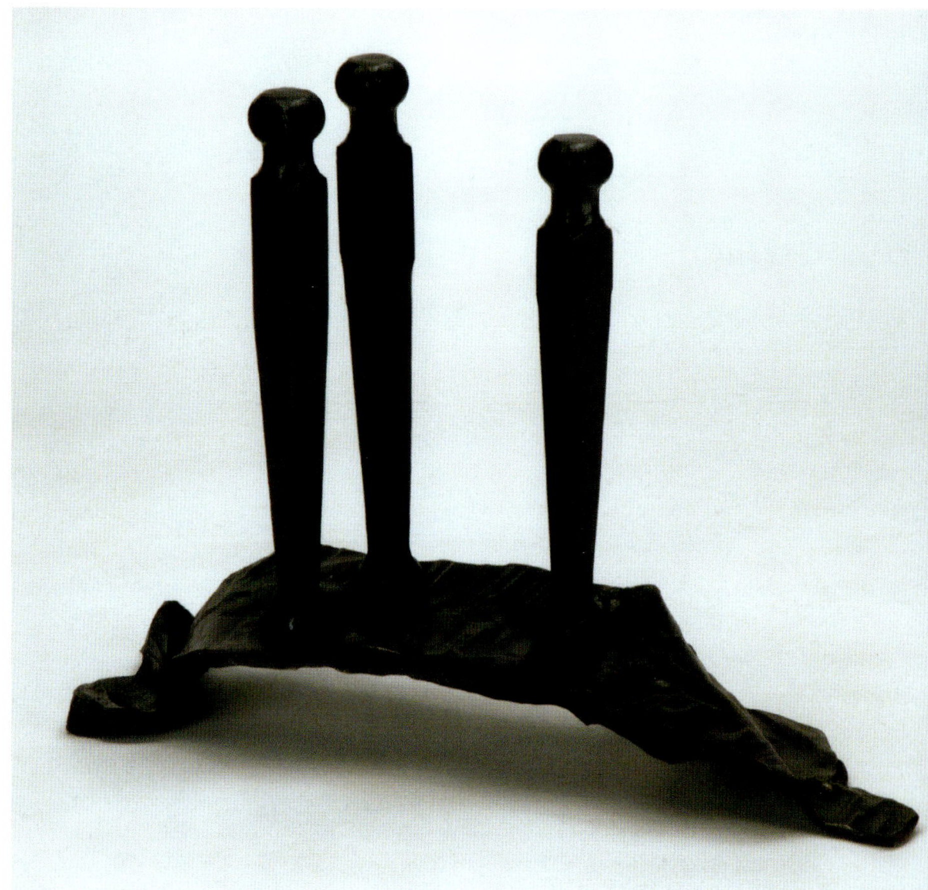

M. Craig Campbell. *Leaving Home,* 2005. Forged and fabricated steel. 13" h x 16" w x 5" d, 18 lbs. *Private collection. Photo Trent Watts*

Inspired by a friend who was leaving her parent's Canadian workshop to travel and work in Europe. Her time as a journeyperson and an artist-blacksmith in her own right had arrived. The three human figures were forged from 1" square bare and the base was forged from an 8" length of heavy bar stock. – M. Craig Campbell

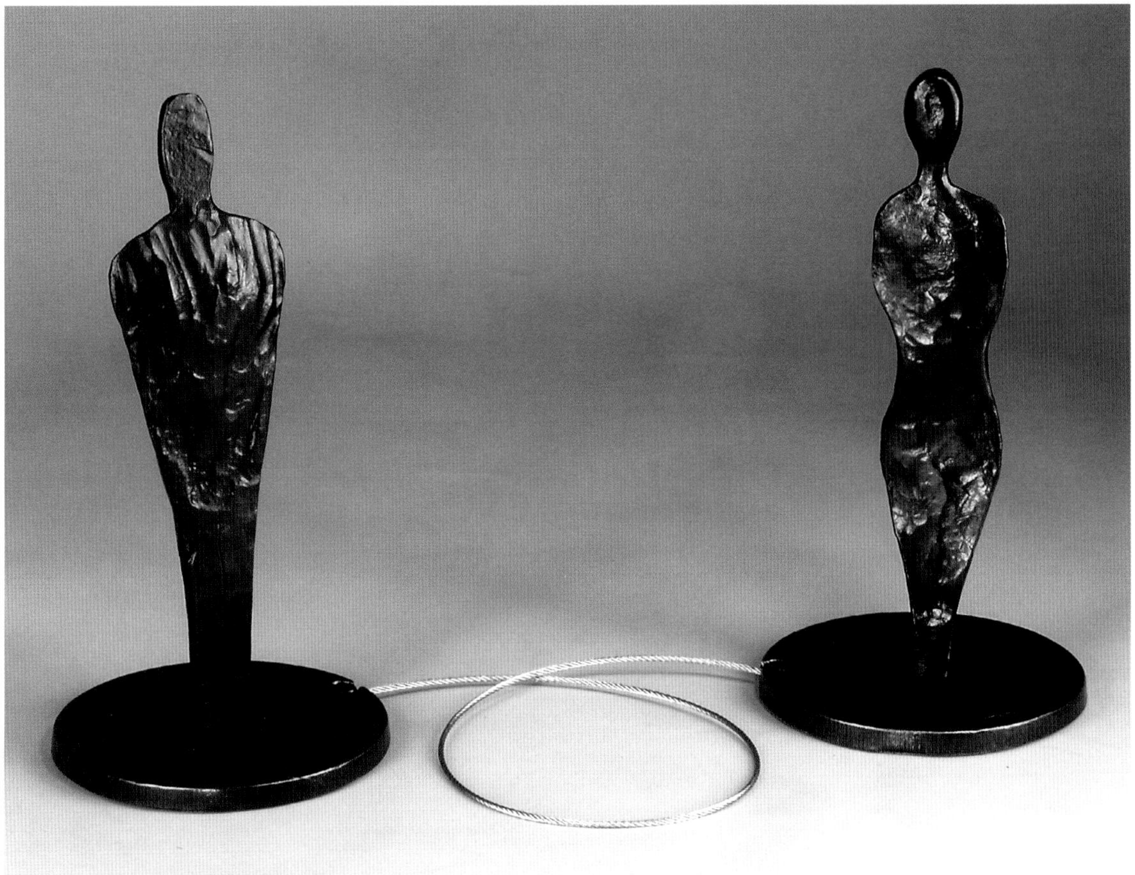

M. Craig Campbell. *He and She*, 2007. Forged and fabricated steel, paste wax, and stainless steel cable. 14" h x 20" w x 8" d, 15 lbs. *Photo Trent Watts*

Playtime at the forge resulted in two figures. Connecting their bases with flexible cable allows them to be a barometer of your relationship. Simply move them together or further apart to represent your feelings today. – M. Craig Campbell

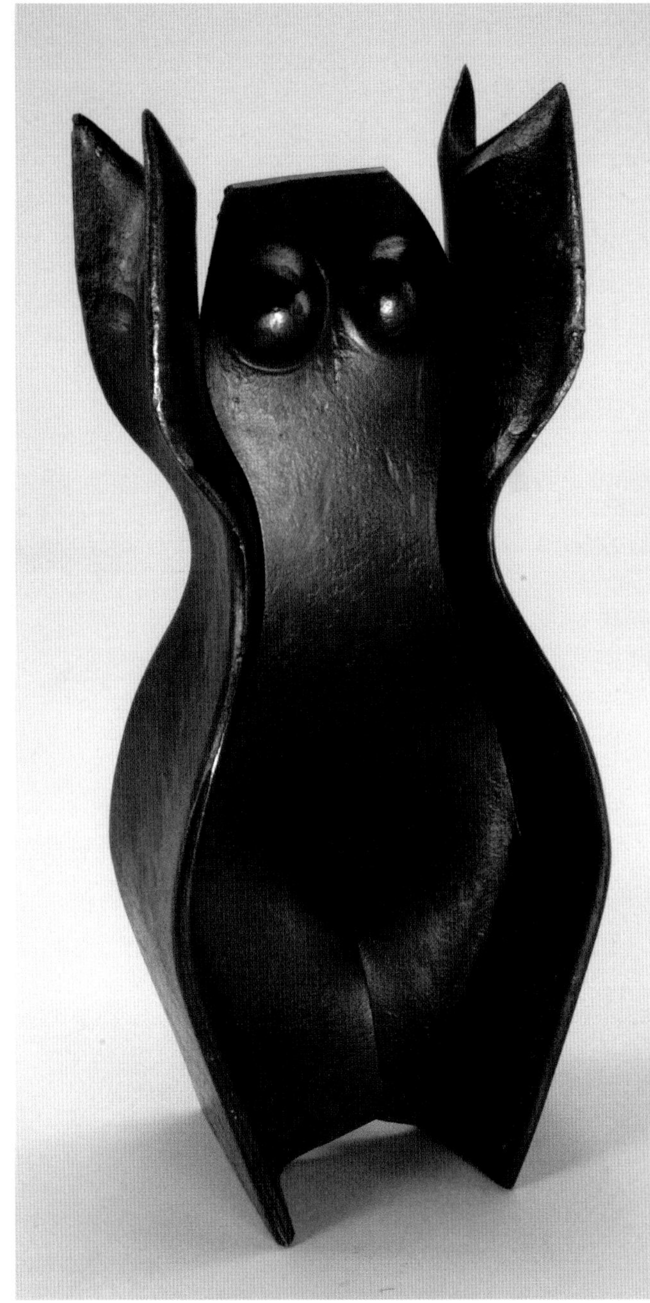

M. Craig Campbell. *I-beam Figure*, 2005. Forged and fabricated steel, paste wax. 14" h x 6" w x 3.5" d, 15 lbs. Once referred to as the prettiest I-beam in Canada. *Private collection. Photo, Trent Watts*

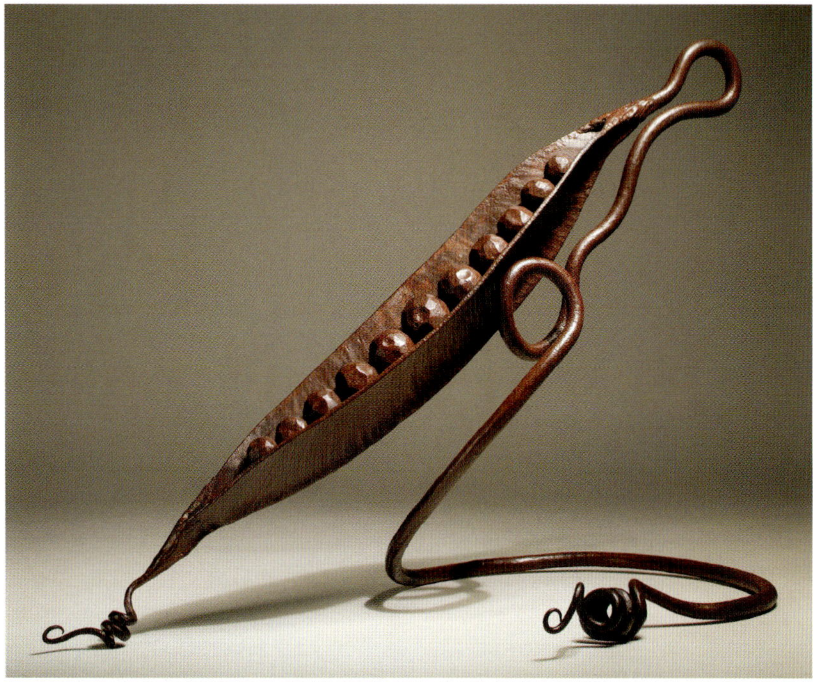

M. Craig Campbell and Daryl Richardson. *Pulse 11-2005 Variety*, 2005. Forged steel rust and wax. 34" h x 36" w x 36" d, 85 lbs. *Private collection. Photo, Hogarth photography*

A wonderful fun and freeing collaboration, the pod was intended to sit horizontally as a boat. Once we held it vertical, we knew it was a seed-pod and commenced forging the vine and peas. – M. Craig Campbell

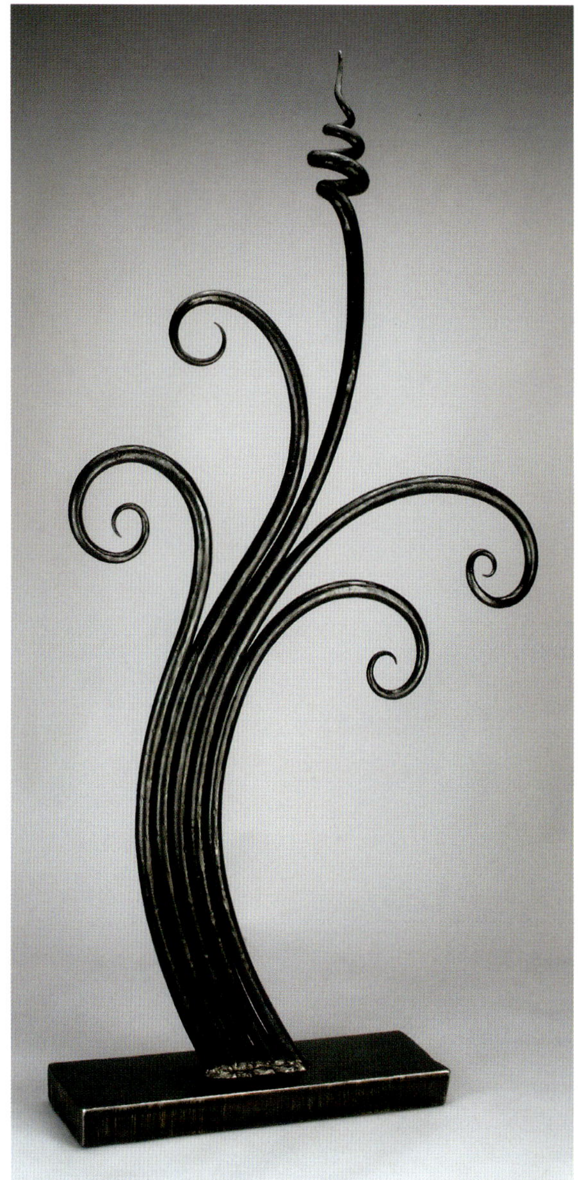

M. Craig Campbell. *Nouveau Spring*, 2007. Forged and fabricated steel, past wax. 56" h x 28" w x 6.5" d. Forged from 1" bar, *Nouveau Spring* evolved from the elements of a sculpture titled Fiddleheads. *Photo, Trent Watts*

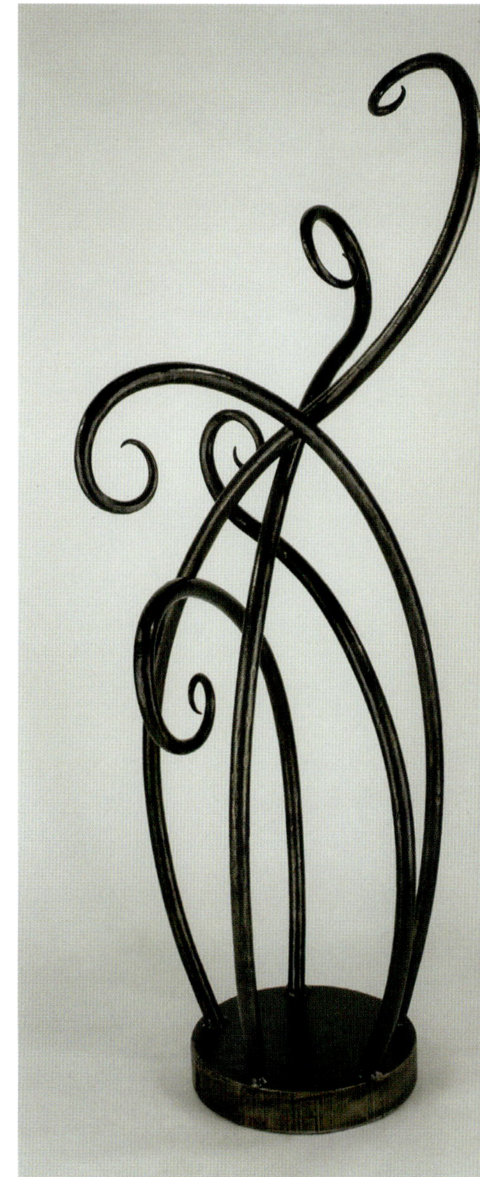

M. Craig Campbell. *Fiddleheads*, 2007. Forged and fabricated steel, paste wax. 45" h x 24" w x 24" d. *Private collection. Photo, Trent Watts*

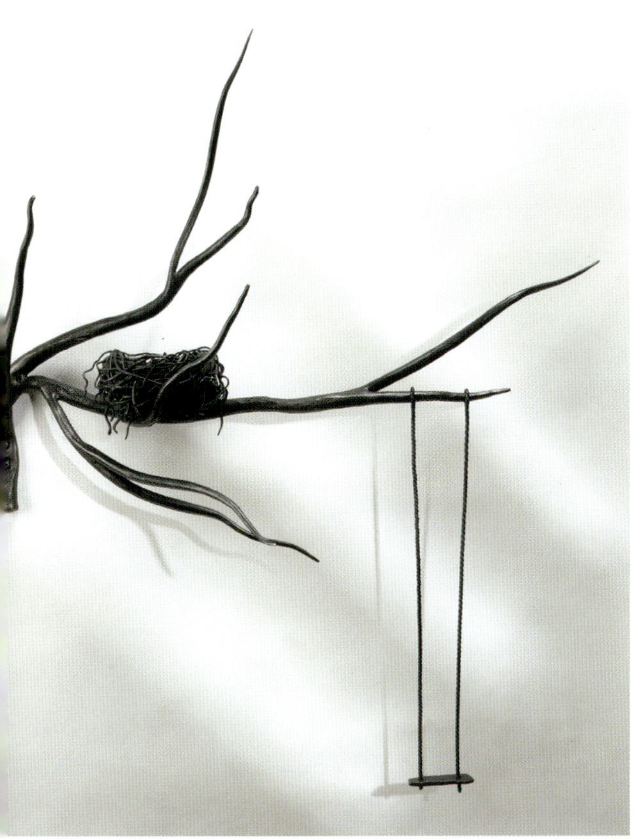

olly Fisher. *Another Divine Dichotomy*. Forged steel, wall hung, aphite encaustic patina. 36" l. *Photo, David Kamm*

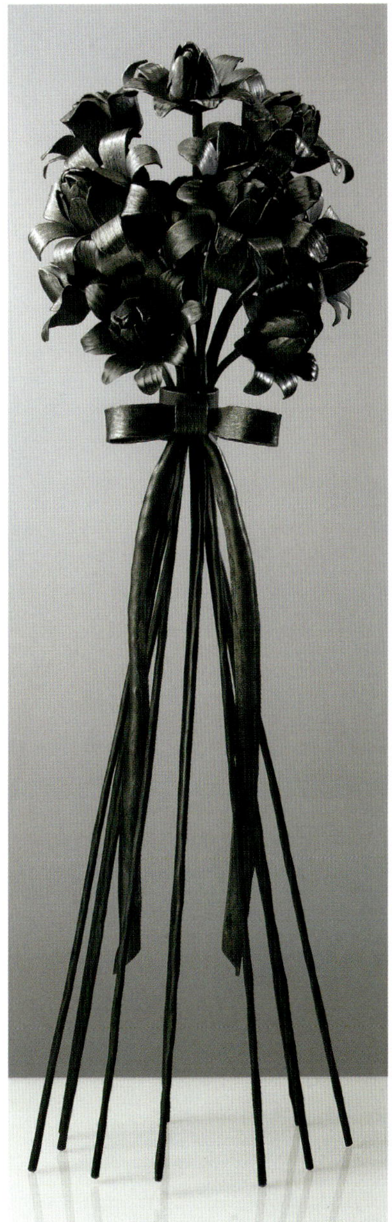

Holly Fisher. *Black Beauties Bouquet*. Forged and fabricated steel, graphite encaustic patina. 36" h. *Photo, David Kamm*

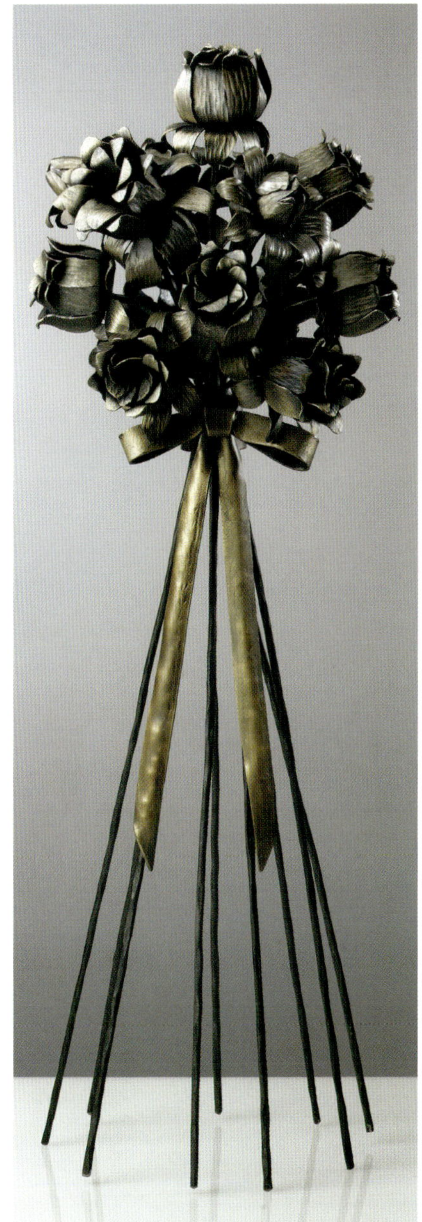

Holly Fisher. *Bronzed Beauties Bouquet*. Forged and fabricated steel, bronze abrasion plating. 36" h. *From the collection of Rob Keeler. Photo, David Kamm*

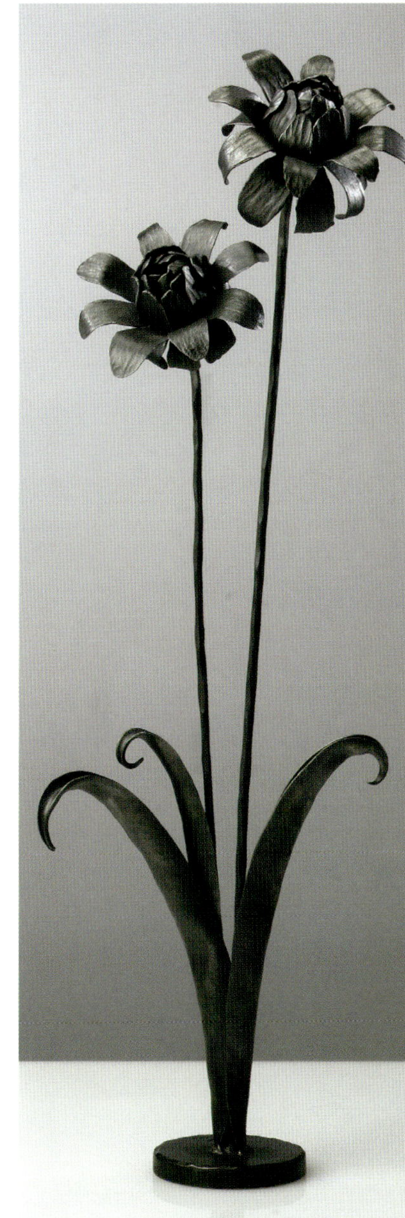

Holly Fisher. *Forged Duet*. Forged and fabricated steel, graphite encaustic patina. 36" h. *Photo, David Kamm*

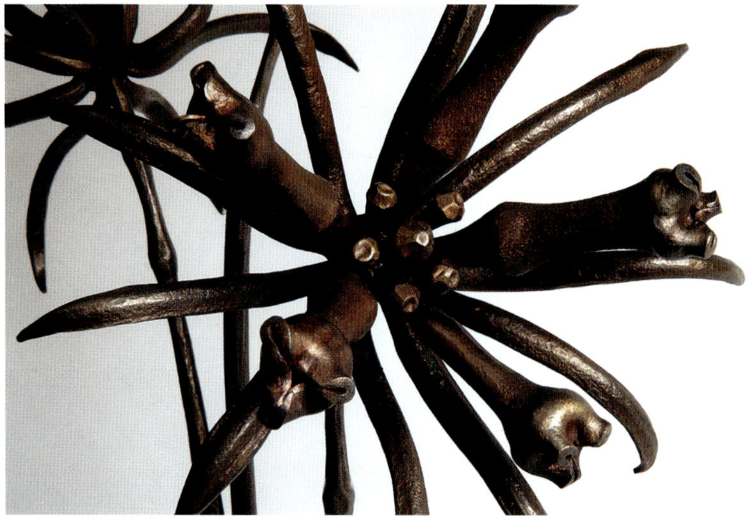

Maegan E. Crowley. *Multiplied*, 2006. Detail. *Photo, Dale Anderson*

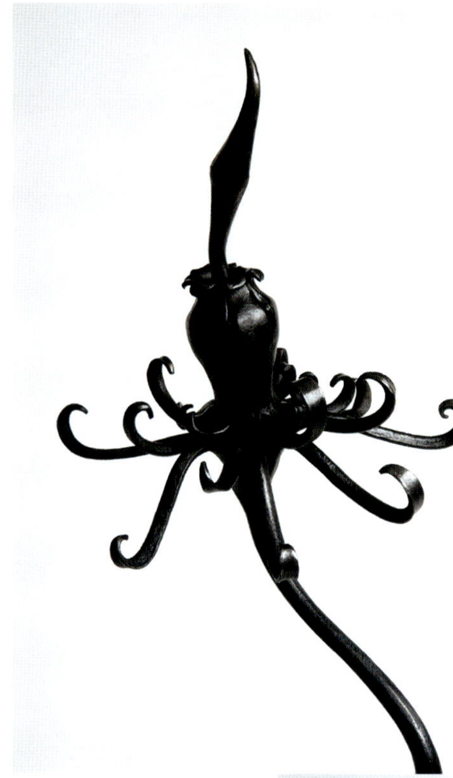

Maegan E. Crowley. *Seven*, 2006. Detail. *Photo, Dale Anderson*

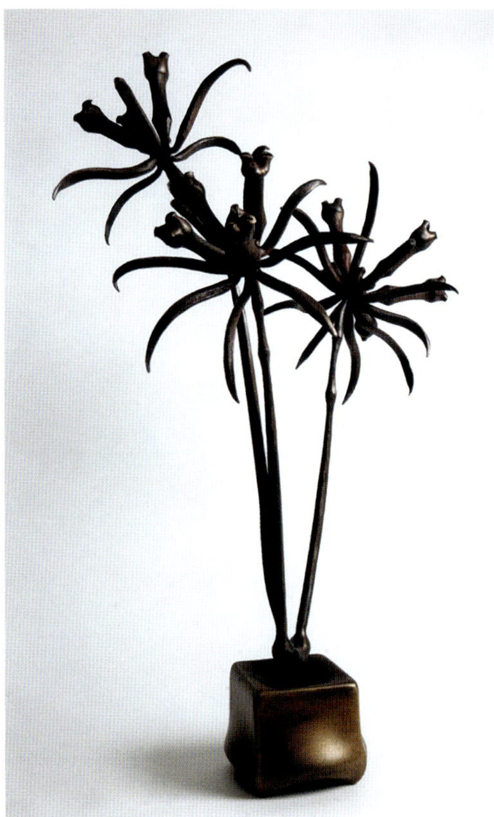

Maegan E. Crowley. *Multiplied*, 2006. Forged and fabricated steel, brass brush finish. 19" x 19" x 29". *Photo, Dale Anderson*

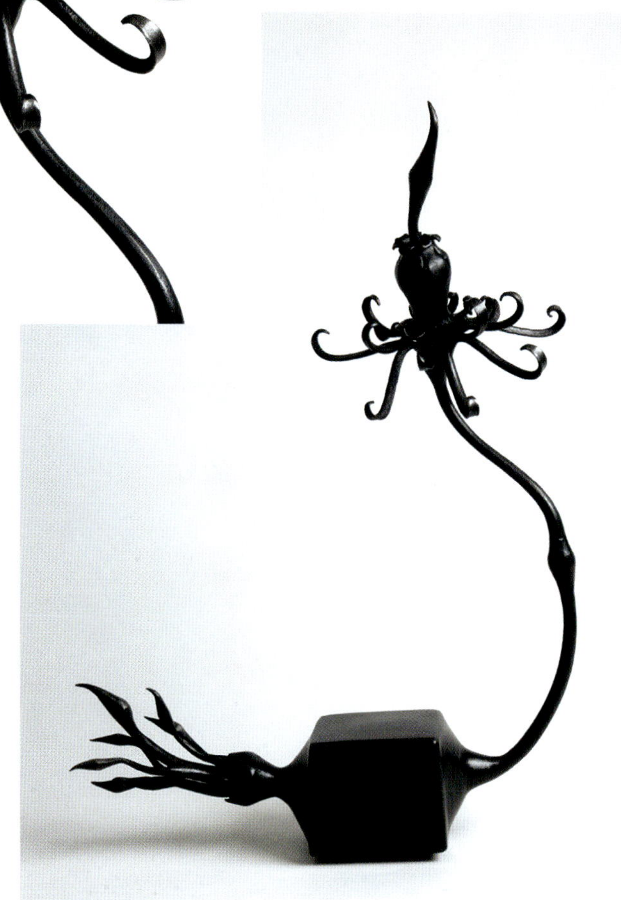

Maegan E. Crowley. *Seven*, 2006. Forged and fabricated steel. 19" x 9" x 25". *Photo, Dale Anderson*

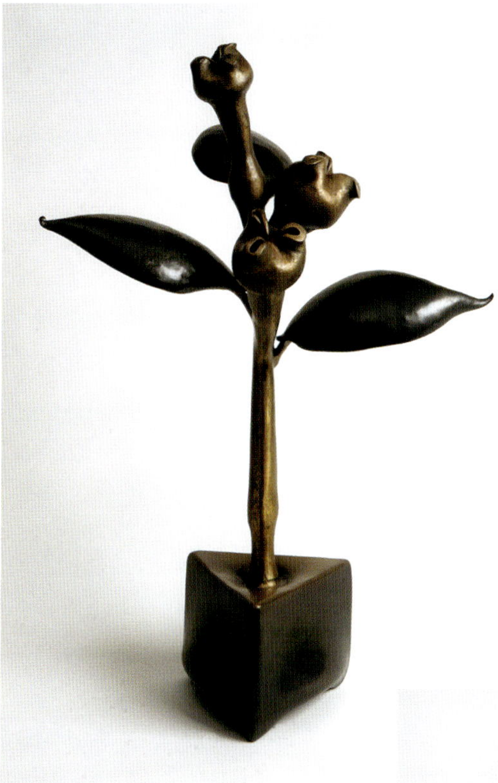

Maegan E. Crowley. *Three,* 2006. Forged and fabricated steel, brass brush finish, 14" x 14" x 24". *Photo, Dale Anderson*

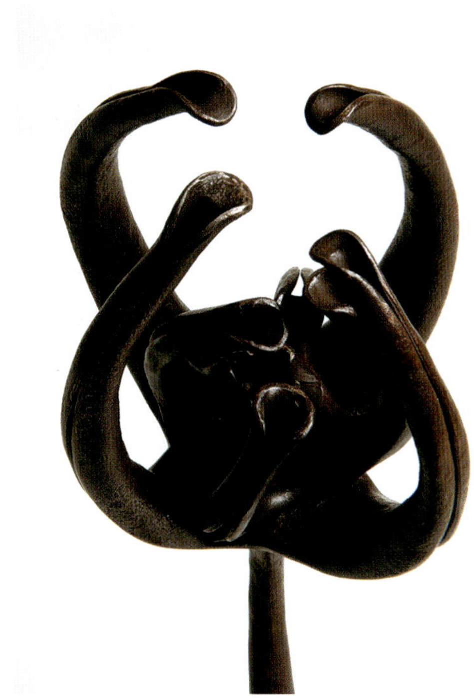

Maegan E. Crowley. *Four*, 2006. Detail. *Photo, Dale Anderson*

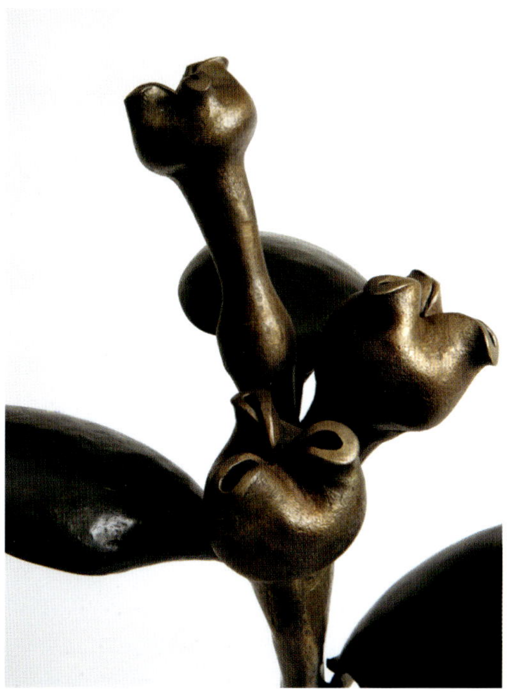

Maegan E. Crowley. *Three*, 2006. Detail. 14" x 14" x 24". *Photo, Dale Anderson*

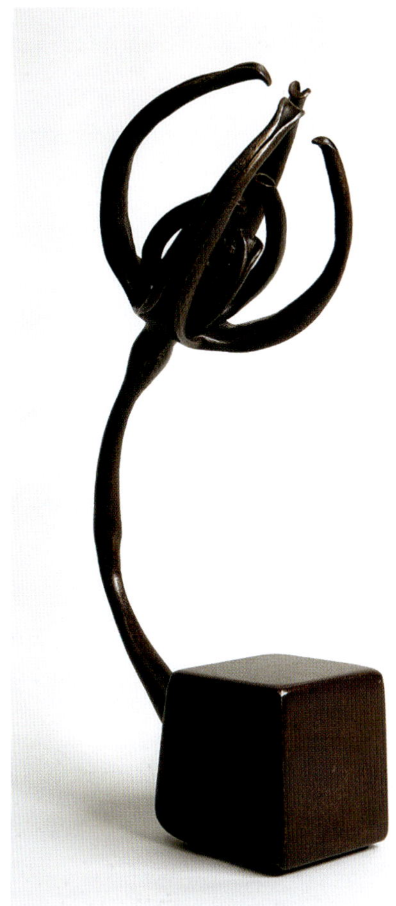

Maegan E. Crowley. *Four*, 2006. Forged and fabricated steel. 10" x 7" x 21". *Photo, Dale Anderson*

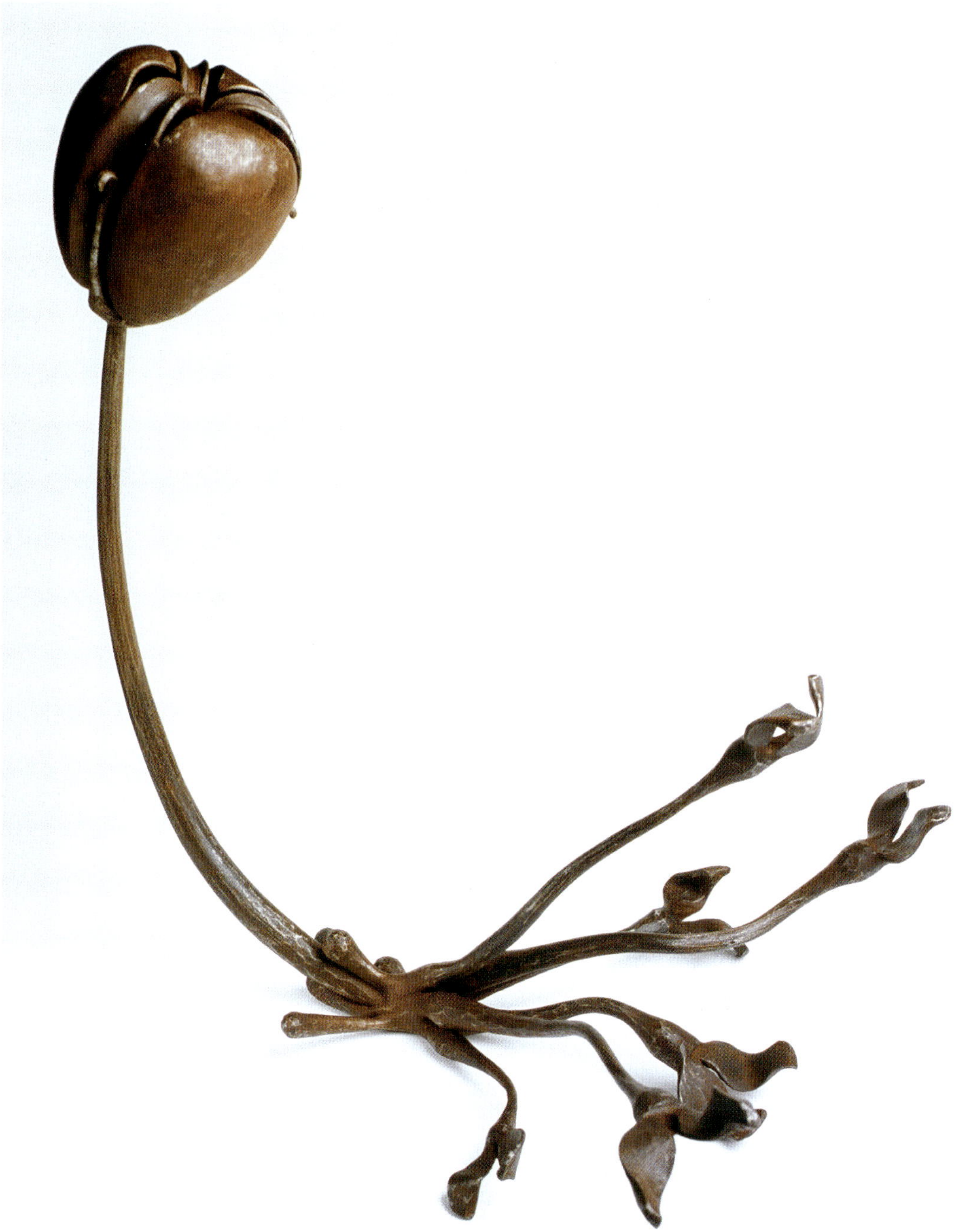

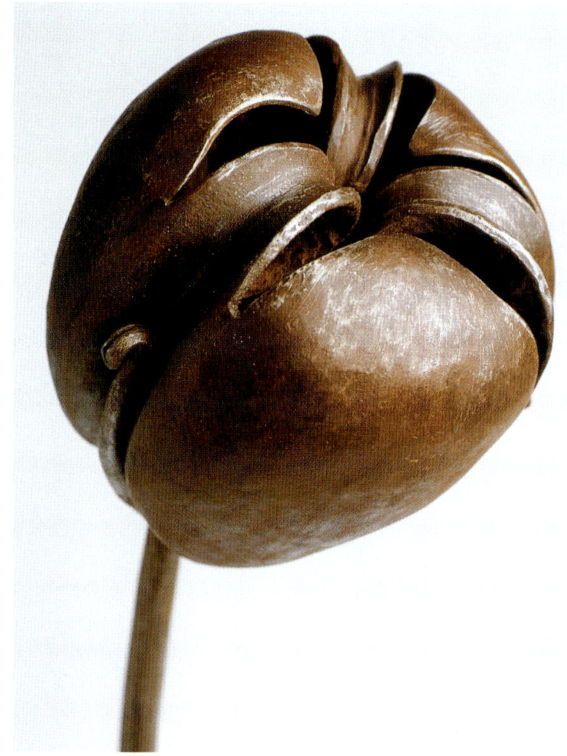

Maegan E. Crowley. *The Lucky One*, 2004. Detail.
Photo, Dominic Episcipo

Maegan E. Crowley. *The Lucky One*, 2004.
Forged and fabricated steel. 28" x 20" x 10".
Photo, Dominic Episcipo

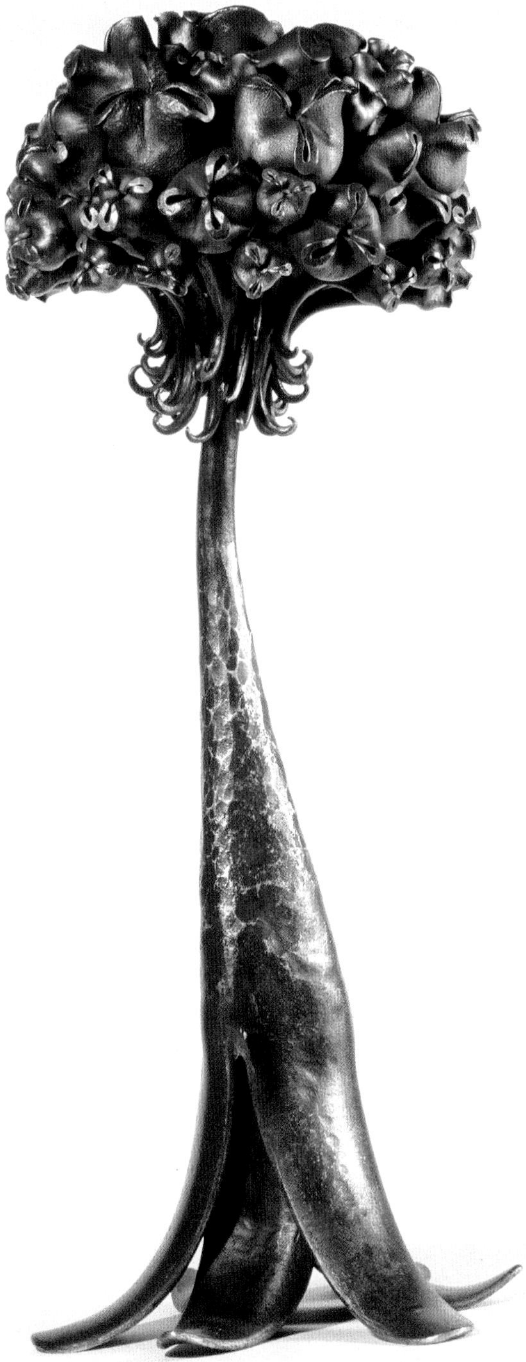

Maegan E. Crowley. *Full Bloom*, 2005. Forged and fabricated steel. 28" x 12" x 12". *Photo, Dominic Episcipo*

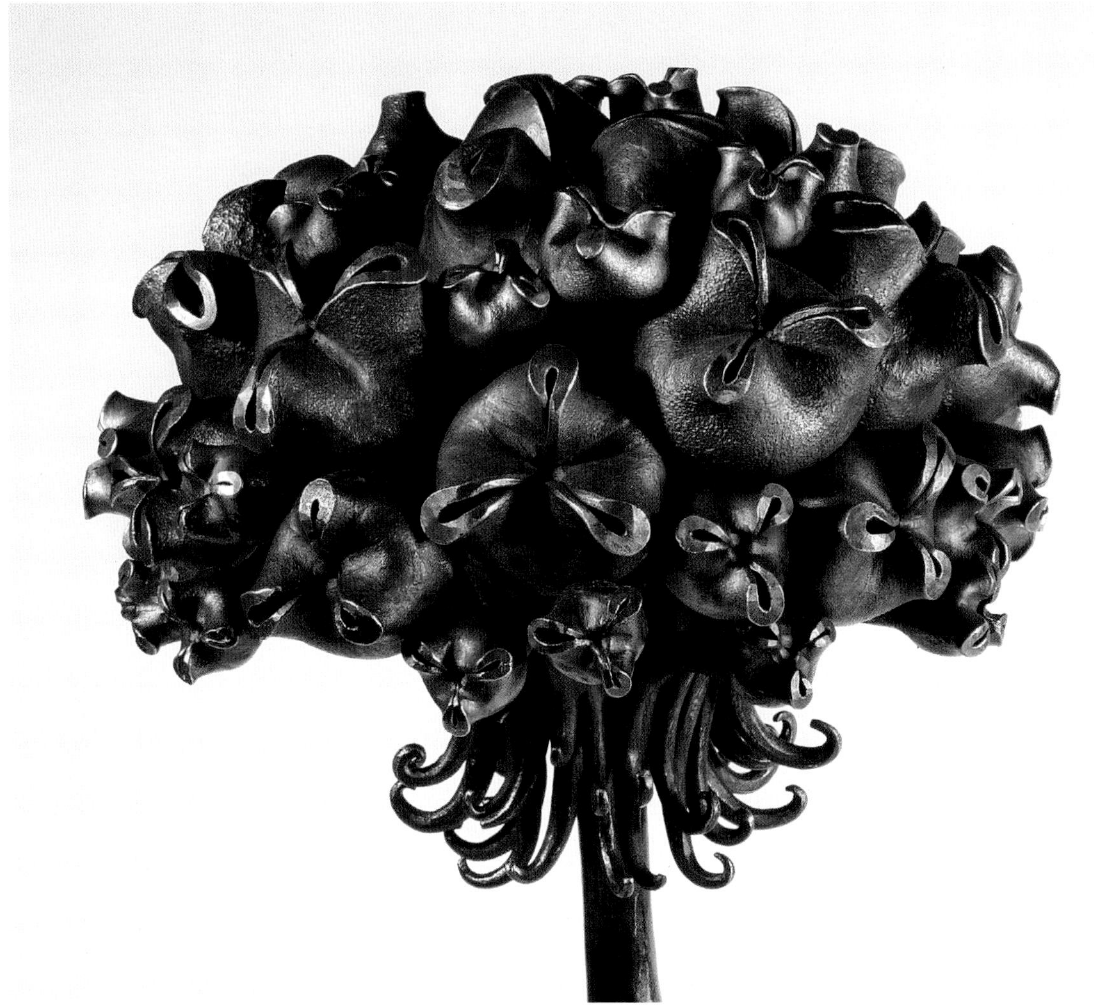

Maegan E. Crowley. *Full Bloom*, 2005. Detail. *Photo, Dominic Episcipo*

Ben Tandler. *Flowers*. Forged and fabricated mild steel. *Photo, Lior Zelberstein*

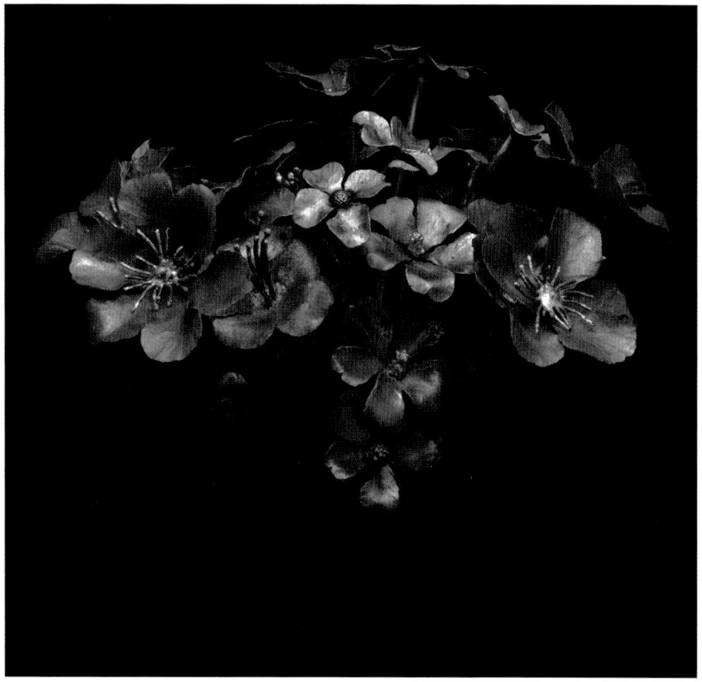

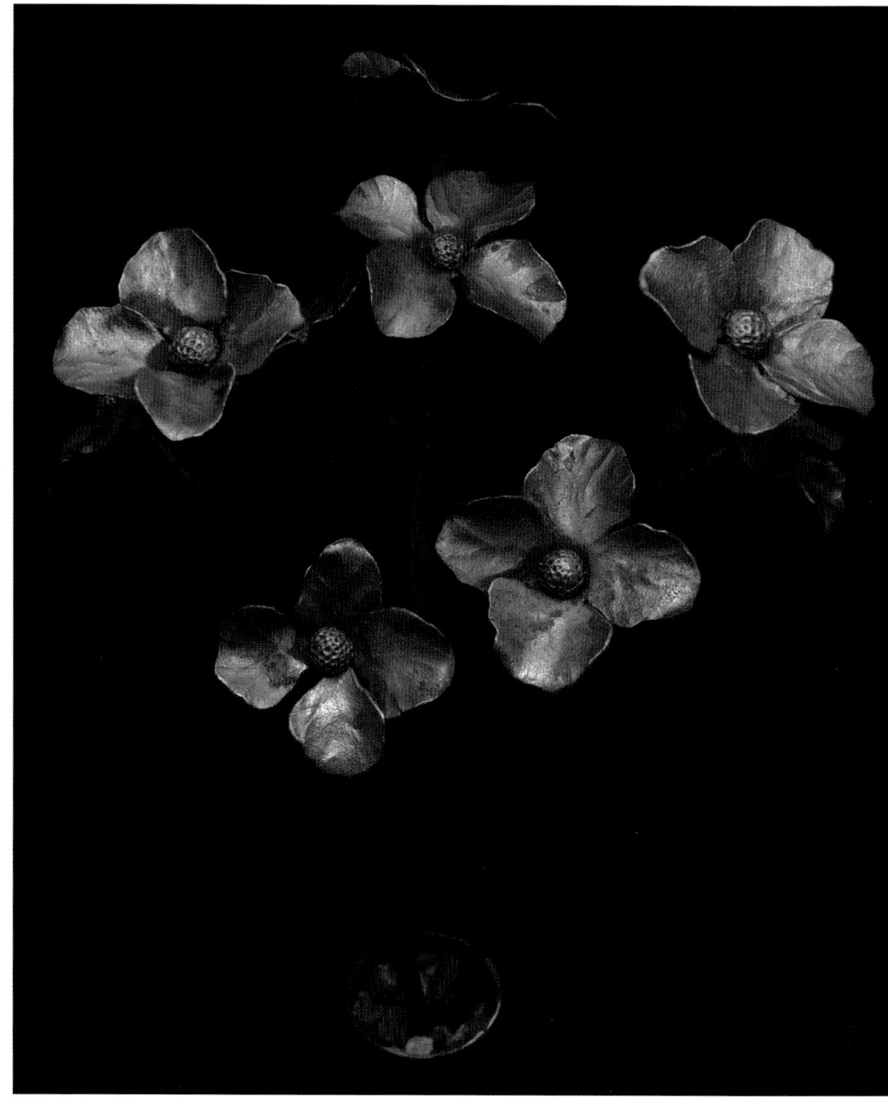

Ben Tandler. *Flowers*. Forged and fabricated mild steel, 16" h. *Photo, Lior Zelberstein*

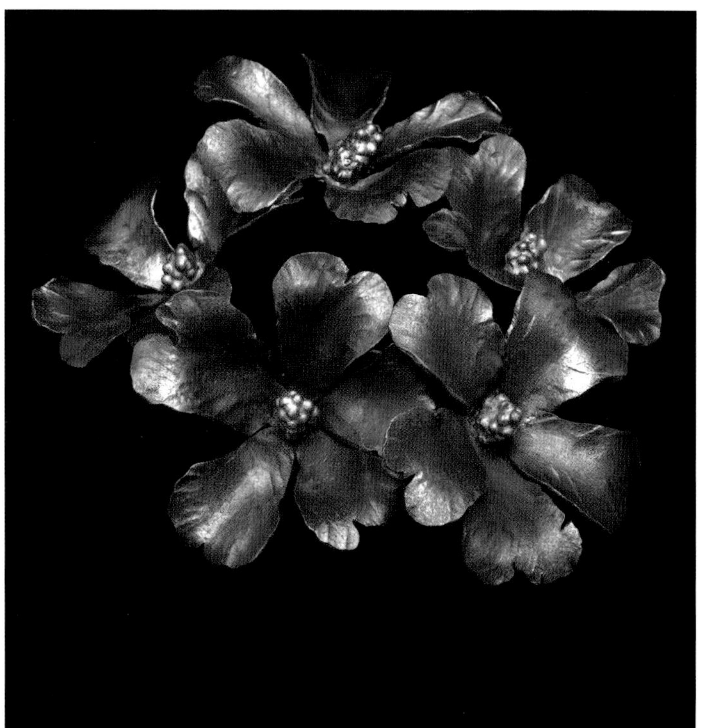

Ben Tandler. *Flowers*. Forged and fabricated mild steel, 10" h. *Photo, Lior Zelberstein*

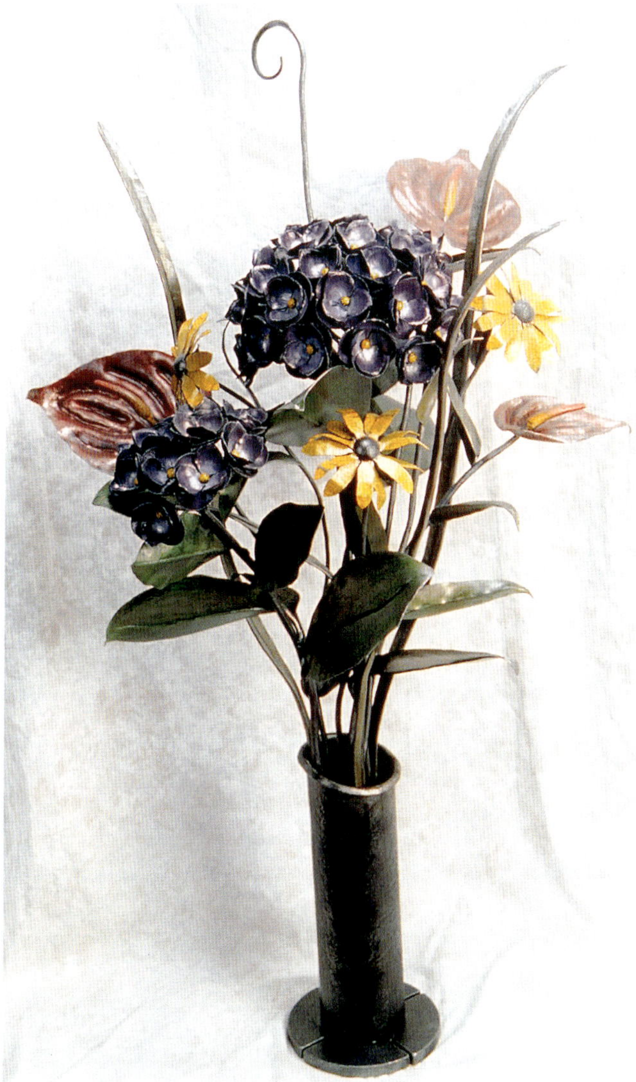

Mike Selinsky. *Right of Spring*. Forged mild steel with pigmented wax finish, 28" h. *Photo, artist*

The flowers were created to mimic nature using various forging processes as well as a repousse process. I tend to enjoy creating works of art that are organic in nature as forging realistic organic pieces from metal is a challenging process that fulfills my creative side. – Mike Selinsky

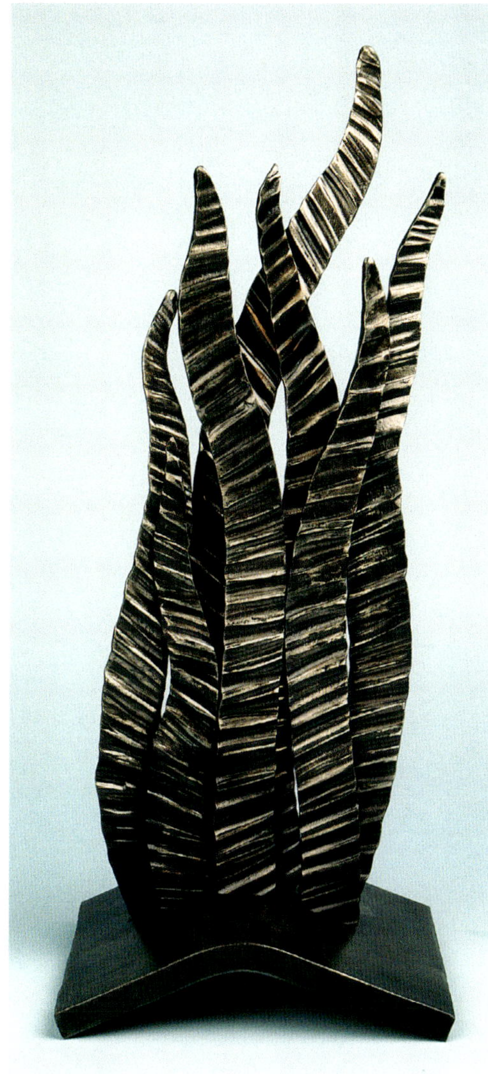

Jeff Fetty. *Alaria*. 20" h x 12" w x 6" d. *Photo, Mike Keller*

Inspired on a scuba diving trip in the red sea. This seaweed forms a band near the low tide mark and in shallow tide pools. – Jeff Fetty

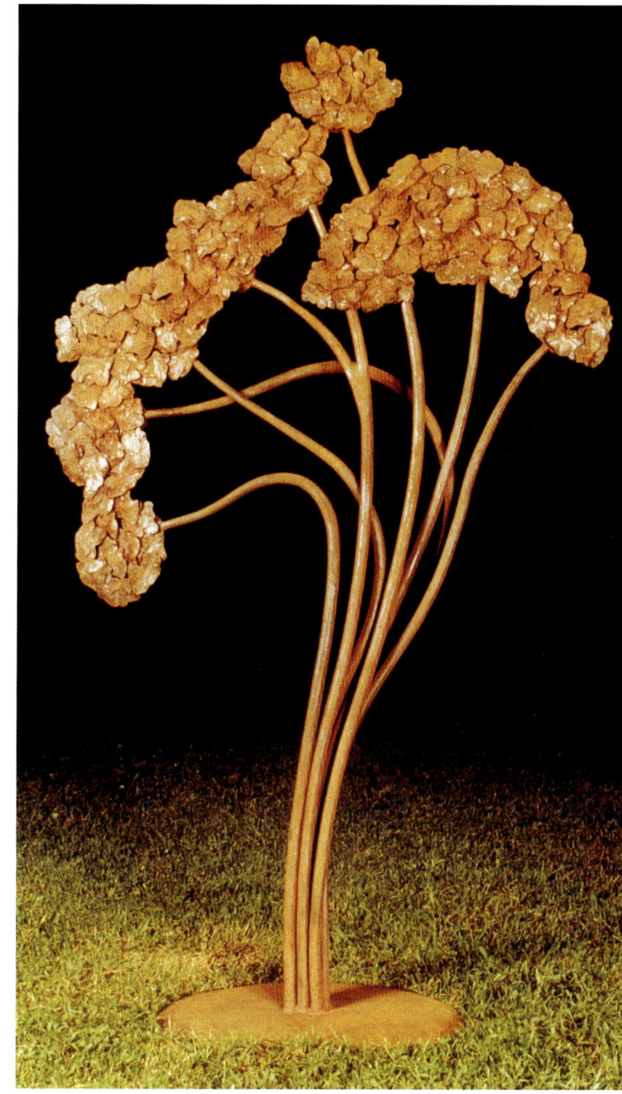

Jeff Fetty. *Joe Pye*. 93" h x 62" w x 18" d. Eupatorium purpureum (Joe Pye Weed) is an ubiquitous plant in the meadows of West Virginia and dominates the late summer flora. *Photo, Gefeti*

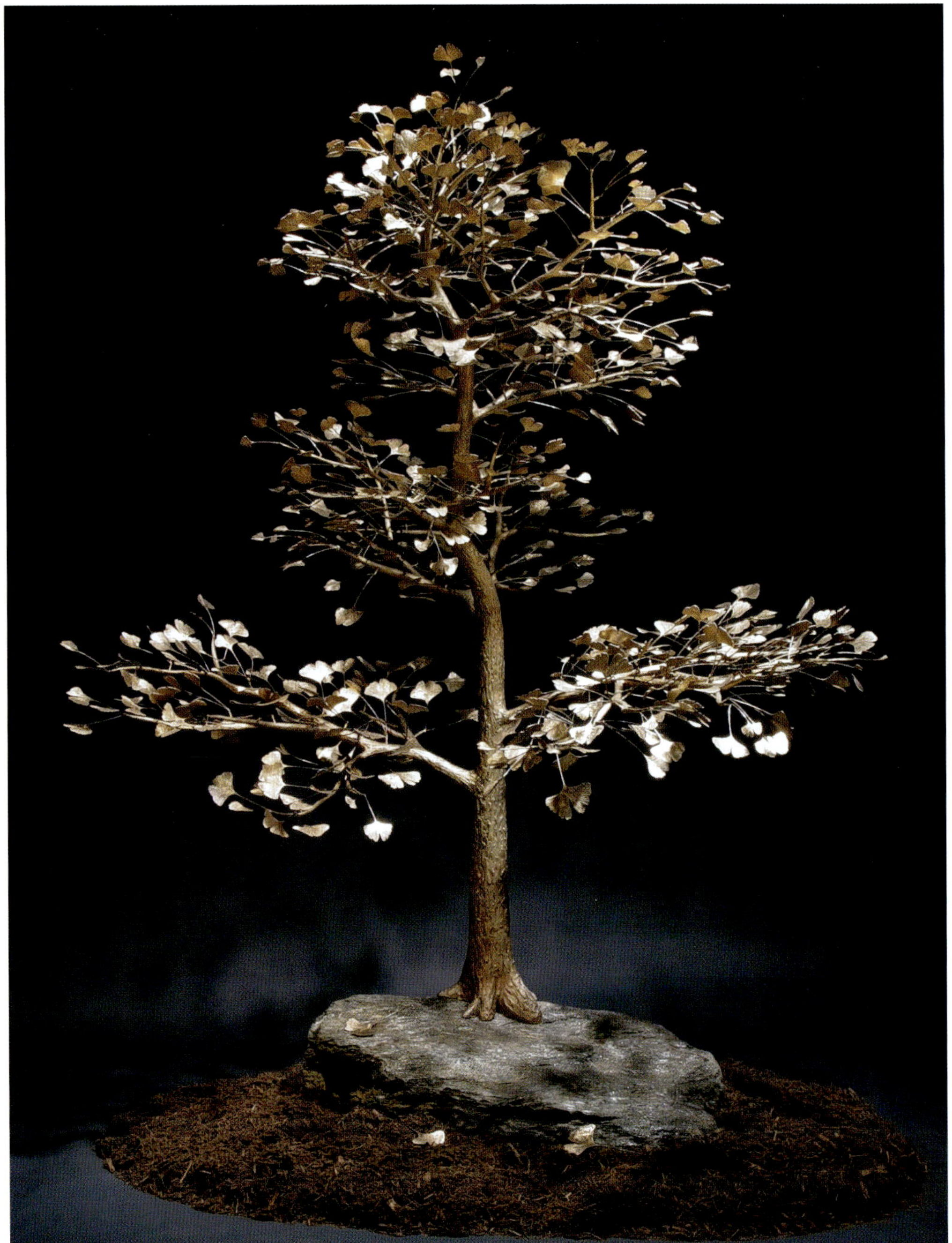

Chris Gavin. *Bonsai Gingko Tree*, 2003. Forged and cast bronze, rock. 84" x 72" x 72". *Collection, Willard 2007, Photo Mark Lee*

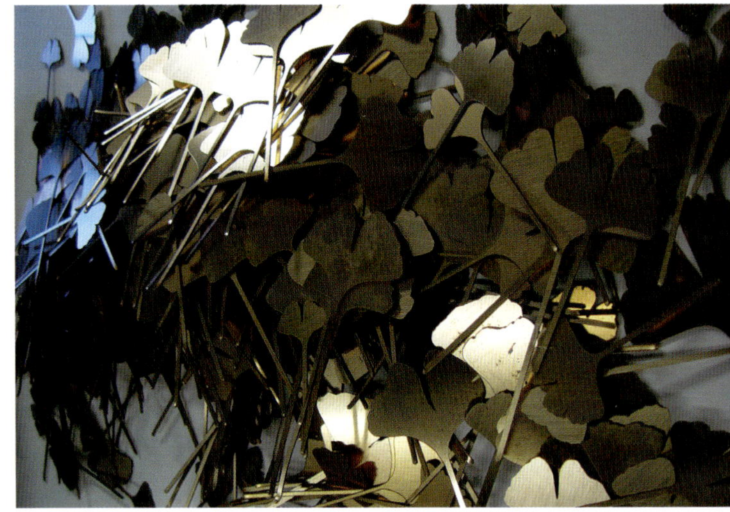

Chris Gavin. *Bonsai Gingko Tree*. Water jet cut leaves from sheet material. *Photo, Mark Lee*

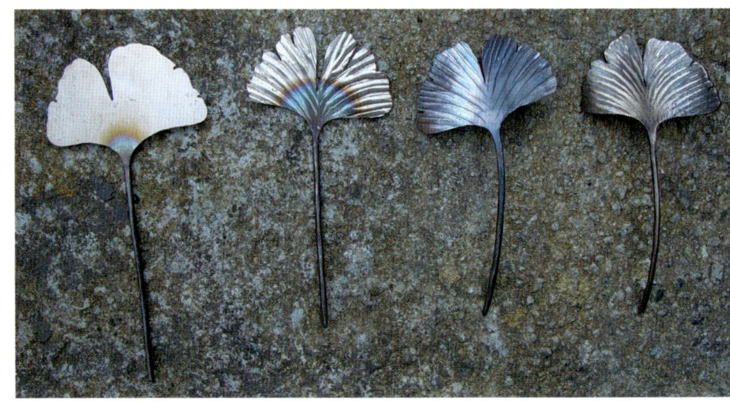

Chris Gavin. *Bonsai Gingko Tree*. Leaf development. *Photo, Mark Lee*

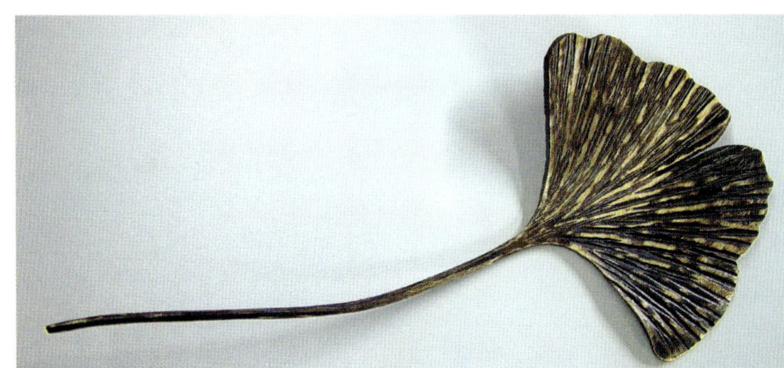

Chris Gavin. *Bonsai Gingko Tree*. Leaf completed. *Photo, Mark Lee*

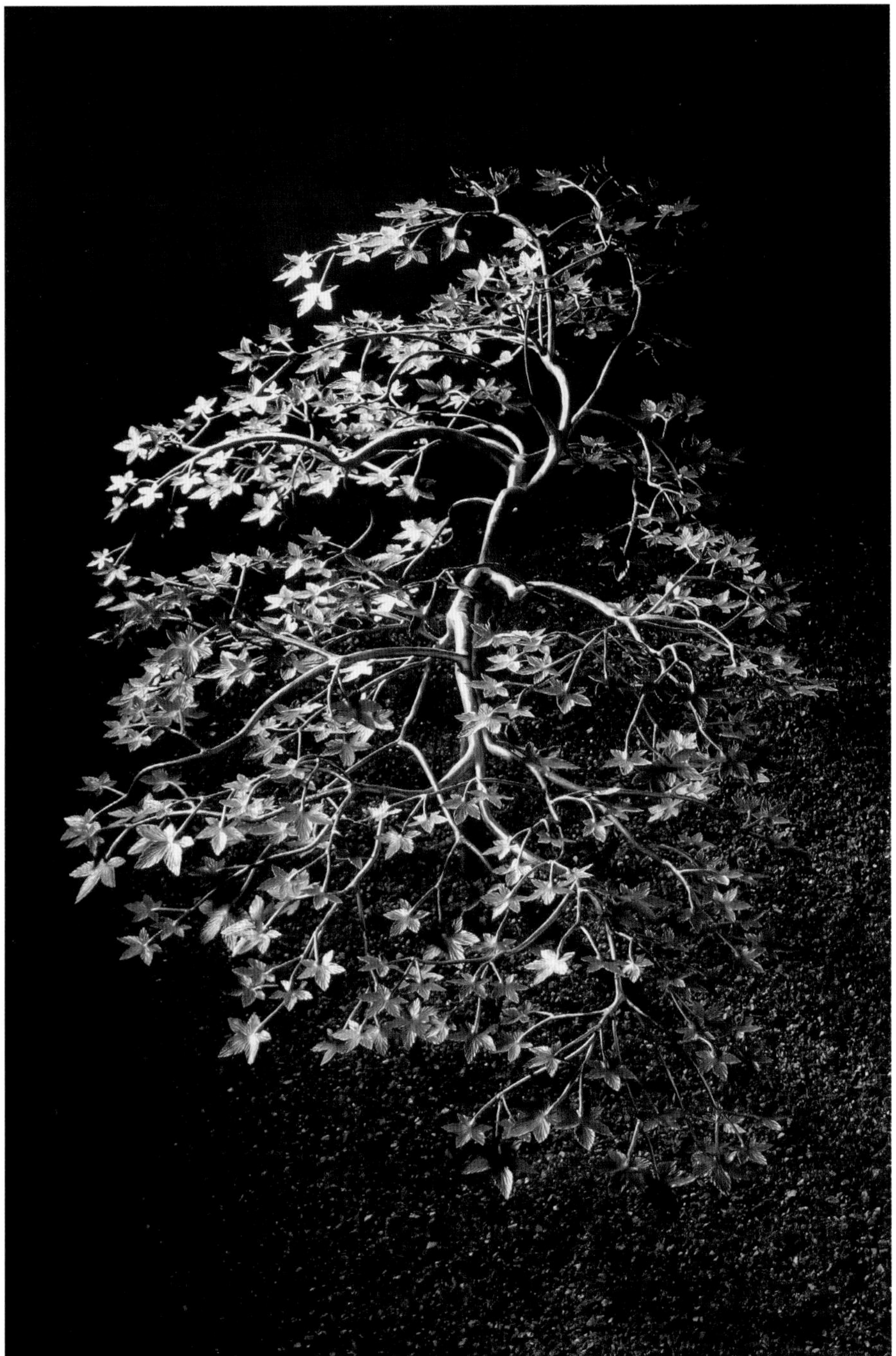

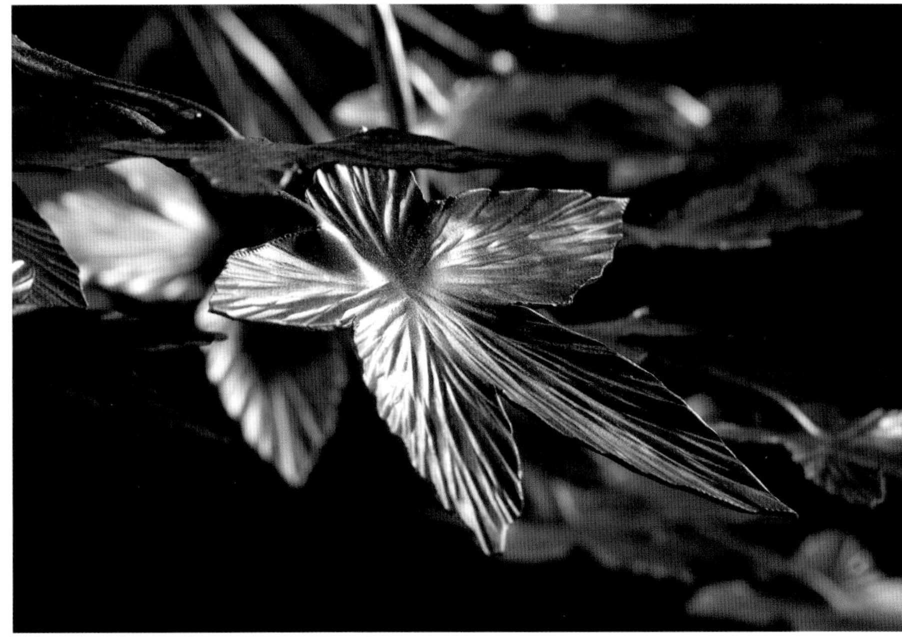

Matt Waldrop. *Japanese Maple*, 2007. Detail. *Photo, Patrick Lefebvre*

Matt Waldrop. *Japanese Maple*, 2007. Forged mild steel, mig welded. 72" w x 24" h. *Photo, Patrick Lefebvre*

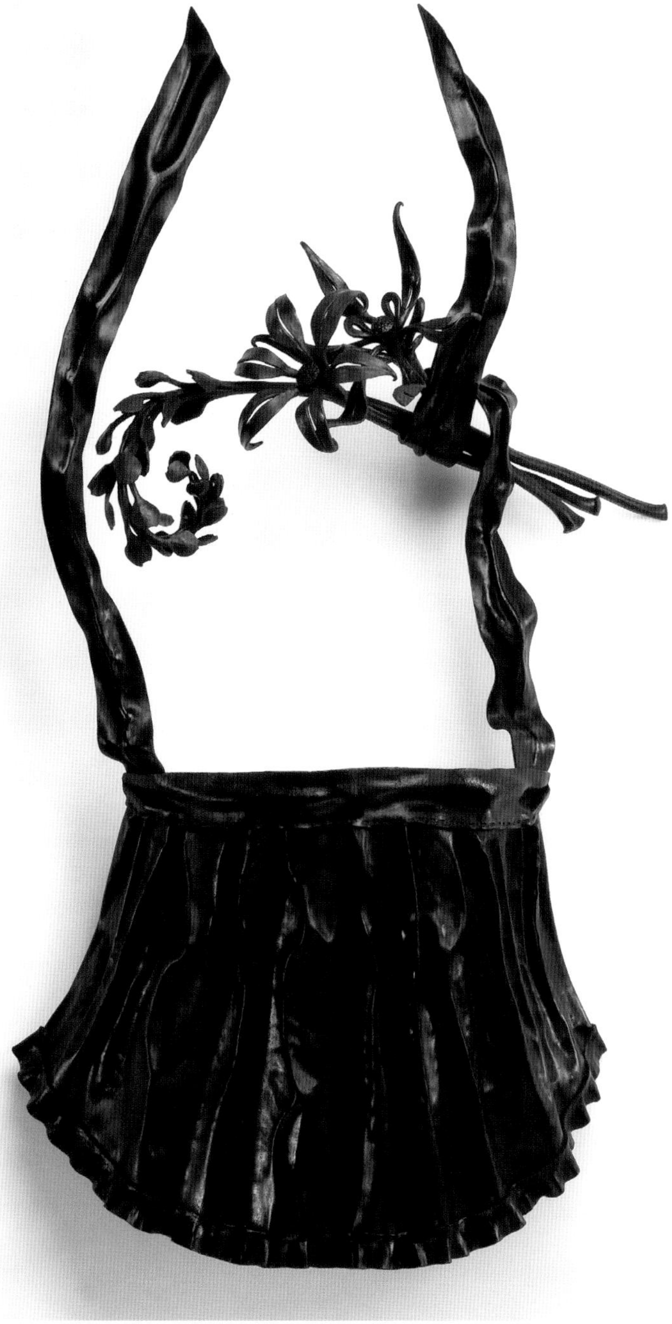

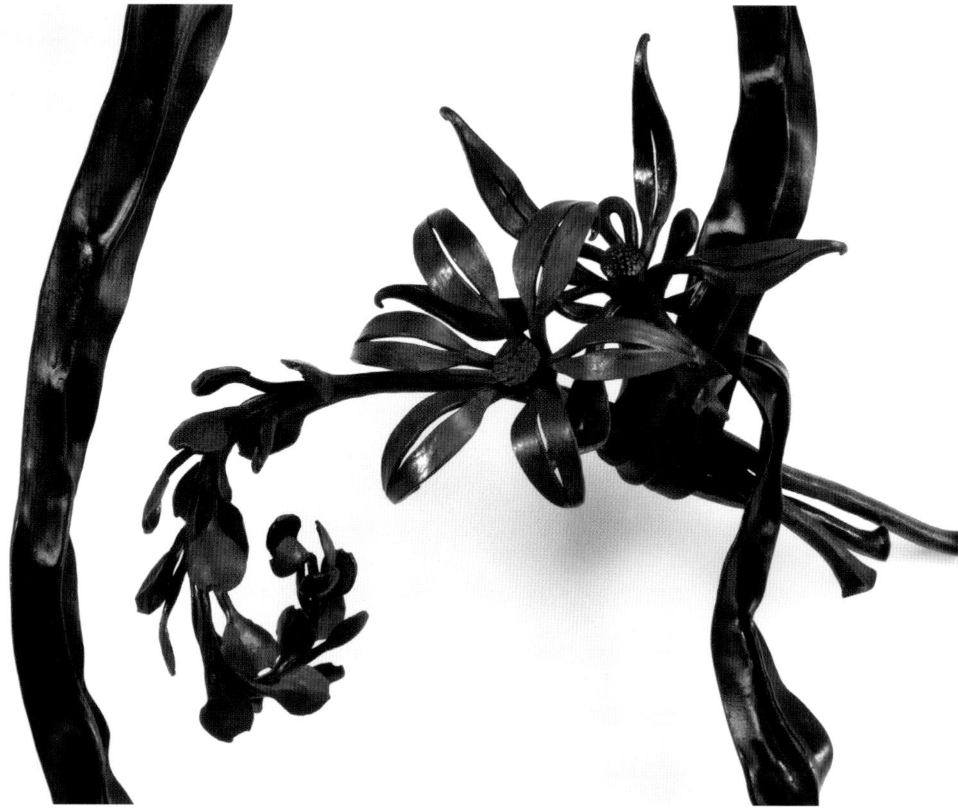

Elizabeth Brim. *Catch*. Detail. *Photo, Tom Mills*

Elizabeth Brim. *Catch*, 2002. Forged and fabricated steel. 36" h x 8" d x 24" w. *Photo, Tom Mills*

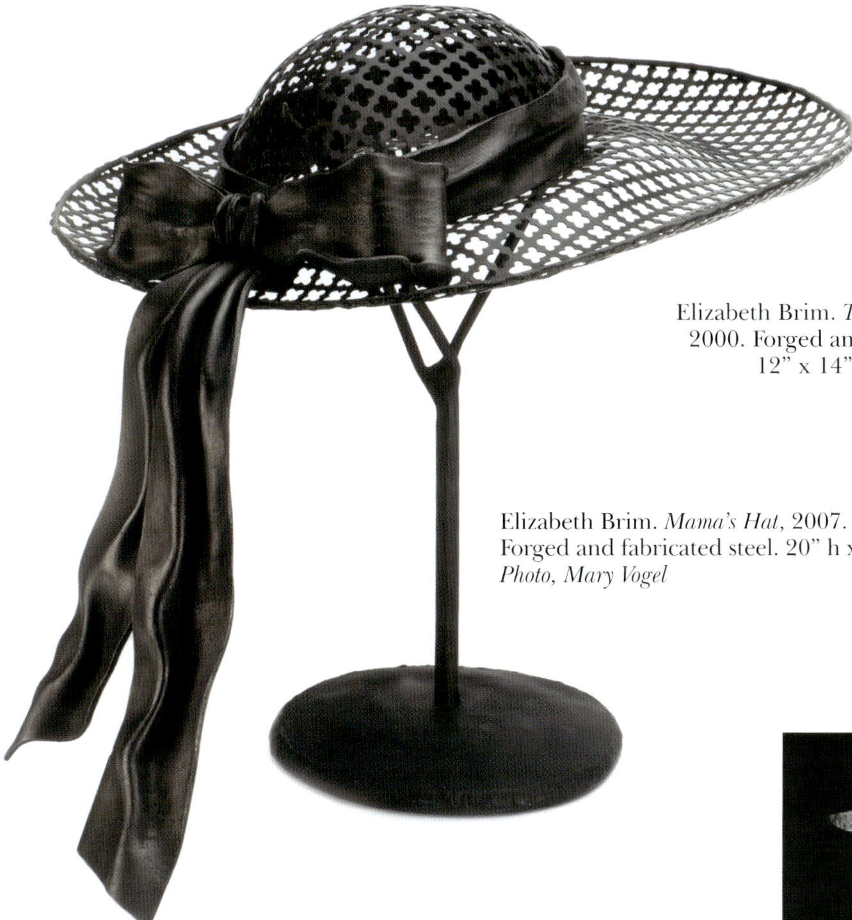

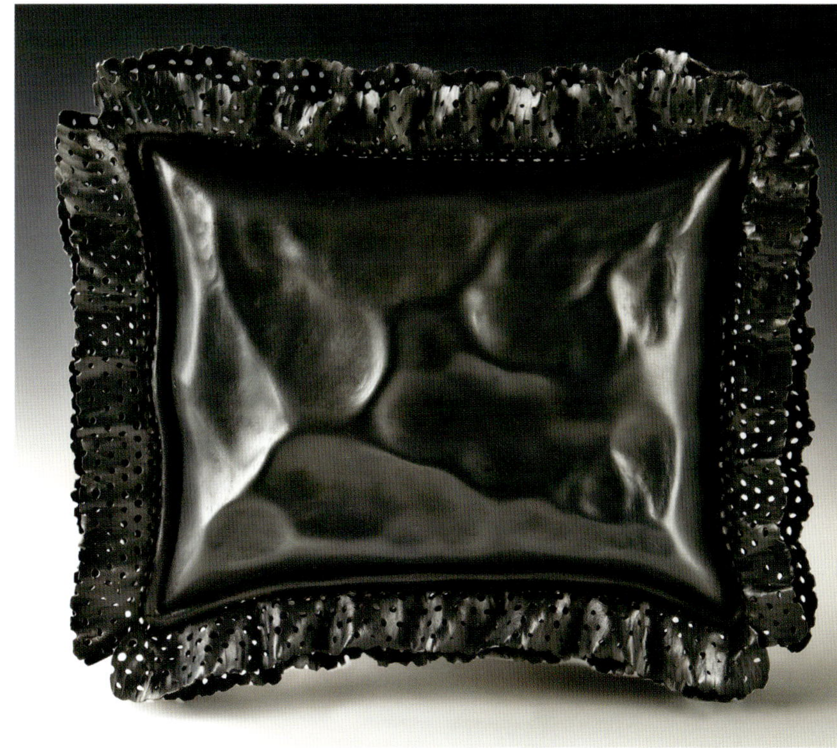

Elizabeth Brim. *The Wedding Pillow*, 2000. Forged and fabricated steel. 12" x 14". *Photo, Mary Vogel*

Elizabeth Brim. *Mama's Hat*, 2007. Forged and fabricated steel. 20" h x 14" d. *Photo, Mary Vogel*

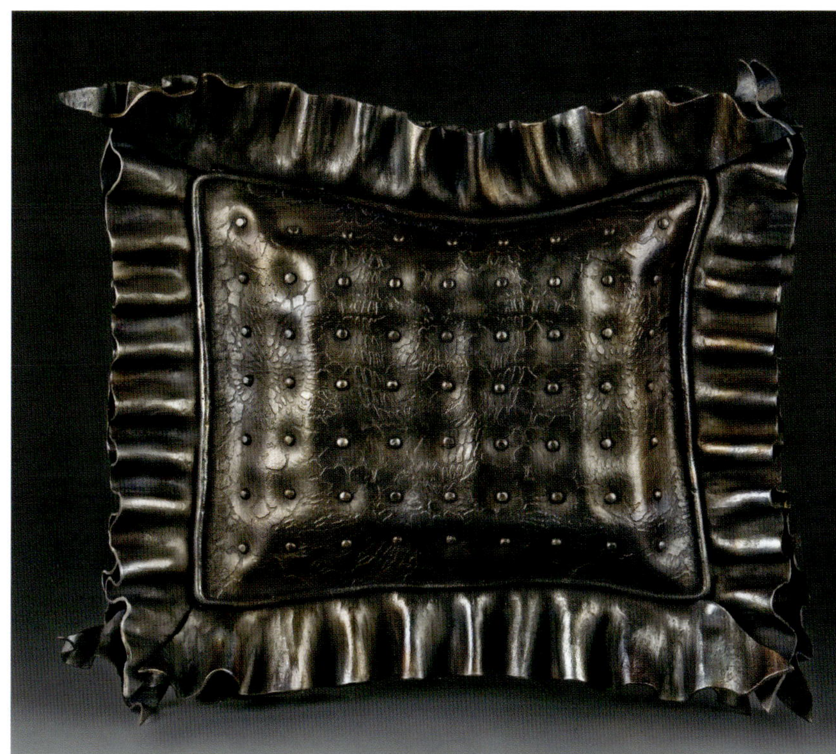

Elizabeth Brim. *The Excess*. Forged, fabricated, and inflated, etched with nitric acid, heat colors, wax, and oil paint. 12" x 14". *Photo, Mary Vogel*

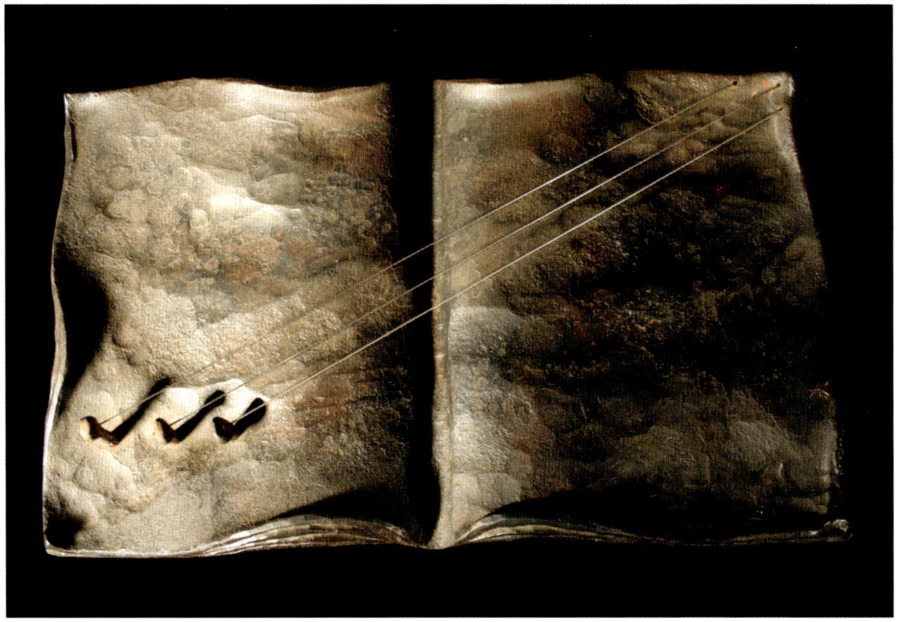

Achim Kühn. *Little Book of Sounds*. Forged steel, stainless steel wire. 3" x 15" x 9". Sound sculpture. *Photo, artist*

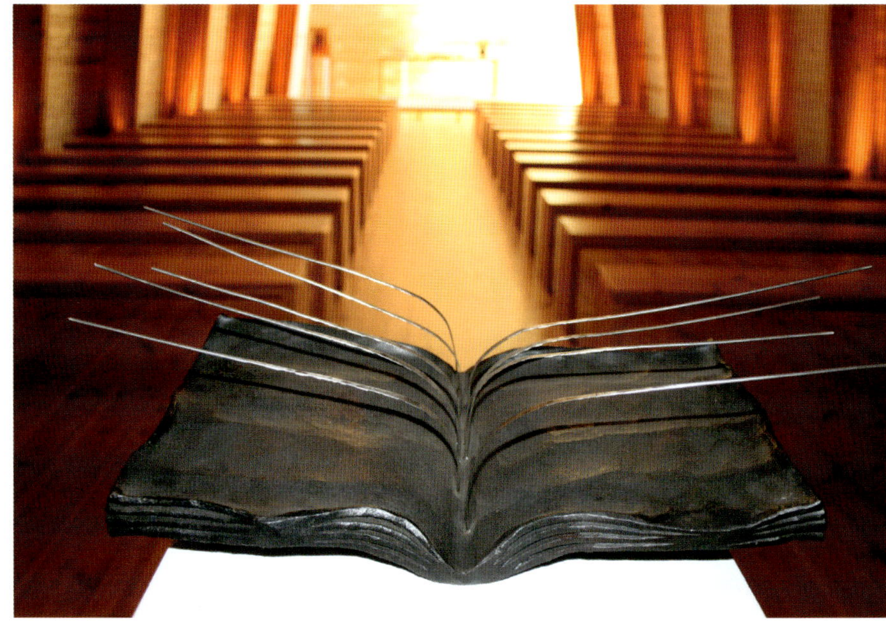

Achim Kühn. *Read Between the Lines*. Forged steel, stainless steel. 1.5" x 20" x 9". *Photo, artist*

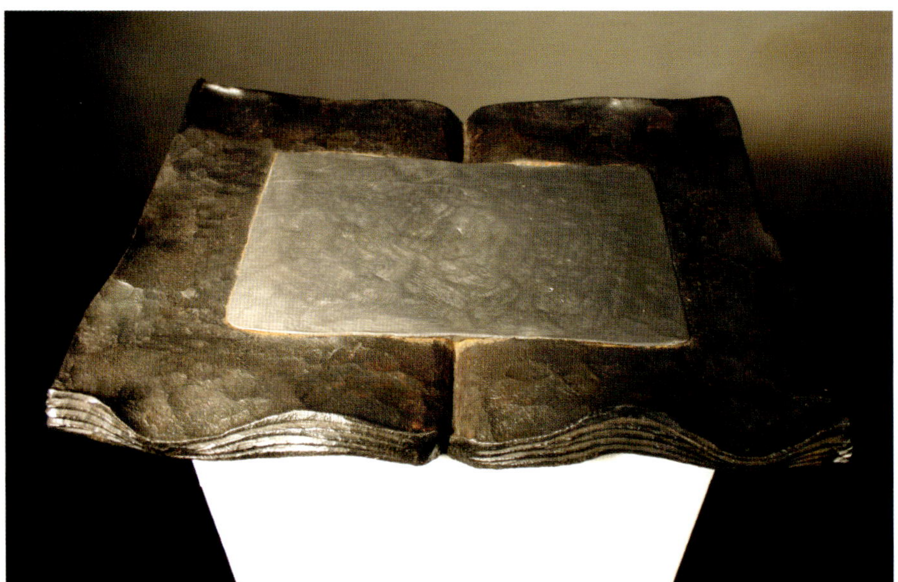

Achim Kühn. *Book of Silence*. Forged steel. 1" x 11" x 9". *Photo, artist*

Achim Kühn. *Book Full of Thoughts*. Forged steel, transparent paper. 6" x 5" x 5". *Photo, artist*

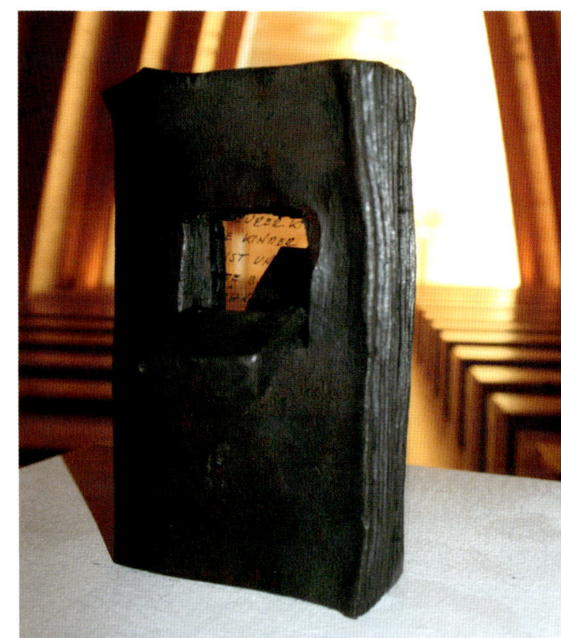

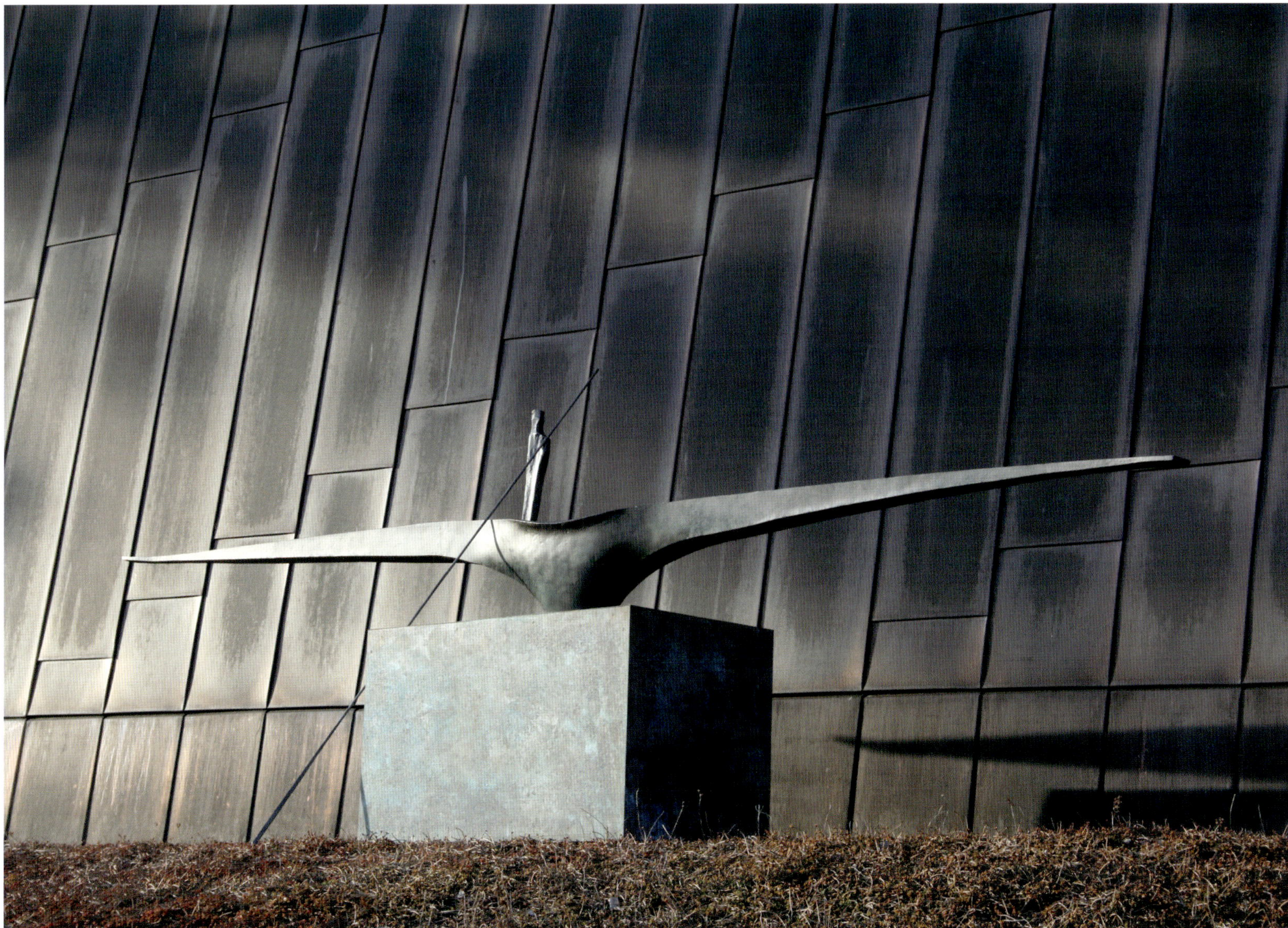

Achim Kühn. *Where We Are? Boat and ferryman*—forged steel, ocean-copper sheet, patina. 53" x 24" x 157". *Photo, artist*

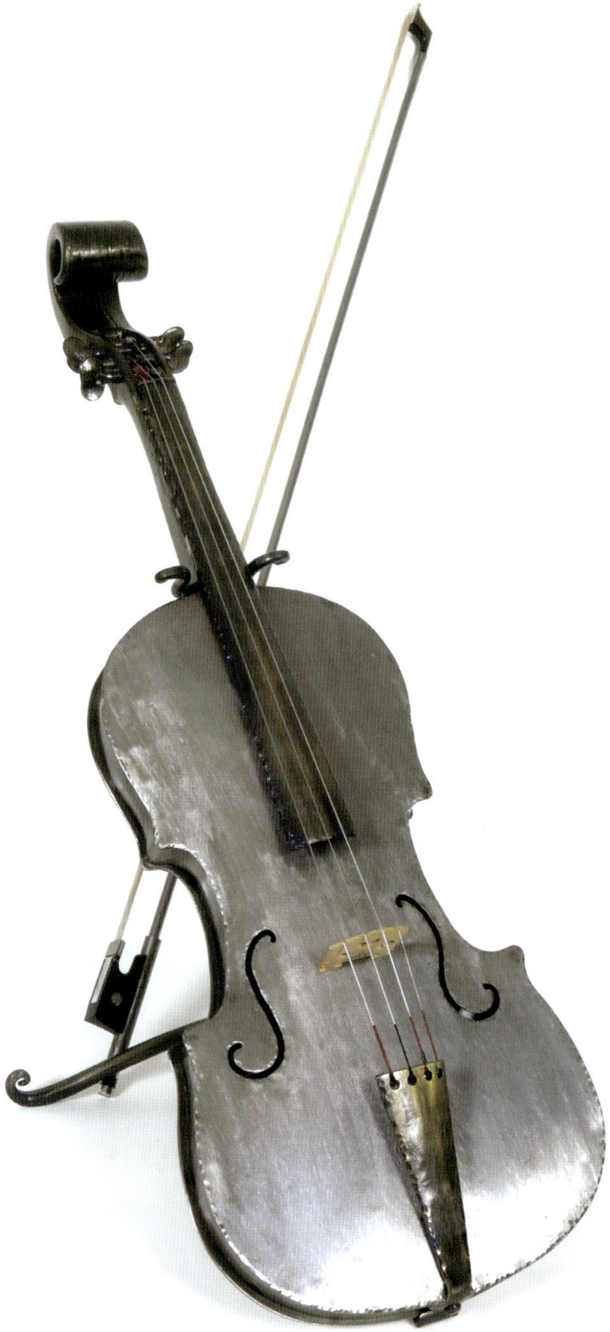

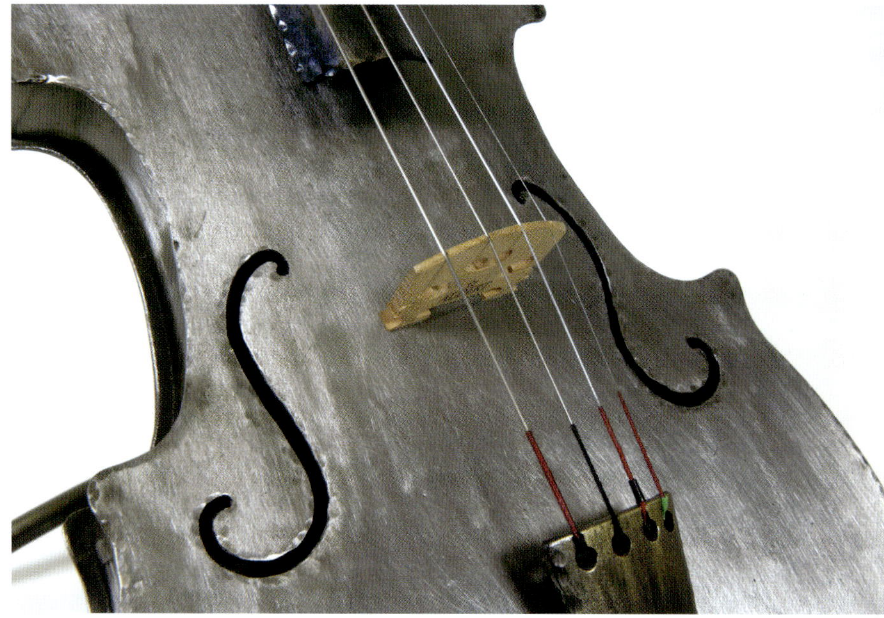

Peter Schlotthauer. *Tribute to Strauss*. Detail. *Photo, Ron Kuzyk*

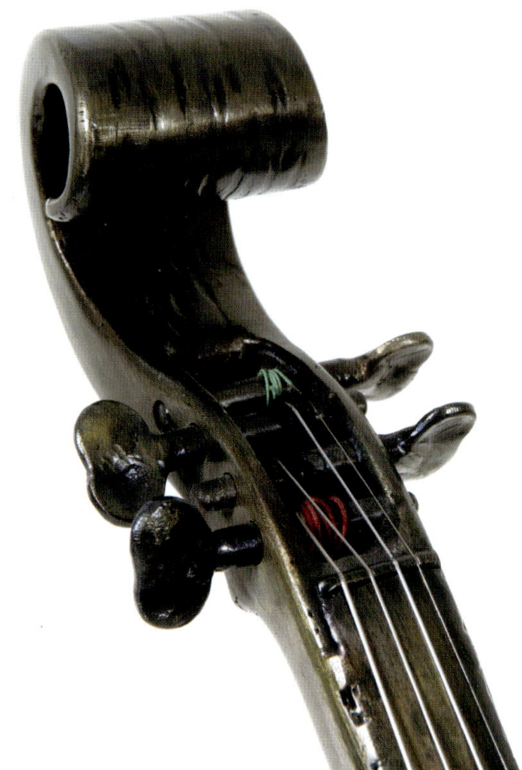

Peter Schlotthauer. *Tribute to Strauss*. Detail. *Photo, Ron Kuzyk*

Peter Schlotthauer. *Tribute to Strauss*. Steel and steel tubing. 23" h x 8" w. *Photo, Ron Kuzyk*

Growing up in my native Australia, the music of the violin was a staple of life. Today, it still evokes the romanticism of a bygone age, where couples waltzed at the Opera Ball in the imperial Palace. I wanted to create my own version of a violin as a remembrance of that wonderful music. This life-sized violin was fashioned from steel to which a wooden bridge and authentic strings were added. When tuned and played, it gives a very distinctive sound. The bow is made of steel tubing and parts of an original bow. Strauss was the great master of this instrument in Vienna; therefore I dedicate this work to him.
– Peter Schlotthauer

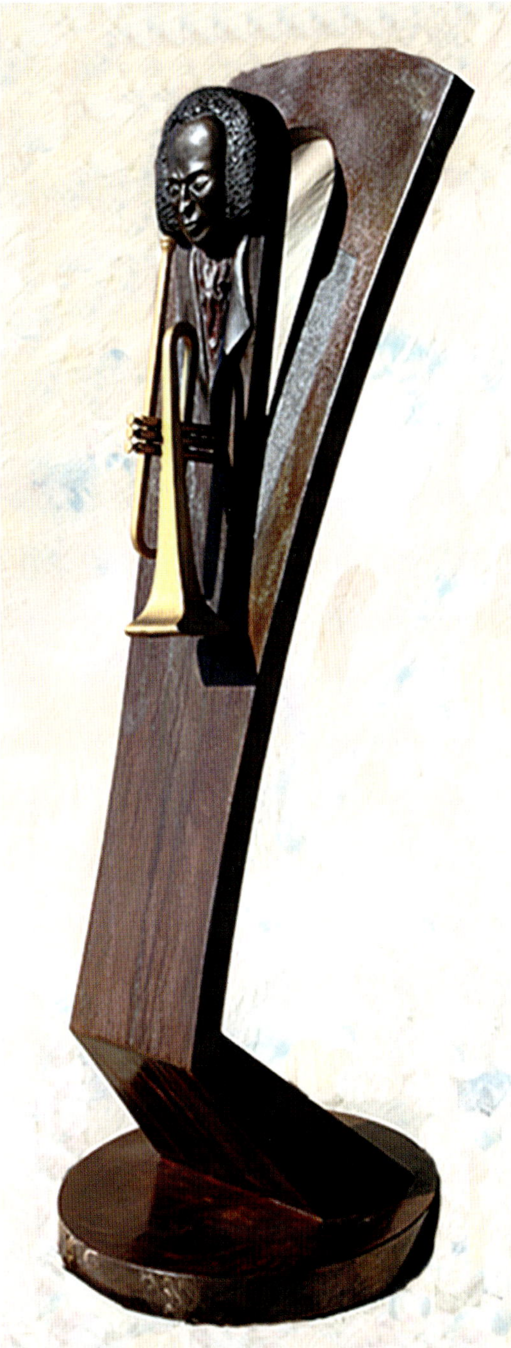

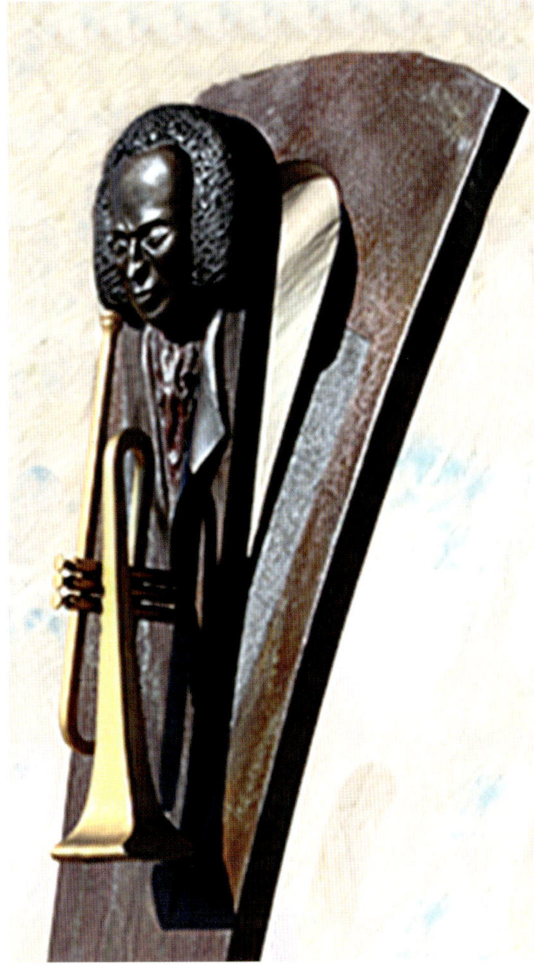

Jan Pearson. *Miles Davis*. Detail.
Photo, Dale W. Anderson

Jan Pearson. *Miles Davis*. Mild steel, rust finish. 76" h. Hand sculpted using "blown steel" technique for the face.
Photo, Dale W. Anderson

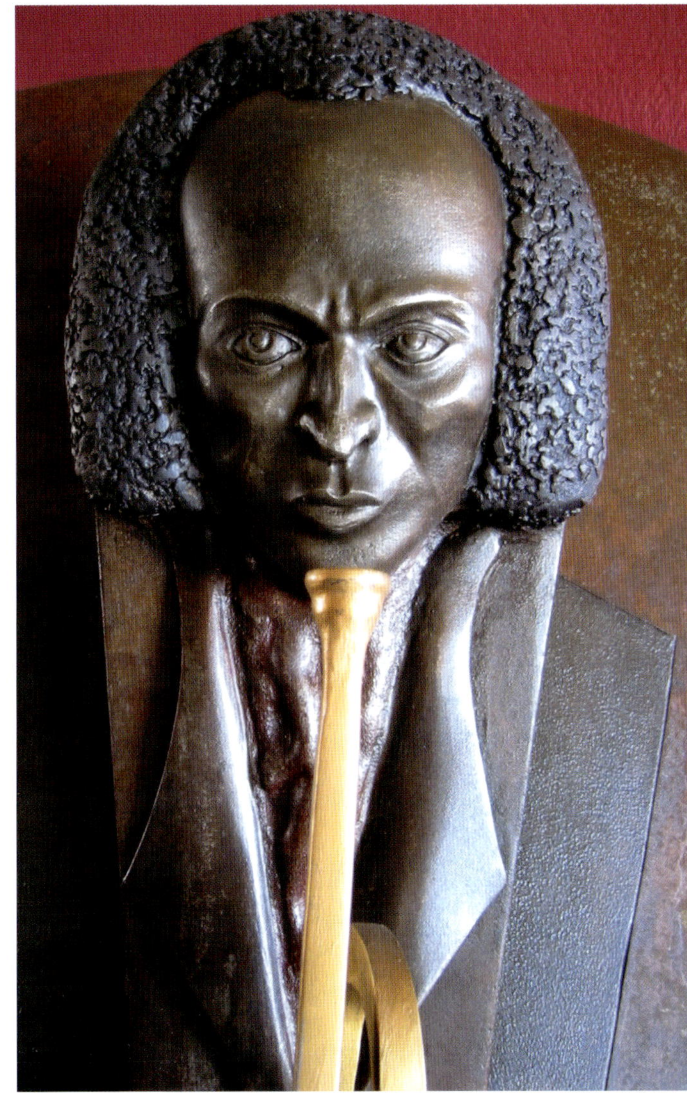

Jan Pearson. *Miles Davis*. Detail. *Photo, Dale W. Anderson*

Matt Weber. *Copper Fishing Lure.* Copper, Aluminum. 28" h x 36" l. Inspired from a fishing catalog received in the mail, this copper lure started as a sketch. The sketch was projected on white poster board and a template was made for the body. Two body halves were cut from copper and were formed into shape on a panel beater bag and an English Wheel. The halves were brazed together and mounted in place. The fins were fold formed and the hook was forged from a solid piece of 3/4 inch copper rod. The eyes are Aluminum and riveted in place. *Gallery Credits: Vision Gallery, Art on Boston, Chandler Sculpture Walk. Photo, artist*

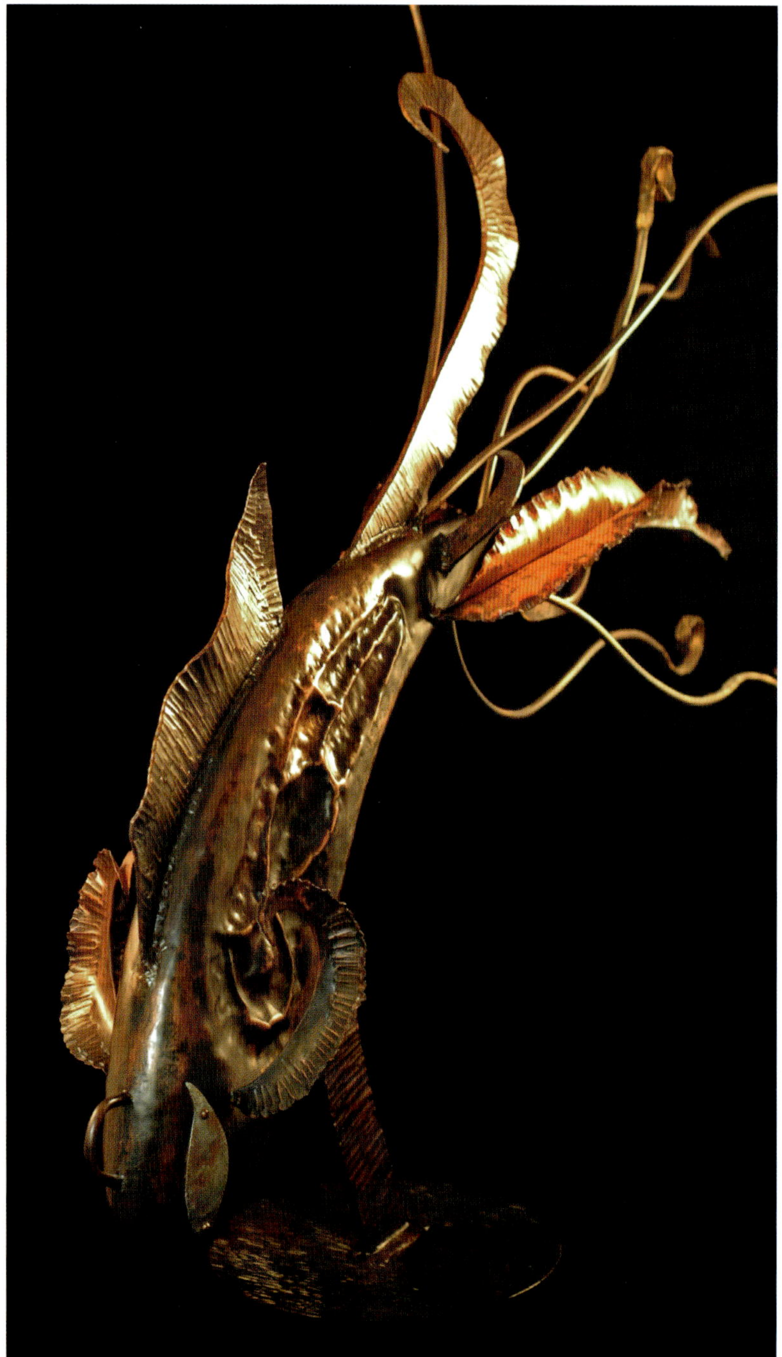

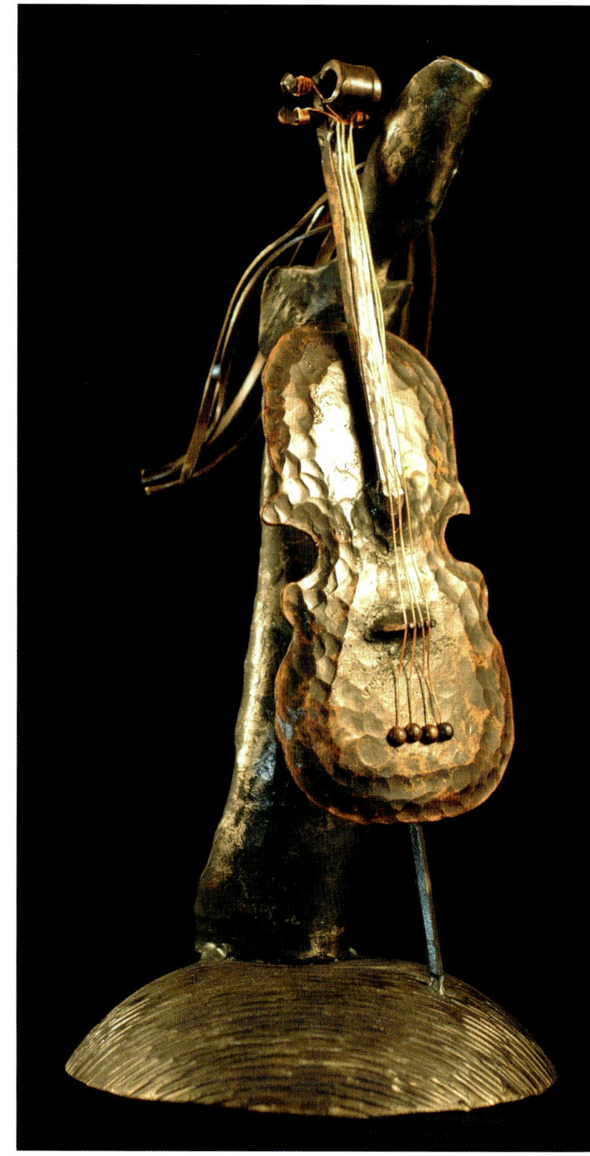

Matt Weber. *The Cellist*. Forged copper and steel. 14" h. *The Cellist* was forged from hot roll steel. Her hair was a 2-inch wide strip of cold roll steel cut into strips with a Beverly shear. The Cello was forged from a 1/4 inch thick piece of copper. *The Cello* neck was brazed onto the body as well as the pegs. The base texture was chisel cut and formed into a dish with a Fly press. *Photo, artist*

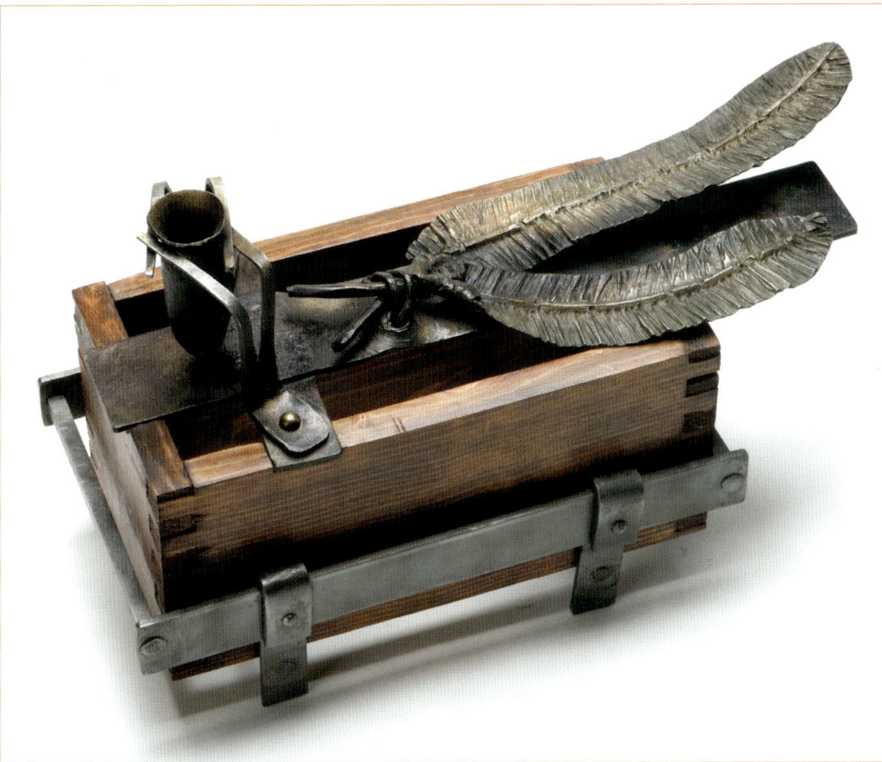

Laura Lea Parker. *The Journey*, 2007. Forged steel and wood. 11" h x 18" w x 7" d. Photo, Kent Lacin

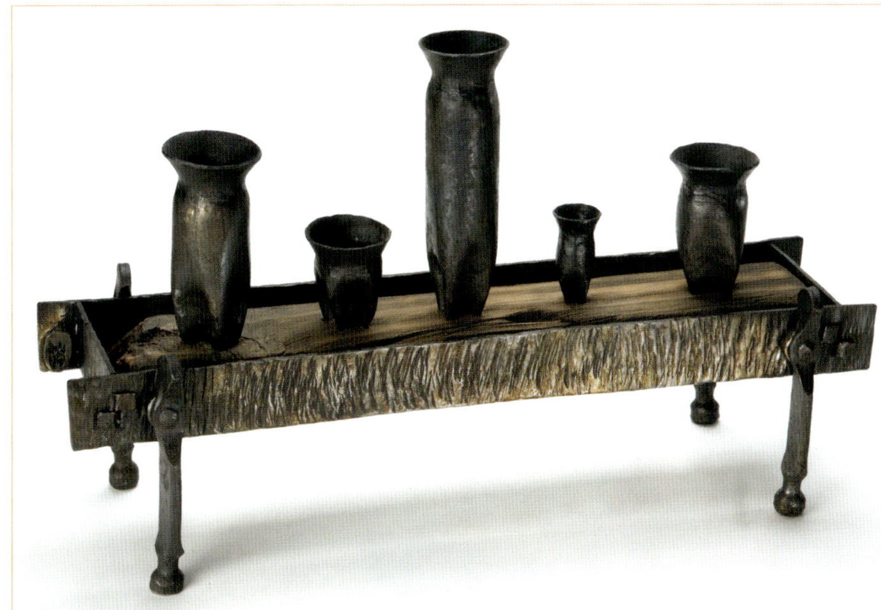

Laura Lea Parker. *Choices*, 2007. Forged steel and wood. 15.5" h x 27" w x 9" d. *Photo, Kent Lacin*

Several of our friends get together for lunch almost daily. For around four months, the topic of conversation always came around to what decision to make for the next step in our lives. We all felt we had lived through several choices we would have done differently and we didn't want to suffer a similar fate. The vessels represent that when you are making a choice all options must be considered even if it seems obvious that one is superior to another. – Laura Lea Parker

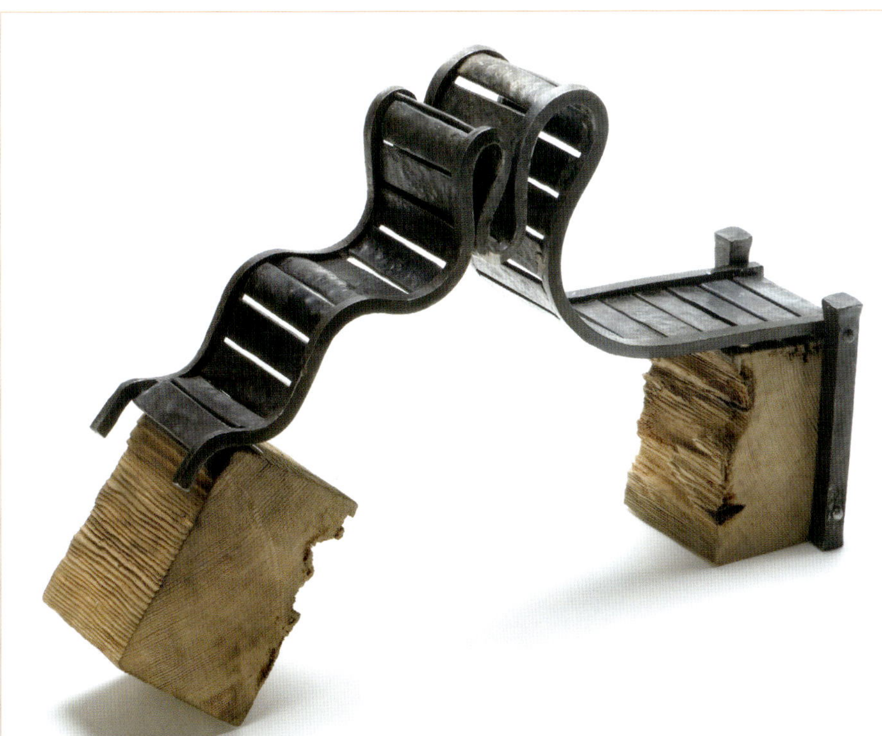

Laura Lea Parker. *Crossing The Bridge*, 2007. Forged steel and wood. 13" h x 21" w x 5.5" d. *Photo, Kent Lacin*

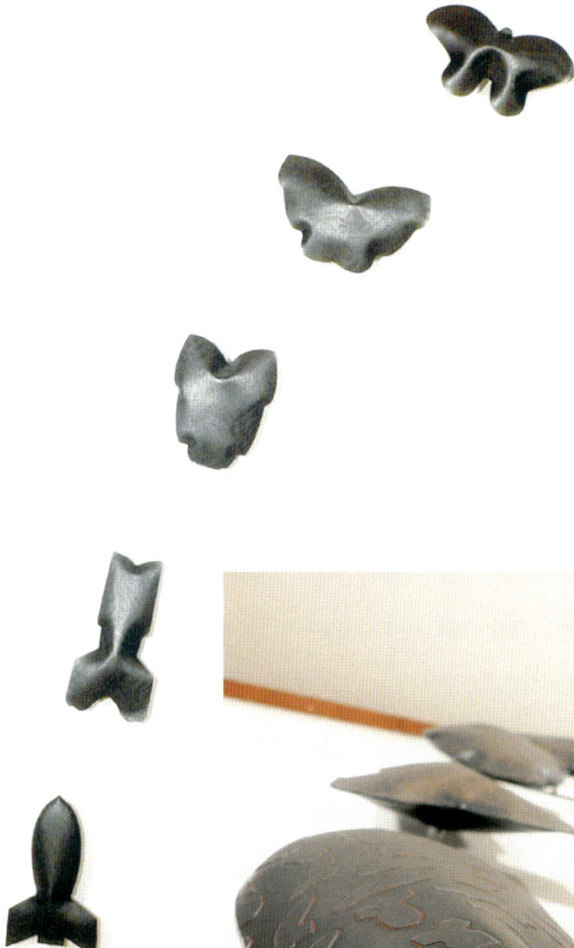

Eric A. Ryser. *Bombs and Butterflies*, 2006. Inflated mild steel, acid etched. *Photo, artist*

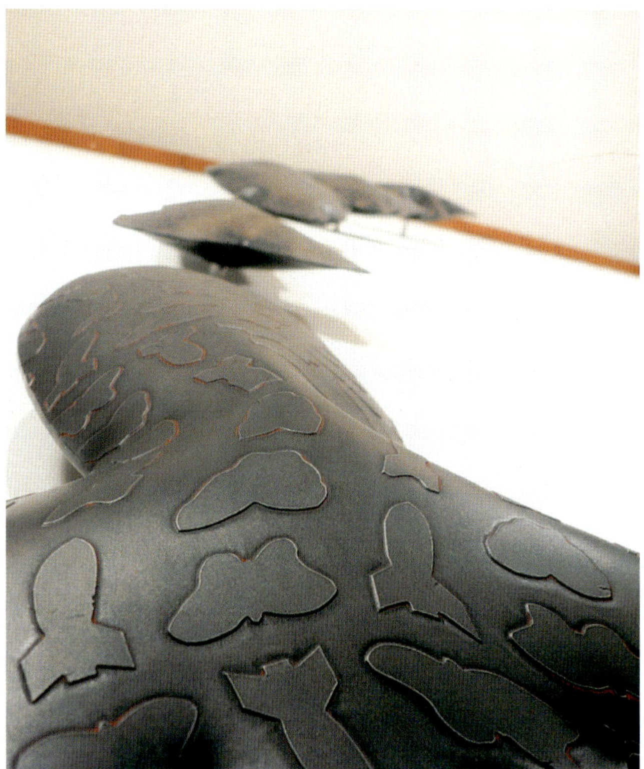

Eric A. Ryser. *Bombs and Butterflies*, 2006. Pattern detail. *Photo, artist*

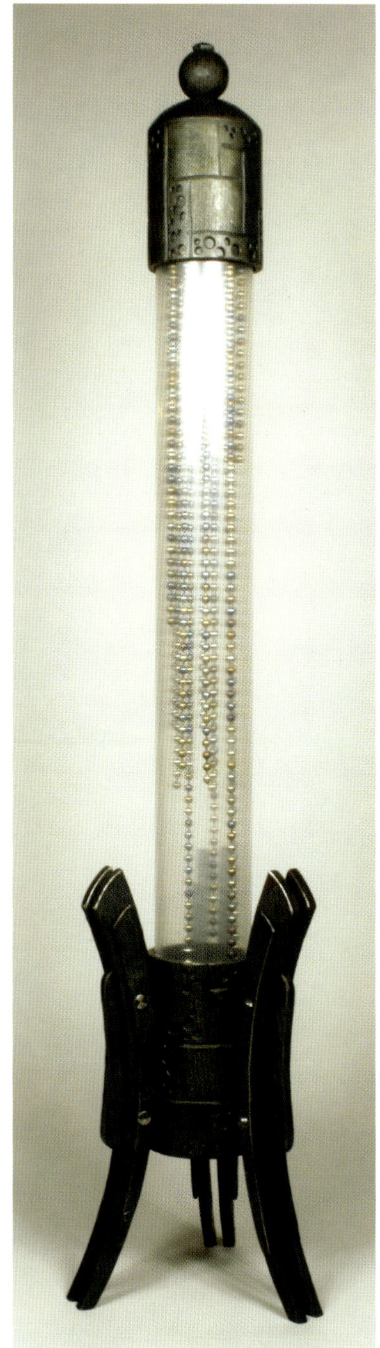

Jennifer Gilbert. *Supermodel*, 2008. Forged steel, Plexiglas tube, and ball chain. 38" h x 8" d. *Photo, artist*

This combination of materials in an experiment that result in an otherworldly feeling.

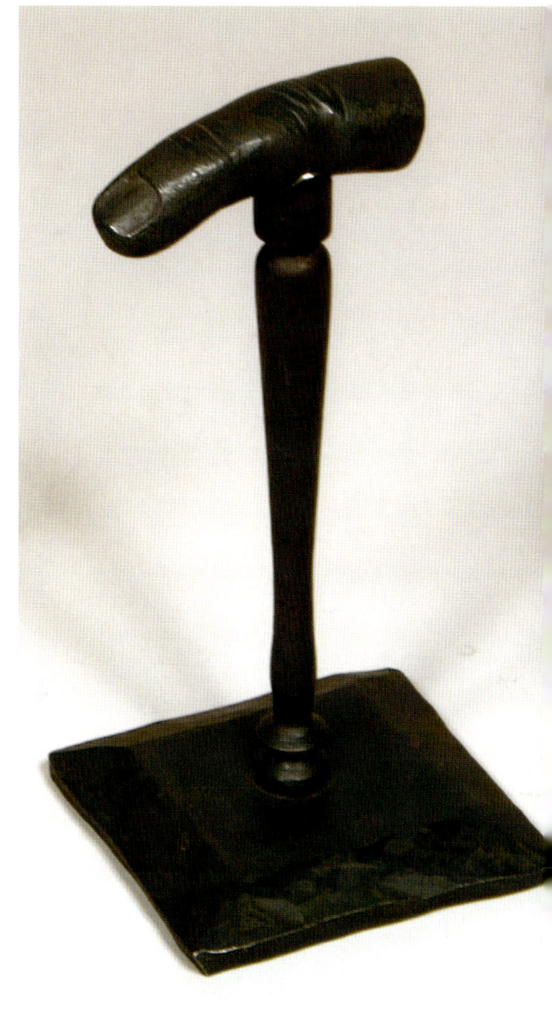

Jennifer Gilbert. *Oops*, 2005. Forged steel. 7.5" h x 3.5" x 3.5". *Photo, artist*

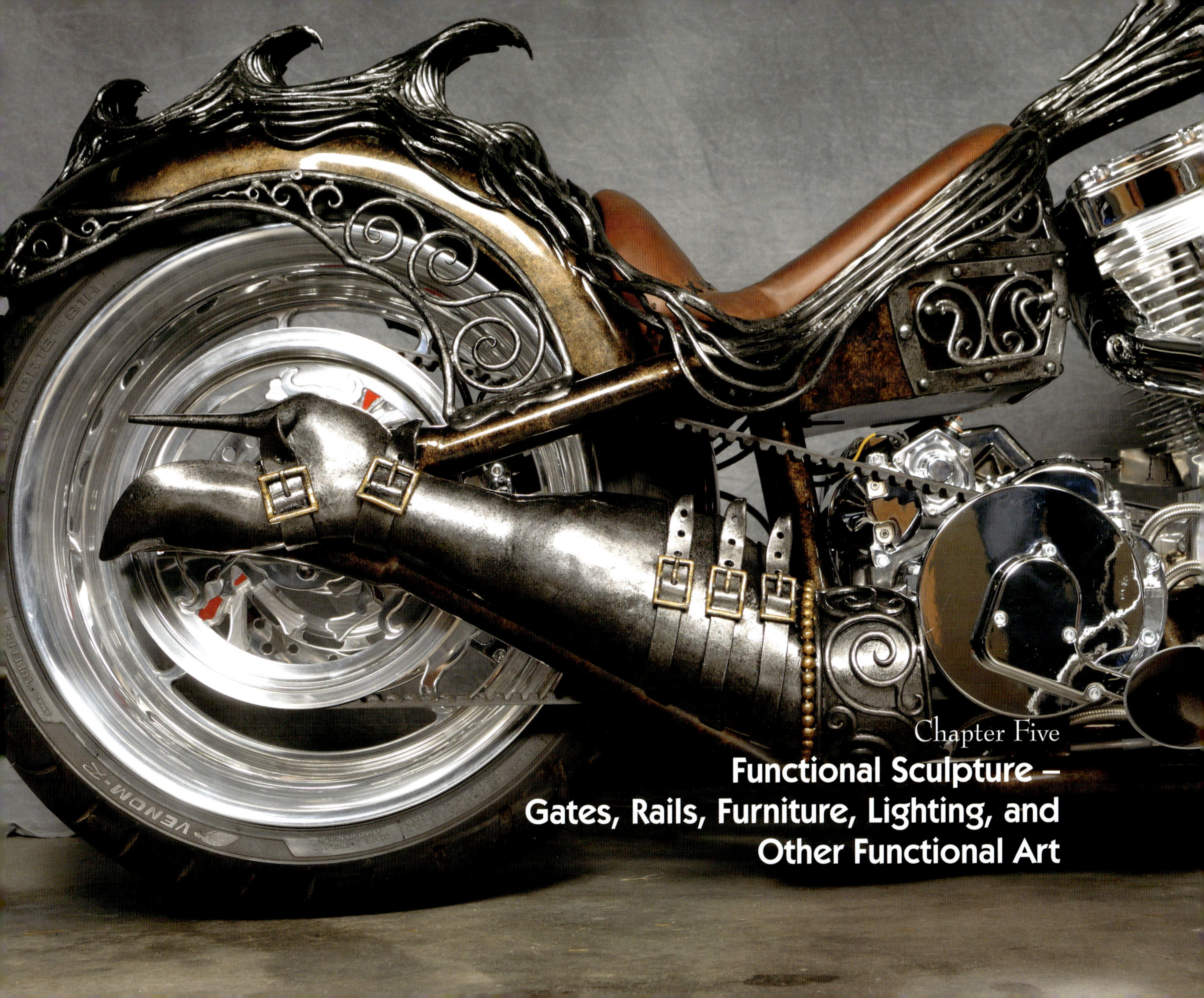

Chapter Five

Functional Sculpture – Gates, Rails, Furniture, Lighting, and Other Functional Art

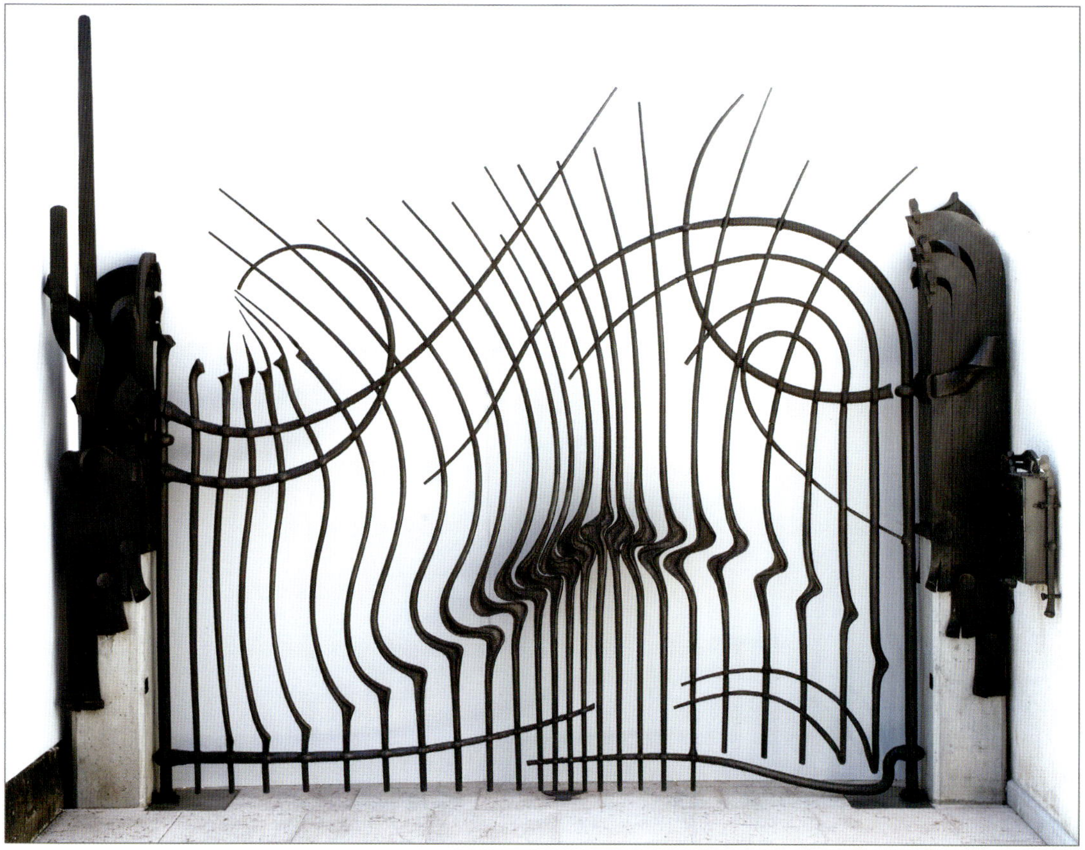

Claudio Bottero. Entrance gate in front of the house of Claudio Bottero. Forged wrought iron. 149" x 118". Piombino Dese (PD) Italy. *Photo, artist*

Claudio Bottero. Entrance gate. Details of left post. *Photo, artist*

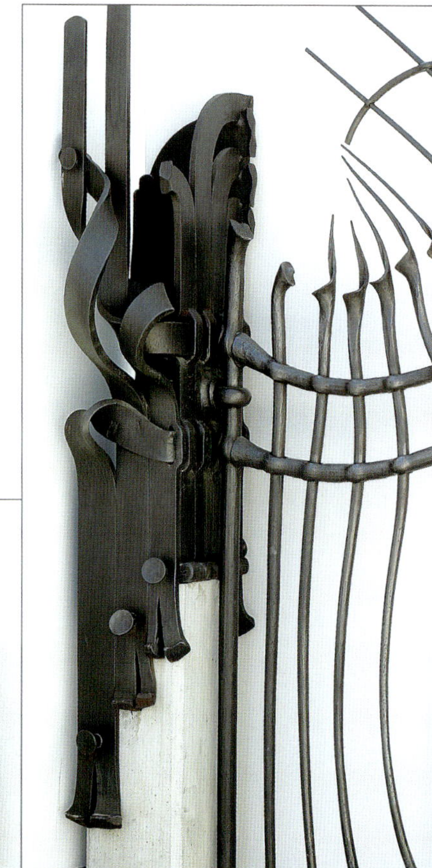

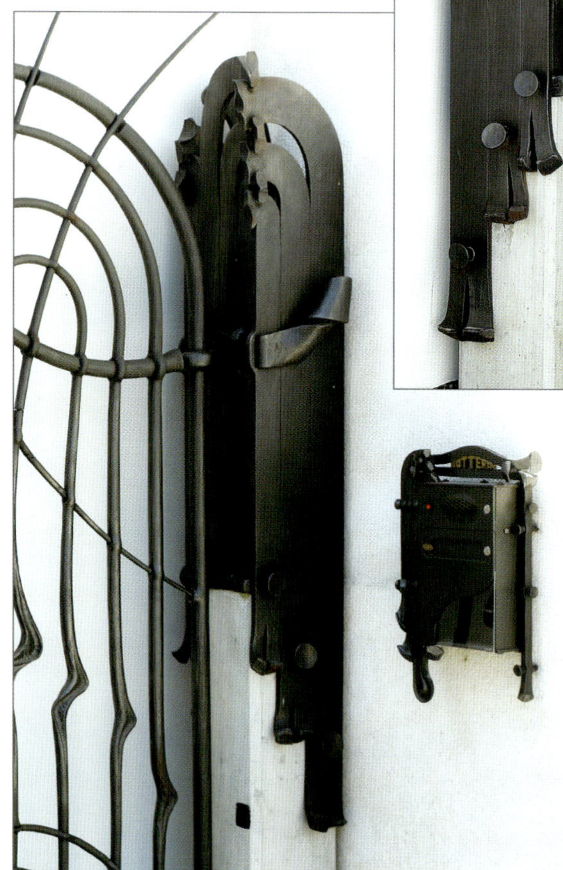

Claudio Bottero. Entrance gate. Details of the right post and letterbox. *Photo, artist*

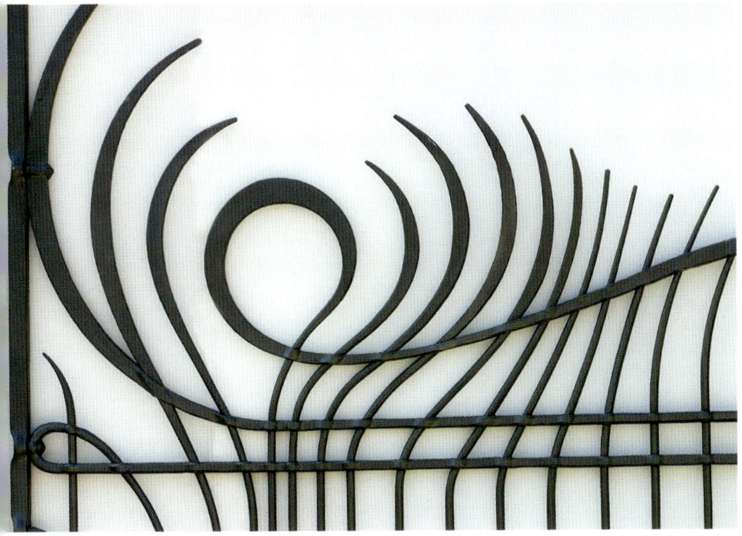

Claudio Bottero. Wrought-iron entrance gate. Central detail. *Photo, artist*

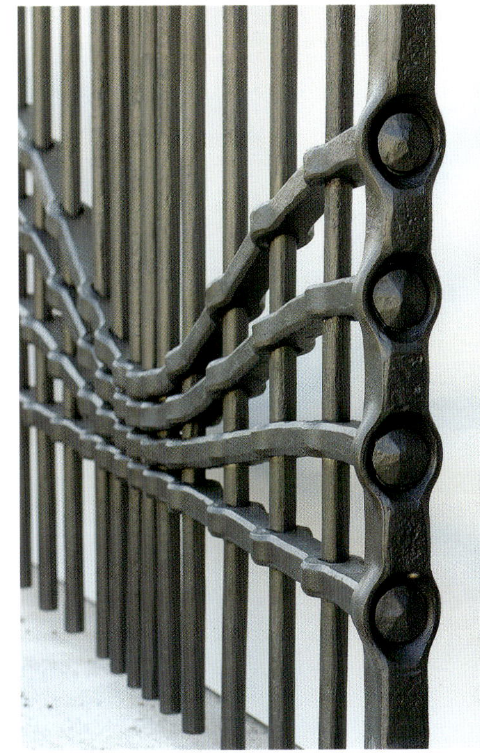

Claudio Bottero. Wrought-iron entrance gate. Detail of central wing. *Photo, artist*

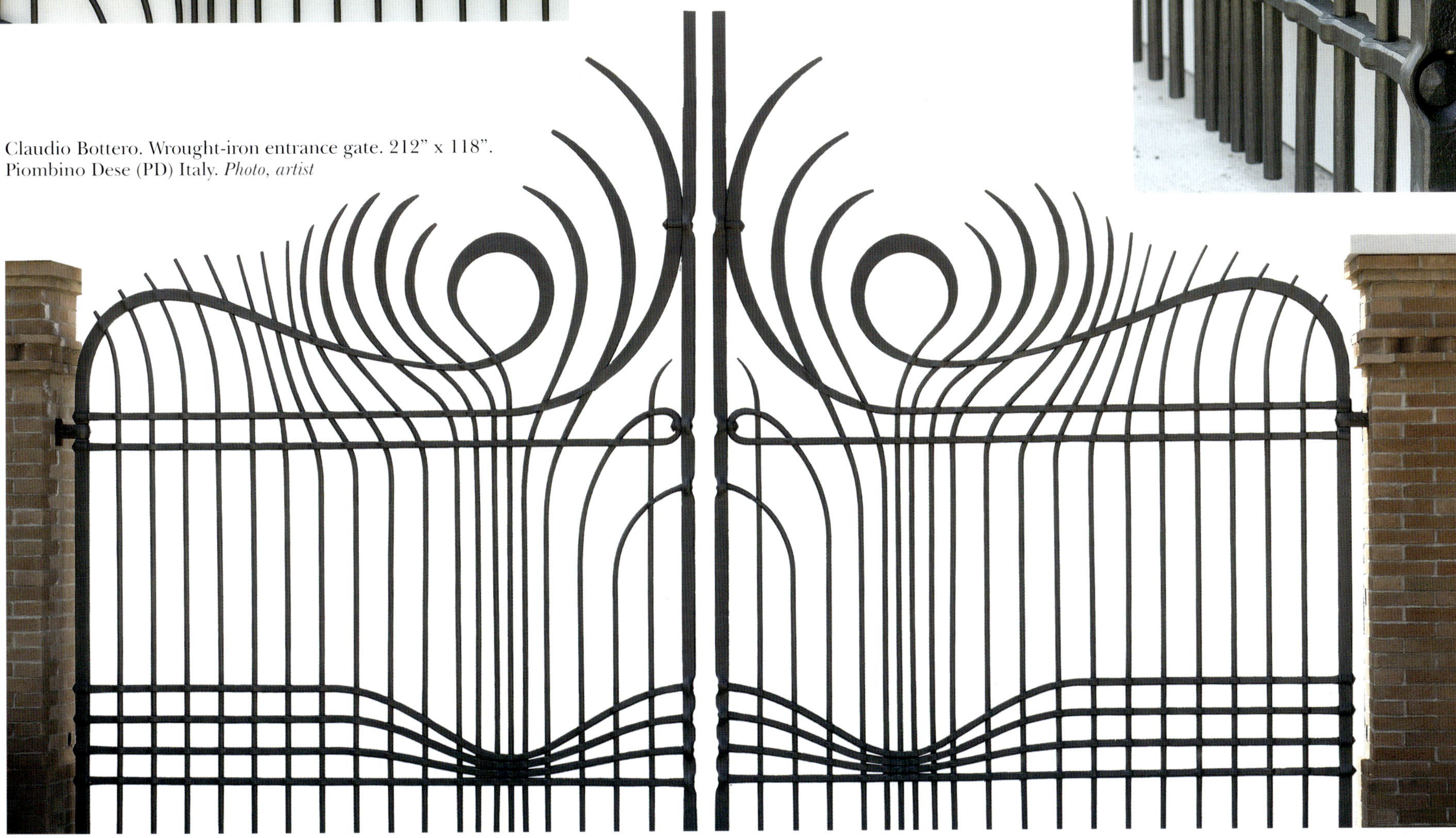

Claudio Bottero. Wrought-iron entrance gate. 212" x 118". Piombino Dese (PD) Italy. *Photo, artist*

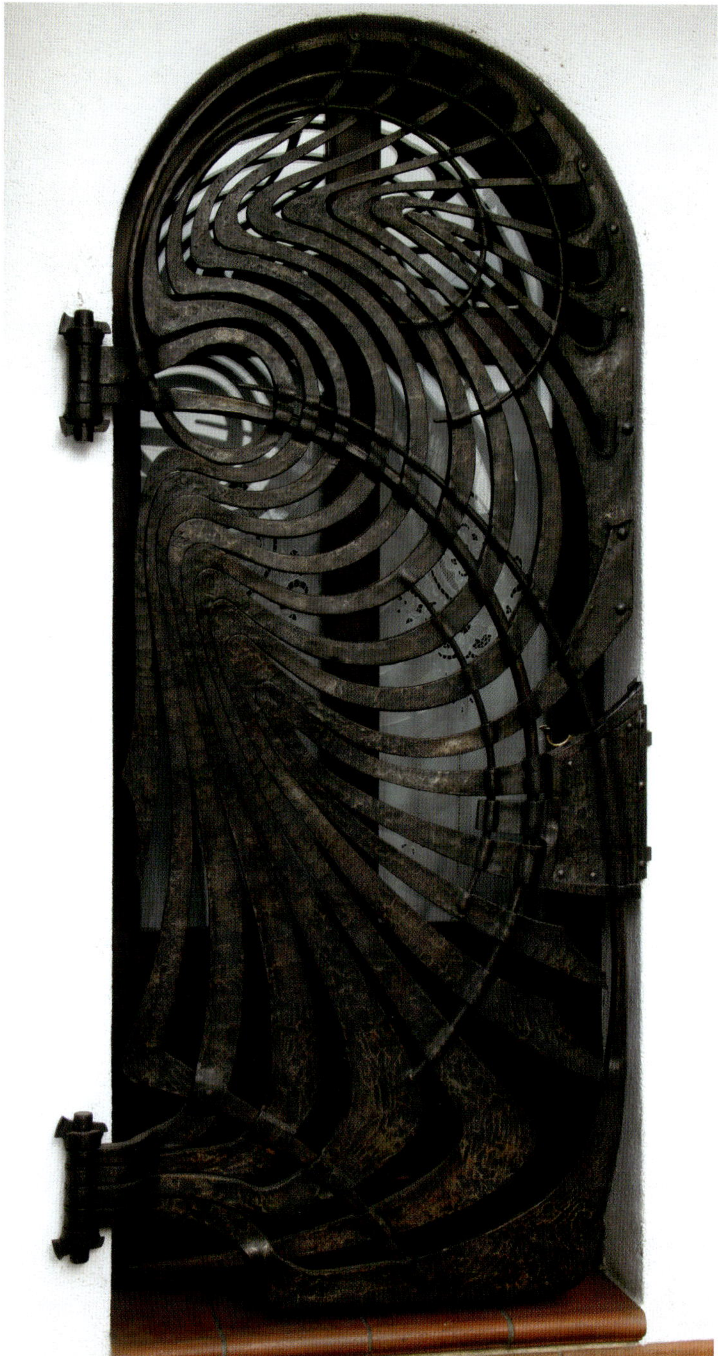

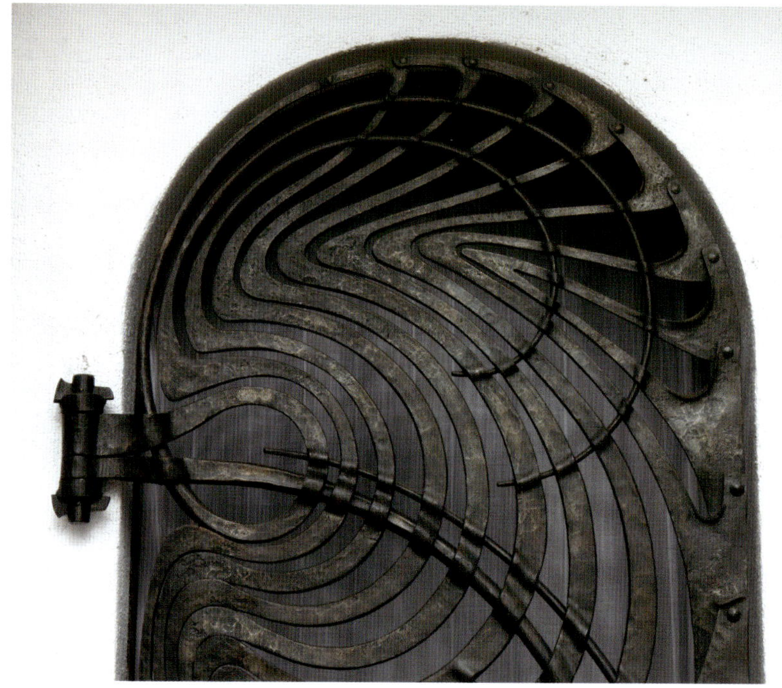

Claudio Bottero.
Cancello per porta,
Detail. Photo, artist

Claudio Bottero. Cancello per porta. Forged iron. 39" x 90". *Photo, artist*

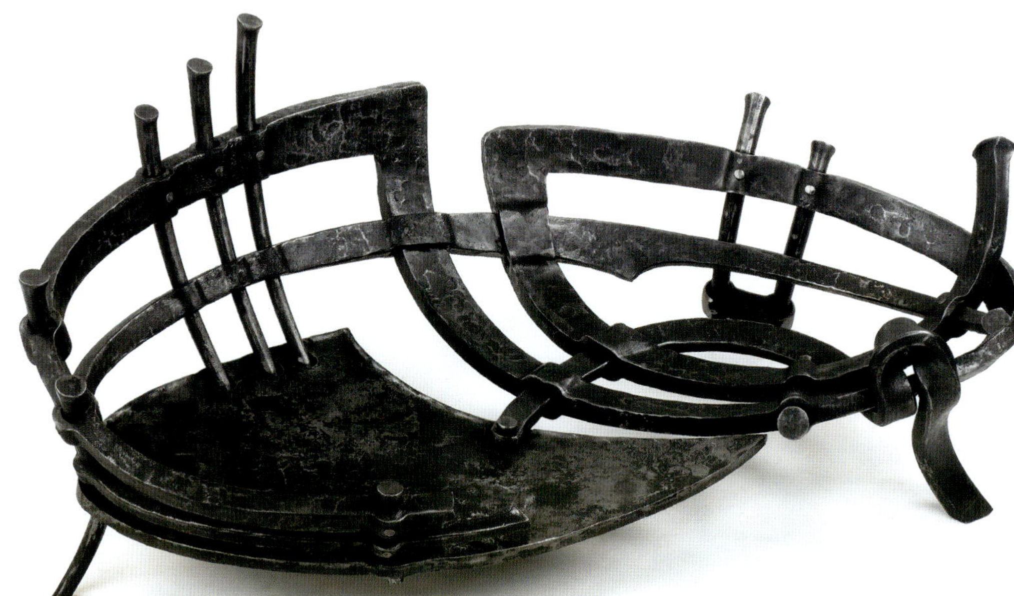

Claudio Bottero. Braciere per caminetto, Forged iron. 39" x 17" x 17" h. Photo, artist

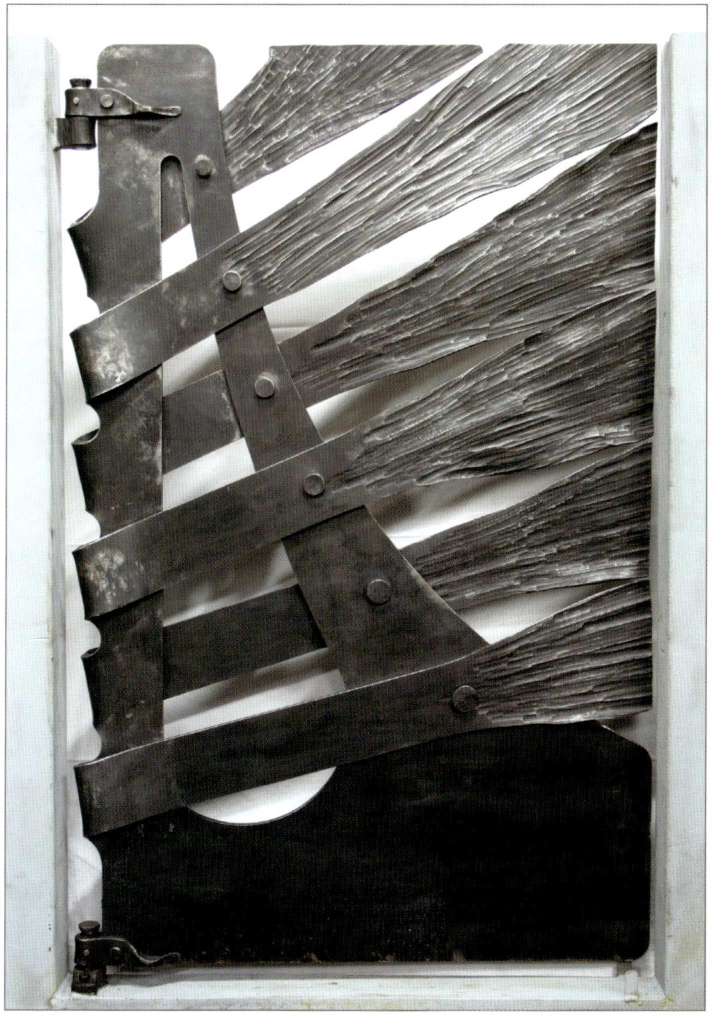

Roberto Giordani. Footgate. Created from a single sheet of half-inch thick steel. 51" h x 31" w. Property of the Galleria D'Arte, il Parco del Chianti- Siena. Photo, artist

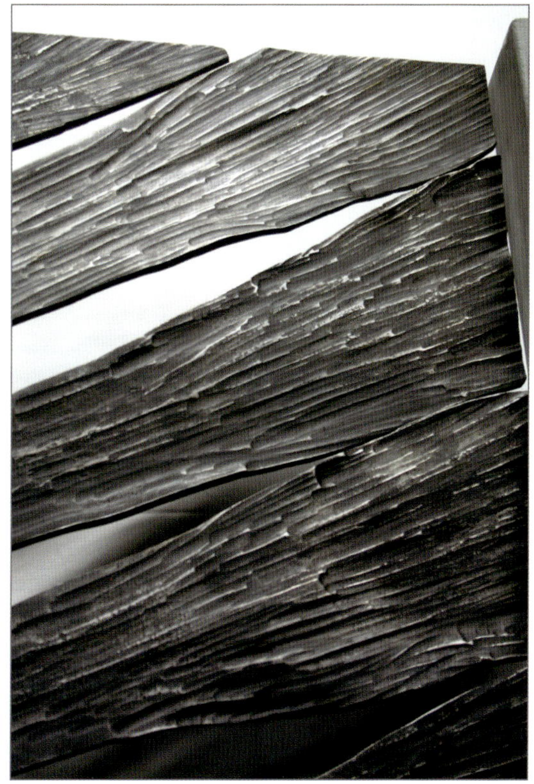

Roberto Giordani. Footgate. Detail. Photo, artist

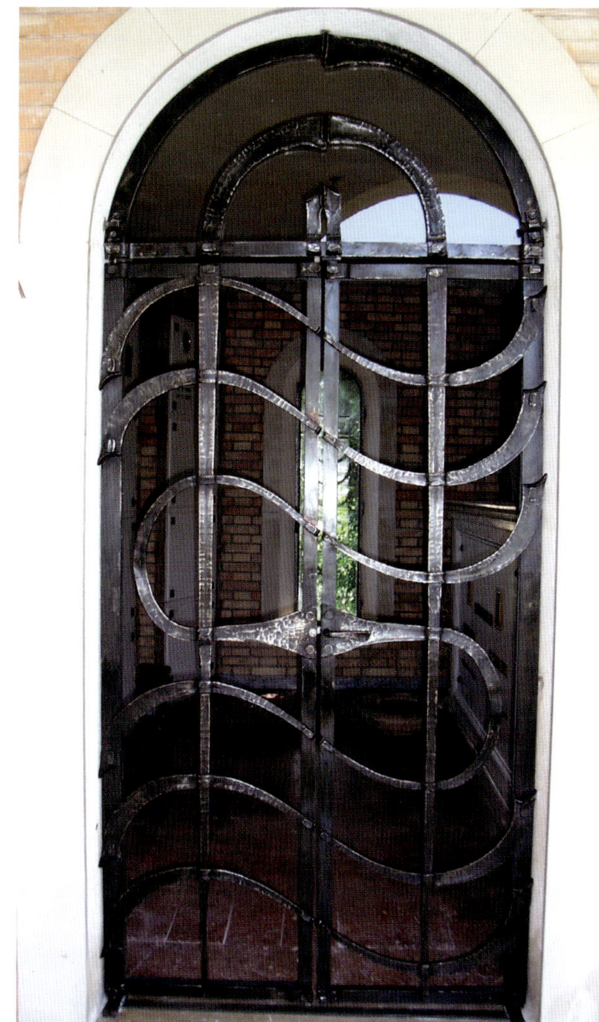

Roberto Giordani. Gate, 2003. Forged iron, in the cemetery of Sarsina. Property of Arnaldo Satanassi. Photo, artist

Pavel Tasovský. The front door to the charnel house of Saint Jacob in Brno. 74" x 33". Photo, artist

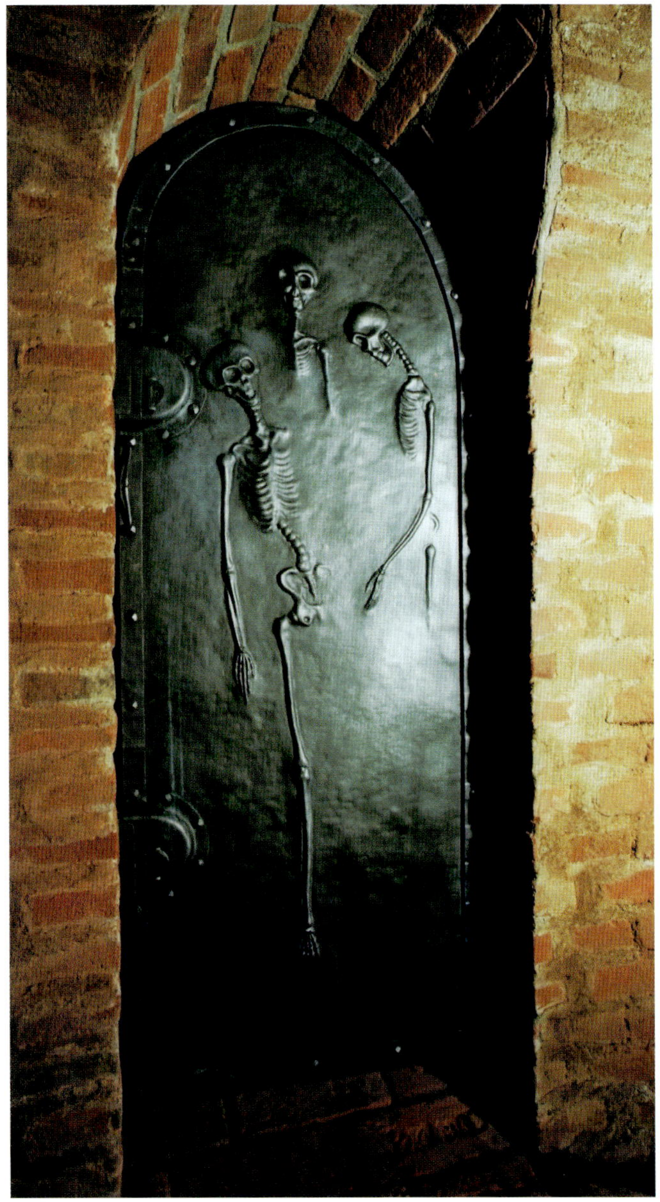

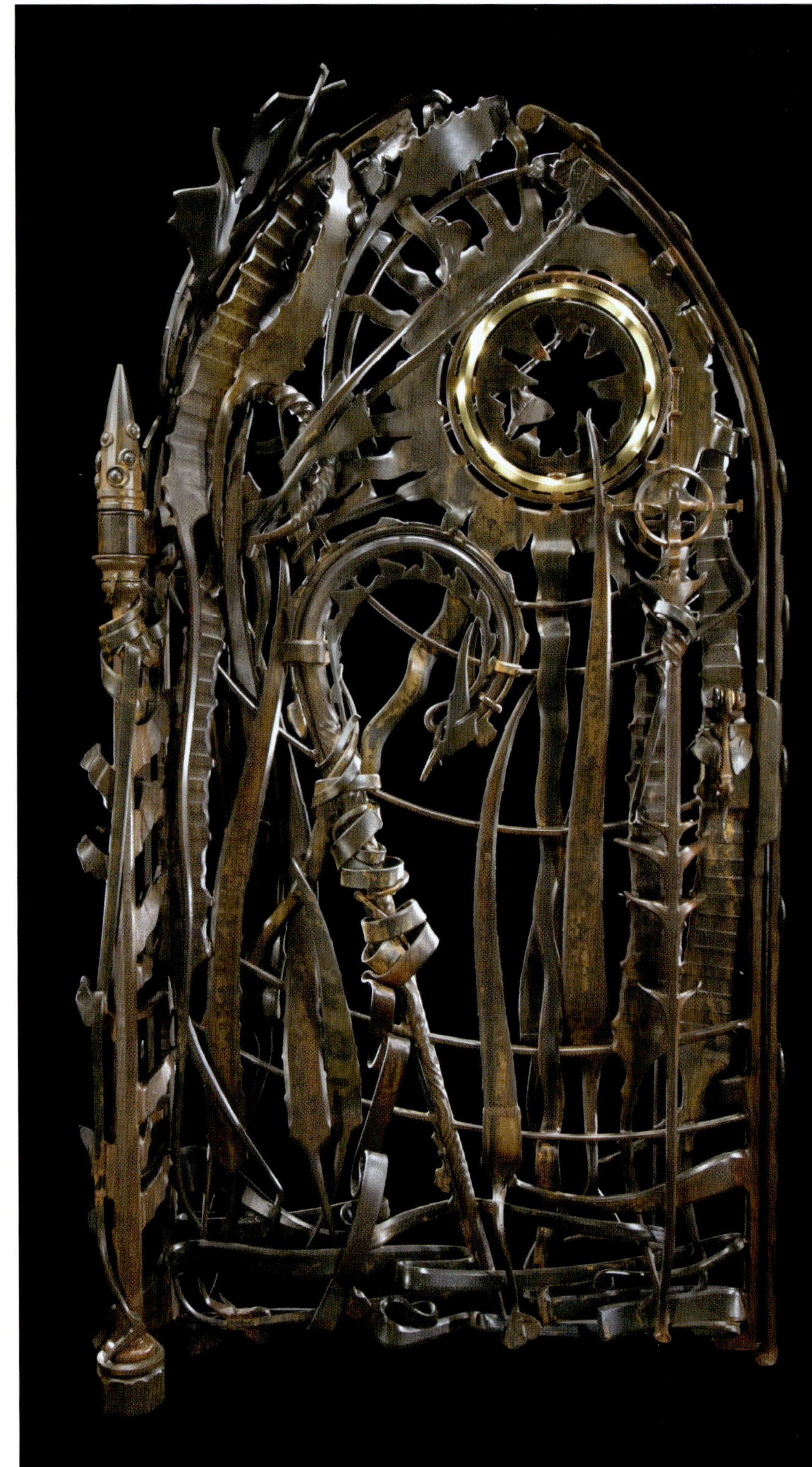

Albert Paley. National Cathedral Gate, 2007. Photo, Courtesy of Paley Studios Archive

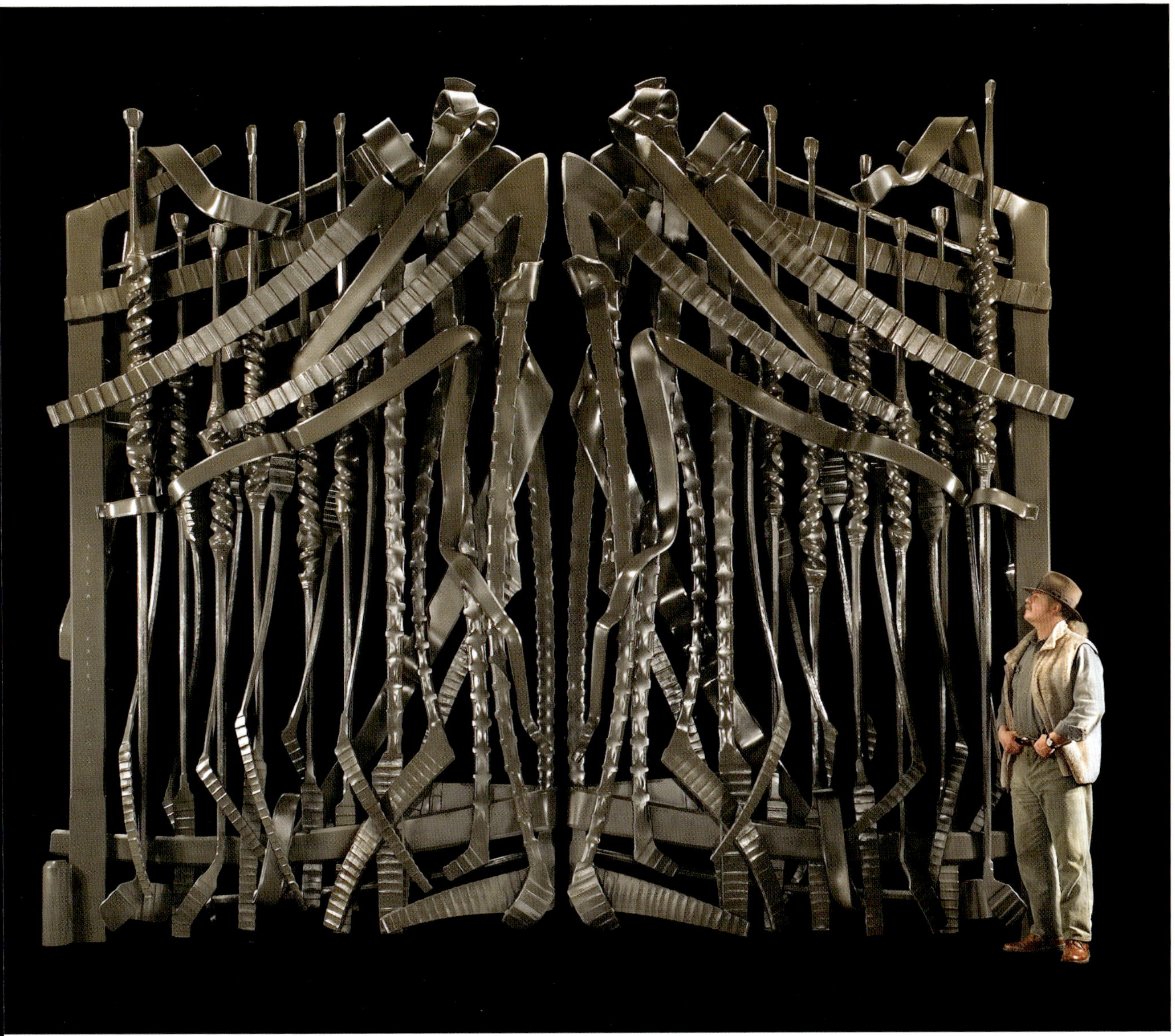

Albert Paley. Memphis Portal Gate, 2005. Forged and fabricated steel. 207" x 12" x 175". For the Brooks Museum of Art, Memphis, Tennessee. Photo, Courtesy of Paley Studios Archive

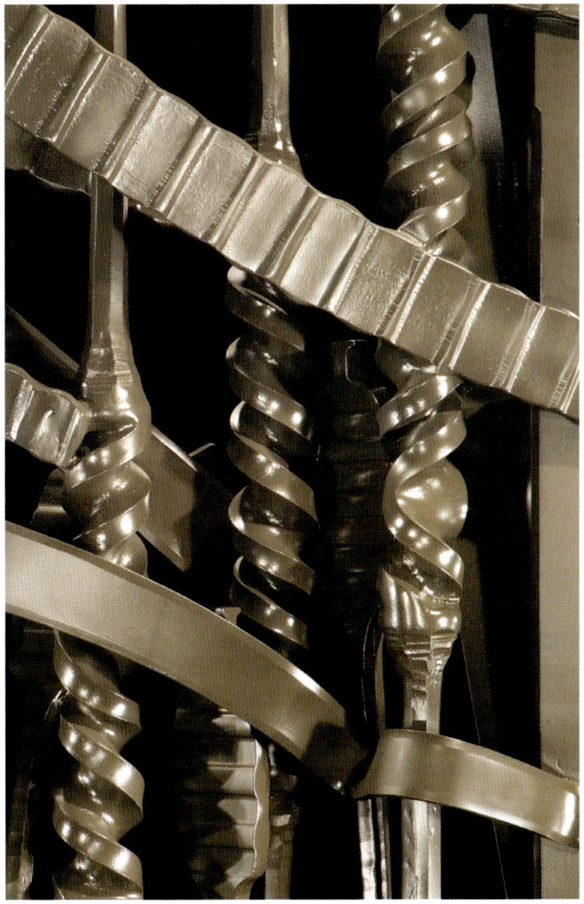

Albert Paley. Memphis Portal Gate, 2005. Detail. Photo, Courtesy of Paley Studios Archive

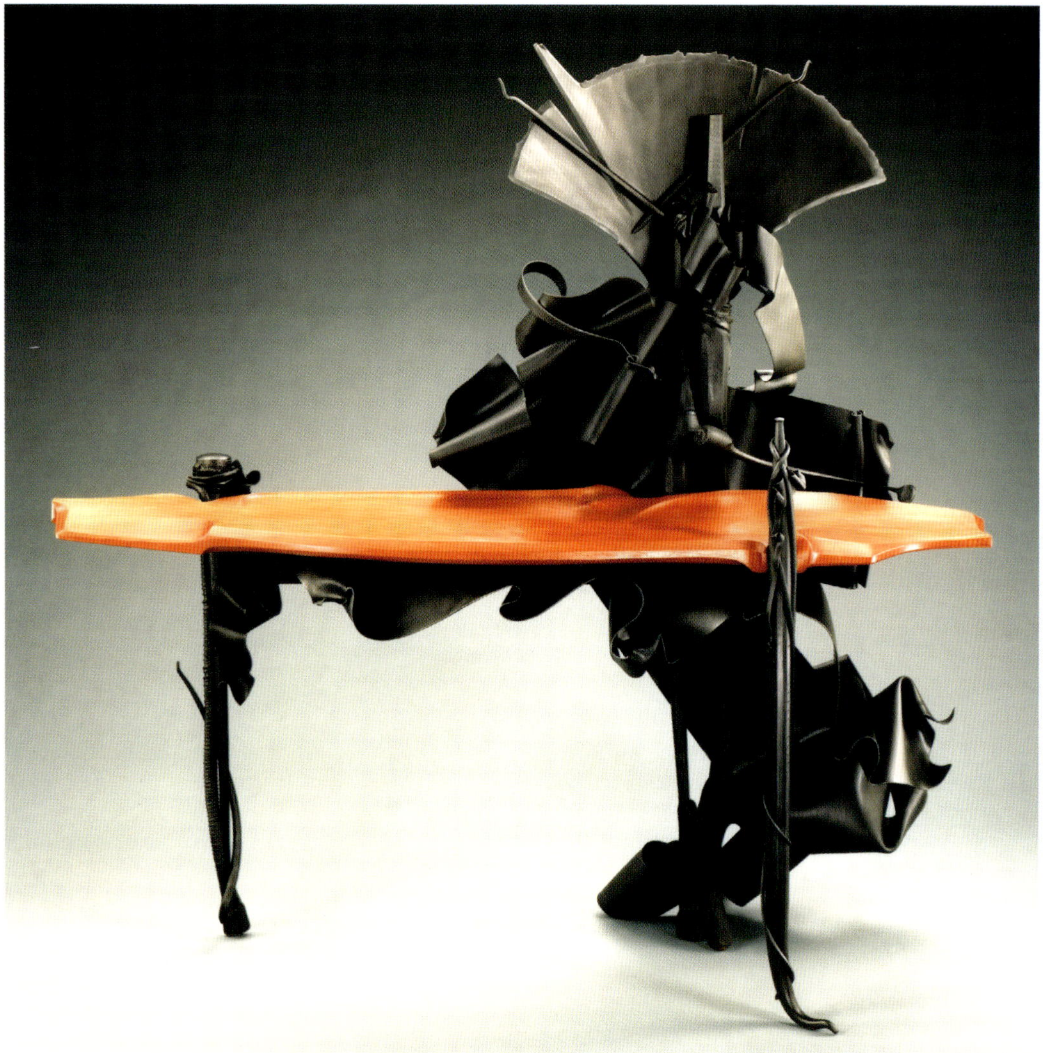

Albert Paley. Demilune, 1992. Photo, Courtesy of Paley Studios Archive

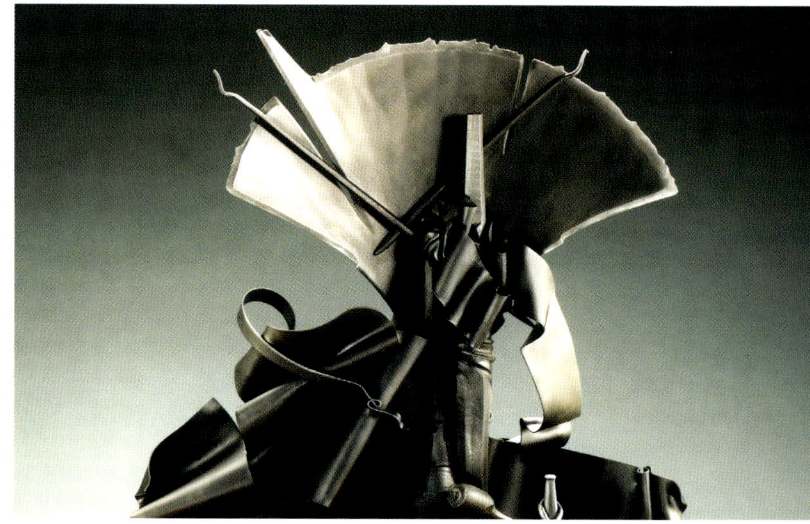

Albert Paley. Demilune, 1992. Detail. Photo, Courtesy of Paley Studios Archive

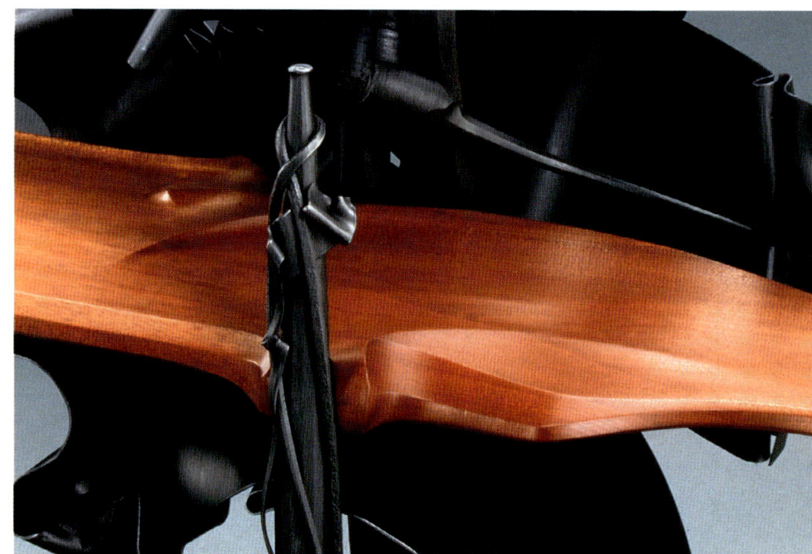

Albert Paley. Demilune, 1992. Detail. Photo, Courtesy of Paley Studios Archive

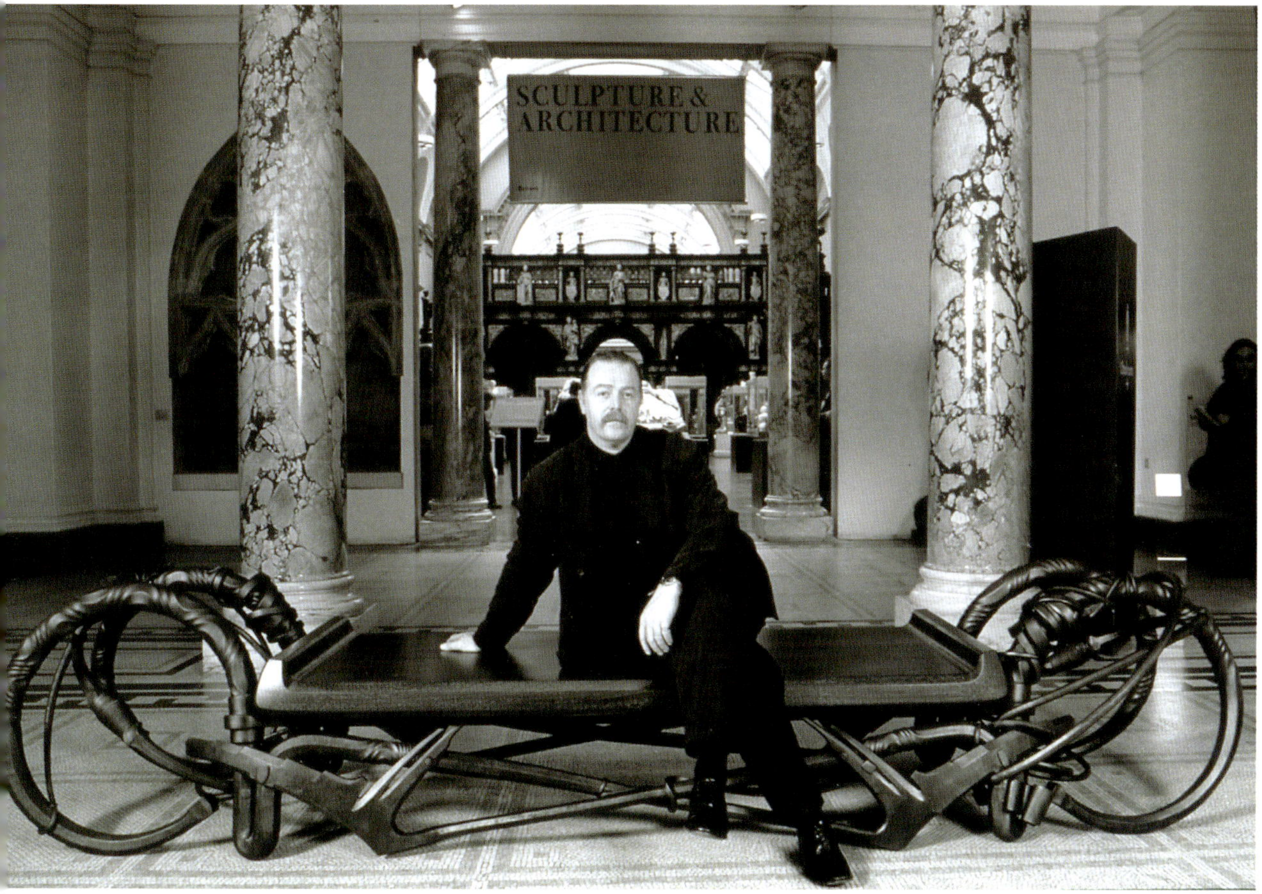

Albert Paley. Museum Bench, 1994. 36" w x 145" l. The artist, Mr. Albert Paley, with his Bench for the Victoria and Albert Museum. Photo, Courtesy of Paley Studios Archive

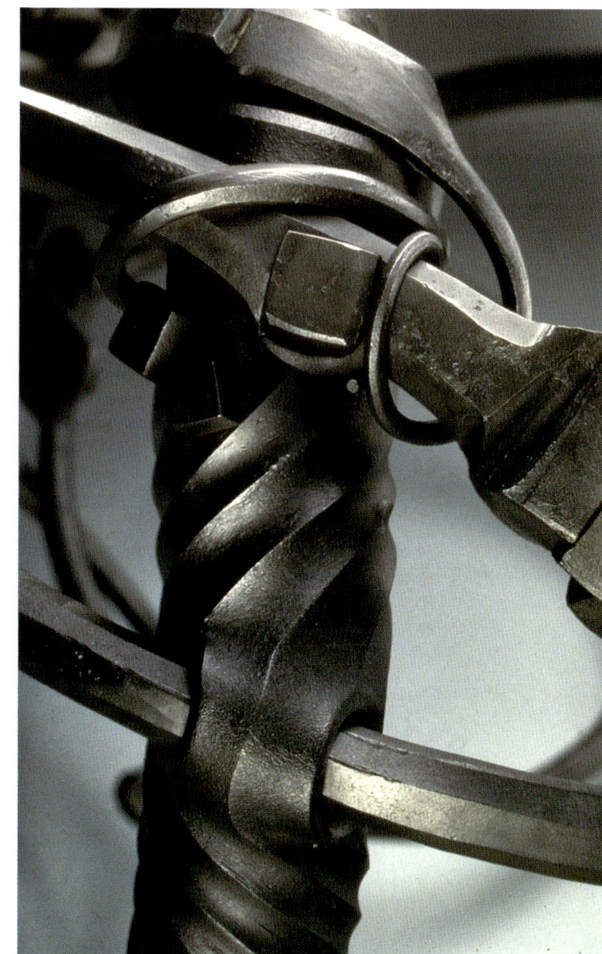

Albert Paley. Museum Bench, 1994. Detail. Photo, Courtesy of Paley Studios Archive

Albert Paley. Viennese Compromise, 1992. Formed and fabricated steel, glass. Photo, Courtesy of Paley Studios Archive

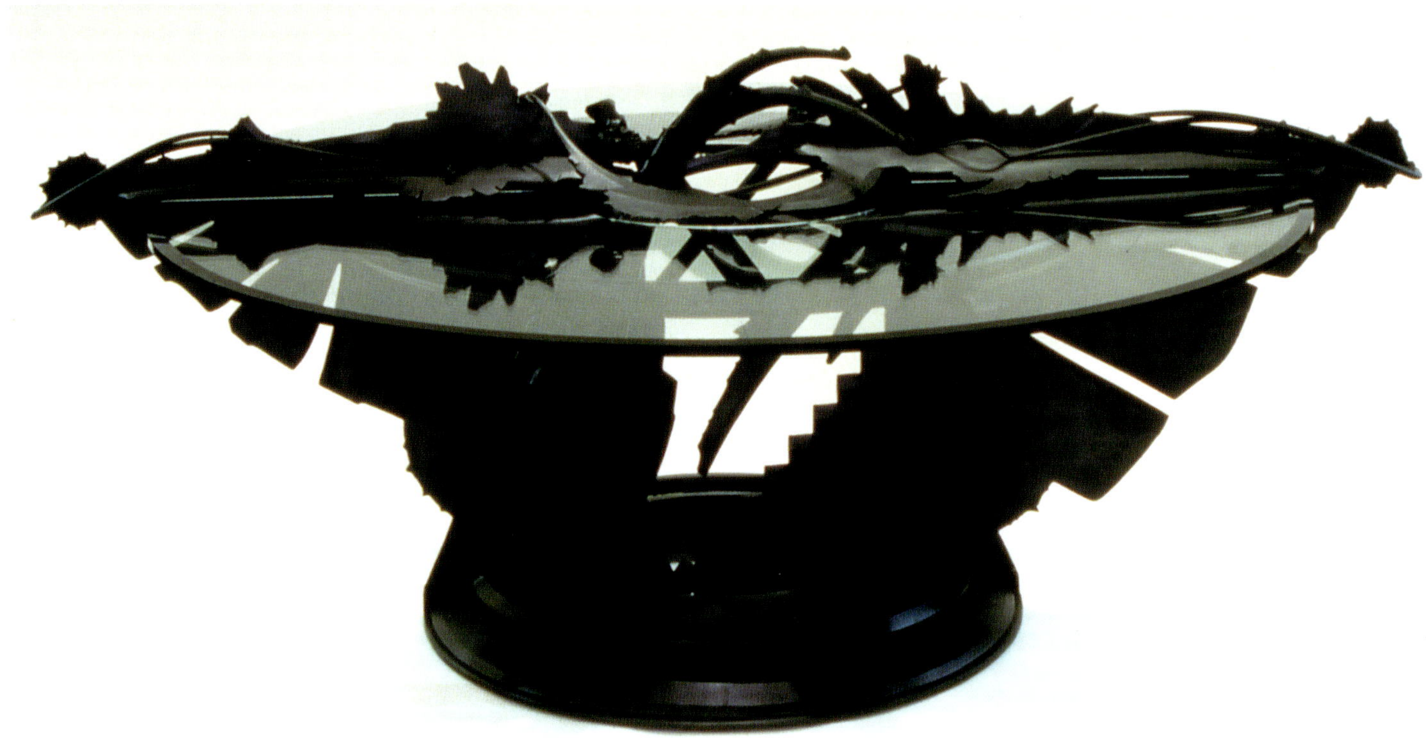

Below:
Albert Paley. Viennese Compromise, 1992. Detail. Photo, Courtesy of Paley Studios Archive

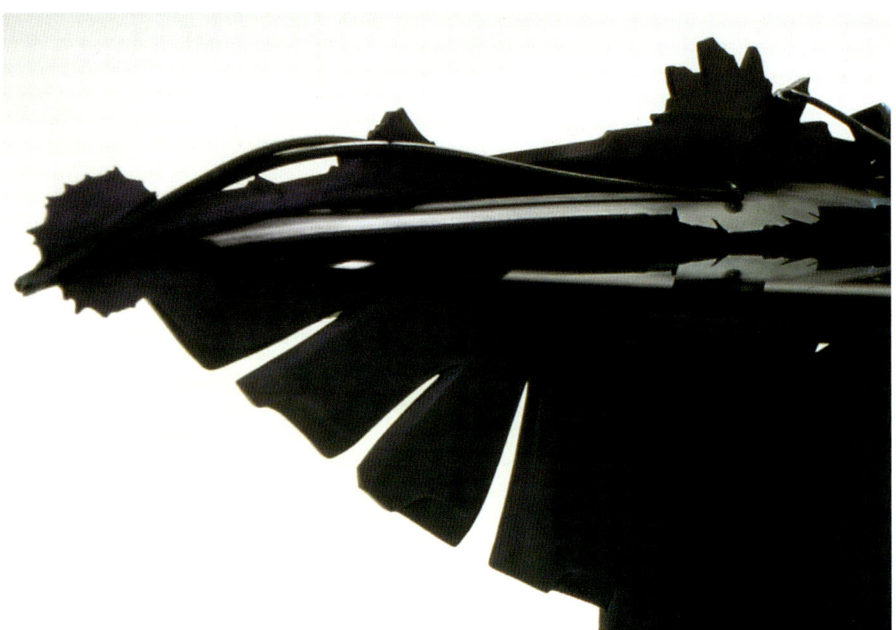

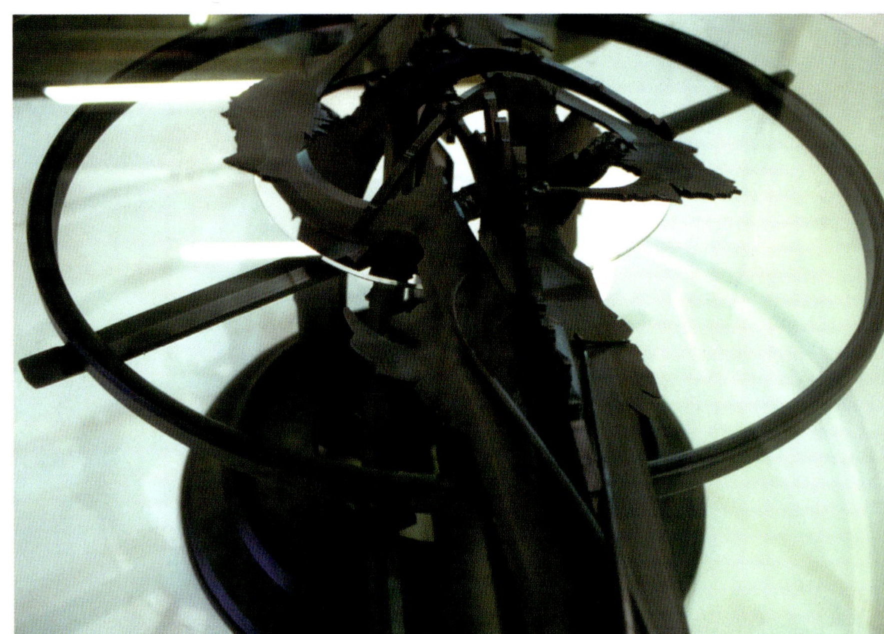

Albert Paley. Viennese Compromise, 1992. Detail. Photo, Courtesy of Paley Studios Archive

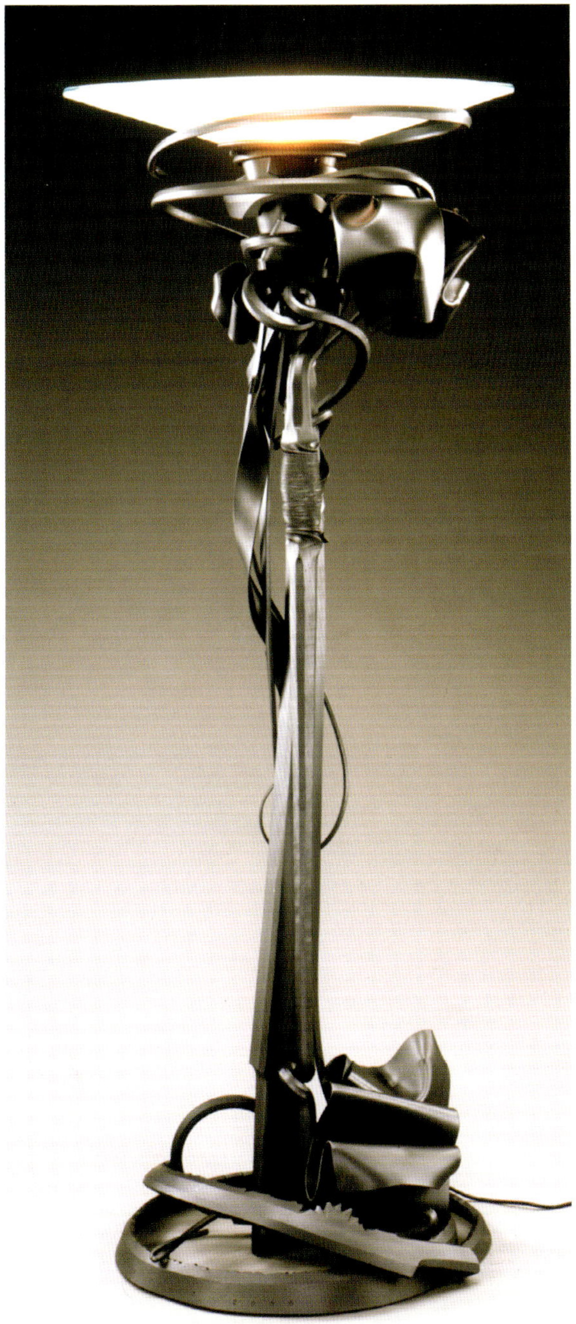

Albert Paley. Dragon's Back Floor Lamp, 2006. Formed and fabricated steel, glass shade. 80" x 32". Photo, Courtesy of Paley Studios Archive

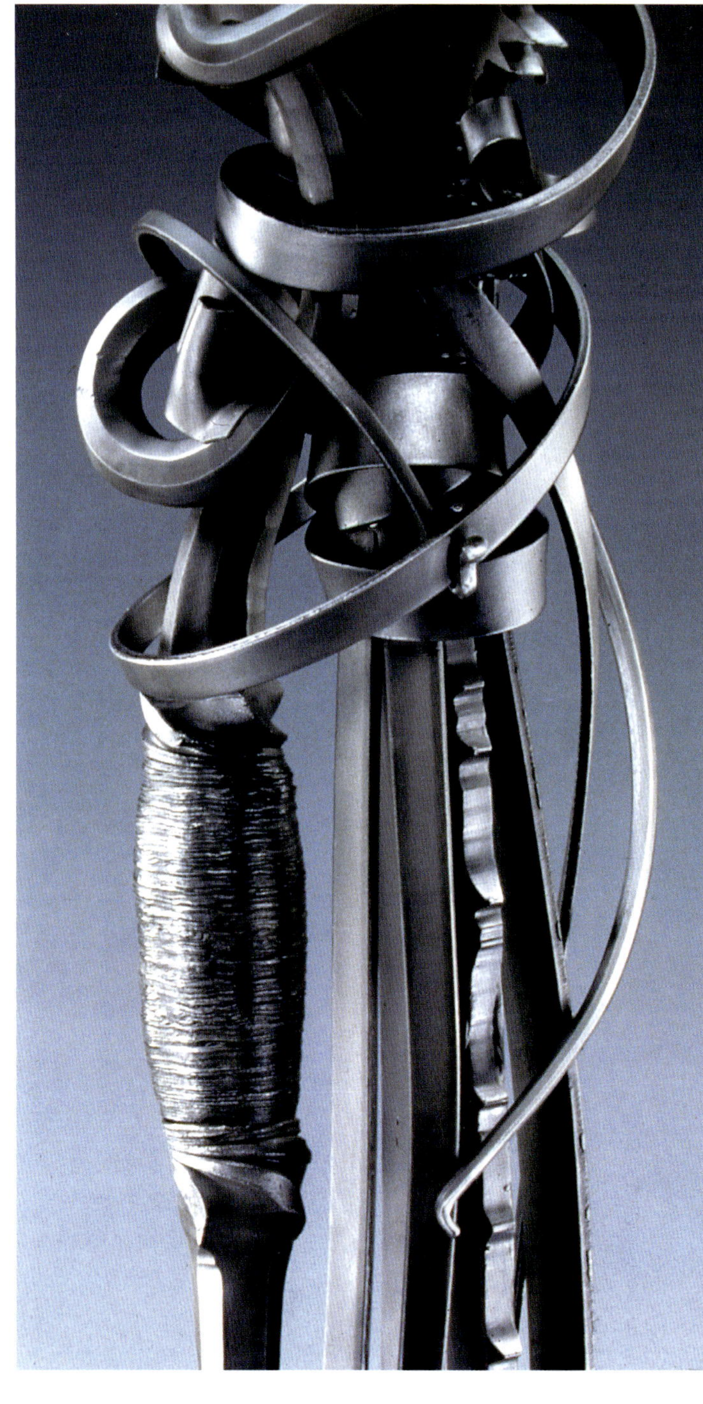

Albert Paley. Dragon's Back Floor Lamp, 2006. Detail. Photo, Courtesy of Paley Studios Archive

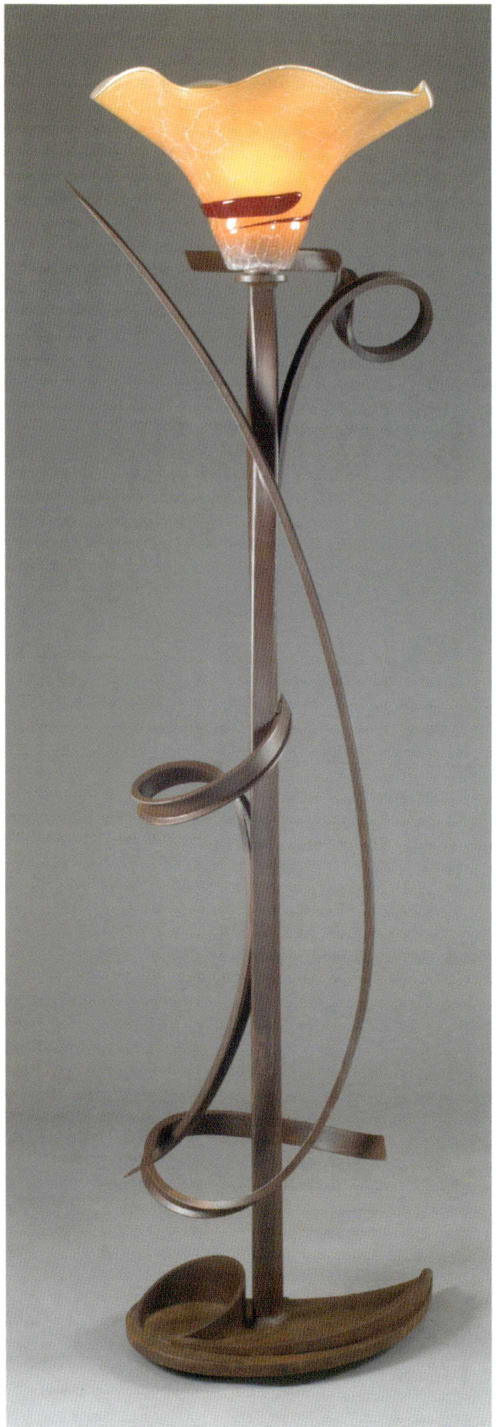

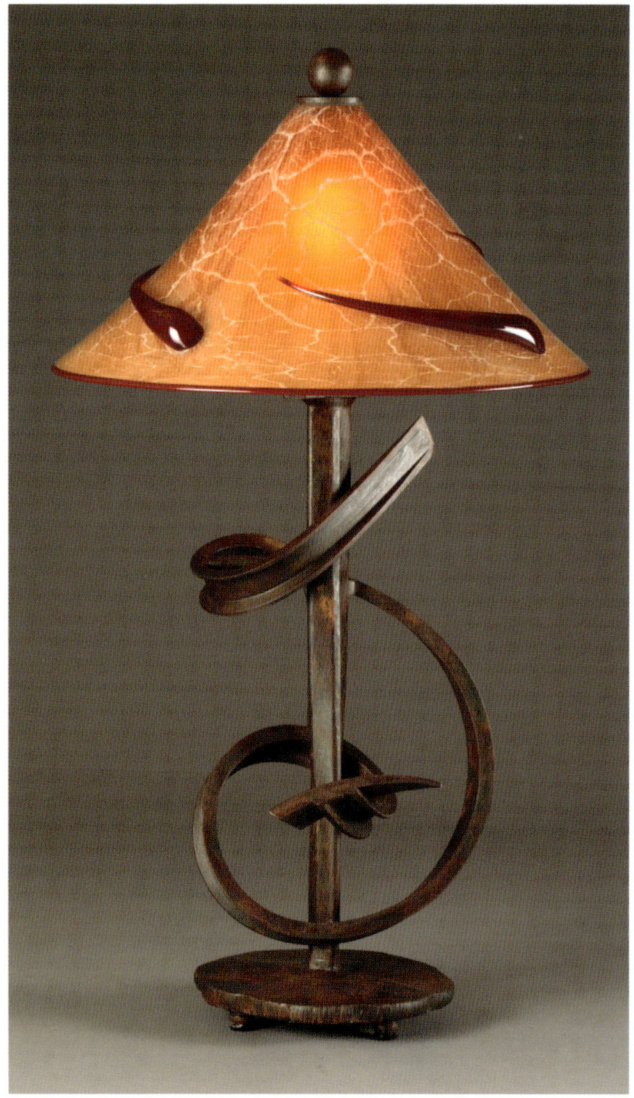

Bill Brown. Lamp #1, 2007. Steel and glass. 28" x 15". Photo, Fanjoy-Labrenz

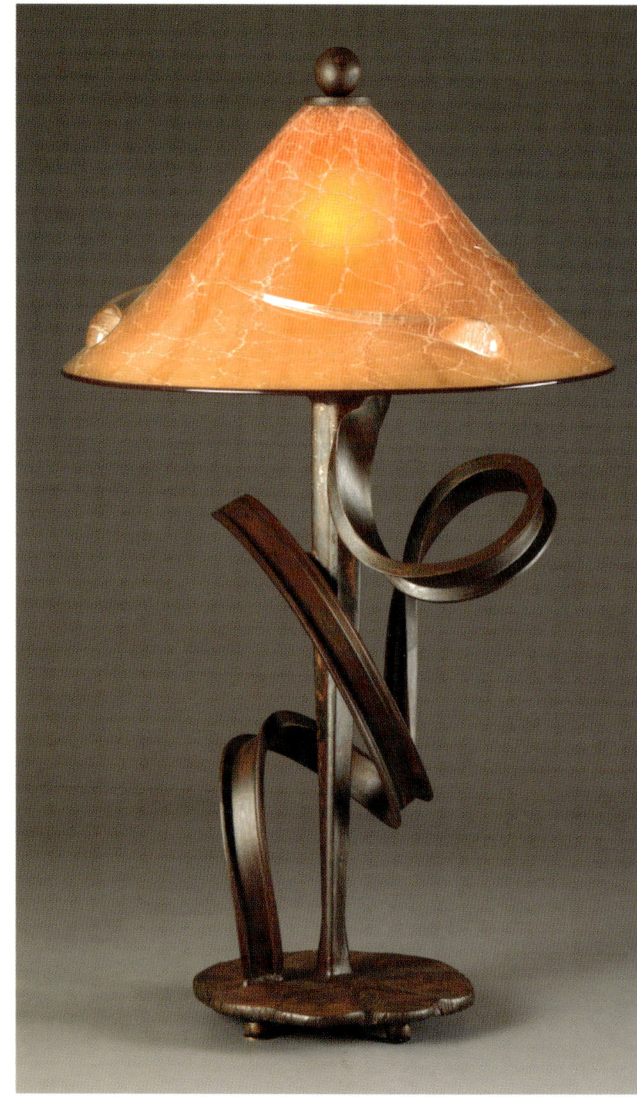

Bill Brown. Lamp #2, 2007. Steel and glass. 28" x 15". Photo, Fanjoy-Labrenz

Bill Brown. Torchiere with scalloped globe, 2007. Steel and glass. 72" x 21" x 15". Photo, Fanjoy-Labrenz

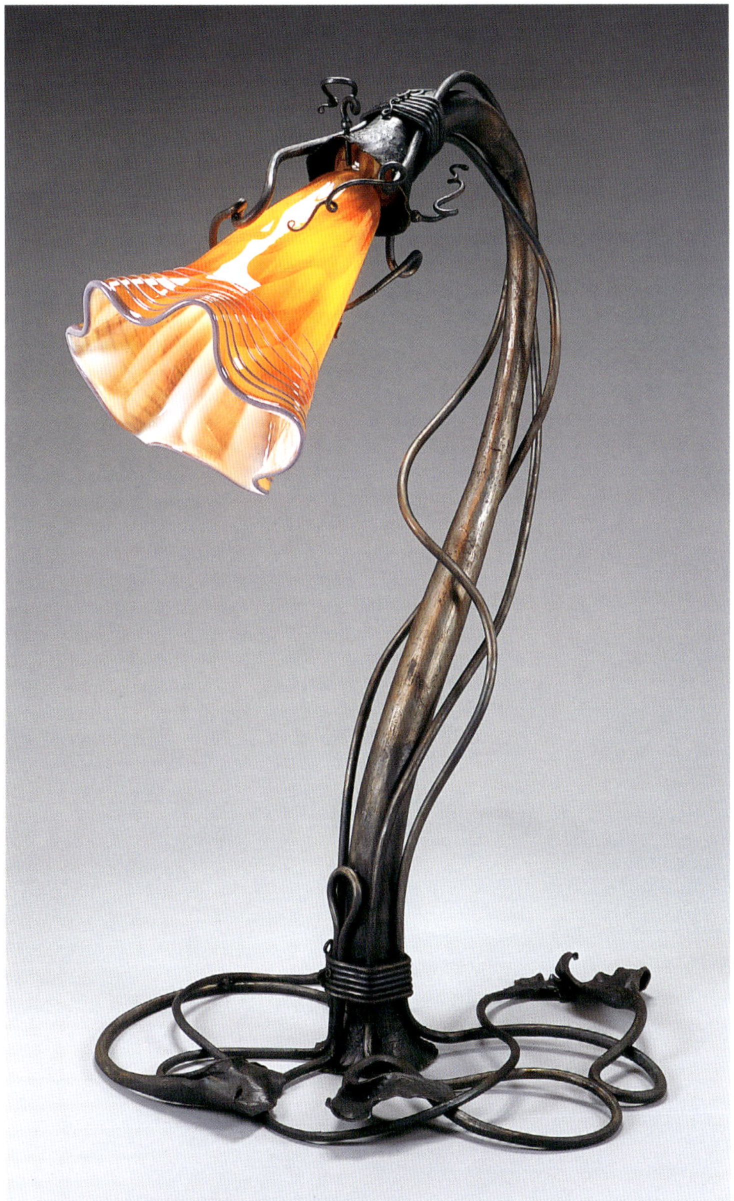

Roberta Elliott, La Waltz. Electric table lamp. Seamed steel pipe, hot rolled strap, blown glass, 32" x 20" x 18". The central stem is pipe, flared on the ends and collapsed in the middle. Strap is flared on one end then tapered to fine points to form the tendrils that cradle the shade. Photo, Larry Sanders

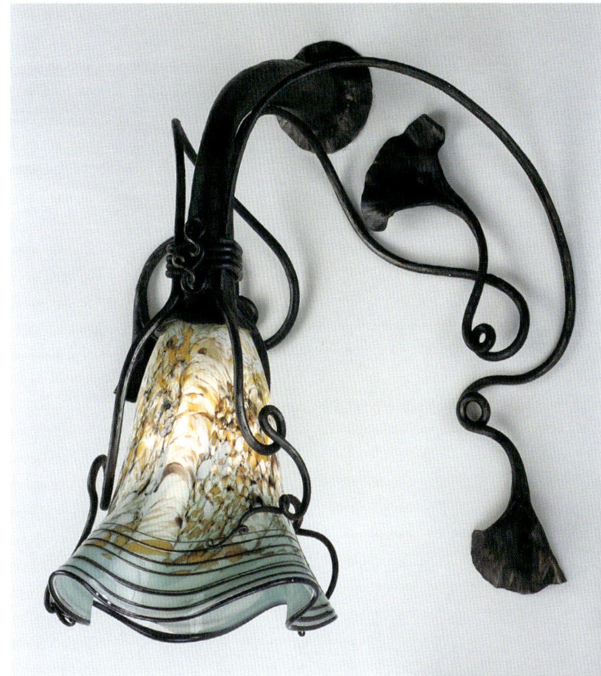

Roberta Elliott, Off the Wall. Electric sconce. Seamed steel pipe, hot rolled strap, blown glass. 19" x 12" x 9". The central stem is pipe, flared on the ends and collapsed in the middle. Strap is flared on one end then tapered to fine points to form the tendrils that cradle the shade. Photo, Jerry Anthony

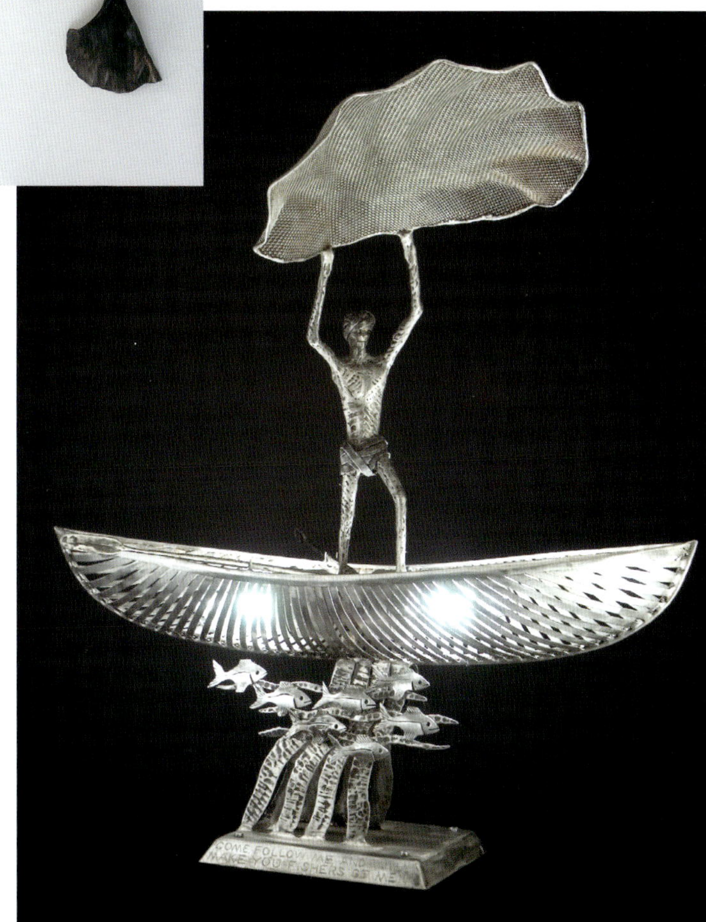

Paul M. Thorne. Fisherman Entrance Light. Forged stainless steel. 24" x 24". Photo, Peter Kuhnlein

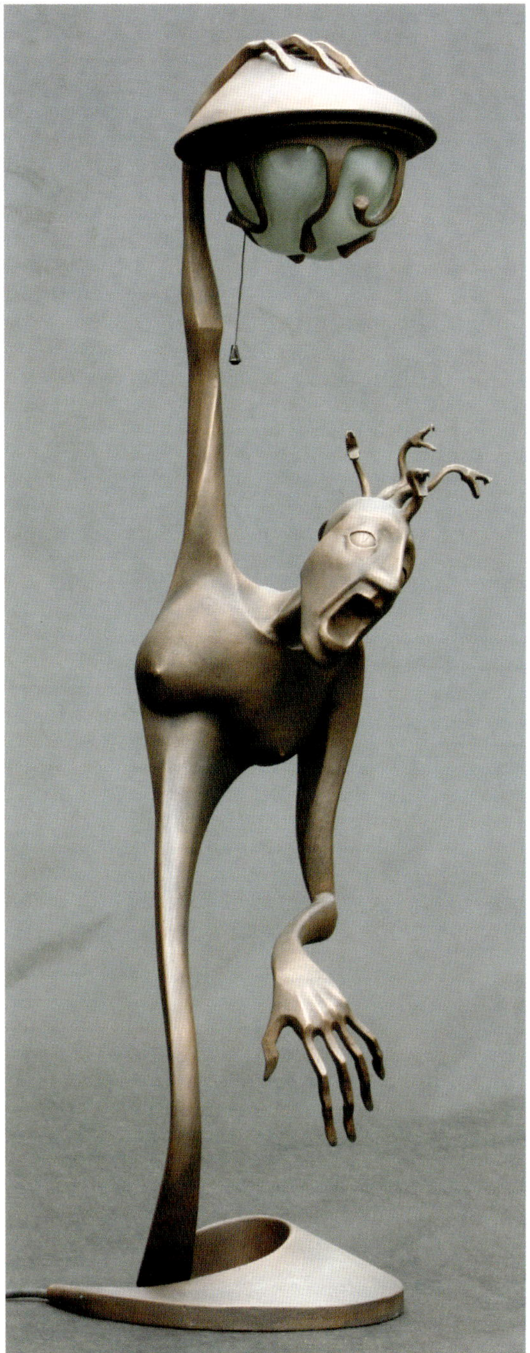

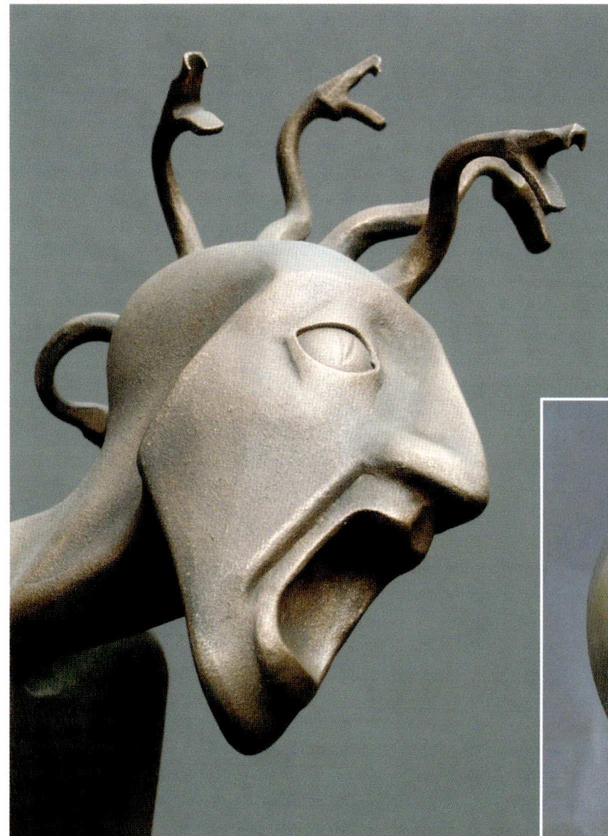

Libor Hurda, Medusa Lamp. Detail. Photo, artist

Libor Hurda, Medusa Lamp. Mild steel, bronzing, and blown glass. 43" h. Photo, artist

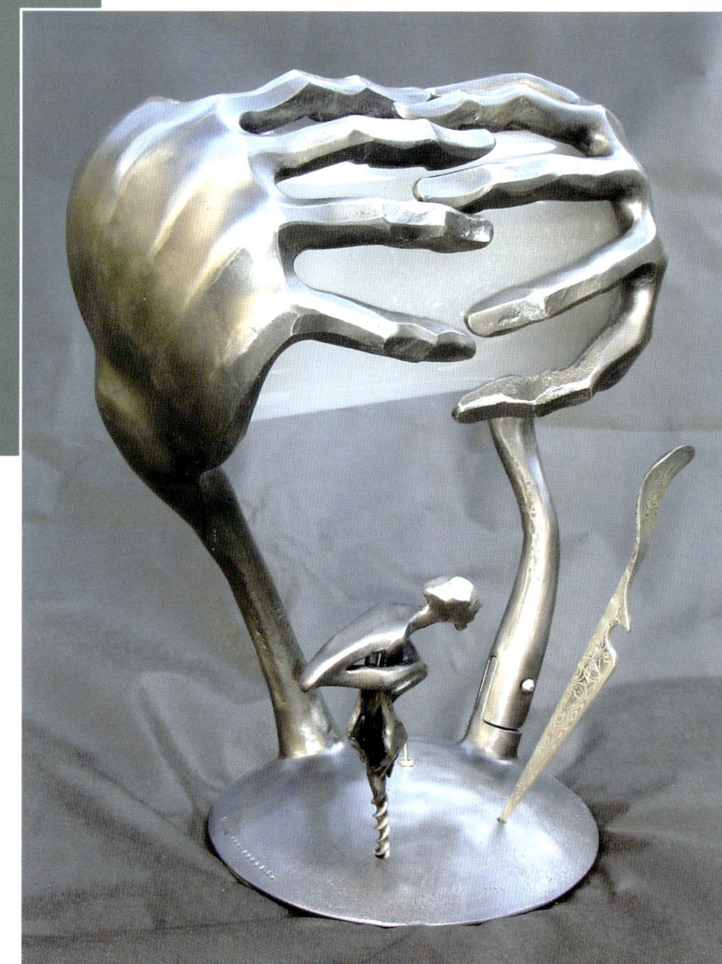

Libor Hurda, Manager Set Lamp. Mild steel and glass. 14" h. Photo, artist

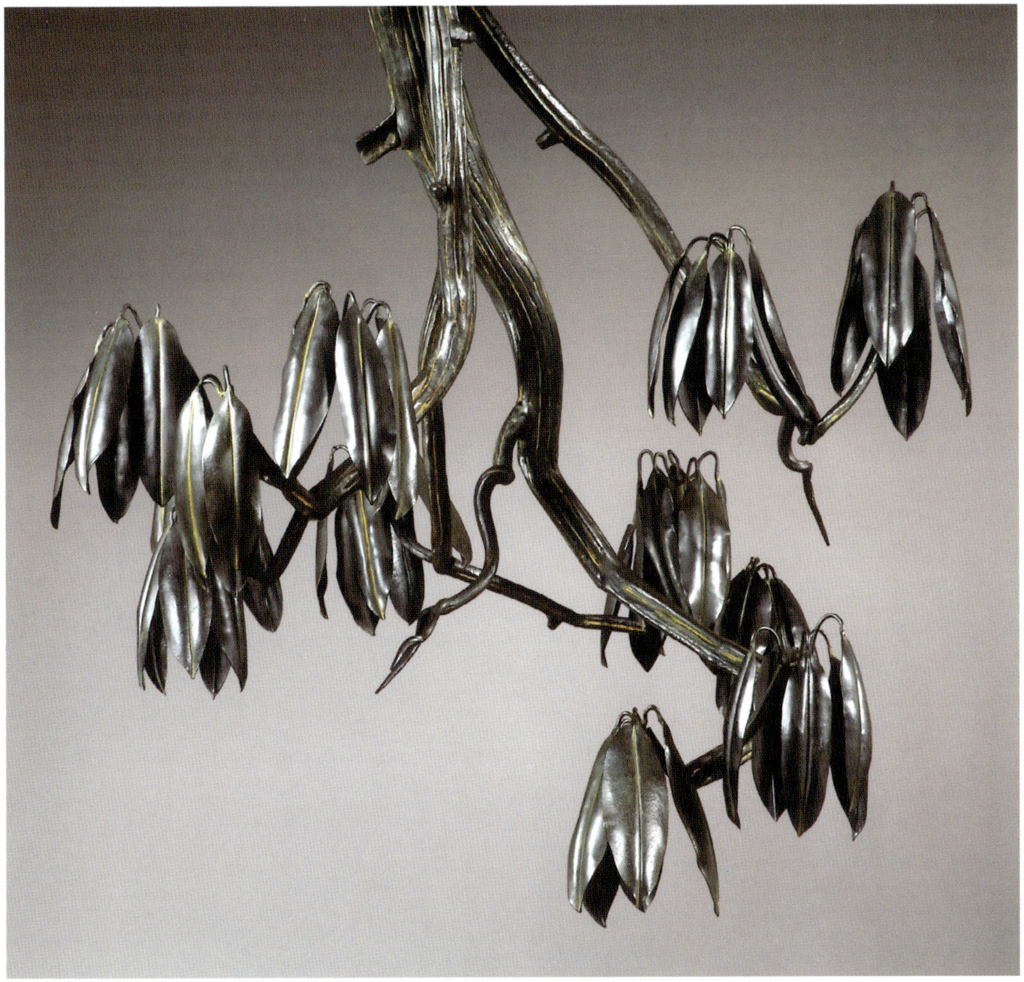

Elizabeth Brim. Rhododendron Chandelier, 2006. 36" h, finished with black paint, brown shoe polish, and oil paint. Photo, Tom Mills

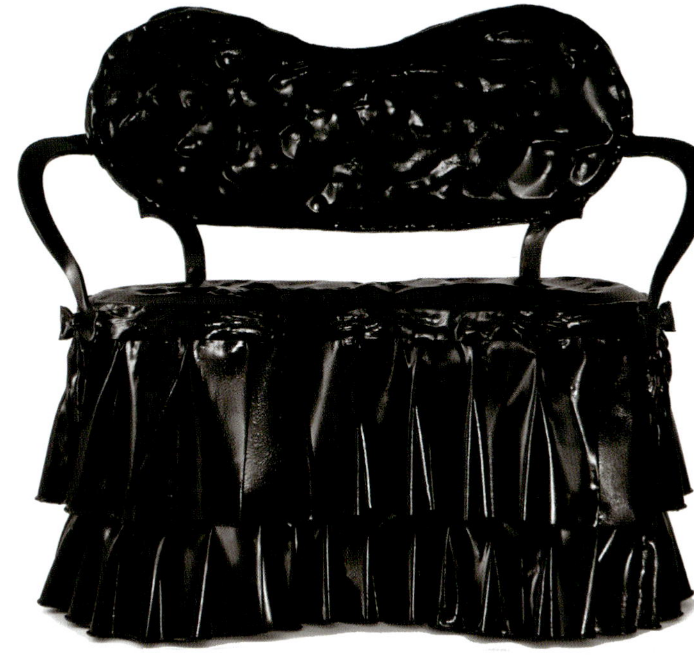

Elizabeth Brim. The Morgan Bench, 2008. The bench parts are forged (ribbons around the seat and back, also the bows at the bottom of the arm rests), the seat and back "cushions" are inflated. The parts are fabricated together with gas and mig welding, sand blasted and painted with epoxy paint. Made for Morgan Park in Spartanburg, South Carolina. 48" w x 42" h x 30" d. Photo, Mary Vogel

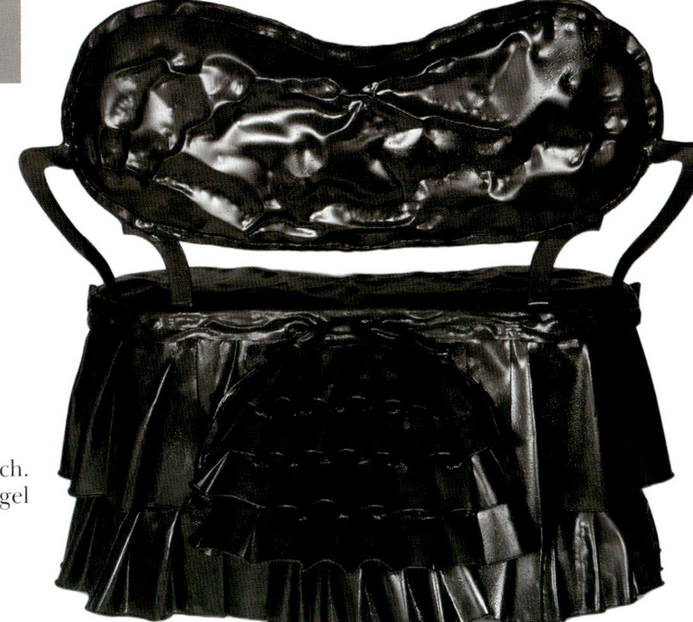

Elizabeth Brim. The Morgan Bench. Back view. Photo, Mary Vogel

Daniel Miller. The Couplers Will, 2004. Wrought iron oil lamp. 22" x 12" x 12". Photo, Steven Keull

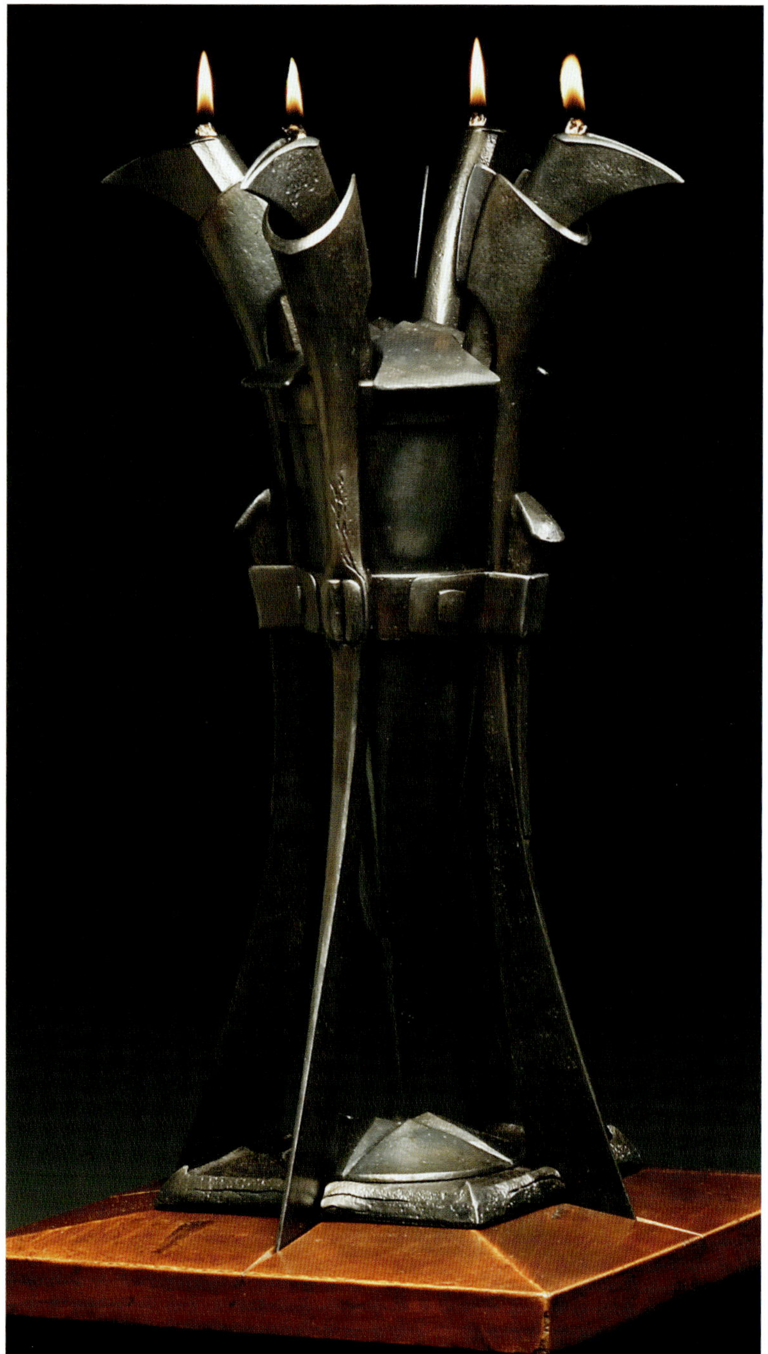

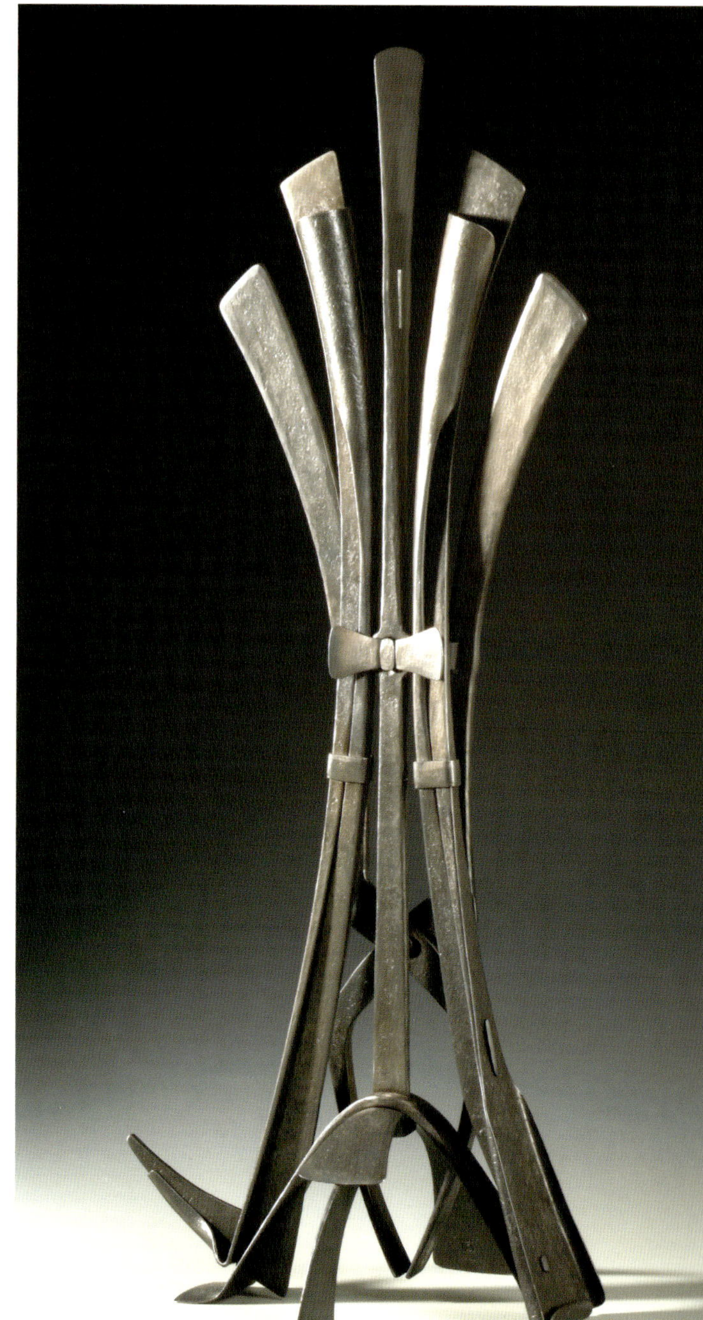

Daniel Miller. Ariadne's Crown, 2002. Mild steel set of fire tools. 32" x 13" x 12". Photo, Steven Keull

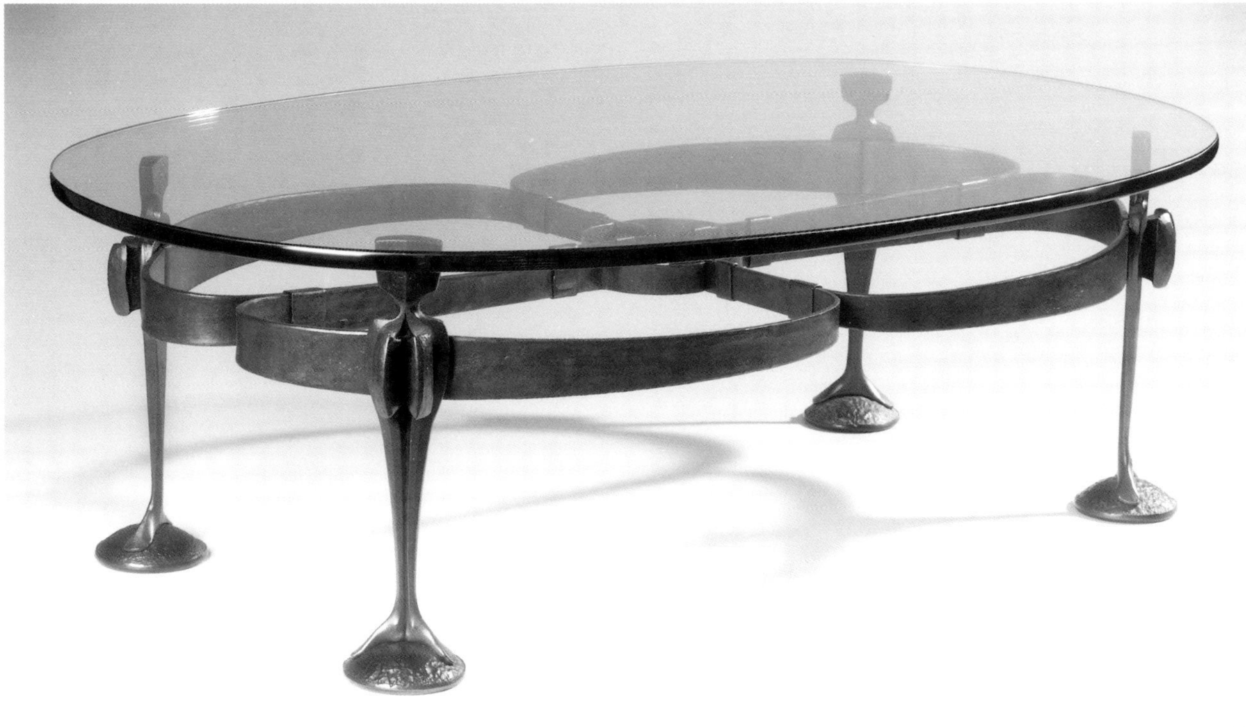

Daniel Miller. Table for my Brother: Sweet Mary, and Her Sons in Her Seas, 2007. Wrought iron and glass. 17" h x 53" x 35". Photo, Steven Keull

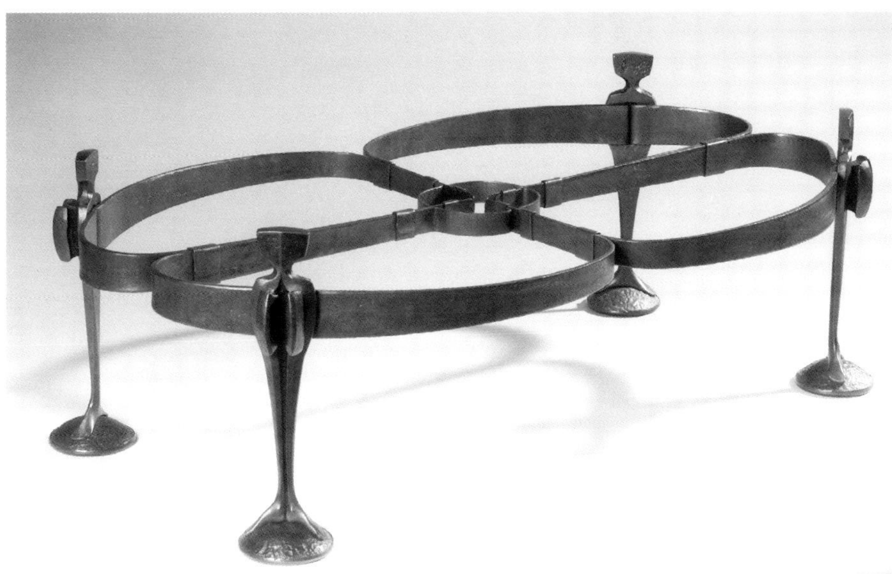

Daniel Miller. Table for my Brother: Sweet Mary, and Her Sons in Her Seas. Second view. Photo, Steven Keull

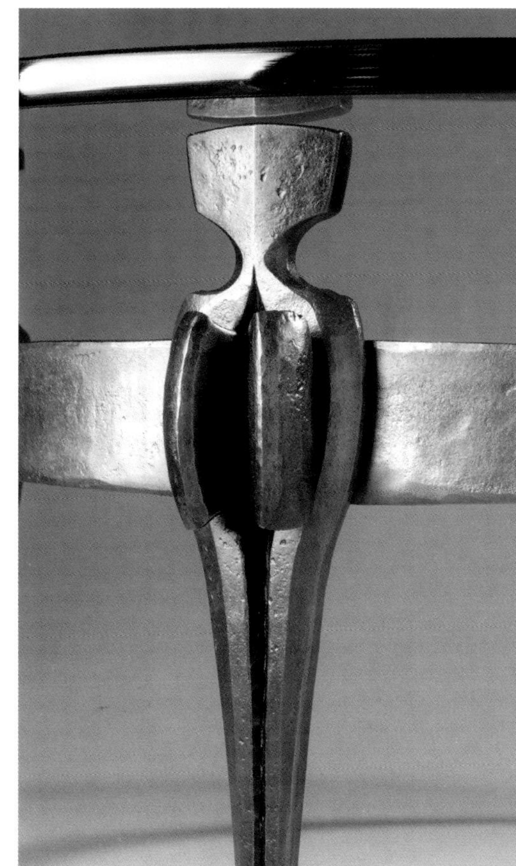

Daniel Miller. *Table for my Brother: Sweet Mary, and Her Sons in Her Seas.* Detail. *Photo, Steven Keull*

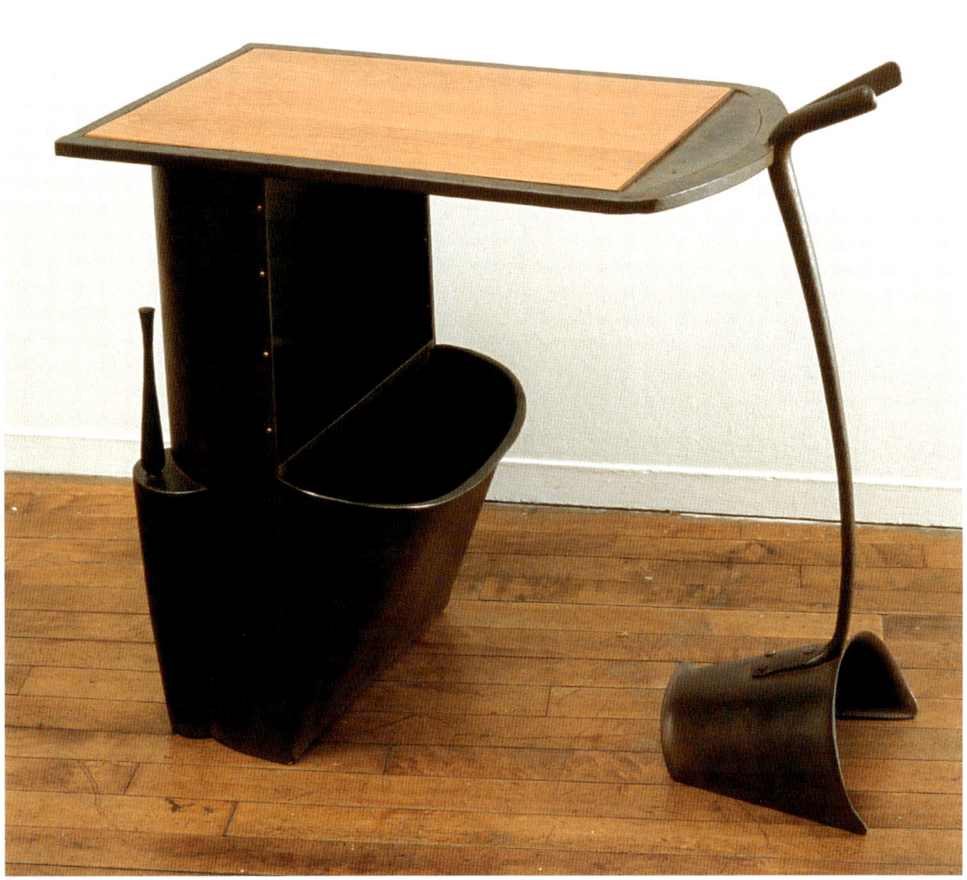

John Rais. *Transfer Table,* 2002. Forged steel, cherry patina, 34" x 45" x 21". *Photo, D. James Dee*

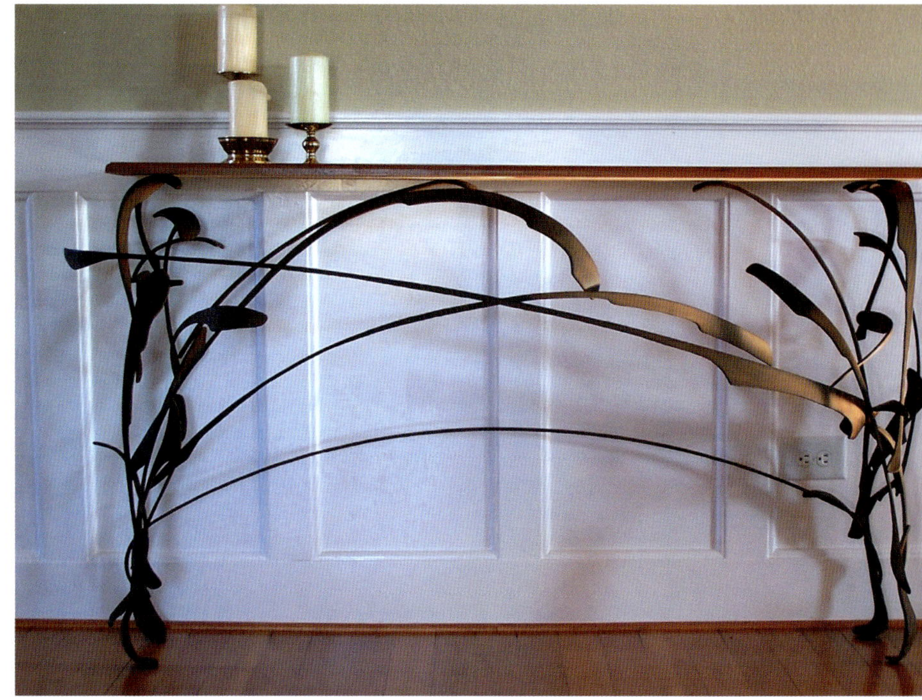

Mike Suri. *Side Table*. Forged steel. 60" x 40" x 15". *Photo, artist*

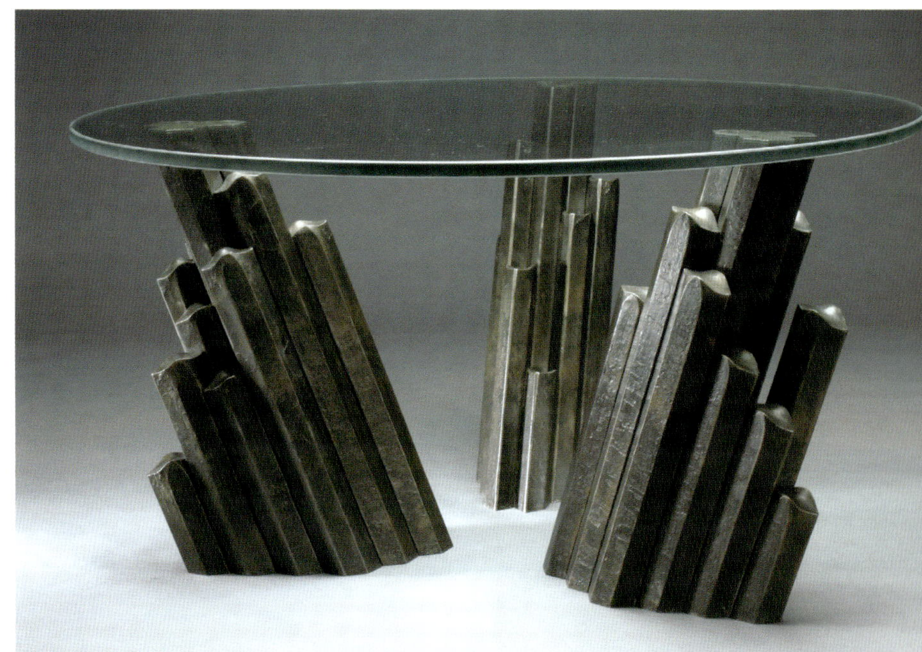

Chris Gavin. "*Thrust*" table base, 2007. Forged and fabricated 1.5" square bars. Each unit 12" x 5.5" x 16" with 32" round glass top. *Photo, Mark Lee*

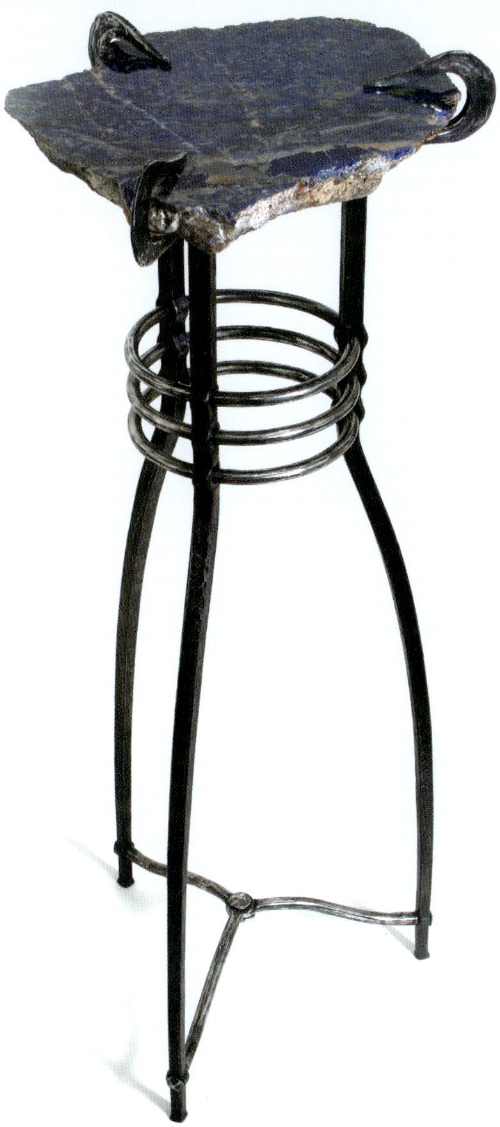

Pavel Tasovský. Table, 2005. 41" x 15" x 17". *Photo, artist*

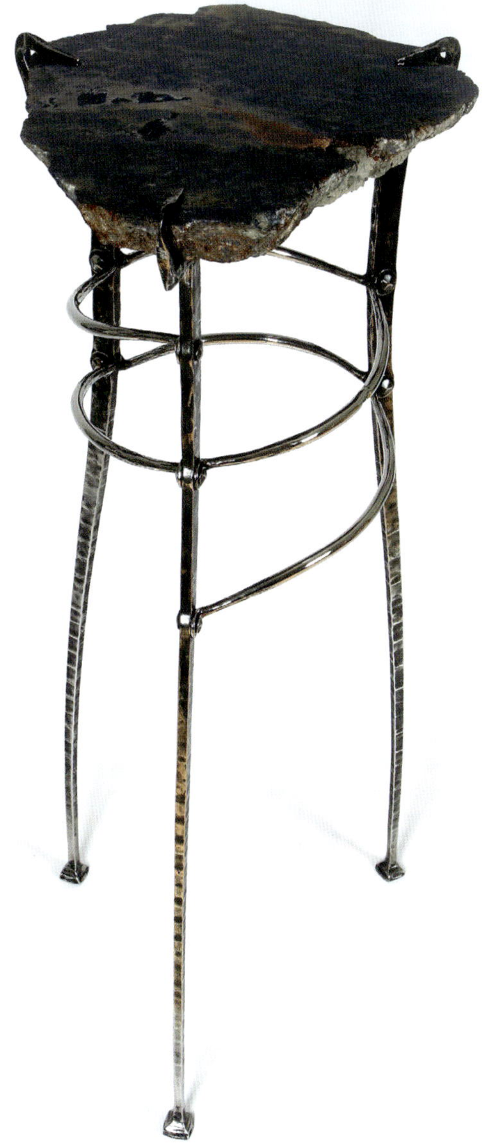

Pavel Tasovský. Table, 2006. Forged steel, 40" x 15" x 16.5". *Photo, artist*

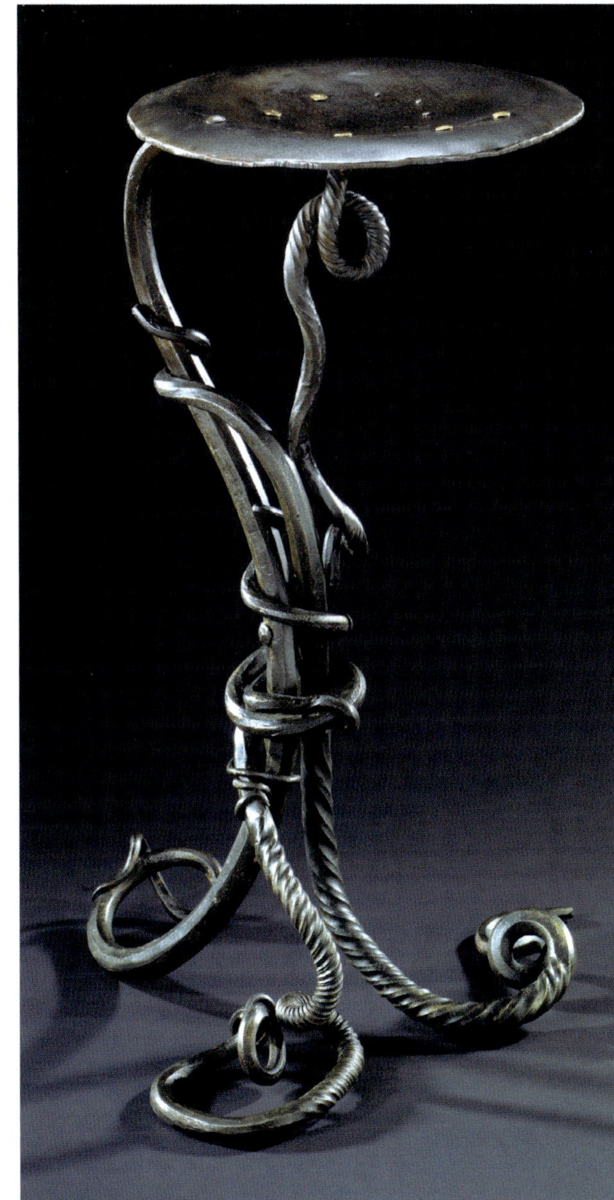

George Rousis. *Root Down*, 2001. Forged steel, steel and brass rivets, orange oil. Designed as part of an organic bar set, from the collection of the artist. *Photo, Chris Dennis*

Using the traditions of blacksmithing as a stepping off point, my organic aesthetic enlivens the fluid movement of the functional and sculptural artwork I create. Via the fire, metal becomes an almost fluid substance influenced easily by the strike of a hammer, snap of the wrist or twist of the body, thus allowing the potential of the material to grow, move, and be free, creating a visual and textural language different from other media. – George Rousis

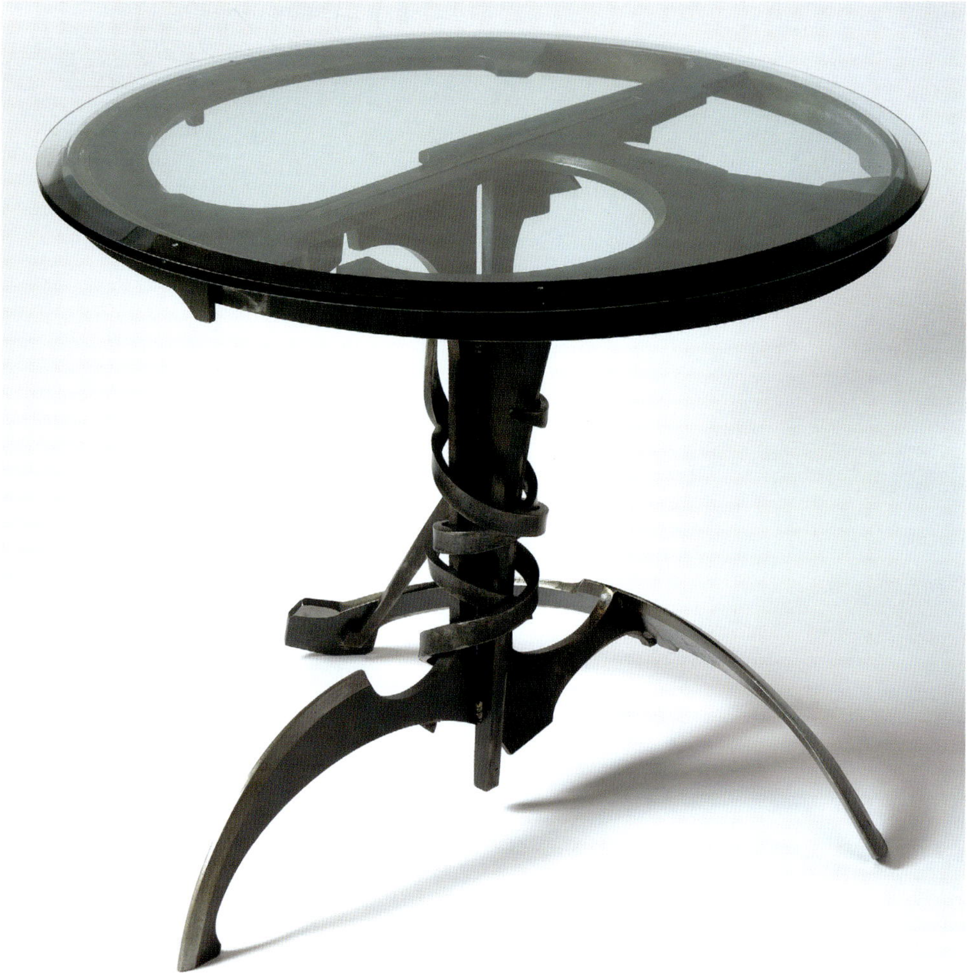

Bushy Park Ironworks. Coffee Table. Forged and fabricated, mild steel, copper and glass, 20" h x 27.5" w. *Photo, Edward Bisgood*

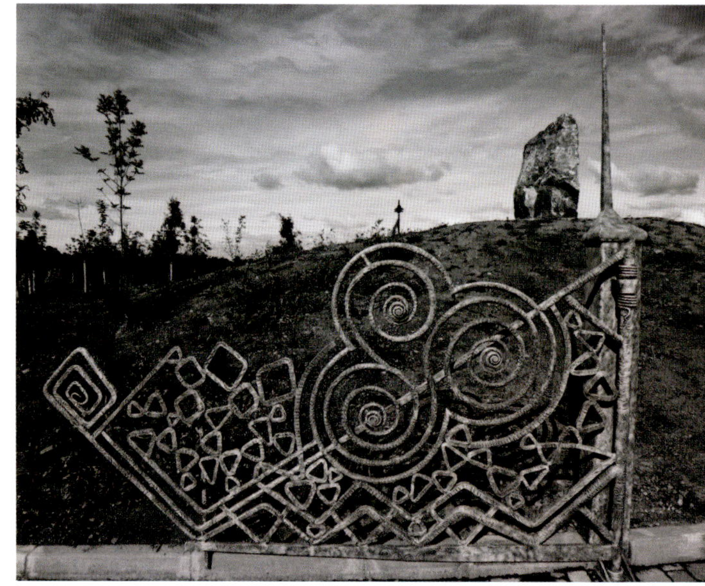

Shawn Lovell. *Tree Bed*. Forged and fabricated steel, leaves and branches are fire welded, trunks are fabricated. Queen size, 90" h. *Photo, Anita Bowen*

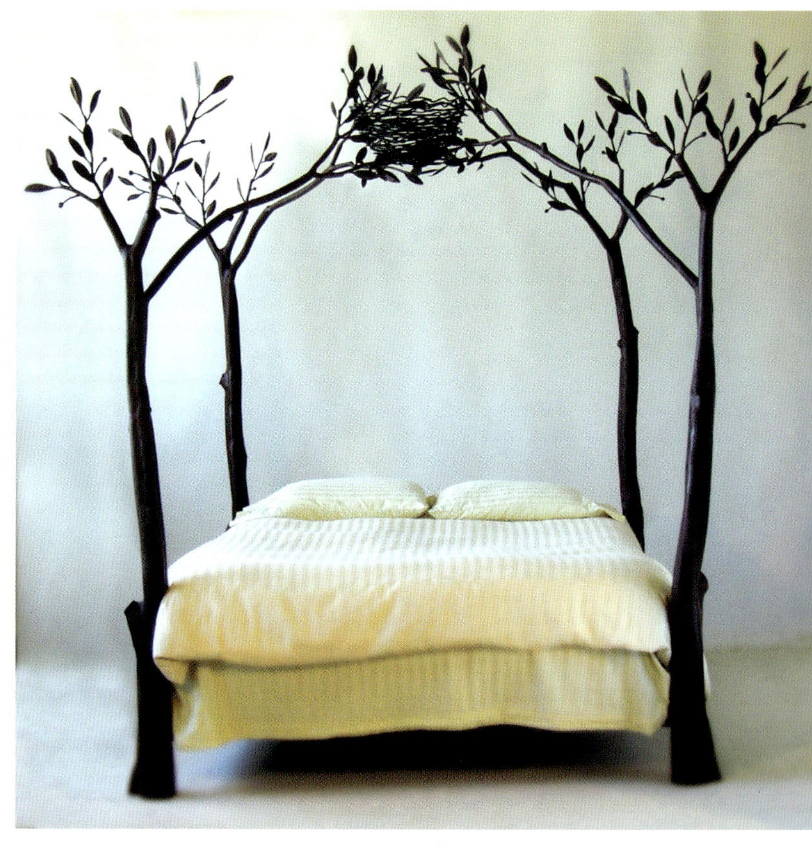

Bushy Park Ironworks. *Newgrange Visitors Center Entrance Gate*. Forged and fabricated, mild steel with verdigris paint finish. 59" h x 118" w. *Photo, Edward Bisgood*

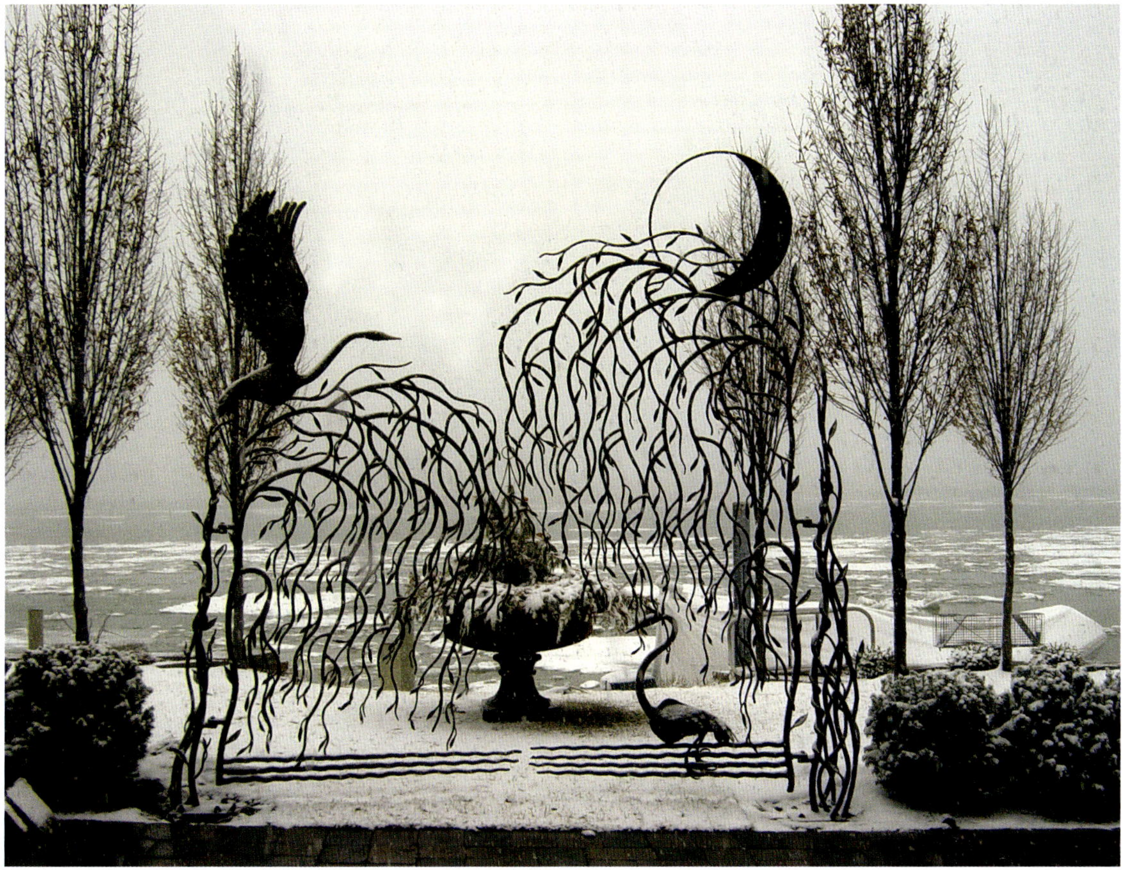

John Boyd Smith. *Swan Moon Gate*. Free-formed gate forged of mild steel, 120" w x 120" h. It depicts two life-sized Trumpeter Swans (one flying, one swimming) also featured are two weeping willow trees and the rising moon. Located at a private residence on the Michigan/Canadian border. *Photo, Rhonda Nelle Fleming*

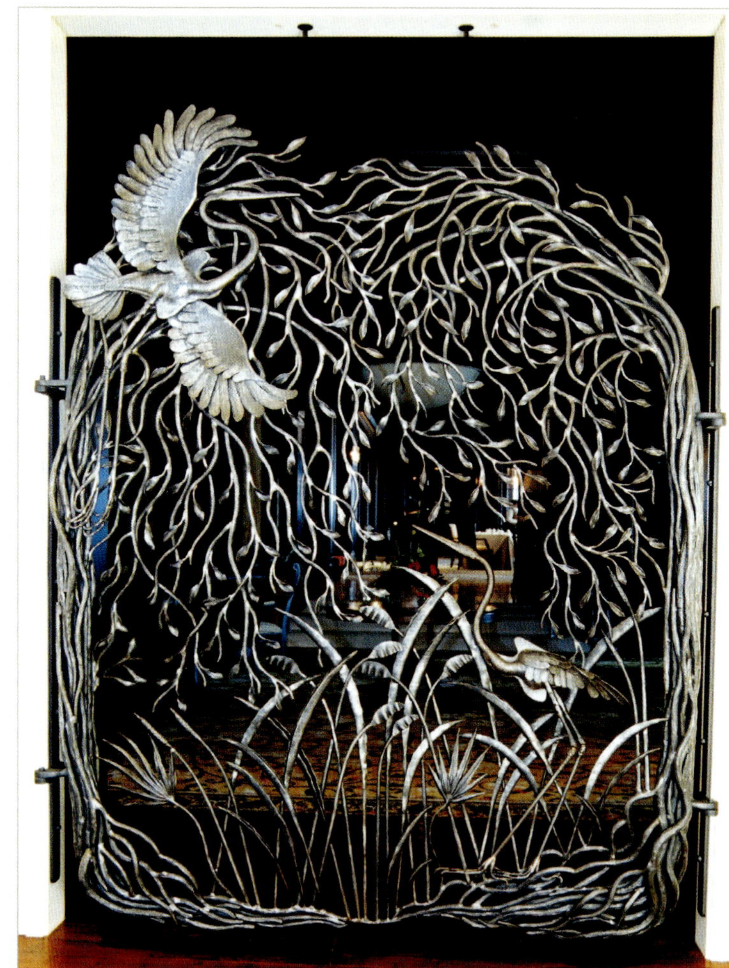

John Boyd Smith. *Sculptural Gate*. This sculptural gate is the entrance to the Ocean Room, an exclusive restaurant at The Sanctuary, a five star luxury hotel, on Kiawah Island, South Carolina. The double gate is eight feet high, and eight feet wide, depicting wildlife of the southern region. The double gate, when fully opened 180 degrees, is designed to serve as two sculptures against neutral wall as a background. This was a design feature that the owner insisted upon, so that the gate could be enjoyed in both closed and opened positions. *Photo, Rhonda Nelle Fleming*

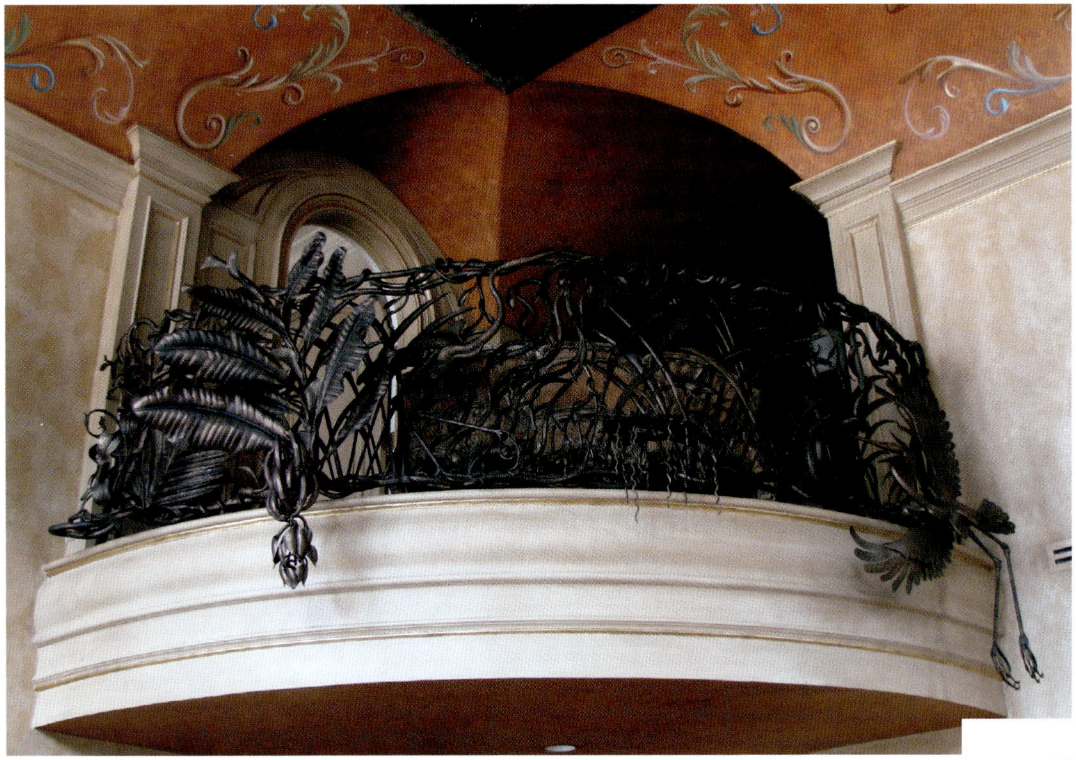

John Boyd Smith. *Low Country Railing*. Forged mild steel. Realistically depicts egrets, mangrove vines, and banana palms. This railing was created for a private estate in Hilton Head Island, South Carolina. *Photo, Rhonda Nelle Fleming*

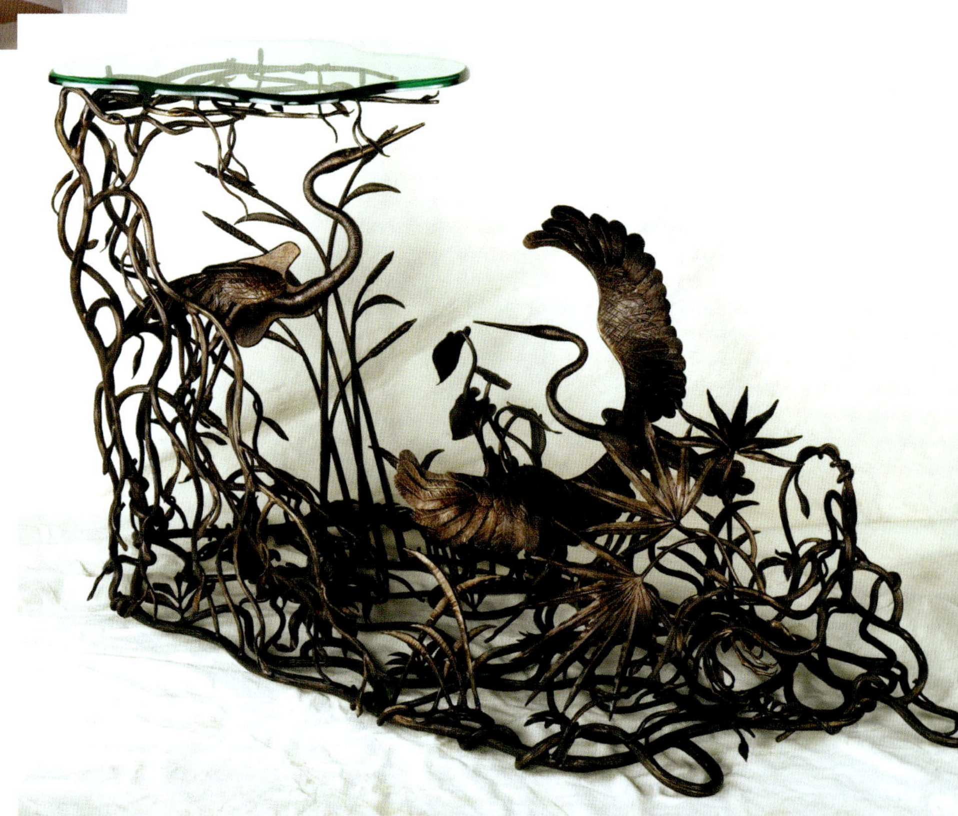

John Boyd Smith. *Savannah Low Country Table*. Forged mild steel. 30" x 84" x 42" h and weighs approximately 600 lbs. Realistically depicts egrets, mangrove vines, ferns, marsh grass, cat-tails, palmetto palm fronds, and other flora indigenous to southern marshlands. *Exhibited at the National Craft Gallery of Ireland in Kilkenny, Ireland. Photo, Paul Nurnberg*

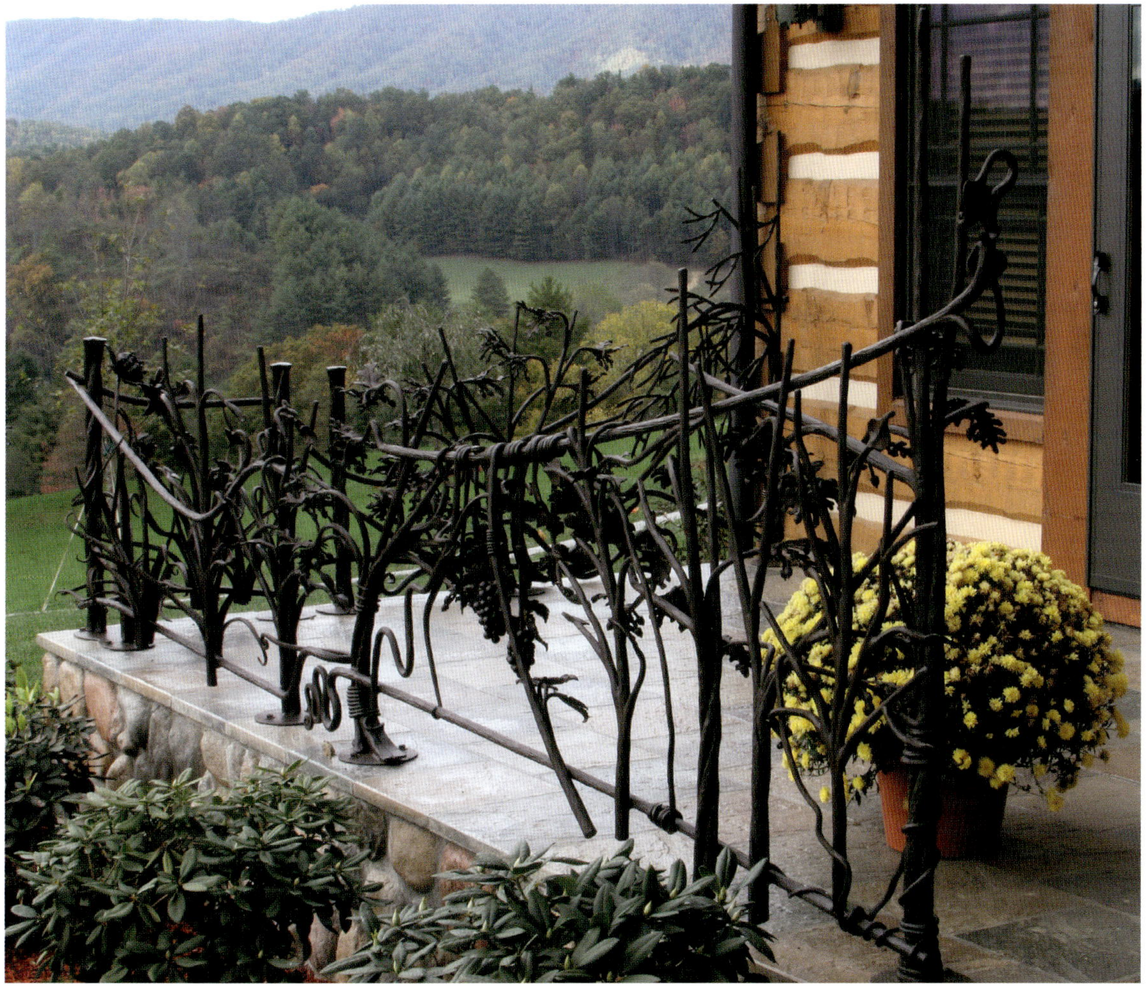

John Winer. *Wildwoods*. Railing, forged and fabricated mild steel. *Photo, Tom Payne*

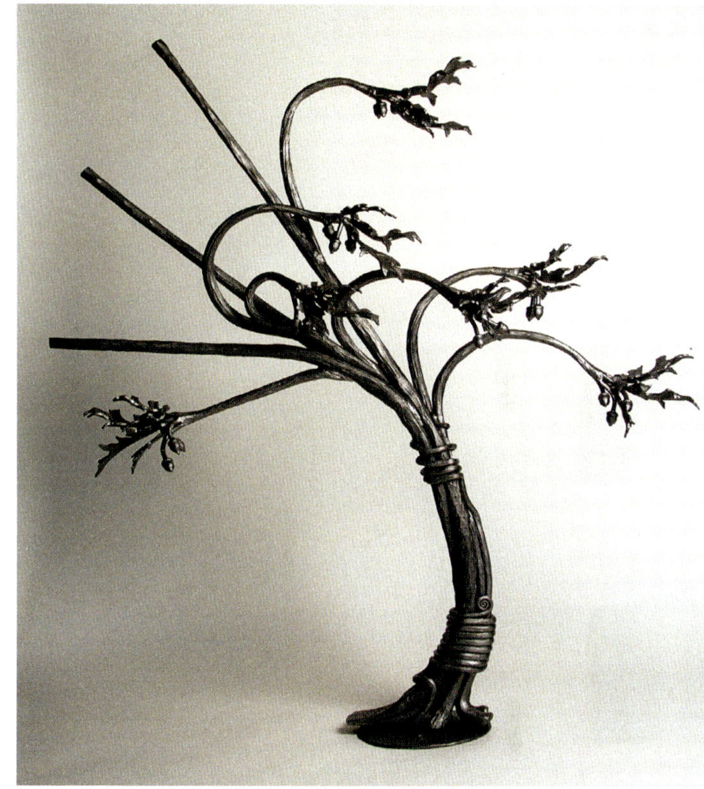

John Winer. *Wildwoods*. Railing test piece. *Photo, Tom Payne*

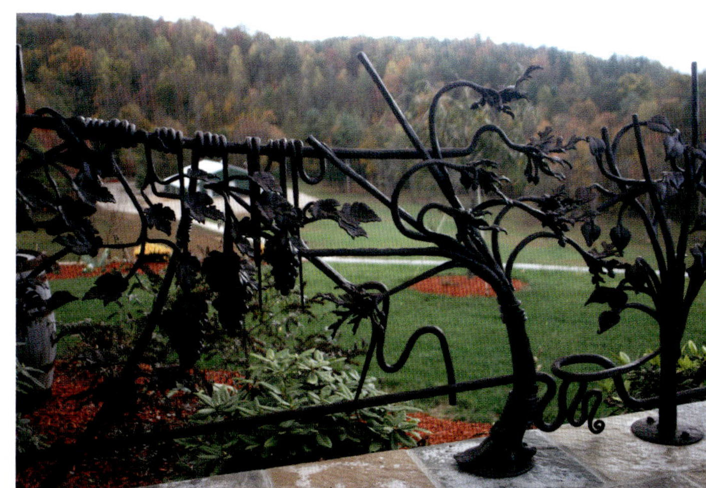

John Winer. *Wildwoods*. Railing, second view. *Photo, Tom Payne*

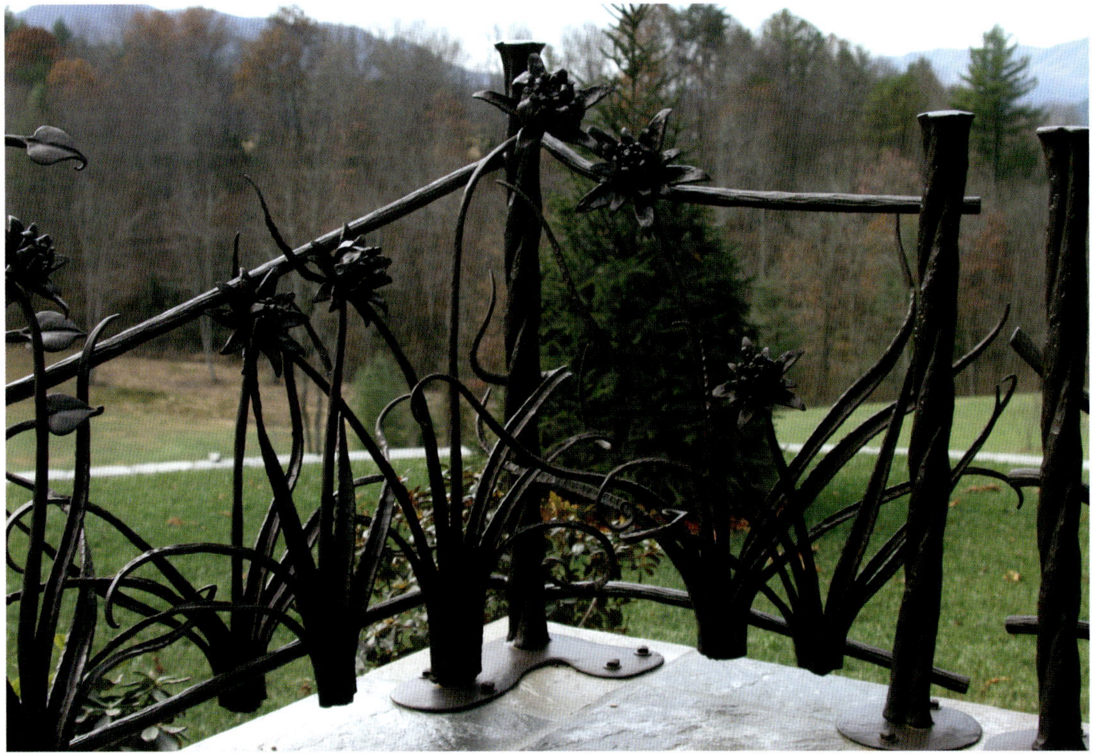

John Winer. *Wildwoods*. Railing, forged and fabricated mild steel. *Photo, Tom Payne*

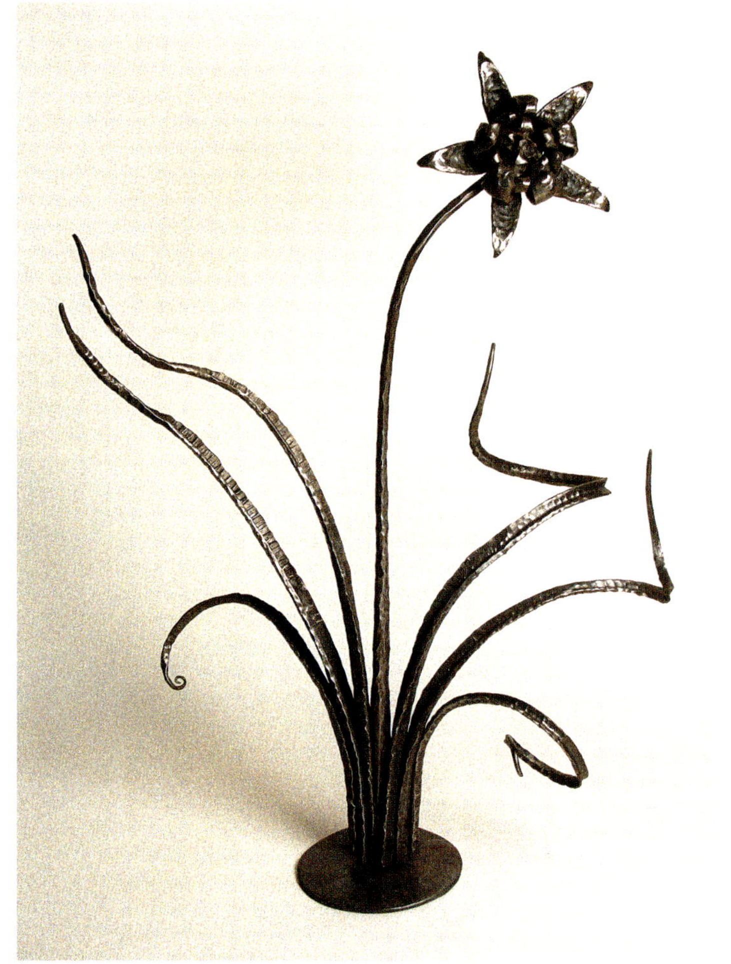

John Winer. *Wildwoods*. Railing test piece. *Photo, Tom Payne*

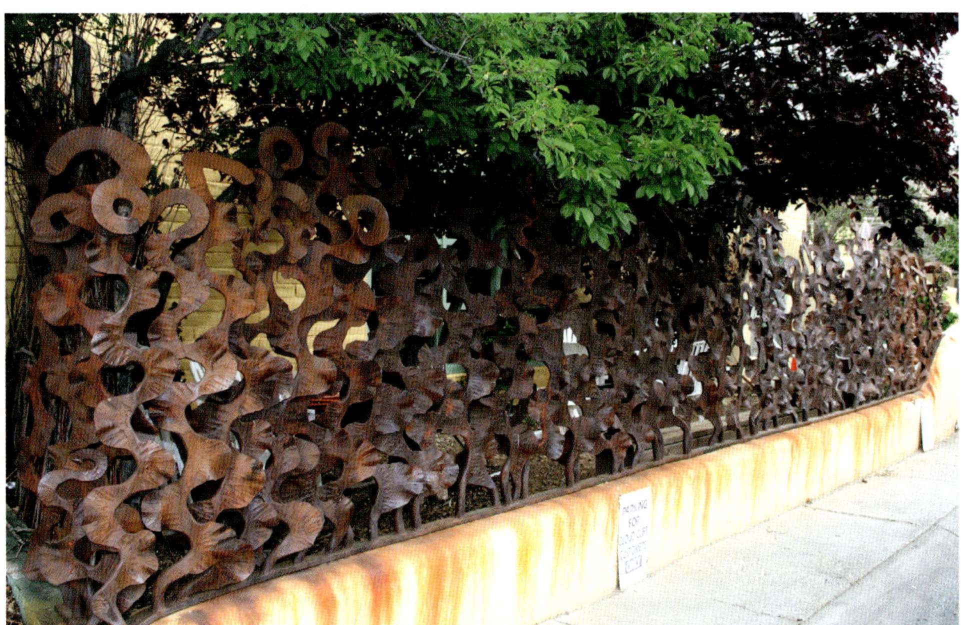

Helmut Hillenkamp. *Cloud Cliff Divider*. Forged steel, 420" long. *Photo, Fausto Cardoso*

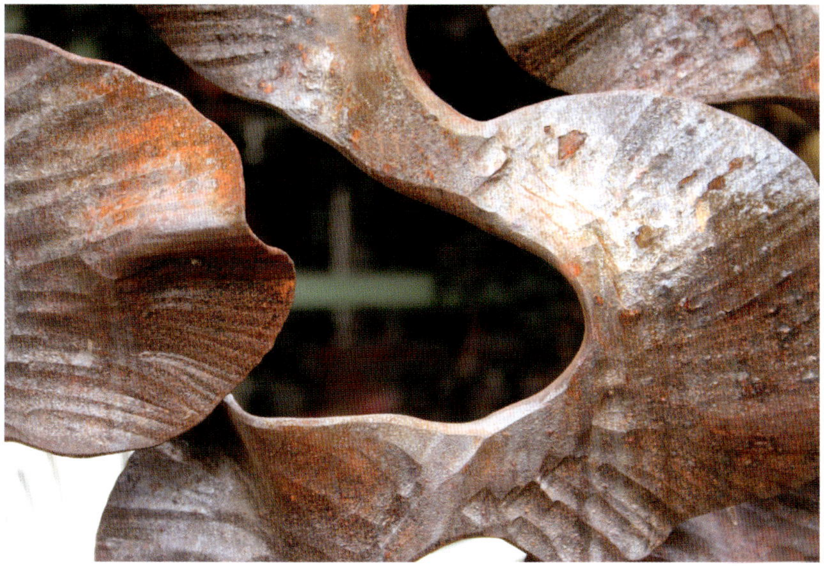

Helmut Hillenkamp. *Cloud Cliff Divider.* Detail. *Photo, Fausto Cardoso*

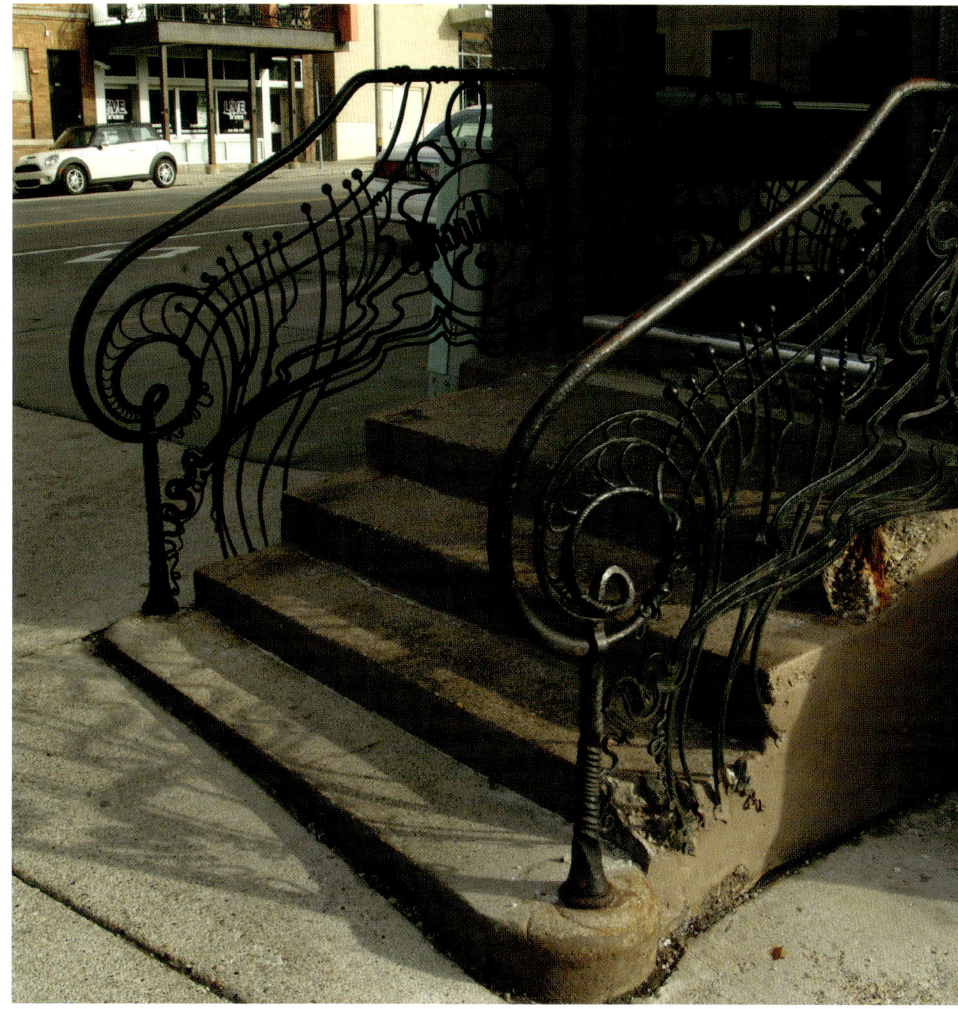

Thomas Wilson. *Hooligans Railing*. Main railing and newel post, one and a half inch thick round bar. Central elements, one half inch square bar. Wavy elements, three quarter by quarter inch flat stock, tapered in areas. Quarter inch square in the chambered nautilus design in newel area. Wall bracket, two and one half by half flat bar stock. End on newel extends 41 inches from brick wall. *Photo, Brian Gumieny*

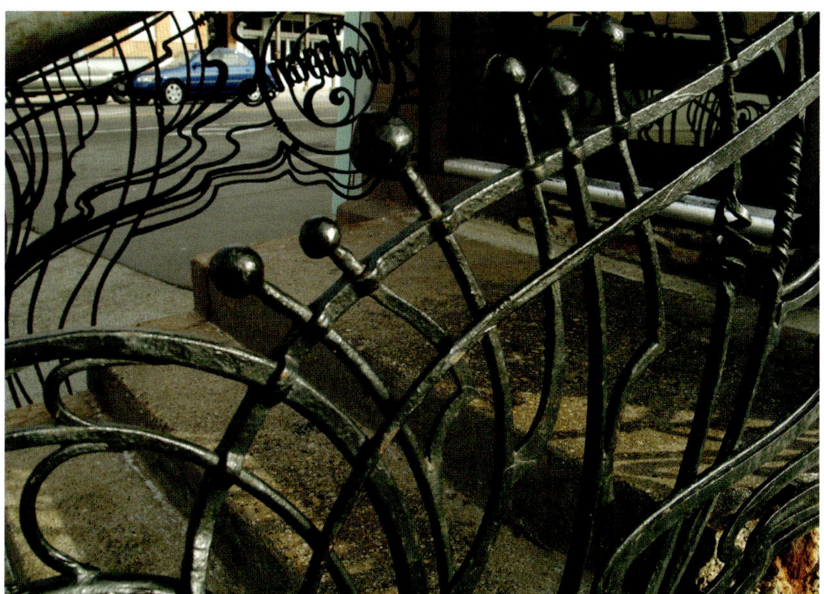

Thomas Wilson. *Hooligans Railing*.
Detail. *Photo, Brian Gumieny*

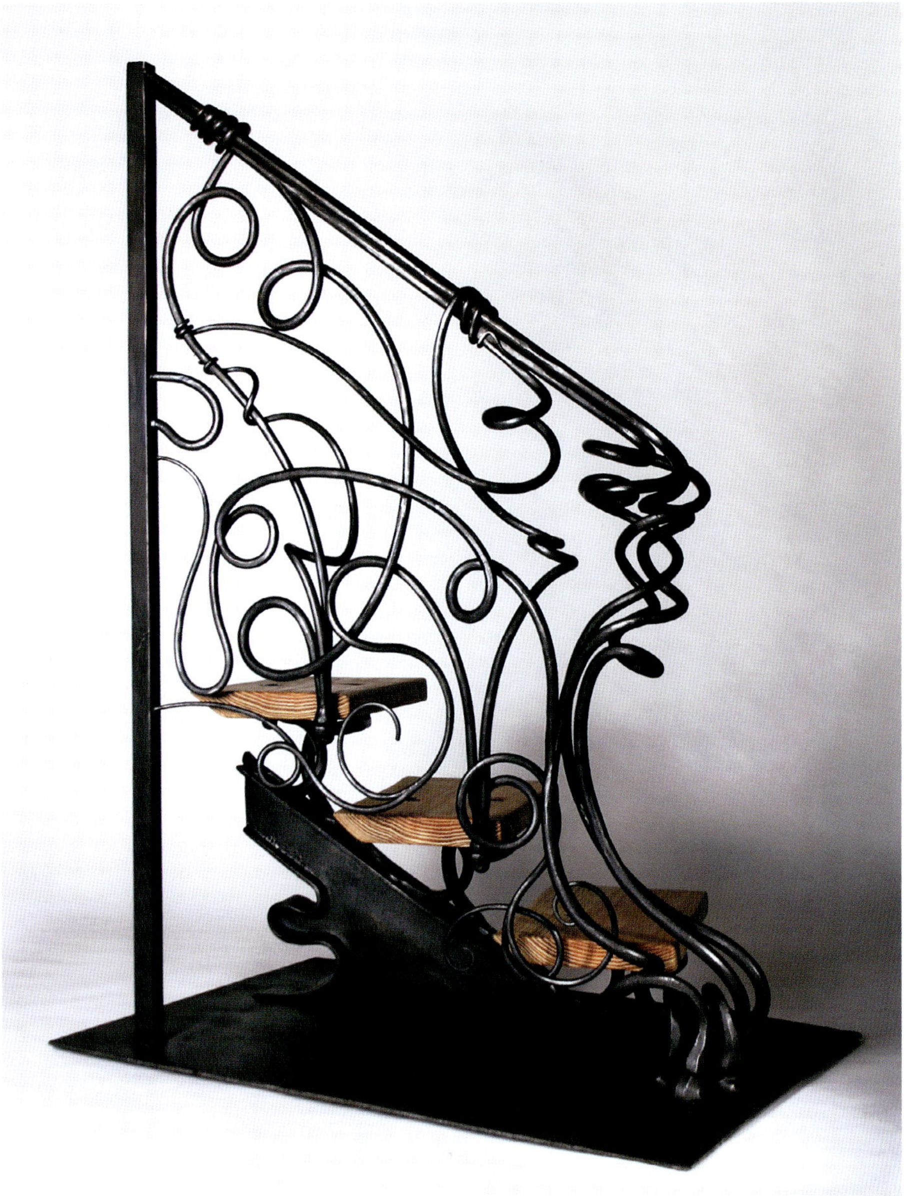

Jake James. *Staircase Study*. Built as a sample for a developer, this is a half width study for a freestanding staircase. Designed to appear almost to be growing up out of the ground, the pattern of the stair rail infill was all totally free formed, starting with the newel post section and working upwards. Every part of the staircase is forged in house, from the ball nuts connecting the staircase to the structural I-beam support. *Photo, Doug Gilbert*

Jake James. Coat Rack. Mild steel. Built to give the feeling of a tree in fall, the coat rack is made of three elements forged from three-quarter inch square bar. Each end was flattened to a long broad taper and manipulated to form the curves and spirals at the top and bottom. These three elements were then interwoven and fastened at the top with a collar. The overall structure has a flex to it so that it not only looks, but also moves, as if windswept. *Photo, Doug Gilbert*

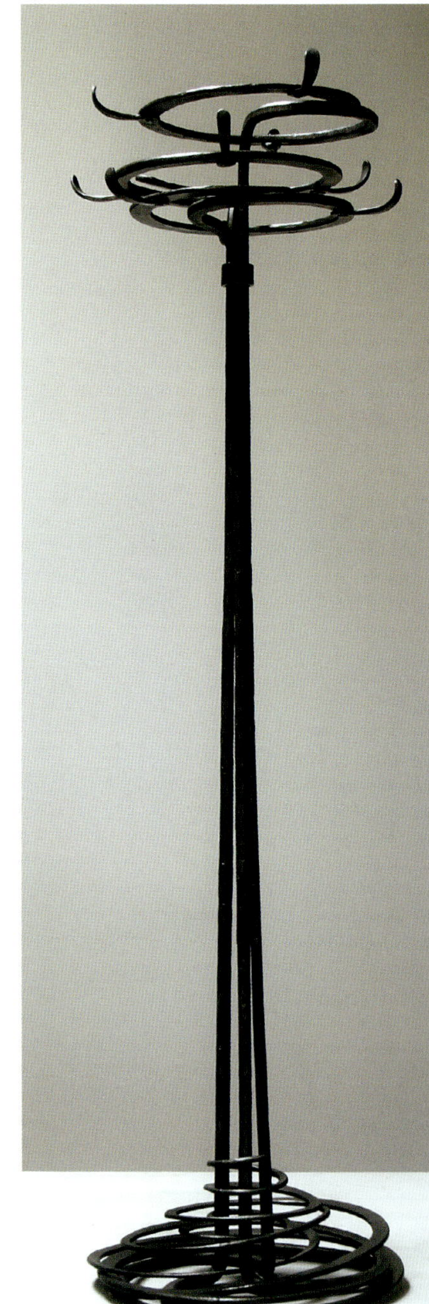

Jake James. Birdbath. Forged steel, glass. *Photo, Doug Gilbert*
Commissioned for a private garden in Vancouver, the clients were keen to have inspiration drawn from their magnolia tree.
I had a 22" fused glass bowl made for the birdbath. My work is all forged steel, mixing solid bar and pipe so I could hide a feed to supply the bowl with fresh water. The "magnolia" buds and flowers are all fire welded, as are all the branching joins. The birdbath is rusted and oiled. I try not to paint my ironwork as it greatly detracts from the detail of the forging. – Jake James

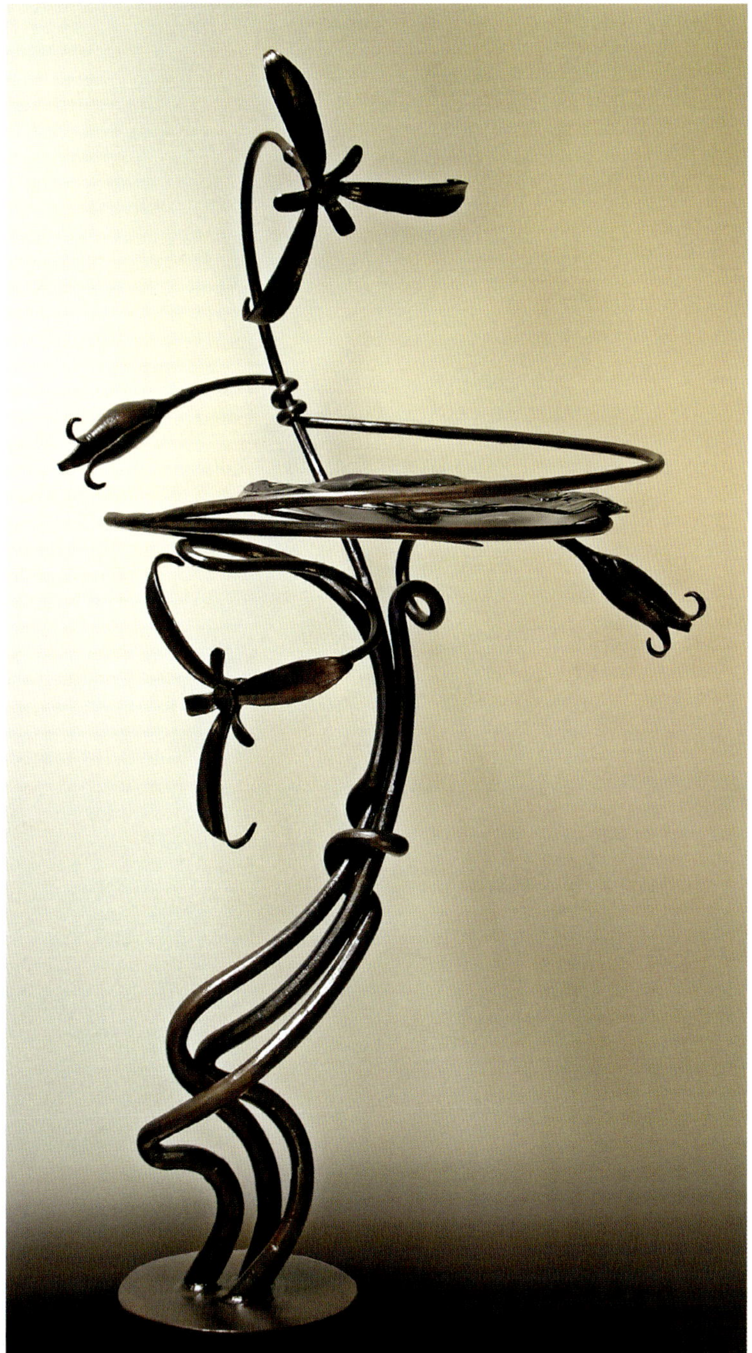

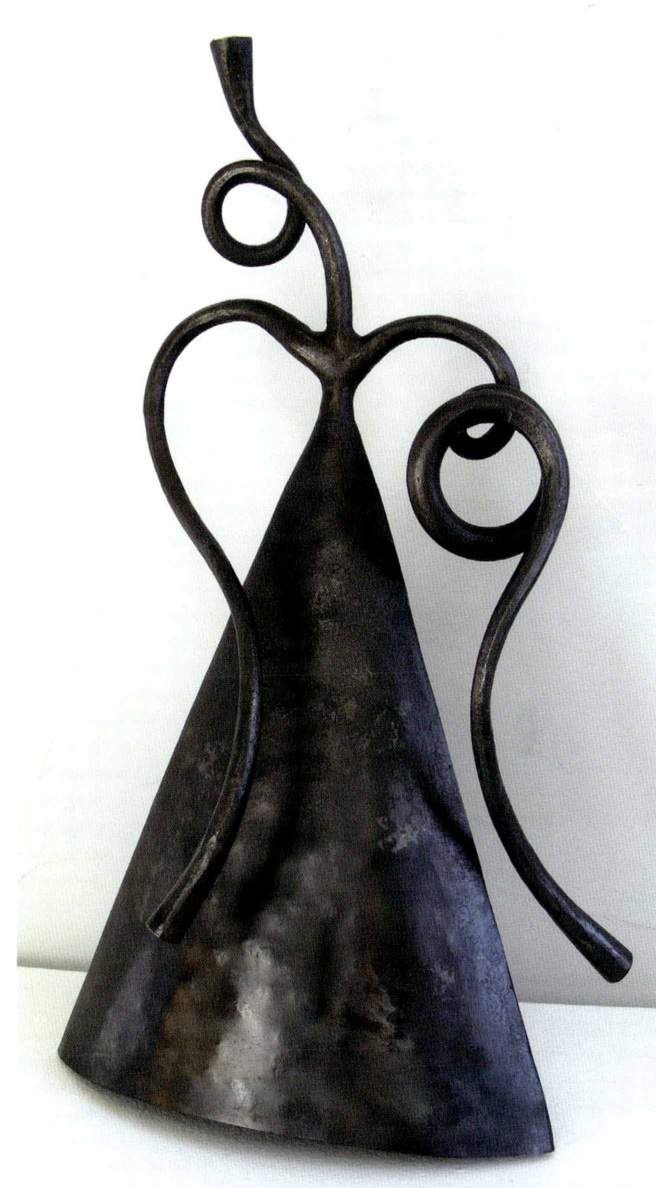

John Little. *Hand Bell 3*, 2008. Forged steel. 17" h x 10" w x 5" d. *Photo, artist*
This is one of a series of percussionist's hand bells. This design makes a wide variety of sounds depending on how it is held, and where, and by what, it is hit.

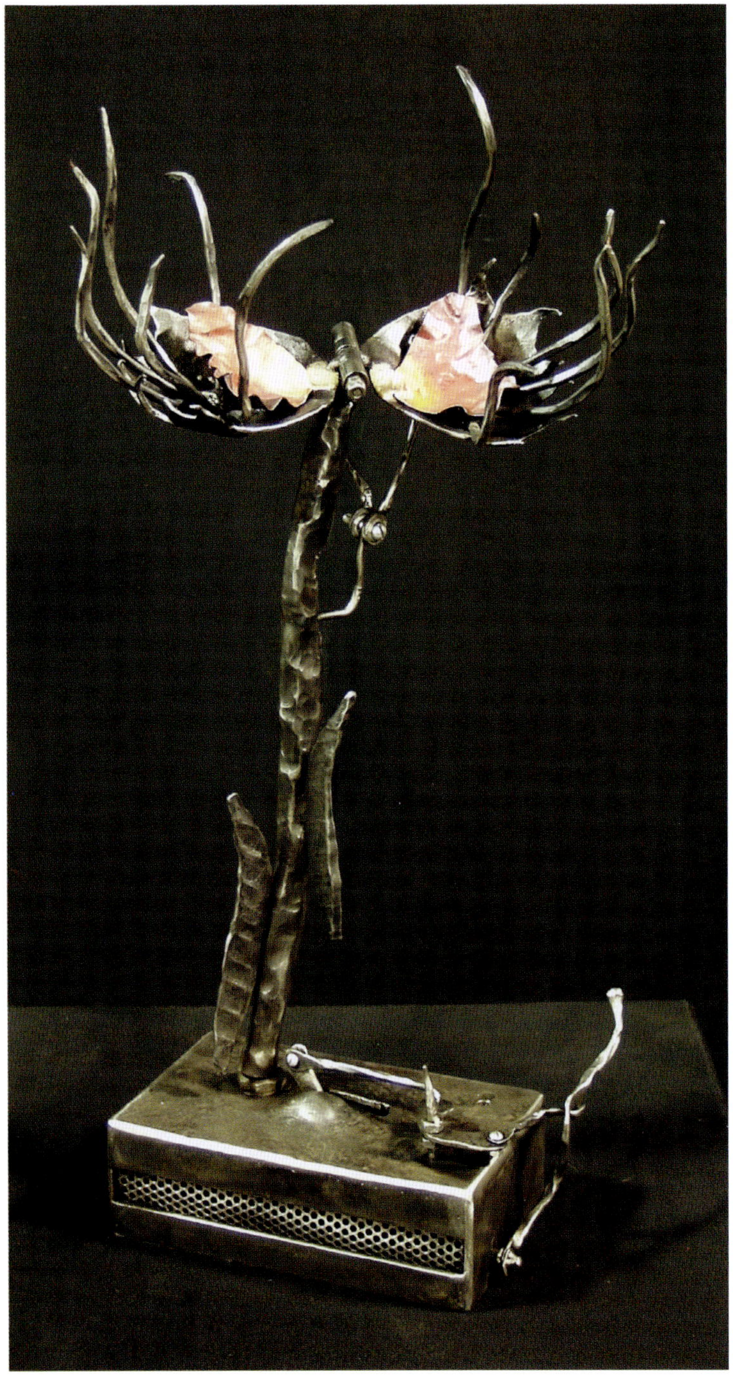

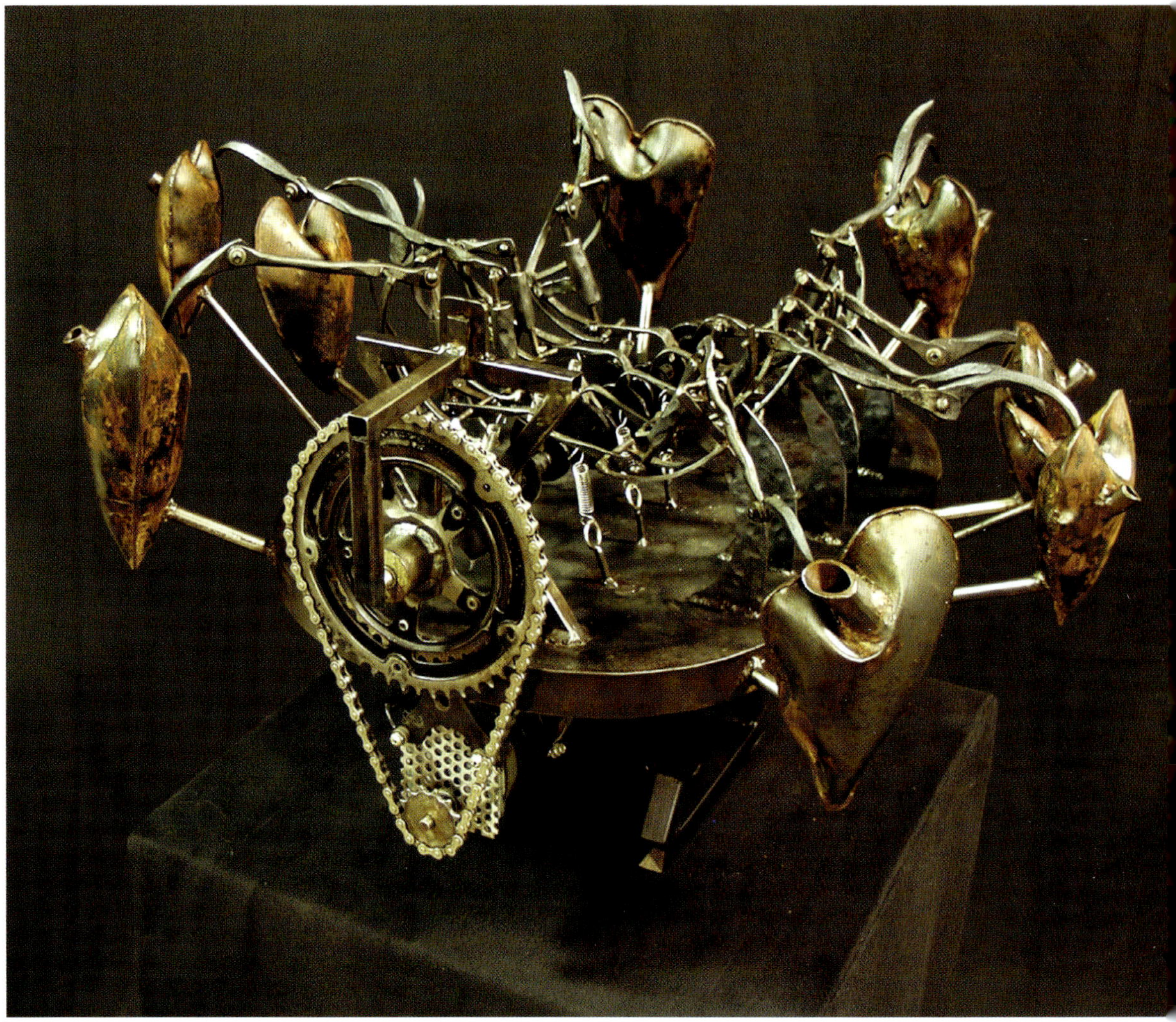

Christina Sporrong. *Nine Beating Hearts*, 2005. Forged steel, fabricated mechanical parts, sprocket, and motor. This is an acoustic piece. Pushing a pedestal-mounted button initiates the action of the piece nine times. A central rotating cam causes forged claws to tap on hearts in a disjointed rhythm. *Photo, artist*

Christina Sporrong. *Venus Fly Trap*, 2007. Forged steel, brazed copper. Pulling the side leaver makes the piece "snap." A variety of forged mechanical components create irregular and naturalistic movement. *Photo, artist*

Arthur H. Johns. *UFO Detector Generation 2 #2*. Forged steel. 15" x 20" x 20". *Photo, artist*

The pieces that I am currently working on are based on energy, gravity, and movement. These pieces are conceived first as stationary sculptures utilizing geometric designs with the primary emphasis being balance, stability, and form. Of course the kinetic aspects of these sculptures are planned for from conception, but the primary emphasis of the work is on the overall form of the sculpture. The kinetic elements of the sculpture are defined during the primary design phase as potential forms. I define these "potential forms" as the shape or shapes that the element will define while in motion. It is these potential forms that I am primarily interested in, thus causing the kinetic aspects of the work to be of secondary importance during the design stages. However, the kinetic forms on the finished piece when not in motion must be interesting in their own right.

My current sculptures require interaction with the observer, so the kinetic elements spend much more time at rest than they do in motion. I believe that these pieces should be enjoyable as a sculpture whether they are kinetic or not. Thus my designs often are intentionally vague in the drawing stages of their conception. This subordinates the kinetic elements of a given sculpture in favor of the definition of the overall form, which the sculpture will take. I want the viewer of my work to become interested in the form of the sculpture before they discover that the piece is kinetic. Once the observer has become interested in the piece, then the kinetic aspects can come into play. The kinetic elements of the work are intended to augment the enjoyment of the work by the observer, not dominate the aesthetic experience. – Arthur H. Johns

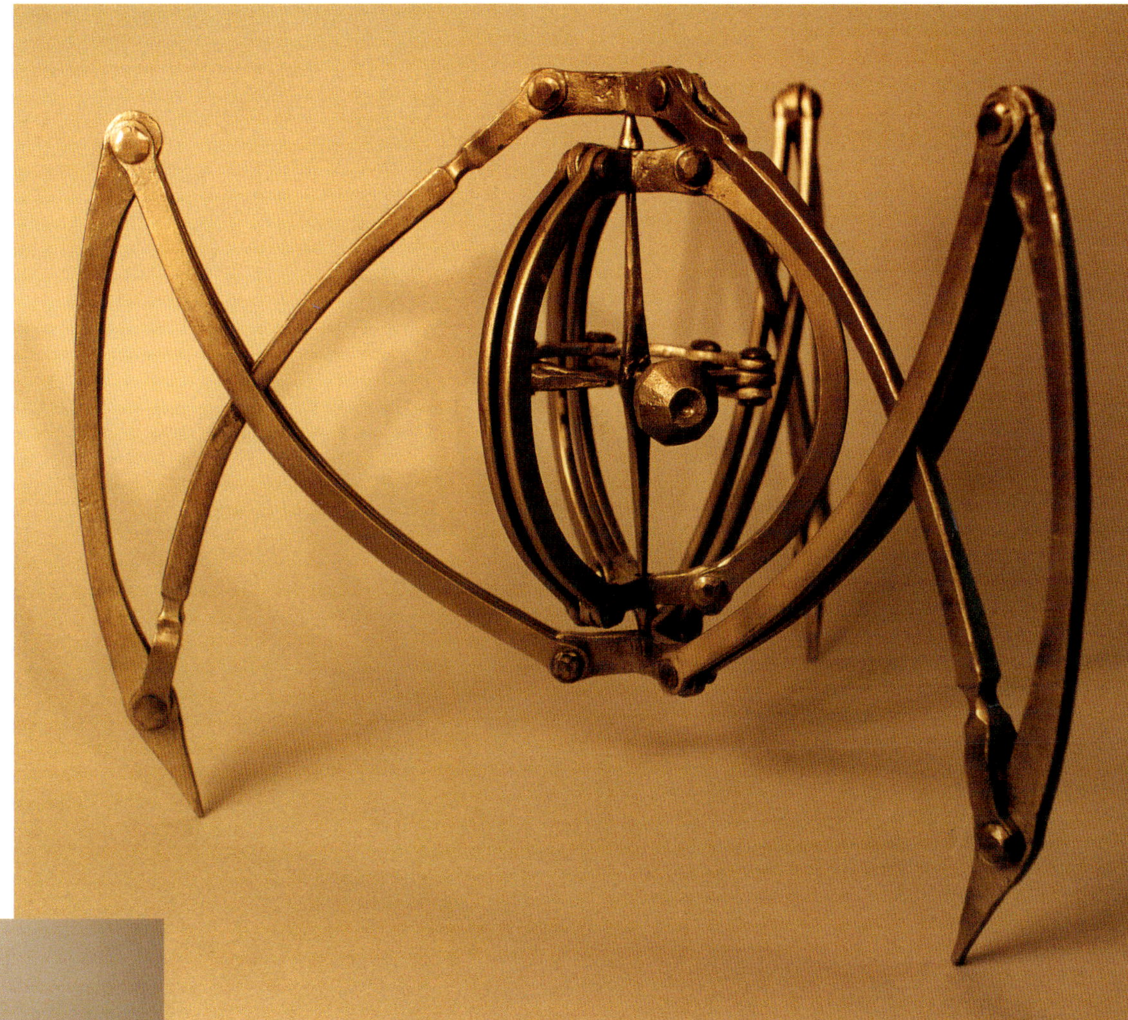

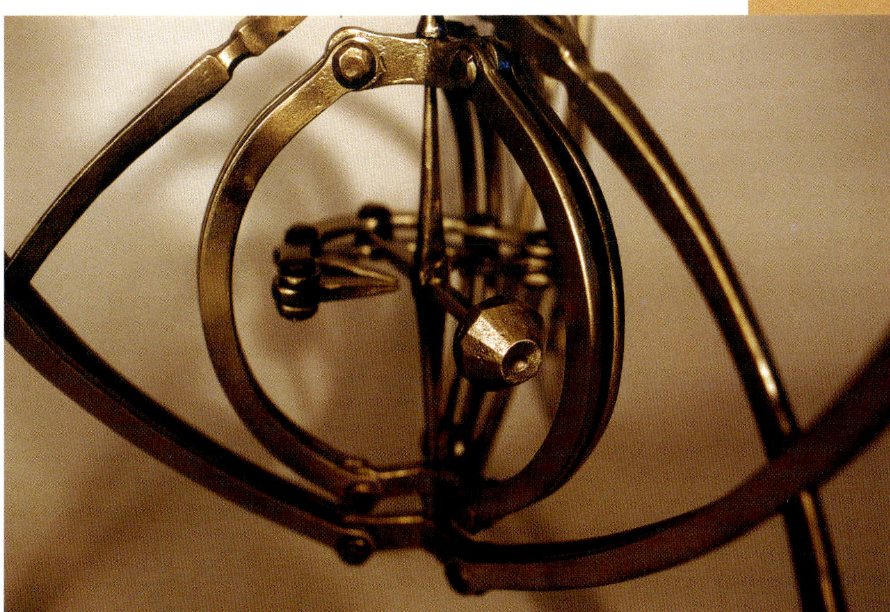

Arthur H. Johns. *UFO Detector Generation 2 #2*. Detail. *Photo, artist*

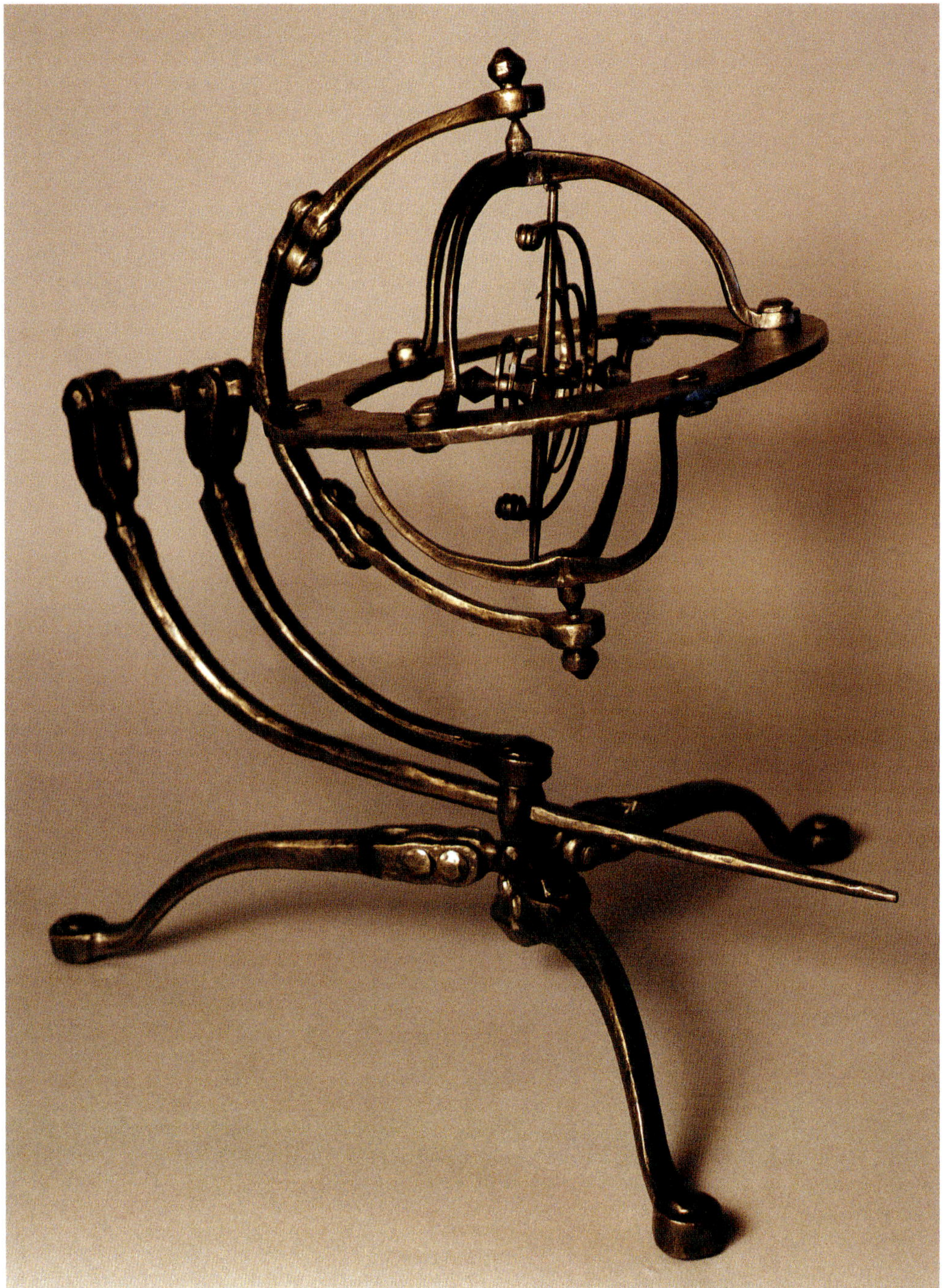

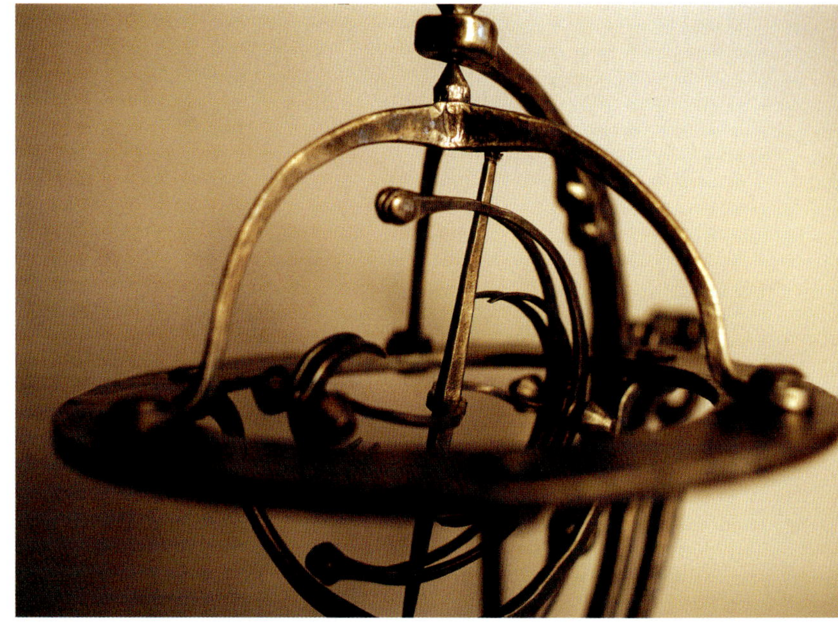

Arthur H. Johns. *UFO Detector Generation 3*. Detail. *Photo, artist*

Arthur H. Johns. *UFO Detector Generation 3*.
Forged steel. 18" x 20" x 24". *Photo, artist*

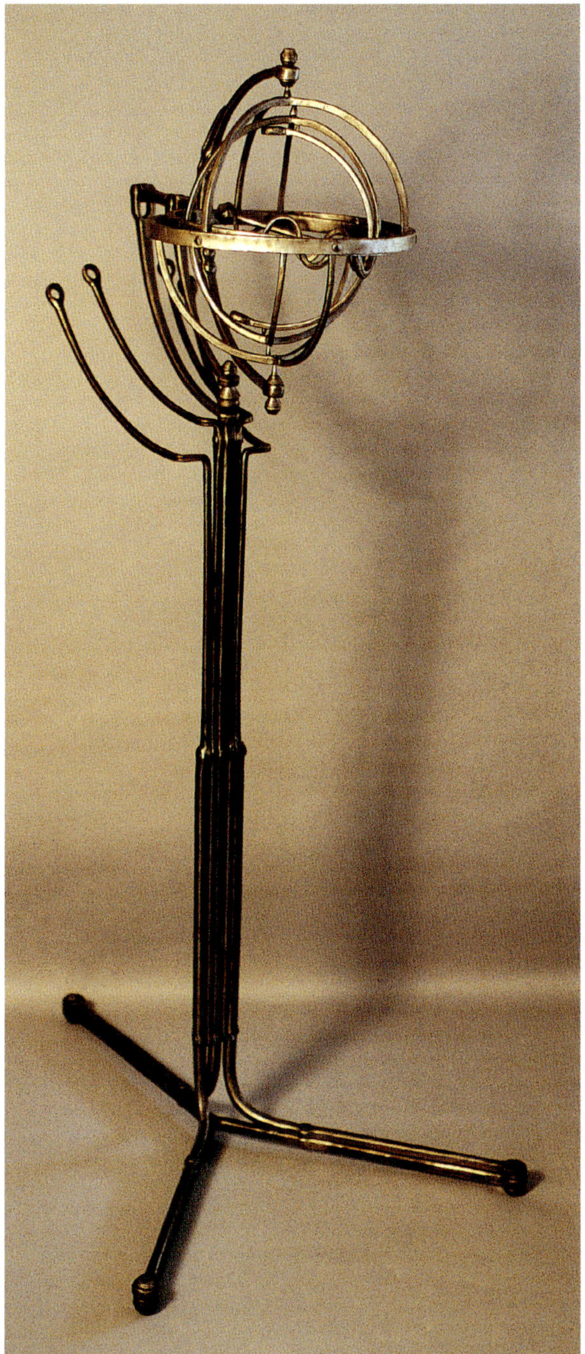

Arthur H. Johns. *Geocentric Universe Model 5*. Forged steel. 50" x 32" x 23". *Photo, artist*

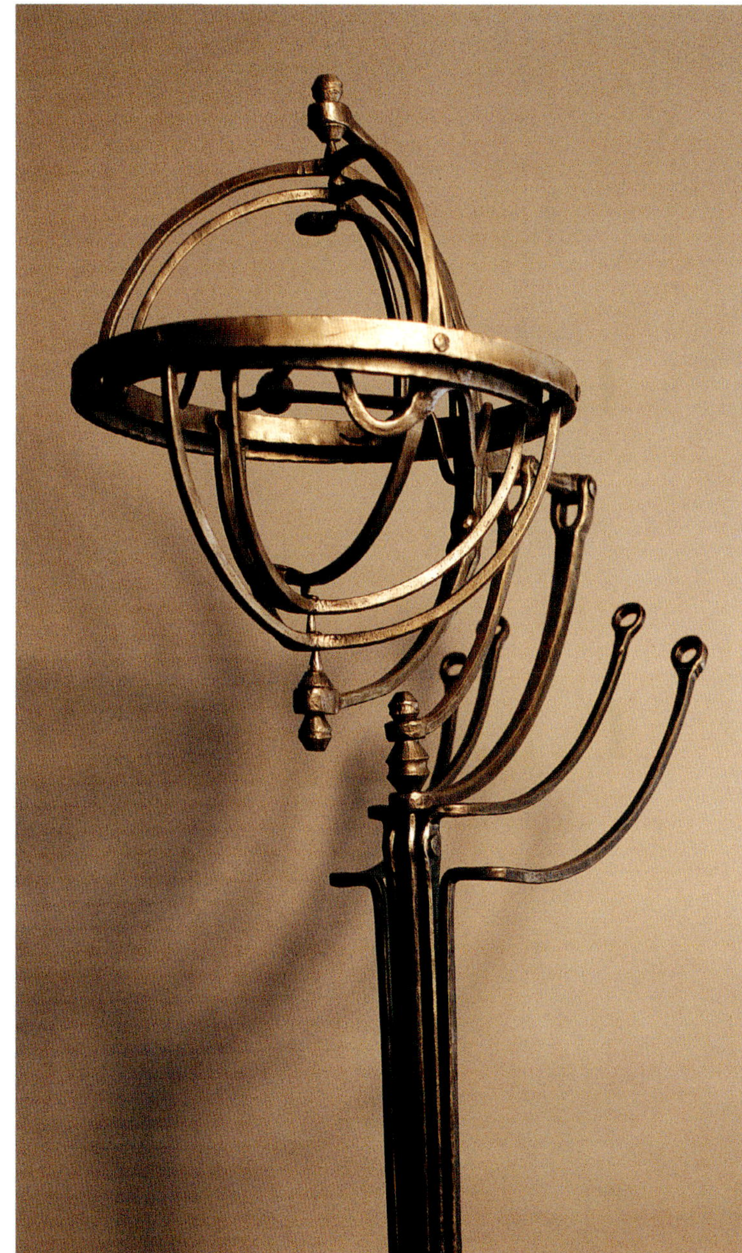

Arthur H. Johns. *Geocentric Universe Model 5*. Detail. *Photo, artist*

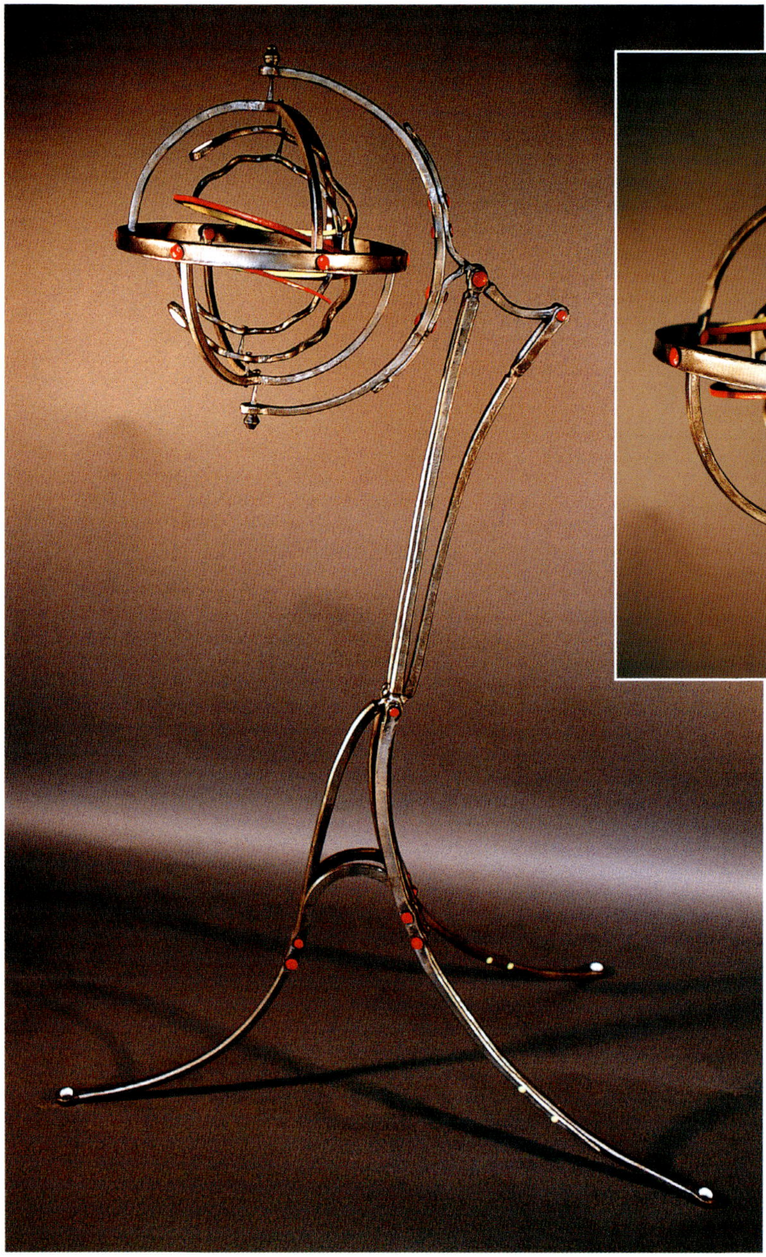

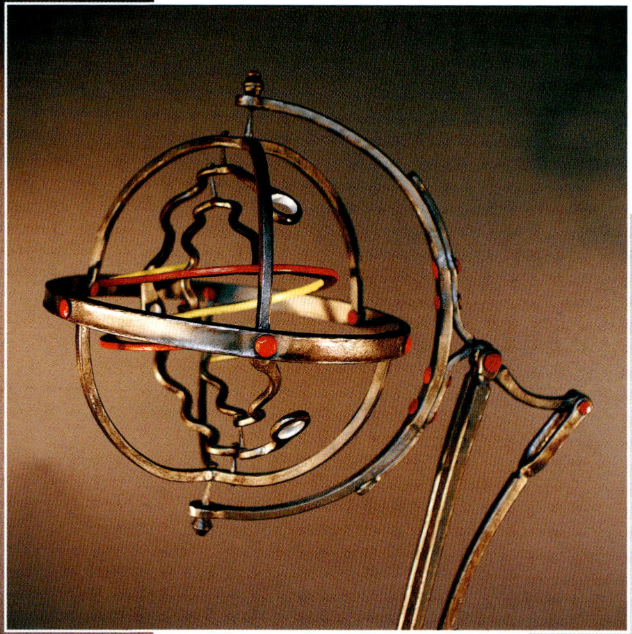

Arthur H. Johns. *Self Centering Universal Locator*. Detail. *Photo, artist*

Arthur H. Johns. *Self Centering Universal Locator*. Forged steel. 53" x 3" x 2". *Photo, artist*

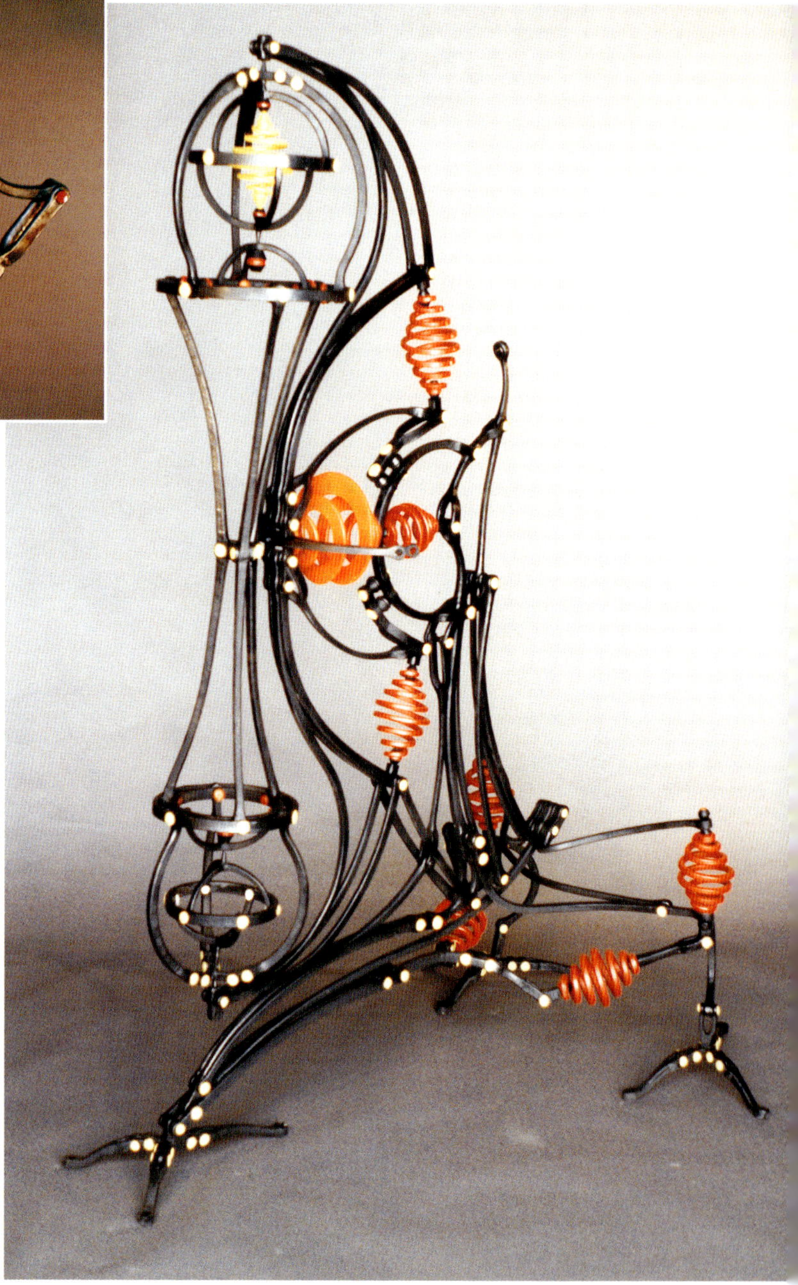

Arthur H. Johns. *Telekinetic*. Forged steel. 72" x 54" x 26". *Photo, artist*

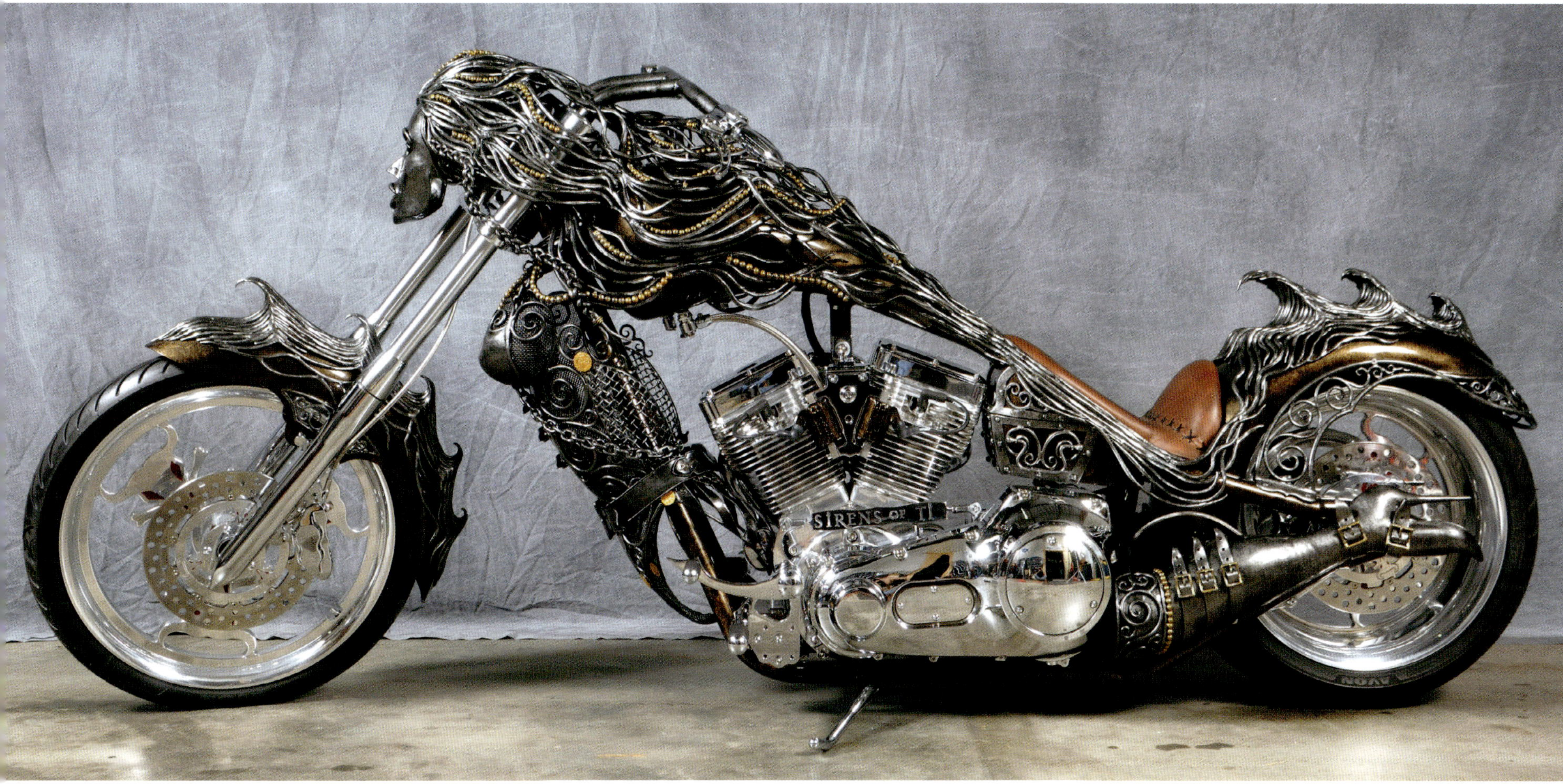

Scott Cawood. *Sirens Of TI Chopper*. Life-sized. *Photo, C. Kurt Holter*

The Siren of TI Chopper is a motor-sculpture I designed, then created in my studio as a collaboration with a local chopper shop. The piece was commissioned by Treasure Island Casino in Las Vegas to capture the essence of their Sirens Of TI show, which is played out daily on the Las Vegas strip.

The project took six months to complete. I attempted to take the raw energy of the powerful motorcycle and transform it into the motion of a seductive Siren rising out of the sea and beckoning to unsuspecting sailors. I cut, forged, bent, shaped, and welded mild steel to create the sculpture. I envision her as an ancient but dynamic force rising up out of the ocean.

The Siren chopper is now on permanent display to the public on the casino floor at Treasure Island Hotel & Casino in LV. — Scott Cawood

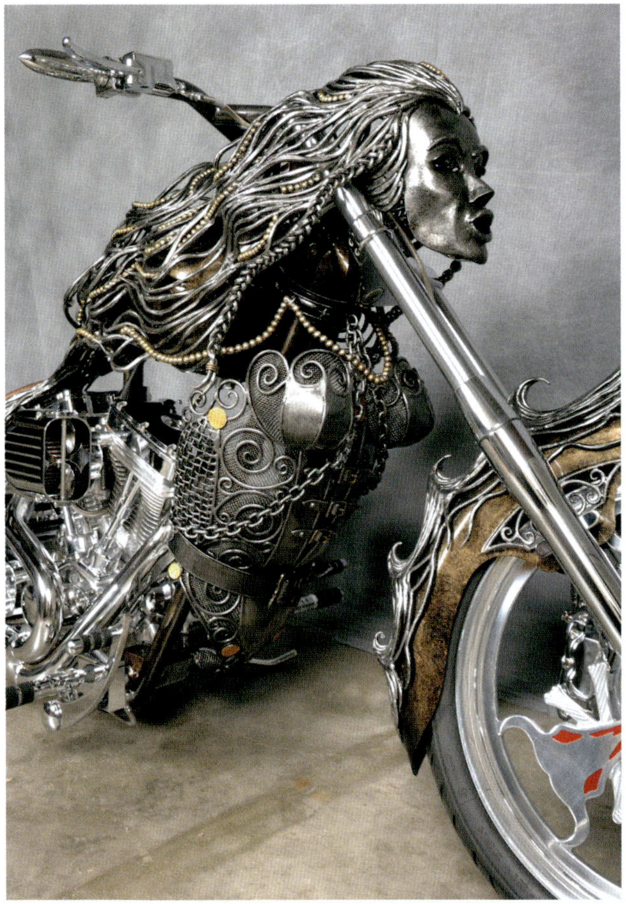

Scott Cawood. *Sirens Of TI Chopper*. Detail.
Photo, C. Kurt Holter

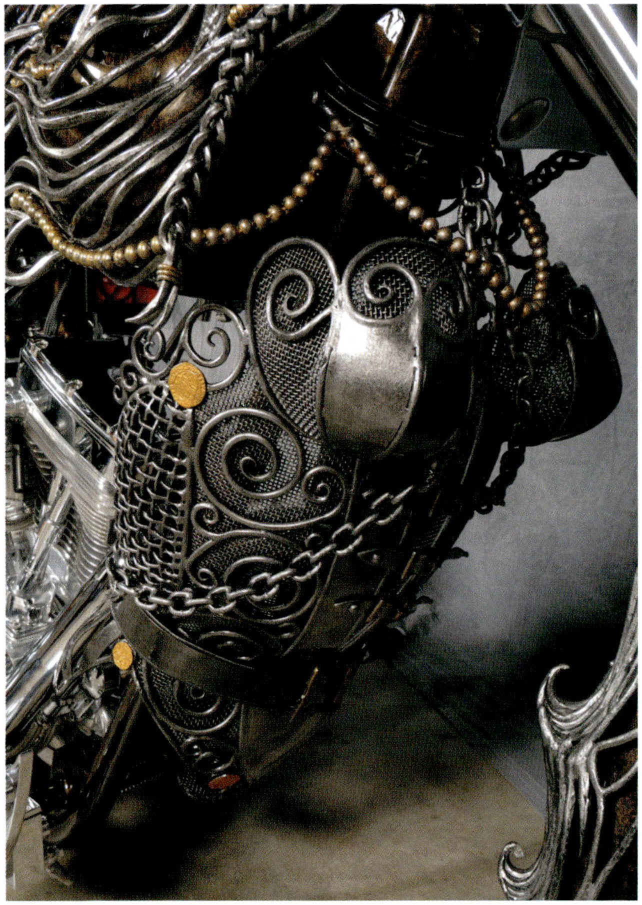

Scott Cawood. *Sirens Of TI Chopper*. Detail.
Photo, C. Kurt Holter

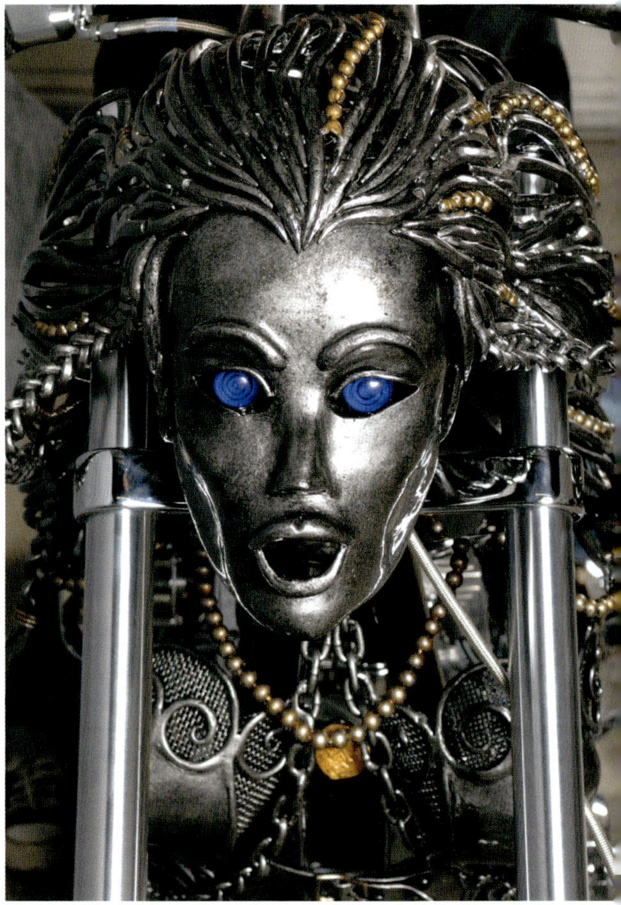

Scott Cawood. *Sirens Of TI Chopper.* Detail.
Photo, C. Kurt Holter

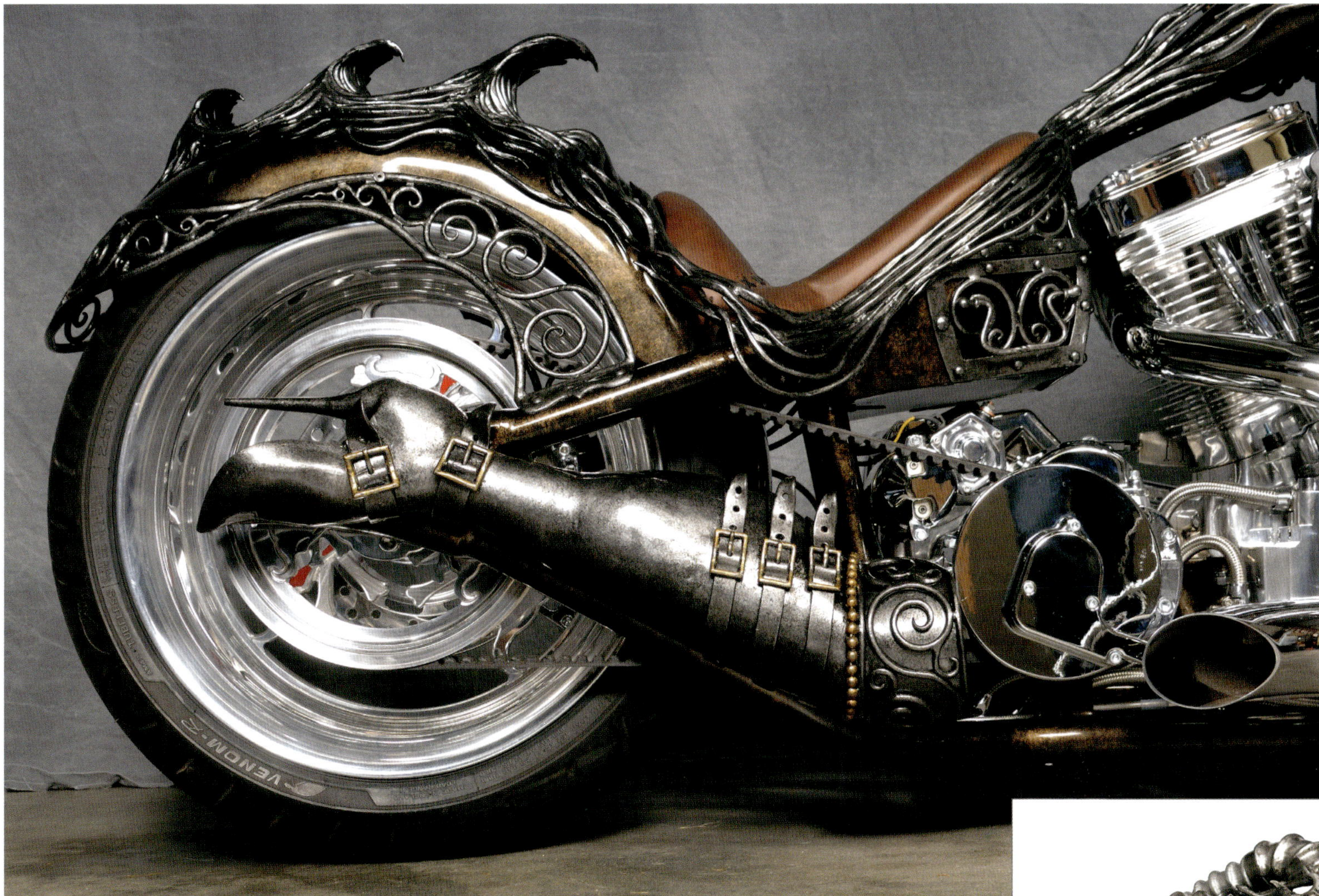

Scott Cawood. *Sirens Of TI Chopper*. Detail. *Photo, C. Kurt Holter*

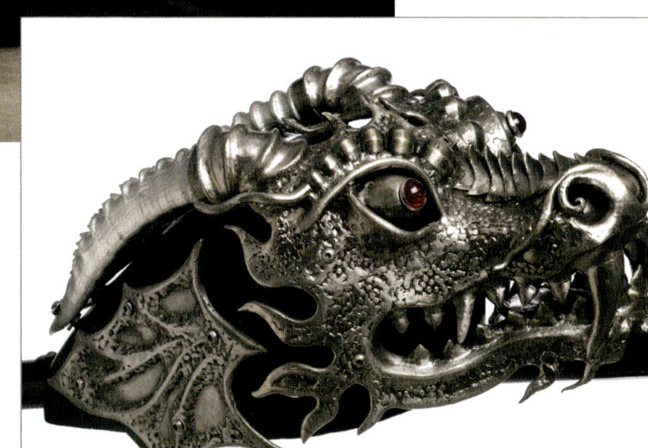

Scott Cawood. *Fire Breather.* Detail. *Photo, C. Kurt Holter*

Index

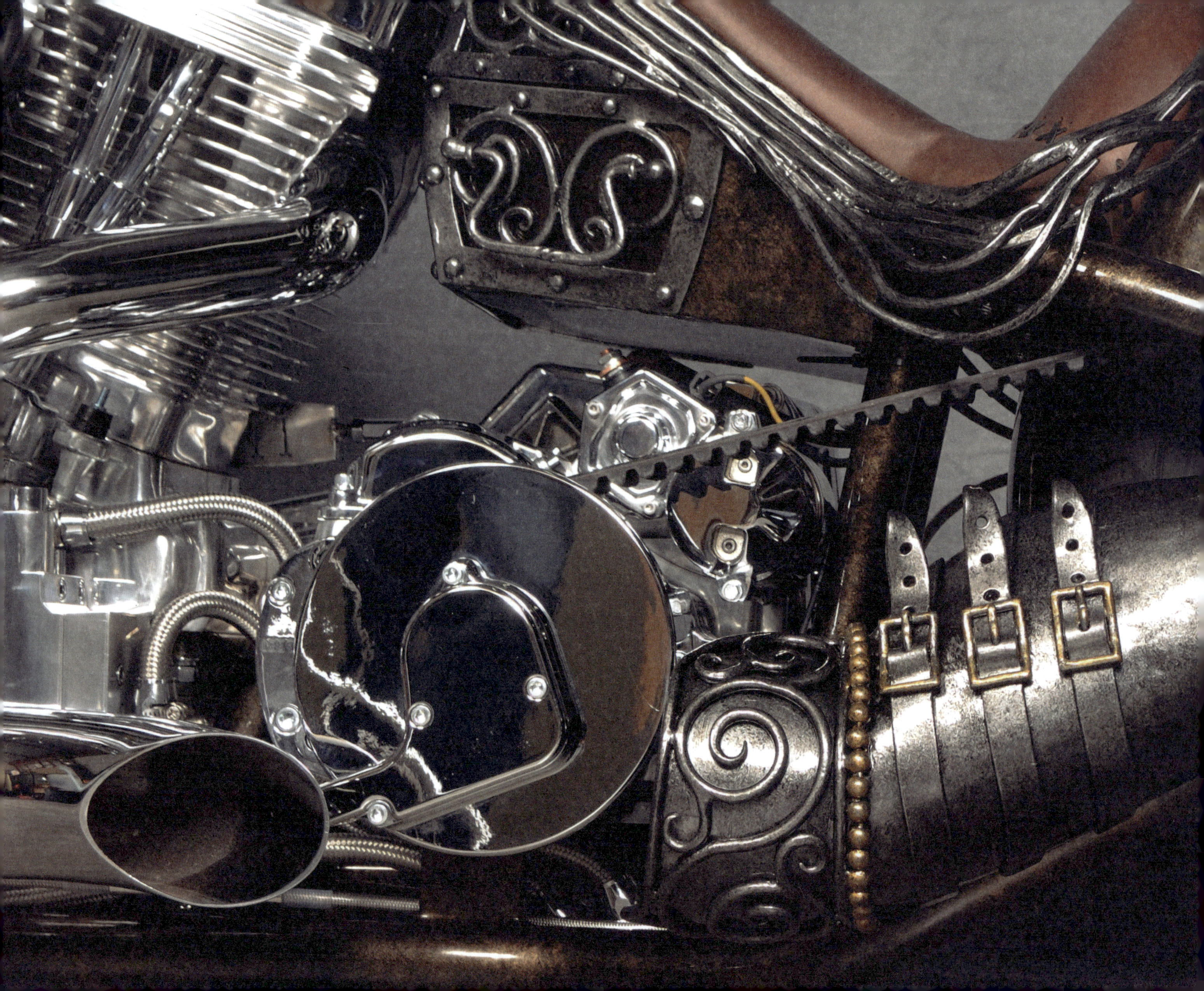